THE ORTHO HOME GARDENER'S PROBLEM SOLVER

THE ORTHO HOME GARDENER'S PROBLEM SOLVER

Created by the Editorial Staff of Ortho Books

Editor
Cheryl Smith

Ortho Books

Publisher:	Robert B. Loperena
Editorial Director:	Christine Jordan
Production Director:	Ernie S. Tasaki
Managing Editors:	Robert J. Beckstrom
	Michael D. Smith
	Sally W. Smith
System Manager:	Linda M. Bouchard
Editorial Assistants:	Joni Christiansen
	Sally J. French

Address all inquiries to:
Ortho Books
Box 5006
San Ramon, CA 94583-0906

	9	10	11	
97	98	99	2000	

ISBN 0-89721-255-X
Library of Congress Catalog Card
Number 92-61734

Acknowledgments

Material from The Ortho Problem Solver *Written by:*	Clare A. Binko
	Rick Bond
	Gene Joyner
	Wayne S. Moore
	Robert D. Raabe
	Deni Stein
	Bernadine Strik
	Lauren B. Swezey
Contributing Author:	L. Patricia Kite
Indexer:	Elinor Lindheimer
Copyeditor:	Toni Murray
Associate Editor:	Sara Shopkow
Editorial Assistants:	Deborah Bruner
	Theresa Lewis
Proofreader:	David Sweet
Composition:	Laurie A. Steele
Illustrator:	Ellen Blonder
Editorial Coordinator:	Cass Dempsey
Photographic Editor:	Pamela Peirce
Computing Services:	Mark Zielinski
Production by:	Indigo Design & Imaging
Designers:	John A. Williams
	Barbara Ziller
Color Separations by:	Color Tech. Corp.
Printing by:	Banta Book Group

Printed in the U.S.A.

THE SOLARIS GROUP
2527 Camino Ramon
San Ramon, CA 94583-0906

PREFACE

All gardeners have problems with pests or diseases from time to time. *The Ortho Home Gardener's Problem Solver* was created to help you solve those problems. In a straightforward way, it will help you discover what kind of problem you have and what's causing it, and it will tell you more about the problem—such as how serious it can get if you don't do anything. Then it will tell you how to solve the problem.

The photographs at the top of the page are arranged so that similar symptoms are grouped together. Select the picture that looks most like your problem. The small map under the photograph shows how likely the problem is to affect your part of the country. If your region is colored red, the problem is commonplace or severe. If it is colored yellow, the problem is occasional or moderate. If it is uncolored, the problem is nonexistent or minor.

A word of explanation is needed about the solutions offered. The "Solutions" section of each discussion of a specific problem assumes that you have seen the problem when the symptoms first become obvious. Our solution begins by telling you what you can do immediately to alleviate that problem. Then it tells you what changes you can make in the environment or in your gardening practices to prevent the problem from returning. In many cases, the text suggests a chemical spray as an immediate solution and a cultural change or a resistant variety as a long-range solution.

We offer several solutions for most of the problems in this book, leaving it to your judgment to choose those most appropriate to your situation. For example, we tell you that you can protect your sycamore tree from anthracnose by spraying

One solution for lawn weeds, such as ground ivy, is to spray with a selective herbicide. Another is to learn ways to improve the care you give your lawn, so the healthier lawn will be better able to crowd out weeds.

it with a fungicide in the spring. If your sycamore is 6 feet high, you might choose to spray it when spring comes. But if it is 40 feet high, you will find that hiring an arborist to spray it will be expensive. From our description of the problem, you know that anthracnose seldom does permanent harm to a tree, so you may choose to do nothing.

When choosing a chemical product, read the label carefully. Although all malathion is the same, all products containing it are not. Even though we know malathion will solve a particular problem and tell you so, some products that contain malathion may be manufactured for a problem different from yours. Using an inappropriate product—even if it contains an appropriate ingredient—can injure your plant. Be sure the plant you wish to spray is included in the list on the product label.

This book is based in large part on research done for *The Ortho Problem Solver* and its revisions. *The Ortho Problem Solver* is a professional reference tool for solving plant problems. We have drawn on that research to create this book to help you, as a home gardener, solve the problems you are most likely to encounter. The pages of both problem solvers present the experience of many experts, most of them members of cooperative extension services of various states. These men and women have shared the most current and practical information available. If you follow their advice in terms of immediate solutions and long-term prevention, you will approach the realization of every gardeners dream: to garden in such a way that you have no problems at all, but are free to fully enjoy the beauty and bounty of your garden.

PREFACE

CONSULTANTS

Many gardening experts contributed to this book, by both writing material and checking work for accuracy. We are indebted to these consultants for their careful work. Since this book relies heavily on information developed for *The Ortho Problem Solver*, we remain grateful to all those who gave their expertise to that book. The following names are those of major consultants—people who spent many hours checking manuscripts for accuracy and patiently answered our questions about fine points of garden care.

Dr. Jan Abernathie
Plant Pathologist
Chesapeake, VA

Dr. James Beutel
Extension Pomologist
University of California, Davis

Dr. Darrel R. Bienz
Professor of Horticulture
Washington State University

Dr. Eugene Brady
Professor of Entomology
University of Georgia

Dr. Jerome Brezner
Department of Environment &
    Forest Biology
State University of New York, Syracuse

Bartow H. Bridges, Jr.
Landscape Architect and
    Horticulturist
Virginia Beach, VA

Dr. Jack Butler
Department of Horticulture
Colorado State University

Dr. Ralph S. Byther
Extension Plant Pathologist
Washington State University

Dr. Robert Carrow
Agronomy Department
University of Georgia Experiment Station
Griffin, GA

Sharon J. Collman
County Extension Agent
Seattle, WA

Dr. Samuel D. Cotner
Extension Horticulturist
Texas A&M University

Dr. G. Douglas Crater
Extension Horticulturist,
    Floriculture
University of Georgia

Dr. T. E. Crocker
Professor of Fruit Crops
University of Florida

Dr. J. A. Crozier
Chevron Chemical Company
San Francisco, CA

Dr. Spencer H. Davis, Jr.
Horticultural Consultant
North Brunswick, NJ

Dr. August De Hertogh
Department of Horticultural Science
North Carolina State University

Dr. Clyde Elmore
Extension Weed Scientist
University of California, Davis

Barbara H. Emerson
Senior Product Specialist
Union Carbide Agricultural
    Products Co.
Research Triangle Park, NC

Dr. James R. Feucht
Extension Professor,
    Department of Horticulture
Colorado State University

Dr. Ralph Garren, Jr.
Small Fruit Specialist
Cooperative Extension Service
Oregon State University

Cathy Haas
Master Landscapes
Salinas, CA

Dr. M. Ali Harivandi
Cooperative Extension
University of California, Berkeley

Duane Hatch
Cooperative Extension Service
Utah State University

Dr. Sammy Helmers
Area Extension Horticulturist
Stevenville, TX

Kermit Hildahl
Cooperative Extension
University of Missouri

Everett E. Janne
Landscape Horticulturist
Texas Agricultural Extension Service
College Station, TX

Dr. Ron Jones
Department of Plant Pathology
North Carolina State University

Gene Joyner
Palm Beach County Extension
West Palm Beach, FL

Caroline Klass
Senior Extension Associate
Department of Entomology
Cornell University

N. S. Mansour
Extension Service
Oregon State University

Dr. Charles Marr
Extension Horticulturist
Kansas State University

Frederick McGourty
Mary Ann McGourty
Hillside Gardens
Norfolk, CT

Bernard Moore
Extension Plant Diagnostician, Retired
Oregon State University

Lester P. Nichols, Professor
Emeritus of Plant Pathology
The Pennsylvania State University

Dr. Norman F. Oebker
Vegetables Specialist
Cooperative Extension Service
University of Arizona

Dr. Howard Ohr
Plant Pathologist
Cooperative Extension Service
University of California, Riverside

Dr. Albert O. Paulus
Plant Pathologist
University of California, Riverside

Dr. Charles C. Powell, Jr.
Department of Plant Pathology
Ohio State University

Dr. Robert D. Raabe
Plant Pathologist
University of California, Berkeley

Dr. Charles Sacamano
Professor of Horticulture
University of Arizona

Professor Donald Schuder
Extension Entomologist
Purdue University

Dr. Arden Sherf
Professor, Department of Pathology
Cornell University

Dr. Gary Simone
Extension Plant Pathologist
University of Florida

Arthur Slater
Environmental Health and Safety
University of California, Berkeley

Dr. Walter Stevenson
Associate Professor of Plant Pathology
University of Wisconsin

Dr. Steven Still
Department of Horticulture
Ohio State University

Bernadine Strik
Department of Horticulture
Oregon State University

Dr. O. Clifton Taylor
Statewide Air Pollution Research Center
University of California, Riverside

William Titus
County Coordinator
Cooperative Extension Service
Plainview, NY

Dr. John Tomkins
Associate Professor of Pomology
Cornell University

Carl A. Totemeier
Director
Old Westbury Gardens
Old Westbury, NY

Marian Van Atta
Editor
Living Off the Land
Melbourne, FL

John White
County Extension Agent –Horticulture
El Paso, TX

Dr. Gayle Worf
Extension Plant Pathologist
University of Wisconsin

SPECIAL CONSULTANTS

Many other gardening professionals and gifted amateurs have shared their experience and wisdom with us. The people on the following list are specialists in particular problems. They were able to supply answers when nobody else could, and we are deeply indebted to them for their contribution to *The Ortho Home Gardener's Problem Solver*.

Dr. Maynard Cummings
Extension Wildlife Specialist
University of California, Davis

Phil Horne
Mosley Nurseries
Lake Worth, FL

Joseph R. Konwinski
Turfgrass Consultant
Lake Worth, FL

Dr. Lloyd A. Lider
Professor of Viticulture
University of California, Davis

Dr. Wayne S. Moore
Entomologist
Berkeley, CA

John Pehrson
Extension Agent
Parlier, CA

Warren G. Roberts
U.C. Davis Arboretum Superintendent
University of California, Davis

Donald Rosedale
Cooperative Extension Service
University of California, Riverside

Dr. Terrel P. Salmon
Extension Wildlife Specialist
University of California, Davis

Ross R. Sanborn
University of California
Farm Advisor
Contra Costa County, CA

Joseph Savage
Entomologist
Cooperative Extension Service
Cornell University

Arthur Slater
Senior Environmental Health and
   Safety Technologist
University of California, Berkeley

Richard Tassan
Staff Research Assistant
University of California, Berkeley

PREFACE

PHOTOGRAPHERS

We wish to thank the following photographers for their invaluable assistance in supplying these photographs.

After each photographer's name, we have listed the pages on which their photographs appear. The letter that follows the page number shows the position of the photograph on the page, from left to right. A lowercase letter "i" refers to an insert photograph.

Ralph J. Adkins: 138C, 149A, 160A, 162B, 163C, 168A, 194A, 196A, 210B, 272i, 273C, 277A, 300B, 302C

Scott T. Adkins: 281A

William W. Allen: 220B, 236B

American Phytopathological Society:
K. Hickey: 204C
A.A. MacNab: 282i
J.R. McGrew: 287A
T.B. Sutton: 217A
K. Yoder: 229A

Max E. Badgley: 25A, 130R, 140R, 196C, 208C, 230A, 253A, 253B, 278B, 286A, 292B, 307L, 309TL, 311A, 313A, 318C, 320B, 324B, 326A, 327C, 330B

Ray R. Bingham: 285C

Laurie Black: 191A, 191B

Allen Boger: 50A, 53B, 59B, 66C, 75B, 83B, 84A, 132B, 143A, 144C, 147A, 152A, 155C, 157A, 164B, 169C, 175C, 207A, 207C, 211A, 250C, 252A, 252C, 255B, 255C, 256A, 285A, 286B, 287B, 291B, 297B, 301C, 302A

R. Harper Brame: 234C, 256C, 266i, 279A

Bartow H. Bridges, Jr.: 132C, 145A, 151B, 153B, 155B, 162A, 179C

Jackie D. Butler: 51B

Ralph S. Byther: 82C, 84B, 110i, 112C, 121C, 122A, 137C, 142, 156A, 156B, 158B, 163B, 166B, 170A, 177B, 178A, 181A, 184A, 184i, 192A, 208i, 214B, 216C, 222C, 227C, 228B, 235B, 256B, 266B, 266i, 270B, 270C, 283C, 290B, 296A, 298C, 299C

Kristie Callan: 27B, 28B, 71B, 80B, 81A, 81C, 82B, 83A, 85A, 85C, 86A, 86B, 88B, 90B, 90C, 91A, 92A, 92B, 93B, 93C, 94A, 94B, 95C, 96A, 97A, 97B, 99A, 100B, 100C, 101A, 101C, 102A, 102B, 103B, 104A, 104C, 105A, 107A, 107B, 107C, 108A, 108B, 110A, 110B, 112A, 113A, 113B, 117B, 117C, 118B, 119A, 120C, 121A, 121B, 123B, 287C, 288A

Chevron Chemical Company: 55B, 60C, 259B

Dick Christman: 12, 262C, 310C

Jack K. Clark: 67C, 210C, 224i, 295i, 310B, 316C, 319C, 327A, 327B, 329A

Jack K. Clark, Bio-Tec Images: 319B

Clemson University: 278C, 315A

James S. Coartney: 23C

Sharon J. Collman: 56C, 65, 82A, 92C, 105C, 135C, 137A, 139B, 139C, 143B, 144A, 144B, 146C, 148B, 148C, 153A, 166C, 167B, 167C, 182B, 183B, 184C, 190A, 191C, 205B, 301B

Alan Copeland: 26B

David M. Coppert: 254C

Larry Costello: 40

Samuel Cotner: 260A, 274A, 275C, 276C, 282A, 282B, 284B, 294i

Rosalind Creasy: 244

David J. Cross: 325C

J.A. Crozier: 42R, 56i, 58B, 61A, 69C, 69i, 116C, 137B, 170C, 192B, 204B, 259C, 272B, 272C, 296C, 305B

Maynard W. Cummings: 205C, 226B, 315C, 316B, 317B, 317C

Margery Daughtrey: 100A, 102C, 116A

The Davey Tree Expert Company: 56A, 149B, 185C, 185i

Spencer H. Davis, Jr.: 114B, 122B, 125, 149A, 164C, 167A, 173B, 178B, 179i

Jim DeFilippis: 135A, 209B, 224B

August A. De Hertogh: 111C

James F. Dill: 153C, 158A, 164A, 173A, 176B, 177C, 180C, 181C, 207B, 217B, 252B, 259A, 260B, 263C, 263i, 264C, 270A, 272A, 275B, 277B, 279i, 281C, 282C, 295A, 296B, 303A, 303C, 313B, 313C, 320C, 321C, 324C, 325B, 331B

Michael A. Dirr: 119B, 133B, 165C, 183C, 189A, 197C

Walter Ebeling: 314A, 320A, 321i, 322C, 328A, 329C

C.W. Ellett: 160B

C.L. Elmore: 5, 41B, 44, 57C, 58A

Thomas E. Eltzroth: 78, 127, 202T, 238, 241T, 245, 247

Barbara H. Emerson: 60B, 64

Derek Fell: 36, 38L, 38R, 39, 79, 124

James Feucht: 24B, 68B, 89A, 91C, 101B, 109C, 110C, 115A, 134B, 134C, 150C, 154B, 158C, 168C, 180B, 185A, 186C, 187B, 193B, 193C, 197A, 211B, 261A, 282i, 302B, 316A, 318A, 325A

Charles Marden Fitch: 24A

Paul F. Frese: 114C

Mal Furniss: 179B

Raymond J. Gill: 25B

David Goldberg: 19, 20L, 20R, 21, 34T, 74T, 75T, 77, 198, 240R, 248, 306

Pete Gumas/Sierra Sod and Supply Co., Davis, CA: 35

John E. Hafernik, Jr.: 312C

Dennis H. Hall: 263B, 268C, 283B, 283i, 300A, 304A

PREFACE

Sherman V. Thomson: 89C, 160i, 161B, 178i, 206C, 231A

USDA: 276B, 328B

USDA Forest Service, Southern Forest Experiment Station: 321A, 322A, 322B

University of California: 60A, 188B, 212C, 217C, 232B, 294i, 331C

University of California, Berkeley, Co-operative Extension: 70C, 159C, 172C, 180A, 187C, 299B

University of California, Riverside, Cooperative Extension: 297A

University of Illinois, Champaign-Urbana: 30C, 106C, 122i

Van Waters & Rogers: 131B, 308L, 309BL, 309C, 318B, 324A, 329B

Wolf von dem Bussche: 63

George Waters: 128B

John A. Weidhaas, Jr.: 173C, 187A

Ron West: 1229, 199, 200R, 201, 307R, 308BR, 309R

Robert L. Wick: 162C

John A. Wott: 87B, 141A

Thomas A. Zitter: 275i

TABLE OF CONTENTS

SOLVING PLANT PROBLEMS

The Ortho Home Gardener's Problem Solver is designed to help you diagnose a problem with a plant, then provide potential solutions to that problem.

Diagnosing such problems requires careful observation of the plants and their environment. The key to an accurate diagnosis is knowing how to look for clues to a problem and the type of clues to look for. The checklist on the following two pages gives a step-by-step procedure for gathering clues and diagnosing a problem. The list will help you develop a case history, eliminate unlikely causes of the symptoms, and find the real cause.

HOW TO OBSERVE

Begin your observations by examining the plant from a distance. Note its general condition. Is the entire plant affected, or only a few stems, branches, or leaves? If the entire plant shows symptoms, the cause will probably be found on the trunk or roots or in the soil. Look for patterns and relationships with other plants. Is the problem confined to the sunny side of the plant? Is only the young growth affected? Are many sick plants clustered in one spot? Locate a part of the plant that shows obvious symptoms and take a closer look. Mottled or discolored leaves may indicate an insect or disease problem. A 5- to 15-power hand lens will allow you to see insects or fungus spores that are not easily visible to the naked eye.

If the initial inspection does not reveal any obvious reason for the symptoms, developing a case history for the plant may lead you to a less conspicuous cause of the problem. What has the weather been like recently? Has the temperature been fluctuating drastically? What kind of winter was it? For tress and shrubs, an unusually dry, cold winter can cause dieback that may not become apparent until new growth begins in spring.

Consider the recent care of the plant. Has it received water and fertilizer regularly? All plants require fertilizer. Without regular feeding, their leaves turn yellow and growth is poor.

When you are observing the area around the plant, be aware of changes in the environment. Construction around established plants can be damaging to them, although symptoms of decline may not appear for several years. Drastic changes in light—caused by moving a houseplant from a sunny window to a dark corner or pruning a fruit tree severely, for example—may cause problems that appear many days later.

You may have to dig into the plant or the soil to find the cause of the problem. If there is a hole in a stem, cut into it. Or slice off a piece of bark from a wilting branch to determine whether the wood is discolored or healthy.

The only way to learn about the roots of sick plants is to dig up a small plant or to carefully dig a hole to examine the roots of a large plant. The key to a root problem may be the soil. Investigate the drainage, probe the soil with a soil auger to determine the soil depth and the type of soil, or test the pH of the soil with a soil-testing kit. Look at all sides of the question and explore each clue.

Particular types of plants are susceptible to typical problems at certain times of the year. For example, cherries are usually plagued with fruit flies in the spring, when the fruit is ripening, and snapdragons are most likely to be infected with rust in spring and summer, when the weather is warm and moisture is present.

PUTTING IT ALL TOGETHER

After studying the ailing plant or plants, read the introduction to the pertinent chapter in this book. The introduction may contain information that relates directly to your problem or give you a tip about where to look next. Then look through the general problem headings at the tops of the pages of the problem-solution section for that chapter. Find the heading that applies to your problem, then look for your specific plant and see if its problem is listed. If you know the name of your plant, the problem it has, or the insect that is bothering it, you can look up the name in the index at the back of the book. For uncommon problems, you may want to refer to *The Ortho Problem Solver*—found in many nurseries and in garden and home improvement centers—but these pages will discuss most of the problems you will encounter.

When you are reading about a plant problem in the *The Ortho Home Gardener's Problem Solver*, read carefully. Every word and phrase is important for understanding the nature of the problem. "May" means that the symptom develops only sometimes. And certain phrases offer clues about the problem, such as the time of year to expect it ("In spring to midsummer . . .") and where to look for the symptom (" . . . on the undersides of the leaves").

Unfortunately, plants frequently develop more than one problem at a time. When a plant is weakened by diseases or insects, its defenses are lowered and other problems are able to affect it. For instance, borers are often responsible for a tree's decline but are seldom a serious problem on healthy trees. A borer problem may indicate another problem, such as a recent severe winter or root rot.

A hand lens is useful for finding and identifying the pests that harm the plants in your garden.

THE CHECKLIST

Use this checklist to help develop a case history for the problem and to identify symptoms that will lead to an accurate diagnosis. Answer each question that pertains to your plant carefully and thoroughly. When looking for symptoms and answering questions about the condition of the plant, begin with the leaves, flowers, or fruit (unless it is apparent that the problem is elsewhere), because they are the easiest to examine. Once you've eliminated those possibilities, move down the plant to the stems, or branches and trunk. Inspect the roots after all other possibilities have been rejected.

INFORMATION ABOUT THE PLANT

	WHAT TO LOOK FOR
Kind of plant	☐ What type of plant is it?
	☐ Does it prefer moist or dry conditions?
	☐ Can it tolerate cold or does it grow best in a warm climate?
	☐ Does the plant grow best in acid or alkaline soil?
Age	☐ Is the plant young and tender, or old and in a state of decline?
Size	☐ Is the plant abnormally small for its age?
	☐ How much has the plant grown in the last few years?
	☐ Is the size of the trunk or stem in proportion to the number of branches?
Time in present site	☐ Was the plant recently transplanted?
	☐ Has it had time to become established, or is it still in a state of shock from transplanting?
	☐ Is the plant much older than the housing development or buildings nearby?
Symptom development	☐ When were the symptoms first noticed?
	☐ Have symptoms been developing for a long period of time, or have they appeared suddenly?
Condition of plant	☐ Is the entire plant affected, is the problem found on only one side of the plant, or are symptoms scattered throughout the plant?
	☐ What part or parts of the plant are affected?
	☐ Are all of the leaves affected, or only the leaves on a few branches?
	☐ Are the leaves abnormal in size, color, shape, or texture?
	☐ Do the flowers and fruit show symptoms?

	WHAT TO LOOK FOR
Condition of plant	☐ Are there any abnormal growths, discolorations, or injuries on the branches, stems, or trunk?
	☐ Is there anything wrapped around and girdling the plant or nailed into the wood?
	☐ Does the trunk have a normal flare at the base, or is it constricted or entering the ground straight like a pole?
	☐ If the entire plant is affected, what do the roots look like? Are they white and healthy, or are they discolored? (Use a trowel to dig around the roots of large plants; pull up small, sick plants to investigate the roots; and examine roots of container plants by removing the container.) Is the bark brown and decayed?
	☐ Have the roots remained in the soil ball, or have they grown into the surrounding soil?
	☐ Are there insects on the plant, or is there evidence of insects, such as holes, droppings, sap, or sawdustlike material?
	☐ What other symptoms are visible on the plant?
	☐ Has the problem appeared in past years?

SOLVING PLANT PROBLEMS

PLANT ENVIRONMENT

	WHAT TO LOOK FOR		WHAT TO LOOK FOR
Location of property	☐ Is the property near a large body of fresh or salt water?	Soil conditions	☐ Is the soil hard and compacted?
	☐ Is the property located downwind from a factory, or is it in a large polluted urban area?		☐ Has the soil eroded away from around the roots? (For information about erosion, see the Controlling Erosion section of the "Vegetables, Berries, and Grapes" introductory text.)
	☐ Is the property part of a new housing development that was built on land fill?	Soil coverings	☐ Is there asphalt, cement, or other solid surface covering the soil around the plant? How close is it to the base of the plant? How long has it been there?
Location of plant	☐ Is the plant growing next to a building?		
	If so, is the location sunny or shady? Is the wall of the building light in color? How intense is the reflected light?		☐ Has the soil surface been mulched or covered with crushed rock?
	☐ Has there been any construction, trenching, or grade change nearby within the past several years?		☐ Was the mulch obtained from a reputable dealer?
	☐ Have there been any natural disturbances?		☐ Are weeds or grass growing around the base of the plant? How thickly?
	☐ How close is the plant to a road? Is the road de-iced in the winter?	Recent care	☐ Has the plant or surrounding plants been fertilized or watered recently? (For information about fertilizers and watering, see the Providing Fertilizer and Watering sections of the "Vegetables, Berries, and Grapes" introductory text.)
	☐ Is the plant growing over or near a gas, water, or sewer line, or next to power lines?		
	☐ Is the ground sloping or level?		
Relationship to other plants	☐ Are there large shade trees overhead?		
	☐ Is the plant growing in a lawn or ground cover?		☐ If fertilizer was used, was it applied according to label directions?
	☐ Are there plants growing nearby that are also affected? Do the same species show similar symptoms? Are unrelated plants affected? How close by are they?		☐ Has the plant or the area been treated with a fungicide or insecticide?
			☐ Was the treatment for this problem or another one?
Weather	☐ Have you had unusual weather conditions recently (cold, hot, dry, wet, windy, snowy, etc.), or in the past few years?		☐ Was the pesticide registered for use on the plant (is the plant listed on the product label)?
Microclimate	☐ What are the weather conditions in the immediate vicinity of the plant?		☐ Was the pesticide applied according to label directions?
	☐ Is the plant growing under something that prevents it from receiving moisture?		☐ Did it rain right after spraying, so the spray was washed off?
	☐ How windy is the location?		☐ Did you repeat the spray if the label suggested it?
	☐ How much light is the plant receiving? Is it the optimum amount for the type of plant? (For information about supplying extra light to houseplants, see the Providing Light section of the "House-plants" introductory text.)		☐ Have weed killers (herbicides) or lawn weed and feeds been used in the area in the past year? How close by? (For information about applying herbicides, see the Using Chemical Controls section of the "Lawns" introductory text.)
Soil conditions	☐ What kind of soil is the plant growing in? Is it clayey, sandy, or loamy?		☐ Did you spray on a windy day?
	☐ How deep is the soil? Is there a layer of rock or hardpan beneath the topsoil? (For information about hardpan, see the Hole Preparation section of the "Trees, Shrubs, and Vines" introductory text.)		☐ Has the plant been pruned heavily, exposing shaded areas to full sun?
			☐ Were stumps left after pruning, or was the bark damaged during the pruning process? (For information about pruning, see ORTHO's book *All About Pruning*.)
	☐ What is the pH of the soil? (For information about testing the soil for pH, see the Assessing and Improving Soil section of the "Annuals, Perennials, and Bulbs" introductory text.)		
	☐ Does the soil drain well, or does the water remain on the surface after a heavy rain or irrigation? Does the soil have a sour smell?		

GLOSSARY OF HORTICULTURAL TERMS

Abscission   A natural dropping of leaves, flowers, and other plant parts.

Acaricide   A chemical that kills spider mites and other types of mites. Acaricides are also known as miticides.

Acid soil   Soils with a pH below 7.0. Acid soils can cause problems when their pH is below 5.5. For more information about acid soils, see page 76.

Adventitious   Plant parts that form in unusual locations. For example, roots that grow from leaves or aboveground stems.

Aeration   To increase the amount of air space in the soil by tilling or otherwise loosening the soil.

Algae   Simple plants without visible structure that grow in wet locations. Some types of algae form a slippery black or green scum on wet soil, plants, walkways, and other surfaces.

Alkaline soil   Soil with a pH above 7.0. Alkaline soils slow the growth of many plants when their pH is above 8.0. For more information about alkaline soils, see page 76.

Annual plant   A plant that grows, flowers, produces seeds or fruit, and dies in a year or less. Many herbaceous flowers and vegetables are annual plants.

Axil   The location on a stem between the upper surface of a leaf or leafstalk and the stem from which it is growing.

Axillary buds   Buds that form in leaf axils.

Balled and burlapped plants   Trees and shrubs that are dug out of the ground with the intact soil ball surrounding the roots; the soil ball is then wrapped in burlap or plastic.

Bare-root plants   Trees and shrubs that are dug out of the ground and sold with their roots bare of soil. Roses and fruit trees are commonly sold in this manner. Bare-root plants are available in the winter.

Biennial plant   A plant that grows, flowers, produces seeds or fruit, and dies in two years. Some herbaceous flowers and vegetables are biennial. Most biennial plants produce foliage the first year and bloom the second year.

Bolting   Rapid development of flowers and seedheads in vegetables. Premature bolting may be stimulated by hot weather, drought, or lack of nutrients.

Bract   A modified leaf that is sometimes brightly colored, resembling a petal.

Bud   A condensed shoot consisting mainly of undeveloped tissue. Buds are often covered with scales, and develop into leaves, flowers, or both.

Callus   A mass of cells, often barklike in appearance, that forms over wounded plant tissue.

Cambium   A thin ring of tissue within the stem, branch, and trunk that continually forms nutrient and water-conducting vessels.

Canker   A discolored lesion that forms in stems, branches, or trunks as a result of infection. Cankers are often sunken, and may exude a thick sap. For more information about cankers, see page 127.

Chlorophyll   The green plant pigment that is necessary for photosynthesis.

Chlorosis   Yellowing of foliage due to a loss or breakdown of chlorophyll. Chlorosis may result from disease or infestation, poor growing conditions, or lack of nutrients.

Cold frame   A protective structure that uses the sun's energy to provide heat for plants. Plants may be grown in cold frames early in the spring before all danger of freezing is past.

Complete fertilizer   A fertilizer containing nitrogen, phosphorus, and potassium, the three nutrients in which plants are most commonly deficient.

Compost   Partially decomposed organic matter used to amend the soil. Compost is often made from grass clippings, leaves, and manure.

Conifers   Woody trees and shrubs that produce cones. Common conifers include pines, firs, spruces, junipers, redwood, and hemlocks.

Conks   Mushroomlike fruiting bodies of several different kinds of tree-decaying fungi.

Corm   A short, solid, enlarged, underground stem from which roots grow. Corms are food-storage organs. They contain one bud that will produce a new plant.

Dead-heading   The removal of old blossoms to encourage continued bloom or to improve the appearance of the plant.

Deciduous   Plants that shed all of their leaves annually, usually in the fall.

Defoliation   Leaf drop that often results from infection, infestation, or adverse environmental conditions.

Desiccation   Dehydration or loss of water.

Dormant   A state of rest and reduced metabolic activity in which plant tissues remain alive but do not grow.

Dormant oil   Oil sprayed on deciduous trees while they are dormant. Dormant oils are used to kill overwintering insects or insect eggs on plant bark.

Espalier   To train a plant (usually a tree or vine) along a railing or trellis so that the branches grow flat against the rail or trellis that supports them.

Evergreen   A plant that retains all or most of its foliage throughout the year.

Fasciation   An abnormal fusion of stems, leaves, or flowers, or the production of distorted growth.

Fertilizers   These substances contain plant nutrients. Fertilizers may be liquid or dry, and may be formulated in many different ways. For more information about fertilizers, see pages 21, 77, 125, and 242.

Formulation   The form in which a compound may be produced. For example, a pesticide may be powdered, liquid, granular, or in an oil solution.

GLOSSARY OF HORTICULTURAL TERMS

Frass   Sawdustlike insect excrement.

Fruiting body   A fungal structure that produces spores.

Fungicide   A chemical that kills fungi or prevents them from infecting healthy plant tissue.

Galls   Abnormal growths that form on plant roots, shoots, and leaves. Galls often result from infection or insect infestation. For more information about galls, see page 129.

Germination   The sprouting of seeds.

Girdle   Encircling of plant roots, stems, trunks, or branches resulting in a constriction of the plant part, or a reduction of water and nutrient flow through the girdled plant part.

Graft   To unite a stem or bud of one plant to a stem or root of another plant.

Gummosis   Oozing of plant sap, often from a plant wound or canker. Gummosis may occur as a result of infection or insect infestation.

Hardening off   The process of plant adjustment to cold temperatures.

Hardiness   The ability of a plant to withstand cold temperatures.

Heartwood   The inner core of wood inside a woody stem or trunk.

Herbaceous   Plants that are mainly soft and succulent, forming little or no woody tissue.

Herbicide   A chemical that kills or retards plant growth. Herbicides may kill the entire plant; or they may kill only the aboveground plant parts, leaving the roots alive.

Host   An organism that is parasitized by another organism, such as a plant that is infected by a fungus, or infested by an aphid.

Humidity   The amount of water vapor (moisture) in the air.

Hybrid   The offspring of two distinct plant species; a plant obtained by crossing two or more different species, subspecies, or varieties of plant. Hybrids are often made to produce a plant that has the best qualities of each parent.

Immune   A plant that is not susceptible to a disease or insect.

Infiltration (soil)   The process by which water moves into the soil.

Insecticide   A chemical that kills insects.

Internode   The section of stem between two nodes.

Interveinal   Between the (leaf) veins. Interveinal yellowing, or chlorosis, refers to a discoloration occurring between the leaf veins.

Juvenile   An early growth phase differentiated from later growth by a distinctly different leaf shape, habit of growth, or other characteristics.

Larva   An immature stage through which some types of insects must pass before developing into adults. Caterpillars are the larvae of moths and butterflies, and grubs are the larvae of beetles. Larvae are typically wormlike in appearance.

Lateral bud   A bud forming along the side of a stem or branch rather than at the end.

Leaching   The removal of salts and soluble minerals from the soil by flushing the soil with water.

Leader   The main stems or trunk of a tree or shrub from which side stems or branches are produced.

Leaf margins   The edges of a leaf. Variations in the shape of leaf margins are used to help identify many plants and differentiate among them.

Leaf scar   The tiny scar left on a twig or stem after a leaf or leafstalk (petiole) drops off.

Leafstalk   A stalk that attaches a leaf to the stem; a petiole.

Lesion   A wound, discoloration, or scar caused by disease or injury.

Macronutrients   Nutrients required by plants for normal growth. Macronutrients such as nitrogen, phosphorus, and potassium are needed in large quantities by most plants.

Metamorphosis   Changes in body shape undergone by many insects as they develop from eggs into adults.

Microclimate   The environment immediately surrounding a plant; very localized climate conditions. Many different microclimates may occur at the same time in different areas of a garden.

Micronutrients   Nutrients required by plants for normal growth. Micronutrients (also called minor nutrients) such as iron, zinc, and manganese are needed in small quantities by most plants.

Mites   A group of tiny animals related to spiders, many of which feed on plants.

Mulch   A layer of organic or inorganic material on the soil surface. Mulches help to moderate the temperature of the soil surface, reduce loss of moisture from the soil, suppress weed growth, and reduce run-off. For more information about mulches, see page 244.

Mycelium   Microscopic fungal strands that form the major part of a fungal growth.

Nematode   Microscopic worms that live in the soil and feed on plant roots. Some nematodes feed on plant stems and leaves.

Node   The part of a stem where leaves and buds are attached.

Nymph   An immature stage through which some types of insects must pass before developing into adults. Nymphs usually resemble the adult form, but lack wings and cannot reproduce.

Oedema   Watery blisters or swellings that form on many herbaceous plants. These swellings may burst open, forming rust-colored lesions.

Organic matter   A substance derived from plant or animal material. For more information about organic matter, see page 33.

Ozone   A common air pollutant that may cause plant injury. For more information about ozone, see page 125.

Palisade cells   A layer of columnar cells located just beneath the upper surface of a leaf.

PAN (peroxyacetyl nitrate)   A common air pollutant that may cause plant injury. For more information about PAN, see page 125.

Parasite   An organism that obtains its food from another living organism. Parasites live on or in their host.

Pathogen An organism (such as a fungus, bacterium, or virus) capable of causing a disease.

Peat Partially degraded vegetable matter found in marshy areas. Peat is commonly used as a soil amendment.

Perennial plant A plant that lives for more than 2 years, often living for many years. Almost all woody plants and many herbaceous plants are perennials.

Permanent wilting point The point of soil dryness at which plants can no longer obtain water from the soil. Once plants have reached the permanent wilting point they do not recover, even if they are supplied with water.

Pesticide A chemical used to kill an organism considered a pest.

Petiole A stalk that attaches the leaf to the stem; a leafstalk.

pH A measure of the acidity or alkalinity of a substance; a measure of the relative concentration of hydrogen ions and hydroxyl ions. For more information about pH, see page 75.

Phloem Nutrient-conducting vessels found throughout the plant. Phloem vessels transport nutrients produced in the foliage down through the stems, branches, or trunk to the roots.

Photosynthesis The process by which plants use the sun's light to produce food (carbohydrates).

Plant disease Any condition that impairs the normal functioning and metabolism of a plant. A plant disease may be caused by a fungus, bacterium, or virus, or by an environmental factor such as lack of nutrients or sunburn.

Propagation Means of reproducing plants, such as by seeds, cuttings, budding, or grafting.

Protectant A chemical that protects a plant from infection or infestation.

Pupa An immature resting stage through which some types of insects must pass before becoming adults.

Resistant plant A plant that can overcome the effects of a disease or an insect infestation, or a plant that is not very susceptible to attack by a pathogen.

Rhizome An underground stem from which roots grow. Rhizomes function as storage organs, and may be divided to produce new plants.

Rootstock 1. The roots and crown, or roots, crown, and trunk of a plant upon which another plant is grafted. 2. The crown and roots of some types of perennial herbaceous plants, also known as rhizomes.

Root zone The volume of soil that contains the roots of a plant.

Runners Aboveground, trailing stems that form roots at their nodes when they make contact with moist soil.

Sapwood The outer cylinder of wood in a trunk between the heartwood and the bark.

Saturated soil Soil that is so wet that all the air pores in the soil are filled with water.

Sclerotium A compact mass of fungal strands (mycelium) that functions as a resting stage for a fungus. Sclerotia are usually brown or black, and can usually withstand adverse conditions.

Slow-release fertilizers Fertilizers that release their nutrients into the soil slowly and evenly, over a long period of time.

Soil heaving Expansion and contraction of soil during periods of freezing and thawing. Plant roots may be sheared off, or plants may be lifted out of the ground during soil heaving.

Solubility The degree to which a compound will dissolve in water. Compounds with high solubility will dissolve in water more readily than compounds with low solubility.

Soluble fertilizers Fertilizers that dissolve easily in water and are immediately available for plant use.

Spore A microscopic structure produced by fungi, mosses, and ferns that can germinate to form a new plant or a different stage of the same plant.

Spur A short lateral branch bearing buds that will develop into flowers and then into fruit.

Stomates Tiny pores located mainly on the undersides of leaves. Oxygen, carbon dioxide, water vapor, and other gases move in and out of the leaf through these pores.

Sucker A shoot or stem that grows from an underground plant part.

Surfactant A substance added to a spray that increases its wetting and spreading properties (also called wetting agents or spreader-stickers).

Systemic pesticide A pesticide that is absorbed into part or all of the plant tissue.

Tender plant A plant that cannot tolerate freezing temperatures.

Terminal bud A bud at the end of a stem or branch.

Toxin A poisonous substance produced by a plant or an animal.

Translocation The movement of a compound from one location in a plant to another.

Transpiration Evaporation of water from plant tissue to the atmosphere. Transpiration occurs mainly through the stomates in the leaves.

Vascular system The system of tissues (phloem and xylem) that conducts nutrients and water throughout the plant.

Vein clearing A lightening or total loss of color of leaf veins. This often results from plant infection or nutrient deficiency.

Vernalization A cooling period required by many plants in order to germinate, grow, or flower properly.

Vigor The health of a plant. A vigorous plant grows rapidly and produces healthy, normal amounts of foliage and flowers. A nonvigorous plant grows slowly, if at all, and produces stunted, sparse growth.

Wetting agent A substance that changes the surface tension of water or other liquid, causing it to wet a repellent surface more thoroughly. Wetting agents are often used when spraying pesticides on waxy or fuzzy foliage.

Xylem Water-conducting vessels found throughout the plant. Xylem vessels transport water and minerals from the roots upward through the plant.

HOUSEPLANTS

When a houseplant stops blooming or drops its leaves, the home gardener may be tempted to discard the plant rather than seek out the problem. Bud failure or leaf drop may be due to low temperature, poor soil, drafts, lack of fertilizer, too much or too little water, or too much or too little light. All these problems may be correctable. Saving the plant is entirely possible.

PURCHASING HOUSEPLANTS

When you go to a nursery or garden center to buy a houseplant, you want a specimen that is appropriate for the conditions you can provide. And, of course, you want a healthy plant that is pest-free.

Appropriate Plants

The most important factor in choosing an appropriate species is the amount of light it will receive in your home. To learn how to evaluate indoor lighting, read the section called Providing Light, which appears later in this chapter. Note whether the proposed growing area receives bright, medium, or low light. Take a houseplant reference book with you when you shop, or make sure your nursery has references available on-site. Look up your intended purchase to see whether the site can provide the light the plant needs. Flowering plants and cacti need the most sunlight. Pothos, cast-iron plants, and some ivies grow slowly but well in indirect light. Prima donnas such as orchids and gesneriads have specific light requirements for optimum bloom; make sure your site can meet their needs before selecting such plants.

Healthy Plants

How can you tell if a plant is healthy? The leaves of a healthy plant are green unless they are naturally variegated or multicolored, as are some pothos, Chinese evergreens, zebra plants, and others. Unhealthy leaves may have tips or edges that look burnt, brown spots, or a yellowish cast. Unhealthy leaves may appear crumpled or tend to droop. Readily apparent leaf problems can be due to

powdery mildew, aphids, whiteflies, spider mites, or other insects. Inspect leaf undersides and leaf-to-stem junctions for signs of disease or insects. Of the plants that appear healthy, select the most compact and fully leafed.

When buying a flowering plant for indoor use, look for a specimen with ample buds as well as flowers. Minimal buds on a plant usually mean it has passed the peak of blooming; it will be another year before it blooms copiously again. A plant with many buds will be colorful throughout the current season. If you find a sturdy, well-budded plant with some flowers, give it a gentle shake. If many flowers drop off, the plant has been subjected to severe stress. Select a healthier specimen.

After bringing your purchase home, set it off by itself for about a week. Even though you did not see any insect pests, the plant may harbor insect eggs, which are microscopic. Check the plant carefully after the quarantine period. If you see even a few insects, treat the new plant with insecticide before placing it near any other plant.

PURCHASING THE PERFECT POT

Among the many choices available for indoor plant potting are unglazed clay, plastic, and glazed ceramic in designs to match every decor.

A clay pot is especially appropriate on a porch or in a rustic atmosphere. Since moisture evaporates quickly through clay pot sides, use clay pots as containers for

plants such as succulents, which tolerate dryness. If you place other types of plants in clay pots, they will need more moisture than normal. Since water tends to seep through clay pot bottoms, place a nonporous saucer underneath to prevent rug or counter stains.

Plastic pots have the advantage of being lightweight and are often used for hanging plants. Plastic pots hold water longer than clay pots, so be careful not to overwater. Many plastic pots are sold with removable saucers underneath.

Glazed ceramic pots are as effective in water control as plastic pots. However, many ceramic pots do not have drainage holes, a deficiency that can cause overwatering. Place a plastic pot with drainage saucer inside the glazed pot.

PROVIDING SOIL

In nature, plant roots can spread out to seek nutrients. In a pot, what's there is what the plant gets. If vitamins and minerals are lacking, the plant fails to thrive. Nutrients are as important to the plant as adequate light and sufficient moisture.

Most houseplants can thrive in all-purpose potting soil. Fussier plants, such as African violets, may grow better in a commercial potting soil formulated especially for the species. Other types of commercial soils are formulated for specific situations—for example, terrariums. Soilless growing mediums are also available.

You can make your own potting mix, using varying proportions of garden soil, sand, peat moss, vermiculite, and leaf

Opposite: Houseplants can be an appealing and inexpensive decor for any room. Here, lace-cap hydrangea, palms, English ivy, and a pelargonium fill the room with color and interest.
Right: Select a plant with a profusion of buds, rather than blooms, to provide color for weeks to come.

Pots are made of many sorts of materials. Make sure your watering routine suits the pot you've chosen for your plant.

mold. Without a dependable means of sterilization, however, the gardener who uses homemade potting mix runs the risk of bringing in pests and disease. Commercial potting soil is inexpensive, convenient, and thoroughly sterilized.

PROVIDING WATER

Water causes more plant problems than any other single factor. These problems include overwatering, underwatering, and using inappropriate water techniques or tainted water.

Too Much Water

A water overdose without adequate drainage rots roots slowly but steadily, causing plant death. One sign of overwatering is green moss that grows on the surface of the soil. Plant symptoms include lower leaf wilting, faded leaf colors, and poor growth. The lower portion of the plant's main stem, right above the soil line, may darken. Roots are brown and mushy.

If damage has not totally destroyed the roots, rescue attempts can include removing standing water, trimming brown roots, and repotting the plant in good soil. An alternative is to take cuttings from healthy stems and start over again.

Too Little Water

Many gardeners worry so much about overwatering that they underwater. A water-stressed plant conserves moisture by slowing or stopping new growth. Without adequate water, green leaves turn dull green or yellow. Drooping

occurs. If buds are present, they may fall off.

When to water? Poke your finger about ½ inch into the potting soil. It should feel moist but not wet. If it feels dry or barely moist, water immediately and thoroughly. Ensure drainage, or standing water will turn the underwatering problem into a case of overwatering.

Watering Techniques and Tainted Water

Water most houseplants from the top. Within an hour pour off excess water from the saucer underneath the pot.

Most drinkable tap water is adequate for plants. Use it at room temperature. The sodium in some types of artificially softened water can prove a problem, however, if used consistently over a long period. Some tap water may also contain salts, which accumulate quickly in plant containers. Salt damage is evidenced by brown leaftips or edges. Damage occurs on older leaves first, and affected leaves eventually die. The plant may also be stunted, with brittle leaves that curl downward. An accumulation or overdose of fertilizer salts causes similar damage. If you see symptoms of salt accumulation, flush the plant thoroughly with water. If salts are built up on the rim or at the soil line in the pot, repot the plant in fresh soil to dilute salt levels.

Some gardeners collect rainwater for indoor plant use. Rainwater may carry pollutants, depending on where you live. In a pot, pollutants may accumulate quickly and deter plant growth.

PROVIDING LIGHT

The secret to providing appropriate light is to match the plant to the site.

Site Evaluation

How do you evaluate light? During prime light time, place a sheet of white paper on the table or sill where a plant will reside. Hold your hand about 12 inches above the paper. If a clearly defined dark shadow results, the site receives bright light. If a muted but clearly definable shadow results, the light is medium. If your hand shadow is barely visible, the amount of light is low. Make sure any plants you purchase can prosper in the lighting conditions you can provide.

Symptoms of Inappropriate Light

Inadequate lighting produces a leggy, weak plant that may suddenly drop its leaves. Growth slows. The lower leaves turn a lighter green, and the plant does not flower. Plants lean toward the light source; rotating the plants regularly prevents sideways growth.

An African violet that does not bloom is probably not receiving enough light. These plants require about 12 hours of bright light daily.

Although most complaints are about insufficient light, some rooms are too sunny. Dry patches on leaves may be symptoms of sunburn. If the site gets hot enough, buds and flowers drop off and the entire plant may wilt. To prevent further damage, try moving the plant away from the window; shading the window with filmy curtains; or replacing the plant with a heat-tolerant species, such as a cactus.

Cacti are the plants of choice for sunny locations. Watering them once a week will do, except when you want them to flower. Do not allow cacti to dry out totally during the flowering season.

The strong shadow indicates that this location is receiving bright light.

Artificial Light

In sites that receive little sun, artificial light may be the only answer. Fluorescent bulbs and incandescent bulbs provide different types of light. Cool-white fluorescent bulbs give off little heat. They do not bake the moisture out of plants, even if placed within 4 inches of the foliage. With adequate fluorescent lighting, you need no outdoor light; you could grow plants in a closet if you provided a fan for air circulation.

To help support plant growth with incandescent light, you must use a bulb of at least 100 watts. Such a bulb produces a lot of heat; keep incandescent light at least 2 feet above plant tops to keep from burning the foliage and baking the soil.

PROVIDING FERTILIZER

Outdoors, soil is constantly improved with leaf mold, earthworm castings, decaying plants, and animal droppings. Indoors, once a plant has used up the nutrients in the pot, there's nowhere for it to get more unless the gardener adds some type of fertilizer.

Symptoms of Nutrient Shortage

Plants quickly reflect a nutrient shortage. A nitrogen shortage shows up as yellowing leaves and poor growth. If a plant has leaves a darker green than normal, poor growth, and leaf stems with a purplish tinge, a shortage of phosphorus is probably the cause. A potassium shortage appears as yellowing leaves with brown tips and edges. A lack of iron appears as the yellowing of older leaves, on the bottom portions of stems. This yellowing starts at leaf edges and progresses inward.

Fertilizer Selection and Application

Many types of indoor plant fertilizer are available. The numbers on the container describe the relative proportions of nitrogen (N), phosphorus (P), and potassium (K). The designation "20-20-20" means the fertilizer contains equal portions of each element. A 5-10-5 mixture is higher in phosphorus than in nitrogen or potassium.

Phosphorus encourages a strong root system as well as luxuriant flowers. Potassium aids in disease resistance, promotes plant vigor, increases bloom, and

strengthens stems. Nitrogen helps make healthy green leaves. In addition, plants need trace elements, such as iron—nutrients essential, in minute amounts, for chlorophyll production and enzyme functioning. Note that plants grown in synthetic mediums, such as sand or vermiculite, need a dose of one-third-strength fertilizer with each watering, because they contain no soil nutrients.

A little bit of fertilizer may be fine, but a lot of fertilizer is almost always too much. Extra fertilizer accumulates in soil, causing tip burn or browning. Too much nitrogen causes rapid growth at the expense of plant vigor. The plant becomes large and spindly, does not set flowers, and is prone to insect invasion.

If you have applied too much fertilizer, take action quickly. Repot the plant in fresh soil or rinse and drain the current soil to wash out fertilizer residue. When applying fertilizer, always follow label instructions.

GROWING OUTDOOR PLANTS INDOORS

Outdoor potted plants purchased for indoor bloom—such as hydrangeas, chrysanthemums, hyacinths, freesias, and narcissus—may be subject to rapid bud withering if kept in areas with continual hot, dry air. Avoid placing these plants in extremely sunny kitchen windows and sites around microwaves, ovens, and heating vents.

Given appropriate light, sufficient water, and ample air circulation, outdoor plants will bloom indoors for several weeks. Dry soil during blooming season, even for a short time, can stop all future flowers, even though foliage may recuperate.

When bulbs and other basically outdoor plants cease flowering, they probably will not do so again indoors. Take them out of their pots and plant them outdoors in appropriate surroundings, however, and they will bloom normally.

Holiday plants, such as poinsettias and Christmas cacti, are reared under controlled conditions to produce blooming during specific seasons. Gardeners often expect them to bloom again next year at the same time. This will probably not happen unless light is strictly regulated.

Extended periods of light encourage foliage rather than flowers. For poinsettias and Christmas cacti to reflower, you

This Christmas cactus was forced into bloom at an unusual time of year, with spectacular results.

must provide total uninterrupted darkness during evening and night hours. After poinsettias bloom the first time, cut back stems to 8 inches long and repot the plants in fresh houseplant soil. Beginning in October, cover both poinsettias and Christmas cacti with a large carton from sundown to sunup. Remove the carton every morning. Do this until flowers appear.

Gift plants, such as azaleas, may lose their flowers quickly indoors if placed in hot direct sun. Do not let them dry out. Place them away from drafts, and keep them moist and cool. Getting azaleas to bloom indoors a second time is extremely difficult. Even with the best care, it may take several years. After the plants bloom the first time, some gardeners place them outdoors in appropriate surroundings, where the azaleas may do well. Others keep azaleas as foliage plants indoors.

Other gift plants that generally do not bloom again indoors are cineraria and cyclamen. Try placing them outdoors in good soil and growing conditions, and after the first or second spring they may surprise you with flowers.

PROBLEMS COMMON TO MANY HOUSEPLANTS

Salt damage to a spathiphyllum.

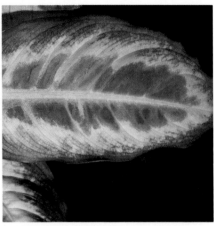

Sunburn on dieffenbachia.

PROBLEM: The leaf edges of plants with broad leaves or the leaftips of plants with long, narrow leaves turn brown and die. This browning occurs on the older leaves first, but when the condition is severe, new leaves may also be affected. Plants may be stunted, with brittle leaves that curl downward. On some plants, the older leaves may yellow and die.

ANALYSIS: Salt damage

Salt damage is a common problem on container-grown plants. Soluble salts may be dissolved in water, in the form of fertilizer, or in potting soil. The roots pick up the salts, and the veins conduct them to the foliage, where they accumulate. When concentrations become high enough, the tissues are killed. Salts build up faster and do more harm if plants are not watered thoroughly. Water high in lime does not cause as much salt damage as water that is high in other salts.

SOLUTION: Leach excess salts from the soil by flushing with water. Water thoroughly at least 3 times in a row, letting the water drain from the pot each time. This is most easily done if the pot is in the bathtub, in a basin, or outside in the shade. If you use a saucer to catch the water, empty the saucer 30 minutes after each watering. If the plant is too large to lift, empty the saucer with a turkey baster. Never let a plant stand in the drainage water.

PROBLEM: Leaf tissue exposed to direct sunlight lightens or turns gray, or dead tan or brown patches develop on leaves. In some cases, the plant remains green but growth is stunted. Damage is most severe when the plant is allowed to dry out.

ANALYSIS: Bleaching or sunburn

Bleaching or sunburn occurs when a plant is exposed to sunlight more intense than it can tolerate. Plants vary widely in their ability to tolerate direct sun. Some plants can tolerate full sunlight; others bleach or burn if exposed to any direct sun. Bleaching occurs when light and heat break down chlorophyll (green plant pigment), causing a lightening or graying of the damaged leaf tissue. On more sensitive plants or when light and heat increase in intensity, damage is more severe; plant tissues are sunburned and turn brown and die. Sometimes tissue inside the leaf is damaged, but outer symptoms do not develop. Instead, growth is stunted. Susceptibility to bleaching and sunburn increases when plants are allowed to dry out, because the normal cooling effect that results when water evaporates from leaves is reduced. Plants that are grown in conditions of little light burn easily if they are suddenly moved to a sunny location.

SOLUTION: Move plants that cannot tolerate direct sun to a shaded spot. Or cut down the intensity of light by closing the curtains when direct sun strikes the plants. To improve their appearance, prune off badly damaged leaves or trim away damaged leaf areas. Keep plants well watered.

Overwatering damage to schefflera.

Nitrogen-deficient Swedish ivy plant.

Spider mite damage to prayer plant.

PROBLEM: Plants fail to grow and may wilt. Leaves lose their glossiness and may become light green or yellow. Roots are brown and soft and do not have white tips. The soil in the bottom of the pot may be wet and have a foul odor. Plants may die.

ANALYSIS: Too much water or poor drainage

Although all parts of a plant need water to live, the roots need air as well as water. If the soil is kept too wet, the air spaces fill with water and the roots are weakened and may die. Weakened plants are susceptible to root-rotting fungi, which wet soils favor. Plants with diseased roots do not absorb as much water as they did when they were healthy, so the soil remains wet. If roots are damaged or diseased, they cannot transport the water and nutrients needed for plant growth.

SOLUTION: Discard severely wilted plants and those without white root tips. Do not water less severely affected plants until the soil is barely moist. Use a light soil with adequate drainage.

PROBLEM: The oldest leaves—usually the lower leaves—turn yellow and may drop. Yellowing starts at the leaf edges and progresses inward without producing a distinct pattern. The yellowing may progress up the plant until only the newest leaves remain green. Growth is slow, new leaves are small, and the whole plant may be stunted.

ANALYSIS: Nitrogen deficiency

Nitrogen is a nutrient that is used by the plant in large amounts and in many ways, including the production of chlorophyll (the green pigment in leaves and stems). When there is not enough nitrogen for the entire plant, it is taken from the older leaves for use in new growth. Nitrogen is easily leached from soil during regular watering. Of all the plant nutrients, it is the one most likely to be lacking in the soil.

SOLUTION: For a quick response, spray the leaves with a liquid plant food rated 23-19-17. Add a plant food fertilizer at regular intervals, as recommended on the product label.

PROBLEM: Leaves are stippled, yellowing, and dirty. Leaves may dry out and drop. There may be cobwebbing over flower buds, between leaves, on the growing points of shoots, or on the undersides of the leaves. To determine if a plant is infested with mites, hold a sheet of white paper underneath an affected leaf and tap the leaf sharply. If mites are present, minute green, red, or yellow specks the size of pepper grains will drop to the paper and begin to crawl around. The pests are easily seen against the white background.

ANALYSIS: Spider mites

These mites, related to spiders, are major pests of many houseplants. They cause damage by sucking sap from the undersides of the leaves. As a result of feeding, the green pigment (chlorophyll) disappears, producing a stippled appearance. Under warm, dry conditions, which favor mites, they can build up to tremendous numbers.

SOLUTION: Spray infested plants with a miticide containing acephate (ORTHENE®) or resmethrin, plus spray oil. Plants need to be sprayed weekly for several weeks to kill the mites as they hatch from the eggs. Isolate infested plants. To avoid introducing mites into the house, inspect newly purchased plants carefully.

PROBLEMS COMMON TO MANY HOUSEPLANTS

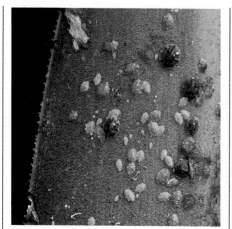

Scale on dracaena (life size).

Aphids on ivy (½ life size).

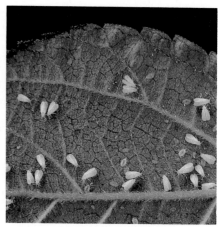

Greenhouse whiteflies (2 times life size).

PROBLEM: Nodes, stems, and leaves may be covered with white, cottony, cushion-like masses. Or portions of the plant may be covered with brown crusty bumps or clusters of somewhat flat reddish, gray, or brown scaly bumps. The bumps can be scraped or picked off easily. Leaves turn yellow and may drop. A shiny or sticky material may cover the leaves. Mold may be growing on the sticky substance.

ANALYSIS: Scale insects
Several different types of scale insect attack houseplants. Some types can infest many different plants. Scales hatch from eggs. The young, called crawlers, are small (about $\frac{1}{10}$ inch) and soft bodied, and they move about on one plant and to other plants. After crawling about for a short time, they insert their mouthparts into a plant, withdrawing the sap. At this point, crawlers' legs usually atrophy, and the scales remain in the same area for the rest of their lives. Some develop a soft covering over their bodies; others develop a hard covering. Some species are unable to digest fully all the sugar in the plant sap. They excrete the excess in a fluid called honeydew, which may cover the leaves or drip onto surfaces below.

SOLUTION: Spray with an insecticide containing acephate (ORTHENE®) or with household plant spray oils that have resmethrin added. Spraying is more effective against crawlers than against adults. Repeated applications will be necessary. Isolate infested plants. Discard badly infested plants.

PROBLEM: Leaves are curling, discolored, and reduced in size. A shiny or sticky substance may coat the leaves. Tiny ($\frac{1}{8}$-inch) nonwinged, green soft-bodied insects cluster on the buds, young stems, and leaves.

ANALYSIS: Aphids
Aphids do little damage in small numbers. However, they are extremely prolific and populations can rapidly build up to damaging numbers on houseplants. Damage occurs when the aphid sucks the juice from the leaves. The aphid is unable to digest fully all the sugar in the plant sap and excretes the excess in a fluid called honeydew, which often drops onto leaves below. Furniture below the plants may become coated with honeydew.

SOLUTION: Use an insecticide containing acephate (ORTHENE®) or resmethrin. Follow label directions.

PROBLEM: Tiny, winged insects $\frac{1}{12}$ inch long feed mainly on the undersides of leaves. Nonflying, scalelike larvae may also be present on the undersides of leaves. The insects are covered with white waxy powder. When the plant is touched, the winged bugs flutter rapidly around it. Leaves may be mottled and yellow.

ANALYSIS: Greenhouse whiteflies
(*Trialeurodes vaporariorum*)
These insects are common pests of many houseplants. The four-winged adult female lays eggs on the undersides of leaves. A larva, which is the size of a pinhead, is flat, oval, and semitransparent, with white waxy filaments radiating from the body. Larvae feed for about a month before changing into adults. Both the larval and adult forms suck sap from the leaves. The larvae are more damaging because they feed more heavily. Adults and larvae cannot fully digest all the sugar in the sap, so they excrete the excess in a fluid called honeydew, which coats the leaves and may drop from the plant. Black, brown, or white mold may grow on the honeydew.

SOLUTION: Spray with an insecticide containing acephate (ORTHENE®), insecticidal soap, or resmethrin. Make sure your plant is listed on the product label. Be sure to spray the undersides of leaves thoroughly. Spray weekly as long as the problem continues. Isolate infested plants and remove heavily infested leaves.

Citrus mealybugs on coleus (2 times life size).

Longtailed mealybugs (2 times life size).

PROBLEMS OF INDIVIDUAL HOUSEPLANTS

This section is arranged alphabetically by the botanical name of each plant.

PROBLEM: White cottony or waxy insects are on the undersides of leaves, on stems, and particularly in crotches or where leaves are attached. The insects tend to congregate, giving a cottony appearance. Cottony masses that contain the insects' eggs may also be present. A sticky substance may cover the leaves or drop onto surfaces below the plant. Infested plants are unsightly, do not grow well, and may die if severely infested.

ANALYSIS: Mealybugs

Mealybugs are one of the more serious problems of houseplants. There are many different types of mealybugs, and virtually all houseplants are attacked by one or more of them. Female mealybugs have soft bodies that appear to have segments. They are covered with waxy secretions, giving them a cottony appearance. The female may produce live young or deposit hundreds of yellow to orange eggs in white cottony egg sacs. The young insects, called nymphs, crawl about the same plant or to nearby plants. Males do no damage because they do not feed and are short-lived. Female mealybugs feed by sucking sap from the plant. They take in more than they can use and excrete the excess in a sugary fluid called honeydew, which coats the leaves and may drop to surfaces below the plant. This fluid may mar finished furniture.

SOLUTION: Control of mealybugs on houseplants is difficult. The waxy coverings on eggs and insects and mealybugs' tendency to congregate protect them from insecticides. As soon as the insects are sighted, spray with an insecticide containing acephate (ORTHENE®) or resmethrin, plus spray oil. Make sure your plant is listed on the product label. Repeat applications at intervals of 2 weeks, and continue for a little while after control seems established. Or, if only a few mealybugs are present, wipe them off with a damp cloth or use cotton swabs dipped in rubbing alcohol. Carefully check all parts of the plant to make sure all insects are removed. Search for egg sacs under the rims or bottoms of pots, in cracks or on the undersides of shelves, and on brackets or hangers. Wipe off sacs; they are a constant source of new insects. Discard severely infested plants, and avoid taking cuttings from them. With soapy water thoroughly clean the growing area before introducing new plants. Inspect new plants thoroughly before putting them in the house. Be on a constant vigil for mealybugs, and start control measures immediately if they appear.

CHLOROPHYTUM (SPIDER PLANT) ■

Dead leaftips.

Salt damage.

PROBLEM: Tips of leaves turn brown or tan. The damage spreads slowly along each leaf. Older leaves are most severely affected.

ANALYSIS: Dead leaftips
There are several reasons why spider-plant leaftips die. Frequently the problem is due to a combination of causes.
1. *Salt damage:* Salts accumulate in the soil from irrigation water or fertilizer. Excess salts are carried through the roots and stems and deposited in the tips of pointed leaves like those of spider plants. When enough salts accumulate there, the leaftip dies. Salts are taken into the plant more rapidly when the soil is dry.
2. *Too dry:* The leaftip, being farthest from the roots, is the first part of the leaf to die when the plant is not getting enough water.
3. *Toxic salts:* Some chemicals, usually in the form of soluble salts, are damaging in extremely small amounts. They accumulate in leaftips as other salts do, killing the tissue there. The most common of these chemicals are chloride and borate.

SOLUTION: Remove the dead tips by trimming the leaves to a point with a pair of scissors. Take these measures to correct the condition or control the problem.
1. Leach excess salts from the soil by flushing with water. Water the plant at least 3 times, letting the water drain through each time. This is done most easily in a bathtub or laundry sink or outside. Always water spider plants from the top of the pot. If you have placed a saucer under the pot, empty it after the pot has finished draining. If the plant is too large to lift easily, use a turkey baster to remove the drainage water. Do not overfertilize.
2. Water the plant regularly.
3. Regular tap water is not a problem for most houseplants, unless it is extremely hard (a pH of 8.0+) or run through a water softener. In that case, you may need to use distilled water on your houseplants.

Chlorophytum cultural information
Light: Medium light
Water: When soil just below surface is dry

CODIAEUM (CROTON) ■

New leaves are green.

PROBLEM: New leaves are green, instead of brightly colored. Stems may be thin and bend toward a light source. The lower leaves may drop.

ANALYSIS: Insufficient light
Plants use light as a source of energy, and they grow slowly in light that is too dim for their needs. If most of the available light is coming from one direction, the stems and leaves bend in that direction. Although foliage plants generally need less light than plants grown for their flowers or fruit, brightly colored plants like croton need fairly bright light to produce the pigments that color their leaves.

SOLUTION: Move the plant to a brighter location. A lightly curtained sunny window is ideal. If a brighter location is not available, provide supplemental lighting. Crotons may be grown outside in the summer. When moving them from indoors to outdoors, place the plants in light shade for at least 2 days before putting them in full sun. If you wish to grow a houseplant in a dim location, select a plant that is tolerant of dim light.

Codiaeum cultural information
Light: Needs bright light
Water: When top inch of soil is barely moist

CYCLAMEN

CYCLAMEN

LIGHT: Flowering plants need more light than foliage plants. To keep cyclamens in flower, place them in a south-facing window.

SOIL: Grow cyclamen in a loose, well-drained soil mix. For more information about soil mixes, see the section on Providing Soil in the introductory text for this chapter.

FERTILIZER: Once each month apply a fertilizer rated higher in nitrogen. Follow the directions on the label.

WATER:
How much: Add enough water to the pot so that a little water drains from the bottom.
How often: Water whenever the top inch of soil is slightly moist. Do not let soil get dry.

TEMPERATURE: Cyclamen continue to flower when daytime temperatures are warm and nighttime temperatures are cool. In mild climates, put plants outside at night. In areas with extremely cold winters, put plants in a cool area but do not allow them to freeze. When days and nights are warm, the leaves eventually yellow and plants stop flowering.

SPECIAL CONDITIONS: Do not allow cyclamen to become dry. In bright light, plants that are dry usually sunburn. Avoid overwatering. Cyclamen are very susceptible to root rot.

High-temperature damage.

PROBLEM: Outer leaves turn yellow. Leaves may die and turn brown, and their stems become soft. Plants stop flowering.

ANALYSIS: High temperature
Although cyclamen are cool-weather plants, they tolerate warm days as long as the nights stay below 55° F. Cool temperatures initiate flower buds. Constant high temperatures inhibit flower buds, and plants stop flowering. High temperatures also prevent the plant from growing well, causing leaves to lose their green color and die.

SOLUTION: Grow cyclamen plants in a cool room with as much light as possible. Use curtains to filter sunlight. If a cool room is not available, put them near a window at night. If temperatures are not below freezing, put the plants outside at night. When grown in warm days and cool nights, cyclamen flower for long periods. Keep plants adequately watered and fertilized.

Cyclamen mite damage.

PROBLEM: In scattered areas of the plant, leaves become curled, wrinkled, or cupped. New leaves may be more severely affected than older growth and remain small. Affected foliage may have a bronze discoloration and be severely misshapen. Flower buds are distorted, and they may drop or fail to open.

ANALYSIS: Cyclamen mites
(*Steneotarsonemus pallidus*)
These insects are extremely small mites that are related to spiders. The mites attack a number of houseplants and can be quite damaging to cyclamen. The insects' feeding injures the plant tissues, causing the leaves and flower buds to be malformed and stunted. Cyclamen mites infest new growth most heavily but do crawl to other parts of the plant or to other plants. Cyclamen mites reproduce rapidly.

SOLUTION: At intervals of 2 weeks or until new growth is no longer affected, spray plants with a miticide containing hexakis. Discard severely infested plants. Isolate houseplants showing cyclamen mite damage until the mites are under control. Closely observe plants that were exposed to the mites but seem healthy; if symptoms appear, treat the newly infested plants with a miticide. Avoid touching leaves of infested plants and then touching leaves of other plants.

Dieback caused by low humidity.

FERN

LIGHT: Ferns prefer bright, indirect light but can usually adapt to moderate light. They burn in direct sun.

SOIL: Use a standard potting mix and add an equal amount of peat moss. For information on potting mixes, see the section on Providing Soil in the introductory text for this chapter.

FERTILIZER: Apply fertilizer once a month during the growing season (early spring through late summer); use a good fish emulsion or a fertilizer rated 10-8-7.

WATER:
How much: Add enough water so that 10 percent of the water drains through the pot.
How often: Water when the top inch of soil is still moist but not wet. For additional information on watering houseplants, see the section on Providing Water in the introductory text for this chapter.

TEMPERATURE: Ferns do well in average house temperatures.

SPECIAL CONDITIONS: Ferns are sensitive to salts, and salts must be flushed from the soil with extra water. Do not let ferns stand in drainage water.

PROBLEM: Small leaves turn yellow and eventually die; large leaves may die from the tips down. The center parts of the plant are more severely affected than the outer portions.

ANALYSIS: Low humidity
Most ferns need higher humidity than homes provide. The ferns used as houseplants are adapted to forest floors and creeksides, where the air is usually moist. In the winter, when homes are heated, indoor air can become as dry as desert air. Home humidity is particularly low near heater vents or radiators. The problem is made more severe if the soil in which the fern is growing is allowed to dry out.

SOLUTION: Move the fern to a more humid location, such as a well-lighted bathroom. Place several plants together and keep them away from drafts. Misting does not help relieve stress on the fern—the mist only dampens the leaves for a few minutes at a time. Placing the plant in a tray of gravel in which some water is kept raises the humidity around the plant only if the damp air is not allowed to escape; if the air moves freely around the plant, the practice is of little value. A portable humidifier will raise the humidity in the immediate vicinity while the machine is operating. Plant ferns in a potting mix that drains quickly and contains a high proportion of organic material, such as peat moss or ground bark. Never allow the potting mix to dry out.

FICUS (ORNAMENTAL FIG)

LIGHT: Grow most ornamental fig plants in the best light available. Fiddle-leaf fig can tolerate somewhat less light.

SOIL: Any standard houseplant mix. For information on soil mixes, see the section on Providing Soil in the introductory text.

FERTILIZER: To plants in full sunlight, apply fertilizer once a month; use a good fish emulsion or a fertilizer with fairly balanced proportions. To plants in less light, apply the same fertilizer once every 2 months.

WATER:
How much: Add enough water so that some drains out the bottom of the pot.
How often: Water when soil under the surface is moist but not wet. Do not allow ornamental fig plants to dry out.
For additional information on watering houseplants, see the section on Providing Water in the introductory text for this chapter.

TEMPERATURE: Keep ornamental fig plants as warm as possible under house conditions.

SPECIAL CONDITIONS: Avoid moving plants to areas where light levels are different. Abrupt changes in light cause leaf yellowing and dropping in some species. If moving plants to different intensities of light, move them gradually into the new location to give them time to adjust.

Yellow leaves.

Leaf drop.

Virus.

PROBLEM: Leaves of weeping fig drop from many branches or, in severe cases, the entire plant. Affected leaves may be green and healthy looking or yellow and discolored.

ANALYSIS: Leaf drop

Weeping figs may drop their leaves in response to any of the following conditions.

1. *Overwatering:* When plants are watered too frequently or soil drainage is poor, the roots are susceptible to root-rotting fungi. Weak and decaying roots cannot provide enough water and nutrients for proper plant growth.

2. *Underwatering:* Weeping figs need constantly moist soil. If plants are not watered frequently enough or if the soil is not thoroughly soaked at each irrigation, they respond by dropping their leaves.

3. *Insufficient light:* Weeping figs need bright indirect light or direct sunlight for best growth. They may drop their leaves even in locations that are bright enough for most other foliage plants.

4. *Transplant shock:* Transplanting always results in some disturbance to the rootball. Weeping figs are likely to drop some leaves even when the disturbance is minimal.

5. *Changes in environment:* Drafts and extreme fluctuation in temperature, light level, and watering pattern are likely to cause leaf drop. When a greenhouse-grown plant is brought into a drier, darker, cooler home environment, it often responds by dropping many leaves.

SOLUTION: Take these measures to correct the condition or control the problem.

1. Allow the plant to dry out slightly between waterings. The soil just beneath the surface should be moist but not wet when you water. Empty the saucer after the container has drained. If the container is not draining well, choose a new container with an adequate drainage hole; add to it a light, well-draining soil mix; and transplant the weeping fig into it.

2. Check the soil periodically. Water when the soil just below the surface is still moist but no longer wet.

3. Move plants to a location in bright, indirect light or direct sunlight. If the plants have been growing in a dark area, first move them for 2 weeks to a location that receives bright, indirect light or only 1 to 2 hours of morning sun; then place them in direct sunlight.

4. Transplant weeping figs carefully to minimize rootball disturbance. Some leaf drop after transplanting is normal. If given proper care, leaf drop will stop after a few weeks.

5. Avoid drafty areas and sudden environmental changes. Place new plants where conditions are as similar as possible to those in which they were grown. Some leaf drop is normal for a few weeks, until the plant becomes acclimated to its new location.

PROBLEM: Leaves are mottled with yellow blotches, or they have yellow streaks or flecks that later turn dark brown or black. Leaves may have partial, complete, or concentric rings of dark-colored tissue. New leaves may be stunted and cupped. Flowers may be mottled and the colors broken. The blossoms may be moderately or severely distorted and have brown flecks or streaks in them. Affected flowers do not last long.

ANALYSIS: Viruses

Several viruses infect orchids. Some infect many different types of orchids; others infect only a few. Viruses cause a plant to manufacture new viruses from the plant's protein. In the process the metabolism of the plant is upset. Different symptoms appear, depending upon the orchid and the virus present. Viruses are easily transmitted on tools used in cutting orchid plants.

SOLUTION: If flowers are badly malformed or discolored, discard them. Keep plants that are virus-free separate from those showing virus symptoms, because viruses are highly contagious. Before moving from one plant to another, sterilize cutting tools by dipping them in rubbing alcohol. Do not purchase plants that show virus symptoms.

Orchid cultural information

Light: Filtered to bright, depending on species

Water: In soil, water when surface is barely moist; in other mediums, water once a week during growing season—less in winter

SAINTPAULIA (AFRICAN VIOLET)

SAINTPAULIA (AFRICAN VIOLET)

LIGHT: African violets need abundant light to produce flowers. Grow them in bright light, but not in direct sunlight.

SOIL: Any standard houseplant mix. For information on potting mixes, see the section on Providing Soil in the introductory text for this chapter.

FERTILIZER: During the summer or when plants are growing, apply fertilizer monthly; use a product rated higher in phosphorus.

WATER:
How much: Add enough water so that some water drains out the bottom of the pot.
How often: Water plants when soil just under the surface is moist but not wet. For additional information on watering houseplants, see the section on Providing Water in the introductory text for this chapter.

TEMPERATURE: Average house temperatures are adequate for African violets, but do not leave them in rooms where the temperature falls below 50° F at night.

SPECIAL CONDITIONS: Avoid getting cold water on the leaves when watering, and don't let African violets sit in drainage water. Do not expose plants to cold drafts.

Failure to flower.

PROBLEM: Although the plant seems healthy, it does not bloom.

ANALYSIS: Insufficient light
Violets, like other flowering plants, won't bloom unless they are properly fed and watered. But if the plant is a healthy-looking green and growing well but not blooming, it is probably not receiving enough light. Plants use light as a source of energy and will not bloom unless they can afford the energy to do so. African violets bloom at lower levels of light than most other plants, but they do require a fairly bright location to bloom well.

SOLUTION: Move the plant to a brighter location. The ideal light for African violets is as bright as possible without being direct sun. If the light is coming through a window exposed to the sun, the window should be curtained so that the sunlight coming through is not quite bright enough to make shadows. If the light is too bright, the leaves will lose their bright green color and become pale, with an orange or yellow cast. If the light is both bright and hot, the leaves will burn. If you don't have an indoor location bright enough, give the plants supplemental light. Use fluorescent fixtures, and place them as close to the top of the plants as possible.

Water spots.

PROBLEM: White to light yellow blotches in various patterns, including circles, occur on older leaves. Small islands of green may be separated by the discolored areas. Brown spots sometimes appear in the colored areas.

ANALYSIS: Water spots
African violets are quite sensitive to rapid temperature changes. Water spots occur most commonly when cold water is splashed on the leaves while the plant is being watered. If this happens in light, the chlorophyll (green pigment) is destroyed. In this plant family, all the chlorophyll in the leaves is found in a single layer of cells near the upper surface. If the chlorophyll in that layer is broken down, the green color disappears, and the color of the underlying leaf tissue is exposed.

SOLUTION: Avoid getting cold water on African violet leaves when watering. Or use tepid water, which will not cause spotting if it touches the leaves. Spotted leaves will not recover. Pick them off if they are unsightly.

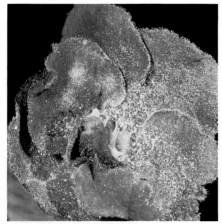

Powdery mildew.

Virus.

Dieback.

PROBLEM: White or gray powdery patches appear on leaves, stems, buds, and flowers. Leaves and flowers may be covered with the powdery growth. This material usually appears first on the topsides of the older leaves. The affected plant parts may turn yellow or brown and shrivel and die.

ANALYSIS: Powdery mildew
Powdery mildew on African violet is caused by one of several fungi (*Oidium* species). The powdery patches consist of fungal strands and spores. The spores are carried by air currents to healthy leaves and flowers of the same plant and to other African violets. The fungi sap plant nutrients, causing yellowing or browning of the tissues. Dim light, warm days, and cool nights encourage the growth of powdery mildew.

SOLUTION: Spray with a fungicide containing benomyl every 2 weeks until the disease is gone. Remove infected flowers and flower buds and badly infected leaves. Keep plants in bright, indirect light, away from cold drafts.

PROBLEM: All leaves have blotches of various shades of yellow and green. Plants with blotched foliage fail to grow as rapidly as green plants of the same type. Affected plants are of a variegated variety.

ANALYSIS: Viruses
Several viruses have been found in variegated piggyback plants. The most common is cucumber mosaic virus. Viruses disrupt the normal functioning of the cells and, as a result, not as much green pigment (chlorophyll) is produced. This causes different shades of green and yellow to appear in the leaves. Aphids and other insects transmit the virus from one plant to another. Although viruses have been shown to be present in variegated piggyback plants, it has not been proven that viruses are the cause of the variegation.

SOLUTION: Keep variegated piggyback plants isolated from other plants because aphids can transmit the virus to susceptible plants. Control aphids by spraying with an insecticide containing acephate (ORTHENE®) or resmethrin; follow label directions.

Tolmiea cultural information
Light: Bright
Water: When soil surface is moist but not wet

PROBLEM: Tips of older leaves turn yellow, then die and turn brown. This condition occurs more frequently on long stems than on short stems. The longer the stem, the more tip burn is found.

ANALYSIS: Dieback
The cause of dieback is unknown. It looks like salt damage (see page 26) but often occurs on plants that have been leached regularly. As wandering-Jew stems grow long, the plant does not support the old leaves, and they turn yellow and die, starting at the tips.

SOLUTION: Remove dead leaves as they appear. Keep pinching the tips of the stems so they do not become too long. This will force new buds to grow farther back on the stems. New leaves will not show symptoms of dieback. Plants may occasionally need to be cut back severely so that only several inches are left on each stem. After cutting back, reduce the amount of water and fertilizer given until the plant is actively growing again.

Tradescantia cultural information
Light: Medium light
Water: When soil is just barely moist

LAWNS

Replanting the lawn is often the first phase of landscaping for a newly purchased home. Out goes the old yellow weedy eyesore of the past. In goes seed or sod. A thick green lawn carpet is many a homeowner's dream. Besides being attractive, lawns provide regular outdoor exercise in the form of applying fertilizer, mowing, watering, removing thatch and clippings, weeding, and inspecting and treating for pests.

INSTALLING A NEW LAWN

Putting in a new lawn involves removing the old one, preparing the soil, then planting seed or installing sod.

A new lawn placed over a still-viable old lawn results in holdover weeds rapidly supplanting delicate seedlings. Before sodding or seeding, spray with a glyphosate compound to kill any growing vegetation—you will avoid much weed hand-picking later.

Soil pH

Before seeding or laying sod, test the soil in the lawn area to determine pH. The pH scale ranges from 0 to 14, with neutral at 7.0. The ideal pH for grass is between 6.5 and 6.8. What difference does it make? pH determines the rate at which nutrients are released from the soil, if these nutrients are already present.

Acidic soil   In soil that is acidic, or has a pH up to 5.5, magnesium, phosphorus, and calcium are less available for plant use than in neutral soil. Nitrogen is only partially released in acidic soil because the soil organisms that free it are less active. When soil has a pH of 5.0 or lower, these organisms cease working altogether and no nitrogen is released. Acidic soil is sometimes called sour soil.

Lawns in overly acidic soil may grow slowly. Leaves may be pale and root development may be poor. Overly acidic soil promotes disease mechanisms. Applying fertilizer may not help because the low pH stops or slows nutrient release. Neutralize acidic soil by applying finely ground dolomitic limestone, working it into the soil.

Alkaline soil   Sometimes called sweet soil, alkaline soil has a pH above 8.0. When pH exceeds 8.0, iron and manganese are no longer available to the grass. The lawn becomes pale or yellow. To correct alkaline soil, spade in iron and sulfate compounds.

Opposite: A luxuriant lawn is the aim of many a homeowner.

pH tests   How do you know the pH of your soil? In general, acidic soils are high in organic material and subject to annual rainfall of 30 inches or more. Alkaline soils are high in calcium or are in areas where rainfall is minimal.

To measure pH precisely, take soil samples to a professional testing service. In some states, soil testing is offered by universities. To find a soil-testing service, look under "Soil" in the local telephone directory or ask the local cooperative extension agent for advice.

Take samples from about 15 areas within a prospective lawn site. A soil-sampling tube, available at your local nursery, works best, but the hollow shaft of an old curtain rod will do. Insert the tube in the soil to a depth of 6 inches. If your home is on an established property, mix the various samples together in a freshly cleaned nonmetal container. You should now have about 2 cups of soil. Remove any stones, roots, or debris. If your home is on land subject to recent construction activities, keep the samples separate. This allows identification of areas that need special work. Label all containers, cover them, and keep them dry. In an accompanying letter, tell the service about land slope and any other details that pertain to the immediate growing area.

An alternative to professional testing is purchasing a home soil-testing kit at a nursery and doing the analysis yourself. Though this is not as accurate as a professional analysis, it is inexpensive, easy, and is usually adequate. When you know the pH of the lawn area, you can correct it, if necessary, when you add organic additives.

Organic Amendments

Although some grasses do well enough in poor soil (see the section Choosing a Lawn Type), none is at its best. Seedlings may fail to thrive or even emerge. Mature grass remains straggly, bare spots emerge, and insect pests can attack the weakened blades.

For the lawn to thrive, you must improve poor soil. Topsoil may be touted as a soil amendment; however, only use it when you must raise the land grading. Ascertaining the origin of topsoil is difficult. The soil may be poor; contain numerous weed seeds, disease organisms, destructive nematodes, or insect pests in larval or egg form; or have a high chemical content. Purchase topsoil carefully.

Organic amendments actually do improve poor soil. Adding ample organic material to clay soil can lessen the problems of compaction and runoff (see the section Soil Type, later in this chapter). This causes the particles to form small crumbs rather than a sticky stiff configuration. Ample organic matter mixed into sandy soil helps hold moisture and nutrients in the root zone. Five organic amendments are most often used: compost, manure, peat moss, ground bark, and sawdust.

Compost   From a compost pile or purchased by the bag or truckload at a nursery, compost is any organic material that has begun to decompose. By decomposing, dead plant parts release their nutrients. In addition, compost makes clay or compacted soil crumblier. When soil particles have air spaces between them, water penetrates better, nutrients reach root zones, and drainage is improved. In sandy soil, compost acts like a sponge to hold moisture and nutrients in the root zone. All this bodes well for delicate grass seedlings, which need all the help they can get.

Manure   Cow and horse manure, if treated to remove insect eggs and weed seeds, is an effective soil conditioner. It is used by itself or with compost. The amount of nutrients in the manure varies with what the donor animals have been eating. Manure may have a high salt content, which can prevent seedling germination. Avoid cow or horse manure additives if the soil is already high in salt or is alkaline. If obtained directly from farm or stable, compost manure first to destroy undesirable organisms. Other forms of manure—such as chicken, sheep, or swine—are sometimes available; as with cow or horse manure, compost them first. Fresh manure cannot be used safely on or around a new or established lawn. Gases given off by the ammonia in fresh manure may severely damage grass and grass roots.

Peat moss   A possible organic amendment to lawn areas, peat moss is usually better off being used for acid-loving plants such as azaleas. Few lawn grasses do well in soil heavily fortified with peat moss, although it can be used sparingly. By itself peat moss has an acidic pH of 3.5 to 4.5. If acidic soil is fortified with peat moss, the highly acidic result may not release valuable plant nutrients, even if they are present. Also, peat moss sheds water if allowed to dry out, so a soil high in peat moss may be detrimental to drought-sensitive seedlings. If your lawn already has a high peat moss component, add a wetting agent to the water. Wetting agents are available at most nurseries.

Ground bark and sawdust   Although less expensive than compost or soil mix, ground bark and sawdust are wood by-products. In the soil, sawdust decomposes with the aid of bacteria that use nitrogen. This takes nitrogen away from growing grass. If sawdust or ground bark is the only organic amendment alternative, add a 10-10-10 general-purpose plant food while incorporating the wood by-products into the soil.

Amendment Application
Regardless of which organic amendment or amendments you choose, a sprinkling will not solve your soil problems. You must add an amendment layer 1 to 4 inches deep to effect a change in soil structure. Work the new material in thoroughly with a rotary tiller, spade, or rake.

Rocks or large dirt clods can cause problems by altering water flow. Rake them out of the top 2 inches of soil. Make certain the ground is level. Water the soil, then go over it with a garden roller; do this several times to see how the soil settles. Make any corrections necessary to avoid puddling and runoff.

Lawns From Seed
Successful seed sowing is a matter of seed quality, timing, effective distribution, and proper care.

Seed quality   Always check the date on the seed container before purchasing grass seed. Buy only seed that is produced for sale in the current year. If the box is a holdover from the previous year, individual seeds may have sprouted in the container. After planting, the others may sprout poorly or not at all.

Sowing time   Planting at the right time helps prevent seedling death. Fall and spring planting give the best results. Fall sowing is preferred by many experienced gardeners. It reduces the problem of heat damage to seedlings. Allow 6 weeks of growing time before the weather turns cold. Seed sown later than that may not germinate. Fall seeding is usually done no later than mid-September. Estimates are that for every day after this, 10 percent of the seeds are lost, except in areas of continual warm weather.

The benefits of spring lawn planting include ample sunlight. Combined with ample water, the result may be a deep cushiony lawn. However, weed growth is quite active in spring. Even the most dense mature grass cannot crowd out weeds while in the seedling stage.

Summer heat is also hard on seedlings. Most grasses do best between 50° and 70° F. A successful springtime planting requires careful watering. Make sure the sprinkler system irrigates the entire planted area. Water it for 20 minutes in the morning; 20 minutes in the evening; and, if the air temperature rises above 80° F, an additional 20 minutes in the afternoon. If you must use a hose to water, provide a fine spray or mist to avoid washing seeds away. In dry weather, keep seedlings moist by covering them with a ¼- to ½-inch-deep sawdust or straw mulch. Do not use peat moss, which promotes water runoff when dry.

Seed distribution   Use a drop or broadcast spreader to sow seeds. Hand-distribution tends to be irregular, resulting in both bare and overly seeded areas. As soon as seeds are distributed, rake the planting area lightly. Then roll the earth with a light roller. This avoids wind drift by pressing the seeds firmly into the soil. Seeds should be no more than ½ inch deep. Improper planting depth may slow or stop seed germination. Seeds spread on top of thatch, or left on top of soil instead of being pressed into the soil, may dry out without sprouting.

Care of newly planted areas   Keep foot and animal traffic off a newly seeded lawn to avoid uncovering or disturbing germinating seeds. Insert small brightly colored flags to warn off pedestrians. To keep animals off, put up some type of temporary barrier.

Improper watering is a common cause of seed failure. Once a seed has germinated and the protective seed coat is broken, adequate moisture is a must. If the soil around the seedling dries out, so does the seedling.

However, overly wet soil with a high nitrogen component encourages the proliferation of the fungi that cause damping-off. These fungi are a major cause of seed failure to thrive. The infection may attack seeds before germination. If they do germinate, the fungi infect the growing tips of the grass and kill the seedlings before they emerge from the soil. Even after seedling emergence, the fungi remain a problem. Fungi may attack stems and roots at or just below soil level. The

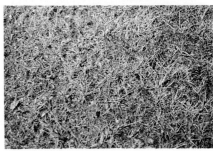

Top: A whirlybird-type spreader is being used to seed a small lawn.
Bottom: Damping-off may result if the seedbed of a new lawn is kept too moist. The seedlings that do come up will often lie on the ground and fail to thrive.

lawn seedlings lie on the ground instead of standing upright. Surviving seedlings may have stunted roots, lessening their nutrient retention. If damping-off causes lawn seed failure, improve drainage before reseeding. Do not add nitrogen fertilizer until seedlings have fully sprouted.

Sod Lawns
Gardeners who do not have time to plant seed and monitor seedlings or who want an immediate lawn thick enough to forestall wind-carried weed seeds often prefer to lay sod.

What to install   Sod comes in strips from 6 to 9 feet long. It should be uniformly green, moist, and ¾ to 1 inch thick. Overly thick sod roots slowly. Overly thin sod dries out too fast, depriving leaves and roots of necessary water. If sod falls apart when handled, reject it. Do not put down sod that is wet, dry, spotted with brown, or yellowing. Sod with any of these characteristics has not been grown under healthy conditions, is old, has been stored improperly, or has been injured in transit.

Installation time   Lay cool-season sod—such as bluegrass or bentgrass—in early spring or in late summer to early fall. Lay

Laying sod provides an instant lawn, but proper preparation and installation are extremely important.

warm-season grass sod—such as bermudagrass, bahiagrass, centipedegrass, or St. Augustine grass—in late spring or early summer.

Sod installation   Healthy sod can be expensive and must be carefully handled to avoid ruining it. Prepare the soil before sod installation to avoid problems from inappropriate pH, holdover weeds, uneven ground, insects, nematodes, and disease. Install the sod as soon as possible after it has been cut.

Unroll one strip of sod at a time. Lay the strips so that the seams are staggered from row to row, as the cement lines between bricks in a walkway are staggered. The sod strips should fit snugly against each other, but be careful not to stretch them. Sod tends to shrink, and stretching increases that tendency and results in yellow stripes that run through the lawn. For 2 weeks, you may have to water daily to keep the soil moist but not wet at all times. Pay special attention to pathway and driveway borders—these are the first to dry out and the last to knit with the soil. Test for sod rooting by tugging gently at the corner of a strip. If it resists, the sod has taken hold. A sod lawn can be functional in as little as 2 weeks, although heavy foot traffic should be routed elsewhere initially.

Warning signals   Symptoms of sod failure include newly laid areas turning yellow, then brown. Instead of meshing with the underlying soil, failing sod rolls up easily, like a carpet. When you roll it, no roots are visible on the bottom of the sod. If your sod exhibits these symptoms, it may have been subjected to heat or water stress either in the field or in storage; sod may be damaged within 2 days of digging and initial rolling if the weather is hot. To try to save failing installed sod, water it diligently. Damaged sod can recover partially with good care.

Sod failure can also occur if the soil dries out. This may occur from direct water lack or if sod is placed directly on thatch. If sod is placed directly on hard soil, the roots cannot penetrate well. Soil preparation prevents these problems.

Once the sod is well established, the next issue is when to begin mowing it.

MOWING NEW LAWNS

Cutting a new lawn too early may pull out young plants. Begin mowing when grass is at least 3 inches high. Before that, seedlings are not well rooted. After the initial mowing, mow to the height recommended for your grass variety; see the next section, Mowing Mature Lawns, for discussion of lawn height and grass clippings.

MOWING MATURE LAWNS

You may be blaming those yellow lawn patches on insects or fungus. Instead, your mower or mowing technique may be the culprit. Like most chores, mowing can be done correctly or incorrectly.

Mower Types

To mow correctly, you must use quality equipment appropriate for the job.

Reel mowers   These mowers work with a scissorslike motion. They are precise and recommended for grass that must be short and well tended—golf course–type grass. If you have zoysiagrass or hybrid bermudagrass or bentgrass, you must use a reel mower.

The disadvantage of reel mowers is that their cutting does not follow the lay of the land. The results may be slightly longer grass in a sunken area and slightly shorter grass on a rise. Reel mowers are not as effective as rotary mowers in lawns that contain high weeds, high grass, or rough ground. To avoid problems with a reel mower, have it serviced 3 times during the growing season. Signs of dull reel blades are an overly "striped" effect after mowing, untouched grass blades, or lawn areas that appear rough.

Rotary mowers   These mowers are easier to maintain than reel mowers. Also, the rotary models are lighter and easier to handle. They are effective on high grass, plant stalks, and tall weeds. Rotary mowers can trim close to trees, walls, fences, and other standing objects. In addition, they chop up lawn leaves effectively. Rotaries work well if you cannot mow your lawn on a precision timetable; however, do not expect that precision look. Rotary mowers give a knifelike cut, fraying and bruising leaftips more than reel mowers. This is particularly true if you neglect to have the blades sharpened often enough.

Dull mower blades shred grass tips, and the result is a lawn with a sickly brownish or grayish tinge. This is particularly noticeable in dry weather. Also, shredded tips act as entry points for lawn diseases. Sharpen the blades of a rotary mower after every 6 to 8 mowings. Some gardeners do the sharpening themselves. For any major work, hire a professional.

Push mowers   Small hand-powered push mowers are time-effective for lawns under 2,000 square feet. You do not have to hunt for fuel, check the parts, and so on; you just have to oil the bearings and get the mower sharpened once a year to keep it in top form. But hand-powered mowers do require more muscle to operate than the power varieties.

Electric mowers   Those with large lawns often consider electric mowers. The major disadvantage of an electric mower is that it remains anchored to a power outlet. This creates a maneuvering problem when you are cutting around trees, for example. However, electrics are quiet and easy to start. Never use a corded electric mower or edger on wet grass.

Frequency of Mowing

Cutting a lawn too often, particularly with the blade set low, exposes the lower portions of grass leaves to bright sun, burning them. If this happens repeatedly, grass reacts by developing shallow roots. Shallow-rooted lawns are particularly prone to disease and weed problems. In addition, poor rooting does not provide enough nutrients to the grass leaves. A lawn with shallow roots may eventually die out.

Mowing too seldom often means taking off too much grass at one time. There is a direct relationship between root depth and usual lawn height. Long roots are to your advantage. They not only reach out for more lawn nutrients, they help the grass resist drought periods. If you let grass grow too long and then lop off more than half of it, the roots go into shock. Do this often enough, and your lawn may develop a thin, spotty, or burned look. For best results, never remove more than one third of the height of the grass.

The table that follows gives recommended grass heights according to grass type. If your lawn is a mixture of various types, cut to the length recommended for the dominant type. Mow whenever grass is ⅓ to ½ higher than the height given.

Recommended Grass Heights

Type of Grass	Recommended Height (inches)
Bahiagrass	2–3
Bentgrass	⅜–¾
Bermudagrass	½–1½
Bluegrass	2–3
Centipedegrass	1–2
Dichondra	½–1½
Fescue	
Chewing	1–2
Red	2–3
Tall	3–4
Ryegrass	
Annual	1½–2
Perennial	1–2½
St. Augustine grass	1–2½
Zoysiagrass	½–1½

CHOOSING A LAWN TYPE

Given all available lawn grasses, you can choose from over 40 varieties. There are also grass substitutes, such as dichondra, to consider. Basically, grass is categorized as a hardy, or cool-season, variety for cold-winter areas or as a subtropical, or warm-season, variety for areas where frost is a rare phenomenon. Whether you are installing a new lawn or caring for the lawn you already have, knowing the needs of the grass is important. If you are installing a lawn, you must choose a type that is appropriate for the climate and has maintenance requirements you can satisfy. Knowing the variety of an existing lawn helps you provide the care it needs and diagnose problems.

Most lawns are a blend of grasses. Blends are more resistant to disease and infestation than lawns of a single type, because the problems that inflict one grass may not affect another.

Bahiagrass

Warm season. Makes a coarse, open lawn. So tall and fast growing that in finer lawns it is thought of as a weed. Spreads by runners. Most varieties are grown for hay; Pensacola and Argentine are lawn varieties. Easy to maintain, drought resistant, shade tolerant, and has little need for fertilizer. Problems are chlorosis (yellowing), dollar spot (see page 50), and mole cricket invasion (see page 53).

Bentgrass

Cool season. Leaves are small, well textured, fine, fairly flat, and upright. Color may be bluish green, medium green, or apple green. Several varieties are available. Spreads by rooting at the joints. If well cared for, bentgrass presents an exceptionally uniform appearance. Often used on golf courses and putting greens. Offers some shade tolerance. Problems arise when bentgrass is not mowed often enough or cut short enough. Bentgrass builds a heavy thatch layer quickly. A few varieties require mowing three times per week. Bentgrass is fussy. It suffers under drought conditions and requires regular, heavy applications of fertilizer. In hot, muggy weather or cool, damp conditions, it is susceptible to several fungus diseases. Because of these factors, bentgrass is not recommended for most home lawns.

Bentgrass becomes a weed when it is accidentally introduced into lawns of other types that do not require such stringent mowing. In bluegrass, fescue, or ryegrass lawns, bentgrass looks matted. In areas between the other grasses, bentgrass may appear dead with long straggly stems. In the spring, it remains brown much longer than the surrounding grasses. It may also take over the lawn, because it grows quickly.

If you do not want the high maintenance of a predominantly bentgrass lawn or do not like its appearance in your chosen lawn type, use a systemic herbicide containing glyphosate. The treatment does not affect roots of surrounding trees or shrubs. Bentgrass areas die out within 4 weeks of treatment, and you can sow selected lawn seed within 7 days.

Bermudagrass

Warm season. Regional names include devilgrass, manienie, and wiregrass. Color differs with variety; bermudagrass may be grayish green, bright deep green, deep bluegreen, light green, yellowgreen, or dark green. Leaf blades range from ⅛ to ¼ inch wide. Common bermudagrass has bronze seed spikes. Stolons, or stems, creep along the soil surface. Stolons range from 6 to 18 inches long. Bermudagrass requires sun. It roots deeply and is drought tolerant. In general, bermudagrass lawns are dense. New varieties are medium to fine textured.

Bermudagrass is usually pest- and disease-free if well tended. When thick, it resists weed sprouting. Provides rapid coverage and withstands a lot of foot traffic. Is used for play areas and athletic

This bentgrass lawn is exceptionally well tended and shows the uniform appearance for which bentgrass is known.

fields. In winter, expect bermudagrass to turn brown or straw-colored. Help it stay green longer by applying fertilizer in late fall and removing thatch, which blocks sunlight. Some gardeners dye dormant bermudagrass green in winter. Once bermudagrass is fully dormant (without naturally green stems or leaves) in winter, use contact weed killer to kill a wide range of grassy weeds and broadleaf weeds.

Before extensive hybridization, early varieties of bermudagrass were considered a worse lawn pest than crabgrass. Even modern "common" varieties can occasionally become a lawn problem. Bermudagrass spreads rapidly by surface and underground runners. If it gets in nonbermudagrass lawns or flower beds, its deep root system may make it difficult to eradicate. Bermudagrass is sometimes confused with quackgrass (see page 56), a weed, because both spread in the same stolen-creeping manner. Control consists of spot-treating with a glyphosate compound. Visible effects appear within 1 week, and unwanted bermudagrass dies out in 2 weeks. Control invasive bermudagrass in ground cover or shrubs with the selective herbicide fluazifop, which kills grassy weeds but does not affect most broadleaf plants.

Kentucky Bluegrass

Cool season. Despite its name, Kentucky bluegrass is not a Kentucky native; English settlers brought it to the state in packing hay. There is "common" Kentucky bluegrass and "improved" Kentucky bluegrass. Both spread by rhizomes. Bluegrass is generally dark green and fine textured. Density is moderate to thick. It is considered the best of all lawn grasses in appearance. The improved version, usually sold as a blend of varieties, has deeper color, higher density, and better heat resistance. Improved Kentucky bluegrass is also more resistant to diseases such as leaf spot (see page 55), stripe smut, and fusarium blight (see page 49).

When considering bluegrass for your lawn, select varieties carefully to avoid problems. Delta, Kenblue, Newport, and Park are susceptible to leaf spot. Delta and Park have problems with chlorosis (yellowing) in alkaline soils. Newport, Fylking, and Park seem susceptible to fusarium blight. Merion does not do at all well in shade and is prone to mildew, stripe smut, and rust. All bluegrass requires ample water; the grass goes dormant and turns brown in even short drought periods, but it does recover if watered well. Bluegrass needs regular applications of a medium to large amount of fertilizer. The grass does not prosper if mowed severely.

Top: Because of its somewhat untidy appearance and winter dormancy, bermudagrass is used mainly in public play areas.
Bottom: This lush bluegrass lawn is a fine example of the rich color and texture that makes bluegrass one of the most popular grass varieties.

Left: Although not a grass, dichondra is an excellent lawn substitute in situations such as this, where mowing would be difficult and foot traffic is minimal.
Right: Fescue can appear wild and windswept, but in the right location it is the perfect grass for a lawn.

Do not confuse perennial Kentucky bluegrass with its pest relative, annual bluegrass (see page 56), which is also called annual speargrass, dwarf speargrass, and walkgrass. Annual bluegrass, which is generally considered a weed, is pale green. In mid- to late spring, white seed heads appear.

Centipedegrass

Warm season. Medium green with a tendency toward yellowing from chlorosis. Needs iron supplements. Centipedegrass has a coarse texture and will grow in some shade. Adaptable to poor soil, it does well in acidic conditions. Is aggressive enough to crowd out weeds. Spreads by runners. Centipedegrass needs little general maintenance, though its shallow root system makes it drought sensitive. With sufficient watering, however, a centipedegrass lawn recovers quickly. This hardy grass is resistant to chinch bug attack and rhizoctonia disease. If centipedegrass gets into ornamental plant areas, control it selectively with a spray containing fluazifop.

Dichondra

Warm season. Dichondra is not a grass, but a soft, ground-hugging broadleafed plant that can make a lush bright green carpet. It spreads by reseeding and from underground runners. Because it needs little mowing, it is used in lieu of grass for many small to medium-sized areas that are not subject to foot traffic. The plant thrives in heat but tolerates some shade. Dichondra needs much water and fertilizer. The ground cover stays green throughout the year. Weeds are hard to control in dense dichondra.

Dichondra is susceptible to a few diseases, including brown patch and alternaria leaf spot. Chlorothalonil is the treatment for both. Dichondra is also susceptible to cutworms, snails, slugs, red spider mites, gnats, flea beetles, and

nematodes. To rid dichondra of nematodes (see page 54), you may have to remove the entire lawn, cultivate deeply, and then replant. Because nematodes can be brought in with flats of dichondra, treat new plants with a soil fumigant before installing them.

Fescue

Cool season. Types of fescue include chewing fescue, red fescue, and tall fescue. Most fine fescue spreads slowly; but tall fescue can spread rapidly. Fescue tends to present a rather stiff and windswept appearance. Grass remains medium to dark green all year. Fescue makes a rugged lawn. Tall fescue is used for play areas. Fescue can survive in city conditions, including smog. Fescue adapts to dry growing conditions and poor soil and needs little fertilizer. During World War II tall fescue was used to cover emergency landing fields. Tall fescue produces bunchy clumps that may be considered a lawn nuisance. Occasionally it does so well it becomes a weed. Red fescue tolerates acidic soil, dry areas, and some shade. In moist fertile soil and in hot climates, it is prone to summer diseases such as red thread. This disease, also

called pink patch, affects ryegrass, bluegrass, and bentgrass, as well as fescue. Infected grass turns light tan to pink in areas ranging from 2 inches in diameter to 3 feet in diameter. Pink webs, almost resembling tangled sewing thread, bind the leaves together. Though seldom fatal, red thread does affect lawn appearance. Try adding nitrogen to the soil as a control, or use chlorothalonil.

Ryegrass (Annual)

Cool season. Also called Italian ryegrass and common ryegrass, the annual type of this grass is coarse, with leaves far apart. It does not make a tightly knit lawn. Annual ryegrass is often used for quick lawn cover. It needs a lot of water but tolerates some shade. Annual ryegrass does not survive cold winters or extremely hot summers. It must be replanted each year.

Ryegrass (Perennial)

Cool season. This grass is somewhat coarse with a waxy shine on the leaves, which are far apart. Perennial ryegrass tolerates some shade and needs only moderate applications of fertilizer and water. Traditionally, its bunchy growth habit did not create the lush lawn look, but selective breeding has developed ryegrass with a fine leaf resembling bluegrass. This improved ryegrass creates a beautiful lawn that is tough enough to plant in play areas. And it is an easy grass to grow, though it can be hard to mow in summer.

St. Augustine Grass

Warm season. A dark blue-green coarse grass with hard flat stems and flat broad leaves. Grows quickly and tolerates salty soil and shade. St. Augustine grass is not always durable under heavy traffic, however, and it turns brown in winter. The coarse texture of this grass makes cutting with a power mower a necessity. This type of lawn needs much iron. It tends to creep into flower beds; fortunately, however, it is shallow rooted and easily removed by hand. Unfortunately, chinch bugs (see page 51) find this grass a favorite food.

Zoysiagrass

Warm season. The several varieties of this grass have wiry blades that may be broad at the base and taper to a point at the tips. Zoysiagrass is dark green and easy to maintain. It requires a moderate amount of water and fertilizer. This grass tolerates heavy foot traffic and is drought and weed resistant. Few pests trouble it. This grass is almost winter hardy. Winter dormancy turns it straw-colored except in mild-winter areas. Zoysiagrass does not turn green again until warm weather. Lawns of this grass are slow to establish. Without regular rotary mowing it becomes difficult to cut. Zoysiagrass tends to build thatch (see page 54).

GRASS CLIPPINGS

Some say grass clippings are good for a lawn; some say they shade a lawn too much; and others say they foul the mower. There's truth in all three views. If you mow regularly and the clippings are less than 1 inch long, you can leave them on the lawn without causing a problem. When grass is mowed properly, the clippings take about a day to disappear. They are 90 percent water and dry up to almost nothing; therefore, they cannot pile up or entangle with thatch and impede the mower. Since as much as one third of a lawn's nitrogen requirements may be supplied by decomposing lawn clippings, they can certainly be beneficial. This is welcome news because many communities now ban yard wastes and grass clippings from normal trash collection, to slow down the rapid filling of available landfills.

But in dry-summer areas or with infrequent mowing, clippings do not decay quickly enough to prevent problems. The clippings can mound, entangling in thatch and making mowing difficult. Excess clippings are not only unsightly, but they shade growing grass underneath. They provide an excellent source of nutrition and humidity for disease fungi, which may soon attack living grass underneath the matting. Some of the new rotary mowers effectively chop clippings small and scatter them so they do not build up into a problem.

Clipping disposal is not difficult if you have an active compost pile. Just gather up the clippings, scatter them in the pile with other garden leaves and waste material, and turn the pile regularly to provide aeration. An alternative is spreading clippings no more than 1 inch thick as a mulch in dahlia, rose, or shrubbery beds.

Clippings can create a problem if you pile them up, however—especially if the pile is near the house. Grass has a high water content. Piled up, no room remains for air movement or water evaporation. Smell-producing bacteria thrive, turning the grass into yellow-brown slime in which flies lay eggs. The pile becomes a breeding place for houseflies, false stable flies, soldier flies, and little houseflies. Turning over just one small section of decaying piled grass may expose as many as 3,000 fly maggots.

WATERING MATURE LAWNS

Even the most drought-tolerant lawns—such as bermudagrass, zoysiagrass, or fescue—cannot live with prolonged lack of water (see page 53). Other grasses suffer from even brief water deprivation. The first sign of a drought problem is the dark bluish green tinge caused partly by leaf folding. The lawn loses its springiness, and footprints remain following any foot traffic. Most lawns go dormant about three days after drought-caused wilting begins.

Many factors determine a proper watering program. These include turf type, soil, climate, temperature, wind velocity, humidity, rain, and maintenance practices. If only the top few inches of soil are regularly watered, roots do not seek water any deeper down. Shallow roots force you to water more often to maintain a green lawn. But frequent watering keeps soil constantly wet, encouraging weeds and disease. Watering should regularly penetrate 6 to 8 inches deep to encourage deep lawn rooting. This enables lawns to go longer between waterings, cutting down on disease potential.

In warm-winter areas that are prone to drought, zoysia is an attractive choice for a lawn.

Sprinkler Efficiency

Inefficient sprinkler head placement causes overwatering in some areas, underwatering in others. Test the sprinkler by setting containers of the same size at regular intervals throughout the lawn area. Put some close to the sprinkler heads and some at the farthest reach of the water. Make a diagram of your container layout, then record the amount of water in each container after a normal sprinkling. Over its entire surface, a lawn needs 1 to 2 inches of water per week. Adjust sprinkler heads accordingly.

Soil Type

The type of soil in your lawn area affects how much water the grass actually receives. Two soil extremes cause watering problems: clay soil and sandy soil.

Clay soil   This type of soil is composed of individual mineral particles of less than $\frac{1}{125000}$ inch. Because of their extremely small size, clay particles tend to pack together and become dense. Dense soil slows water penetration.

Water clay soil slowly to avoid water runoff. Many gardeners believe they are giving ample water to lawns growing in clay soils, but runoff is causing a water shortage that results in brown or yellow grass. Clay soil packing and subsequent runoff becomes even worse if the grass is subject to traffic when wet, a situation common to lawns.

Once wet, clay subsoil holds water for quite a while. This is true even if the topsoil looks dry and cracks. Waterlogged soil decreases air penetration and may lead to a myriad of fungus diseases. But because the topsoil is dry, you may mistakenly continue watering.

Sandy soil   This type of soil provides quick drainage and effective air circulation, but it does not retain moisture well. You may be giving enough water, yet still see lawn yellowing or browning. Water moves rapidly through sand particles, which range in size from $\frac{1}{500}$ inch for fine sand to $\frac{1}{12}$ inch for coarse sand.

Type Determination

To determine the type of soil in your lawn, fill a quart jar about two-thirds full of water. Fill the jar with soil until it is almost full. Add a bit of commercial dispersing agent, such as Calgon, to get best results. Replace the jar top tightly. Shake the jar vigorously. Now let the soil settle. A sand layer becomes visible in a short time, the heaviest sand settling out first. Clay and silt take hours to settle; fine clay may remain suspended indefinitely. Many soils are a mixture of types, but one type usually predominates.

Effectiveness Tests

If your watering schedule is not producing desired results, purchase a soil-moisture tester, or coring tube. The coring tube takes up a long earth plug and lets you see and feel the deep-down moisture level. A simple test, but not as diagnostic, is poking a long screwdriver into the ground. If it pokes through 6 soil inches easily, the lawn is usually wet enough. Test soil moisture 12 hours after watering. Soil should be moist 6 to 8 inches down.

Changes in Water Availability

Since lawn brownout can occur quickly, the response must be prompt. When water availability becomes restricted (see page 53), do not apply fertilizer except during the fall rainy season. Fertilizer promotes growth now unsupported by adequate moisture. Remove all weeds, which compete for water. Do not cut grass as short, and mow less often. But do not let it grow higher than one third over the recommended mowing height. Less

frequent mowing may mean clipping cleanup is now necessary.

With restricted watering, a lawn does not look lush. It may develop a spotty, thin appearance. Some gardeners under mandatory water rationing prefer to let a lawn die out altogether. If drought is a recurrent phenomenon, replant with drought-tolerant turf or drought-resistant ground cover.

If your lawn suddenly becomes spongy, the cause may be thatch buildup. Some gardeners confuse thatch with loose grass clippings. Clippings can be raked out (see page 54).

PREVENTING WEEDS

Weeds produce huge numbers of seeds. The seeds are lightweight and often have built-in travel mechanisms that allow them to stick to fur or be wafted by the wind. In addition, weed seeds travel by means of transported soil, soil amendments, and garden seeds that are not weed-free; birds and other animals; rain; equipment; and the gardener who unknowingly has weed seeds on his or her clothing. Some planted grasses become weeds when they invade nonlawn areas or lawns of different types.

In general, lawn weeds are a sign that growing conditions are not optimal for grass. In nature, the strongest vegetation usually survives in an area for which it is best suited. The correct lawn grass for the area, put in properly and given prime care, can usually preclude newly arriving weeds. Conversely, weeds thrive in an area where ground preparation has been poor, soil unimproved, water minimal, and fertilizer scarce.

In the ongoing lawn weed battle, your primary strategy in lawn weed control is creating optimal growth conditions for planted grass, thereby crowding out weeds. To grow the healthiest grass possible, consider the questions that follow.

• Is soil acidity slowing grass growth?
• Does poor drainage affect grass growth adversely?
• Is soil compaction inhibiting roots?
• Have you planted the grass types best suited to the climate?
• Is fertilizer application timed to meet the needs of the lawn throughout its seasonal life cycle?
• Is your mowing technique and frequency appropriate for the type of grass?
• Are you watering deeply enough?
• Are you overwatering intermittently and creating soggy soil?
• Are trees and shrubs blocking necessary sunlight?
• Have pest insects, nematodes, or disease weakened the grass?
• Are you attempting to grow lawn where foot traffic prevents the grass from thriving?

If your analysis shows that growing conditions are hindering the grass, correct the conditions by following the suggestions in the appropriate sections of this book. Time spent encouraging grass will be time saved from pulling weeds.

In addition, reduce the opportunity for weed seeds to take hold by purchasing weed-free seed and treating the ground with a preventative before planting. During prime lawn-growing season, consider spraying emerging weeds before they send out roots or runners or create seeds. Control measures to prevent weed seed formation, keep new seed from finding a place to set roots, and quickly eliminate any seedlings that do take hold, form an effective prevention trio.

Note that weed seeds are extremely durable. Some seeds may germinate quickly upon finding a satisfactory site; others may lie dormant for a year, or even two, before germinating. Repeat weed-control measures each season. If you are thorough, weeds will not invade your lawn or your free time.

IDENTIFYING WEEDS

Correctly identifying lawn weeds allows you to plan thorough effective control measures. Knowing whether your weeds reproduce from roots, rhizomes, stolons, seeds, or a combination thereof allows you to take appropriate action. For example, the dandelion multiplies not only from seeds, but from its long root system. If you leave even a fairly small portion of root in the ground, way down, the dandelion will re-emerge with vigor.

To check on irrigation coverage, the homeowner has spaced containers around this lawn.

In general, weeds are categorized as annuals or perennials and as warm-season or cool-season plants.

Warm-season Annuals

About 80 percent of lawn weeds are annuals. Summer, or warm-season, annual weeds peak at midsummer, when heat slows the growth of competing cool-season grass. Warm-season annuals include foxtail, crabgrass (see page 57), goosegrass, quackgrass (see page 56), barnyardgrass (see page 57), sandbur, and shepherdspurse. All these begin as seeds that germinate as soon as soil temperature reaches 60° to 65° F. These seeds are not shade tolerant. If perennial lawn grasses are present and growing strongly, warm-season annual weeds have problems germinating because of lack of light. Even tree shade gives them pause. But where lawn is thinning, whether because of care problems or pest problems, weed seedlings establish rapidly. They then aggressively crowd out lawn grass.

In warm climates, apply fertilizer early in the season according to grass requirements. This causes grass to make a growth spurt before annual summer weeds germinate. Letting the lawn grow a little tall before cutting, particularly in spring, provides shade that slows annual weed seedlings. Watch watering practices carefully. Light frequent watering helps weeds and discourages grass growth. Water deeply and only when needed for your grass type.

In cool climates, apply fertilizer and mechanically improve the growing area at the end of summer. Follow this with an application of fertilizer in early spring. Leave the grass longer throughout spring and summer, letting established lawn smother out emerging weed seedlings.

Common warm-season annual weeds include foxtail, goosegrass, sandbur, and shepherdspurse.

Foxtail Types of foxtail include green, yellow, and giant. Alternate names are bristlegrass and pigeongrass. Annual foxtail is found throughout the United States and in parts of Canada. Foxtail leaves are 2 to 6 inches long, flat, ¼ to ½ inch wide, and sometimes appear twisted. The topsides of green foxtail leaves are hairy. Yellow foxtail leaves are smooth. Foxtail thrives in sunny bare lawn spots. It grows best in damp well-fertilized soil. If a lawn is kept mowed, foxtail forms a low mat. If unmowed, hairy flower spikes resembling bristles appear between June and September. Each bristle may be 2 to 4 inches long and somewhat resemble a fox's tail. Foxtail is often confused with crabgrass because both grow

in clumps. However, foxtail clumps are not as wide as crabgrass clumps. Since foxtail reproduces from seeds only, rather than from reproductive stems or runners, foxtail can be removed successfully with a trowel or by hand. Keep foxtail under control by removing mowing clippings that contain seed heads. Controls for foxtail include sprays containing calcium acid methanearsonate, fluazifop, or a glyphosate compound.

Goosegrass Also called yardgrass and silver crabgrass, this warm-season annual resembles crabgrass but is a darker green and has a silver center. Goosegrass stems are smooth and flat. They form a rosette resembling wheel spokes. Leaf blades are 2 to 10 inches high and ⅕ inch wide. Goosegrass germinates when soil temperature is between 60° and 65° F, several weeks after crabgrass. Goosegrass multiplies from seeds and expands by spreading. It has an extensive root system. It does not root at stem joints. Seeds are produced on stalks 2 to 6 inches high. Stalks appear from July to October. Mature plants die with first frost. Seeds are dormant over winter. Goosegrass prefers compacted soils with poor drainage and light frequent watering. To control this weed, use a treatment containing calcium acid methanearsonate or a glyphosate compound.

Sandbur Also called burgrass and sandburgrass, this annual grassy weed has yellow-green leaf blades that are 2 to 5 inches long and ¼ inch wide. The topsides of weeds may be rough. In mowed lawns, sandbur tends to form low mats. In unmowed lawns, it may reach 2 feet tall. Spiked straw-colored seed burrs ½ inch tall appear from July to September. Sandbur grows best in sandy dry soil. Begin control by improving soil with organic matter and encouraging strong lawn growth. If weeds persist, spot-treat with controls containing calcium acid methanearsonate, fluazifop, or glyphosate.

Shepherdspurse Also called shepherd's-bag and lady's-purse, this annual weed may appear throughout the year in warm-winter areas. Its arrow-shaped leaves are toothed or lobed and form a rosette. Tiny white flower clusters appear on stems that can reach up to 18 inches high. Seeds are in triangular pods resembling small sacklike purses. Seeds can remain dormant in soil for several years before germinating in spring. In warm-weather areas, seeds may germinate in fall. Shepherdspurse is not fussy about

Top: These foxtails are easily identifiable in an unmown area. When kept mown, foxtail resembles narrow clumps of crabgrass. Bottom: The odd silver center identifies this weed as goosegrass.

soil, but it will not grow in shade. Mechanical control consists of hand-pulling. Chemical control consists of a treatment containing MCPP. Treat when plants are actively growing.

Cool-season Annuals

This category includes downy brome, prostrate knotweed, black medic, common chickweed (see page 59), common groundsel, henbit (see page 59), mallow (see page 60), and annual bluegrass (see page 56). Cool-season annual weeds generally start growth from seeds in late summer or fall. They grow rapidly until the first solid frost, then go into a partial resting phase. With spring, cool-season annual weeds grow rapidly again. This time they set seeds. These weeds die out in early summer.

Cool-season weeds have the advantage of growing when most grasses are partially or entirely dormant. They thrive in early spring, when desired grasses are just getting started, and in fall, when desired grasses are already slowing down for winter. Unrestricted, cool-season annual weeds may ruin a lawn before it gets into full spring growth.

If your lawn has just a few cool-season weeds, eliminate them completely before any flowers or seeds appear. In southern states, plant a winter grass in fall that crowds weeds out. In northern states, leave the grass slightly higher in spring and fall to shade out weed seedlings. Rake up grass clippings if weed seeds are

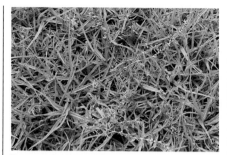

Prostrate knotweed is a ground-hugging plant that forms dense mats as large as 2 feet across.

Black medic resembles clover, but it can be distinguished by its many tiny yellow flowers.

Dallisgrass is a particularly unattractive weed that thrives in wet, untended lawns.

present. Chemical controls are quite effective when cool-season grasses are not responsive to manual measures.

Downy brome   Other names for this weed include downy bromegrass, cheatgrass, and militarygrass. It grows throughout the United States except for in some southeastern areas. Downy brome is a slender, upright annual weed growing to 2 feet tall. Light green coarse, hairy leaves are 2 to 6 inches long. Drooping, loose purple flower clusters appear in spring. Seeds can remain viable in soil for more than two years. Germination is in fall or early spring. Downy brome weeds turn purplish when mature. They prosper in poor sandy or gravelly soil and cool growing conditions. Remove individual weeds by hand-pulling. To control the plants by using chemicals, spray with fluazifop or glyphosate compounds. To keep downy brome from returning, apply an herbicide containing trifluralin, eptam, or chloral dimethyl.

Prostrate knotweed   Also called knotweed and doorweed, this plant grows quite low to the ground. Prostrate knotweed has smooth bluish green oval leaves. Each leaf is about 1 inch long and ¼ inch wide. The leaves attach to wiry stems at visible joints. The stems range from 4 to 24 inches long. Knotweed is an annual that forms mats that can reach 2 feet wide. These mats crowd out lawn grasses. Knotweed grows throughout the United States and in southern Canada. The weed is usually found in compacted soil. The fastest growth period for prostrate knotweed is from early spring to early fall. Tiny greenish white flowers bloom in clusters at the leaf and stem joints from June to November. Knotweed reproduces from seeds, which are plentiful. Though knotweed cannot get started in healthy dense turf, it is common in areas of heavy foot traffic. Aeration helps control prostrate knotweed. Pull out young plants. There is no preemergent control. If necessary, treat the lawn with a spray containing MCPP.

Black medic   Other names for black medic include *yellow trefoil* and *black clover.* It is sometimes confused with clover. Black medic has three-leaflet cloverlike leaves that are slightly toothed at the tips. Its low-growing stems are slightly hairy. Black medic is common in lawns throughout the United States from May through September. It forms thick mats that crowd out desirable lawn grasses. Small bright yellow flowers bloom in late spring and early summer. In warm-weather areas, black medic can bloom until December. Blooms are followed by black kidney-shaped pods containing seeds. Black medic is an annual that multiplies from seeds only. It is prevalent in nitrogen-deficient lawns. To eliminate small black medic patches, try hand-pulling. Increase lawn nitrogen with fertilizer where appropriate. Control with a spray containing MCPP if necessary.

Common groundsel   This weed is also known as grimsel. It grows 6 inches to 1½ feet tall. The weed has 4-inch-long toothed leaves of medium green. Yellow flowers 1 inch long appear from April to October. Common groundsel reproduces by seeds and by stems that may take root at the lower joints. The plant grows best in moist rich soil. Hand-pull groundsel before it produces seeds. Spot-treat with a control containing glyphosate.

Warm-season Grassy Perennials

These weeds are more difficult to control than annual weeds. Since they are a different color and texture than lawn grasses, they stand out, possibly ruining a lawn's appearance. If grassy perennial weeds take over, it may be necessary to pull out the present lawn and replace it.

Warm-season grassy perennials include dallisgrass, bermudagrass, zoysiagrass, nimblewill, nutsedge, and quackgrass (see page 56). The most common is dallisgrass.

Dallisgrass   A clumpy rosette-type weed, dallisgrass has coarse-textured leaves. Each leaf is 4 to 10 inches long and ½ inch wide. Stems 2 to 6 inches long emerge from the plant center in a starlike pattern. Dallisgrass reproduces from seeds and underground stems. This perennial has extremely deep roots. Dallisgrass has a tendency to turn brown in the center. Although it is primarily a summer weed in cool areas, it grows all year in mild climates. Growth begins quite early in spring. Dallisgrass grows best in warm weather; low, wet ground; and high-cut lawns. However, once established, it spreads rapidly in low-cut lawns. Dallisgrass is a severe problem in the southern United States. There is no preemergent control. Try draining soil to eliminate dallisgrass. If the weed persists, treat it in early spring or summer with glyphosate. Repeated treatments are often necessary.

Nimblewill   Also termed nimbleweed and dropseed, nimblewill has smooth, flat light green or bluish green leaves up to 2 inches long. Wiry stems grow up to 10 inches tall. In spring nimblewill turns green after other grasses. The result is brown patches in nimblewill-infested lawns. Nimblewill stems root at lower nodes as the plants reach outward. Nimblewill thrives in hot dry areas and in thin turf during drought. For small infestations, dig out patches of the weed. Eliminate nimblewill in lawns with an herbicide containing fluazifop. Begin control in early spring.

Nutsedge   Other names for nutsedge are nutgrass, cocosedge, and cocograss. The most common nutsedge forms are yellow or purple. There are annual varieties as well as perennial. Nutsedge has greenish yellow leaves emerging from triangular stems. In flower, nutsedge has umbrella-like clusters topping its stems. Seed heads are yellow-brown. In summer, nutsedge grows more rapidly than lawn grass, is easily seen, and disfigures lawns. It can

Plantain is fairly easy to recognize but can be difficult to control.

be extremely difficult to eliminate, because it multiplies from tubers, seeds, and underground stems. The tuber stores nutrients. If any tuber is left in the ground after the rest of the plant is removed, nutsedge can regrow. This weed prefers overly watered soil. Control includes changing lawn-watering techniques or increasing soil drainage. To treat nutsedge chemically, use a spray containing MCPP. Begin spraying in early spring and repeat the treatment according to label instructions.

Cool-season Perennial Broadleaf Weeds

The leaves of these weeds can be lance-shaped, arrow-shaped, scalloped, or oval. Basically, they are not grasslike. All make a ragged appearance in lawns. This category includes broadleaf plantain, dandelion (see page 60), mouse-ear chickweed, ground ivy, speedwell, and white clover (see page 58).

Broadleaf plantain   Also called common plantain, broadleaf plantain has thick egg-shaped wavy-edged leaves growing in a ground-hugging rosette. This weed grows throughout the United States and southern Canada. The gray-green leaves of the broadleaf plantain range from 2 to 10 inches long. From May to September seed heads appear in a long cluster from a central upright stem. Plantain multiplies from seeds and from resprouting roots. The weed germinates best in rich, moist, compacted soil. As broadleaf plantains grow, they suffocate surrounding lawn grass. To mechanically control plantain, dig out roots with a trowel. Do not let flowers or seeds form. Aerate the lawn. There is no preemergent control. To treat major infestations, control with a spray containing DCPA.

Mouse-ear chickweed   This plant can appear in the finest of well-kept lawns. Not directly related to the annual common chickweed, this broadleaf perennial multiplies rapidly and can crowd out desired grasses. Mouse-ear chickweed has a different color and texture than grass.

The ½-inch-long leaves of the weed are both fleshy and fuzzy. Stems are low and spreading. Small white flowers appear from April through June. The period of fastest growth is in early spring. Mouse-ear chickweed multiplies from seeds and runners, which root easily at the nodes. This prevalent weed thrives in moist, poorly drained soil in sun or shade. Mechanical control consists of keeping runners and stems off the ground so they cannot take root. Mouse-ear chickweed is extremely difficult to eliminate by hand-pulling, since it can resprout from pieces left in the soil. To discourage mouse-ear chickweed, cut the lawn short. Remove clippings containing runners and discard them. Apply chemical controls when this weed is emerging and actively growing; there is no preemergent control. Be certain to apply the correct amount of postemergent product. The controls should contain DCPA.

Ground ivy   This plant is also called creeping ivy and gill-over-the-ground. It is a cool-season perennial weed that also functions as a sturdy ground cover in moist, shady or partial-sun areas where little else can grow. Plant height is 3 to 6 inches. Bright green leaves are scalloped, round, and about 1 inch wide. Tiny light blue to purple trumpet-shaped flowers appear from spring through summer. Reproduction is from seeds and creeping stems that root easily upon soil contact. Ground ivy does well in sun or shade as long as soil is damp. Plants form a dense mat that can completely crowd out desired lawn grass. There is no preemergent control. Cut grass short and rake to keep runners from touching the ground. Hand-pulling must be thorough because pieces left in the ground can resprout. Postemergent sprays may contain DCPA.

Speedwell   Another name for speedwell is creeping veronica. In a few years it can cover an entire lawn. This perennial weed has bright green, roundish, scallop-edged leaves ½ inch long. Each plant is about 4 inches high. Tiny bluish white flowers bloom on stalks that grow somewhat above leaves. Heart-shaped seedpods form on stems below flowers. Speedwell reproduces from creeping stems that root easily upon touching ground. The weed usually stays out of well-drained sunny areas that receive fertilizer regularly. It grows best in moist, shady lawn and acidic soil, but it can grow in sunlight if soil remains moist. To discourage speedwell, cut grass short and remove all clippings to avoid stem rooting. If necessary, spray with a control containing DCPA or MCPP.

Cool-season Perennial Grassy or Grasslike Weeds

This category includes bermudagrass, zoysiagrass, quackgrass (see page 56), tall fescue (see page 57), wild garlic and wild onion, timothygrass, and velvetgrass.

Bermudagrass   This plant can be a valued warm-season turfgrass or a nasty weed in cool season lawns. It is also called devilgrass, wiregrass, and dog's tooth grass. Bermudagrass is often confused with quackgrass because both spread in the same creeping fashion and form mats. Bermudagrass blades are about ⅛ inch wide. Stems are gray-green, hairy, and 6 to 18 inches long. This grass reproduces from seeds, aboveground stems, and underground stems. Roots may grow several feet deep. Seeds are formed on 3-inch-wide fingerlike segments that grow slightly above stems. From three to seven of these segments grow on each plant. Bermudagrass is a fast-growing perennial that turns brown when temperatures drop below 50° F. It is slow to turn green in spring, creating brown patches throughout the lawn.

Though drought and heat tolerant, this annual does not grow vigorously in shade. In sunny areas, however, bermudagrass may quickly crowd out desirable lawn. Mechanically control bermudagrass by hand-pulling. Remove all roots—any piece of root left can resprout. The best time to begin chemical control is in spring, when shoots are just appearing; use glyphosate or fluazifop according to label instructions. Six weeks later, retreat any new green stems and leaves. Bermudagrass can be spot-treated with glyphosate or fluazifop any time grass is actively growing. After 1 week, mow as close as possible and reseed the area. Multiple treatments may be needed. There is no preemergent treatment. To prevent bermudagrass invasion in cool-season areas, apply a heavy dose of fertilizer in the fall. Give the lawn adequate water during the summer.

Zoysiagrass   Like bermudagrass, zoysiagrass is a valued lawn grass in warm-weather areas but a weed in other regions. In cold areas, this perennial becomes dormant with the first fall frost and remains so until late spring. The result is that small to large irregular patches of brown suddenly develop amidst cool-weather grasses that stay green, such as bluegrass, fescue, or bentgrass. The browning is often attributed to insect invasion, but the zoysiagrass is still perfectly healthy. Its tops have died back, but its

The bright green velvetgrass stands out against the duller green of this lawn.

roots are merely resting. Though it grows slowly, zoysiagrass is hardy. It often takes hold in a lawn in areas of heavy traffic, then invades the surrounding area. Mechanical control consists of digging up clumps and reseeding. If zoysiagrass is a continuing problem, some gardeners let it take over lawns growing in full sun, then spray it with green dye in winter. Chemical control consists of spot treatment with glyphosate. Treat while zoysiagrass is still green; once it turns brown, anything but digging is ineffective.

Wild garlic and wild onion Wild garlic is often mistaken for wild onion and vice versa. Though they are similar in habits, they are not the same. Both are often the first growth seen in spring. They resemble grasses but are not. Both grow from small underground bulbs and have a garlicky or oniony odor. Leaves are slender, hollow, and round, joining together near the plant base. Greenish purple or white flowers appear at leaf height. Germination occurs in spring and fall. Bulblets may appear at leaftips. The bulblets fall to the ground and sprout. Wild garlic and onion spread rapidly from spring to midsummer. They thrive in heavy, wet soil. They are drought and cold hardy. There is no preemergent control. Mowing when wild garlic and wild onion first appear can lessen infestation, but bulbs must be totally removed for full control. Postemergent control is most effective in late fall, when wild garlic or onion is still small and vulnerable. Once these perennial weeds take hold, they can be extremely difficult to eliminate. Spray with a control containing DCPA.

Timothygrass This weed thrives in thin, poorly fertilized lawns. Its leaves are broad and pointed. This blue-green bunching grass grows best in spring and fall. To control timothygrass dig up all visible clumps.

Velvetgrass This perennial can grow to 4 feet tall in unmowed areas. In mowed areas, the bright green velvety leaves stay flat. The plants root wherever joints touch

the soil. Seed heads 2 to 4 inches long appear from July to August. Seeds remain dormant over winter and germinate in spring. Perennial velvetgrass thrives in damp areas with good soil, but it tolerates partial shade. To eliminate velvetgrass, use a control containing glyphosate at any time, but spraying before seed heads mature will be most effective.

Eliminating Moss

An invasion of moss can disfigure lawn areas. Moss mats consist of thousands of tiny plants. Moss grows to a maximum of 2 inches tall, forming a green, velvet-like covering on bare ground. The presence of moss usually indicates poor drainage, high soil acidity, too much shade, ground compaction, low soil fertility, or excess moisture. To eliminate moss, find which conditions apply in your situation and correct them. If moss begins growing under trees in lieu of lawn, try pruning tree branches and applying fertilizer under the trees. To eliminate standing water, dig up the ground in springtime; fill depressions with organic matter; if necessary, correct soil pH; level the area; and reseed it.

Small moss patches can be raked from lawns, but the moss will reappear if the cause is not remedied. Treat large moss patches with ferrous ammonium sulfate in early spring. This treatment may cause surrounding grass to darken for about a week, but it will recover.

Using Chemical Controls

Herbicides are powerful formulations that must be used on the appropriate plants at the proper time. In fact, the time of application defines into which of two major categories a chemical fits. These categories are for preemergent herbicides and postemergent herbicides.

A preemergent herbicide is most effective when placed in or on soil before weed seedlings poke out of the ground. A preemergent control stops sprouting at an early stage. If applied properly, few, if any, of the targeted weeds emerge. A postemergent control is effective after the weeds have emerged and begun growth.

Many modern preemergent and postemergent controls are quite specific as to what weeds they eliminate. Used improperly, these herbicides can create more problems than the weeds themselves. Desired grass and surrounding plants can be temporarily or permanently harmed. Read the herbicide label before purchasing the product. Make sure the chemical is appropriate for the plant you want to treat, and see if using the product requires special precautions. Use all controls at the appropriate time. Post-

emergent controls are not effective during the weed's dormant season. Use them on lawn grasses when soil is moist and weeds are growing strongly. Avoid spraying or dusting on windy days. Wind can waft weed killer to nearby plants. If they are susceptible to the control, they may soon brown or die. Apply chemical controls early in the morning or early at dusk, when the air is generally calm. If the herbicide label lists a nearby plant as particularly sensitive to the control, protect the plant with a cardboard or wood barrier.

Lack of patience may result in control overdose. A treatment can take from 3 to 10 days to produce visible results. Do not reapply the product because weed browning does not occur a day or two after spraying or dusting. Herbicide overdoses are dangerous to surrounding grasses.

Weed killers do not gain effectiveness if mixed at a concentration stronger than the instructions recommend. Using too strong a mixture can damage or kill desirable plants.

Do not use a weed killer on newly seeded lawns, even if the control is not supposed to affect grass of the type that is planted. Any type of weed control used around seedling grasses can kill them. Seedlings are far more sensitive to control ingredients than mature plants. If you want to use a postemergent control, do so far in advance of reseeding the grass; this will give the control ingredients time to weaken in the soil. The time required differs for different controls. Read the label of the product you buy to determine a safe time for treatment.

Sometimes desirable plants brown long after the application of a weed control but soon after the application of an insecticide. If the same applicator was used for both, the cause could be herbicide contamination. If even a little bit of an herbicide remains in the applicator, it can affect plants. Wash all applicators thoroughly with water and detergent to remove herbicide remnants. Better yet, use separate applicators for herbicides and insecticides.

Solving Tree-Related Lawn Problems

When trees and grass grow in the same area, two problems often develop: surface roots and excess shade from tree canopies and fallen foliage.

Surface Roots

Because of their marked natural tendency to develop surface roots, some trees are best left out of lawn areas. These include acacia, ailanthus, silver maple, alder, Pacific dogwood, fig, evergreen ash, honey-locust, mulberry, sycamore, poplar, elm, sumac, black locust, and willow. If you move into a home whose lawn has severe surface root problems, consider removing the trees and replacing them with more appropriate species. Those include maple; silk tree; smoke tree; hawthorn; Modesto ash; goldenrain tree; crape myrtle; saucer and star magnolia; and flowering cherry, peach, and plum.

Surface rooting is caused by external factors as well as natural tendencies. One of the most common factors is lawn watering. Tree roots need regular watering that penetrates from 6 inches to 3 feet into the soil—the depth necessary depends on the tree species. Sprinkler systems tend to water shallowly. Tree roots, suffering from drought in deeper, unirrigated soil, move upward instead of downward to get the moisture they need.

Excess standing water around lawn trees is another cause of surface rooting. Water fills the air spaces in the soil. As a result, the only readily available oxygen is near the surface, so the tree roots move upward. If a natural or created basin is around the tree, you might want to dig a drainage area. Irrigate less often near the tree base so soil dries out between waterings. When you do irrigate the tree, water it deeply, perhaps using a root irrigator.

Compacted soil can also cause tree roots to move upward, seeking oxygen. To allow deeper oxygen penetration, loosen soil around tree roots. Try not to impact the roots themselves. Severe root injury can permit disease and insect attack.

Like compacted soil, fertilizer application practices can encourage surface rooting. If nutrients remain at the surface, the roots do too. To prompt downward growth, place fertilizer in 12-inch-deep holes or borings. Space the holes evenly under the full expanse of the leaf canopy.

If surface rooting remains a problem after watering, drainage, soil compaction, or fertilizer application has been adjusted, root pruning may be necessary. Some root pruning can be done without harming the tree. If you prize the tree, consider hiring a professional to do the job.

If surface roots are allowed to remain, you may have to adjust your mowing practices. If you do not want to leave the root area bare, consider placing a ring of bark mulch around the tree, or planting a hardy ground cover.

Regardless of tree type and maintenance practices, some lawn upheaval may occur near old or large trees. Their big roots, even at a depth, displace ground. Adding good weed-free soil as a yearly topdressing can improve appearance.

Tree Shade
The fact that your lawn is shaded by trees does not necessarily mean the grass gets too much shade. Trees with naturally sparse canopies, such as birch, can allow enough filtered light to permit shade-tolerant grass to grow fairly well. If the lawn thins and turns dark green, however, or if moss and algae take hold, corrective action is necessary.

To increase the amount of sun under deciduous or nondeciduous trees, try trimming back or cutting off all limbs that extend below or grow less than 6 feet from the ground. Thinning a dense tree crown can also help. If the lawn does not improve after the pruning, you may have to replant the area.

In an area that receives less than 2 hours of direct sunlight each day, consider planting a shade-tolerant nongrass species such as vinca; wild ginger; sweet woodruff; mondograss; winter creeper; ajuga; Japanese spurge; or even ivy, if it can be controlled.

If the area receives at least 2 hours of direct sun daily, a shade-tolerant grass can probably survive. Under deciduous trees in cool-winter areas, put in shade-tolerant lawns in late summer or early fall. This gives the grass time to establish during the tree's leafless period.

Under nondeciduous trees in cool climates, reseed or resod in early spring. Consider creeping, red, or chewing fescue. Some of the bluegrass varieties also tolerate partial shade. Where warm-season grasses can grow, replant just after the grass-growing season begins in early spring. Among the shade-tolerant, warm-season choices are zoysiagrass, centipedegrass, St. Augustine grass, and carpetgrass. Since tree roots interfere with deep soil preparation, adding a thin layer of topsoil will help make a healthy seedbed.

Always remove fallen leaves under deciduous trees planted in lawn areas. Fallen foliage shades grass even when light is available. When removing leaves from newly seeded areas, take care not to damage the seedlings or seedbed.

Shady areas call for care in mowing as well. When light is scarce, grass grows a bit taller in its reach for the sun. Close mowing of shaded grass can be harmful since it reduces the productive leaf blade area. Adjust your lawn mower accordingly when moving from turf in sun to turf in tree shade; let the shaded grass grow a little taller than the grass in the sun.

In lawn areas that have been overplanted with trees, regardless of tree type, shading will eventually become a problem. Overplanting is fairly common in new-home areas where owners want, in a short time, to establish the leafy look of an old neighborhood. In addition to creating too much shade, overplanting impedes air flow. Lack of air circulation discourages grass growth and encourages lawn diseases. If the planting is extremely thick, pruning is not enough; trees must be removed to alleviate the shading problem.

CONTROLLING ANIMAL PESTS
Gardeners usually think of lawn pests in two categories: insects and larger animals.

Lawn Insects
Insect pests do an ample share of lawn destruction. At varying times of the year, chiggers (see page 319), chinch bugs (see page 51), billbugs (see page 52), armyworms, cutworms, European crane flies, grubs (see page 51), sod webworms (see page 50), flea beetles (see page 69), fiery skipper butterfly larvae, fleas (see page 318), fire ants, fruit flies, grasshoppers, greenbugs, leafhoppers, mites, scales, wireworms, and mole crickets (see page 53) can invade in small or large numbers. Healthy lawns can tolerate more insect damage than poorly maintained lawns. Some perennial ryegrasses are not attractive to pests such as armyworms, billbugs, cutworms, and sod webworms. Large populations of any pest insect species usually call for intervention by the gardener. Predators—such as birds, parasitic wasps, *Bacillus thuringiensis* (Bt), ladybugs, and green lacewing larvae—can help the gardener control insect pests without chemicals.

Armyworms These pests chew grass blades and stems, causing circular bare patches in lawns. In large numbers, armyworms can chew a lawn to the ground in three days. Found throughout the United States except in the coldest areas, the fall armyworm is one of the worst southern lawn pests. These worms move from lawn to garden, then perhaps return to do more damage. Newly hatched worms are white with black heads. Mature worms are green, tan, or brown with dark or orange back and side stripes. Adult size is 1½ inches long. Parents are 1-inch-wide tan or mottled gray moths. Like the adults, armyworms are most active at night and on overcast days. In daylight, they hide in the soil around grass roots. The first generation, which appears in spring, causes the most damage. *Bacillus thuringiensis* is partially effective as a natural control of larvae. Other controls include sprays containing chlorpyrifos, diazinon, acephate (ORTHENE®), or carbaryl (SEVIN®). Lawn granules containing diazinon or chlorpyrifos also work effectively.

Cutworms   The larvae of moths, cutworms feed on grass stems and leaf blades. Cutworms are brown, gray, or nearly gray; there are spotted and striped varieties. A full-sized larva can be up to 2 inches long. Cutworms curl up when touched. Adults are dark 2-inch-wide night-flying moths. Often called miller moths, they are common at night around outdoor lights. Cutworms feed at night. During the day, they hide in the upper soil layers. Some types never emerge, feeding only on grass roots. Their feeding causes 2-inch-wide bare spots in the lawn. A closer look shows grass sheared off at or below ground level. Birds often seek out cutworms as food. *Bacillus thuringiensis* sprays and parasitic wasps help destroy cutworms. Apply chemical controls in late afternoon or early evening; use lawn sprays or granules containing diazinon or chlorpyrifos. Control can be difficult.

European crane fly larvae   These larvae eat grass roots, causing yellow-brown patches in summer dry seasons. Damage often begins at the lawn periphery and moves inward. The brownish wormlike maggots develop a tough skin and are sometimes called leatherjackets. A larva is about 1 inch long. Crane flies are found throughout the United States. Adults look like long-legged mosquitoes. An adult's body size, not including the legs, is about 1 inch long. Crane flies do not sting or do other harm. To ascertain whether damage is caused by crane fly larvae or other lawn pests, water damaged areas thoroughly, then cover them overnight with black plastic. If crane fly larvae are present, they will be lying on the soil surface under the plastic the next morning. Crane fly feeding stops naturally in mid-May. Treatment is most effective in early April; use diazinon or chlorpyrifos.

Fiery skipper butterfly larvae   By destroying grass blades, these insects create isolated brown spots in lawns. Initially these dead areas are 1 inch wide, but they can expand to cover larger lawn areas. The adult butterfly is orange, brown, or both. It is usually seen during warm weather, flying over lawns in midday. The larvae are small brownish yellow worms that may be found within affected grass blades. White cottony masses may appear in the lawn—these are the cocoons of a butterfly parasite. The parasites can sometimes control an infestation. If not, use a control containing chlorpyrifos.

Fire ants   Infestations of fire ants are becoming increasingly serious as their territory moves from southern states to other warm-winter areas. Their tunnels and mounds can obstruct mowers, and tunneling can eliminate a lawn. Their bites are painful and, if numerous, can severely injure animals and people. Fire ants are more of a problem in sunny clay soils than other areas. Control fire ants by using acephate (ORTHENE®), chlorpyrifos, diazinon, or various baits.

Fruit fly larvae   These pests live in young grass stems. They eat and gradually destroy the central shoots. Grass then sends out side shoots. Parents are tiny black flies. The females lay eggs on the grass blades. As many as 10 larvae can live inside a single blade. Control is difficult because larvae are so well protected by the stems. Diazinon granules can be partially effective as a control.

Grasshoppers   These insects can become lawn problems in areas near farmland; they migrate to yards when crop sustenance is insufficient. Dry windy weather encourages grasshopper populations. In large numbers, grasshoppers can eat grass to the base. If the number is small, handpicking can be effective. This job is easier early in the morning, when grasshoppers move slowly. If grasshopper lawn invasions occur repeatedly, slow down the next infestation with a bran bait containing *Nosema locustae*, a grasshopper disease organism. This may take several years to achieve full effect. Seasonal controls include an acephate (ORTHENE®) or a chlorpyrifos spray applied with a lawn sprayer over the entire lawn.

Greenbugs   Small light green aphids that feed on plant sap, greenbugs usually infest Kentucky bluegrass lawns. Their damage appears as rusty-looking lawn areas. These areas expand as greenbug populations increase. Greenbugs do not do much damage in lawns with enough sun; in shaded areas, they can become pests. To control greenbugs, use an insecticidal soap or a control containing acephate (ORTHENE®) or diazinon.

Leafhoppers   These ⅛-inch wedge-shaped yellow, green, or gray insects live on most lawns. They hop and fly easily from one leaf blade to another and suck out leaf sap. As a result, individual leaves develop white spotting. With large infestations, leafhopper damage is demonstrated by lawn fading. Severe infestations can eradicate an emerging lawn. Leafhoppers are most abundant in warm weather. The appearance of damaged seedlings may mimic drought injury. However, if leafhoppers are present, they are almost surely doing the damage. Small infestations are usually not bothersome to plants. Leafhoppers hop about in groups when disturbed, however, and their presence may annoy gardeners. Use acephate (ORTHENE®), diazinon, malathion, or carbaryl (SEVIN®) as a control measure if necessary.

Mites   Grass turns straw-colored as mites suck sap from the blades. The lawn then becomes brown and sparse. Some gardeners working in areas where mites are about may experience skin irritation. Three types of mites generally infest lawns: bermudagrass mites, which prey on bermudagrass only; clover mites; and winter grain mites, which attack bluegrass, fescue, and bentgrass. Most mites are too small to be seen without a microscope. Under magnification, these ⅟₅₀-inch pests vary in color depending on species. They have eight legs and are insect relatives rather than insects. Bermudagrass mites may be seen by shaking an infested plant over a sheet of dark paper. The mites are visible as creamy specks that begin crawling around. Mites thrive in hot, dry weather. Adequate watering keeps populations down. Controls include insecticidal soap, diazinon, or chlorpyrifos.

Scales   Infestations of scales on lawns are difficult to control. Scales are legless insects with hard shells. They are extremely small and look like bumps on leaves or roots. Pearl scales attack the roots of centipedegrass, bermudagrass, and St. Augustine grass. Bermudagrass scale feeds on bermudagrass stems, giving the plant a moldy appearance. Rhodesgrass scales attack grass crowns, causing blades to wither and die. Control consists of spot-treating with diazinon every 7 to 14 days from May 1st through June.

Wireworms   These brown hard-shelled larvae are the offspring of click beetles. A full-sized larva is 1½ inches long. Wireworms feed in groups on grass roots, causing irregular areas of wilted grass. The larvae are most prevalent in soggy soil. Create an organic control by digging several 3-inch-wide by 3-inch-deep holes in the lawn. Bury a potato in each hole and mark each one by inserting a stake or

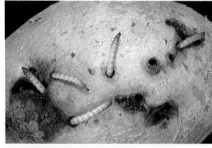

This potato was buried to attract wireworms.

some other device in the ground. In a few days the potatoes will be filled with feeding wireworms. Remove and destroy the potatoes; do not compost them. Chemical controls include diazinon and chlorpyrifos. In areas of serious wireworm infestation, use diazinon or chlorpyrifos as a preventive before seeding the lawn. This treatment will help keep wireworms from destroying seedlings.

Other Lawn Pests

Moles, rabbits, and gophers top the list of lawn-destroying animals, although in certain areas armadillos, skunks, crayfish, birds, voles (meadow mice), and field mice can cause significant damage.

Moles   In digging tunnels that serve as feeding pathways, moles create raised ridges that may eventually crisscross a lawn. Ridges range from 3 to 5 inches wide. Because mole tunneling destroys grass roots, ridge areas brown quickly. Moles build new tunnels constantly and may not use the same one twice. If you look carefully, you may find the mole entry and exit mounds. These are round, conical, fan-shaped, or irregular in appearance. The hole usually has dirt in it but is still visible. The mounds are connected to the main runways. These are 6 to 10 inches underground and not usually visible above ground. Moles use these repeatedly.

Moles are 6 to 8 inches long with gray to black velvety fur. They have slender hairless snouts and small eyes and ears. Moles' front feet are large with long claws, and they function for digging much like a hoe. Despite the many tunnels, one lawn is usually home to only one mole. Except for breeding season, in early spring, moles tend to live solitary lives. Moles eat insects and earthworms. Before you try any other control, consider using diazinon to eliminate pest bugs in the lawn. Without ample food, a resident mole may seek supplies elsewhere. Other controls include trapping, bait, repellents, and fumigation. Bait and repellents are not as effective as other controls. Above- and below-ground mole traps are available. Move tunnel traps daily if a mole is not caught.

Gophers   These rodents are occasionally seen poking their heads out of newly constructed dirt mounds early in the morning. Gophers are brown, have small eyes and ears, and have conspicuous pouches on both sides of their mouths. Gophers protect their territories. The number of mounds in your lawn may seem to indicate the presence of a gopher colony; however, each lawn usually contains just one gopher. The mounds consist of finely pulverized soil that is quite visible in a green lawn. Each mound may contain a visible hole, or an earth clump may camouflage the hole. Tunnels 6 to 8 inches below the lawn surface connect the mounds. Gophers do not create lawn ridges. The rodents eat roots of grass and other plants, pulling them down into underground burrows. Traps are the most efficient form of gopher control. Both wire traps and box traps are sold at many hardware stores and plant nurseries. Dig down to an active horizontal tunnel, and place two traps in it. Follow the instructions that accompany the trap.

Rabbits   When hungry, rabbits eat almost every type of green plant, including lawn grass. They can be minor pests or major ones, depending on the supply of food in the area. The most effective control is keeping rabbits out. Owning a cat or dog that annoys animal pests is sometimes a solution. Another control is a fence made of 1-inch-wide wire mesh. This should be 2 feet high and extend 6 inches underground to avoid rabbit jumping and tunneling. Keeping jackrabbits out requires an even higher fence. Rabbit repellents are sometimes effective. They repel rabbits by making grass taste unpleasant. Repellents must be reapplied as grass grows or is mowed.

Field mice and voles   These rodents sometimes take up residence in abandoned gopher and mole burrows or create their own. If they make a lawn their winter residence, they may work under snow cover. Lawn runways become visible when snow disappears. Voles feed on grass during the winter and can cause extensive damage. A cat that annoys these rapidly multiplying pests can be an effective control. Other controls include mousetraps, rattraps, and box traps. If children or pets are in the area, do not use poison bait in the open.

Skunks and armadillos   In residential areas adjacent to woodland or farmland, skunks and armadillos can cause lawn damage as they dig up grass to feed on insects, particularly grubs. Lawn grubs from an infestation of pest beetles, such as Japanese beetles or June beetles, act as an attractant. If the problem becomes serious, apply a pest-beetle control. Removing their food supply usually causes skunks and armadillos to go elsewhere.

Birds   Lawns containing earthworms, chinch bugs, sod webworms, cutworms, and caterpillars are a valuable food source

A mole trap has been set out for the maker of these unsightly burrows.

for birds. Birds do not cause many problems in high-cut lawns; the insects they eliminate would do much more damage. However, in low-cut lawns, mass feeding may create an abundance of pecking holes that detract from appearance. Since pest bugs are a prime attractant, using a pest-insect control containing diazinon or chlorpyrifos usually causes the birds to turn elsewhere. Be certain to treat lawns in late afternoon so insecticides are dry by the following day when birds return—freshly applied insecticide may be harmful to birds.

Crayfish   Also called crawfish and craw-dads, crayfish are water-loving creatures that resemble miniature lobsters. Crayfish become a lawn problem only if a lawn is constantly soggy. This can be due to watering practices, poor drainage, or a high water table. Crayfish construct soil mounds around a hole about 1 inch wide. In severe infestations, these mounds must be leveled out to permit mowing. Control consists of correcting drainage problems or easing up on watering. Without hospitable surroundings, crayfish usually go elsewhere. If the growing site is not fully correctable, consider using crayfish bait. Spring treatment is most effective, particularly after a rain.

Snails and slugs   The silvery trails of snails and slugs wind across lawns and are visible in the morning and on overcast days. These familiar lawn pests hide under ground cover or leaves during the day to avoid sunlight. Both animals eat grass. Control snails and slugs by using liquid or pellet baits. Place the bait near the animals' hiding places and in the same areas each time.

DEAD PATCHES

Dog urine spots.

Burn caused by a fertilizer spill.

Dead annual bluegrass.

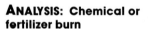

PROBLEM: Circular spots, straw brown in color and 8 to 10 inches in diameter, appear in the lawn. A ring of deep green grass may surround each patch. The lawn may also contain other patches, dark green in color, without any dead areas in them. No spots or webby growth appear on the grass blades, and the grass does not mat down. Dogs have been in the area.

ANALYSIS: Dog urine injury
Dog urine burns grass. The salts in the urine cause varying stages of damage, from slight discoloration to outright killing. The nitrogen in the urine may encourage immediately surrounding grass to grow rapidly, resulting in a dark green, vigorously growing ring. Lawns suffer the most damage in hot, dry weather.

SOLUTION: Water the affected areas thoroughly to wash away the urine. This reduces but does not eradicate the brown discoloration. Surrounding grass eventually fills in the affected areas. For quick repair, spot-sod. If possible, keep dogs off the lawn.

PROBLEM: Grass dies and turns yellow in irregular patches or definite regular stripes or curves. Grass bordering the areas is a healthy green color. Yellow areas do not spread or enlarge. They appear within two to five days after fertilizer is added or after a chemical is spilled on the lawn.

ANALYSIS: Chemical or fertilizer burn
Chemicals such as pesticides, fertilizers, gasoline, and hydrated lime may burn the grass if applied improperly or accidentally spilled. When excessive amounts of these materials contact grass, they cause the blades to dry out and die.

SOLUTION: Damage can be prevented or minimized by picking up the spilled material, then washing the chemical from the soil immediately. If the substance is water-soluble, water the area thoroughly—3 to 5 times longer than usual. If the substance is not soluble in water, such as gasoline or weed oil, flood the area with liquid dishwashing detergent diluted to about the same strength as used for washing dishes. Then water the lawn as indicated above. Some substances, such as preemergent herbicides, cannot be washed from the soil. Activated charcoal can be worked into the soil to deactivate or tie up the herbicide. Prevent further damage by filling gas tanks, spreaders, and sprayers on an unplanted surface, such as a driveway. Apply chemicals according to the label instructions. Apply fertilizers when the grass blades are dry and the soil is moist. Water thoroughly afterward to dilute the fertilizer and wash it into the soil. Keep drop spreaders closed when stopped or turning.

PROBLEM: Areas of grass that were once lush and green die and turn straw brown. In places where the grass had a whitish appearance in late spring, irregular patches appear with the onset of hot summer weather.

ANALYSIS: Annual bluegrass
(*Poa annua*)
Annual bluegrass is one of the most troublesome but least-noticed weeds in the lawn. This member of the bluegrass family is lighter green, more shallow rooted, and less drought and heat tolerant than Kentucky bluegrass. Annual bluegrass, as its name suggests, usually lives for only one year, although some strains are perennials. The seeds germinate in cool weather from late summer to late fall. Annual bluegrass grows rapidly in the spring, especially if fertilizer is applied then. Seed heads appear in mid- to late spring, at the same height the grass is cut. The seed heads give the lawn a whitish appearance. When hot, dry weather arrives, the plants die. The seeds fall to the soil and do not germinate until cooler weather. Annual bluegrass is most serious where the soil is compacted.

SOLUTION: Weed killers are only partially effective in controlling annual bluegrass. In early to midfall prevent seeds from germinating by applying an herbicide containing bensulide or DCPA. Do not use this herbicide if you plan to reseed the lawn in the fall. Replace the dead areas with sod. Do not cut the lawn too short. Lawns more than 2½ inches tall seldom contain much annual bluegrass. Aerate the lawn by coring in compacted areas (see page 54).

Dead crabgrass.

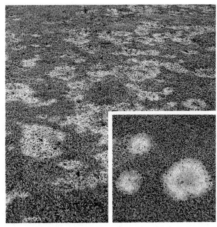

Fusarium patch. *Insert:* Close-up.

Fusarium blight.

PROBLEM: Brown
patches develop in the
lawn with the first frost in
the fall. Close examination of the dead
spots reveals that it is not the lawn grass
that has died, but a weed.

ANALYSIS: Crabgrass dying out
Crabgrass (*Digitaria* species) is an annual
grassy weed. It forms large flat clumps,
smothering lawn grass as it spreads. Crabgrass dies with the first killing frost in the
fall or with the onset of cold weather,
leaving dead patches in the lawn. Crabgrass sprouts from seeds in early spring. It
is a prolific seed producer; a single plant
can make thousands of seeds during the
course of the summer.

SOLUTION: In early spring, 2 weeks be-
fore the last expected frost, treat the lawn
with an herbicide containing DCPA or si-
duron. These preemergent weed killers
kill the seed as it germinates. Kill actively
growing crabgrass with a herbicide containing methanearsonate. Maturing plants
are harder to kill, so repeat the treatment
2 more times, at 4- to 7-day intervals, if
necessary. To control crabgrass growing in
cracks in sidewalks and driveways, use an
herbicide containing glyphosate and oxyfluorfen or fluazifop-butyl. A thick lawn
seldom contains much crabgrass. For
more information on crabgrass, see
page 57.

PROBLEM: Pale yellow
areas, 2 inches to 1 foot in
diameter and pink along
the edges, occur in the lawn in the late
winter and early spring. Blades are light
tan and stick together. A white cottony
growth may cover the blades.

ANALYSIS: Fusarium patch
This grass disease is caused by a fungus
(*Fusarium nivale*) that attacks lawns when
the turf remains wet from snow, rain, or
poor surface drainage in the fall, winter,
or spring. The disease, also called pink
snow mold, is most severe on bentgrass,
but it also occurs on other grasses. Fusarium patch is most prevalent in humid
weather when daytime temperatures remain below 65° F or when snow falls on
unfrozen soil. Fusarium-patch fungi often
grow beneath the snow or as it melts.
Usually, only the grass blades are affected;
when the disease is severe, however, the
crowns also are attacked, killing the plants.

SOLUTION: Treat the lawn in early
spring, at the first sign of the disease,
with a fungicide containing benomyl,
iprodione, or methyl thiophanate. Repeat
the treatment in 10 to 14 days. Treat the
lawn again in mid- to late fall when the
daytime temperatures remain below 60° F
and the weather is wet. Make 2 applications, 10 to 14 days apart. To discourage
fusarium patch, avoid applying high-nitrogen fertilizers late in the fall. To prevent matting, keep mowing the lawn
until the grass stops growing in the fall.
Reduce the thatch layer if necessary.

PROBLEM: From June
through August, patches
of grass turn light green,
then straw-colored. Hot spots in the
yard—areas along driveways, sidewalks,
and buildings—usually discolor first.
These circular, crescent-shaped, or
streaked patches range from a few inches
to several feet in size. Often the center of
the patch remains green, resulting in a
"frog-eye" pattern. The bases of dead
stems dry out and turn brown or black.

ANALYSIS: Fusarium blight
This lawn disease is caused by several
fungus organisms (*Fusarium* species and
others) that are active during 75° to
100° F summer weather and primarily attack bentgrass, Kentucky bluegrass, and
other grasses. Lawns under stress from
lack of moisture, hot dry winds, low pH
(6.0 or less), thick thatch, and close mowing are most susceptible to the disease.
Lush, dense growth from excessive use of
nitrogen fertilizer is readily attacked. In
cool fall weather new grass fills in the
dead areas, but the disease may recur
there the following year.

SOLUTION: Rake out the dead grass. Re-
seed with resistant varieties. A mixture of
15 percent or more perennial ryegrass and
85 percent or less bluegrass greatly reduces the occurrence of fusarium blight.
Next year in late May, before the disease
occurs, treat the whole lawn with a fungicide containing benomyl or iprodione. At
10- to 14-day intervals, repeat the treatment 2 more times. Water thoroughly the
day before; water again immediately afterward. Complete control is difficult to
achieve.

DEAD PATCHES

Brown patch.

Dollar spot damage. *Insert:* Close-up.

Damage. *Insert:* Sod webworm (2 times life size).

PROBLEM: Circular patches of dead grass a few inches to a few feet in diameter appear in the lawn during periods of high humidity and 75° to 85° F temperatures. Brown areas are sometimes surrounded by dark purplish smoky rings. Filmy white tufts cover blades in the early morning before the dew dries. After two to three weeks, the brown grass in the center of the patches may recover and turn green, giving brown areas a doughnut shape.

ANALYSIS: Brown patch
Brown patch is caused by a fungus (*Rhizoctonia solani*). It is one of the most prevalent diseases in warm, humid areas; it attacks all turfgrasses. Lush, tender growth caused by excessive nitrogen fertilizer is the most susceptible to attack. Sometimes only the blades are affected, and the grass recovers in two to three weeks. When the infection is severe and warm weather continues, the disease attacks plant crowns and kills the grass.

SOLUTION: Control brown patch with a fungicide containing chlorothalonil. Spray the lawn when the disease is first noticed and at least 3 more times at 7- to 10-day intervals. Continue to repeat the treatments as long as warm, humid weather continues. Keep grass as dry as possible to slow down disease spread. Water only in the morning, 1 or 2 times a week.

Resistant varieties of ryegrass: Birdie, Citation, Derby, Diplomat, Omega, Pennfine, Yorktown II. *Other resistant grasses:* Bluegrasses, tall fescue.

PROBLEM: During the warm, wet weather of May to June and September to October, the grass turns light brown to straw-colored in circular areas from the size of a silver dollar to 6 inches in diameter. The small dead areas may merge to form large irregular patches. Small, light brown blotches with reddish brown borders appear on the leaf blades. These spots extend across the entire width of the blade. In the early morning before the dew dries, a white cobwebby growth may cover the infected blades.

ANALYSIS: Dollar spot
This lawn disease, also called small brown patch, is caused by a fungus organism (*Sclerotinia homeocarpa*). They are most active during moist days from 60° to 85° F and nights that are moist and cool. They attack many kinds of lawn grasses but are most severe on bentgrass, bermudagrass, and Kentucky bluegrass. Lawns troubled by dollar spot are usually under stress from lack of moisture and nitrogen. An infection seldom causes permanent damage, although it takes the lawn several weeks or months to recover. The fungus organisms are spread by shoes, hoses, mowers, and other equipment.

SOLUTION: Control dollar spot with a fungicide containing chlorothalonil. Make 2 applications, 7 to 10 days apart, beginning when the disease is first evident. The grass recovers quickly if treated promptly. Keep grass as dry as possible. Water only in the morning, 1 or 2 times a week. Maintain proper nutrient levels and apply nitrogen if the lawn suffers from nitrogen deficiency.

PROBLEM: From mid-May to October, in the hottest and driest areas of the lawn, the grass turns brown in patches the size of a saucer. These areas may expand to form large irregular patches. Grass blades are chewed off at the soil level. Silky white tubes nestle in the root area. Inside are light brown or gray worms, from ¼ to ¾ inch long, with black spots. White or gray moths fly in a zigzag pattern over the lawn in the evening. When a moth lands, it folds its wings along the body, rather than letting them spread like most moths.

ANALYSIS: Sod webworms
Several different moths with similar habits are called sod webworms, or lawn moths. These night-flying moths are the adults of this pest. Female moths drop eggs into the grass as they fly. The eggs hatch into worms that feed on grass blades at night or on cloudy, rainy days. In the daytime the worm hides in white silky tubes in the soil. Sod webworms can kill an entire lawn in a few days.

SOLUTION: First rake out all the dead grass; mow the lawn; rake again. Water thoroughly, then spray with an insecticide containing chlorpyrifos, acephate (ORTHENE®), diazinon, or isofenphos. For best results, apply the insecticide in the late afternoon or evening, when the worms and moths are most active. Do not cut or water the lawn for 1 to 3 days after the treatment. To avoid recurring damage, treat the lawn again every 2 months, beginning in late spring or early summer. Damaged lawns may recover rapidly if the insects are controlled early.

Damaged lawn. *Insert:* White grub (2 times life size).

Pythium blight on seedlings.

Damage. *Insert:* Chinch bug (15 times life size).

PROBLEM: In August and September the grass turns brown in large irregular patches. Brown areas of grass roll up easily, like a carpet. Milky white grubs from ⅛ to 1 inch long, with brown heads and three pairs of legs, lie curled in the soil.

ANALYSIS: Grubs
Grubs are the larvae of different kinds of beetles, including May and June beetles (also called white grubs) and Asiatic, Japanese, and masked chafer beetles. The grubs feed on turf roots and may kill an entire lawn. The adult beetles do not damage the lawn, but the females do lay eggs in the soil. May and June beetles lay their eggs in the spring and summer. The Asiatic, Japanese, and masked chafer beetles lay eggs in mid- to late summer. The eggs hatch and the grubs feed on roots 1 to 3 inches deep in the soil. In late fall, they move deep into the soil to overwinter and resume feeding in the spring.

SOLUTION: The younger the grubs are, the easier they are to kill. Apply an insecticide containing diazinon, isofenphos, or chlorpyrifos when you first notice damage and grubs. For preventive control, apply the insecticide just after eggs are laid. Contact the cooperative extension office to learn the correct time in your area. Water the lawn thoroughly within 1 hour after application to help carry the insecticide into the root zone, where the grubs are feeding. The grubs may be active for up to 35 days after treatment. Some grubs appear to be resistant to pesticides, so retreatments may be necessary. To save areas just beginning to fade, keep the soil moist but not wet.

PROBLEM: In hot weather from April to October, the grass wilts, shrivels, and turns light brown in irregular spots ½ to 4 inches in diameter. Spots enlarge rapidly, forming streaks 1 foot wide or wider or patches 1 to 10 feet in diameter. Infected blades mat together when walked on. Blades are often meshed by white cobweblike threads, in the early morning before the dew dries. Grass sometimes dies within 24 hours.

ANALYSIS: Pythium blight
This lawn disease, also called grease spot and cottony blight, is caused by a species of fungus (*Pythium* species). The fungi attack lawns under stress from heat (above 85° F), poorly drained soil, and excessive moisture. Dense, lush grass is the most susceptible. All turfgrasses can be infected, ryegrasses the most severely. The fungus spores spread easily in free-flowing water, on lawn-mower wheels, and on the soles of shoes. The disease is hard to control because it spreads so rapidly, killing large areas in hours. Pythium blight is common in the fall on topseeded ryegrass.

SOLUTION: As soon as the disease appears, treat the lawn with a fungicide containing chloroneb or ethazole. Repeat treatments every 5 to 10 days until symptoms disappear or cooler weather resumes. Keep traffic off the diseased area to avoid spreading spores. Don't overwater in hot, humid weather. Severely infected areas often do not recover, so reseed or resod to re-establish the lawn. Treat the new lawn during hot, humid weather.

PROBLEM: The grass wilts, turns yellowish brown, dries out, and dies in sunny areas and along sidewalks and driveways. To check for chinch bugs, select a sunny spot on the edge of an affected area where yellow grass borders healthy green grass. Cut out both ends of a tin can. Push one end of the can 2 to 3 inches into the soil. Keep it filled with water for 10 minutes. Black to brown insects with white wings, ⅛ to ¼ inch long, float to the surface in 5 to 10 minutes. Pink to brick-red nymphs with a white stripe around the body may also be numerous.

ANALYSIS: Chinch bugs
(*Blissus* species)
These insects feed on many kinds of lawn grasses, but St. Augustine grass is a favorite. Both the adults and the nymphs suck the juices out of the blades. At the same time, they inject a poison that causes the blades to turn brown and die. Heavy infestations may completely kill a lawn in several days. These sun- and heat-loving insects seldom attack shady lawns.

SOLUTION: As soon as damage is seen, water the lawn with ½ to 1 inch of water to bring the insects to the surface. Then apply an insecticide containing chlorpyrifos, isofenphos, or diazinon. To prevent recurring damage from newly hatched nymphs, treat every 2 months until frost. In southern Florida, repeat the applications the year around.

DEAD PATCHES

Scalped spot.

Lawn pale, or yellow.

Billbug damage. *Insert:* Close-up.

PROBLEM: Grass has yellow patches after mowing. A few days later, patches may turn brown and die.

ANALYSIS: Improper mowing

Too much grass was removed from the damaged places when the lawn was mowed. This can happen in two ways:
1. *Scalping:* Mowing near the soil level, or scalping, occurs when the mower cuts too low in some areas. This can happen if the lawn is bumpy, in which case the high spots get scalped. Where the grass has been cut too short, the lower parts of the grass blades are exposed to sunlight, which burns them. If the base of the grass plant was damaged by the scalping, the grass may die. Otherwise, it will probably recover in a week or so.
2. *Insufficient mowings:* If the mower is cutting at the proper height but the grass has grown too long between mowings, the lower parts of the grass blades are exposed and burned. The grass is seldom killed from being mowed when it is too long, but it remains unsightly for a week or two.

SOLUTION: The damaged spots need no special care. To prevent further damage:
1. If the lawn surface is uneven, level the high spots. If the lawn is spongy from an accumulation of thatch, follow the procedure described on page 54. Raise the mower blade to the suggested height.
2. Mow frequently enough so that you don't remove more than half the grass blade. If the grass is very tall when you mow, raise the mower blade to half the grass height and lower it gradually over the next few mowings.

PROBLEM: Irregular patches of grass are yellow. Individual blades are yellow between the veins; the veins remain green. If the condition persists, the leaves may become almost white and die back from the tips. In severe cases, the grass is stunted.

ANALYSIS: Iron deficiency

This is a common problem in many plants and is usually caused by high soil pH. In acidic conditions iron in the soil may form compounds that plants cannot use. Lack of iron may also be caused by a deficiency of iron in the soil, excess phosphorus in the soil, a poor root system, overwatering, or the use of water that contains large amounts of bicarbonate salts. Plants use iron in the formation of the green pigment (chlorophyll) in the leaves. When it is lacking, new growth is yellow. Many turfgrass species—including Kentucky bluegrass, perennial ryegrass, fine fescue, creeping bentgrass, and bermudagrass—are susceptible to iron deficiency.

SOLUTION: Spray the lawn with a liquid iron supplement. Lower the pH of the soil by adding ferrous sulfate or ferrous ammonium sulfate. Water the lawn thoroughly after applying one of these amendments. Never add lime to soil in which iron deficiency is a problem. Some turfgrass varieties are resistant to iron deficiency; when replanting, ask for one of these at your nursery.

PROBLEM: The grass turns brown and dies in expanding patches from mid-June to late August. When pulled, the grass lifts easily. Lying in the soil are fat, humpbacked white grubs with brown heads, without legs, and from ¼ to ½ inch long. Black, slow-moving snouted weevils, ¼ to ½ inch long, occasionally walk on sidewalks and driveways in May and October.

ANALYSIS: Billbugs

(*Sphenophorus* species)
The larvae of this pest damage lawns by hollowing out the grass stems and chewing off the roots. They can destroy an entire lawn. In May, the adults lay eggs in holes they chew in grass stems. The newly hatched larvae feed inside the stems, hollowing out the stem and crown, leaving fine sandlike excrement. Large larvae feed on roots. Once the larvae move down to the roots and inside the crown, chemical control can't reach them.

SOLUTION: Control billbugs with an insecticide containing diazinon or isofenphos. Young larvae can be controlled if treated while still feeding on the grass blades. If the larvae have already moved down to the roots, then water and fertilize the lawn to stimulate new growth. Repeated treatments are not usually necessary unless the billbugs are migrating from your neighbors' yards. Small damaged areas usually recover if the larvae are killed. Reseed or resod large areas. Next year, treat the lawn in early May to kill the adults as they lay eggs. Maintain proper soil moisture and nutrients.

Damaged lawn. *Insert:* Mole cricket (¾ life size).

Dead patches caused by salt accumulation.

Lawn damaged by drought.

PROBLEM: Small mounds of soil are scattered on the soil surface. The lawn feels spongy underfoot. Large areas of grass turn brown and die. To determine if the lawn is infested with mole crickets, make a solution of 1 ounce of liquid dishwashing detergent in 2 gallons of water. With the mixture, drench 4 square feet of turf. If present, mole crickets—greenish gray to brown insects, 1½ inches long, with short front legs and shovellike feet—will come to the surface within 3 minutes.

ANALYSIS: Mole crickets
(*Scapteriscus* species)
Several species of mole crickets attack lawns. They prefer bahia- and bermudagrass but also feed on St. Augustine, zoysia, and centipedegrass. They damage lawns by tunneling through the top 1 to 2 inches of soil, loosening it and uprooting plants and causing them to dry out. They feed also on grass roots, weakening the plants. Mole crickets feed at night and may tunnel as far as 10 to 20 feet before the sun rises. In the daytime, they return to their underground burrows. Adults migrate from their burrows to new areas twice a year: in the spring from March to July and again from November to December.

SOLUTION: In June or July, after the eggs hatch and before the young nymphs cause much damage, mow and water the lawn, since mole crickets are not active in dry soil. Then treat the lawn with a chemical containing chlorpyrifos, acephate (ORTHENE®), or diazinon. Do not water for 36 hours after application. If damage continues, treat again in late summer to early fall. Keep the lawn watered to encourage new root growth.

PROBLEM: Grass slowly dies, especially in the lowest areas of the lawn. A white or dark crust may be on the soil.

ANALYSIS: Salt damage
Salt damage occurs when salt accumulates to damaging levels in the soil. This can happen in two ways: The lawn does not receive enough water from rainfall or irrigation to wash the salts from the soil, or the drainage is so poor that water does not pass through the soil. In either case, as water evaporates from the soil and grass blades, the salts that were dissolved in the water accumulate near the surface of the soil. A white or dark brown crust of salts may form. Salts can originate in the soil, in the irrigation water, or in applied fertilizers.

SOLUTION: The only way to eliminate excess salts is to wash them through the soil with water. If the damage is only at a low spot in the lawn, fill in the spot to level the lawn. If the entire lawn drains poorly, improve the soil or improve the drainage by aerating according to the directions on page 54. If the soil drains well, increase the amount of water applied at each watering by 50 percent or more, so excess water will leach salts below the root zone of the grass. Apply fertilizer according to label instructions.

PROBLEM: Footprints in the lawn make a long-lasting imprint instead of bouncing right back. The grass blades turn a bluish green or slate gray and wilt. In the cool of the evening, the grass recovers until the sun and heat of the following day make it darken and wilt. Areas begin to thin out, and after a few days the lawn begins to look and feel like straw and dies.

ANALYSIS: Drought
A lawn suffers from drought damage when water evaporates from the lawn faster than it is absorbed. Drought damage occurs first in the hottest and driest areas of the lawn—along sidewalks, driveways, south- or west-facing slopes, south sides of reflecting buildings, and areas with sandy soil. Grass blades don't wilt like broadleafed plants do. They don't droop; instead they roll or fold up lengthwise.

SOLUTION: Water the lawn immediately. If the grass has turned yellow, affected areas will take several weeks to recover. If you are not very conscientious about watering your lawn, consider planting a drought-tolerant turfgrass.

Drought-tolerant turfgrasses: Bahiagrass, bermudagrass, red fescue, tall fescue, zoysia.

GRASS THIN

Thatch.

Lawn damaged by soil compaction.

Nematode damage.

PROBLEM: Grass thins out in sunny or shady areas of the lawn. Weeds invade the sparse areas. Grass may suddenly die in large patches during summer heat and drought. Cut and lift several plugs of grass 2 to 3 inches deep. Look to see if the stringy, feltlike material between the grass and soil surface is thicker than ½ inch.

ANALYSIS: Thatch
Thatch is a tightly intermingled layer of partially decomposed stems and roots of grass, which develops between the actively growing grass and the soil surface. Thatch slows grass growth by restricting the movement of water, air, and nutrients in the soil. Thatch in a lawn is normal, but when thatch is thicker than ½ inch, the lawn begins to suffer. As the layer accumulates, the grass roots grow in the thatch instead of down into the soil. Thatch accumulation is encouraged by overly vigorous grass growth caused by excessive use of fertilizer and frequent watering. Grass clippings do not contribute to thatch.

SOLUTION: To reduce the thatch and increase lawn vigor, power-rake or dethatch it. Dethatch cool-season grasses in the fall; dethatch warm-season grasses in the early spring, before new growth begins, and in late spring or early summer. Avoid dethatching while new growth is turning green. The machines for the job can be rented, or hire a contractor. Dethatchers have vertical rotating blades that slice through the turf, cutting out thatch. Before dethatching, mow the lawn as short as possible. Go over it 1 to 3 times with the dethatcher. Take up the debris (which can be a considerable amount!), fertilize the lawn, and water the grass to hasten lawn recovery.

PROBLEM: In heavily traveled areas, the grass becomes thin and develops bare spots. Water runs off quickly.

ANALYSIS: Compacted soil
Soil is easily compacted, or pressed together, in areas of frequent foot or vehicular traffic. Clay soils are more likely to become compacted than loamy or sandy soils. Compaction prevents air, water, and nutrients from penetrating into the soil and reaching the grass roots. This results in a shallow root system and stress on the grass because of insufficient water and nutrients.

SOLUTION: Water daily during hot periods, and apply fertilizer as needed to keep the grass alive until you can relieve the compacted soil. Aerate the compacted soil with a coring machine. These machines can be rented, or hire a contractor to do the coring for you. Coring machines remove cores of soil, allowing water and nutrients to pass into the soil. Water the lawn a few days before aerating, so the soil is moist. Do not aerate dry or wet soil. After aerating, allow the removed soil cores to dry a few days in the sun, then rake them up or break them by mowing with a rotary mower or dragging a heavy flat board over them. In a few weeks the grass will begin to fill in the holes in the lawn. Tools for coring by hand are available for aerating small areas. Aerate heavily trafficked areas annually. Reduce foot traffic in the area by installing a walk or patio, erecting a fence, or planting a hedge to divert traffic.

PROBLEM: The grass grows slowly, thins out, and turns pale green to yellow. In hot weather the blades may wilt. Main roots are short with few side roots, or many roots may grow from one point.

ANALYSIS: Nematodes
Nematodes are microscopic worms that live in the soil. There are various types, some highly beneficial and some highly destructive. They are not related to earthworms. Destructive nematodes feed on grass roots. The damaged roots can't supply sufficient water and nutrients to the leaf blades, and the grass is stunted or slowly dies. Nematodes are found throughout the United States but are most severe in the South. They prefer moist, sandy loam soils. They can move only a few inches each year on their own, but they may be carried long distances by soil, water, tools, or infested plants. Testing roots and soil is the only method for confirming the presence of nematodes. Contact the local cooperative extension office for sampling instructions and addresses of testing laboratories. Soil and root problems—such as poor soil structure, drought stress, nutrient deficiency, and root rots—can produce symptoms of decline similar to those caused by nematodes. Eliminate these problems as causes before sending soil and root samples for testing.

SOLUTION: Chemicals to kill nematodes in planted soil are not available to homeowners. However, before planting a new lawn, nematodes can be controlled by soil fumigation.

LAWN PALE OR YELLOW

■ POWDERY MATERIAL ON GRASS

Unfertilized lawn with green clover.

Septoria leaf spot.

Rust.

PROBLEM: Grass is pale green to yellow and grows more slowly than usual. If the condition persists, the grass becomes sparse and weeds invade the lawn.

ANALYSIS: Nitrogen deficiency

Nitrogen is a key element in maintaining a healthy lawn with few insect and disease problems. Clover stays green because it obtains nitrogen from the air, but grasses must absorb it through their roots. Maintain a level of nitrogen in the soil that (1) does not stimulate excessive leaf growth, which reduces mowing frequency; (2) does not encourage shoot growth at the expense of root growth; and (3) varies according to the cultural and environmental conditions present. Because heavy rains and watering leach nitrogen from the soil, periodic feedings are necessary throughout the growing season. Acidic soil may cause nitrogen to be unavailable to the grass.

SOLUTION: Apply a lawn fertilizer rated 16-16-16 (16 percent each of nitrogen, phosphorus, and potash) according to the instructions on the label. You can also use a liquid lawn food rated 27-0-1 plus iron or a soluble lawn food rated 36-4-8. Adequately fertilized lawns exhibit acceptable density and color without excessive growth. To prevent burning and to move the nutrients into the soil, water thoroughly after application. Grass begins using the nitrogen in the fertilizer within 15 to 24 hours. For the most efficient utilization of applied nitrogen, leave grass clippings on the lawn if they are not extremely long. If the soil is acidic (below pH 5.5), liming is necessary for effective nitrogen utilization.

PROBLEM: In the spring and fall, the lawn has a gray cast. The tips of the blades are pale yellow to gray, with red or yellow margins. Pale areas may be ⅛ to 1 inch long. Tiny black dots are scattered in the diseased spots on the blades.

ANALYSIS: Septoria leaf spot

This lawn disease, also called tip burn, is caused by a fungus (*Septoria* species) that infects most northern grass species and bermudagrass. It is most prevalent in the cool, wet weather of spring and fall. Lawns in unfertilized soil are most susceptible. The disease usually attacks in the spring, declines during the hot summer months, and returns in the fall. Because the disease infects the leaftips first, frequent mowing removes much of the diseased part of the grass blades.

SOLUTION: As soon as the discoloration appears, treat the infected lawn with a fungicide containing maneb. Repeat the treatment 3 more times, 7 to 10 days apart, or as long as weather favorable for the disease continues. Mow the lawn regularly. Since no variety is completely resistant, plant a blend of 2 or 3 disease-tolerant varieties.

Disease-tolerant bluegrass varieties: A-20, A-34, Adelphi, Birka, Bonnieblue, Glade, Ruby, Sydsport, Touchdown, Victa.

PROBLEM: Grass turns light green or yellow and begins to thin out. An orange powder coats the blades and rubs off on fingers, shoes, and clothing. Reddish brown lesions under the powder do not rub off.

ANALYSIS: Rust

This lawn disease is caused by one of a number of fungi (*Puccinia* species) that occur most frequently on Merion Kentucky bluegrass, ryegrass, and zoysia. The fungi are most active during moist weather from 70° to 75° F, but they can be active all winter in mild areas. Heavy dew favors its development. Grasses under stress from nitrogen deficiency, lack of moisture, and close mowing are most susceptible to attack. Rust is more severe in the shade. The orange powder is composed of millions of microscopic spores that spread easily in the wind. Lawns attacked severely by rust are more likely to suffer winter damage.

SOLUTION: Rust develops slowly, often more slowly than the grass grows. Apply a high-nitrogen fertilizer to maintain rapid growth. Mow frequently, removing the clippings. If the disease is severe, treat with a fungicide containing chlorothalonil. Repeat the application every 7 to 14 days until the lawn improves. A blend of 2 or more rust-resistant varieties is more resistant than a single variety.

POWDERY MATERIAL ON GRASS ──■ **GRASSLIKE WEEDS**

Powdery mildew.

Seed heads. *Insert:* Annual bluegrass plant.

Quackgrass.

PROBLEM: Whitish gray mold develops on the topsides of grass blades during cool rainy weather. The lawn looks as if it has been dusted with flour. The leaf tissue under the mold turns yellow and then tan or brown. Severely infected plants wither and die.

ANALYSIS: Powdery mildew
This lawn disease is caused by a fungus (*Erysiphe graminis*) that thrives when the nights are damp and from 65° to 70° F and the days are warm and humid. The infection is most severe on Merion Kentucky bluegrass, but powdery-mildew fungi also attack other varieties of bluegrass, fescue, and bermudagrass. Lawns growing in the shade are the most affected. Powdery mildew slows the growth of leaves, roots, and underground stems, causing gradual weakening of the grass and making it more susceptible to other problems. Lawns growing rapidly because of excessive use of nitrogen fertilizer are extremely susceptible. The fine white mildew on the blades develops into powdery spores that spread easily in the wind. The spores can infect a grass plant in two to four hours.

SOLUTION: Treat the lawn with benomyl when the mildew is first seen. Repeat the application every 7 to 10 days, until the mildew is no longer apparent. Reduce the shade and improve air circulation by pruning surrounding trees and shrubs.

Mildew-resistant varieties of Kentucky bluegrass: A-20, A-34, Aquila, Baron, Birka, Glade, Nugget, Rugby, Sydsport, Touchdown.

PROBLEM: In midspring the grass has a whitish appearance. Pale green grassy weeds grow among desirable grasses.

ANALYSIS: Annual bluegrass
(*Poa annua*)
Annual bluegrass is one of the most troublesome but least-noticed weeds in the lawn. This member of the bluegrass family is lighter green, more shallow rooted, and less drought and heat tolerant than Kentucky bluegrass. As its name suggests, annual bluegrass usually lives for only one year, although some strains are perennial. The seeds germinate in cool weather from late summer to late fall. Annual bluegrass grows rapidly in the spring, especially if fertilizer is applied then. Seed heads appear in mid- to late spring, at the same height the grass is cut. The seed heads give the lawn a whitish appearance. When hot, dry weather arrives, the plants die. The seeds fall to the soil and do not germinate until cooler weather. Annual bluegrass is most serious where the soil is compacted.

SOLUTION: Weed killers are only partially effective in controlling annual bluegrass. Prevent seeds from germinating by applying an herbicide containing DCPA or bensulide as a preemergent treatment in early to midfall. Do not use if you plan to reseed the lawn in the fall. Replace the dead areas in the summer with sod. Do not cut the lawn too short. Lawns more than 2½ inches tall seldom contain much annual bluegrass. Aerate the lawn by coring in compacted areas (see page 54).

PROBLEM: A grassy weed with hollow stems grows in a newly seeded lawn. Wheatlike spikes grow at the tips of the stems. The narrow leaf blades are bluish green and rough on the topside. A pair of "claws" occurs at the junction of the blade and the stem. Rings of root hairs grow every ¾ to 1 inch along the underground stems.

ANALYSIS: Quackgrass
(*Agropyron repens*)
This cool-season perennial, also called couchgrass or witchgrass, spreads extensively through the lawn by means of long white underground stems. It reproduces from seeds and by developing from the underground stems. Quackgrass is found most frequently in fertile, newly seeded lawns. It grows much more rapidly than grass seedlings, often crowding them out.

SOLUTION: Kill clumps of actively growing quackgrass with a chemical containing fluazifop-butyl or glyphosate. If regrowth occurs, repeat the treatment.

Crabgrass.

Tall fescue.

Barnyardgrass.

PROBLEM: A grassy weed forms broad, flat clumps in thin areas of the lawn. It grows rapidly through the summer, rooting easily at the stem joints. The pale green blades are 2 to 5 inches long and ⅓ inch wide. Seed heads 2 to 6 inches tall grow from the center of the plant.

ANALYSIS: Crabgrass

(*Digitaria* species)
Crabgrass sprouts from seeds in the early spring, growing rapidly and producing seeds all summer until the first killing frost in the fall. Then the plants turn brown and die. The seeds lie dormant over the winter and sprout in the spring. Crabgrass is one of the most common lawn weeds in its area of adaptation. When a lawn begins to thin out from insects, disease, or poor maintenance, crabgrass is one of the first weeds to invade the area.

SOLUTION: Kill actively growing crabgrass with an herbicide containing fluazifop-butyl, glyphosate, or methanearsonate. Older plants are harder to kill; repeat the treatment 2 more times at 4- to 7-day intervals, if necessary. To kill crabgrass seeds as they germinate, apply a weed killer containing DCPA in the early spring, 2 weeks before the last expected frost or about the time the forsythia bloom. A thick lawn seldom contains much crabgrass.

PROBLEM: Clumps of coarse, tough grass invade thin areas of the lawn. The medium-dark green blades, each ½ inch wide, are ribbed on the topside and smooth on the underside. In the spring and fall, the lower parts of the stems turn reddish purple. The blades tend to shred when mowed.

ANALYSIS: Tall fescue

(*Festuca arundinacea*)
This cool-season, perennial, bunch-type grass is durable. It is commonly used on athletic fields because it holds up well under hard wear. Tall fescue makes an attractive turf when grown by itself. However, when it is seeded with or invades bluegrass, bermudagrass, or ryegrass lawns, it is considered a weed. It becomes clumpy and makes an uneven turf. When insects and diseases attack the desirable grasses in the lawn, the tall fescue is usually not affected. It resists diseases and grubs, and sod webworms attack it only if they've eaten everything else. Also, tall fescue is somewhat heat tolerant, and its deep roots help it survive periods of heavy moisture and drought.

SOLUTION: While it is actively growing, from early summer to early fall, kill clumps of tall fescue with a weed killer containing glyphosate or fluazifop-butyl. Omit a regular mowing before treating, to ensure that the grass blades have enough tissue to absorb the chemical. The weed killer will also kill desirable grasses. One week after spraying, mow the tall fescue and reseed the area. The tall fescue may still be green when it is removed, but the roots will die in 3 to 4 weeks and will not resprout.

PROBLEM: In summer and fall, a low-growing grassy weed with reddish purple stems 1 to 3 feet long grows in the lawn. The smooth leaves are ¼ to ½ inch wide, with a prominent midrib.

ANALYSIS: Barnyardgrass

(*Echinochloa crus-galli*)
Barnyardgrass, also called watergrass, is a warm-season annual weed that is usually found in poorly managed lawns of low fertility. It reproduces from seeds and develops into a plant with a shallow root system. Although the natural growth habit of barnyardgrass is upright, when mowed regularly it forms ground-hugging mats.

SOLUTION: Kill mats of actively growing barnyardgrass with a chemical containing methanearsonate or fluazifop-butyl. Repeat the treatment 2 more times, at intervals of 7 to 10 days, until the plants die. The chemical may discolor the turf for 2 to 3 weeks. To kill barnyardgrass seedlings as they sprout, apply a weed killer containing DCPA in the early spring, 2 weeks before the last expected frost.

BROADLEAF WEEDS

Clover.

Oxalis.

Spotted spurge.

PROBLEM: A weed with leaves composed of three round leaflets at the top of a hairy 2- to 4-inch-tall leafstalk grows in the lawn. The leafstalks sprout from the base of the plant. White or pink-tinged flowers, ½ inch in size, bloom from June to September. They often attract bees.

ANALYSIS: Clover
(*Trifolium* species)
Clover is a common perennial weed in lawns throughout the United States. Some people like it in a lawn; others consider it messy, or they don't like the bees that are attracted to the flowers. Clover reproduces from seeds and aboveground root stems. The seeds can live in the soil for 20 years or more. The plant, which has a creeping, prostrate habit, suffocates lawn grasses, resulting in large patches of clover. When buying a box of grass seed, be sure to read the label carefully; clover seeds are sometimes contained in seed mixtures. Since clover produces its own nitrogen, it thrives in lawns that are low in this plant nutrient.

SOLUTION: In the spring and early fall, treat the lawn with a weed killer containing 2,4-D and mecoprop. Repeat treatments are often necessary.

PROBLEM: A weed with pale green leaves divided into three heart-shaped leaflets invades thin areas of the lawn. The leaves are ¼ to ¾ inch wide and are similar to clover. The stems root at the lower joints and are often thinly covered with fine hairs. Small, bright yellow flowers are ½ inch long with five petals. Cucumber-shaped, light-green seedpods develop from the fading flowers. Plants may be 4 to 12 inches high with a prostrate or erect growth habit.

ANALYSIS: Oxalis
(*Oxalis stricta*)
Oxalis, also called yellow woodsorrel, is a perennial plant that thrives in dry, open places. It invades lawns that are beginning to thin because of insect, disease, or maintenance problems. Oxalis reproduces from the seeds formed in the seedpods. When the pods dry, a light touch causes them to explode, shooting their seeds several feet in all directions. Oxalis leaves contain oxalic acid, which makes them sour.

SOLUTION: Control oxalis with a weed killer containing 2,4-D and mecoprop or dicamba. The most effective time to spray is when the weeds are actively growing, in the spring or late summer to fall. Oxalis is not easy to kill; several treatments are usually needed. Check the soil pH level (see page 33). A healthy lawn helps control oxalis by smothering it.

PROBLEM: A low-growing weed with oval pale to dark green leaves ¼ to ¾ inch long appears in the lawn. Each leaf may have a purple spot. Stems ooze milky white sap when broken. The leaves are slightly hairy on the underside and smooth on the topside. Tiny pinkish white flowers bloom in midsummer. The numerous pale green stems fan out on the soil surface and over the top of the grass, forming mats up to 2 feet in diameter.

ANALYSIS: Spotted spurge
(*Euphorbia maculata*)
Spotted spurge, also called milk purslane, invades thin areas of the lawn, smothering the grass. Spurge sprouts from seeds in the spring and dies with the first frost. This weed commonly invades lawns that are dry and infertile, but it can also be found in well-maintained lawns.

SOLUTION: In the late spring or early summer, treat the lawn with a weed killer containing dimethylamine salt of 2,4-D and mecoprop or dicamba. Keep the lawn well watered to discourage spurge from invading dry areas.

Common chickweed.

Henbit.

Purslane.

PROBLEM: A weed with small (½-inch-long) heart-shaped leaves and starlike white flowers grows in thin spaces in the lawn. A row of hairs projects from the leafstalk that attaches the leaves to the stems. The stems root easily at their joints.

ANALYSIS: Common chickweed
(*Stellaria media*)
This weed grows from seeds that sprout in the fall and live for less than a year. Common chickweed grows primarily in damp shady areas under trees and shrubs and on the north side of buildings. The weed invades home lawns when they begin to thin out from insects, disease, mechanical damage, or shade. It reproduces from seeds and the creeping stems that root at their joints wherever they touch the soil. Common chickweed has a low prostrate growing habit and forms a dense mat that crowds out the grass.

SOLUTION: When common chickweed is growing actively in the early spring or late fall, treat the lawn with a weed killer containing 2,4-D and mecoprop. Repeated applications may be necessary. Do not water for 2 days after a treatment.

PROBLEM: A weed with rounded, toothed leaves, ¾ inch wide, grows in the lawn. The lower leaves are attached to the four-sided upright stems by short leafstalks; upper leaves attach directly to the stems. Stems root easily at lower joints. Lavender ½-inch flowers appear from April to June and again in September.

ANALYSIS: Henbit
(*Lamium amplexicaule*)
This weed, also known as dead nettle or bee nettle, is found in lawns and flower and vegetable gardens across the United States. It is a winter annual that sprouts from seeds in September and grows rapidly in the fall and the following spring. Henbit also reproduces by stems that root easily wherever the stem joints touch the soil. The weed most frequently invades thin areas in lawns with rich soil.

SOLUTION: In early spring, when henbit is growing most rapidly, treat the lawn with a weed killer containing 2,4-D and mecoprop. Do not water for 24 hours after treating. A few small plants can be hand-pulled.

PROBLEM: A low-growing weed with reddish brown, thick, succulent stems is found in thin areas or newly seeded lawns. The leaves are thick, fleshy, and wedge-shaped. Small yellow flowers sometimes bloom in the leaf and stem joints. Stems root wherever they touch the soil.

ANALYSIS: Purslane
(*Portulaca oleracea*)
Purslane—a summer annual weed that thrives in hot, dry weather—is seldom found in the spring when the lawn is being treated for other weeds. Purslane grows vigorously, forming a thick mat. The small yellow flowers open only in the full sunlight. Purslane primarily invades bare spots in lawns or thin lawns that have not been watered properly. Purslane stores water in its thick fleshy stems and leaves; therefore, it survives longer than grass during dry weather.

SOLUTION: When the weed is actively growing, spray the lawn with a weed killer containing 2,4-D and mecoprop. On St. Augustine grass, use a weed killer containing atrazine. If the lawn has just been reseeded, do not treat it until the seedlings have been mowed 3 times. Wait 3 to 4 weeks after a treatment before seeding bare areas.

BROADLEAF WEEDS

Dandelion.

Sheep sorrel.

Mallow.

PROBLEM: From spring to fall, a weed with bright yellow flowers blooms in the lawn. In some southern states, it may bloom all winter. Flower stems grow 2 to 10 inches above the plants. The medium-green leaves, 3 to 10 inches long, are lobed along the sides. The plant has a deep, fleshy taproot.

ANALYSIS: Dandelion
(*Taraxacum officinale*)
This perennial is the most common and easily identified weed in the United States. It reproduces from seeds and shoots that grow from the fleshy taproot. This taproot grows 2 to 3 feet deep in the soil, surviving even the severest of winters. Dandelions grow in any soil and are most numerous in full sunlight. In the early spring, new sprouts emerge from the taproot. As the yellow flowers mature and ripen, they form white puff balls containing seeds. The wind can carry the seeds for miles. The tops of the plant die back in late fall, and the taproot overwinters to start the cycle again in the spring. Dandelions prefer wet soil and are often a sign of overwatering.

SOLUTION: Treat an entire lawn with a weed killer containing propionic acid; for spot treatment, apply an herbicide containing 2,4-D and mecoprop. For best results make 2 applications, one in the early summer and another in the early fall. Do not water or mow for 2 days after treatments. Hand-digging and removal is not only time-consuming and tedious, but impractical, since pieces of root that are broken off and left in the soil will sprout into new plants.

PROBLEM: Arrow-shaped leaves, 1 to 4 inches long, with two lobes at the base of each leaf, form a dense rosette. Erect stems grow 4 to 14 inches tall. Two types of flowers appear in midspring: one is reddish green and the other, yellowish green.

ANALYSIS: Sheep sorrel
(*Rumex acetosella*)
This cool-season perennial is also called red sorrel or sour grass because of its sour taste. It grows in dry, sterile, sandy or gravelly soil and is usually an indication of acidic soil or low nitrogen availability. Sheep sorrel reproduces from seeds and red underground rootstalks. The root system is shallow but extensive, and it is not easily removed.

SOLUTION: In spring or fall treat with a weed killer containing 2,4-D and mecoprop. In the southern parts of the United States, use a weed killer containing atrazine. Don't mow for 5 days before or 2 days after treating. Sheep sorrel is difficult to control, so several treatments may be necessary. To discourage sheep sorrel, test the soil pH (see page 33); correct it to between 6.0 and 7.0 if necessary.

PROBLEM: A weed with hairy stems, 4 to 12 inches long, spreads over the lawn. The stem tips turn upward. Round, heart-shaped, hairy leaves, ½ to 3 inches wide and slightly lobed along the edges, are attached to the stems by a long leafstalk. White to lilac flowers, 2½ inches in diameter with five petals, bloom singly or in clusters at the leaf and stem junction. Mallow is often mistaken for ground ivy but, unlike ground ivy, the spreading branches do not root when they touch soil.

ANALYSIS: Mallow
(*Malva* species)
Mallow, also called cheeseweed, is found throughout the United States in lawns, fields, and along roadways. It is usually an annual, though sometimes a biennial, and it reproduces from seeds. It has a straight, nearly white taproot that is difficult to pull from the soil. Mallow is most commonly found in poorly managed lawns and in soils high in manure content.

SOLUTION: Any time from midspring to early summer, treat the lawn with a weed killer containing 2,4-D and mecoprop. Don't water for 5 days before treating or 2 days after. Maintain a thick, healthy lawn.

■ MISCELLANEOUS ■

Field bindweed.

Mushrooms.

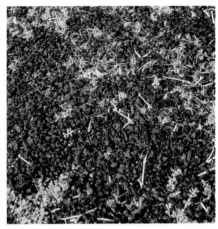
Algae.

PROBLEM: A plant with long twining stems grows across the lawn. The leaves are arrowhead-shaped and up to 2 inches long. White to pink funnel-shaped flowers, about 1 inch across, appear from spring to fall.

ANALYSIS: Field bindweed
(*Convolvulus arvensis*)
This deep-rooted perennial weed, also known as wild morning glory, is found throughout most of the United States in lawns, gardens, fields, and along roadways. It is one of the most troublesome and difficult weeds to eliminate, because of its extensive root system. The roots may grow 15 to 20 feet deep. Roots or pieces of roots left behind from hand-pulling or spading easily resprout. Field bindweed, which reproduces from seeds and roots, twines and climbs over shrubs and fences and up into trees. It prefers rich, sandy, or gravelly soil but will grow in almost any garden soil.

SOLUTION: In late spring to early summer or in early to late fall, treat broad areas with a weed killer containing 2,4-D and mecoprop or dicamba. Spot-treat bindweed with a spray containing glyphosate, wait one week, then reseed. Because of the deep roots, repeated treatments may be necessary. Treat again whenever new growth appears.

PROBLEM: Mushrooms sprout up in the lawn after wet weather. They may be growing in circles of dark green grass. When the weather gets colder or the soil dries out they disappear.

ANALYSIS: Mushrooms
Mushrooms, also called toadstools and puffballs, live on organic matter buried in the soil. The mushroom is the above-ground fruiting, or reproductive, structure of a fungus. The organic matter mushrooms help to decay buried logs, lumber, roots, or stumps. Most mushrooms do not damage a lawn, but they are objectionable because they are unsightly. Mushrooms growing in circles of dark green grass, called fairy rings, may make the soil impervious to water and cause injury to the lawn.

SOLUTION: There is no practical or permanent way to eliminate mushrooms. When the buried wood is completely decayed, the mushrooms will disappear. The easiest solution, although it is only temporary, is to break the mushrooms with a rake or lawn mower.

PROBLEM: A green to black slimy scum covers bare soil and crowns of grass plants. When dry, it becomes crusty, cracks, and peels easily.

ANALYSIS: Algae
(*Symploca* species or *Oscillatoria* species)
Algae are freshwater plants that invade shady, wet areas of a lawn. They injure grass by smothering or shading it as they grow over the crowns of the plants. Invaded areas become slippery. Algae live in compacted soil and soil that is high in nitrogen and organic matter. They need constantly or frequently wet conditions to survive. Organic fertilizers encourage algae, especially in the cool seasons. Algae may be carried from place to place by animals, equipment, people, and birds. Water taken from ponds, lakes, or streams and used for irrigation usually contains algae.

SOLUTION: Spray patches of algae with wettable sulfur 2 times, 1 month apart, in early spring. This is only a temporary solution. Algae will soon return if the conditions promoting them are not corrected. Reduce soil compaction as instructed on page 54. Improve drainage and prune nearby trees to reduce shading. Do not apply high-nitrogen fertilizers in late fall and winter. Maintain a healthy, vigorous lawn.

GROUND COVERS

Ground covers shade out weeds and add both texture and color to small or large areas. They can be remarkably drought resistant. But ground covers, like other lawn and garden plants, require nurturing to stay lush.

CONSIDERING THE SOIL

The first step in establishing ground cover is to ensure that the soil can provide plants with the aeration, nutrients, and pH they need.

Dense Soil

Some soils, such as clay, tend to be naturally dense. Clay soil cracks and becomes quite hard when dry. Water may run off rather than sinking in, creating drought-like conditions.

To tell if you have dense soil, dig a hole 2 feet deep. Fill the hole with water. If the water level drops less than $\frac{1}{10}$ inch per hour, your soil is dense and has a drainage problem.

Correcting dense soil is hard work but necessary. The most permanent solution is to dig the entire planting area to a depth of 6 inches and work in such soil amendments as gypsum and organic matter. This is also a good time to correct soil pH (see the Inappropriate pH section).

Compacted Soil

Some soils are naturally compact. Others are compacted by construction work or foot traffic. Whatever the cause, the result can be hardpan and struggling ground cover unless the gardener corrects the situation.

Hardpan

A planting hole in hardpan, even when backfilled with organic amendments, collects water, creating a basin where roots rot. If your ground cover site contains hardpan, you must correct the soil before planting. In mild cases, correction consists of using a soil auger to bore deep

holes in the soil. The holes allow air and water to flow downward and ease the way for growing roots. If the planting area is small but the soil is quite compact, use a hand-operated aerating tool to make 3-inch-deep holes about 3 inches apart. The practical approach to breaking up hardpan in large areas is deep plowing—you may have to hire a contractor to do the job. Working gypsum into the soil can also be effective. Talk to a knowledgeable nursery professional or a landscape gardener about the best approach to your situation.

If you have an area subject to constant foot traffic, consider installing paving stones or constructing a paved pathway. Plant shrubbery to prevent pedestrians from taking shortcuts.

Nutrient Shortage

Slow growth is often a sign of a nutrient shortage. Other symptoms are yellowing or pale green leaves that remain small. To correct the soil, apply a general-purpose fertilizer regularly, according to label instructions. If leaves turn pale but leaf veins remain normal, supplemental iron may be needed.

In some cases, the soil contains sufficient nutrients but its pH keeps plants from absorbing them. Read the next section to determine if your planting site is too acidic or alkaline.

Inappropriate pH

Kits for testing soil pH are available at nurseries. The kits are easy to use and supply valuable information.

Opposite: Two ground covers, foam flower (*Tiarella cordifolia*, foreground) and sweet woodruff (*Galium odoratum*, left with white flowers), are combined with *Lunaria annua* (pink flowers) and wood hyacinth (*Endymion*) to create an enticing landscape.
Right: Ivy can be particularly invasive; if uncontrolled, it will soon cover this fence.

Ivy is not the only invasive ground cover. Mugwort (*Artemisia vulgaris*), a chrysanthemumlike plant widely sold in the East, spreads wildly.

Acidic soil   Plants unsuited to acidic soils (see page 66) grow slowly. Their leaves turn yellow or pale green. To improve acidic soils, apply a ground dolomitic limestone additive formulated especially for gardens.

Alkaline soil   Plants grown in overly alkaline soil develop yellow areas between the veins on new leaves. This yellowing may be due to the lack of iron and manganese, which alkaline soil keeps plants from absorbing. To remedy the problem, make soils more acidic by applying aluminum sulfate, ferrous sulfate, or other sulfur. Use a fertilizer that creates an acidic reaction, such as a fertilizer formulated for azaleas.

Supplementary Soil

If you decide to add topsoil to your planting site, make sure the new soil is free of weeds and weed seeds. Soil delivered by the truckload from construction sites is particularly suspect. Buy supplementary topsoil from a reputable nursery, and make sure you specify a weed-free product. If it saves you from weed control, clean topsoil is worth the extra cost.

CONSIDERING GROUND COVERS

In selecting a ground cover, consider its growth habit, its ability to crowd out weeds, and its requirements for sun or shade and water.

Invasive Ground Covers

A ground cover is often selected for its rapid growth habit. But this can turn the ground cover into a nuisance that moves into areas reserved for other plants. Any ground cover marked "Rapid growth, very hardy" might be invasive given the right environment. Included in the possibly invasive list are honeysuckle, some mints, goutweed, sweet woodruff, crown vetch, Indian mock strawberry, gill ivy, Aaron's beard, and dwarf bamboo. If a ground cover becomes too energetic and regular cutting does not deter it, treat it as a weed and kill it by applying a systemic herbicide.

Weed-shading Ground Covers

Some ground covers eventually grow thick enough to shade the ground below them. This decreases weed germination. Given the best environment, essentially weed-free ground covers include ajuga, chamomile, Irish moss, snow-in-summer, wild strawberry, cinquefoil, lamb's-ears, and vinca.

Sun and Shade Requirements

A shade-loving ground cover, such as Irish moss, does not grow well where sunlight plays on it most of the day. A sun-loving ground cover, such as chamomile, tends to die out in shady areas.

Study the planting area before rushing out to buy plants. You must know what the environment can support. If you live in or near an established area, one way to find out what will grow is to walk past thriving gardens in your neighborhood. If a neighbor's planting area faces the same direction yours does, given the same care, the same ground cover will probably do well for you. Do not limit yourself by choosing a ground cover that is already established nearby, however. If you see a thriving ground cover, research its growing requirements. Then find other plants that thrive in similar conditions.

Signs of inadequate sunlight include poor growth, leggy growth, leaf drop, unusually dark green leaves, and insect attack. Increase the sunlight the ground cover receives by trimming adjacent shrubbery or tree limbs. If providing more sunlight is impossible, carefully transfer the affected plants to a more suitable area. Replant with a shade-tolerant species.

Signs of too much sun include faded leaves. In severe situations, leaves may turn yellowish white. Growth slows. Too much sun breaks down plant tissue. Chlorophyll (green leaf pigment), which is necessary for leaf functioning, disappears. Wind and drought make the problem more severe. Place affected plants in a shadier location with sufficient water. Replace them with a more sun-tolerant species.

Resilient Ground Covers

If your planting site is subject to heavy foot traffic, choose a ground cover that can tolerate it. The list of such plants includes dichondra, chamomile, Korean grass, Irish moss, lippia, and mazus.

Drought- and Moisture-tolerant Ground Covers

If you live in a drought area, consider using a drought-tolerant ground cover. The selection includes woolly yarrow, coyotebrush, ground cover ceanothus, low-growing California buckwheat, and lippia.

Quite a few ground covers can prosper in damp soil, as long as you provide adequate drainage. These include mint, ajuga, wild ginger, bunchberry, and Japanese spurge.

PREVENTING WEEDS

Unfortunately, prime conditions for ground cover also encourage weeds. Hand-picking weeds from ground cover is difficult; getting a firm grip on a weed usually means tearing out some ground cover, too. Practical solutions include plastic or fabric sheets that block weeds—weed blocks—and herbicides.

Weed Blocks

If it is thick enough to block sunlight, a black plastic sheet spread over the planting area can be an effective weed preventive. Holes cut in the plastic allow the ground cover to grow. In addition to preventing weeds, weed blocks conserve soil moisture. Weed block fabric, a fairly new innovation, is even better than black plastic because it allows water, air, and nutrients to pass into the soil but does not allow weed growth.

Weed blocks present a few disadvantages, however. Plastic cracks with age and needs to be replaced. Weeds may sprout through cracked plastic or through the holes intended for ground cover. Though a weed block is an excellent defense against weeds, you may need to use herbicides as well.

Herbicides

One way herbicides are classified is according to the time they are applied.

Preemergent herbicides   Weed killers of this type are applied before weeds sprout; these herbicides prevent weed germination while allowing desirable plants to grow normally. Preemergent herbicides, which are usually applied in granular form, permeate the top inch or so of soil. When applied under a weed block, these products contribute to highly effective weed control. Check the label to ensure that the product is safe for your ground cover.

Preemergent herbicides do not kill existing weeds, which must be treated separately. The products lose some of their effectiveness if the soil is used as a path or disturbed by feeding birds, digging animals, or cultivation.

Postemergent herbicides   If weeds emerge, consider postemergent herbicides. Some are systemic, which means they work throughout the plant (including the root). Some can be applied without injury to specific ground covers. Others must be applied to weeds only; they will kill your desirable plants as well as weeds.

Before selecting a postemergent herbicide, read the label instructions carefully. Find out if your ground cover is susceptible to the product and how you need to apply it to protect garden plants. In lush ground cover you may have to use a narrow paintbrush to treat weeds. Use postemergent herbicides on windless days only, when chemicals cannot drift on the breeze. Shield susceptible ground cover to protect it from inadvertent exposure.

WATERING GROUND COVERS

Soil that is too dry or soggy may be due to factors other than too little or too much rain. Soil permeability and irrigation systems affect the amount of water plants actually absorb.

Drought Conditions

In drought conditions, plants begin to yellow. Leaf edges may turn brown. Bare spots may appear. If you have been watering adequately, dryness can occur because compacted soil is prohibiting water penetration. Rapid watering causes run-off rather than allowing moisture to sink in. Hand-watering is often the culprit—

which is not to say that sprinkler systems are perfect. Sprinkler heads may fall out of adjustment and leave some areas dry. To test the coverage, put a few small cans throughout the watering area. All areas should get an equal amount of water, appropriate to the type of ground cover. If the cans contain different amounts, correct the system.

Overwatered Ground Covers

Too much water causes root rot. Ground cover may die in spots or fail to thrive. Lower leaves turn yellow, then upper leaves. If too much rain is the cause—not excess watering—install drain tile.

This ajuga is suffering badly from too much sun and should be transplanted to a shadier location.

PROBLEMS COMMON TO MANY GROUND COVERS — DISCOLORED LEAVES

PROBLEMS COMMON TO MANY GROUND COVERS

Iron deficiency in pachysandra.

Leaf yellowing on vinca, caused by acidic soil.

PROBLEM: Leaves turn pale green or yellow. The newest leaves (those at the tips of the stems) are most severely affected. Except in extreme cases, the veins of affected leaves remain green. In extreme cases, the newest leaves are small and completely white or yellow. Older leaves may remain green.

ANALYSIS: Iron deficiency
Plants frequently suffer from deficiencies of iron and other trace nutrients, such as manganese and zinc, that are essential to normal plant growth and development. Deficiencies can occur when one or more of these elements is lacking in the soil. Often these nutrients are present, but alkaline (pH 7.5 and higher) or wet soil conditions cause them to form compounds that cannot be used by plants. An alkaline condition can result from over-liming or from lime leached from cement or brick. Alkaline soil usually exists in regions where soil is derived from limestone and in those with low rainfall.

SOLUTION: Spray the foliage with a liquid iron treatment, and also apply it to the soil around the plants. Check the soil pH (see the instructions on page 33). If necessary, correct the pH of the soil by treating with ferrous sulfate and watering it in well. Maintain an acidic pH by applying a fertilizer rated 10-7-7.

PROBLEM: Plants grow slowly and the leaves turn pale green to yellow. Plants don't improve much, even after fertilizer is added. A soil test shows a pH below 6.0.

ANALYSIS: Acidic soil
Soils with a pH of less than 6.0 are common in areas of heavy rainfall. Heavy rains leach lime from the soil, making it more acidic. The amounts and types of nutrients available to plants are limited in acidic soils. Below a pH of 5.5, the availability of nitrogen, phosphorus, potassium, calcium, and other nutrients is decreased. These nutrients are essential for healthy plants. Plants vary in their tolerance for acidic soils; most plants grow best with a soil pH between 6.0 and 7.5.

SOLUTION: Test your soil pH with an inexpensive test kit available in garden centers. Many county extension offices also test soil pH. To make a soil less acidic, apply lime; follow the directions given with the soil-testing kit. Soil acidity corrections are only temporary. Add lime to your soil every year or two if you live in an acidic-soil area. Adding iron can also help to correct the situation. Also make sure that there is good drainage, as wet plant roots can add to the difficulty.

Acid-tolerant ground covers: Creeping gardenia, epimedium, ferns, gaultheria, heathers, heaths, hosta, pachysandra, sarcococca, tiarella, vancouveria.

■ **INSECTS**

Scorched ivy leaves.

Powdery mildew on euonymus.

Spider mite (50 times life size).

PROBLEM: Tips and edges of leaves are brown and dead. Leaves may fall.

ANALYSIS: Scorch

Leaf scorch may be caused by any of a number of conditions.
1. *Heat scorch:* This condition occurs in hot weather, when water evaporates rapidly from the leaves. If the roots can't absorb and convey water fast enough to replenish this loss, the leaves turn brown and wither. This condition is often seen when shade-loving plants receive too much sun.
2. *Winter injury:* This type of injury occurs on plants growing in full sun. On a clear winter day, the sun heats the leaf surface, increasing the need for water. If the ground is frozen or if it has been a dry fall and winter, the roots can't absorb enough water.
3. *Salt injury:* This condition results from excess salts in the soil. These salts can come from irrigation water, de-icing salts, or fertilizers. Salt injury is worse in poorly drained soils, where salts can't be easily leached.

SOLUTION: Follow these guidelines to prevent scorching.
1. Keep ground covers well watered during hot weather. Check that you have planted a sun-tolerant ground cover.
2. To prevent winter injury, be sure the soil is moist before the ground freezes. Provide shade during clear, cold weather.
3. Leach the salts from the soil by administering heavy waterings. If your irrigation water is salty, leach regularly to keep salt from accumulating in the soil. When you apply fertilizer, use only the amounts recommended on the label; water thoroughly afterward.

PROBLEM: Leaves and stems are partially or entirely covered with grayish white powdery patches. Leaves die and may drop off. The patches occur primarily on the topsides of the leaves.

ANALYSIS: Powdery mildew

This common plant disease is caused by one of several fungi that thrive in both humid and dry weather. The powdery patches consist of fungal strands and spores. The spores are spread by the wind to healthy plants. The fungi sap plant nutrients, causing yellowing and sometimes the death of the leaf. A severe infection may kill the plant. Since powdery mildew attacks many different kinds of plants, the fungi from a diseased plant may infect other types of plants in the garden. Under conditions favorable to infection, powdery mildew can spread through a ground cover in a matter of days or weeks.

SOLUTION: Spray with a fungicide containing benomyl or triforine. Make sure your plant is listed on the product label. These fungicides do not kill the fungi on leaves that are already diseased; they do, however, protect healthy leaves by killing the mildew spores as they germinate. Follow label directions regarding frequency of application. Remove infected leaves and debris from the garden.

PROBLEM: Leaves are stippled, yellowing, and dirty. Leaves may dry out and drop. There may be cobwebbing over flower buds, between leaves, or on the undersides of leaves. To determine if the plant is infested with mites, hold a sheet of white paper underneath an affected branch and tap the branch sharply. If mites are present, minute green, red, or yellow specks the size of pepper grains will drop to the paper and begin to crawl around. The pests are easily seen against the white background.

ANALYSIS: Spider mites

Mites, related to spiders, are major pests of many garden and greenhouse plants. They cause damage by sucking sap from the undersides of the leaves. As a result of this feeding, the green leaf pigment (chlorophyll) disappears, producing a stippled appearance. Some mites are active throughout the growing season, but they are favored by dry weather above 70° F. By midsummer, they build up to tremendous numbers; other mites are most prolific in cooler weather. Cool-weather mites feed and reproduce primarily during spring and, in some cases, fall. At the onset of weather above 70° F, these mites have caused their maximum damage.

SOLUTION: When the mites first appear, treat infested plants with a miticide such as hexakis. Make sure your plant is listed on the product label. Repeat the treatment 2 more times at 7- to 10-day intervals. Continue the treatments if the mites reappear.

GROUND COVERS

Greenhouse whiteflies (10 times life size).

Aphids on ivy (2 times life size).

Snail and slug damage to ivy.

PROBLEM: Tiny, winged insects $\frac{1}{12}$ inch long are found mainly on the undersides of leaves. The insects are covered with white, waxy powder. When the plant is touched, the insects flutter rapidly around it. Leaves may be mottled and yellowing. In warm-winter areas, black mold may cover the leaves.

ANALYSIS: Greenhouse whiteflies
(*Trialeurodes vaporariorum*)
These insects are common pests of many garden and greenhouse plants. The adult females lay eggs on the undersides of leaves. A larva is the size of a pinhead and looks quite different from the adult. In its immature form the whitefly is flat, oval-shaped, and semitransparent, with white waxy filaments radiating from the body. Larvae feed for about a month before changing into adults. Both the larval and adult forms suck sap from leaves. The larvae are more damaging because they feed more heavily. Adults and larvae cannot fully digest all the sugar in the plant sap, so they excrete the excess in a fluid called honeydew. Sooty mold, a black fungus, grows on the honeydew. In warm-winter areas, greenhouse whiteflies can be active the year around, with eggs, larvae, and adults present. Whiteflies are unable to live through freezing winters. Spring reinfestations in freezing-winter areas result from migrating whiteflies and the introduction of infested plants into the garden.

SOLUTION: Control whiteflies by spraying with an insecticide containing either diazinon, malathion, or acephate (ORTHENE®). Make sure your plant is listed on the product label. Treat every 7 to 10 days as necessary. Spray the foliage thoroughly, covering both surfaces of the leaves.

PROBLEM: Leaves are curled, distorted, and yellow. A shiny, sticky substance may coat them. Tiny ($\frac{1}{8}$-inch) pale green to black soft-bodied insects cluster under leaves and stems. Ants may be present. If the infestation continues, plants may become stunted.

ANALYSIS: Aphids
Aphids do little damage in small numbers. However, they are extremely prolific and populations can rapidly build up to damaging numbers during the growing season. Damage occurs when the aphid sucks the juice from the leaves of the ground cover. The aphid is unable to digest fully all the sugar in the plant sap and excretes the excess in a fluid called honeydew. Ants feed on honeydew and are often present where there is an aphid infestation.

SOLUTION: As soon as aphids appear, spray with an insecticide containing acephate (ORTHENE®). Respray if the plant becomes reinfested.

PROBLEM: Stems and leaves may be sheared off and eaten. Silvery trails wind around on the plants and soil nearby. Snails or slugs move around or feed on the plants, especially at night; look for them at night by flashlight.

ANALYSIS: Snails and slugs
These pests are mollusks and are related to clams, oysters, and other shellfish. They feed on a wide variety of garden plants. Like other mollusks, snails and slugs need to be moist all the time. For this reason they avoid direct sun and dry spots and hide during the day in damp places, such as under flowerpots or in thick ground cover. They emerge at night or on cloudy days to feed. Snails and slugs are similar, except that the snail has a hard shell into which it withdraws when disturbed. In protected places female slugs lay masses of white eggs encased in slime. Female snails bury their eggs in the soil, also in a slimy mass. The young look like miniature versions of their parents.

SOLUTION: Scatter bait or pellets containing metaldehyde or methiocarb in bands around the areas you wish to protect. Also scatter the bait in areas where snails or slugs might be hiding, such as in dense ground cover, weedy areas, compost piles, or pot storage areas. Before spreading the bait, wet down the areas to be treated, to encourage snail and slug activity that night. Repeat the application every 2 weeks as long as snails and slugs are active. Remove scrap lumber and other debris near the ground cover that create cool, damp breeding places.

— AJUGA ———————— ■ DICHONDRA —————

PROBLEMS OF INDIVIDUAL GROUND COVERS

This section is arranged alphabetically by the botanical name of each plant.

Crown rot.

PROBLEM: Lower leaves turn yellow. White cobwebby strands may cover stems and spread over the soil. Large patches suddenly wilt and die during the first few warm, humid days of spring. Plants pull up easily; most of the roots and crown (where stem and roots meet) are rotted away. Tiny, hard, yellow-brown and white pellets are found in the soil.

ANALYSIS: Crown rot
This plant disease is caused by one of several fungi (*Sclerotium* species) that occur mostly in wet, poorly drained soil. These fungi attack many kinds of plants and cause the only serious disease of ajuga. The fungi enter through the roots and crown and spread into the stem, rotting it and causing the plant to wilt and die. In mild infections new growth sometimes sprouts from buds that have not been killed. The tiny fungal pellets found in the soil survive winters and other unfavorable conditions to infect other plants. The infection most frequently enters the garden originally in infested soil or plants, and it lives for years in the soil.

SOLUTION: Remove and destroy all infected plants. Do not replant in the area until the infected soil has either been removed or drenched with a fungicide containing PCNB. To prevent crown rot, plant ajuga in well-drained soil.

Ajuga cultural information
Light: Light shade
Water: Do not allow soil to dry out
Soil: Rich, loamy, well drained
Fertilizer: Medium

Flea beetle damage. *Insert:* Flea beetle (life size).

PROBLEM: From May to October, dichondra leaves turn brown, first along the edges of the lawn, then toward the center. Small round holes are in the leaves. To determine if the cause is an insect, spread a white handkerchief on the border between a damaged area and a healthy area. If black insects, about $\frac{1}{16}$ inch long, hop onto the white cloth, flea beetles are present.

ANALYSIS: Flea beetles
Adult flea beetles are the most damaging pests of dichondra. Although these insects hop like fleas, they are true beetles. Adults spend the winter in garden trash and weeds, emerging with the warm spring weather. Damage is spotty at first, because the number of beetles is small. In a short time, a new generation of grubs hatches and the increased population can destroy a lawn. The discoloration of the leaves is often mistaken for drought damage or fertilizer burn.

SOLUTION: At the first sign of damage, water the infested area, then spray dichondra with a chemical containing diazinon or chlorpyrifos; follow label directions. Repeat the treatment once a month throughout the growing season. A healthy planting of dichondra is more resistant to flea beetles than an unhealthy one, and healthy grass recovers more quickly if it does become infested. Apply fertilizer once a month from March to September.

Dichondra cultural information
Light: Sun or light shade
Water: While soil is still moist
Soil: Heavy or light
Fertilizer: Medium to heavy

FRAGARIA (WILD STRAWBERRY) ■

Leaf spot.

PROBLEM: Spots and blotches appear on leaves. The spots may be yellow, red, tan, gray, or brown, ranging in size from barely visible to ¼ inch in diameter. Several spots may join to form blotches. Leaves often turn yellow, die, and fall off. Leaf spotting is most severe in warm, humid weather. In damp conditions a fine gray mold sometimes covers the affected leaf tissue.

ANALYSIS: Leaf spot
Several different fungi cause leaf spot on wild strawberry. Some of these fungi eventually kill the plant. Others merely spot the leaves and are unsightly but not harmful. The fungi are spread from plant to plant by splashing water, wind, and contaminated tools. They survive the winter on diseased plant debris not cleaned out of the garden. Most leaf-spot fungi do their greatest damage in humid conditions between 50° and 85° F.

SOLUTION: Every 3 to 7 days, spray the infected planting with a fungicide containing chlorothalonil or maneb. Because leaf-spot fungi are most active during warm, humid weather, spray more frequently during those conditions. These fungicides protect the new healthy foliage but do not kill the fungi on leaves that are already infected.

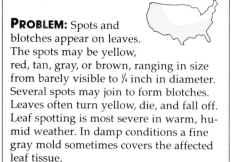

Strawberry cultural information
Light: Full sun
Water: While soil is still moist
Soil: Sandy, well drained
Fertilizer: Medium

HEDERA (IVY) ■

Brown soft scale (2 times life size).

PROBLEM: The stems or the undersides of leaves are covered with raised tan to reddish black crusty or waxy bumps. The bumps can be picked off; their undersides are usually soft. Leaves may turn yellow and fall. In some cases, a sticky substance coats them. A black sooty mold often grows on the sticky material. Ants may be present.

ANALYSIS: Scales
Scales are insects that spend the winter on the trunk and twigs of plants. The females lay eggs in spring and in early summer (late spring in the southern United States); the young scales, called crawlers, settle on leaves and twigs. The small (⅒-inch), soft-bodied young feed by inserting their mouthparts and sucking sap from the plant. Their legs usually atrophy, and a hard crusty or waxy shell develops over their bodies. The mature female scales lay their eggs underneath their shells. Some species of scale that infest English ivy are unable to digest all the sugar in the plant sap, so they excrete the excess in a fluid called honeydew. A black sooty mold fungus may develop on the honeydew. Ants feed on the sticky substance and are often present where scales cluster. An uncontrolled infestation of scales may kill the vines after one or two seasons.

SOLUTION: In early summer (late spring in the South), when the young are active, spray with an insecticide containing acephate (ORTHENE®), malathion, or carbaryl (SEVIN®). The following spring, before new growth begins, spray the vines with a dormant oil spray to control overwintering insects.

MESEMBRYANTHEMUM (ICE PLANT) ■

Mesembryanthemum scales (2 times life size).

PROBLEM: White sacs appear on the new growth, stems, and undersides of leaves in early spring and late summer to midfall. Lime green or yellow flecks almost the same color as the plants, are on the stems and leaves. Plants may turn reddish purple.

ANALYSIS: Scales
(*Pulvinaria delottoi* or *Pulvinariella mesembryanthemi*)
The two insects that attack ice plant are a serious problem in home gardens and in highway plantings along the California coast. They damage and kill plants by sucking the sap from the leaves and stems. Both scales feed actively the year around, but they cause much less damage in the winter. The females mature and lay their eggs in white sacs from February to May and August to October. The eggs are spread from plant to plant by the wind. The fall generation causes the most damage because the plants are already under stress from summer heat and dryness.

SOLUTION: These pests are difficult to control. Once the plants have turned reddish purple, it is too late to spray. Discard them and plant new ones. Treat mildly infested plants with malathion or acephate (ORTHENE®) mixed with a summer oil spray. Do not spray when the white sacs are first present, because the eggs are protected. Spray shortly afterward, when the young have hatched and begin feeding. For best control, spray both surfaces of the plants. Beetles and wasps have been successful in keeping scales under control on highway plantings.

VINCA (PERIWINKLE)

Root and stem rot.

Gray mold.

PROBLEM: Shoot tips wilt and die. There are no black specks on the affected stems. Plants pull up easily, and most of the roots and the lower stems are soft and rotted away. Individual plants are affected first, and within several weeks entire clumps wilt and die.

ANALYSIS: Root and stem rot

This plant disease is caused by a fungus (*Pellicularia filamentosa*). It is the most serious disease affecting periwinkle. Root and stem rot occurs mostly in heavy, poorly drained soil and during periods of wet weather. It can be found throughout the growing season in most periwinkle plantings. The fungi enter the plant through the roots and crown. Infection rots the cells, causing the plant to wilt and die. The fungi persist indefinitely in the soil and spread from plant to plant on contaminated tools and in splashing water.

SOLUTION: Remove and destroy badly infected plants. Allow the soil to dry between waterings. If the area is replanted, improve the drainage. To prevent recurrence of the disease, allow the soil to dry between waterings until it is barely moist.

Vinca cultural information
Light: Light shade
Water: While soil is still moist
Soil: Well drained
Fertilizer: Medium

PROBLEM: Brown or black spots appear on the edges of leaves and spread inward, sometimes covering entire leaves. Flowers may be discolored or spotted. As the disease progresses, a fuzzy brown or grayish mold forms on affected tissue during cool, wet weather.

ANALYSIS: Gray mold

This widespread plant disease is caused by a fungus (*Botrytis cinerea*) found on most dead plant tissue. Fungi of this species initially attack foliage and flowers that are weak or dead, causing spotting and mold. The fuzzy mold that develops is composed of fungal strands and millions of microscopic spores. Once gray mold has become established on plant debris and weak or dying leaves and flowers, it can invade healthy plant tissue. The fungi are spread by splashing water or by contact between infected tissue and healthy tissue. Cool temperatures and high humidity favor gray mold. Rain and overhead watering enhance the spread of the fungi. Infection is more of a problem in spring and fall, when temperatures are lower. In mild-winter areas, where freezing is rare, gray mold can be a year-round problem.

SOLUTION: Remove and discard all fading flowers and diseased leaves. Treat plants with a fungicide containing benomyl, captan, chlorothalonil, or zineb after removing affected plant parts. For best control, add a spreader-sticker to the spray.

ANNUALS, PERENNIALS, AND BULBS

Flowers can turn a drab yard into a show-place. Indoors, a bouquet of cut flowers—whether a formal arrangement in a porcelain vase or a bunch of black-eyed-susans in a jar—seems to bring sunlight and a touch of elegance into the house. Home gardeners usually turn to annuals, perennials, biennials, and bulbs to provide a supply of blooms. Each type requires a different approach in terms of planning, planting, and care.

PICKING PLANTS TO SUIT THE JOB

Buying plants always calls for research. What climate does each species need? What requirements does it have for sunlight, drainage, or fertilizer? (Before purchasing plants and fertilizer, read the section called Assessing and Improving Soil, which appears later in this chapter.) Buying plants that flower takes special attention in terms of learning the blooming patterns and life cycle of each species. In addition, be aware of the limitations of labels and catalogs as information sources.

Climate

Passion flowers are from South America, a climate that stays warm most of the year. Logically, a warm climate is what this showy vine needs to be at its best. Peonies hail from China and range into northern Siberia; hot climates do not always promote their flowering. Agapanthus and pelargoniums originally hail from South Africa, so while they will take some drought, they are also accustomed to warmth. Though a plant may be available for purchase in your area, it may not be well suited to grow there. Research growing conditions carefully, keeping your microclimate in mind.

Time of Purchase

Outdoor plants are seasonal. Each may flower for a week, or a month, but then enter a foliage-only phase, or may die back altogether. If you buy a plant in full bloom, it may be at the close of its blooming season. Buy flowering plants at the beginning of the blooming season.

Time of Flowering

Plan ahead for color areas by checking full flowering period of each plant in your growing zone. Go beyond learning whether the species you are considering is an annual, perennial, or biennial;

Opposite: This attractive border is composed of *Oenothera* (yellow flowers), two kinds of *Campanula* (blue flowers), and *Anthemis* (white flowers).

ascertain the habits of this particular variety.

Some plant species, such as pinks and bellflowers, have biennial, perennial and annual varieties. Labels don't always identify which a plant is. If you unknowingly plant an annual variety, you may think you have a plant problem when the plant dies after a single blooming period. To prevent such surprises, bring a reference book with you to the nursery or garden center, or consult one there. Make sure the habits of the variety you choose suit the plans you have for your garden.

If you are buying through a catalog, be aware that the catalog description may not jibe with what happens in your neighborhood. A catalog may state clearly that a certain plant is a perennial, but in your garden it may turn out to be an annual. Blooming time given in the catalog is usually dictated by weather where the catalog originates, and may be far from what you experience in your part of the country. Bacteria and viruses found in local soil can markedly change flower color, so the red tulips you bought may come up streaked. Talk with your neighbors and gardening professionals to learn how specific plants behave in your area.

Containerized Camouflage

If you have a highly visible site that is homely unless kept color camouflaged, select containerized flowering plants. Chrysanthemums, daylilies, and many other vivid plants thrive this way. The containers can be hidden with a natural mulch or redwood chips, or you can use large decorative pots. When the plants' blooming period is over, move the containers elsewhere, and replace them with another set of full-flowered containerized plants.

Buying Seeds

Packets of seeds can provide an ample rainbow of beauty for a small amount of money. Patient gardeners may find planting seeds more satisfying than installing transplants, and seed packets often offer a greater variety of plant species than local nurseries. Take care when buying seeds, however. Buy only from a reputable dealer and always check the package date to be sure the seeds are fresh. Stale seeds don't germinate as well as fresh ones. In addition, the information given on the packet is often sparse and fairly generic. Read up on whatever varieties you have chosen to determine appropriate sowing and transplanting times, and proper garden conditions.

PLANTING AND GROWING ANNUALS

Annual plants—such as pansies, marigolds, impatiens, or phlox—live and die in a year or less. If annuals get through this period, grow, flower, and produce seed, their disappearance is a natural phenomenon, not a problem. You have wisely satisfied their requirements for direct sun, ample water, effective drainage, and soil of at least average quality.

If you want flowers in your garden on a continuous basis throughout the season, plant annuals. Healthy annuals may bloom for months, one flower following another, from the moment of first bud to the first severe cold spell. Gardeners living in an area with no frost or only occasional frost can plant a series of annuals to provide flowers almost all year long.

Annuals do have disadvantages, however. You might not have abundant flower production unless you prepare soil beforehand, preferably a month in advance. This gives added ingredients—such as compost, manure, or fertilizers—a chance to blend and mellow. The roots of most annuals tend not to reach out as much as other plants, so they must generally draw on the nutrients provided where they are placed. If the vitamins and minerals are not there, an annual might continue blooming for a time after purchase, drawing on nutrients already within the leaves. However, flowers will become smaller and smaller and finally cease altogether. As a result of their relatively limited root systems, annuals are susceptible to transplant shock.

If you are planning on bouquets of summer annuals, do not wait for summer weather to buy the plants. Summer weather may seem prime for planting, but it is often too hot for newly transplanted annuals. The summer sun encourages top growth before the annuals' meager root systems can support it. The result may be stunted plants and minimal flowering. Solve the problem by planting summer flowering annuals when spring weather is still a bit on the cool side but not cold enough to risk frost damage.

PLANTING AND GROWING PERENNIALS

Perennials—such as begonias, foxgloves, bergenias, and asters—bloom for a limited time per year, but they make up for it by having a longer life. Unlike shrubs, which are woody plants, perennials are nonwoody, or soft-stemmed, plants.

Top: These nursery transplants were placed in the ground the day before the photo was taken. Because of root damage and inadequate water, they coped poorly with hot, sunny weather. Bottom: Divide perennials before they show obvious signs of being crowded, or you may find division quite a chore.

Division

Some perennials, such as chrysanthemums, require division every few years, when the plant grows into a crowded unattractive clump. Other signs that you need to divide perennials include extra-tall growth, weak stems, and few blooms. Divide perennials in the spring. Simply expose the rootball and divide its segments to create separate plants. Transplant the newly formed perennials to a site where they do not have to compete for light and nutrients. To increase the number of flowers, pinch plants back after transplanting. Do this every few weeks until the plants become quite bushy and full.

Transplant Shock

To ease transplant shock in divided or new perennials, work when the weather is cool, in early mornings or late evenings. Try not to damage roots. Each root is valuable in water acquisition. After transplanting, nip back about one third of the old growth. Water well, utilizing a vitamin booster with a liquid plant food. Despite the best of care, you may still see some symptoms of transplant shock, including leaf, flower drop, and wilting.

PLANTING AND GROWING BIENNIALS

Biennial plants have two-year lives. They start their life cycle one year, go dormant in winter, then bloom and complete their lives the following year. Many gardeners think something is wrong with plants like foxgloves, hollyhocks, and Canterbury bells because the first year after being set out they grow but do not flower. Waiting for these plants to flower takes patience. If you want blooming biennials on a continual basis, plant some new ones each year to flower the following year, being careful not to disturb those planted previously.

PLANTING AND GROWING BULBS

Bulbs should be as easy to grow as annuals, biennials, and perennials, but some gardeners seem to have no luck with them. The most frequent problems are caused by unhealthy bulbs, poor drainage, and improper care.

Bulb Selection

Some problems are inherent with bulb purchase. With bulbs, you tend to get what you pay for. In many cases, bargain bulbs are "bargains" for a reason. They may be undersized, diseased, poorly stored, inaccurately labeled, improperly matured, or of inferior stock.

Examine bulbs carefully before purchase. Do a light squeeze test. Healthy

Each perennial usually blooms once a season. This can be for a week or a month. Some perennials completely die back and disappear after flowering, then emerge the following year. Their disappearance can be a problem if you forget to mark their planting site. Resting perennials often get chopped up when enthusiastic gardeners think they have empty space and begin planting something new. Avoid this problem by marking perennial plant sites with small labeled stakes. Or, if you live in a warm area, purchase perennials that stay green the entire year, forming a leafy backdrop despite winter.

You may see the phrase "Perennial treated as an annual" on plant labels or in reference books. The phrase refers to perennials such as wax begonia, snapdragon, and coleus, which may not survive winter in cold climates. Gardeners who live in areas where winters are harsh should treat such a plant as an annual and plan to replace it each year.

bulbs, regardless of type, are quite firm and feel heavy for their size. They are free of deep, dark areas; cuts; or soft spots. No mold grows on the outside covering.

Bulb Diseases

The bulb holds nutrients much as a storage tank does. The nutrients enable the plant to send up flowers in spring or early summer. Viruses and fungi can interfere with the scenario, however.

Viruses If soil- or insect-borne viruses enter the bulb, they move quickly throughout the entire plant, affecting every stage of growth. The many different types of viruses can only be seen with a special microscope. Virus damage is highly visible, however, and accounts for much plant damage.

Fungi Root and stem rots are extremely common causes of failure to thrive. They are caused by fungi, which standing water attracts. Plant fungi invade and plug the nutrient channels. The infection remains long after standing water has finally disappeared. Sometimes plant descriptions can help you avoid bulb infection. Be wary of bulbs whose labels say "Needs well-drained soil," "Keep on dry side," or "Requires good aeration." Standing water suffocates plant roots of all kinds by filling necessary air spaces with water. Roots cannot absorb water and nutrients unless oxygen is present. A plant top can wilt from drought while its roots are standing in water.

Do not confuse standing water with ample water. If soil is permeable to air and water, the danger of overwatering is slight. Standing water, however, offers an open invitation to fungi.

Hole Preparation

In poorly drained areas, improve drainage and minimize the chance of disease by digging planting holes at least 1½ to 2 feet deep. Place a layer of stones and gravel at the bottom of the holes, and slant the excavation so it leads water away from the site. If you are placing a great number of bulbs in the same poorly drained area, install drain tiles to keep excess water from accumulating.

Proper soil preparation encourages bulb longevity and increase. If you have clay or some other heavy soil, dig planting holes 12 inches deep. Plant the bulbs, then backfill the holes with commercial potting soil.

Bulb Foliage

The health of the bulb through the dormant season is related to the longevity of the foliage. Do not cut back the leaves of a bulb plant until after the foliage dies

Top: These daffodil bulbs are firm, free from mold, a uniform healthy color, and ready to plant. Bottom: A soil-sampling tube, or corer, is being used to obtain samples for testing.

back naturally. Cutting leaves before they wither or cutting off many leaves when you cut flowers can impede the storage of nutrients and cause bulbs to decline.

ASSESSING AND IMPROVING SOIL

In terms of soil, annuals, perennials, biennials, and bulbs need a growing site that provides an appropriate pH and essential nutrients.

Soil pH

The pH of soil reflects the concentration of hydrogen ions in it; this determines how acidic or alkaline the soil is. pH is measured on a scale from 0.0 to 14.0. A soil that measures pH 7.0 is neutral; it is neither acidic nor alkaline.

In terms of plant growth, acidity or alkalinity is important because it determines how quickly the soil can release nutrients—or whether the nutrients can be released from the soil at all. For

Hydrangea show extreme color variation in response to varying soil pH. The plant at top is in acidic soil; the one at the bottom, in alkaline soil.

take soil samples to a professional testing service. The local cooperative extension office can tell you about such services in your area. Or try looking under "Soil" in the telephone directory. The testing service will give instructions about taking the samples. Most services ask you to take samples from different garden areas by digging to a depth of 6 inches and taking a thin soil slice from the edge of each hole. Then you mix the various samples together in a freshly cleaned nonmetal container. You should now have about 2 cups of soil. Remove any stones, roots, or debris. Cover the container, and keep it dry until analysis.

An alternative to professional testing is using a home soil-testing kit, which you can buy at a nursery or garden center. A home test is not as accurate as a professional analysis, but a kit is inexpensive, easy to use, and usually adequate.

Acidic soil   Most plants placed in acidic soil grow slowly and have pale green or yellow leaves. Roots are few and small. Overly acidic soil promotes disease. Adding fertilizer does not help the plants, because low pH slows nutrient release.

To correct acidic soil, apply finely ground dolomitic limestone. This not only raises soil pH, but supplies needed calcium and magnesium. The heavier the soil, the more limestone you need. Liming to increase alkalinity is especially helpful to clay soils, making them more friable, or crumbly. Liming is not permanent. You will have to recheck pH every 2 years and reapply limestone as necessary.

If you have acidic soil and are unable to correct it, consider planting rhododendrons, azaleas, hydrangeas, camellias, or other acid-loving plants. These plants do not have to depend on soil organisms to release nitrogen from soil. A beneficial fungus species on the plants' roots can convert soil nitrate into usable nitrate; these plants do not have to rely on soil organisms. If you put acid-loving plants in nonacidic soil, sufficient iron may not be released for their needs. Yellow areas may appear between the veins of new leaves, affecting plant appearance. Leaves weakened in this way cannot support normal flowering.

Alkaline soil   Soil with a pH over 7.0 is alkaline. Some plants thrive at this level. When pH reaches 8.0, however, the soil does not release certain nutrients. Iron and manganese are no longer available to plants. Older leaves remain green, but

example, in acidic soil—that with a pH of 5.2, say—magnesium, phosphorus, and calcium are less available for plant use than in neutral soil. Nitrogen is released only partially because soil organisms that create it are less active in acidic soil. When soil has a pH of 5.0 or lower, these organisms often cease working altogether so that no nitrogen is released. Conversely, at a pH below 5.0, manganese and aluminum may become available in harmful amounts.

How do you know the pH of the soil you have? Generally, acidic soils are found in areas of high rainfall; alkaline soils are found in desert areas or areas of low rainfall. However, every region contains microclimates, so the general principle may not provide an accurate assessment. To get a precise pH reading, new leaves have yellow areas between their veins. Flowering plants do not generally tolerate alkaline soil. If you live in a highly alkaline region and want to put in annuals, perennials, or bulbs, consider using raised beds or containers in the garden. Fill these with a commercial soil mix.

To correct mildly alkaline soil, apply acidic peat or an acidic mulch made of pine needles. Use a fertilizer that promotes acid-loving plants, which will create reactions that lower soil pH. Ordinary powdered sulfur corrects alkalinity, but you must strictly regulate the rate of application according to soil needs. Use commercial aluminum sulfate instead of powdered sulfur; the combination product is less prone to application error. For the first treatment, use 2 pounds of aluminum sulfate per 100 square feet. Applying lime-sulfur spray is also helpful.

Soil Nutrients and Fertilizers

Buying the wrong type of fertilizer may cause as many flowering plant problems as overfertilizing. The "big three" fertilizer elements are nitrogen, phosphorus, and potassium. Other elements, present in trace amounts, are also important to plant growth.

Nitrogen This element is a vital component of plant protein. Symptoms of nitrogen shortage include slow growth and yellowing leaves. Too much nitrogen forces lush foliage as opposed to structural growth. The plant becomes vulnerable to weather variables, attacks by insects, and diseases.

Phosphorus Only with phosphorus can plants create stiff stems to hold leaves and flowers up to sunlight and pollination. A phosphorus shortage slows root growth, flowering, and seed production. Leaves turn purplish or become dark gray-green. Symptoms appear in older leaves first. With severe phosphorus deficiencies, plant flowering is minimal.

Potassium In North American soils potassium tends to be plentiful but in a form difficult for plants to use. Potassium is necessary for photosynthesis; without photosynthesis, plants starve. In addition, potassium is essential for stiff stems on flowering plants and for the formation of bulbs and tubers. Symptoms of potassium shortage include mottled yellow or pale green mature leaves with scorched edges. Flower yield is minimal.

Removing spent blooms encourages a plant to continue blossoming. Spent dahlia blooms close up and resemble unopened buds, but a close look often reveals brown petals sticking out.

Other soil nutrients Fertilizer labels often list elements in addition to nitrogen, phosphorus, and potassium. These include iron, calcium, magnesium, zinc, manganese, and sulfur. Though plants use them in minuscule amounts, these trace elements have significant growth effects. Of the secondary nutrients, iron is the one usually in shortest natural supply. Iron deficiency causes yellowing plant leaves, though leaf veins generally remain green. The newest leaves are the most severely affected. Applying an iron-containing fertilizer to the soil corrects yellowing. If necessary, also spray foliage and soil with an iron solution.

Fertilizer selection To correct nitrogen, phosphorus, or potassium imbalance, purchase a fertilizer that meets your immediate and long-term needs. Fertilizer labels look complex, but they are not. The numbers on the container tell you, in relative terms, how much of each of the three major elements is present. If the label says "20-20-20," the fertilizer contains equal portions of nitrogen, phosphorus or phosphate, and potassium or potash. A 5-10-5 mixture is higher in phosphorus than in nitrogen or potassium.

PREVENTING AND SOLVING PROBLEMS

Cultural techniques such as disbudding, pinching back, and staking can prevent many growth problems. When growth is healthy, plants are in the best position to fend off external threats, such as frost and insects.

Cultural Techniques for Problem Prevention

Plants—like people—have a finite energy supply. By using cultural techniques to direct a plant's energy toward healthy growth, you can save the energy you would otherwise have to expend on treating disease or replacing plants.

Flower removal Make certain poor flowering isn't caused by old flowers left on the stems. In many plants, especially roses, flower production slows when older blossoms use energy to create seed. To encourage continual flowering, cut off flowers past their prime.

Disbudding If your plants produce many flowers, but they are not large enough to be attractive in cut displays, try the technique of disbudding. Disbudding involves removing some flower buds while they are about the size of a bean. With fewer buds to develop, the plant has more energy to use in creating larger blooms from the remaining buds. Disbudding is a common practice on peonies, dahlias, carnations, chrysanthemums, and roses.

Pinching back Snapdragons, chrysanthemums, dahlias, fuchsias, blood leaf, salvias, and garden geraniums tend toward ranginess, though the problem can strike just about any plant. To encourage sturdy, bushy growth, pinch back the stems by using your thumb and forefinger to nip them off just under the flower buds. Pinching back does delay blooming, but the long-term result is a stronger, more attractive plant. Snapdragons do well with just one pinching. Chrysanthemums may need up to four.

Stem support Long-stemmed flowering plants may fall over because of stem or blossom weight. Grabbing a handful of stems and tying them to a pole is not the answer to this problem. If the plants have just a few slim stems, such as delphiniums or carnations, loosely tie each stem to a slender stake. If the plants are bushy, provide support by surrounding them with metal hoops that are made for the purpose. Be sure to anchor the hoops securely in the ground. Whether using hoops or stakes, always maintain the natural growth habit of the plants.

Problems in the Environment

Encroaching shade, burning sun, sudden frosts, and hungry insects threaten flowering plants. With a little help from you, your flowers can survive, thrive, and reward you with an array of blossoms.

Insufficient sunlight Flowering plants need plenty of sun. Though they may continue to grow in less than optimum conditions, they may not flower or flowering may be sparse. In some cases, just enlarging the open space around the plants may give them the boost of

These delphinium are staked correctly and inconspicuously.

sunlight they need to prosper. Sometimes the remedy is to cut back overhanging branches that shade the garden. (Before cutting, make sure the limbs are not critical to the survival of the tree or shrub. Read about pruning techniques or consult an arborist to prevent damage.) In other cases, the only course is to move the struggling plants to a sunnier spot. Though transplanting is always a risk, continuing shade could mean certain failure.

Sunburn Though plenty of sunlight encourages flowering plants, too much sunlight can damage them. Symptoms of sunburn include faded and bleached leaves or leaves that turn pale and yellowish. Foliage may become brittle. To prevent sunburn, temporarily shade the plants with some sort of loose cover. Make sure they get all the water they need during periods of sunburn danger.

Frost Whenever it occurs, frost is a danger to plants because it can damage plant cells. Symptoms of frost damage include blackened leaf parts and failure to thrive.

Some perennials and biennials must survive frost during the dormant season. Protect them with a covering of mulch. Mulch vulnerable plants before the first hard frost; the layer of insulation protects them from low temperatures. Mulch hardy perennials and biennials after the ground freezes. Because the plants are hardy, they are likely to begin spring growth after the first significant thaw. The first thaw is often a false spring, and the frost that follows may damage or kill delicate shoots. By mulching hardy perennials after the ground freezes, you insulate them from weather fluctuations. In this case, the mulch keeps the plants cold until sprouting is safe.

Evergreen branches, wood chips, straw, pine needles, and corn stalks are effective mulches because they allow air circulation. Avoid using fallen leaves as mulch unless the leaves are well composted. Uncomposted leaves tend to form a thick soggy mass that compacts and smothers most plants.

A 3-inch layer of mulch usually provides the needed protection. The layer should be loose so air can penetrate to the soil. Through the winter, some of the mulch decomposes. By spring, the soil is clear enough for plants to sprout but still sufficiently covered to get some protection from drying and weed encroachment.

Pests Among the hungry horde of insects that plague flowering plants are thrips, leafminers, leafhoppers, aphids, ants, spittlebugs, mealybugs, bulb flies, cutworms, and a multiplicity of caterpillars. Correct diagnosis is 90 percent of cure. Consult the problem-solving section of this book for photographs and a detailed discussion of insect pests.

Some problems are easily recognizable. Look closely and you can see budworms of varying ages hiding in your decimated petunia blossoms. Cut the stem of a dying hollyhock or aster and 1-inch-long yellow or pale pink corn borers are suddenly out in the open. The 1½-inch-long green cabbageworm can eliminate your entire nasturtium bed and then move over to your alyssum, carnations, and geraniums. The band around the body of the 2-inch-long woolly-bear caterpillar is supposed to predict winter weather: the narrower the band, the colder the season. True or not, one accurate prediction is that hungry caterpillars can defoliate and deflower an entire flower bed. Woolly bears like canna, dahlias, violets, petunias, hollyhocks, and verbena, among many other perennials and annuals. Caterpillar parents are moths and pretty butterflies. The sight of parents flying about each spring should make you alert to potential caterpillar problems in the flower garden.

Earwigs are familiar to gardeners in all but the coldest parts of the country. Normally they are beneficial scavengers, eating waste materials such as decaying fruit and plant litter. But sometimes they multiply and become pests, feeding on flowers and seedlings. Since earwigs like to hide in dark damp places, try trapping them in rolled-up newspapers and overturned flowerpots. Each morning shake the catch out into a pail of soapy water. Continue trapping until no new earwigs appear. If that does not work, use a 2-percent propoxur bait according to label directions.

Grasshoppers emerge only during certain weather conditions, but their appearance can signify disaster to flowering plants. They often move into planted areas from nearby fields in dry weather. Seedlings disappear first. Then grasshoppers begin chewing large holes around leaf edges. They often begin work in areas near weed patches. Begin your control program as soon as you see grasshoppers, because the first few act as scouts for the rest. Spray with acephate (ORTHENE®), after reading the container label to ensure that the spray is suitable for your crop. Pay attention to the preharvest interval specified in the instructions. You may have to repeat the treatment until grasshoppers disappear from the area.

Like insect pests, animal pests can endanger the flower garden. Bulbs sometimes seem particularly vulnerable to attack by animal pests.

Mice use mole runs to get at bulbs underground. Tulip, lily, and crocus bulbs are particular favorites. Bulbs wilt rapidly after being gnawed, and they may be completely destroyed. Adding a liberal load of stone chips or pebbles to the soil when planting discourages mice. Another solution is encircling the entire bulb bed with 12-inch-high fine-mesh netting. Bury this vertically so that only about 3 inches extend above the ground surface. Do not mulch the bulb bed in winter until the ground is quite frozen. If depredations continue, plant bulbs that mice do not like as well, such as narcissus.

Deer often seek out spring bulbs. Since keeping high-jumping deer out of a garden is extremely difficult, one solution is to plant more than you need so you have enough to share. Keep deer favorites close to the house, where the wild animals may be somewhat reluctant to venture. Place tinned mothballs around the perimeter of the yard if children or pets are not nearby. The mothballs may act as a deer repellent. On yard outskirts, plant narcissus. Deer normally will not touch this bulb, and you can choose from many beautiful varieties.

Rabbits can be a garden menace. They eat almost any growing thing they can reach. Rabbits devour all parts of crocus plants and can finish a tulip bed off while it is still in bud form. For emergency protection, apply a thick layer of blood meal around bulb plants. Cover early spring bulbs with evergreen limbs from your holiday tree—a nice recycling project. Leave the green covering over crocus bulbs until the spring sprouts leaf out. Keep tulips covered until stems are 12 inches high. Though dogs and cats can cause garden problems, they do help keep rabbits away.

This *Lavandula* is being protected for the winter with a mulch of pine needles.

PROBLEMS COMMON TO MANY FLOWERS

Transplant shock on cineraria.

PROBLEM: Recently transplanted flowers drop their flower buds before they open. In some cases, blossoms and leaves also drop prematurely. The plant may wilt during the hot part of the day, even if the soil is moist.

ANALYSIS: Transplant shock
Even under ideal conditions, many plants drop some of their buds, flowers, and leaves when they are transplanted. Bud and leaf drop result from root damage that occurs during transplanting. Hairlike rootlets that grow at the periphery of the root system absorb most of the water the plant uses. When these rootlets are damaged during transplanting, the amount of water that can be supplied to the foliage and flowers decreases. Flower buds, flowers, and leaves fall off, and the plant wilts. The more the roots are damaged during transplanting, the greater the leaf and bud drop will be. Also, because plants lose water rapidly during hot, dry, windy periods, transplanting at these times causes plants to undergo greater shock. They will not recover as quickly. As the root system regrows, new flower buds will form.

SOLUTION: Transplant when the weather is cool—in the early morning, in the late afternoon, or on cloudy days. When transplanting, disturb the soil around the roots as little as possible. Preserve as much of the root system as possible. If the roots have been disturbed or if the plant is large or old, pinch off about a third of the growth to reduce the amount of foliage needing water. Water immediately after transplanting with a plant starter containing vitamin B-1.

Thrips damage to gladiolus.

PROBLEM: Flower buds turn brown and die before they open. There are often silvery white streaks on the leaves. Flowers that have opened are often streaked and distorted. If a flower bud is peeled open, tiny ($\frac{1}{20}$-inch) insects resembling brown or straw-colored wood slivers can be seen moving around at the base of the petals.

ANALYSIS: Thrips
Several species of this common insect pest attack garden flowers. Thrips are found in protected parts of the plant, such as inside flower buds. They feed by rasping the soft plant tissue and then sucking the released plant sap. The injured tissue dies and turns white or brown, causing the characteristic streaking of the leaves and flowers. Because thrips migrate long distances on wind currents, they can quickly infest widespread areas. In cold climates, thrips feed and reproduce from spring until fall. With the onset of freezing weather, they find sheltered areas, such as grass clumps, and hibernate through the winter. In warm climates, thrips feed and reproduce all year. These pests reach their population peak in late spring to midsummer. They are especially troublesome during prolonged dry spells.

SOLUTION: Thrips cannot be eliminated completely, but they can be controlled. As soon as damage is noticed, spray infested plants with an insecticide containing acephate (ORTHENE®), carbaryl (SEVIN®), malathion, or diazinon. Spray 1 or 2 more times at intervals of 10 days. Make sure your plant is listed on the product label. Repeat the treatment if reinfestation occurs. Pick off and destroy old or infested flowers.

■ **SLOW GROWTH** ■

Chrysanthemums that weren't disbudded.

Zinnias planted too late.

Phosphorus-deficient columbine.

PROBLEM: The plant produces many small flowers rather than a few large, showy flowers. The leaves are healthy.

ANALYSIS: Many small flowers
Certain plants—such as chrysanthemums, dahlias, and carnations—do not produce large, showy flowers unless most of the flower buds are removed. Generally, these plants produce long stems with a terminal flower bud at the end and secondary flower buds at the base of each leaf on the flower stem. The plant has only a limited amount of nutrients with which to nourish each bud. If there are many buds, each bud receives only a small amount of nutrients and develops into a small flower.

SOLUTION: Pinch off the side flower buds as soon as they are large enough to be handled. The earlier they are removed, the larger the terminal flower will be.

PROBLEM: Plants fail to grow or grow quite slowly. There are no signs of insects or diseases.

ANALYSIS: Poor growth
There are many reasons why plants might grow slowly.

1. *Improper planting time:* Many plants require warm temperatures and long hours of sunlight to grow well. If transplants that need warm weather are set out too early in the spring or too late in the fall, when temperatures are cool, they will not grow.

2. *Unseasonable cool spell:* If the weather is unseasonably cool or cloudy, the growth rate of most plants slows—even plants adapted to cool temperatures.

3. *Natural dormancy:* Many perennials and all bulbs undergo a period of no growth, which usually occurs soon after they have flowered. Although it may seem that the plant is inactive during this period, it is actually developing roots, bulbs, or rhizomes. The foliage of many perennials and bulbs eventually dies back completely, and the plant becomes entirely dormant.

4. *Phosphorus deficiency:* Phosphorus is a plant nutrient essential to normal plant growth and development. Many garden soils are deficient in phosphorus. When plants do not receive enough phosphorus, they usually grow slowly or stop growing altogether. Sometimes their foliage turns dark green or reddens slightly.

SOLUTION: Take these measures to correct the condition or control the problem.

1. Check a list of common flowers and their growing seasons to determine planting time. As the weather warms up, plants that have been set out too early will probably start to grow.

2. Plants will start to grow again when unseasonable cool spells have passed. If the weather is especially cloudy and moist, check for signs of disease. Fungal and bacterial infections are especially troublesome during periods of moist weather.

3. Check a plant list to see if your plant is a bulb or a perennial with a natural dormancy period. If it is, growth will resume during the growth period.

4. For a quick response, treat leaves with a spray rated 23-19-17. Apply phosphate according to label directions.

PROBLEMS COMMON TO MANY FLOWERS — DISCOLORED OR SPOTTED LEAVES

Discolored iris leaves caused by lack of water.

Dried-out crocus.

Nitrogen-deficient impatiens.

PROBLEM: Leaves turn pale green to yellow. The plant may be stunted. In many cases, leaf edges turn brown and crisp; some of the leaves shrivel and die. There are no signs of disease or pests. Unlike nitrogen deficiency, the leaves do not discolor from the base of the plant upward. For information on nitrogen deficiency, see the third column.

ANALYSIS: Leaves discolored
There are several reasons why leaves discolor.

1. *Frequent stress:* Plants require water to remain healthy and grow properly. When they are allowed to dry out once or twice, they usually survive. However, plants that suffer from frequent drought stress undergo metabolic changes that result in leaf discoloration, stunting, and lack of growth. If the soil is allowed to dry out repeatedly, the plant will die.

2. *Salt buildup in the soil:* Leaf discoloration and browning occur when excess salts dissolved in the soil water are taken up into the plant and accumulate in the leaf tissue. Soil salts build up to damaging levels in soils that are not occasionally flushed. Salt buildup commonly occurs in arid regions.

3. *Sun bleaching and sunburn:* Shade-loving plants placed in a sunny location develop discolored leaves. Sun-bleached leaves turn yellow to white or gray; sun-burned leaves turn brown and die. Leaves not directly exposed to the sun usually remain green and uninjured.

SOLUTION: Take these measures to correct the condition or control the problem.

1. Do not let plants wilt between waterings. Look in the alphabetical section that begins on page 93 to determine the moisture requirements of your plant. Provide plants with adequate water.

2. Flush out soil salts periodically by watering deeply and thoroughly.

3. Look in the alphabetical section that begins on page 93 to determine the sunlight requirements of your plant. Transplant shade-loving plants to a shaded location.

PROBLEM: Beginning with the older foliage, leaves turn pale green, then yellow. Growth is slowed. Older leaves may drop. New leaves are small. Severely affected plants may die.

ANALYSIS: Lack of nitrogen
Garden soils are frequently deficient in nitrogen, the most important nutrient for plant growth. Nitrogen is essential in the formation of plant protein, chlorophyll (green leaf pigment), and many other compounds. When a plant becomes deficient in nitrogen, it breaks down proteins and chlorophyll in the oldest leaves to recover nitrogen for new growth. This loss of chlorophyll causes the older leaves to turn yellow. A continuing shortage of nitrogen results in overall yellowing. Because nitrogen is leached from the soil more readily than other plant nutrients and because it is needed in larger quantities, nitrogen must be added to almost all garden soils and for all flowers. Nitrogen leaches from sandy soil more readily than from clay soil, and it leaches more quickly when rainfall or irrigation is heavy.

SOLUTION: For a quick response, spray the leaves with a soluble plant food rated 23-19-17. Apply a plant food rated 12-6-6 or 10-10-10. Repeat applications according to label directions. Fertilize more frequently in sandy soils or where rainfall is heavy.

Fungal leaf spot on impatiens.

Leaf spot.

Iron-deficient pelargonium.

PROBLEM: Spots and blotches appear on leaves and flowers.

ANALYSIS: Leaf and flower spots

Several disease and environmental factors contribute to spotting and blotching of leaves and flowers.

1. *Fungal leaf spot:* Spots caused by fungi are usually small and circular and may be found on all the leaves. The spots range in size from barely visible to ¼ inch in diameter. They may be yellow, red, tan, gray, brown, or black. Often the leaves are yellow and dying. Infection is usually most severe during moist weather from 50° to 85° F.

2. *Bacterial leaf spot:* Spots caused by bacteria are usually tiny and angular. They are usually dark and sometimes accompanied by rotting and oozing. Bacterial spots may be found on all parts of the plant and are most often favored by warm, moist conditions.

3. *Sun bleaching and sunburn:* Shade-loving plants placed in a sunny location may develop spots and blotches. Sun-loving plants may develop bleaching and sunburn symptoms if they are allowed to dry out. Initially, sun-bleached leaves develop a whitish or yellowish appearance. If the leaves develop sunburn, large, dark, angular blotches form on the damaged tissue. Leaves that are not directly exposed to the sun remain green and uninjured.

4. *Spray damage:* Spotting of foliage and flowers may be caused by insecticide, fungicide, or herbicide sprays. Such spots are usually irregular in shape. Spray injury includes distortion, browning, and death of flowers and young leaves. Sprays may drift in from other areas.

SOLUTION: Take these measures to correct the condition or control the problem.

1. Generally, picking off the diseased leaves gives adequate control. Clean up plant debris, especially during the winter. If plants are severely infected, spray them with a fungicide containing chlorothalonil, mancozeb, or zineb. Make sure your plant is listed on the fungicide label before spraying. Water early in the day so that the foliage can dry thoroughly.

2. If practical, pick off and destroy spotted leaves. If the plant is severely infected, discard it. Clean up plant debris. Avoid overhead watering. Dip contaminated tools in rubbing alcohol.

3. Pick off the injured leaves and plant parts. Look in the alphabetical section that begins on page 93 to determine the sunlight requirements of your plant. Transplant shade-loving plants to a shaded location, or provide shade. Provide plants with adequate water, especially during hot, sunny, or windy days.

4. Once damage has occurred, there is nothing you can do. Read and follow directions carefully when spraying. Avoid spraying on windy days when the spray can drift. If spray drifts onto the wrong plant, rinse off the leaves immediately. Pick off dead or badly injured plant parts.

PROBLEM: Leaves turn pale green or yellow. The newest leaves (those at the tips of the stems) are most severely affected. Except in extreme cases, the veins of affected leaves remain green. In extreme cases, the newest leaves are small and completely white or yellow. Older leaves may remain green.

ANALYSIS: Iron deficiency

Plants frequently suffer from deficiencies of iron and other trace nutrients, such as manganese and zinc, that are essential to normal plant growth and development. Deficiencies can occur when one or more of these elements are lacking in the soil. Often these nutrients are present, but alkaline (pH 7.5 or higher) or wet soil conditions cause them to form compounds that cannot be used by plants. An alkaline condition can result from overliming or from lime leached from cement or brick. Alkaline soil usually exists in regions where soil is derived from limestone and in those with low rainfall.

SOLUTION: Spray the foliage with a liquid iron treatment, and also apply it to the soil around the plants. Check the soil pH. If necessary, correct it before planting; use a fertilizer containing aluminum sulfate. Maintain an acidic pH by applying a fertilizer rated 10-7-7.

PROBLEMS COMMON TO MANY FLOWERS — DISCOLORED OR SPOTTED LEAVES

Powdery mildew.

Rust on geranium.

Nasturtiums damaged by ozone.

PROBLEM: Leaves and stems are covered with grayish white powdery spots and patches. In many cases, these patches occur primarily on the topsides of the leaves. Infected leaves eventually turn yellow.

ANALYSIS: Powdery mildew
This common plant disease is caused by one of a number of closely related fungi that thrive in both humid and dry weather. The powdery patches consist of fungal strands and spores. The spores are spread by the wind to healthy plants. The fungi sap the plant nutrients, causing the leaves to turn yellow and sometimes to die. A severe infection may kill the plant. Since some powdery mildews attack many different kinds of plants, the fungi from a diseased plant may infect other types of plants. Under conditions favorable to powdery mildew, the infection can spread through a closely spaced planting in a matter of days. In the late summer and fall, the fungi form small, black, spore-producing bodies, which are dormant during the winter but which can infect more plants the following spring. Powdery mildew is generally most severe in the late summer and under humid conditions.

SOLUTION: Look up your specific plant in the alphabetical listing beginning on page 93 to determine which fungicide to use. Spray at regular intervals of 10 to 12 days or as often as necessary to protect new growth. Remove and destroy severely infected plants. Where practical, pick off diseased leaves. Clean up and destroy plant debris.

PROBLEM: Yellow or orange spots appear on the topsides of leaves. Yellowish orange, rust, or chocolate-colored pustules of spores develop on the undersides. Infected leaves usually wilt and either hang down along the stem or drop prematurely. The plant may be stunted.

ANALYSIS: Rust
This plant disease is caused by any of a number of related fungi. Most rust fungi spend the winter as spores on living plant tissue and, in some cases, in plant debris. Some rust fungi infect various weeds and woody trees and shrubs during part of their life cycle. Flower infection usually starts in the early spring as soon as conditions are favorable for plant growth. Splashing water and wind spread spores to healthy plants. Some rust fungi cannot infect the flower host unless the foliage is wet for six to eight hours. Rust is favored by moist weather, cool nights, and warm days.

SOLUTION: Several different fungicides are used to control rust. Look up your specific plant in the alphabetical listing beginning on page 93 to determine which fungicide to use. Spray infected plants thoroughly, covering both surfaces of the leaves. Some plants are so susceptible to rust that you may need to spray at weekly intervals throughout the summer. Water in the morning rather than the late afternoon or evening. This will allow wet foliage to dry out more quickly. Remove and destroy all infected plants in the fall to prevent them from infecting new plantings. Plant rust-resistant varieties, if available.

PROBLEM: The topsides of leaves may be bleached, with white flecks or reddish brown spots. Sometimes the leaves are distorted. Older leaves are more affected than younger ones.

ANALYSIS: Air pollution
Some gases released into the atmosphere from cars and factories damage plants. The most common type of pollution is smog. Air pollution damage is most common in urban areas, but it also occurs in rural areas where gardens are downwind from factories. Some plants are severely affected and may even die. Pollution-damaged plants produce fewer flowers than healthy plants. The three most common pollutants are ozone, PAN, and sulfur dioxide. Many different environmental factors affect plant susceptibility to air pollution, including temperature, air movement, light intensity, and soil and air moisture.

SOLUTION: Air-pollution injury is usually a localized problem. Check with neighbors to see if the same kinds of plants in their gardens have been affected the same way. Because injury from air pollutants is similar in appearance to injury from nutrient deficiencies, insects, diseases, and mites, eliminate these problems as causes before attributing the damage to air pollution. Nothing can be done about air pollutants. If you live in a smoggy area, select plants that are smog resistant.

Leafminer damage to dahlia.

Virus-damaged gladiolus.

Mite damage to columbine.

PROBLEM: Light-colored irregular trails wind through leaves. Blotches may eventually appear on infested leaves. Some of the trails and blotches are filled with black matter. Severely infested leaves may dry up and die.

ANALYSIS: Leafminers

Most of the insects that cause this type of damage belong to the family of leaf-mining flies. The tiny adult female flies lay their eggs on the undersides of leaves. The maggots that hatch from these eggs penetrate the leaves and live between the surfaces. They feed on the inner leaf tissue, creating winding trails and blotches. Their dark excrement may dot or partially fill sections of the trails. Generally, the larvae emerge from the leaves to pupate. Leafminers are present from the spring until the fall. The last generation of maggots pupates in the soil or plant debris through the winter, to emerge as adult flies the following spring.

SOLUTION: Spray infested plants with an insecticide containing acephate (ORTHENE®). Pick off and destroy infested leaves. Remove and destroy all plant remains in the fall.

PROBLEM: Leaves may be mottled yellow-green or uniformly yellowing. In some cases, the foliage develops yellow rings; in others, the veins turn yellow. Flowers and leaves may be smaller than normal and distorted. The plant is usually stunted, and flowering is generally poor.

ANALYSIS: Viruses

Several different plant viruses infect flowering plants. These viruses include mosaics, yellows, and ring-spots. The severity of virus infections depends on the plant and on the strain of virus. In some cases, symptoms of infection may not show up unless several viruses are present at the same time. Virus infections do not generally kill a plant, but they may greatly reduce its overall vigor and beauty. Many viruses are spread by aphids, which feed on diseased plants and transfer the virus to healthy plants. Touching or pruning diseased plants may transfer viruses to hands and equipment, which in turn can transfer the viruses to healthy plants. Viruses usually persist in a plant indefinitely. Cuttings or divisions made from diseased plants will be infected.

SOLUTION: There are no chemicals that control or eliminate plant virus diseases. Remove and destroy weak, infected, and stunted plants. Wash your hands thoroughly and dip pruning shears in rubbing alcohol after working on infected plants. Purchase only healthy plants. Keep aphid populations under control. Remove any nearby weeds that may attract and harbor aphids.

PROBLEM: Leaves are stippled, yellowish, bronze-colored, or reddish and are often dirty. There may be cobwebbing over flower buds, between leaves, or on the undersides of leaves. To determine if the plant is infested with mites, hold a sheet of white paper underneath an affected leaf and tap the leaf sharply. If mites are present, minute green, red, or yellow specks the size of pepper grains will drop to the paper and begin to crawl around. These pests are easily seen against the white background.

ANALYSIS: Spider mites

These common pests of many garden and greenhouse plants are related to spiders. They cause damage by sucking sap from the undersides of the leaves. As a result of feeding, the green leaf pigment (chlorophyll) disappears, producing a stippled, discolored appearance. Spider mites are active throughout the growing season, but most are favored by dry weather above 70° F. By midsummer, they build up to tremendous numbers. During cold weather, spider mites hibernate in the soil, on weeds and plants retaining foliage, and on tree bark.

SOLUTION: As soon as damage is noticed, spray infested plants with a miticide containing hexakis. Make sure your plant is listed on the product label. Spray plants thoroughly, being sure to cover both surfaces of the leaves. Respray at least 2 more times at intervals of 5 to 7 days. If the plant can tolerate heavy watering, heavy irrigation of the foliage can also help to reduce the number of spider mites.

PROBLEMS COMMON TO MANY FLOWERS — WILTING PLANTS

Wilting snapdragons.

Wilting pincushion flowers.

Wilting hosta.

PROBLEM: The plant is wilting. The leaves are discolored to yellow or brown, and they may be dying. The soil may be moist or dry.

ANALYSIS: Root problems
These symptoms are caused by one of several root problems.

1. *Stem and root rot:* Many fungi and bacteria decay plant roots and stems. In addition to leaf wilting and discoloration, they frequently cause spots and lesions on the leaves and stems. The infected tissue may be soft and rotted, and the plant pulls out of the ground easily to reveal rotted roots. Most of the disease-causing organisms thrive in wet soil.

2. *Fertilizer burn:* Excessive fertilizer causes leaves to wilt and become dull and brown. Later they become dark brown or black and dry up. When too much fertilizer is applied and not watered well, a concentrated solution of fertilizer salts is formed in the soil. This concentrated solution makes it difficult for plants to absorb the water they need and may even draw water out of plants.

3. *Nematodes:* These microscopic worms (which are not related to earthworms) live in the soil and feed on plant roots. While feeding, they inject a toxin into the roots. The result is that roots can't supply adequate water and nutrients to the aboveground plant parts, so the plant slowly dies. Infested plants are weak and slow growing; often turn bronze or yellowish; and wilt on hot, dry days, even when the soil is wet. Pulling the plant up reveals stunted roots that are often dark and stubby. There may be nodules on the roots.

SOLUTION: Take these measures to correct the condition or control the problem.

1. Look up your plant in the alphabetical section that begins on page 93 to determine which root- and stem-rot diseases may affect it. Treat accordingly.

2. Dilute the fertilizer in the soil and leach it below the root zone by watering the soil heavily. Soak the affected area thoroughly with plain water, let it drain, then soak it again. Repeat 3 or 4 times. Cut off dead plant parts. Follow directions carefully when applying fertilizer.

3. If you have a chronic problem with wilting, yellowing plants that slowly die and you've eliminated all other possibilities, test for nematodes. Testing roots and soil is the only method for confirming the presence of these pests. Contact the local cooperative extension office for sampling instructions, addresses of testing laboratories, and control procedures for your area.

PROBLEM: The plant wilts frequently, and the soil is frequently or always dry. The leaves turn brown, shrivel, and may be crisp.

ANALYSIS: Lack of water
The most common cause of plant wilting is dry soil. Water in the soil is taken up by the plant roots. It moves up into the stems and leaves and evaporates into the air through microscopic breathing pores in the surfaces of the foliage. Water pressure in the plant cells keeps the cell walls rigid and prevents the plant from collapsing. When the soil is dry, the roots are unable to furnish the leaves and stems with water, the water pressure in the cells drops, and the plant wilts. Most plants will recover if they have not wilted severely; however, frequent or severe wilting curbs plant growth and may eventually kill the plant.

SOLUTION: Water thoroughly, applying enough water to wet the soil to the bottom of the root zone. If the soil is crusted or compacted, cultivate the soil around the plant before watering. To help conserve soil moisture, apply a mulch around the plant or incorporate peat moss or other organic matter into the soil. Do not allow the plant to wilt between waterings.

Transplant shock on begonias.

Poor drainage on impatiens.

Cucumber beetle feeding on zinnia (½ life size).

PROBLEM: The plant is wilting, but the foliage looks healthy. There are no signs of disease or insects. The soil is moist.

ANALYSIS: Heat or acute root damage
These symptoms are the typical results of one of several causes.

1. *Intense heat or wind:* During hot, windy periods, plants may wilt even though the soil is wet. Wind and heat cause water to evaporate quickly from the leaves. The roots can't take in water as fast as it is lost.

2. *Transplant shock:* Plants frequently wilt soon after being transplanted. Transplant shock, or wilt resulting from root injury during transplanting, occurs because damaged roots are unable to supply the plant with enough water, even when the soil is wet. As the root system restores itself, its water-absorbing capacity increases. Unless the roots are severely injured, the plants will soon recover.

3. *Rodents:* The roots, underground stems, and bulbs of many plants are often disturbed or fed upon by various rodents, including pocket gophers and field mice. Root, bulb, and stem damage result in rapid wilting and sometimes the death of a plant.

4. *Mechanical injury:* Cultivating, digging, hoeing, thinning, weeding, and any other kind of activity that damages plant roots can cause wilting.

SOLUTION: Take these measures to correct the condition or control the problem.

1. As long as the soil is kept moist during periods of intense heat and wind, the plants will probably recover without harm when the temperature drops or the wind dies down. Recovery may be hastened by shading the plants and by sprinkling them with water to cool off the foliage and reduce the rate of water evaporation from the leaves.

2. Preserve the root system when transplanting. Keep as much soil around the roots as possible. Transplant when the weather is cool, in the early morning, in the late afternoon, or on cloudy days. If the roots have been disturbed or if the plant is large and old, prune off about a third of the growth. Water immediately after transplanting with a plant starter containing vitamin B-1. If possible, transplant when the plant is dormant.

3. Rodents may be trapped or baited.

4. Prevent mechanical injury to plants by working around them carefully.

PROBLEM: Insects chew holes in leaves and flowers. Their hard wing covers are folded across their backs, meeting in a straight line down the center of the insects' bodies. The insects may be shiny and brightly colored.

ANALYSIS: Beetles
Many different species of beetle infest flowers. In the spring or summer, beetles fly to plants to feed on flowers, buds, and leaves. Punctured flower buds usually fail to open, and fully open flowers are usually soon eaten. Because many beetles feed at night, only their damage may be noticed, not the insects. Female beetles lay their eggs in the soil or in the flowers in late summer or fall. The emerging larvae crawl down into the soil to spend the winter, or they mature and pass the winter in plant debris. The larvae of some beetles feed on plant roots before becoming mature beetles in the fall or spring.

SOLUTION: At first signs of infestation, spray with an insecticide containing carbaryl (SEVIN®), diazinon, acephate (ORTHENE®), or malathion.

PROBLEMS COMMON TO MANY FLOWERS — INSECTS

Damaged zinnias. *Insert:* Japanese beetle (life size).

PROBLEM: Leaf tissue has been eaten between the veins, making the leaves lacy. Flowers are eaten. Winged-metallic green and bronze beetles, ½ inch long, feed in clusters on the flowers and foliage.

ANALYSIS: Japanese beetles
(*Popillia japonica*)
As their name suggests, these beetles are native to Japan. They were first seen in New Jersey in 1916 and have since become a major pest in the eastern United States. They feed on hundreds of different plant species. The adult beetles are present from June to October. They feed only in the daytime and are most active on warm, sunny days. The female beetles live for 30 to 45 days. Just before they die, they lay their eggs immediately under the soil surface of lawns. The grayish white grubs that hatch from these eggs feed on grass roots. As the weather turns cold in the late fall, the grubs burrow 8 to 10 inches into the soil, where they hibernate. When the soil warms up in the spring, the grubs migrate back to the surface and resume feeding. They pupate and re-emerge as adult beetles in late May or June.

SOLUTION: Spray infested plants with an insecticide containing acephate (ORTHENE®), carbaryl (SEVIN®), or malathion when beetles first appear or as soon as you notice damage from their feeding.

Caterpillar (life size).

PROBLEM: Holes appear in leaves and buds. Leaves, buds, and flowers may be entirely sheared off. Caterpillars feed on the plants.

ANALYSIS: Caterpillars
Many species of these moth or butterfly larvae feed on garden plants. Usually the female adult moths or butterflies begin laying eggs on garden plants with the onset of warm spring weather. The larvae that emerge from these eggs feed on the leaves, flowers, and buds for two to six weeks, depending on the weather and the species. Mature caterpillars pupate in cocoons buried in the soil or attached to leaves, tree bark, or buildings. Some caterpillar species produce only one generation each year. With these species, all the caterpillars hatch, grow, and pupate at the same time. Other species pupate numerous generations yearly, so caterpillars of various sizes may be present throughout the growing season. The last generation of caterpillars in the fall survives the winter as pupae. The adult moths and butterflies emerge the following spring.

SOLUTION: Spray infested plants with an insecticide containing acephate (ORTHENE®), carbaryl (SEVIN®), or diazinon. Make sure your plant is listed on the product label. If the number of caterpillars is small, remove them by hand. If the caterpillars are small in size, Bt (*Bacillus thuringiensis*) may be effective.

Ants on euphorbia (½ life size).

PROBLEM: Ants crawl on plants and soil. In many cases, these plants are infested with aphids, scales, mealybugs, or whiteflies.

ANALYSIS: Ants
These insects, familiar to gardeners throughout the country, do not directly damage plants. Ants may be present for any of several reasons. Many ants feed on honeydew, a sweet, sticky substance excreted by several species of insects, including aphids, scales, mealybugs, and whiteflies. Ants are attracted to plants infested with these pests. To ensure an ample supply of honeydew, ants may actually carry aphids to healthy plants. Aphid infestations are frequently spread in this manner. Ants may also feed on flower seeds and nectar. Although they do not feed on healthy plants, ants may eat decayed or rotted plant tissue. Ants generally live in underground nests. Certain species may form colonies in trees or in building foundations.

SOLUTION: Destroy ant nests by treating anthills with granules containing diazinon or by spraying the nest and surrounding soil with a diazinon solution. Control aphids, scales, mealybugs, and whiteflies by spraying infested plants with malathion, carbaryl (SEVIN®), or diazinon. Make sure your plant is listed on the product label.

Aphids on ornamental pepper (½ life size).

Aster leafhopper (4 times life size).

Whiteflies on fuchsia (2 times life size).

PROBLEM: Leaves are curled, distorted, and yellowing. In many cases, the flowers are malformed. Tiny (⅛-inch) yellow, green, or dark-colored soft-bodied insects cluster on the leaves, stems, and flowers. A shiny, sticky substance may coat the leaves. Ants may be present.

ANALYSIS: Aphids
These common insects do little damage in small numbers. However, they are extremely prolific and populations can rapidly build up to damaging numbers during the growing season. Damage occurs when the aphid sucks the juices from the leaves and buds. The aphid is unable to digest fully all the sugar in the sap and excretes the excess in a fluid called honeydew, which often drops onto the leaves below. Ants feed on this sticky substance and are often present where there is an aphid infestation. A sooty mold fungus may develop on the honeydew, causing the leaves to appear black and dirty. In warm areas, aphids are active the year around. In cool climates, where winter temperatures drop below freezing, the adults cannot survive. However, the eggs females lay in the fall on tree bark, old leaves, and plant debris can survive the winter to cause reinfestation in the spring. Aphids transmit plant diseases such as mosaics and viral yellows.

SOLUTION: As soon as aphids appear, spray with an insecticide containing acephate (ORTHENE®), diazinon, or malathion. Clean up plant debris in the fall.

PROBLEM: Spotted, pale green insects up to ⅛ inch long hop or fly away quickly when the plant is touched; nymphs crawl away sideways like crabs. The leaves are stippled and may be yellowing.

ANALYSIS: Aster leafhoppers
(*Macrosteles fascifrons*)
This insect, also known as the six-spotted leafhopper, feeds on many vegetable and ornamental plants. It generally feeds on the undersides of leaves, sucking the sap, which causes stippling. This leafhopper transmits aster yellows, a plant disease that can be quite damaging. Leafhoppers at all stages of maturity are active during the growing season. They hatch in the spring from eggs laid on perennial weeds and ornamental plants. Even areas where the winters are so cold that the eggs cannot survive are not free from infestation, because leafhoppers migrate in the spring from warmer regions.

SOLUTION: Spray plants whenever feeding damage appears with an insecticide containing acephate (ORTHENE®), diazinon, carbaryl (SEVIN®), or malathion. Check to make sure your plant is listed on the product label. Eradicate nearby weeds—especially thistles, plantains, and dandelions—that may harbor leafhopper eggs and aster yellows.

PROBLEM: Tiny, winged insects ¹/₁₂ inch long feed on the undersides of leaves. The insects are covered with white waxy powder. When the plant is touched, they flutter rapidly around it. Leaves may be mottled and yellowing. In warm-winter areas, black mold may cover the leaves.

ANALYSIS: Greenhouse whiteflies
(*Trialeurodes vaporariorum*)
These insects are common pests of many garden and greenhouse plants. The four-winged adult females lay eggs on the undersides of leaves. A larva, which is the size of a pinhead, is flat, oval-shaped, and semitransparent, with white waxy filaments radiating from the body. Larvae feed for about a month before changing into adults. Both the larval and adult forms suck sap from the leaves. The larvae are more damaging because they feed more heavily. Adults and larvae cannot fully digest all the sugar in the plant sap, so they excrete the excess in a fluid called honeydew, which often drops onto the leaves below. A sooty mold may develop on the honeydew. In warm-winter areas, these insects can be active the year around, with eggs, larvae, and adults present at the same time. Whiteflies are unable to live through freezing winters. Spring reinfestations in freezing-winter areas result from migrating whiteflies and the introduction of infested greenhouse-grown plants into the garden.

SOLUTION: As soon as insects are noticed, spray infested plants with an insecticide containing acephate (ORTHENE®), diazinon, or malathion. Make sure your plant is listed on the product label. When spraying, be sure to cover both surfaces of the leaves.

INSECTS ━━━━━━━━━━━━━━━━━━━━ ■ **LEAVES, FLOWERS CHEWED** ━━━━━━━━━━━━━━━━━━━━ ■

Spittlebug froth.

Cineraria damaged by nocturnal insects.

Snails feeding on hosta (¼ life size).

PROBLEM: Masses of white, frothy foam are clustered between leaves and stems. If the froth is removed, small, green, soft-bodied insects can be seen feeding on the plant tissue. The plant may be stunted.

ANALYSIS: Spittlebugs

These insects, also known as froghoppers, appear in the spring. Spittlebug eggs, laid in the fall, survive the winter to hatch when the weather warms. The young spittlebugs, called nymphs, produce a foamy froth that protects them from sun and predators. This froth envelops the nymphs completely while they suck sap from the tender stems and leaves. The adult spittlebugs are not as damaging as the nymphs. The adults are ¼ inch long, pale yellow to dark brown, and winged. They hop or fly away quickly when disturbed. Spittlebugs seldom harm plants; but, if the infestation is heavy, the plant may be stunted. Their presence is usually objectionable for cosmetic reasons only.

SOLUTION: Use a garden hose to wash spittlebugs from plants. If plants are heavily infested, spray with an insecticide containing malathion, acephate (ORTHENE®), or methoxychlor. Make sure your plant is listed on the product label. Repeated treatments are usually not necessary.

PROBLEM: Holes appear in leaves and flowers. Some of the leaves, stems, and flowers may be sheared off. There are no insects to be seen feeding on the plants during the day. When the affected plants are inspected at night with a flashlight, insects may be seen feeding on the foliage and flowers.

ANALYSIS: Nocturnal insects

Several kinds of insect feed on plants only at night, including some beetles, weevils, and caterpillars and all earwigs and cutworms. Beetles are hard-bodied insects with tough, leathery wing covers. The wing covers meet in the middle of the back, forming a straight line. Weevils look like beetles, except they have elongated snouts. Earwigs are reddish brown, flat, elongated insects, up to 1 inch long, with rear pincers. Caterpillars and cutworms are smooth or hairy soft-bodied worms. These insects usually hide in the soil, in debris, or in other protected locations during the day.

SOLUTION: Control these insects by spraying with an insecticide such as acephate (ORTHENE®). Follow the directions on the product label.

PROBLEM: Holes are chewed in the leaves, or entire leaves are sheared from the stems. Flowers are partially eaten. Silvery trails wind around on the plants and soil nearby. Snails or slugs move around or feed on the plants, especially at night; check for them by inspecting the garden at night by flashlight.

ANALYSIS: Snails and slugs

These pests are mollusks and are related to clams, oysters, and other shellfish. They feed on a wide variety of garden plants. Like other mollusks, snails and slugs need to be moist all the time. For this reason they avoid direct sun and dry places and hide during the day in damp places, such as under flowerpots or in thick ground covers. They emerge at night or on cloudy days to feed. Snails and slugs are similar in appearance, except that the snail has a hard shell, into which it withdraws when disturbed. In protected places female slugs lay masses of white eggs encased in slime. Female snails bury their eggs in the soil, also in a slimy mass. The young look like miniature versions of their parents.

SOLUTION: Scatter bait or granules containing metaldehyde or methiocarb in bands around the areas you wish to protect. Also scatter the bait in areas where snails or slugs might be hiding, such as in dense ground covers, weedy areas, compost piles, or pot storage areas. Before spreading the bait, wet down the areas to be treated, to encourage snail and slug activity that night. Repeat the application every 2 weeks as long as snails and slugs are active.

SEEDLINGS DIE

Damping-off on petunia.

Damping-off on snapdragon.

Damping-off of marigold seedlings.

PROBLEM: Seedlings fail to emerge.

ANALYSIS: Germination problems
Seeds may fail to emerge for several reasons.

1. *Dehydration:* Once the seeds have started to grow, even before they have emerged from the soil, they die easily if allowed to dry out.

2. *Damping-off:* Germinating seedlings are susceptible to damping-off, a plant disease caused by fungi. These fungi inhabit most soils, decaying the young seedlings as they emerge from the seeds. Damping-off is favored by wet, rich soil.

3. *Slow germination:* Seeds of different kinds of plants vary considerably in the amount of time they require to germinate.

4. *Poor seed viability:* Seeds that are old, diseased, or of inferior quality may fail to germinate.

5. *Wrong planting depth:* Seeds of different kinds of flowers vary in their planting depth requirements. If planted too deep or shallow, the seeds may fail to germinate.

6. *Seeds washed away:* If a seedbed is flooded or watered with a forceful spray, the seeds may wash away. Heavy rains can also wash seeds away.

7. *Cold weather:* Cold weather may delay seed germination considerably or prevent germination entirely.

SOLUTION: Take these measures to correct the condition or control the problem.

1. Do not allow the soil to dry out completely. Check the seedbed and seed flats at least once a day. Water when the soil surface starts to dry slightly.

2. Allow the soil surface to dry slightly between waterings. Do not start seeds in soil that is high in nitrogen. Add nitrogen fertilizers after the seedlings have produced their first true leaves.

3. Check the seed packet or a plant book to see if seeds of the type you have planted germinate slowly.

4. Purchase seeds from a reputable nursery or seed company. Plant seeds packed for the current year.

5. Plant seeds at the proper depth. For the proper depths, follow the instructions on a commercial seed packet or consult with a reputable nursery.

6. Water seedbeds gently. Do not allow the water to puddle and run off. Use a watering can or hose nozzle that delivers a gentle spray.

7. Even though germination may be delayed, many of the seeds will probably sprout when the weather warms up. Next year, plant seeds later in the season, after the soil has warmed.

PROBLEM: Seedlings die soon after emerging from the soil and are found lying on the ground.

ANALYSIS: Wilted seedlings
Seedlings may wilt and die from lack of water or from disease.
1. *Dehydration:* Seedlings are soft stemmed and have shallow roots. If the soil dries out even an inch below the surface, the plants may die.
2. *Damping-off:* Young seedlings are susceptible to damping-off, a plant disease caused by fungi. Damping-off is favored by wet soil with a high nitrogen level. Damping-off can be a problem when the weather remains cold or cloudy and wet while seeds are germinating or if seedlings are too heavily shaded.

SOLUTION: Take these measures to correct the condition or control the problem.
1. Do not allow the soil to dry out completely. Water when the soil surface is slightly dry. During warm or windy weather, you may need to water several times a day.
2. Allow the soil surface to dry slightly between waterings. Do not start seeds in soil that is rich in nitrogen. Add nitrogen fertilizers after the seedlings have produced their first true leaves. Protect seeds during germination by coating them with a fungicide containing captan. Add a pinch of fungicide to a packet of seeds (or ½ teaspoon per pound), and shake well to coat the seeds with the fungicide.

PROBLEMS COMMON TO MANY FLOWERS — SEEDLINGS DIE ∎

Seedlings sheared off by snails.

Cutworm damage to petunia seedlings.

Rabbit.

PROBLEM: Seedlings are sheared off and eaten, with only the stems emerging from the ground. Silvery trails wind around on the plants and soil nearby. Snails or slugs move around or feed on the plants, especially at night; check for them by inspecting the garden after dark with a flashlight.

ANALYSIS: Snails and slugs
These pests are mollusks and are related to clams, oysters, and other shellfish. They feed on a wide variety of garden plants. Like other mollusks, snails and slugs need to be moist all the time. For this reason, they avoid direct sun and dry places and hide during the day in damp places, such as under flowerpots or in thick ground covers. They emerge at night or on cloudy days to feed. Snails and slugs are similar in appearance, except that the snail has a hard shell into which it withdraws when disturbed. In protected places female slugs lay masses of white eggs encased in slime. Female snails bury their eggs in the soil, also in a slimy mass. The young look like miniature versions of their parents.

SOLUTION: Apply baits containing metaldehyde or methiocarb in bands around the areas you wish to protect. Also use the bait in areas where snails or slugs might be hiding, such as in dense ground covers, weedy areas, compost piles, or pot storage areas. Before applying the bait, wet down the areas to be treated, to encourage snail and slug activity that night. Repeat the application every 2 weeks as long as snails and slugs are active.

PROBLEM: Seedlings are chewed or cut off near the ground. Gray, brown, or black worms, 1½ to 2 inches long, may be found about 2 inches deep in the soil near the bases of damaged plants. The worms coil when disturbed.

ANALYSIS: Cutworms
Several species of cutworm attack plants in the vegetable garden. The most likely pests of seedlings planted early in the season are the surface-feeding cutworms. A single surface-feeding cutworm can sever the stems of many young plants in one night. These pests hide in the soil during the day and feed only after sundown. Adult cutworms are dark, night-flying moths with bands or stripes on their forewings. In the southern United States cutworms may also attack fall-planted seedlings.

SOLUTION: Apply an insecticide containing carbaryl (SEVIN®), chlorpyrifos, or diazinon around the bases of undamaged plants when stem cutting is observed. Since cutworms are difficult to control, weekly reapplications will probably be necessary. Before transplanting in the same area, apply a preventive treatment of a carbaryl or diazinon product and work it into the soil. In late summer and fall cultivate the soil thoroughly to expose and destroy eggs, larvae, and pupae. Further reduce damage by setting a "cutworm collar" around the stem of each plant. Make collars from stiff paper, aluminum foil, tin cans, or milk cartons. Collars should be at least 2 inches high and pressed firmly into the soil.

PROBLEM: Plants and seedlings may be partially or entirely eaten. Mounds of soil, ridges, or tunnels may be clustered in the yard. There may be tiny holes in the soil and small, dry, rectangular brown pellets on the ground near the damaged plants. Various birds and animals may be seen feeding in the garden, or their tracks may be noticed around the damaged plants.

ANALYSIS: Animal pests
A number of different animals feed on flowers. Pocket gophers (found primarily in the West), field mice, rabbits, and deer cause major damage by eating seedlings or mature plants. Certain birds feed on seedlings. Moles, squirrels, woodchucks, and raccoons are generally less damaging but may feed on flower roots, bulbs, and seeds. Even if these animals are not observed directly, their tunnels, burrows, droppings, and tracks usually signal their presence.

SOLUTION: Fences, cages or screens, traps, repellents, or baits can greatly reduce plant damage caused by animals.

■ AGERATUM (FLOSSFLOWER) ■

PROBLEMS OF INDIVIDUAL ANNUALS, PERENNIALS, AND BULBS

This section is arranged alphabetically by the botanical name of each plant.

Gray mold.

PROBLEM: Brown spots and blotches appear on leaves and possibly on stems. As the disease progresses, a fuzzy brown or grayish mold forms on the infected tissue. Gray mold and spots may appear on the flowers, especially during periods of cool, wet weather. The leaves and stems may be soft and rotted.

ANALYSIS: Gray mold
This widespread plant disease is caused by one of several fungi (*Botrytis* species). Fungi that cause gray mold initially attack foliage and flowers that are weak or dead, causing spotting and mold. The fuzzy mold that develops is composed of millions of microscopic spores. Once gray mold has become established on plant debris and weak or dying leaves and flowers, it can invade healthy plant tissue. Splashing water spreads the fungi, as can bits of infected plant debris that land on the leaves. Crowded plantings, rain, and overhead watering enhance the spread of the disease. Cool temperatures and high humidity favor gray mold growth. In warm areas where freezing is rare, gray mold can be a year-round problem.

SOLUTION: At intervals of 10 to 14 days, spray infected plants with a fungicide containing maneb. Continue the treatment as long as mold is visible. Remove old flowers and dying or infected leaves and stems. Clean up and destroy plant debris. Avoid wetting the foliage.

Ageratum cultural information
Light: Full sun
Water: When soil is still moist
Soil: Rich, well drained
Fertilizer: Medium to heavy, applied after plants begin growing

---

Corn earworms (⅛ life size).

PROBLEM: Striped green, brown, or yellow caterpillars chew holes in leaves and buds. The caterpillars range in size from ¼ inch to 2 inches.

ANALYSIS: Tobacco budworms and corn earworms
(*Heliothis* species)
These closely related caterpillars are the larval stages of night-flying moths. In addition to feeding on many different ornamental plants, both moths are major agricultural pests. The corn earworm, in particular, is one of the most destructive pests of corn in the United States. The moths survive the winter as pupae in the soil, emerging in the spring to lay their pale yellow eggs singly on the undersides of leaves. The caterpillars hatch in two to eight days and feed for several weeks on leaves and buds, then crawl into the soil and pupate. One to three weeks later the new adults emerge. The females lay eggs in the evenings and on warm, overcast days. In cooler areas, the caterpillars are present from early spring to the first frost. In warmer areas, the feeding caterpillars are present the year around.

SOLUTION: When the caterpillars first appear, control tobacco budworms and corn earworms on ornamentals with an insecticide containing acephate (ORTHENE®) or carbaryl (SEVIN®). Repeat the treatment every 10 to 14 days as needed. Deep cultivation in the fall and winter helps destroy some of the overwintering pupae.

ALCEA (HOLLYHOCK)

Rust.

PROBLEM: Yellow or orange spots appear on the topsides of leaves in the early spring. Reddish brown pustules develop on the undersides of the leaves and possibly on the stems. These pustules may turn brown as the growing season progresses. Severely infected leaves shrivel, turn gray or tan, and hang down.

ANALYSIS: Rust

This disease is caused by a fungus (*Puccinia mulvacearum*) and is the most serious and widespread disease of hollyhock. Fungi of this species spend the winter as spores on living plant tissue and plant debris. Infection starts in the early spring as soon as conditions are favorable for plant growth. Splashing water and air currents spread the spores to healthy plants. A number of weeds known as cheeseweeds, or mallows (*Malva* species), are frequently infected with rust and are a source of spores. Wet conditions favor rust.

SOLUTION: In the spring, as soon as the first signs of infection are noticed, spray with a fungicide containing chlorothalonil. Spray the foliage thoroughly, being sure to cover both surfaces of the leaves. This fungicide protects the new, healthy foliage but will not eradicate the fungus on diseased leaves. Spray once every 7 to 10 days or as often as necessary to protect new growth until the end of the growing season. Remove and destroy all infected foliage and any nearby cheeseweed in the fall, when the plant has stopped growing, and again in early spring. Pick off and destroy infected plant parts during the growing season. Water early in the day so that foliage will dry thoroughly.

ANTIRRHINUM (SNAPDRAGON)

Rust.

PROBLEM: Pale yellow spots appear on the topsides of leaves. Reddish brown pustules of spores develop on the undersides. Often these pustules form concentric circles. There may be spores on the stems. Severely infected leaves dry up. The plant is stunted and may die prematurely.

ANALYSIS: Rust

This common disease of snapdragons is caused by a fungus (*Puccinia antirrhini*). Fungal spores are spread by wind and splashing water. Rust can survive only on living plant tissue and as spores on seeds. It does not persist on dead plant parts. Plants must be wet for six to eight hours before rust fungi can infect the leaf surfaces. The disease is favored by moist conditions, nights from 50° to 55° F, and days from 70° to 75° F. Temperatures above 90° F kill the spores.

SOLUTION: At intervals of 5 to 18 days, spray infected plants with a fungicide containing chlorothalonil. Avoid wetting the foliage. Water in the morning, rather than the late afternoon or evening, to give foliage a chance to dry out. Pick off and destroy infected plant parts during the growing season. Remove all snapdragon plants at the end of the growing season to prevent infected plants from reinfecting new plantings. Space plants far enough apart to allow adequate air circulation.

Root and stem rot.

PROBLEM: The plant may suddenly wilt and die, or it may die slowly from the top down. The leaves turn yellow, and overall growth is stunted. There may be lesions on the stems. The roots are decayed.

ANALYSIS: Root and stem rot

This plant disease is caused by any of a number of different fungi that live in the soil. They thrive in waterlogged, heavy soils. The fungi can attack the plant stems and roots directly or enter them through wounds. Infection causes the stems and roots to decay, resulting in wilting, yellowing leaves and plant death. These fungi are generally spread by infested soil and transplants, contaminated equipment, and moving water. Many of these organisms also cause damping-off of seedlings.

SOLUTION: Let the soil dry out between irrigations. Improve soil drainage. Before planting next year, apply PCNB to the soil and work it in to a depth of 6 inches.

Antirrhinum cultural information
Light: Full sun
Water: When soil just below surface is barely moist
Soil: Reasonably good
Fertilizer: General plant food

ASTILBE ■ BEGONIA

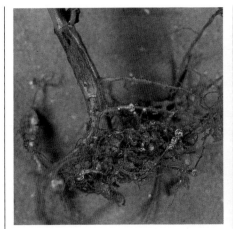

Root nematodes.

PROBLEM: The plant is stunted and growing poorly. Leaves are curled and may be yellowed. The plant can be pulled out of the ground easily. Roots are sparse, short, and dark. Small (⅟₁₆-inch) knots may be visible on the roots.

ANALYSIS: Root nematodes

Root nematodes are microscopic worms that live in the soil. There are many varieties, some highly beneficial and some highly destructive. The destructive types feed on plant roots, damaging, stunting, or causing them to become enlarged. Such roots can't supply sufficient water and nutrients to the aboveground plant parts, and the plant becomes stunted or slowly dies. Nematodes are found throughout the United States, especially in areas with moist, sandy loam soil. The worms can move only a few inches each year on their own, but they may be carried long distances by soil, water, tools, or infested plants. Laboratory testing of roots and soil is the only method for confirming the presence of nematodes. Contact the local cooperative extension office for sampling instructions and addresses of testing laboratories. Problems such as poor soil structure, drought stress, overwatering, nutrient deficiency, and root rot can produce symptoms of decline similar to those caused by nematodes. Root weevils, such as the black vine weevil, may also cause similar symptoms. Eliminate these problems as causes before sending soil and root samples for testing.

SOLUTION: Chemicals to kill nematodes in planted soil are not available to homeowners. However, nematodes can be controlled by soil fumigation with metam-sodium (VAPAM®) before planting.

BEGONIA

ADAPTATION: Throughout the United States.

FLOWERING TIME:
Tuberous: Early to late summer.
Fibrous: Spring to late fall.

LIGHT:
Tuberous: Filtered light to full shade.
Fibrous: Full shade to half-day sun. Dark-colored plants can tolerate full-day sun.

PLANTING TIME:
Tuberous: Start indoors in the spring in zones 1 through 9. To determine your zone, see the map on page 348. You may start tuberous begonias outdoors in zone 10.
Fibrous: Start all year round in zones 9 and 10. Start fibrous begonias in spring through summer in zones 2 through 8.

SOIL: Well drained, rich in organic matter. pH 6.0 to 7.0.

FERTILIZER:
Tuberous: Every 2 weeks apply a fertilizer rated 8-12-4; use half the amount recommended by the label instructions. Stop applying fertilizer about 6 weeks before the first fall frost.
Fibrous: Every 2 weeks, apply a fertilizer rated 8-12-4.

WATER:
How much: Apply enough water to wet the soil 6 to 8 inches deep.
Containers: Apply enough water so that 10 percent of the water drains from the bottom of the container.
How often: Water when soil 1 inch below the surface is moist but not wet.

Gray mold.

PROBLEM: Brown spots and blotches appear on leaves and possibly on stems. As the disease progresses, a fuzzy brown or grayish mold forms on the infected tissue. Gray mold and spots often appear on the flowers, especially during periods of cool, wet weather. The leaves and stems may be soft and rotted.

ANALYSIS: Gray mold

This widespread plant disease is caused by a fungus (*Botrytis cinerea*) found on most dead plant tissue. Fungi of this species initially attack foliage and flowers that are weak or dead, causing spotting and mold. The fuzzy mold that develops is composed of millions of dark microscopic spores. Once gray mold has become established on plant debris and weak or dying leaves and flowers, it can invade healthy plant tissue. Splashing water spreads the fungi, as can bits of infected plant debris that land on the leaves. Cool temperatures and high humidity favor the growth of gray mold. Crowded plantings, rain, and overhead watering also enhance the spread of the disease. Infection is a greater problem in spring and fall, when temperatures are lower. In warm-winter areas where freezing is rare, gray mold can be a year-round problem.

SOLUTION: Control gray mold with a fungicide containing benomyl or chlorothalonil. Spray every 1 to 2 weeks as long as the mold is visible. Clean up plant debris, and remove dying or infected leaves, stems, and flowers. Provide enough space between plants to allow adequate air circulation. Try to avoid wetting the foliage when watering.

BEGONIA

Leaf spot.

Bacterial leaf spot.

Leaf nematode damage.

PROBLEM: Spots and blotches appear on leaves. The spots may be yellow, red, tan, gray, or brown. They range in size from barely visible to ¼ inch in diameter. Several spots may join together to form blotches. Leaves may be yellowing and dying. Leaf spotting is most severe in warm, humid weather.

ANALYSIS: Fungal leaf spot
Begonias are susceptible to several fungi that cause leaf spots. Some of these fungi may eventually kill a plant or weaken it so it becomes susceptible to attack by other organisms. Others merely cause spotting that is unsightly but not harmful. Leaf-spot fungi are spread by splashing water, wind, insects, tools, and infected transplants and seed. The fungi survive the winter in diseased plant debris. Some leaf-spot organisms affect a large number of plants. Most of these fungi do their greatest damage during temperatures from 50° to 85° F. Moist conditions favor infection.

SOLUTION: At intervals of 7 to 10 days, spray with a fungicide containing zineb, chlorothalonil, or benomyl. Because leaf spot is favored by warm, humid conditions, spray frequently during such periods. Fungicides protect new, healthy foliage; however, they will not eradicate the fungus on leaves that are already infected. Clean up and destroy infected leaves and debris.

PROBLEM: Small, blisterlike spots appear on leaves. The spots are translucent, then turn brown with yellow, translucent edges. The spots enlarge and run together, giving the leaf a blotched appearance. Sometimes a slimy substance oozes from the infected areas, turning light brown as it dries. Infected leaves often die prematurely. If the stems become infected, the entire plant may collapse.

ANALYSIS: Bacterial leaf spot
This plant disease is caused by a bacterium (*Xanthomonas begoniae*) that infects tuberous and fibrous begonias. The slimy substance that oozes from infected lesions is composed of bacterial cells, which can live for three months or more. The bacteria are spread by splashing water, contaminated equipment, and infected transplants. Infection is favored by high humidity. Localized leaf infection causes early leaf drop. If the water-conducting tissue of the plant is infected, the whole plant softens and collapses.

SOLUTION: Remove and destroy severely infected plants and the soil immediately surrounding them. Spray remaining plants with basic copper sulfate or streptomycin at intervals of 7 to 10 days to prevent the spread of the disease. Infected tissue will not recover, but new growth and healthy leaves will be protected. Cut off and discard infected plant parts. After working with diseased plants, disinfect tools by dipping them in rubbing alcohol. Avoid wetting or splashing the leaves. Space plants far enough apart to allow adequate air circulation.

PROBLEM: Angular brown leaf blotches develop on the lower leaves first, then on the upper leaves. The blotches enlarge and eventually the leaves curl up, wither, and drop off. The plant is stunted, and new leaf buds may not develop.

ANALYSIS: Leaf nematodes
(*Aphelenchoides olesistus*)
This plant condition is caused by nematodes, microscopic worms that live and feed inside leaf tissue. Infestation occurs when the foliage is wet. Nematodes migrate in the thin film of water on the outside of the leaf to infest healthy tissue. Water splashing on foliage encourages infestation. Leaf nematodes are most severe in warm, humid areas. The pests can survive for three or more years in plant debris and in the soil.

SOLUTION: Remove and destroy severely infested plants. Pick off and destroy all the infested leaves and the 2 leaves directly above them. As much as possible, avoid wetting the foliage. Inspect new plants carefully to be sure they are not diseased, and do not plant in infested soil. Spray weekly with an insecticide containing malathion or dimethoate. Continue the treatment until the symptoms stop spreading.

Begonia cultural information
Light: Full shade to partial sun
Water: When soil just below surface is barely moist
Soil: Rich, well drained
Fertilizer: Medium

■ **CALENDULA** ━━━━━━━━━ ■ **CALLISTEPHUS (CHINA ASTER)** ━━━

Mealybugs (½ life size).

Cabbage loopers (⅛ life size).

Aster yellows.

PROBLEM: Oval, white insects up to ¼ inch long cluster in white cottony masses on stems and leaves. Leaves may be deformed and withered. The infested leaves are often shiny and sticky.

ANALYSIS: Mealybugs
Several mealybug species feed on begonias. Mealybugs damage plants by sucking sap, causing leaf distortion and death. Adult female mealybugs may produce live young or deposit eggs in white, fluffy masses of wax. The immature mealybugs, called nymphs, are active and crawl all over the plant. Soon after the nymphs begin to feed, they exude filaments of white wax that cover their bodies, giving them a cottony appearance. As they mature, their mobility decreases. Mealybugs cannot fully digest all the sugar in the sap, so they excrete the excess in a fluid called honeydew, which coats the leaves. Mealybugs can be spread when they are brushed onto uninfested plants, or when young, active nymphs crawl to nearby plants. They may also be spread by the wind, which can blow egg masses and nymphs from plant to plant. Mealybug eggs and some adults can survive through the winter in warm climates. Spring reinfestations in colder areas come from introducing infested plants into the garden.

SOLUTION: Spray infested plants with an insecticide containing acephate (ORTHENE®). Respray at intervals of 7 to 10 days until the mealybugs are gone. Gently hose down plants to wash off honeydew. Remove and destroy severely infested leaves and plants.

PROBLEM: Foliage and flower buds are chewed. Leaves have ragged edges and irregular or round holes. White-striped green caterpillars up to 1½ inches long feed on the leaves.

ANALYSIS: Cabbage loopers
(*Trichoplusia ni*)
These destructive caterpillars feed on many garden ornamentals and vegetables. With the warm weather of spring, the brownish adult female moths lay tiny, pale green eggs at night on the topsides of leaves. The eggs hatch into active green larvae, which feed extensively on buds and foliage for two to four weeks. Looper damage can occur from early spring through late fall. The caterpillars spend the winter as pupae attached to plant leaves or objects near plants.

SOLUTION: When the caterpillars first appear, spray with an insecticide containing diazinon or carbaryl (SEVIN®). Respray 10 to 14 days later if reinfestation occurs. In the fall, remove plant debris and weeds that may harbor pupae. A solution containing *Bacillus thuringiensis*, a biological control, is effective when sprayed on young loopers.

PROBLEM: Leaf veins pale and may lose all their color. Part or all of the foliage yellows. The flowers are distorted and may turn green. The plant may grow many thin stems bearing pale, spindly leaves. The plant is usually dwarfed.

ANALYSIS: Aster yellows
This plant disease is caused by mycoplasmas, microscopic organisms similar to bacteria. The mycoplasmas are transmitted from plant to plant by leafhoppers. The symptoms of aster yellows are more severe and appear more quickly in warm weather. Although the disease may be present in the plant, aster yellows may not manifest symptoms in temperatures below 55° F. The disease also infects many ornamental plants, vegetables, and weeds.

SOLUTION: Aster yellows cannot be eliminated entirely, but it can be kept under control. Remove and destroy infected China asters. To remove sources of infection, eradicate nearby weeds that may harbor aster yellows and leafhopper eggs. Spray leafhopper-infested plants with an insecticide containing acephate (ORTHENE®). Respray whenever leafhoppers are seen.

Callistephus cultural information
Light: Full sun
Water: When soil just below surface is barely moist
Soil: Good, well drained
Fertilizer: Medium

CANNA ■ CENTAUREA (DUSTY-MILLER) ■ CHRYSANTHEMUM

Bud rot.

Root and stem rot on dusty-miller.

PROBLEM: Newly opened leaves may be partially or entirely black or covered with tiny white spots. Older leaves may be distorted. In many cases older leaves are covered with yellow or brown spots and streaks. Flower buds may turn black and die before they open. Entire stalks are often decayed. A sticky substance may coat affected leaf tissue.

ANALYSIS: Bud rot
This plant disease is caused by bacteria (*Xanthomonas* species) that usually attack young canna leaves and flowers while they are still curled in the buds. The bacteria can spread from the leaves and flowers into the stems, causing plant death. Some of the infected tissue may exude a sticky ooze filled with bacteria. The bacteria are spread by splashing water and rain and by direct contact with contaminated equipment, hands, and insects. Wet conditions enhance the spread of the disease. Bacteria that cause bud rot survive through the winter in diseased rhizomes, contaminated soil, and infected plant debris to reinfect young plants the following spring.

SOLUTION: There are no effective chemical controls for this disease. To control bud rot, reduce excess moisture around infected plants. Water in the morning so the foliage will dry out during the day. Try to avoid wetting the foliage. Space plants far enough apart to allow sufficient air circulation. Pick off infected leaves and flowers. Remove severely diseased plants and the soil immediately surrounding them. Clean up plant debris. Plant only healthy plants and rhizomes.

PROBLEM: Leaves turn yellow, wilt, and eventually die. The roots and lower stems may be soft and rotten. There may be white fungal strands on infected stems and around the base of plants.

ANALYSIS: Root and stem rot
This plant disease is caused by any of a number of different fungi, also known as water molds, that persist indefinitely in the soil. They thrive in waterlogged, heavy earth. Some of these fungi attack the plant stems at the soil level; others attack the roots. Infection causes the roots and stems to decay. This results in wilting, then yellowing, leaves and eventually the death of the plant. These fungi are generally spread by infested soil and transplants, contaminated equipment, and splashing or running water. Many of these organisms also cause damping-off of seedlings.

SOLUTION: Allow the soil around the plant to dry out. Remove and discard severely infected plants. Avoid future root rot by planting in well-drained soil.

Centaurea cultural information
Light: Full sun
Water: Let soil dry between waterings
Soil: Very well drained
Fertilizer: Medium

CHRYSANTHEMUM (SHASTA DAISY, MARGUERITE, MUM)

ADAPTATION: Throughout the United States.

FLOWERING TIME:
Chrysanthemums: Late summer to late fall.
Shasta daisies: Late spring to late summer.
Marguerites: Spring to fall.

LIGHT: Full sun.

SOIL: Any good garden soil. pH 6.0 to 7.5.

FERTILIZER: According to label directions, apply a general-purpose fertilizer rated 10-10-10, or one rated higher in phosphorus, such as 8-12-4.

WATER:
How much: Apply enough water to plants in the ground to wet the soil 8 to 12 inches deep.
How often: Water when soil 1 inch below the surface is just barely moist.

HANDLING:
Chrysanthemums: Pinch plants frequently during the spring to encourage bushy growth. For more information, see page 99.
Shasta daisies: Divide clumps every 2 to 3 years. Pinch off old flowers to encourage continued bloom.
Marguerites: Replace plants every 3 years. Do not cut marguerites back; they will not resprout.

Weak, leggy growth.

Rust.

Foliar nematode damage.

PROBLEM: Mums are leggy, and many of the stems are thin and spindly. Some plants topple and may need to be tied.

ANALYSIS: Leggy growth
Legginess in mums can be caused by two things.
1. *Natural growth pattern:* Most mum varieties grow tall and leggy naturally.
2. *Too much shade:* Mums are sun-loving plants. Chrysanthemums planted in a shaded area produce thin, leggy growth even when pinched back. Under shaded conditions, the plants may not flower well.

SOLUTION: To prevent leggy growth, follow these guidelines.
1. Plants that are leggy may be pinched back to encourage bushier growth as long as they have not yet formed flower buds. Next year, when the new plants are 6 to 8 inches tall, carefully pinch, or nip off, the young growing tips just above a leaf. The tiny side bud that is between this leaf and the stem will grow into a new branch. Every 2 weeks, pinch back all the new growing points that have formed as a result of the previous weeks' pinching. Stop pinching the plant by August. Purchase short-growing mum varieties.
2. Move or transplant chrysanthemums to a location that receives at least 4 hours of direct sun daily.

PROBLEM: Pale spots appear on the topsides of leaves. Chocolate brown pustules of spores form on the undersides of leaves and on the stems. Infected leaves may wither and fall prematurely. The plant is stunted and may die.

ANALYSIS: Rust
This common disease of chrysanthemums is caused by a fungus (*Puccinia chrysanthemi*). The fungal spores are spread by wind and splashing water. Rust can survive only on living plant tissue and as spores on seeds; it does not persist on dead plant parts. Plants must remain wet for six to eight hours before the fungus can infect leaf surfaces. The disease is favored by moist conditions, cool nights, and warm days. Temperatures above 90° F kill the spores. Rust can survive the winter on infected plants.

SOLUTION: As soon as the disease is noticed, spray infected plants with a fungicide containing chlorothalonil; repeat the treatment weekly. Continue spraying throughout the growing season. Water in the morning, rather than the late afternoon or evening, to allow wet foliage to dry out more quickly. Pick off and destroy infected plant parts during the growing season. Space plants far enough apart to allow adequate air circulation. Remove and destroy all infected plants in the fall to keep them from reinfecting new plantings. Next year, grow only rust-resistant varieties.

PROBLEM: Fan-shaped or angular yellow-brown to gray leaf blotches progress upward from the lower leaves. The blotches join together, and leaves turn brown or black. Affected foliage then withers, dies, and hangs down along the stem. The plant is stunted and new leaf buds do not develop. In the spring, young, succulent, leafy growth becomes thickened, distorted, and brittle.

ANALYSIS: Leaf nematodes
(*Aphelenchoides ritzema-bosi*)
The cause of this damage is a microscopic worm, or nematode, that lives and feeds inside the leaf tissue. The nematode is restricted in its movement by large leaf veins. This confined feeding range creates the angular shape of the blotch. When the foliage is wet, the nematode migrates in the thin film of water on the outside of the leaf to infect healthy tissue. This pest is spread from plant to plant by splashing water. It penetrates the plant tissue by entering through a small breathing pore on the underside of the leaf. Leaf nematodes are most damaging in regions where summers are warm and wet. The worms can survive for three years or more in plant debris and in the soil.

SOLUTION: Remove and destroy severely infested plants. Pick off and destroy all the infested leaves and the 2 leaves directly above them. Avoid wetting the foliage. Check new plants carefully to be sure they are not diseased, and do not replant them in infected soil. Spray weekly with an insecticide containing malathion. Continue the treatment until the symptoms stop spreading.

CHRYSANTHEMUM

Thrips damage.

Verticillium wilt.

Mosaic virus.

PROBLEM: Silvery white streaks and flecks appear on leaves and flowers. The leaves and flowers may be distorted and brown. If a flower bud is peeled open, tiny (1/20- to 1/16-inch) insects resembling brown or straw-colored wood slivers can be seen moving around at the base of the petals.

ANALYSIS: Thrips
Several species of this common insect attack chrysanthemums, daisies, and many other garden plants. Thrips are generally found in protected locations, such as inside leaf and flower buds, where they feed by rasping the soft plant tissue, then sucking the released plant sap. The injured tissue dies and turns white, causing the characteristic streaking of the leaves and flowers. Because thrips migrate long distances on wind currents, they can quickly infest widespread areas. In cold climates, thrips feed and reproduce from spring until fall. With the onset of freezing weather, they find sheltered areas such as grass clumps and hibernate through the winter. In warm-winter climates, thrips feed and reproduce all year. These pests reach their population peak in late spring to mid-summer. They are especially troublesome during prolonged dry spells.

SOLUTION: Thrips can be controlled, although not eliminated entirely. Before plants bloom spray them with an insecticide containing acephate (ORTHENE®), diazinon, carbaryl (SEVIN®), or malathion. Respray 1 or 2 more times at one-week intervals. Repeat the treatment if reinfestation occurs. Pick off and destroy old, infested leaves and flowers.

PROBLEM: Leaves yellow, wilt, and die, starting with the lower leaves and progressing up the plant. Older plants may be stunted. Leaf wilting and death often affect only one side of the plant. Flowering is poor. There may be dark brown areas on the infected stems. Slicing a stem open near the base of the plant reveals dark streaks and discolorations of the inner stem tissue.

ANALYSIS: Verticillium wilt
This plant disease affects many ornamental plants. It is caused by one of several soil-inhabiting fungi (*Verticillium* species) that persist indefinitely on plant debris or in the soil. The disease is spread by contaminated seeds, plants, soil, equipment, and ground water. The fungi enter the plant through the roots and spread up into the stems and leaves through the water-conducting vessels in the stems. These vessels become plugged and discolored. This plugging cuts off the flow of water to the leaves, causing leaf yellowing and wilting.

SOLUTION: No chemical control is available. The best course is to destroy infected plants. Verticillium can be removed from the soil by fumigation techniques only. The best prevention is usually to plant flowers that are resistant to verticillium.

PROBLEM: Leaves are mottled, and the leaf veins may turn pale. Plants may be dwarfed and bushy. Flowers are small and may have brown streaks. Leaves, stems, and flowers may be deformed.

ANALYSIS: Mosaic virus
This plant disease is caused by several different viruses. Mosaic is primarily transmitted from plant to plant by aphids. The symptoms of mosaic virus can vary considerably in their severity, depending on the type of virus and the plant species and variety. Viruses can be transmitted to chrysanthemums from many weeds and ornamental plants. Some plants may be infected with mosaic virus without showing the typical symptoms.

SOLUTION: Infected plants cannot be cured; remove and destroy them. Spray aphid-infested plants in the area with an insecticide containing diazinon, acephate (ORTHENE®), or malathion. Respray at intervals of 7 days as often as necessary to keep the aphids under control. For spot treatment of a few plants, use a product containing pyrethrins; follow label directions. To reduce the numbers of plants that may harbor viruses, keep your garden free of weeds.

■ COLEUS ■ CYMBIDIUM

Aster yellows.

Mealybugs (2 times life size).

Mosaic virus.

PROBLEM: Leaf

veins pale and may lose all their color. Part or all of the foliage turns yellow. Leaf edges may turn brown. The flowers are dwarfed, distorted, and may turn green. The plant may grow many thin stems bearing pale, spindly leaves. The plant is generally stunted.

ANALYSIS: Aster yellows
This plant disease is caused by mycoplasmas, microscopic organisms similar to bacteria. The mycoplasmas are transmitted from plant to plant primarily by leafhoppers. The symptoms of aster yellows are more severe and appear more quickly in warm weather. Although the disease may be present in the plant, aster yellows may not manifest symptoms in temperatures below 55° F. The disease also infects many ornamental plants, vegetables, and weeds.

SOLUTION: Aster yellows cannot be eliminated entirely, but it can be kept under control. Remove and destroy infected plants. To remove sources of infection, eradicate nearby weeds that may harbor aster yellows and leafhopper eggs. Spray leafhopper-infested plants with an insecticide containing diazinon or malathion. Respray whenever leafhoppers are seen.

PROBLEM: Oval, white insects up to ¼ inch long cluster in white cottony masses on the stems and leaves. Leaves may be deformed and withered. The infested leaves are often shiny and sticky. Ants may be present.

ANALYSIS: Mealybugs
Several mealybug species feed on coleus. Mealybugs damage plants by sucking sap, causing leaf distortion and death. Adult female mealybugs may produce live young or deposit eggs in white fluffy masses of wax. The immature mealybugs, called nymphs, are active and crawl all over the plant. Soon after the nymphs begin to feed, they exude filaments of white wax that cover their bodies, giving them a cottony appearance. As they mature, their mobility decreases. Mealybugs cannot fully digest all the sugar in the sap, so they excrete the excess in a fluid called honeydew, which coats the leaves. Ants may feed on the honeydew. Mealybugs can be spread by the wind, which may blow egg masses and nymphs from plant to plant. Ants may also move them, or young, active nymphs can crawl to nearby plants. Mealybug eggs and some adults can survive the winter in warm climates. Spring reinfestations in colder areas come from introducing infested plants into the garden.

SOLUTION: Spray infested plants with an insecticide containing resmethrin or acephate (ORTHENE®). Respray at intervals of 7 to 10 days until the mealybugs are gone. Gently hose down plants to knock off mealybugs and wash off honeydew. Remove and destroy severely infested leaves and plants.

PROBLEM: Leaves are mottled or streaked. Pale rings may develop on the foliage. As the leaves grow older, black or brown stripes develop along the leaf veins, and irregular, sunken blotches may form. The flowers may be marred with dark green or light-colored rings or streaks.

ANALYSIS: Mosaic virus
This plant disease is caused by a number of closely related viruses. The symptoms of mosaic infections vary in their severity, depending on the strain of virus and the cymbidium variety. Virus infections generally do not kill plants, but they may greatly reduce overall vigor and beauty. Mosaic persists in a plant indefinitely. Cuttings or divisions made from the diseased plant will also be infected. If diseased plants are touched or pruned, the virus can be transferred to healthy plants on contaminated hands and pruning equipment. Aphids and other insects may also transmit viruses.

SOLUTION: There are no chemicals that control or eliminate virus diseases. Discard weak or severely infected plants. Wash your hands and dip pruning shears in rubbing alcohol after working on infected plants. Purchase only healthy plants.

DAHLIA

Tuber rot.

PROBLEM: Tuberous roots in storage develop dark brown, sunken areas that are usually dry and firm but are sometimes soft and mushy. Tufts of pink and yellow mold may cover part or all of the roots. Tuberous roots that have been planted may not produce any foliage. If they do, the foliage turns yellow and wilts. Digging up the plant reveals roots that are rotted and moldy.

ANALYSIS: Tuber rot
This plant disease is caused primarily by one of two types of common soil-inhabiting fungi (*Fusarium* species or *Botrytis* species). The fungi generally don't infect the tuberous roots unless the roots are wounded. If the roots are damaged when they are dug out of the ground, the fungi can penetrate the wounds and rot the tissue. The roots rot rapidly when they are stored in warm, humid conditions. If tuberous roots suffer frost damage while they are in storage, they are also susceptible to fungal invasion. Sometimes tuberous roots in storage are contaminated, but the fungal decay has not progressed far enough to be noticed. When they are planted the following spring, they may not produce foliage. If they do produce foliage, the fungus causes wilting, yellowing, and the eventual death of the plant.

SOLUTION: Infected roots cannot be saved. To prevent tuber rot next year, dig up the roots carefully after they have matured fully. Discard any roots that show decay. Handle them carefully to prevent injuries. Store the roots in peat moss in a cool, dark place safe from frost.

Wilt disease.

PROBLEM: Lower leaves turn yellow, wilt, and die. Or all the foliage turns yellow and then withers. Older plants may be stunted. Yellowing and wilting often affect only one side of a plant. The flower heads droop. There may be dark brown areas on the infected stem. Slicing open the stem near the base of the plant reveals dark streaks and discolorations on the inner stem tissue. The root system may be partially or entirely decayed.

ANALYSIS: Wilt disease
This disease infects many ornamental plants. It is caused by any of a number of soil-inhabiting fungi (*Verticillium dahliae* or *Fusarium* species) that persist indefinitely on plant debris or in the soil. The disease is spread by contaminated seeds, plants, soil, and equipment. The fungi enter the plant through the roots and spread up into the stems through the water-conducting vessels. The vessels become plugged and discolored. This plugging cuts off the flow of water to the leaves, causing leaf yellowing and wilting.

SOLUTION: No chemical control is available. The best course is to destroy infected plants. *Verticillium* and *Fusarium* can be removed from the soil by fumigation techniques only. The best prevention is usually to use plants that are resistant to these fungi.

DELPHINIUM

Cyclamen mite damage.

PROBLEM: Flower buds are deformed and blackened. The leaves are curled, distorted, thickened, and brittle. Dark brown or black streaks and blotches form on the leaves and stems. The plant may be stunted to only a quarter of its normal size.

ANALYSIS: Cyclamen mites
(*Steneotarsonemus pallidus*)
These microscopic plant pests are members of the spider family. Cyclamen mites are $\frac{1}{100}$ of an inch long and can only be seen with a powerful magnifying glass. Although the mites are not visible to the naked eye, their damage is distinctive and is often called the blacks. Mites generally live and feed in leaf and flower buds and rarely venture out onto exposed plant surfaces. These pests spread by crawling from one overlapping leaf to another. They are also spread on contaminated tools, clothing, and hands. Cyclamen mites are not active during the hot summer months; they are most injurious from the early spring until June and again in late summer. The adults live through the winter in the base of the delphinium plant, where the roots and stalks join, about $\frac{1}{2}$ inch deep in the soil.

SOLUTION: Spray the infested plants with a miticide containing hexakis; repeat the treatment 3 more times at intervals of 7 to 10 days. Spray the foliage thoroughly, covering both surfaces of the leaves. Space plants far enough apart so that their foliage doesn't overlap; this prevents the mites from spreading. To prevent spreading mites to healthy plants, wash hands and tools after working on an infested plant.

DIANTHUS (CARNATION, PINK, SWEET WILLIAM)

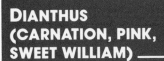

DIANTHUS (CARNATION, PINK, SWEET WILLIAM)

ADAPTATION: Throughout the United States. Carnations may be grown as annuals in zones 3 to 8, but the plants may need winter protection to be grown as perennials in these areas. Carnations do not need protection in zones 9 and 10. To determine your climate zone, see the map on page 348.

FLOWERING TIME: Late spring and summer.

LIGHT: Full sun.

PLANTING TIME: Spring, after all danger of frost is past.

SOIL: Well drained. pH 6.5 to 7.5.

FERTILIZER: According to label directions, apply fertilizer rated 10-10-10.

WATER:
How much: Apply enough water to wet the soil to the bottom of the root zone. For carnations, wet the soil 8 to 10 inches deep. For pinks and sweet william, wet the soil 4 to 6 inches deep.
Containers: Apply enough water to container plants so that about 10 percent of the water drains from the bottom of the container.
How often: Water when soil is just barely moist.

Bacterial wilt.

PROBLEM: Stems or the entire plant may wilt. Leaves dry, turn yellow, and die. The roots are often rotted. Cracks may appear around the base of a stem, with yellow streaks extending up its length. Slicing open a stem reveals yellowish to brownish discolorations. The infected interior portions are sticky.

ANALYSIS: Bacterial wilt
This disease of carnations and pinks is caused by a bacterium (*Pseudomonas caryophylli*) that lives in the soil. Bacteria of this species penetrate the plant stems through wounds or cuts in the roots or the base of a stem. Once inside, the wilt organisms multiply and clog the water-conducting stem tissue, causing the plant to wilt and die. The bacteria can also move down into the root system, causing decay. A sticky fluid, which coats infected stems and roots, contains millions of bacteria. The bacteria are spread to other plants by water, contaminated soil, plant debris, equipment, and handling. Bacterial wilt damage increases as the weather grows warmer.

SOLUTION: Once a plant is infected, it cannot be cured; remove and destroy all infected plants. Clean up plant debris. After handling infected plants, wash your hands thoroughly with soap and hot water. Dip contaminated tools in rubbing alcohol before working on healthy plants. Do not replant healthy carnations or pinks in contaminated soil. Avoid damage to plants when cultivating.

Rhizoctonia stem rot on carnation.

PROBLEM: The leaves turn pale and wilt, sometimes very suddenly. The lower leaves are rotted. The stem is slimy and decayed, and minute black pellets may be just barely visible around the base of the plant.

ANALYSIS: Stem rot
This plant disease is caused by a fungus (*Rhizoctonia solani*) found in almost all soils. Stem-rot fungi penetrate the plant at or just below soil level, rotting through the outer stem bark into the inner stem tissue. Unlike the outer stem, the inner stem tissue becomes dry and corky when it is infected. As the rot progresses up the stem, the lower leaves rot, the foliage pales and withers, and the plant may die. Stem-rot fungi thrive in warm, moist conditions.

SOLUTION: If all the foliage is wilted, replace the plants. Plants not so severely affected can be saved. An effective cultural method to help control the disease is to let the soil dry out between waterings. Next year before planting, spray or dust the soil with a fungicide containing PCNB.

DIANTHUS (CARNATION, PINK, SWEET WILLIAM) ■   DIGITALIS (FOXGLOVE) ■

Virus.

Alternaria leaf spot.

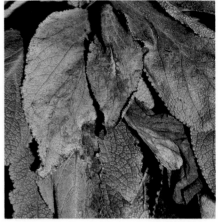

Foxglove anthracnose.

PROBLEM: Leaves are mottled or have yellow to reddish spots, rings, or streaks parallel to the leaf veins. The lower leaves may turn yellow. Sometimes foliage is blotched. Flowers may be streaked or blotched with light or dark colors, or coloring may be uneven.

ANALYSIS: Viruses
Several different viruses infect carnations. Generally, virus infections are not very harmful to the plant. In fact, symptoms of infection may not show up unless several viruses are present in the plant at the same time. However, in severe infections, viruses can cause the lower leaves to turn yellow by suppressing the development of the green pigment (chlorophyll) in the leaf tissue. As a result, the leaves produce less food, causing the plant to be weakened. Certain viruses are spread by aphids, which feed on diseased plants and transfer the virus to healthy ones. Other viruses can be spread when the plants are pruned or handled with contaminated hands or equipment.

SOLUTION: Once plants are infected, no chemical can control the virus. Remove weak and stunted plants. Wash your hands thoroughly and dip pruning shears into rubbing alcohol after working on infected plants. Keep aphid populations low by spraying infested plants with an insecticide containing malathion; follow label directions. For spot treatment of a few plants, use an insecticide containing pyrethrins; follow label directions. Purchase only healthy plants.

PROBLEM: Dark purple spots surrounded by yellow-green margins appear on leaves and stems. Sunken, grayish brown dead areas develop in the center of the spots. Individual spots enlarge and merge to form blotches. Infected leaves turn yellow, blacken, then die. Lesions develop on stems, especially at the bases. Flowers may be spotted. The leaves at the tips of infected stems may become mottled, turn yellow, and wilt. The entire plant may eventually wilt and die.

ANALYSIS: Alternaria leaf spot
This plant disease is caused by a fungus (*Alternaria dianthi*) that infects carnations, pinks, and sweet william. Infection is most severe in wet, humid conditions. Spores are spread by wind and splashing water. Infection occurs when spores germinate on wet leaves, stems, or petals. The fungi survive as spores on plant debris.

SOLUTION: Pick off and destroy infected plant parts and clean up and destroy plant debris. Spray with a fungicide containing captan or chlorothalonil; follow label directions. Water plants in the morning so the foliage has a chance to dry. Try to avoid wetting the foliage when watering.

PROBLEM: Light or purplish brown spots up to ⅛ inch in diameter appear on leaves. The spots are circular or angular and have purplish edges. Rough black areas often develop in the centers of the leaf spots. There may be sunken lesions on the leaf veins and stems, and severely infected leaves turn yellow, wither, and drop off. Often the plants are stunted and die, especially during periods of warm, moist weather. Seedlings may wilt and die.

ANALYSIS: Foxglove anthracnose
This plant disease is caused by a fungus (*Colletotrichum fuscum*) that infects only foxgloves. The fungal spores are spread from plant to plant by splashing water or rain, insects, animals, and contaminated tools. If the leaves are wet, the spores germinate and infect the leaf tissue, creating spots and lesions. Warm temperatures and moist conditions favor foxglove anthracnose. The fungi survive the winter in diseased plant debris and infected seed. This fungus species also causes damping-off of foxglove seedlings.

SOLUTION: Spray diseased plants with a fungicide containing chlorothalonil. Respray throughout the growing season at intervals of 7 to 10 days. Remove and destroy plant debris in the fall. If practical, pick off infected leaves. Water in the morning so the foliage has a chance to dry. Try to avoid wetting the foliage when watering.

Digitalis cultural information
Light: Sun to moderate shade
Water: When soil is just barely moist
Soil: Any good garden soil
Fertilizer: Medium

DIMORPHOTHECA (AFRICAN DAISY) ■ **GLADIOLUS**

Wilt.

PROBLEM: Lower leaves turn yellow, then wilt and die. Or all the foliage turns yellow and then withers. The flower heads may droop. Often, a plant is affected on one side only. Slicing open the stem near the base reveals dark streaks and discolorations of the inner stem tissue. The root system may be partially or entirely rotted.

ANALYSIS: Wilt disease

This disease infects many ornamental plants. It is caused by any of a number of soil-inhabiting fungi (*Verticillium albo-atrum* or *Fusarium* species) that persist indefinitely on plant debris or in the soil. The disease is spread by contaminated seeds, plants, soil, and equipment. The fungi enter the plant through the roots and spread up into the stems and leaves through the water-conducting vessels in the stems. The vessels become plugged and discolored. This plugging cuts off the flow of water to the leaves, causing leaf yellowing and wilting.

SOLUTION: No chemical control is available. The best course is to destroy infected plants. *Verticillium* and *Fusarium* can be removed from the soil by fumigation techniques only.

Dimorphotheca cultural information
Light: Sun
Water: Allow to dry between waterings
Soil: Any good garden soil
Fertilizer: Medium

GLADIOLUS

ADAPTATION: Throughout the United States.

FLOWERING TIME: Summer to fall.

LIGHT: Full sun.

PLANTING TIME: From late winter or spring, when all danger of frost is past, to midsummer.

SOIL: Any good, well-drained garden soil. pH 5.5 to 7.5.

FERTILIZER: Apply a general-purpose fertilizer rated 10-10-10; follow label directions.

WATER:
  How much: Apply enough water to wet the soil 6 to 8 inches deep.
  How often: Water when soil 1 inch below the surface is just barely moist.

HANDLING: For continuous summer bloom, make successive plantings at 2-week intervals from mid-April to mid-July. For cut flowers, harvest when the bottom flower is open. When cutting flowers, allow at least 4 leaves to remain on the plant.

Gladiolus thrips damage.

PROBLEM: Silvery white streaks appear on flowers and foliage. The leaves turn brown and die. Flowers may be deformed and discolored. In the early morning, late afternoon, or on overcast days, blackish brown, slender, winged insects 1/16 inch long can be seen on the foliage and flower petals. On warm, sunny days, these insects hide between leaves and in flower buds. They can be detected only by pulling apart a flower bud or two overlapping leaves.

ANALYSIS: Gladiolus thrips
(*Thrips simplex*)
This insect, one of the most common pests of gladiolus plants, also feeds on many other garden ornamentals. Both immature and adult thrips feed on plant sap by rasping the plant tissue. The injured tissue turns white, causing the characteristic streaking and silvering of the leaves and flowers. The adult female thrips inserts her eggs into growing plant tissue; the emerging young mature within two to four weeks. Thrips actively feed and reproduce from spring until the first frost of fall. They cannot survive freezing temperatures. In warm-winter climates, the adult thrips hibernate in the soil until spring. In cold-winter climates, they overwinter by hibernating on gladiolus corms (bulblike storage organs) in storage. Corms infested by thrips turn brown and corky and may fail to grow, or they may produce only stunted, poor-quality flowers and foliage.

SOLUTION: Spray infested plants with an insecticide containing acephate (ORTHENE®) or diazinon. Respray at intervals of no less than 10 days if reinfestation occurs. Before storing corms, dust them with an insecticide containing malathion. Discard brown corms.

GLADIOLUS

Streaking of gladiolus flowers caused by virus.

Fusarium yellows.

Scab.

PROBLEM: Leaves and flowers are streaked, spotted, or mottled. The leaves may also be yellowing, stiff, or thickened. An affected plant may bloom prematurely, or the flowers open only partially and then fade rapidly. The entire plant may be dwarfed, although sometimes only the flower spike is stunted.

ANALYSIS: Viruses
A number of different plant viruses infect gladiolus. Depending on weather conditions and plant variety, the symptoms of infection can vary from barely noticeable to quite severe. Virus infections rarely cause a plant to die, but they can weaken it seriously. The virus increases in the corms (the "bulbs" of the gladiolus plant) year after year. Successive plantings from diseased corms provide flowers of poor quality. Viruses are spread by aphids. These insects feed on diseased plants and transfer the virus to healthy plants at subsequent feedings.

SOLUTION: Once plants are infected, no chemical can control the virus. To prevent the spread of the disease to healthy plants, remove and destroy infected plants. Infected corms cannot be reused, even if the stem growth is removed. Keep aphid populations under control by spraying infested plants with an insecticide containing diazinon or acephate (ORTHENE®); follow label directions. Because 2 of the viruses that infect gladiolus are common on vegetables in the bean and cucumber families, avoid planting gladiolus near beans, clover, cucumbers, squash, melons, or tomatoes.

PROBLEM: Foliage and flower spikes are stunted, flowers may be small and faded. Yellowing starts on the leaftips and spreads through the entire plant, which finally dies. Pulling a dying plant out of the ground reveals roots that are rotted and a corm (the bulblike storage organ) spotted with circular, firm, brown or black lesions. In some cases, the corm appears normal. However, slicing it open reveals brown or discolored inner tissue.

ANALYSIS: Fusarium yellows
This common and widespread disease of gladiolus plants and corms is caused by a soil-inhabiting fungus (*Fusarium oxysporum* var. *gladioli*). Fungi of this species may penetrate and rot the corms in storage or in the ground. Wet soils and temperatures above 70° F favor the rapid development of this disease. Sometimes corms are contaminated when they are put into storage, but the fungal decay may not have progressed far enough to be noticed. If severely infected, they may not produce foliage after being planted the following spring. If they do produce feeble growth, it soon turns yellow and dies. The fungi survive in diseased corms and soil for many years. Corms that have been removed from the soil prematurely are especially susceptible to infection.

SOLUTION: Destroy all plants and corms that show signs of infection. Dig them up only when they have fully matured. Do not replant healthy corms in soil in which diseased plants have grown. Before storing corms, soak them for 15 minutes in a fungicide containing benomyl; before planting, soak them for another 15 minutes. Store corms in a dry place at 40° to 50° F.

PROBLEM: Sunken black lesions on the corm (the "bulb" of the gladiolus plant) are covered with a shiny, varnishlike material and encircled by raised, brittle rims. Later in the season, after the corms have been planted, many tiny, raised, reddish brown specks develop on the bases of the emerging leaves. These specks become soft, elongated dead spots, which may be covered with and surrounded by a shiny, oozing material in wet weather. The leaves usually fall over.

ANALYSIS: Scab
This plant disease, caused by a bacterium (*Pseudomonas marginata*), earns its name from the scablike lesions it produces on the gladiolus corms. Bacteria of this species penetrate the corm tissue and then move up into the stem base, producing a soft, watery rot. This decay causes the leaves to fall over. The shiny, varnishlike spots that form on the leaves and corms contain millions of bacteria. Wet, heavy soil and warm temperatures favor the rapid development of this disease. The bacteria can live for several years in infected corms and plant debris. The infection is spread by splashing water, and by contaminated corms, soil, tools, and insects. Severely infected plants may die.

SOLUTION: There is no chemical control for this disease. Destroy infected corms and plants. Plant healthy corms in well-drained soil where diseased gladioli have not grown.

Penicillium corm rot.

Dry rot.

Short stems.

PROBLEM: Corky, reddish brown, sunken lesions ½ inch or larger in diameter appear on the corm (the bulb-like storage organ). In cool, moist conditions, the rotted areas of the corm become covered with a blue-green mold. Infected corms that have been planted may not produce any foliage. Foliage that is produced turns yellow and wilts. The corms are rotted and moldy.

ANALYSIS: Penicillium corm rot
This plant disease is caused by a common fungus (*Penicillium gladioli*) that is most often noticed on corms in storage. Fungi of this species infect the corm through wounds or abrasions that usually occur when the corm is dug out of the ground. The rot spreads throughout the corm and up into the stem tissue. Infected corms rot rapidly when they are stored in warm, humid conditions. The fungi form masses of blue-green spores and tiny brown fungus pellets that can survive dry conditions and extremes of temperatures to invade healthy corms. If mildly infected corms are planted, they may or may not produce foliage, depending upon how severely the infection has progressed. Eventually, any foliage produced will turn yellow and die.

SOLUTION: Dig up corms carefully and only when the gladiolus leaves have turned entirely yellow in the fall. Destroy all corms showing decay. Handle healthy-looking corms carefully to prevent injuries. Before storing, dip them in a solution of a fungicide containing captan; dip the corms again before planting. Store corms in a dry location at 40° to 45° F.

PROBLEM: Foliage turns yellow and dies prematurely. Leaf bases are rotted and may be shredded. Black fungal pellets the size of pepper grains may cover the decayed leaf bases and husks of the corms (the "bulbs" of the gladiolus plant). On the corms are dark brown to black sunken lesions, which are dry and corky. They may enlarge and join together, destroying the entire corm.

ANALYSIS: Dry rot
This plant disease is caused by a fungus (*Stromatinia gladioli*) that attacks corms either in storage or in the soil. After the initial infection, the decay spreads up into the leaf bases, killing the leaves prematurely. Corms planted in cold, wet soil or stored in moist conditions are most susceptible to dry rot. The infection is spread by contaminated soil and corms. The tiny black fungal pellets that form on infected tissue can survive for 10 years or more in the soil.

SOLUTION: Discard infected corms and plants. Plant in well-drained soil. Dig corms before the onset of cold, wet weather, and store them in a dry place. If you wish to replant in areas where infected corms have been growing, fumigate the soil with metam-sodium (VAPAM®).

Gladiolus cultural information
Light: Full sun
Water: When soil just below surface is barely moist
Soil: Rich, well drained
Fertilizer: Medium

PROBLEM: Flower stalks are extremely short, and flowers may be smaller than normal. Sometimes only the tip of the flower stalk emerges and blooms at ground level. There are no signs of insects or disease, and the foliage appears to be healthy.

ANALYSIS: Short stems
This condition is the result of inadequate chilling. Hyacinth bulbs contain embryonic flowers and stems. A minimum of six weeks' exposure to temperatures from 45° to 50° F during the winter stimulates the stem cells to elongate, causing the immature hyacinth to emerge from the ground. During spring temperatures from 50° to 55° F, the stems continue to elongate to their full length, at which point the flowers mature and open. In warm-winter areas, the hyacinth stems may fail to elongate properly because of inadequate chilling. Also, during unseasonable spring hot spells, when air temperature reaches 70° F or higher, the hyacinth flowers are stimulated by the heat to mature and open before the stems have entirely emerged from the ground.

SOLUTION: There is nothing you can do to increase the length of the hyacinth stem once the flower has matured. If warm spring temperatures are common in your area, plant hyacinths in locations where they will receive either filtered light or direct sun only in the morning or late afternoon. The lower air and soil temperatures in such areas will help to increase stem lengths. If you live in a warm-winter area, place hyacinth bulbs in paper bags in the fall, and chill them in the crisper section of the refrigerator for 6 weeks before planting.

HYACINTHUS (HYACINTH) ■ IMPATIENS (BALSAM) ■ IRIS

Diseased bulb on left.

PROBLEM: Bulbs that have been planted may not produce any foliage. If foliage is produced, the flower stalk may not form. In some cases, flowers open irregularly and rot off. The entire stalk may rot at the base and fall over. If pulled gently, the leaves and flower stalk may lift entirely off the bulb. The bulb is soft; rotted; and filled with a white, thick, foul-smelling ooze.

ANALYSIS: Bacterial soft rot
This plant disease is caused by a bacterium (*Erwinia carotovora*) that infects hyacinth bulbs both in storage and when planted in the ground. The bacteria initially penetrate and decay the upper portion of the bulb. The disease then progresses upward into the leaves and flower stalks and down through the bulb and roots. The thick ooze that accompanies the decay is filled with millions of bacteria. Bulbs that are infected before they are planted produce little, if any, growth. Even well-established, healthy plants may decay quite rapidly after they are infected, sometimes within three to five days. The bacteria survive in infected plant debris and bulbs and are spread by contaminated insects and tools and by diseased bulbs and plants. Moist conditions favor soft rot. If bulbs freeze while they are in storage, they are especially susceptible to infection.

SOLUTION: There is no cure for this disease. Remove and destroy all bulbs and plants showing signs of decay. Store bulbs in a dry location from 40° to 45° F. Plant only healthy bulbs in well-drained soil. Do not overwater.

Leaf spot.

PROBLEM: Leaves are spotted or blotched with brown spots that range in size from barely visible to ¼ inch in diameter. Several spots may join to form blotches. The leaves may turn yellow and die. Leaf spotting is most severe in wet weather.

ANALYSIS: Leaf spot
A number of different fungi cause leaf spot. Some of these fungi will eventually kill the plant; others merely cause spotting that is unsightly but not harmful. Leaf-spot fungi are spread by wind, insects, splashing water, and contaminated tools. Fungal strands or spores survive the winter in plant debris. Most leaf-spot organisms do their greatest damage in humid conditions from 50° to 85° F.

SOLUTION: Spray infected plants with a fungicide containing captan or benomyl; respray at intervals of 7 to 10 days. Make sure your plant is listed on the product label. Because leaf spot is favored by warm, wet conditions, conscientious spraying during these periods is important. Pick off spotted, diseased leaves, and clean up and destroy plant debris.

Impatiens cultural information
Light: Full shade to filtered sun
Water: When soil just below surface is barely moist
Soil: Rich
Fertilizer: Medium

IRIS

ADAPTATION:
Rhizomatous: Zones 5 through 10.
Bulbous: Zones 7 through 10.
Irises may be grown in colder areas if plants are heavily mulched. To determine your zone, see the map on page 348.

FLOWERING TIME:
Rhizomatous: Early summer.
Bulbous: Late spring through early summer.

LIGHT: Full sun.

PLANTING TIME:
Rhizomatous: Summer.
Bulbous: Fall.

SOIL: Well drained. pH 6.0 to 7.5.

FERTILIZER: Apply a general-purpose fertilizer rated 10-10-10; follow label directions.

WATER:
How much: Apply enough water to wet the soil to 1½ feet deep.
How often: Water when soil 1 inch below the surface is just barely moist.

HANDLING: Mulch irises after the first hard fall frost. Divide rhizomatous iris clumps every 3 to 5 years.

Didymellina leaf spot.

Rust.

Iris borer damage.

PROBLEM: Tiny brown spots from ⅛ to ¼ inch in diameter appear on leaves. The spots have distinct reddish borders and may be surrounded by water-soaked areas that later turn yellow. After the plant has flowered, the spots enlarge rapidly and may join together to form blotches. Spotting is most severe in wet weather. The leaves die prematurely.

ANALYSIS: Didymellina leaf spot
This plant disease is caused by a fungus (*Didymellina macrospora*) that infects only irises and a few other closely related plants. This fungus species attacks the leaves and, occasionally, the flower stalks and buds. It will not affect iris roots, bulbs, or rhizomes (elongated underground stems). Although the fungi do not directly kill the plant, several years of repeated infection result in premature leaf death each summer, greatly reducing rhizome and bulb vigor. Some varieties of iris suffer leaf dieback even when they are only lightly spotted; other varieties can be covered with spots before they start to die. When the leaves are wet or during periods of high humidity, the fungal spots produce spores that are spread to other plants by wind or splashing water. The fungi spend the winters in infected leaves and debris.

SOLUTION: Spray plants with a fungicide containing chlorothalonil. Respray every 7 to 10 days until the foliage starts to die back. Clean up and destroy plant debris, and clip off diseased foliage in the fall. Spray again when new growth appears, and repeat 4 to 6 more times at intervals of 7 to 10 days. Use a spreader-sticker when spraying.

PROBLEM: Rust-colored, powdery pustules appear on both sides of leaves. Later in the season, these pustules turn dark brown. Severely infected leaves may die prematurely.

ANALYSIS: Rust
This plant disease is caused by one of a number of closely related fungi (*Puccinia* species). The rust-colored pustules are composed of millions of microscopic spores. Some of the spores spend the winter on iris leaves that have not died back entirely; others overwinter on other kinds of plants. Infection usually starts in the spring, as soon as conditions are favorable for plant growth. The spores are spread to healthy plants by splashing water and wind. Because iris varieties vary greatly in their susceptibility to rust, some may be killed prematurely, but others may not be affected. Wet weather greatly favors rust.

SOLUTION: Spray infected plants with a fungicide containing ferbam or chlorothalonil. Respray 2 or 3 more times at intervals of 7 to 10 days. Remove and destroy old and dying iris leaves in the fall. Water in the morning to allow the foliage a chance to dry out before nightfall. Plant rust-resistant varieties, if available.

Rust-resistant Dutch iris: Early Blue, Gold and Silver, Golden West, Imperator, Lemon Queen, Texas Gold.

PROBLEM: Dark streaks, water-soaked spots, and possibly slits develop in new leaves in the spring to early summer. The leaf edges may be chewed and ragged. By midsummer, the foliage is wilting and discolored. The leaf bases are loose and rotted. The rhizomes (elongated underground stems) may be filled with holes and may be soft and rotted. Pink caterpillars, from 1 to 2 inches long, feed inside the rhizomes.

ANALYSIS: Iris borers
(*Macronoctua onusta*)
The larva of the iris borer, a night-flying moth, is the most destructive insect pest of iris. In the fall, the adult female moth lays eggs in old leaf and flower stalks. The eggs hatch in late April or early May. The emerging larvae initially feed on the leaf surface, producing ragged leaf edges and watery feeding scars. They then bore into the inner leaf tissue and gradually mine their way down into the rhizome, on which they feed throughout the summer. The damaged rhizome is extremely susceptible to bacterial soft rot. The larvae leave the rhizome, pupate in the soil, and emerge as adult moths in the fall.

SOLUTION: To eliminate overwintering borer eggs, clean up and destroy plant debris in the fall or by April. From the time iris growth starts until the beginning of June, spray the plants weekly with an insecticide containing lindane. In May and June, squeeze the leaves in the vicinity of feeding damage to kill feeding borers inside. To kill the borers in lightly infested rhizomes, poke a wire into borer holes. Destroy heavily infested plants and rhizomes.

IRIS ━━━━━━━━━━━━━━━━━━━━━━━━━━━━━━━ ■   **LATHYRUS (SWEET PEA)** ━━━━━━━ ■

Crown rot.

Bacterial soft rot.

Powdery mildew.

PROBLEM: The leaves of bearded and other irises grown from rhizomes (elongated underground stems) die, starting with the leaftips and progressing downward. The leaf bases and possibly the rhizomes are dry, brown, and rotted. The leaves of Dutch and other irises grown from bulbs are stunted, turn yellow, and die prematurely. The leaves and stems at the soil level are rotted, and the bulbs are soft and crumbly. White matted fungal strands cover the crown (where the stem meets the roots) and soil surrounding both rhizomatous and bulbous irises. Tan to reddish brown pellets the size of mustard seeds form on the infected plant tissue and soil.

ANALYSIS: Crown rot

This plant disease is caused by a widespread fungus (*Sclerotium rolfsii*). This species decays and kills the leaf and stem bases, bulbs, and often part or all of the rhizomes. Crown rot is spread by moving water, diseased transplants, infested soil, and contaminated tools. The fungal pellets can survive for many years in dry soil and extremes of temperature to reinfect healthy plants when conditions are suitable. Crown rot is most severe in overcrowded plantings, warm temperatures above 70° F, and moist conditions.

SOLUTION: Remove and destroy infected plants, bulbs, and rhizomes and the soil immediately surrounding them to 6 inches beyond the diseased area. Drench the area with a fungicide containing PCNB. Next year, redrench the soil at planting time and again when new growth is showing. Plant in well-drained soil with roots covered and tops of rhizomes showing at the soil line. Thin out overcrowded plantings.

PROBLEM: Leaves turn yellow, wilt, and eventually die. Dieback often starts at the leaftips and progresses downward. The entire leaf cluster (fan) may be found lying on the ground. If pulled gently, the leaf fan sometimes lifts off the rhizome (the elongated, jointed, underground stem). Leaf bases and rhizomes are often rotted and foul smelling.

ANALYSIS: Bacterial soft rot

This plant disease is caused by a bacterium (*Erwinia carotovora*). It is a serious and common disease of bearded and other rhizomatous irises. The bacteria enter the plant through wounds in the leaves and rhizomes; the wounds are frequently made by iris borers. As the infection develops, the plant tissue decays into a soft, foul-smelling mass. Finally, the plant dies and the inner rhizome tissue disintegrates. Moist, dark conditions favor infection and rapid decay. Soft-rot bacteria live in the soil and in plant debris. They are spread by contaminated plants and rhizomes, soil, insects, and tools.

SOLUTION: Remove and destroy all diseased plants; they cannot be cured. If only a small portion of a newly acquired rhizome is infected, it may possibly be saved by cutting off the diseased portion; the safest course, however, is to discard all diseased rhizomes before planting. Avoid wounding the rhizomes when digging them up. After dividing them, let the wounds heal for a few days before replanting. Place irises in a sunny, well-drained location. The planted rhizome should be shallow, so the upper portion is exposed. Clean up plant debris in the fall. Control iris borers.

PROBLEM: Leaves and stems are covered with grayish white powdery spots and patches that occur primarily on the topsides of the older leaves. Leaves eventually turn yellow and wither.

ANALYSIS: Powdery mildew

This common plant disease is caused by a fungus (*Erysiphe polygoni*) that can be severe on sweet peas. Powdery mildew thrives in both humid and dry weather. The powdery patches consist of fungal strands and spores. The spores are spread by the wind to healthy plants. The fungi sap plant nutrients, causing yellowing and sometimes the death of the leaves, especially the older ones. A severe infection may occasionally kill the plant. Since this powdery mildew attacks many different kinds of plants, the fungi from a diseased plant may infect other types of plants in the garden. Under conditions favorable to powdery mildew, the infection can spread through a closely spaced planting in a matter of days or weeks.

SOLUTION: Spray infected plants with a fungicide containing benomyl, or dust them with sulfur. These fungicides protect the new, healthy foliage by killing the powdery mildew spores as they germinate on the leaves; they do not eradicate the fungi on leaves that are already diseased. If practical, pick off infected leaves. Remove severely infected plants. Spray or dust at regular intervals of 7 to 10 days or as often as necessary to protect new growth. Clean up plant debris.

LILIUM (LILY)

Root and bulb rot. Diseased plant on right.

Virus.

Leaf scorch.

PROBLEM: Plants are stunted and wilting, and the lower leaves turn yellow. The tips of the lower leaves may be dying and brown, and dead patches may appear along the leaf edges. The flower buds may wither and fail to open. The bulbs and roots are rotted.

ANALYSIS: Root and bulb rot
Rot problems are common with lilies. These plant diseases are caused by various fungi (*Rhizoctonia*, *Phytophthora*, *Pythium*, *Fusarium*, and *Cylindrocarpon* species). These fungi attack and decay the bulbs and roots, causing stunting, wilting, and the eventual death of the foliage and flowers. These bulb- and root-rot organisms live in the soil and stored bulbs and are favored by wet soil. Sometimes bulbs in storage are lightly infected, but the fungal decay hasn't progressed far enough to be easily noticed. When planted, these bulbs may rot so quickly that they do not produce any foliage.

SOLUTION: Remove and destroy infected plants. Check all bulbs carefully and discard any that are moldy, rotted, or dry and crumbly. Before planting, dip clean, healthy bulbs in a fungicide solution containing truban or benomyl. Plant in well-drained soil. Store bulbs in a dry location from 35° to 45° F.

Lilium cultural information
Light: Full to part sun
Water: When soil just below surface is barely moist
Soil: Well drained, rich
Fertilizer: Medium

PROBLEM: The leaves are mottled and streaked light and dark green, and the plant may be stunted and dying. The foliage may be spotted with tiny yellow, brown, or gray flecks. These flecks are elongated and run parallel to the leaf veins. Plants with these flecks are often stunted and have small, streaked flowers that do not open fully. Their leaves may be twisted or curled. In many cases these plants die prematurely, starting from their bases.

ANALYSIS: Viruses
Several virus diseases of lilies cause mottling or flecking of the foliage. Mosaic viruses produce leaf mottling and discoloration. Depending on the species or variety, the symptoms of infection can be mild or severe. Fleck is produced if a plant is simultaneously infected by the symptomless lily virus and the cucumber mosaic virus (which may or may not produce mottling by itself). Leaf flecking is usually accompanied by stunting and poor-quality flowers and foliage. The plant is generally disfigured. Viruses remain in infected bulbs year after year, so successive plantings of diseased bulbs will produce only poor-quality flowers and foliage. All these viruses are spread by aphids, which pick them up while feeding on diseased plants and then transmit them to healthy plants at later feedings.

SOLUTION: There is no chemical control for viruses. Remove and destroy infected plants. Control aphids by spraying infested plants with an insecticide containing malathion or acephate (ORTHENE®); follow label directions. Respray if reinfestation occurs. Plant mosaic-resistant or immune lilies.

PROBLEM: Brown semicircular or crescent-shaped areas develop along leaf edges. Leaftips may be brown. Usually the lower leaves are affected first. Soil pH is acidic.

ANALYSIS: Leaf scorch
Leaf scorch is a condition that may develop in lilies when they are growing in acidic (lower than pH 6.5) soil. In this environment, toxic amounts of aluminum and manganese salts become available and are absorbed by plant roots. Leaf scorch is most likely to occur when the plant is not receiving adequate or balanced supplies of nutrients, such as nitrogen and calcium. During the part of the growing season when growth is most rapid, significant temperature changes can also cause leaf scorch.

SOLUTION: Add ground dolomitic limestone to the soil to decrease its acidity. To all plants apply a balanced fertilizer rated 8-12-4.

LOBULARIA (SWEET ALLYSUM) ▪ NARCISSUS (DAFFODIL, JONQUIL)

Root and stem rot.

PROBLEM: Leaves and stems turn yellow, wilt, and die. The lower leaves and stems may be soft and rotted. White fungal strands may grow around the bases of the plants.

ANALYSIS: Root and stem rot
This plant disease is caused by any of a number of different fungi, also known as water molds, that persist indefinitely in the soil. They thrive in waterlogged, heavy earth. Some of these fungi attack the plant stems at the soil level; others attack the roots. Infection causes the roots and stems to decay. This results in wilting, then yellowing, leaves and eventually the death of the plant. These fungi are generally spread by infested soil and transplants, contaminated equipment, and splashing or running water. Many of these organisms also cause damping-off of seedlings.

SOLUTION: Allow the soil around the plants to dry out. Remove and discard severely infected plants. Avoid future root rot by planting in well-drained soil.

Lobularia cultural information
Light: Part to full sun
Water: When soil is almost dry
Soil: Well drained
Fertilizer: Light

NARCISSUS (DAFFODIL, JONQUIL)

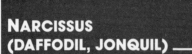

ADAPTATION: Throughout the United States.

FLOWERING TIME: Spring.

LIGHT: Full sun is best for these plants. Daffodils tolerate light shade, but may stop blooming after several years.

PLANTING TIME: Fall.

SOIL: Any good well-drained garden soil. pH 6.0 to 8.0.

FERTILIZER: When planting, mix 1 teaspoon of bone meal or other phosphorus-only fertilizer into the soil at the bottom of the planting hole. During the growing season, apply a general-purpose fertilizer rated 10-10-10; follow label directions.

WATER:
How much: Apply enough water to wet the soil 1½ feet deep.
How often: Water when soil 1 inch below the surface is just barely moist. Stop watering the bulbs after the foliage has turned yellow.

HANDLING: Continue to water and apply fertilizer regularly until the foliage turns yellow; then remove the dead leaves.

Fusarium bulb rot.

PROBLEM: Leaves turn yellow, and the plant is stunted and dies prematurely. If the bulb is unearthed, there may be few or no roots. Bulbs in storage develop a chocolate- or purple-brown spongy decay that is especially noticeable when the outer fleshy bulb scales are pulled away. White fungus strands may grow on the bulbs.

ANALYSIS: Fusarium bulb rot
This plant disease is caused by a fungus (*Fusarium oxysporum* var. *narcissi*) that attacks both growing plants and bulbs in storage. Growing plants are infected through their roots; stored bulbs may be infected through wounds or abrasions in the bulb tissue. Infected bulbs that are planted continue to decay in the ground and produce few or no roots and stunted, yellowing foliage. Fungi of this species persist in the soil indefinitely and are spread by contaminated bulbs, soil, and tools. Generally, bulb rot is most destructive when soil temperatures reach 60° to 75° F. The disease is most common in warm climates where temperatures rarely drop below freezing and in daffodils that are forced for indoor winter use.

SOLUTION: Discard all diseased plants and bulbs and the soil for 6 inches around the bulb. Dig bulbs up carefully to prevent wounds. Prepare a fungicide bath for the healthy bulbs by heating water to 80° to 85° F and stirring in 2 tablespoons of a fungicide containing benomyl. Clean the bulbs, then soak them in the solution for 15 to 30 minutes. Store bulbs in a cool well-ventilated place at 55° to 60° F. Do not replant healthy bulbs in an area where diseased plants have previously grown. In warm climates use fusarium-resistant cultivars.

Failure to bloom.

No flowers due to weak growth.

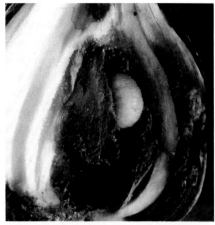

Narcissus bulb fly larva (life size).

PROBLEM: Foliage is healthy but may be sparse. Few or no flowers are produced. Flowers that are produced may be smaller than normal.

ANALYSIS: Failure to bloom
There are several cultural reasons why daffodils fail to flower.

1. *Overcrowding:* Bulbs multiply each year, producing larger clumps the following spring. If the clumps are not divided and transplanted every few years, they become overcrowded.

2. *Too much shade:* Daffodils planted in a shaded spot will usually bloom well the first year. However, they require a sunny location for continued flowering. The leaves use light to manufacture food, which is stored in the bulbs for next year's growth and flowering. Inadequate light reduces the amount of stored food, resulting in few or no flowers.

3. *Overheating:* If a bulb is stored at temperatures above 80° F, the flower embryo inside the bulb is killed. Leaves will grow in the spring, but flowers will not be produced.

4. *Undersized bulbs:* If flower bulbs are much smaller than normal, they may produce only foliage for the first one to two years. Undersized bulbs don't store enough food to produce both leaves and blossoms, but the bulbs will grow larger; finally they will produce flowers.

5. *Foliage removed too soon:* After a daffodil flowers, the remaining foliage continues to use sunlight to manufacture food for new bulbs and next year's flowers. If the foliage is removed before it has a chance to die back naturally, the new bulbs may not have stored enough food to produce a flower.

SOLUTION: Take these measures to correct the condition or control the problem.

1. Divide bulb clumps when flower production drops off—as a general rule, every 3 to 4 years.

2. Grow daffodils where they will receive at least 4 hours of full sun each day. Plants in the shade can be transplanted to a sunny location any time after the flowering period. Try to keep the soil and roots immediately surrounding the bulb intact when transplanting.

3. Store bulbs at 55° to 60° F in a well-ventilated location.

4. Purchase only large, healthy bulbs. Apply fertilizer in the fall and when shoots emerge.

5. Let the foliage turn yellow before removing it.

PROBLEM: Narcissus and daffodil bulbs feel soft and spongy and produce little or no growth after they are planted. Foliage that does emerge is yellow, stunted, and looks grassy. No flowers are produced. In the spring, flying insects that resemble small (½- to ¾-inch-long) bumblebees hover around the plants. These black, hairy insects have bands of yellow, buff, or orange around their bodies.

ANALYSIS: Narcissus bulb flies
(*Merodon equestris*)
This insect, a member of the fly family, is a common pest of many ornamental bulb plants. In the spring, the adult female fly lays her eggs on the leaf bases and soil immediately surrounding a plant. The emerging larvae tunnel through the soil to the bulb and feed on the bulb tissue throughout the summer, making it soft and pulpy. The larvae spend the winter in the bulb as wrinkled, plump, grayish white to yellow maggots ½ to ¾ inch long. In the spring, they either remain in the bulb or move out into the surrounding soil to pupate. After 1 to 2½ months, the adult female bulb fly emerges and starts laying eggs.

SOLUTION: Check all bulbs carefully before planting. If they are soft or spongy, discard them. Dust the remaining bulbs with an insecticide containing trichlorfon. Dust them again after they've been planted but before they're covered with soil. In May, drench the foliage and surrounding soil with a solution containing trichlorfon, to kill the adults and emerging larvae. Make sure your plant is listed on the pesticide label.

PAEONIA (PEONY)

PAEONIA (PEONY)

ADAPTATION:
Herbaceous peonies: Zones 3 through 7.
Tree peonies: Zones 3 through 9. To determine your zone, see the map on page 348.

FLOWERING TIME: Spring.

LIGHT: Full sun or—in hot, dry areas—half-day sun.

PLANTING METHOD: Plant peonies in the fall, placing the eyes of the tubers 2 inches below the soil surface.

SOIL: Well drained, high in organic matter. pH 6.0 to 7.5.

FERTILIZER: When planting, apply a high-phosphorus fertilizer (0-20-0, for example); mix ½ cup of the product into the soil for each plant. During the growing season, apply a general-purpose fertilizer rated 10-10-10; follow label directions.

WATER:
How much: Apply enough water to wet the soil 1½ to 2 feet deep.
How often: Water when soil 1 inch below the surface is just barely moist.

HANDLING: Divide herbaceous peony clumps every 6 to 10 years. When cutting flowers, leave 3 or 4 leaves on each stem. To ensure an ample bloom the next year, pick only a third of the blooms for cut flowers.

Failure to bloom.

PROBLEM: Peonies fail to produce flower buds, or buds fail to develop into flowers.

ANALYSIS: Failure to bloom
There are several reasons why peonies fail to bloom.
1. *Crown buried at wrong depth:* If the crown (where the stems meet the roots) is planted too deep or too shallow, peonies often fail to bloom.
2. *Immature transplants:* Peony roots that have been divided and transplanted usually fail to flower for at least two years. If the divisions were extremely small, the plants may not flower for as long as five years.
3. *Crowded plantings:* Established peony clumps eventually become overcrowded and stop producing flowers.
4. *Too much shade:* Peonies stop blooming when they are heavily shaded by trees, tall shrubs, or buildings.
5. *Lack of nutrients:* Peonies that are not being fed enough fail to bloom.

SOLUTION: Take these measures to correct the condition or control the problem.
1. Carefully dig up and reset the crown so the buds are 1½ to 2 inches below the soil surface.
2. With time, the young plants will mature and start flowering.
3. Peonies usually need to be divided after 6 to 10 years or any time after that when flower production starts to drop off. Dig up and divide old clumps into divisions containing 3 to 5 eyes. Replant the new clumps, providing adequate space.
4. Transplant to a sunny location.
5. Around each plant in early spring apply a handful of plant food rated 10-10-10; work it lightly into the soil.

Gray mold.

PROBLEM: New shoots wilt and die. The bases of the wilted stems are brownish black and rotted. Young flower buds turn black and wither. Older buds and open flowers turn soft and brown and develop a gray or brown fuzzy covering in wet weather. Irregular brown lesions or patches form on the leaves. In severe cases, the plant base and roots may decay.

ANALYSIS: Gray mold
This common disease of peonies is caused by one of two fungi (*Botrytis paeoniae* or *B. cinerea*). Gray mold is most serious in the wet, cool conditions of early spring. Fungal growth on the stems, leaves, and flowers causes spotting, blackening, and decay. The fuzzy growth that forms on infected tissue is composed of millions of tiny spores. This growth, which may develop on all infected plant parts, is distinctive and can be used to help distinguish this disease from those caused by *Phytophthora* species (see page 115). Gray mold is spread by wind; splashing rain or water; or contaminated plants, soil, and tools. The fungi that cause gray mold form small black pellets that survive in plant debris and in the soil for many years.

SOLUTION: Remove and destroy all decayed or wilting plant parts. Clean up plant debris during the growing season and again in the fall. In the spring, spray emerging shoots with a fungicide containing chlorothalonil or benomyl. Respray 2 more times at intervals of 5 to 10 days. Spray again if the infection recurs.

■ PELARGONIUM (GERANIUM)

Peonies infected with phytophthora blight.

PROBLEM: New shoots wilt and turn black. Flowers, buds, leaves, and stems shrivel and turn dark brown and leathery. Black lesions several inches long often appear on the lower sections of the stem. The plant pulls up easily. Roots are black and rotted. The fuzzy mold that is characteristic of gray mold (see page 114) does not occur in this disease.

ANALYSIS: Phytophthora blight

This disease of peonies and many other plants is caused by a fungus (*Phytophthora cactorum*) common in most soils. In the form of tiny pellets, fungi of this species can survive in the soil and in plant debris for many years. Like gray mold, this species is favored by the cool, wet conditions of early spring. Initially the fungi attack either the roots or the developing shoots at the soil level, causing shoot wilting and a dark decay of the stem tissue. This disease is spread by splashing rain or water and by contaminated plants, soil, and tools. Wherever the fungi touch a plant, lesions, spots, and a brown, leathery decay may develop. The blight is most serious in heavy, poorly drained soils.

SOLUTION: Remove and destroy plants with decayed roots. Pick off and destroy infected plant parts. Clean up plant debris. Spray the foliage and drench the bases of infected plants with a fungicide containing zineb, mancozeb, or maneb. Spray 3 times at intervals of 5 to 10 days. Respray if infection recurs. Thin out overcrowded plants. Plant peonies in well-drained soil.

PELARGONIUM (GERANIUM)

ADAPTATION: Throughout the United States.

FLOWERING TIME: Spring and summer. In zones 9 and 10, some geraniums bloom throughout the year. To determine your zone, see the map on page 348.

LIGHT: Full sun or light shade.

PLANTING TIME: Spring, when all danger of frost is past; any time of year in zones 9 and 10.

SOIL: Well drained. pH 6.0 to 8.0.

FERTILIZER: According to label directions, apply a general-purpose fertilizer rated 10-10-10.

WATER:
  How much: Apply enough water to plants in the ground to wet the soil 8 to 10 inches deep.
  Containers: Apply enough water so that 10 percent of the water drains from the bottom of the container.
  How often: Water when soil 1 inch below the surface is just barely moist.

HANDLING: Remove old flower clusters to encourage continuing bloom.

Oedema on ivy geranium.

PROBLEM: Water-soaked spots appear on the leaves. Eventually, these spots turn brown and corky. Affected leaves may turn yellow and drop off. Corky ridges may form on the stems and leafstalks. In most cases, the soil is moist and the air is cool and humid.

ANALYSIS: Oedema

Oedema is not caused by a pest but results from an accumulation of water in a plant. Oedema often develops when the soil is moist or wet and the atmosphere is humid and cool. Under these conditions, water is absorbed rapidly from the soil and lost slowly from the leaves, resulting in an excess amount of water in the plant. This excess water causes cells to burst. The ruptured cells eventually form spots and ridges. Oedema occurs most frequently in late winter and early spring during cloudy weather.

SOLUTION: Plant geraniums in soil that drains well, and avoid overwatering them.

PELARGONIUM (GERANIUM)

Bacterial leaf spot.

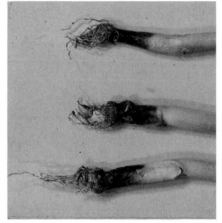

Black stem rot.

Geranium budworm (2 times life size).

PROBLEM: Dark, circular, sunken spots (up to ¼ inch in diameter) or larger, angular dead areas appear on leaves. The leaves wilt and die. They either fall off the plant immediately or hang down along the stem for several weeks. Many or all of the stems shrivel and turn brown or black. The roots are black but not rotted. When an infected stem is sliced open, a thick yellow fluid may ooze from the cut surface. Older diseased plants may retain only a few tufts of leaves, at the stem tips.

ANALYSIS: Bacterial stem rot and leaf spot
This common and widespread disease of geraniums is caused by one of two bacteria (*Xanthomonas pelargonii* or *Pseudomonas* species). The disease develops most rapidly when the plants are growing vigorously and during periods of warm, moist weather. The bacteria decay the leaf tissue, causing the small spots and lesions. Then the organisms may penetrate the entire plant, causing wilting and rotting. The thick fluid that oozes from cut stems is filled with millions of bacteria. Infection is spread to healthy plants when bacteria are splashed onto the leaves or when they make contact with contaminated tools. The bacteria can live in plant debris and in the soil for 3 months or more. Not all plants are killed by this disease. They often remain weak, stunted, and disfigured.

SOLUTION: Remove and destroy infected plants. Clean up plant debris. Avoid overhead watering. Sterilize contaminated tools by dipping them in rubbing alcohol. Wash your hands thoroughly after handling infected plants. Purchase healthy plants only.

PROBLEM: Dark lesions form at the bases of stems. These lesions enlarge and turn black and shiny. The blackening progresses up the stems. The leaves wilt and drop, and the plant may eventually die.

ANALYSIS: Black stem rot
This common disease of geraniums is caused by a fungus (*Pythium* species) that lives in the soil. Wet, poorly drained soil favors black stem rot. Fungi of this species attack the stems at the soil level, then spread upward. The stems decay and the foliage wilts, shrivels, and may eventually die. Black stem rot is spread by contaminated soil, transplants, and tools.

SOLUTION: Remove and destroy infected plants. If they have been growing in containers, throw out the soil in which they grew. Wash contaminated tools and pots, then dip them in a solution of 1 part household bleach to 9 parts warm water for 1 minute or more. Plant healthy geraniums in well-drained soil and let soil dry to a depth of 2 inches between waterings.

PROBLEM: Irregular or round holes appear in leaves and buds. Leaves, buds, and flowers may be entirely chewed off. Worms or caterpillars feed on the plants.

ANALYSIS: Caterpillars
Many species of these moth or butterfly larvae feed on geraniums and other garden plants. Some common caterpillars include budworms, hornworms, and loopers. Usually, the adult female moths or butterflies begin to lay their eggs on garden plants with the onset of warm spring weather. The larvae that emerge from these eggs feed on the leaves, flowers, and buds for two to six weeks, depending on weather and species. Mature caterpillars pupate in cocoons attached to leaves or buildings or buried in the soil. There may be one to several overlapping generations during the growing season. The last generation of caterpillars in the fall survives the winter as pupae. The adult moths and butterflies emerge the following spring.

SOLUTION: Spray infested plants with an insecticide containing acephate (ORTHENE®). Respray if reinfestation occurs, allowing at least 7 to 10 days between applications. A bacterial insecticide containing *Bacillus thuringiensis* may also be used.

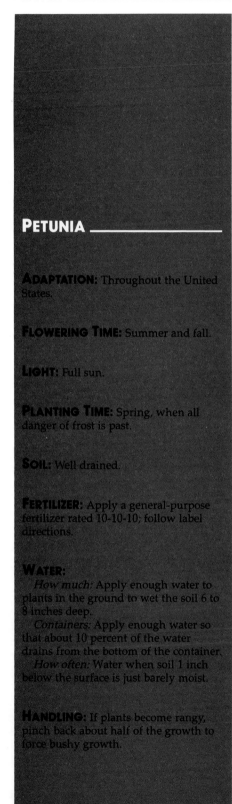

PETUNIA

ADAPTATION: Throughout the United States.

FLOWERING TIME: Summer and fall.

LIGHT: Full sun.

PLANTING TIME: Spring, when all danger of frost is past.

SOIL: Well drained.

FERTILIZER: Apply a general-purpose fertilizer rated 10-10-10; follow label directions.

WATER:
How much: Apply enough water to plants in the ground to wet the soil 6 to 8 inches deep.
Containers: Apply enough water so that about 10 percent of the water drains from the bottom of the container.
How often: Water when soil 1 inch below the surface is just barely moist.

HANDLING: If plants become rangy, pinch back about half of the growth to force bushy growth.

Gray mold.

PROBLEM: Gray or brown spots appear on flowers, especially during periods of wet weather. Brown spots and blotches may appear on leaves and stems. As the disease progresses, a fuzzy brown or grayish mold may form on the infected tissue.

ANALYSIS: Gray mold
This widespread plant disease is caused by one of several fungi (*Botrytis* species) found on most dead plant tissue. Fungi of these species initially attack foliage and flowers that are weak or dead, causing spotting and sometimes mold. The fuzzy mold that may develop is composed of millions of microscopic spores. Once gray mold has become established on plant debris and weak or dying leaves and flowers, it can invade healthy plant tissue. The fungi are spread by the wind, splashing water, or infected pieces of plant tissue that touch healthy tissue.
Cool temperatures and high humidity favor gray mold. Crowded plantings, rain, and overhead watering also enhance the spread of the disease. Infection is more of a problem in the spring and fall, when temperatures are lower. In warm-winter areas, where freezing is rare, gray mold can be a year-round problem.

SOLUTION: At regular intervals of 10 to 14 days as long as mold is visible, spray infected plants with a fungicide containing chlorothalonil. Remove infected flowers and leaves, and clean up plant debris. Try to avoid wetting the flowers when watering.

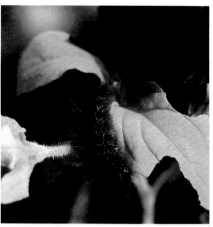
Caterpillar (life size).

PROBLEM: Irregular or round holes appear in leaves and buds. Leaves, buds, and flowers may be entirely chewed off. Smooth or hairy caterpillars, up to 4 inches in length, feed on the plants.

ANALYSIS: Caterpillars
Numerous species of these moth or butterfly larvae feed on petunias and many other garden plants. Some common caterpillars include budworms, armyworms, hornworms, and loopers. As a rule, the adult female moths or butterflies start to lay eggs on garden plants with the onset of warm weather in spring. The larvae that emerge feed on the leaves, flowers, and buds for two to six weeks, depending on weather and species. Mature caterpillars pupate in cocoons attached to leaves and structures or buried in the soil. There may be one to several overlapping generations during the growing season. The last generation of caterpillars in the fall survives the winter as pupae. The adult moths and butterflies emerge the following spring.

SOLUTION: Spray infested plants with an insecticide containing acephate (ORTHENE®). Respray if reinfestation occurs, allowing at least 7 to 10 days between applications. A bacterial insecticide containing *Bacillus thuringiensis* may also be used.

PETUNIA ■   **RANUNCULUS** ■

Cutworm damage.

Bird damage.

Ranunculus mosaic virus.

PROBLEM: Young plants are chewed or cut off near the ground. Many leaves may be sheared from the stems. Gray, brown, or black worms, 1½ to 2 inches long, may be found about 2 inches deep in the soil near the base of the damaged plants. The worms coil when disturbed.

ANALYSIS: Cutworms
Several species of cutworm attack petunias and many other flowers and vegetable plants. The most likely pests of young petunia plants early in the season are the surface-feeding cutworms and climbing cutworms. A single surface-feeding cutworm can sever the stems of many young plants in one night. Climbing cutworms shear the leaves off older plants. Both pests hide in the soil during the day and feed only after sundown. Adult cutworms are dark, night-flying moths with bands or stripes on their forewings.

SOLUTION: Apply an insecticide containing diazinon, carbaryl (SEVIN®), or chlorpyrifos around the bases of undamaged plants when stem cutting is observed. Since cutworms are difficult to control, weekly reapplications will probably be necessary. Before transplanting into the area, apply a preventive treatment of diazinon and work it into the soil. In late summer and fall, cultivate the soil thoroughly to expose and destroy eggs, larvae, and pupae. Further reduce damage by setting a "cutworm collar" around the stem of each plant. Make collars from stiff paper or aluminum foil. They should be at least 2 inches high and pressed firmly into the soil.

PROBLEM: Tender young leaves are torn. Seedlings may be entirely eaten. Birds may be seen feeding in the garden, or their tracks may be evident around the damaged plants.

ANALYSIS: Bird damage
Birds are fond of ranunculus and frequently eat the tender parts. Individual birds may develop the habit of feeding on the plants every day.

SOLUTION: Protect emerging shoots and young transplants with cages or coverings made of 1-inch-mesh chicken wire. Cages about 10 by 10 by 24 inches are self-supporting; larger cages may need to be reinforced with heavy wire. Cheesecloth cages supported with stakes, wire, or string may also be used.

Ranunculus cultural information
Light: Full sun
Water: When soil just below surface is barely moist
Soil: Well drained
Fertilizer: Medium

PROBLEM: Leaves are mottled yellow-green. Plants may be stunted, and flowers may be smaller than normal. In some cases, the petals are streaked.

ANALYSIS: Ranunculus mosaic virus
This virus disease infects ranunculus plants and tubers. The severity of infection varies from plant to plant. Mosaic does not kill ranunculus, but it greatly reduces their overall vigor and beauty. The virus is spread by aphids that, while feeding, transmit the disease from plant to plant. Mosaic persists in a plant indefinitely. Tubers obtained from diseased plants are also infected.

SOLUTION: There are no chemicals that control virus diseases. Discard infected plants. Help prevent the spread of the virus by keeping the aphid population under control.

SALVIA (SAGE) ▪

Verticillium wilt. Diseased plant on right.

PROBLEM: Leaves yellow, wilt, and die, starting with the lower leaves and progressing up the plant. Older plants may be stunted. Yellowing and wilting often affect only one side of the plant. Flowering is poor. There may be dark brown areas on the infected stems. Slicing a stem open near the base of the plant reveals dark streaks and discolorations of the inner stem tissue.

ANALYSIS: Verticillium wilt
This plant disease is caused by one of several soil-inhabiting fungi (*Verticillium* species) that persist indefinitely on plant debris or in the soil. The disease is spread by contaminated seeds, plants, soil, and equipment. The fungi enter the plant through the roots and spread up into the stems and leaves through the water-conducting vessels in the stems. The vessels become plugged and discolored. This plugging cuts off the flow of water to the leaves, causing leaf yellowing and wilting.

SOLUTION: No chemical control is available. The best course is to destroy infected plants. Verticillium can be removed from the soil by fumigation techniques only. The best prevention is usually to use plants that are resistant to verticillium.

Salvia cultural information
Light: Sun
Water: When soil is just barely moist
Soil: Well drained
Fertilizer: Light

TAGETES (MARIGOLD) ▪

Wilt and stem rot.

PROBLEM: Leaves wilt and die. The lower stems have a dark, water-soaked appearance. They eventually shrivel and turn brown near the soil line. The plant pulls up easily to reveal rotted roots. The plant usually dies within one to three weeks.

ANALYSIS: Wilt and stem rot
This plant disease is caused by a widespread fungus (*Phytophthora cryptogea*) that persists indefinitely in the soil. Fungi of this species attack the roots, then spread up into the stems. As the roots and stems decay, the leaves wilt and turn yellow and the plant dies. The fungi thrive in cool, waterlogged soils. This disease is spread by contaminated soil, transplants, equipment, and moving water. African marigolds (*Tagetes erecta*) are quite susceptible, but French marigolds (*T. patula*) and other dwarf varieties are resistant.

SOLUTION: Remove and discard infected plants and the soil immediately surrounding them. With a solution of captan or etridiazole, drench flower beds in which diseased plants grew. Make sure the soil drains well. Plant healthy marigolds of the resistant French or dwarf varieties. Allow the soil to dry between waterings. Drenching the plants with the captan or etridiazole solution immediately after planting helps prevent another infection.

TROPAEOLUM (NASTURTIUM) ▪

Leaf spot.

PROBLEM: Spots and blotches appear on leaves. The spots may be yellow, red, tan, gray, or black. They range in size from barely visible to ¼ inch in diameter. Several spots may join to form blotches. Some of the leaves may be yellow and dying. Leaf spotting is most severe in warm, humid weather.

ANALYSIS: Leaf spot
Nasturtiums are susceptible to several fungi that cause leaf spot. Some of these fungi may eventually kill the plant or weaken it so that it becomes susceptible to attack by other organisms; other fungi merely cause spotting that is unsightly but not harmful. Leaf-spot fungi are spread by wind, insects, tools, splashing water, and infected transplants and seeds. The organisms survive the winter in diseased plant debris. Most of these fungi do their greatest damage during mild weather from 50° to 85° F. Moist conditions favor infection.

SOLUTION: Picking off the diseased leaves generally gives adequate control. If infection is severe, spray with a fungicide containing copper, such as basic copper sulfate. Clean up debris.

Tropaeolum cultural information
Light: Sun to partial shade
Water: When soil is just barely moist
Soil: Any good garden soil
Fertilizer: Light

TULIPA (TULIP)

Old planting.

Undersized bulbs.

TULIPA (TULIP)

ADAPTATION: Throughout the United States. In zones 9 and 10, bulbs must be prechilled (see Handling below for details).

FLOWERING TIME: Spring.

LIGHT: Full sun to filtered light.

PLANTING TIME: Fall.

SOIL: Well drained. pH 6.0 to 7.5.

FERTILIZER: When planting, add 1 teaspoon of bone meal or other phosphorus-only fertilizer to the bottom of the planting hole; mix the fertilizer into the soil. During the growing season, apply a general-purpose fertilizer rated 10-10-10; follow label directions.

WATER:
How much: Apply enough water to wet the soil 1 to 1½ feet deep.
How often: Water when soil an inch below the surface is just barely moist.

HANDLING: In zones 9 and 10, precool bulbs for 6 to 8 weeks before planting. Store bulbs in paper bags in the refrigerator crisper. Tulips usually do not flower as well the second or third year after planting. Either replace them or dig, separate, precool if necessary, and replant.

PROBLEM: Tulip bulbs produce healthy foliage but fail to bloom.

ANALYSIS: Failure to bloom
Healthy tulips may fail to bloom for several reasons.

1. *Lack of cooling:* To flower properly, tulip bulbs require a minimum exposure of 15 weeks to temperatures from 40° to 50° F in fall and winter. Cooling stimulates the embryonic flower stem within the bulb to elongate and emerge from the ground.

2. *Foliage removed too soon:* After a tulip flowers the remaining foliage continues to manufacture food for new bulbs and flowers for next year.

3. *Lack of nutrients:* When tulips are grown in infertile soil for more than one season, they form small, poor-quality bulbs. Such bulbs produce only sparse foliage and few, if any, flowers.

4. *Undersized bulbs:* Bulbs smaller than 2½ inches in circumference may not contain an embryonic flower. They will produce only foliage for one to two years, until they are large enough to produce a flower.

5. *Old plantings:* Tulip flowers are largest and most prolific the first spring after newly purchased bulbs have been planted. After flowering, the original bulb usually disintegrates and several small "daughter bulbs" form. Often these daughter bulbs are too small to provide many flowers. Depending on the variety, a planting of tulips generally continues to flower for only two to four years, each year producing fewer flowers. Tulips are especially short-lived in warm-winter areas (zones 9 and 10; see page 348 for zone map).

SOLUTION: Take these measures to correct the condition or control the problem.

1. In warm-winter areas (zones 9 and 10), precool bulbs before planting or buy precooled bulbs. For details on cooling bulbs, see page 120. Postpone planting until mid-December.

2. Let foliage turn yellow before removing it.

3. Add a phosphorus-only fertilizer when planting, and a general-purpose fertilizer after the new leaves appear on the plants in the spring, and again after they bloom.

4. Purchase only large, healthy bulbs from a reputable nursery or mail-order company.

5. Replace old tulips with fresh bulbs. You may also dig up, separate, and replant old bulbs; however, they may not flower for at least one year. Unless soil and climate conditions are ideal for growing tulips, the bulbs and flowers will never be as large and prolific as they were the first year. You can prolong the flowering life of a tulip bed by planting the bulbs deeper than usual. Place them 12 inches deep in the soil rather than the usual 6 inches. The soil must be well drained to prevent rot.

Poor growth.

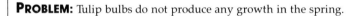

Diseased plants.

Bulb rot.

PROBLEM: Tulip bulbs do not produce any growth in the spring.

ANALYSIS: Failure to grow

Improper cultural techniques, diseases, animal pests, and natural decline can all contribute to lack of growth in tulips.

1. *Lack of cooling:* Tulip bulbs require a period of cooling to develop properly. They need to spend at least six weeks below 50° F to perform ideally. If newly purchased bulbs are not precooled or if winter soil temperatures remain at 55° F or above, root formation, flower emergence, and the production of new daughter bulbs for future flowering will be inhibited.

2. *Foliage removed too soon:* After a tulip flowers, the remaining foliage continues to use sunlight to manufacture food for the developing new bulbs and next year's flowers. If the foliage is removed before it has a chance to turn yellow naturally, the new bulbs will be small or will not form at all.

3. *Lack of nutrients:* After the first year, tulips do not continue to perform well in infertile soil. They form only small bulbs and flowers. After several years, they stop producing growth.

4. *Root rot:* Infected tulip bulbs planted in heavy, poorly drained soil frequently decay.

5. *Rodents:* Mice, pocket gophers, and other rodents may feed on tulip bulbs. Dig in the area where the bulbs were planted and check for underground tunnels and half-eaten bulbs, both of which indicate rodent damage.

SOLUTION: Take these measures to correct the condition or control the problem.

1. In warm-winter areas (zones 9 and 10; see page 348 for zone map), store bulbs in a refrigerator crisper for 6 to 8 weeks before planting.

2. Allow foliage to turn yellow before removing it.

3. Add a bonemeal rated 0-12-0 when planting bulbs. When tulips emerge in the spring, apply a food rated 8-12-4. Reapply it once a month after the plants have flowered until the foliage dies back.

4. Before planting, discard discolored, spongy, or moldy bulbs. Plant in well-drained soil.

5. The most effective method of protecting tulips is to plant them in baskets made of ¼-inch wire mesh. Traps or baits may also be used.

PROBLEM: Foliage is sparse and stunted. Often the leaves turn red, wilt, and die. Digging up the plant reveals rotted bulbs. The bulbs may be either mushy or firm and chalky. Usually they are covered with a white, pink, or gray mold. There may be reddish brown to black pinhead-sized pellets on the bulb husks, leaf bases, and in the soil immediately surrounding the plant.

ANALYSIS: Root and bulb rot

This disease of tulips is caused by one of several different soil-inhabiting fungi that attack and decay the bulbs and roots. The fungi form tiny pellets on the bulbs and in the soil. These pellets survive through dry conditions and extremes of temperature. Wet, poorly drained soils favor bulb and root rots. Bulbs injured during digging or storing are especially susceptible to infection. Sometimes bulbs in storage are lightly infected, but the fungal decay hasn't progressed far enough to be easily noticed. When planted, these bulbs may rot so quickly that they don't produce any foliage.

SOLUTION: Remove and destroy infected plants and the soil immediately surrounding them. Check for infected bulbs before planting; discard them. Avoid wounding bulbs when cultivating around them or handling them. Dip clean, healthy bulbs in a warm (80° to 85° F) solution of benomyl before storing and again before planting. Plant in a well-drained location. Do not replant tulips in infested soil for at least 3 years.

TULIPA (TULIP) ■ ■ VERBENA ■

Botrytis blight. *Insert:* Infected bulbs.

Virus.

Powdery mildew.

PROBLEM: Light-to dark-colored spots appear on leaves and flowers. The spots enlarge to form extensive gray blotches, which may cover the entire leaf and flower. During periods of cool, moist weather, a fuzzy brown or grayish mold forms on the infected tissue. Many of the leaves and stems are distorted, and they often rot off at the base. Infected bulbs have dark, circular, sunken lesions. Dark brown pinhead-sized pellets form on the bulb husks.

ANALYSIS: Botrytis blight
This common disease of tulips is caused by a fungus (*Botrytis tulipae*). Fungi of this species persist through the winter and hot, dry periods as tiny pellets in the soil, plant debris, and bulbs. In the spring, these pellets produce spores that attack foliage and flowers, causing spotting, decay, and mold. Wounded, weak, and dead plant tissues are especially susceptible to infection. The fungi are spread by splashing water. Botrytis blight is most serious during periods of cool, moist weather. Tulip bulbs that are injured when they are dug up to be stored are especially vulnerable to infection.

SOLUTION: Remove and destroy diseased plants, leaves, flowers, and debris. Before planting tulip bulbs, check them for signs of infection, and discard diseased bulbs. Using a spreader-sticker, treat emerging plants when they are 4 inches tall; spray them with a fungicide containing benomyl. Spray plants every 5 to 7 days until the flowers bloom. Remove tulip flowers just as they start to fade, and cut off the foliage at ground level when it turns yellow. Move plants to a new location next year.

PROBLEM: Flowers are streaked, spotted, or mottled in an irregular pattern. The leaves may also be streaked or mottled with light green or white. The plant may be stunted and low in vigor.

ANALYSIS: Viruses
Several plant viruses commonly infect tulips, causing a characteristic streaking or mottling of the flowers and foliage. Infection may be accompanied by stunted growth. Virus infections rarely cause a plant to die, but they can weaken it seriously. The viruses increase in the bulbs year after year. Successive plantings from diseased bulbs yield infected flowers and foliage of poor quality. Some viruses are spread by aphids. These insects feed on diseased plants and transfer viruses to healthy plants at subsequent feedings. Sometimes tulips are intentionally infected to produce showy flowers.

SOLUTION: Once the plant is infected, no chemical can control the virus. To prevent the spread of the virus to healthy tulips, remove and destroy infected plants. Keep aphid populations under control by spraying with a chemical containing acephate (ORTHENE®); follow label directions. Because tulip viruses may also infect lilies, avoid planting tulips near lilies. Parrot tulips may exhibit showy streaked patterns, but the streaking is genetic in origin and cannot be transferred to other tulips and lilies.

PROBLEM: Leaves and stems are covered with grayish white powdery spots and patches. These patches occur primarily on the topsides of the leaves. The infected leaves eventually turn yellow and wither.

ANALYSIS: Powdery mildew
This common plant disease is caused by a fungus (*Erysiphe cichoracearum*) that thrives in both humid and dry weather. The powdery patches consist of fungal strands and spores. The spores are spread by the wind to healthy plants. The fungi sap plant nutrients, causing yellowing and sometimes the death of the leaves. A severe infection may kill whole plants. Since this powdery mildew attacks many different kinds of plants, the fungi from a diseased plant may infect other types of plants in the garden. Under conditions favorable to powdery mildew, infection can spread rapidly in closely spaced plantings.

SOLUTION: Spray infected plants with a fungicide containing dinocap. Respray at intervals of 10 to 12 days or as often as necessary to protect new growth. These fungicides protect the new, healthy foliage but do not eradicate the fungi on leaves that are already infected. Remove and destroy severely infected plants. Where practical, pick off diseased leaves. Clean up and destroy plant debris.

Verbena cultural information
Light: Sun
Water: When soil is just barely moist
Soil: Well drained
Fertilizer: Medium

VIOLA (PANSY, VIOLET) ■ ZINNIA

Spindly growth and poor flowering.

Root and stem rot.

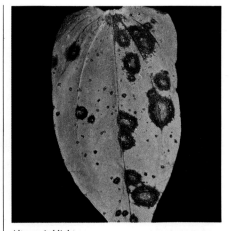

Alternaria blight.

PROBLEM: Leaves are small and thin, and stems are long and spindly. Flowering is poor, and flowers are small.

ANALYSIS: Spindly growth and poor flowering
Several cultural problems may contribute to spindly growth.
1. *Failure to remove old flowers:* If the fading flowers remain on the plant, only a few small new flowers are produced. This is because the plant uses its energy in seed development instead of producing new flowers.
2. *Inadequate light:* Pansies and violas grow lanky and flower poorly when planted in deep shade. At the least they require strong filtered light to grow compactly; they flower most profusely in full sun during mild weather.
3. *Old age:* Pansies and violas are perennials and, theoretically, last from year to year. In cold-winter climates, they are killed by freezing temperatures. In warm-winter areas, they often last for a year or more, but they usually start to produce lanky, unattractive growth after the first growing season.

SOLUTION: Take these measures to correct the condition or control the problem.
1. Pinch off flowers when they start to fade.
2. Grow plants in full sun, partial sun, or strong filtered light.
3. Treat pansies and violas as annuals. Plant them in the spring (or the fall in zones 9 and 10) and replace them when they start to decline in the summer. Rejuvenate rangy plants by pinching back one third of the spindly stems to one third their height.

PROBLEM: Leaves turn yellow, wilt, and die. The roots and lower stems are soft and rotted. There may be white fungal strands on infected stems and around the base of the plant.

ANALYSIS: Root and stem rot
This plant disease is caused by one of a number of different fungi that persist indefinitely in the soil. They thrive in waterlogged, heavy soils. Infection causes the stem and roots to decay, resulting in wilting, yellowing leaves and the eventual death of the plant. These fungi are generally spread by infested soil and transplants, contaminated equipment, and splashing or running water.

SOLUTION: Remove dead and dying plants. Allowing the soil to dry between irrigations is important; waterlogged conditions encourage root and stem rot.

Viola cultural information
Light: Violets need half sun to full shade. Pansies and violas need full sun to partial shade.
Water: When soil just below surface is barely moist
Soil: Rich, well drained
Fertilizer: Medium

PROBLEM: Reddish brown circular or irregular spots up to ½ inch in diameter appear on leaves. The centers of the spots may turn grayish white. The blossoms also are often spotted. Severely infected leaves, stems, and flowers turn brown and die. Dark, sunken lesions may appear at the bases of the stems. The entire plant frequently wilts and dies.

ANALYSIS: Alternaria blight
This common and widespread disease of zinnias is a leaf spot caused by a fungus (*Alternaria zinniae*). Moist conditions favor the disease. The fungal spores are spread from plant to plant by wind and splashing water. The fungi survive on infected debris in the soil and in contaminated seeds. This fungus species also causes damping-off of seedlings.

SOLUTION: Remove dying plants. Spray infected plants with a fungicide containing captan or chlorothalonil. Pick off infected leaves and flowers. Clean up and destroy plant debris. Avoid overhead watering.

TREES, SHRUBS, AND VINES

Unless trees or shrubs start browning drastically or suddenly fall over, many gardeners tend to take them for granted. The shade, color, and serenity trees provide may not be as conspicuous as brilliant flowering anemones or a startlingly large squash.

Given optimal surroundings trees live hundreds or even thousands of years. But sometimes something goes wrong: Insect pests, virus and fungus infections, grading changes, too much or too little water, and pollution take their toll. Unlike flower problems, which are visible merely by looking down, tree problems may begin at the towering top or be hidden amongst the branches. By the time you notice the damage, it may be severe. But, with knowledge and persistence, most trees and shrubs can be saved.

STAYING ALERT FOR SYMPTOMS

Part of effective tree and shrub management is maintaining an awareness of their health. Make a visual inspection each week as you go about your normal gardening chores. Distorted leaf growth is often the first eye-level symptom. The leaves may be crinkled, rolled, or otherwise different from normal. Leaves may or may not change color. Some develop brown spots, others develop red highlights out of season. Since leaf distortion is a clear sign that something is bothering the tree, it is time to play gardener-detective before the problem progresses.

REMEDYING GROUND POLLUTION

If the tree is receiving water but looks as if it is suffering from drought, ground pollution may be the problem. Road salt is one possible cause. Improper herbicide application is another. The wind may carry herbicide from weeds, the intended targets, to garden plants. Damage may also result when spray equipment used to apply an herbicide is not cleaned thoroughly before being used to apply an insect control. Whatever the cause, damage usually appears several days after herbicide spraying.

Symptoms include puckered leaves or twisted needles. Leaves may seem off-color, yet still be green. If garden plants receive a significant dose of herbicide, distorted new growth may continue throughout the growing season.

Opposite: You may think of trees and shrubs as green backdrops for flower beds, but they can provide their own extravagant show of color as well.

To remedy ground-pollution effects, give soil around the tree several ample waterings to flush out chemicals. Prune off twigs or branches with distorted leaves. Apply fertilizer to prevent tree stress and aid recovery.

To prevent future problems, apply herbicide on a windless day and aim the sprayer carefully; follow label directions. Use one sprayer for herbicides and another for pesticides.

MITIGATING AIR POLLUTION

Air pollution is a worsening problem over which the average gardener has little control. Because it begins so gradually, its initial effects are subtle. Yet pollution paves the way for a host of insect annoyances—including the seemingly ever-present bark beetles, which hone in on weak or injured trees.

Most air pollution falls into one of two categories: ozone and smog.

Ozone

This type of air pollution does considerable damage throughout the United States and is the prime culprit on the East Coast. Though the ozone layer in the outer atmosphere is essential to our well-being, ozone at lower elevations is a threat to plants and animals. Ozone forms when the gases produced by an industrialized society combine with each other once they get into the air.

Ozone enters trees and shrubs through leaf pores. Once in foliage, it destroys cell membranes, causing them to collapse. Cell membrane death shows up as white to tan leaf markings. In pine, new needles are flecked with yellow. Older needles may be deep yellow and smaller than normal. Needles may drop. If just some leaves or needles are affected, tree and shrub growth slows. Blossoms may fall. If enough foliage is affected, as has happened in heavily polluted areas, entire trees die.

Smog

On the West Coast, smog is the type of air pollution that causes the most severe damage. The damage-causing component of smog is peroxyacetyl nitrate (PAN), which affects shrubs and smaller plants to a greater degree than it affects trees. Young rapidly growing spring foliage is especially sensitive to smog.

Smog enters leaves through pores. The undersides of leaves turn silver as a result of internal damage. In severe cases, damaged leaves turn light beige and die.

Pollution Solutions

No magic potion can eliminate air pollution, but you can alleviate the damage it causes to your home landscape. If possible, plant European white birch, gray dogwood, American arborvitae, winged eunymus, or Norway maple—these species are more smog and ozone tolerant than others. Apply fertilizer regularly, and make certain that watering is sufficient to reach all tree roots. Avoid overwatering, because sitting in soggy soil makes some species especially prone to pollution damage, particularly in warm climates. Make certain that all or some of the damage is not attributable to insects, disease, or nutrient deficiencies, which are problems you can counter directly.

PROVIDING FERTILIZER

Nutrient deficiencies tend to impact a rapidly growing young tree more than a mature one. For this reason, aid young growth by applying fertilizer in the spring. Providing nutrients early will make the most of growing time so, when winter comes, the new growth has sufficient strength to withstand the cold.

Treating a sapling and a mature specimen to the same fertilizer program is not always wise. A mature ornamental tree with healthy leaf color and a growth rate appropriate for the variety needs little fertilizer. Overfertilizing can increase leaf density to the point where interior leaves do not get enough sun for survival. Any

This white pine shows damage from air pollution.

plants under such a thick leaf umbrella may also fail. In addition, the ground under the canopy remains moist, opening up the path for a variety of fungus infections.

ASSESSING FOLIAGE DROP

Leaf drop causes many gardeners to apply fertilizer with all speed. Falling foliage may be a symptom of tree illness or damage that fertilizer will alleviate; on the other hand, falling leaves may be a natural part of the life cycle. In autumn, for example, the level of green pigment (chlorophyll) in the leaves of deciduous trees changes in preparation for an annual foliage drop. Exquisite reds, golds, and oranges take the place of greens, then the leaves fall. Leaf drop in deciduous trees allows them to enter a resting, or dormant, state in which they can survive the winter.

Evergreens also shed leaves and needles as part of their life cycle. Usually the older leaves are the ones that fall, leaving room for new growth. Pines shed needles the second year after they appear; junipers hold needles 10 years or more before they drop. Evergreen foliage may fall throughout the year or in batches during particular seasons. Many evergreen trees in dry climates routinely lose some older foliage at the beginning of summer. Holly leaves drop in late winter.

If you are worried about what appears to be abnormally heavy leaf shedding, inspect the tree carefully. The most common cause of excessive leaf drop is insufficient sunlight. Perhaps the tree once received enough sun, but changes in surrounding growth have altered the light pattern. Sometimes the shape of the tree blocks sunlight from reaching lower leaves. Pruning may restore the tree's vigor. Always look for signs of insect damage, another cause of abnormal foliage drop, and take control measures if needed. Some climatic conditions, such as drought or heavy rainfall, may cause changes in the amount of leaf fall. Changes in grading or runoff direction can also cause shedding. Reduce tree stress by watering or correcting drainage, and the amount of foliage drop may return to normal.

SOLVING ROOT PROBLEMS

If the full branch spread of a tree is 25 feet wide, the roots reach out at least that far. The large size of trees' root zones often leads to problems.

Far-reaching Roots

If the roots of your tree extend into your neighbor's yard and your neighbor does any construction, your tree may suffer damage over which you have little

control. The practical way to avoid this problem is to research mature tree size before purchase, then pace off the eventual root zone to determine whether there will be encroachment on nearby lots. When in doubt, plant the smaller tree. Many exquisite shrubs, growing no more than 8 to 10 feet high, can be clipped or trained to look like trees.

Of course the opposite can happen: Roots from a neighbor's tree may invade your property and compete with your plants for nutrients. Some trees, such as willow and birch, can be aggressive in seeking needed water, and they can cause dry ground and mineral deprivation around them by removing the water and nutrients they need for survival. Despite numerous tries, you may not be able to grow anything in these areas.

Two antidotes for far-reaching roots are root pruning and root barriers.

Root Pruning

If the amount of needed pruning is extensive, hire a professional arborist to do the work. If the job requires cutting a few small roots only, do the pruning yourself. After the cutting, tree growth may slow for a bit but be unaffected otherwise.

Root Barriers

If root pruning is infeasible, consider installing a root barrier. Dig a trench at least 3 feet deep, just outside the area affected by the invading tree roots. The deeper the trench, the more effective the barrier will be. Cut roots that cross the trench. Insert a thin wall of concrete, sheet metal, or rolled roofing material in the trench, which will inhibit tree roots from reaching into the planted area. Backfill the trench. Even with the best barrier, you may have to remove persistent tree roots every 5 years or so.

If root competition is severe and uncontrollable, your only choice may be to install drought-tolerant plants. Compensate for nutrient loss caused by the invasive roots by applying fertilizer.

Roots in Plumbing Lines

Roots frequently clog plumbing lines. The problem tree may be quite a distance away, on your property or your neighbor's. Some trees are known for their invasive properties. Others become problems because the amount of water they get is inadequate for their needs, so they seek elsewhere for survival. The best way to prevent root-clogged lines is to thoroughly research any tree before putting it into curb strips, near house foundations, next to patios, in lawns, and near any plumbing line. If you are in the position of installing a new line, ask your supplier about pipe that is relatively rootproof.

If a drain is plugged with tree roots, a plumber needs specific equipment to clear it. Some firms specialize in sewer and drain line clearing. To prevent further plugging, pour 1 pound of copper sulfate crystals into the lowest entry point to the sewer line (such as a toilet or basement drain) at a time when drains and sewer lines are not being used (such as just before going to bed). Copper sulfate is highly poisonous; use it with the utmost care. Flush the toilet or wash the crystals into the pipe with a bucket of water. The copper sulfate collects in the root mass and kills the roots, which rot in a few weeks. The copper sulfate is not circulated through the tree, so the tree itself is not harmed. You may have to repeat the treatment from time to time, as long as the invasive tree remains in its current site.

PRUNING AWAY EXCESS SHADE

Too much shade may be a neighbor's complaint, your own, or both. Researching ultimate tree growth before planting prevents this problem. Sometimes, however, a huge problematic shade tree is part of newly purchased property.

Jobs for Professionals

Limbs and large branches—with their thousands of food, water, and sunlight-gathering leaves—are a vital part of a tree's survival system. Cutting limbs off without planning can result in severe shock that may injure or even kill a mature tree. Hire a licensed tree surgeon or arborist to prune limbs. Your garden center or nursery may be able to recommend a local professional. Before the surgeon starts pruning, discuss the specifics of the job to ensure that the final result suits your landscape plan and budget.

Prune-it-yourself Jobs

Home gardeners with the proper equipment and technique can undertake limited branch pruning. The rewards will be immediate and long lasting: In addition to removing undesirable shade, the pruning is likely to slow new growth, extending the time to the next pruning. For growth limitation, do not prune in early spring. The nutrients that would normally feed the removed area will be diverted into other branches, forcing them into a growth spurt. Prune later in the season, when growth has slowed.

In general, you can remove any branch that crosses another, any dead branches, branches growing inward toward the trunk, and branches growing downward. Cut small sections off a large branch before you go after the total. If a branch is really heavy with growth, its falling weight may tear bark all the way to the trunk. Do not get so carried away with pruning that you eliminate the tree. More trees are ruined by incorrect pruning than by complete neglect. After you have cut the most obvious of the branches mentioned previously, stand back; take a rest; and perhaps finish the job another day, when you have a fresh supply of objectivity.

Overzealous pruners can do more than harm the tree; they can hurt themselves. Take the time for safety precautions. Pay attention to the cutting angle so the limb falls away from you. Do only the pruning that allows you to keep both feet on the ground. Pruning shears and saws with extension handles let you reach up quite a distance.

In general, leave pruning cuts open to the air—sealing them may trap fungi inside the tree. If a wound does not appear to be healing well, however, apply a pruning sealer. Available as liquids or foams, sealers protect the tree from dehydration and prevent excess sap flow, which could be an invitation to insects. Apply sealer evenly over the entire cut.

TREATING BARK WOUNDS

Bark protects a tree by covering the xylem and phloem, the system that conveys water, minerals, sugar, and protein. If bark wounds do not heal quickly and properly, the xylem and phloem are exposed to sun and wind and will quickly dry out and die. This deprives the tree of vital nutrition.

Bark wounds can be caused by insects, animals, pruning, or mechanical injury. Monitor bark wounds carefully. If the wound does not heal quickly and properly, apply a pruning sealer as described previously, in the pruning section.

TREATING CANKERS

A tree canker is caused by bacteria or fungi. The infected wood is discolored, sunken, and oozing. If cankers are widespread, consult an arborist for treatment. If cankers are few and isolated, try treating them yourself.

Remove cankered branches by pruning off the branch at the trunk or at least 6 inches below the canker. If the canker is on the main trunk or a main branch, use a chisel and a sharp knife to remove the lesion. Remove all discolored and oozing wood and bark. Sterilize equipment with rubbing alcohol after each cut, to avoid infecting other tree segments. After the area dries, apply pruning sealer. If cankers are extensive and treatment is ineffective, the tree may have to be removed.

REMOVING TREES

A tree may grow too large for its surroundings, be too diseased to save, or must make way for new construction. Removing a large tree is a job for a licensed professional, who has the correct equipment for cutting and climbing. Such a job takes a professional's consideration as well as equipment. Tree weight must be lessened by judicious pruning before it is felled. Limbs must be cut so that they fall without injuring people, pets, plants, equipment, roofs, and power lines.

After a tree has been removed, stump treatment is necessary.

TREATING AND REMOVING STUMPS

The aggressiveness that may have caused you to remove the tree may be evident in its regrowth. Within 30 minutes of tree removal, treat freshly cut stumps with a liquid brush killer such as triclopyr, which acts systemically. Before you begin, remove suckers from the sides of the stump. Then paint or daub the brush killer over the entire stump surface.

If some time has passed before stump treatment, use a hatchet to make multiple notches around the stump, angling downward into the bark. Cut through the bark, without removing it. Pour brush killer into the notches, following label directions. If the herbicide tends to leak from the stump and desirable plants are nearby, cover the stump with a plastic bag secured at the stump base.

You may want to remove a stump altogether. This is best done when the stump, roots and all, is dead. A stump is dead if it fails to resprout the season after the tree has been cut. Digging out the stump yourself is quite a job. If you undertake it, avoid back injury by lifting and prying safely. A landscape contractor with proper equipment can remove a stump in a short time.

PLANTING AND TRANSPLANTING TREES

Many trees fail due to root injury and lack of preparation when planting or transplanting. The tree begins to die back from the outer portions inward and from the top down. With care, however, the home gardener can move small trees successfully. A tree with a trunk up to 1 foot in diameter is in the plant-it-yourself category. The more mature the tree, the more difficult it is to move, though professional tree movers can transplant even large trees successfully.

Deciduous trees are best moved in spring, before leaves begin to appear, or in fall, after leaves drop. Evergreen trees plant best in September.

Hole Preparation

Prepare the receiving hole before moving the tree. The root system of the tree to be moved probably spreads as far as the branches; the hole needs to be twice that width. Dig the hole deep enough to allow the tree to remain at its current level. If soil is sandy or heavy clay, improve it with organic material.

If soil turns out to be hardpan, you have a problem. Sometimes referred to

The suckers being sent up by this recently transplanted crape myrtle are a signal that the roots were damaged in the move.

Top: This crab apple tree is supported by two stakes, shielded wraps connecting them to the trunk.
Bottom: This containerized tree has obviously been suffering from a girdling root for a long time.

as shallow soil or caliche, hardpan is formed by extensive compaction from construction or it may be the natural soil formation in the region. Hardpan may feel like bedrock, but it is not. Bedrock is actually solid rock. If you find it, plant elsewhere or do container gardening.

When you hit hardpan, your shovel feels like it has hit brick. Instead of moving easily through soil, you scrape dirt away, a bit at a time. Eventually, if you scrape down far enough, you may get through the hardpan. But it can extend for quite a distance.

You must provide good soil to allow root penetration to the full depth and width of eventual root growth. This will be approximately equal to the branch spread of the full-grown tree.

Even if you are able to complete the hole, the remaining hardpan can present a problem for the tree planted in it. Rain or irrigation water tends to remain in hardpan for hours or even days. Standing water blocks nutrient absorption and invites fungi and bacteria. To compensate, you should make the hole even larger than normal, difficult as that may be.

If you decide to finish the digging yourself, drill through soil with an auger or posthole digger. Break up the hardpan to a depth of 2 feet for trees, 1 foot for shrubs. A less strenuous option is to hire a contractor to plow the hardpan and complete the digging. Do not put hardpan back into the planting hole. Backfill with topsoil mixed with organic material.

Do not plant a tree in uncorrected hardpan. Not only will it not prosper, its roots will remain shallow, and a heavy windstorm could topple it.

If the work or expense of planting in hardpan does not coincide with your definition of recreational gardening, remember the option of planting the tree in a container. Drought-tolerant species that perform adequately in restricted growing places include silk trees, redbuds, dwarf mungo pines, and strawberry trees.

Tree Preparation for Transplanting

Cut back about one third of the tree before digging it out. This lessens nutrient need until roots take hold and reduces the area exposed to drying sun and wind. Do not just cut from the top down; prune broken and crossing branches and branches that are too close to each other.

To excavate a tree 10 feet high, dig a trench at least 4 feet in diameter and about 18 inches deep. Generally, roots spread as far as branches. If thick roots obstruct the space, move farther away from the trunk and, with a digging fork, carefully remove anchoring soil from around the exposed roots. Leave as much soil around the roots as possible. Sway the plant gently to loosen the tree's hold.

The Move

With a ball of earth surrounding the roots, immediately move the tree into the receiving hole. Do not let the roots dry out. If the move will take some time, purchase a trunk spray to slow down water loss or wrap the trunk of a thin-barked tree, such as birch, with burlap. Leave the burlap on the tree for the first year after transplanting.

Ongoing Care

With careful transplanting, you have given the tree a boost toward a long healthy

life in the new site. The transplant still needs your special attention, however.

Mulch   Place a 4-inch-deep layer of mulch around the transplanted tree to further conserve moisture. To prevent fungus diseases encouraged by moisture buildup, keep mulch away from the trunk. Don't overwater or overfertilize—that may stimulate top growth that the traumatized roots cannot handle.

Sucker pruning   Suckers may appear around the base of a transplanted tree. If this happens and no top growth is evident, the tree has sustained damage that may hinder its survival. In such a situation, suckers indicate root injury and the failure to prune the treetop sufficiently before transplanting. Keeping suckers diligently pruned may help the tree to recover.

Trunk support   In heavy wind areas a transplanted trunk may need support. There are two widely used methods of wind staking. The first is to hammer a strong stake near the center of the hole, then set the tree close to the stake. Since this method presents the possibility of the trunk rubbing the stake, some gardeners prefer the two-stake method. This involves placing a stake at either side of the tree but not touching it. These stakes should be at a right angle to the usual wind direction. Either rot-resistant wood stakes or metal ones serve the purpose.

In the past, experts thought using tall stakes was necessary to prevent any tree movement. Current studies indicate that some trunk movement encourages eventual sturdiness. Using short stakes might be an effective compromise between the two viewpoints. Allow some room for tree sway when installing the stakes, and orient the tree so that the side with the most branches faces into the wind. Place the largest root in the direction of the wind for strongest support. Connect each stake to the tree with a nonabrasive tape in a figure-eight pattern. Do not use rope or wire, which will cut into the tree.

Another option, often used for larger trees, is to hammer 3 or 4 pegs into the ground several feet from the tree base. The tree is then secured to the pegs with shielded wires. A piece of old garden hose makes an excellent shield, or purchase shielded holding wires designed for trunk support. After the first year, if the tree is flourishing and seems well established, remove the stakes of guide wires. Remove all restraints by the second year.

Trunk injury may occur when wires or other restraints are left on a growing tree. Sometimes the restraints become so embedded in the tree that they are almost invisible. Since the nutrient system for the tree is directly under the bark, such a restraint begins to choke off circulation. New leaves may be small and discolored. Twigs and then larger branches may die. Tree growth may slow. The entire tree above the restraint can die. Removing an embedded restraint can be difficult. However, the deeper it gets, the more circulation it impedes. Use wire cutters at exposed sites. If you cannot free the embedded material, consult an arborist.

PREVENTING ROOT PROBLEMS

Girdling is a common root malady that can take two forms: container girdling and girdling roots.

Container Girdling

If the roots of a tree you are considering for purchase meander out of the container or wrap around the outside of the container, choose another plant. This root condition, called container girdling, is a visible sign of problems ahead. So are circling roots at the soil surface. To check for roots circling within the container, stick your finger in the top 2 to 3 inches near the trunk. Brush away a bit of topsoil. Roots that look or feel damaged, broken, or tightly compacted might be circling within the limited space of the container.

If you do buy a containerized tree with a tight or circling rootball, the tree may still be salvageable. Remove any ties around the rootball. Carefully move the roots apart so they spread out normally in the planting hole. To accomplish this, you may have to cut and remove some of the circling roots. Removing one quarter of the roots in the outer inch of the rootball should not damage the tree. Add and firm backfill gradually to get the best root contact.

Girdling Roots

A girdling root is any root that wraps itself completely around the trunk, either above soil level or just below it. Girdling roots may occur if trees are grown in hardpan. They are also common when containerized trees are placed in too small a hole or if the tree suffered from container girdling before it was planted.

As the trunk enlarges, the rootball tightens, effectively cutting off circulation. Tree leaves are small and discolored. They may drop out of season. Twigs, then larger branches, may die. If the girdling is below the soil surface, the problem may become severe before the cause is discovered. One clue to below-ground girdling is a trunk that narrows where it

This gall is large enough that it should probably be pruned away.

enters the soil—a normal trunk exhibits a slight flare at that point. A severely constricted trunk may break in a heavy windstorm.

The girdling root must be completely or partially removed to open up tree circulation. Since you are removing part of the root system, which provides the tree with nutrients, compensate for the loss by pruning back weak, crowded, or excess branches. If constriction at the base is severe, stake the tree for a few years to prevent wind breakage. In serious cases that require professional attention, the tree surgeon can sometimes save a girdled tree by using a procedure called bridge grafting.

TREATING GALLS

Sometimes a tree or shrub develops an odd-looking bump or bumps. They can be quite small or very large. They may appear to be part of the tree or completely separate, almost like a piece of fruit. These strange plant growths are called galls. They occur because a foreign substance has been injected into the tree. As a protective measure, the tree surrounds the substance with firm tissue.

Gardeners tend to worry about gall formation. But aside from changing the appearance of a plant, most galls do no serious damage. Small plants may be stunted if the gall blocks the flow of nutrients, but if the plant is ill, something else is usually causing the problem. The exception is crown gall, which can grow so rapidly that nutrient flow is markedly decreased. A tree with crown gall will usually survive for years but will decline slowly and eventually die.

Each gall is specific to the tree type. In addition, each gall is specific to the insect, bacterium, or fungus causing it. Oaks can develop 805 different galls; rose bushes can develop 133; and maple trees can develop 48. Nematodes cause nodule-like cysts on plant roots. Mite infestation may cause bladder gall and spindle gall. Bacteria cause euonymus crown gall and wartlike galls on oleander. Fungi cause camellia leaf gall; the white thick azalea

leaf gall; and gall rust, the large, rough, round orange swellings on pine trunks and branches.

Insects cause most gall formations. Psyllids cause the cylindrical nipple like growths of hackberry leaf gall. Aphids cause the green pineapple galls seen on spruce and the white cottony galls found on fir. Other gall-forming insects include gall midges, gall wasps, caterpillars, beetles, and thrips.

Galls caused by insects begin when an adult female places an egg in a plant bud. Plant cells begin to close around the egg. Some insects even inject a toxin that stimulates rapid and abnormal cell growth, hastening development of the gall. The egg hatches, and the larva begins development. The plant cells, responding to the larva within, begin to enlarge, forming the gall. When the larva completes its growth, it chews its way out of the gall. A tiny hole remains; so does the gall. Some galls are home to just one larva, others to many.

Oak galls, or oak apples, are most commonly seen as round balls growing on twigs. However, oak galls can be round, spiny, star-shaped, flat, or long. They may be found on leaves and branches as well as twigs. Occasionally the leaf galls slow nutrient use by leaves, resulting in discoloration and premature drop. Some twig galls can cause twig dieback.

Nothing can cure a tree of galls. If they are causing a problem or if you simply do not like their appearance, prune away the affected growth. To help prevent recurrence, cut off the galls and destroy them before the adult insects emerge in spring. If galls are especially numerous or unsightly, controlling the insects or diseases causing them may be necessary. Identification of the insect or disease responsible can be difficult. Take samples to a garden center, or consult an arborist.

CONTROLLING INSECT PESTS

The battle with insect pests seems as old as time. Modern research has provided a new strategy for the fight, however, and understanding the enemy will help protect your garden.

Integrated Pest Management

Today, integrated pest management (IPM) is the buzzword for gardeners seeking healthy trees and shrubs, with an economy of labor and a concern for the environment. IPM includes planting resistant species, using natural controls, supplying fertilizer and water for maximal plant strength, and using pesticides only where necessary and always according to label directions.

Beneficial insects such as ladybugs, lace wings, syrphids (also called flower-flies or hover flies), mantises, and parasitic wasps are part of any IPM program. Encourage their presence by providing thick shrubs. These provide not only shade, but protection from predators such as birds. If you have several large shrubs on your property and want to nurture beneficial bugs, leave the bases of the shrubs untrimmed. That slightly untidy area is a favorite trysting spot for helpful insects, and under its protection they climb up the shrub or tree, often to deposit eggs. Leafy branches then cover both eggs and larvae and keep them high enough off the ground to avoid many predators. (Be aware, however, that this also provides cover for unwanted pests such as rodents. If you are having problems with mice or rats, you may be forced to trim shrubs further.)

Many garden centers offer a variety of beneficial insects; you just purchase them and release them in your garden. Once released, they are of course free to go where they please, but if you have provided appropriate living conditions, it is likely that they will remain to feed on pests.

Hopping Insects

Trees are afflicted with their share of these common pests. Some are extremely small, such as leafhoppers. Others are weirdly shaped, such as treehoppers. And some are large and noisy, such as cicadas.

Cicadas infest both shade and fruit trees. Most of the damage they do results from egg-laying, which damages twigs. The twigs then turn brown and drop. Nymphs chew tree roots, and their feeding may eliminate both flowers and fruit. Adults suck sap from limbs and twigs. Broods of the periodical cicada (*Magicicada septendecim*) may be large and destructive or small and merely an annoyance. Cicadas usually appear where they have appeared before, because trees harbor eggs from prior generations. As

many as 40,000 cicadas have been known to infest a single tree.

Each brood may spend 13 or 17 years underground, feeding on tree roots, before appearing in masses aboveground. The species with the 13-year life cycle is found primarily in eastern states; the 17-year species is found primarily in southeastern states. Cicadas are wedge-shaped and black-bodied. They have red-orange eyes and red wing edges. An adult's full size is about 1½ inches long. Males make the annoying high-pitched droning that sometimes seems to go on forever. The females puncture twigs with knifelike egg-laying organs. Each female deposits up to 600 eggs within the twig.

Cicada young, or nymphs, resemble brown ants when young. They drop to the ground and enter soil. For the 13 or 17 years they take to complete development, nymphs feed on tree roots. In May or June of a breeding year, they crawl up from the ground on tree trunks or almost any other available object. They change to adults and begin breeding.

Cicada control consists of monitoring cicada outbreaks. Where heavy populations are known to occur, avoid planting new trees while cicadas are visibly present. Prune damaged twigs where the female has laid eggs. To protect small trees, cover them with netting or cheesecloth during cicada outbreaks. Carbaryl (SEVIN®) sprays are effective against cicadas. Spray when the males first begin to drone, and respray after one week.

Plant Bugs

Small shield-shaped insects, plant bugs often live with leafhoppers. These insects are extremely mobile—they both run and fly when disturbed. They feed by sucking sap, and several species inject toxins as they feed. The tree parts attacked wither and die.

The plant-bug category includes many species. The four-lined plant bug is greenish yellow with black stripes and ⅟₁₆-inch long. It infests many ornamental

trees and shrubs as well as crop plants. Leaves develop tan to reddish brown spots. The spots may join together to totally discolor the leaf. The sycamore plant bug, ⅛-inch long, is common on sycamore as well as ash, mulberry, and hickory trees. Feeding causes yellowish or reddish leaf spots. Sometimes holes appear where dead leaf tissue drops out. The yucca-plant bug appears only on yucca, causing stippled leaves covered with black waste matter. The adult of the species is blue-black with reddish head and throat. Its nymphs are bright scarlet and may be plentiful on leaves.

Control plant bugs with a malathion or carbaryl (SEVIN®) spray when you first notice damage in spring. Make certain to cover both the topsides and undersides of leaves. Repeat as necessary.

Leaf-destroying Insects

Leaves plagued by insects may seem as if they are punctured with shotgun pellets, cut with scissors, the victims of a hole punch, or suddenly transformed into fine lace. Sometimes leaves disappear almost overnight. Leaf-destroying insects include leafcutter bees, rose slugs, cankerworms, Japanese beetles, alder flea beetles, elm leaf beetles (see page 196), two-banded taxus weevils, bagworms, snails, slugs, mimosa webworm, holly leafminer, tent caterpillars (see page 175), stain moth caterpillars, leaf beetles (see page 196), woolly-bear caterpillars, and gypsy moth caterpillars. See the sidebar or indicated pages for identification and control.

Insect Pests of Pines

The increasing use of pines for reforestation, conservation, city areas, yard ornamentation, and holiday trees has caused an increase in pine-infesting insects. Many times the problem is a direct result of planting pines in clusters rather than mixing species in a natural way. Pine moths, pine sawflies, and other pests move quickly from one pine to another. In such a situation, insect populations quickly build up to numbers that natural predators cannot control. In general, avoid planting new pines near areas that contain pest-infested trees. Do not use bluegrass in pine-planted areas. Bluegrass encourages field mice, which may girdle pine trees.

Regular inspection of pines is crucial. Trouble signs include off-color foliage, unusual leaf drop, distorted growth, and insects. If caught in time, problems can be eased or eliminated. If you remove damaged pine wood, destroy it—prunings are an invitation to bark beetle invasion.

This female cicada is laying her hundreds of eggs in this tree limb.

This boxelder bug is just one of the many varieties of plant bugs that may be feeding on your trees.

LEAF-DESTROYING INSECTS

Leafcutter bees
(*Megachile* species)

Stout-bodied, hairy. Can be black, green, purple, or metallic blue. Females cut precise circles or ovals from leaf edges. Valuable pollinators. Control not recommended.

Rose slugs
(*Endelomyia aethiops*)

About ½ inch long, greenish white to dark green, velvety or covered with bristles. Skeletonize topsides of leaves; leaves turn brown. Damage can be mistaken for rust. Control with carbaryl (SEVIN®) on foliage at first sign of feeding. Repeat as necessary.

Cankerworms
(*Alsophila pometaria* and *Paleacrita vernata*)

Inch-long caterpillars, wingless moth adult females. Chew leaves and can defoliate entire trees. Tree banding with sticky substance such as tanglefoot helps prevent caterpillars from crawling up trunk. Spray with carbaryl (SEVIN®), acephate (ORTHENE®), or diazinon in late April to early May. Respray as leaves expand.

Woolly-bear caterpillars
(*Diacrisia virginica*)

Yellow or black fuzzy 2-inch-long caterpillars. Black type feeds mainly on weeds, but yellow type is destructive to desirable plants. May skeletonize shrubs in fall. If numbers are small try hand-picking; otherwise, try a *Bacillus thuringiensis* (Bt) or carbaryl (SEVIN®) spray.

Taxus weevils
(*Otiorhynchus sulcatus*)

White larvae underground; ⅜-inch black adults with long snouts. Notch leaf edges as if trimmed with a ticket punch. May also chew bark. Spray foliage and soil with acephate (ORTHENE®). Respray as necessary.

Holly leafminers
(*Phytomyza ilicus*)

Minute black flies. Multiple feeding punctures resemble pinpricks and distort leaves. Begin spraying with diazinon as soon as you notice flies.

Alder flea beetle
(*Altica ambiens*)

Hopping, greenish blue or shiny dark blue adults, ⅕ inch long. Produce numerous small holes or pitted areas on leaves. Remove weeds and debris where beetles overwinter. Spray with carbaryl (SEVIN®) when you first notice damage in spring. Respray as necessary.

PINE-DESTROYING INSECTS

Pine engraver beetles
(*Ips* species)

Brown or black beetles, ⅛ inch long. Create small circular holes in branches or trunk. White pine and spruce particularly susceptible. Serious problem in California. Needles turn yellow, then red, then die. Spray foliage and trunks with lindane to form a protective coating. If more than half of foliage has yellowed, remove the tree.

Pitch-mass borers
(*Synanthedon pini*)

Small moth with black metallic wings and orange-banded black body. Large globular masses of pitch emerge from tree, particularly in whorl areas. Remove pitch masses, where borers pupate. Spray foliage and trunk with lindane.

Zimmerman pine moths
(*Dioryctria zimmermani*)

Reddish gray adults, 1 inch long; white to reddish yellow larvae, ¾ inch long. Browning and wilting of new growth. Resin masses near whorls. Prune infested branches before August; destroy them. Spray foliage with lindane in mid-April and mid-August.

Pine webworms
(*Tetralopha robustella*)

Adults are 1 inch long and have purple-black forewings and smoky black hind wings; larvae are yellow-brown, ¾ inch long, and have stripes along their sides. Brown, globular nests of silk, old needles, and brown sawdustlike waste matter. Remove and destroy nests. Spray with BT or carbaryl (SEVIN®) before protective webbing appears.

Insects attacking pine or spruce include the white pine weevil (see page 183), pales weevil, Zimmerman pine moth, pitch-mass borer, European pine shoot moth (see page 182), Eastern pine shoot borer, pine webworm, Nantucket pine tip moth (see page 182), pine root collar weevil, European pine sawfly (see page 182), redheaded pine sawfly (see page 182), white pine sawfly (see page 182), irregular pine scale, pine tortoise scale, southern pine beetles, pine engraver beetles, pine tube moth, white pine aphid (see page 181), pine needle miner, and Saratoga spittlebug (see page 181). Spider mites (see pages 172 and 178) and nematodes (see page 179) also attack pine. See the sidebar or indicated pages for identification and control.

In general, supply optimum water and fertilizer to make trees less appealing to these pests. Frequent inspection will help in early detection, which will allow you to solve the problem by pruning infested branches or spraying with appropriate chemicals.

These two photographs show the obvious visible symptoms of boring insects in pine trees and a close-up look at what these insects actually do inside an attacked tree.

PROBLEMS COMMON TO MANY TREES, SHRUBS, AND VINES

Flowerless dogwood in dark location.

Flower buds pruned off crape myrtle.

PROBLEM: Plants fail to bloom or bloom only sparsely and sporadically.

ANALYSIS: Few or no flowers
Plants produce few or no buds or flowers for any of several reasons.

SOLUTION: Take these measures to correct the condition or control the problem.

1. *Juvenility:* Plants, like people, must reach a certain age or size before they are able to reproduce. They will not develop flowers or fruit until this time.

1. Plants will eventually begin to flower if they are otherwise healthy and adapted to the area. The juvenile stage in some trees and vines may last 15 years.

2. *Inadequate winter cooling:* To produce flowers, many plants must undergo a period of cooling during the winter. The plant must be exposed for a certain number of hours to temperatures between 30° and 45° F. The number of hours needed is different for different plant species. If the cooling requirement is not satisfied, flowering is delayed and reduced and flower buds may drop off. This is a common problem when plants adapted to cold climates are grown in warmer climates.

2. Plant trees and shrubs that are adapted to the area. Consult a local garden center; cooperative extension office; or a book on plant selection, such as Ortho's book *Shrubs & Hedges* or *All About Trees.*

3. *Improper pruning:* If a plant is pruned improperly or too severely, flower and fruit production can be reduced or, in some cases, prevented. Drastic pruning, especially of young plants, stimulates a flush of green growth, which inhibits flowering. Flowering is also reduced if flower buds are pruned off.

3. For instructions on proper pruning techniques, see Ortho's book *All About Pruning.*

4. *Nutrient imbalance:* Plants oversupplied with nitrogen tend to produce a flush of green growth. Some plants do not produce flowers while they are growing vigorously.

4. Do not overfertilize plants or apply nitrogen heavily before plants flower.

5. *Shade:* Flowering plants require a certain amount of light to produce flowers. If these plants are grown in inadequate light, they produce few or no flowers.

5. Thin out shading trees, or move plants to a sunnier area.

Drought.

Bud drop caused by cold injury.

Boxelder seeds create messy litter.

PROBLEM: Many or all of the buds or flowers die or drop off.

ANALYSIS: Buds die or drop

Buds may die or drop for any of several reasons.

1. *Transplant shock:* Whenever a tree or shrub is transplanted, it goes through a period of shock. Dormant plants usually recover more quickly and are injured less than growing plants. However, even when transplanted properly, dormant plants may still lose some of their buds. Plants that have begun growth or are in bloom often drop many of their flower buds or flowers shortly after transplanting. Some buds may remain on the plant but will not open.

2. *Cold or frost injury:* Flower buds or flowers may be killed by cold or freezing temperatures. Many or all of them either fail to open or drop off. Cold injury occurs during the winter when temperatures drop below the lowest point that can be tolerated by buds of that particular plant species. Frost injury is caused by an unseasonal cold snap, in either fall or spring, which damages buds, developing flowers, and tender shoots of growing plants.

3. *Drought:* Flowers or flower buds dry and drop off during a temporary lack of moisture in the plant. This may be due to dry soil, minor root injuries, or anything else that disrupts water movement to the top of the plant.

4. *Insects:* Certain insects, such as thrips and mites, feed on flower buds. When infestations are heavy, their feeding kills flower buds, causing them to dry and drop off. Some infested buds may open but are distorted.

SOLUTION: Take these measures to correct the condition or control the problem.

1. Whenever possible, transplant trees and shrubs during the dormant season. Avoid wounding the roots when planting, and do not let plants dry out.

2. Plant trees and shrubs adapted to the area. Consult a local garden center; cooperative extension office; or a book on plant selection, such as Ortho's book *Shrubs & Hedges* or *All About Trees*. Protect shrubs and small trees from early or late cold snaps by covering them with burlap or a plastic tent. Leaving on a light underneath the covering offers additional protection.

3. Water trees and shrubs regularly. Most plants will recover from minor root injuries. Frequent shallow waterings and a light application of fertilizer may speed the recovery process. Avoid wounding plants.

4. Insects can be controlled with various chemicals. For more information about thrips and mites and their controls, look on pages 153 and 154.

PROBLEM: Trees and shrubs drop flowers, seedpods, or fruit, creating unwanted messy litter.

ANALYSIS: Excess flowers and fruits

All trees and shrubs produce flowers or flower structures that develop into seedpods or fruit. Some plants, such as juniper and boxwood, produce inconspicuous flowers and fruits. Others—such as ornamental crab apple, olive, sweet gum, horse-chestnut, and glossy privet—produce many conspicuous flowers, seedpods, or fruits. The dropping flowers and fruits of such plants create litter that may detract from the beauty of the landscape and increase time spent in garden upkeep.

SOLUTION: Prevent flower and fruit production by spraying with a compound containing the growth regulator *NAA* (napthalene acetic acid), ethephon, or dikegulac-sodium; treat plants when the flower buds are forming. Contact the local cooperative extension office to determine this period for your particular plant. Make sure your plant is listed on the product label, and follow directions carefully. If plants are small enough to be moved, transplant them to a location where their flower and fruit drop will not be a nuisance. If spraying is impractical, replace messy trees and shrubs with plants that do not produce litter.

PROBLEMS COMMON TO MANY TREES, SHRUBS, AND VINES — INSECTS

Long-horned beetle (2 times life size).

Gypsy moth larvae (life size).

Gypsy moth and egg masses (life size).

PROBLEM: Shiny or dull hard-bodied insects with tough, leathery wing covers appear on the plants. Each insect's wing covers meet in the middle of its back, forming a straight line down the insect's body. Leaf tissue is chewed, notched, or eaten between the veins, giving the leaves a lacy appearance. The bark may be chewed, or flowers may be eaten. Holes may be found in branches or the trunk.

ANALYSIS: Beetles

Many different species of beetle feed on ornamental trees and shrubs. In most cases, both larvae (grubs) and adults feed on the plants, so damage is often severe. The insects spend the winter as grubs inside the plants or in the soil or as adults in bark crevices or in hiding places on the ground. Adult beetles lay eggs on the plants or on the soil during the growing season. Depending on the species, the grubs may feed on foliage, mine inside the leaves, bore into stems or branches, or feed on roots. Beetle damage to leaves rarely kills the plant; grubs feeding inside the wood or underground often kill branches or the whole plant.

SOLUTION: Grubs feeding in the soil or inside plants are difficult to detect and control, so control measures usually focus on the adults. Several different insecticides, including ones containing carbaryl (SEVIN®), may be used to control these pests. Make sure your plant is listed on the label. For advice about beetles on specific plants, look up your plant in the alphabetical section beginning on page 157.

PROBLEM: Leaves are chewed; the entire tree may be defoliated by late spring or early summer. Large (up to 2½ inches long), hairy, blackish caterpillars with rows of red and blue spots on their backs feed on the foliage. The caterpillars hide under leaves or bark or crawl on buildings, cars, or other objects outdoors. Insect droppings accumulate underneath infested tree foliage. Trees, especially those defoliated for several consecutive years, may be killed.

ANALYSIS: Gypsy moths (*Lymantria dispar*)

The gypsy moth is a general feeder, devouring over 450 species of plants. Gypsy moth populations fluctuate from year to year. When the number of moths is low, oaks are the preferred host. When their numbers increase, entire forests may be defoliated as the moths spread to other trees and shrubs. Repeated, severe defoliation weakens trees and reduces plant growth. Defoliated deciduous trees are rarely killed unless already in a weakened condition. However, they are more susceptible to attack by other insects and by plant diseases that may kill them. Gypsy moths are also an extreme nuisance in urban areas and in parks and campgrounds, where females attach overwintering masses of eggs, which are covered with beige or yellow hairs, to almost any outdoor object. The eggs hatch from mid- to late spring. The tiny larvae crawl to trees where they feed, or they drop on silken threads to be carried by the wind to other plants. As the caterpillars mature, they feed at night and rest during the day. The larvae may completely cover sides of houses or other objects during these resting periods. When population levels are high, the insects feed continually on a tree and large amounts of excrement accumulate beneath it. The larval hairs may cause allergies. The larvae pupate in sheltered places, and dark brown male or white female moths emerge in midsummer.

SOLUTION: If the insects are bothersome or trees are weak or unhealthy from last year's gypsy moth feeding or from drought, mechanical damage, other insects, or plant diseases, treatment with an insecticide is required. The insecticide should be applied before larvae are 1 inch long, and the tree must be covered thoroughly. Hire a professional arborist to treat large trees. Spray small trees when tiny larvae are first noticed; use an insecticide containing carbaryl (SEVIN®), Bt (*Bacillus thuringiensis*), or acephate (ORTHENE®). Respray at weekly intervals if damage continues. Homeowners can reduce infestations by destroying egg masses during the winter months. During the spring, when larvae are feeding, place burlap bands on trees, leaving the bottom edge unattached. Larvae will crawl under these flaps to hide during the day. Collect and destroy the larvae daily. Keep trees healthy by applying fertilizer regularly and watering during periods of drought. When planting trees, choose species that are less favored by the gypsy moth. These trees will be damaged only slightly by larval feeding. In addition, when interplanted with more favored hosts, they may reduce damage by preventing a large buildup of insects in the area. Do not transport items that may have eggs or larvae attached to them.

Japanese beetle (life size).

Looper (2 times life size).

Western tent caterpillars (¼ life size).

PROBLEM: Leaf tissue is chewed between the veins, giving the leaves a lacy appearance. If the plant is flowering, the flowers are also eaten. The entire plant may be defoliated. Winged metallic green and bronze beetles, ½ inch long, feed in clusters on the plant.

ANALYSIS: Japanese beetles

(*Popillia japonica*)
As their name suggests, these beetles are native to Japan. They were first seen in New Jersey in 1916 and have since become a major pest in the eastern United States. They feed on hundreds of different plant species. The adult beetles are present from June to October. They feed only in the daytime and are most active on warm, sunny days. The female beetles live for 30 to 45 days. Just before they die, they lay their eggs immediately under the surface of lawns. Grayish white grubs soon hatch and feed on grass roots. As weather turns cold in the late fall, grubs move 8 to 10 inches down into the soil, where they remain dormant for the winter. When the soil warms up in spring, the grubs move back up near the soil surface and resume feeding on roots. They soon pupate and re-emerge as adult Japanese beetles in late May or June.

SOLUTION: In late May or June, control the adults with an insecticide containing acephate (ORTHENE®), carbaryl (SEVIN®), or malathion. Respray 10 days later if damage continues.

PROBLEM: Caterpillars are clustered or feeding singly on leaves. The surfaces of the leaves are eaten, giving the remaining tissue a lacy appearance, or leaves are chewed all the way through. Sometimes cobwebs appear on the foliage. The tree may be completely defoliated. Damage appears any time between spring and fall. Repeated heavy infestations may weaken or kill plants.

ANALYSIS: Leaf-feeding caterpillars

Many different species of caterpillar feed on the leaves of trees and shrubs. From early spring to midsummer, female moths lay the eggs from which the caterpillars hatch; the time depends on the species. The larvae that hatch from these eggs feed singly or in groups on buds, on one leaf surface or the other, or on entire leaves. Certain caterpillars web leaves together as they feed. In some years, damage is minimal due to environmental conditions unfavorable to the pest or control by predators and parasites. However, when conditions are favorable, entire plants may be defoliated by late summer. Defoliation weakens plants because no leaves remain to produce food. When heavy infestations occur several years in a row, branches or entire plants may be killed.

SOLUTION: When damage is first noticed, spray with an insecticide containing acephate (ORTHENE®) or carbaryl (SEVIN®) or apply a bacterial insecticide containing *Bacillus thuringiensis*. Spray the leaves thoroughly. Respray if the plant becomes reinfested.

PROBLEM: In the spring or summer, silken nests appear in the branch crotches or on the ends of branches. Leaves are chewed; branches or the entire tree may be defoliated. Groups of caterpillars feed in or around the nests.

ANALYSIS: Tent caterpillars or fall webworms

(*Malacosoma* species or *Hyphantria cunea*)
These insects feed on many ornamental trees. In the summer, female tent caterpillars lay masses of eggs in a cementing substance around twigs. They hatch in early spring as the leaves unfold, and the young caterpillars construct their nests. On warm, sunny days, they emerge from the nests to devour the surrounding foliage. In mid- to late summer, brownish or reddish moths appear. Adult female fall webworms lay many eggs on the undersides of leaves in the spring. In early summer, the young webworms make nests over the ends of branches. They feed inside the nests. As the leaves are devoured, the webworms extend the nests over more foliage. Eventually the entire branch may be enclosed with this unsightly silken webbing. The webworms drop to the soil to pupate. Up to four generations occur between June and September. Damage is most severe in the late summer.

SOLUTION: Spray with an insecticide containing acephate (ORTHENE®) or carbaryl (SEVIN®) or a bacterial insecticide containing *Bacillus thuringiensis*; follow label directions. The bacterial insecticide is most effective against small caterpillars. Remove egg masses found in winter.

PROBLEMS COMMON TO MANY TREES, SHRUBS, AND VINES — INSECTS ▬▬■ SCALES OR POWDER ON PLANT ▬▬

Bagworm case on honeylocust (life size).

Aphids on hawthorn (life size).

Elm bark scale (life size).

PROBLEM: Leaves are chewed; branches or the entire tree may be defoliated. Carrot-shaped cases, or "bags," from 1 to 3 inches long, hang from the branches. The bags are constructed from interwoven bits of dead foliage, twigs, and silk. When a bag is cut open, a tan or blackish caterpillar or a yellowish grub-like insect may be found inside. A heavy attack by bagworms may stunt deciduous trees or kill evergreens.

ANALYSIS: Bagworms
(*Thyridopteryx ephemeraeformis*)
Bagworms eat the leaves of many trees and shrubs. The larvae hatch in late May or early June and immediately begin feeding. Each larva constructs a bag that covers its entire body, and to which it adds as it develops. The worm partially emerges from its bag to feed. When all the leaves are eaten off the branch, the bagworm moves to the next branch, dragging its bag along. By late August, the larva spins silken bands around a twig, attaches the bag, and pupates. In the fall, the winged male moth emerges from his case, flies to a bag containing a female, mates, and dies. After mating, the female lays 500 to 1,000 eggs and dies. The eggs spend the winter in the mother's bag.

SOLUTION: Sometime from late May to mid-July, spray with an insecticide containing acephate (ORTHENE®), Bt (*Bacillus thuringiensis*), or carbaryl (SEVIN®). Respray after 10 days if leaf damage is still occurring. Hand-pick and destroy bags in winter to reduce the number of eggs.

PROBLEM: Tiny (⅛-inch) green, yellow, black, brownish, or gray soft-bodied insects cluster on the bark, leaves, or buds. They may be covered with white, fluffy wax and have wings. Leaves are discolored and may be curled and distorted. Sometimes leaves drop off. A shiny or sticky substance may coat the foliage. A black sooty mold often grows on the sticky substance. Plants may lack vigor, and branches sometimes die. Ants may be present.

ANALYSIS: Aphids
Many different types of aphid infest ornamental trees and shrubs. They do little damage in small numbers. However, they are extremely prolific during a cool growing season. Damage occurs when the aphid sucks the juice from the plant. Sap removal often results in scorched, discolored, or curled leaves and reduced plant growth. A severe infestation of bark aphids may cause branches to die. Aphids are unable to digest fully all the sugar in the plant sap. They excrete the excess in a fluid called honeydew, which often drops below the tree or shrub. Ants feed on this sticky substance and are often present where there is an aphid infestation. A sooty mold fungus may develop on the honeydew, causing the leaves to appear black and dirty.

SOLUTION: When damage is first noticed, spray with an insecticide containing acephate (ORTHENE®) or malathion. Respray if the plant becomes reinfested.

PROBLEM: Leaves, stems, branches, or trunk are covered with crusty or waxy bumps or clusters of somewhat flat, scaly bumps. The bumps can be scraped or picked off; their undersides are usually soft. Leaves turn yellow and may drop. In some cases, a shiny or sticky substance coats them. A black sooty mold often grows on the sticky substance.

ANALYSIS: Scales
Many types of scale infest trees and shrubs. The females lay their eggs on leaves or bark. In spring to midsummer, the young scales, called crawlers, settle on leaves, branches, or the trunk. The small (1/10-inch), soft-bodied young feed by sucking sap from the plant. Their legs usually atrophy, and a hard crusty or waxy shell develops over their bodies. The female scales lay their eggs underneath their shells. Some species of scale are unable to digest fully all the sugar in the plant sap, so they excrete the excess in a fluid called honeydew. A sooty mold fungus may develop on the honeydew, causing the leaves to appear black and dirty. An uncontrolled infestation of scales may kill a plant after two or three seasons.

SOLUTION: When the young are active, spray with an insecticide containing diazinon, malathion, carbaryl (SEVIN®), or acephate (ORTHENE®). Contact the local cooperative extension office to determine the best time to spray for scales in your area. The following early spring, before new growth begins, spray the trunk and branches with a dormant oil spray to control overwintering insects. Make sure your plant is listed on the product label.

Pine bark aphid on white pine (¼ life size).

Powdery mildew on London plane tree.

Rust on Oregon grape.

PROBLEM: Branch crotches, the trunk, or stems and the undersides of leaves are covered with white, cottony masses. Leaves may be curled, distorted, and yellowing. Knotlike galls may form on the stems or trunk. In some cases, a shiny or sticky substance coats the leaves. A black sooty mold may grow on the sticky substance. Twigs and branches may die.

ANALYSIS: Cottonycushion scales, mealybugs, or woolly aphids
The similar appearances of cottonycushion scales, mealybugs, and woolly aphids make separate identification difficult for the home gardener. All produce white, waxy secretions that cover their bodies. Young insects are usually inconspicuous on the host plant. Their bodies range in color from yellowish green to brown, blending in with the leaves or bark. As the insects mature, they exude filaments of white wax, giving them a cottony appearance. Mealybugs and scales generally deposit their eggs in white, fluffy masses. All three insect types feed on plant sap, damaging the leaves, branches, or trunk. Because the pests are unable to digest fully all the sugar in the plant sap, they excrete the excess in a fluid called honeydew, which often drops onto the leaves or plants below. A sooty mold fungus may develop on the honeydew, causing leaves and twigs to appear black and dirty.

SOLUTION: Spray with an insecticide containing acephate (ORTHENE®).

PROBLEM: Leaves, flowers, and young stems are covered with a thin layer or irregular patches of a grayish white powdery material. Infected leaves may turn yellowish or reddish and drop. Some leaves or branches may be distorted. In late fall, tiny black dots (spore-producing bodies) are scattered over the white patches like ground pepper.

ANALYSIS: Powdery mildew
This common plant disease is caused by any of several fungi that thrive in both humid and dry weather. Some fungi attack only older leaves and plant parts; other fungi attack only young tissue. Plants growing in shady areas are often severely infected. The powdery patches consist of fungal strands and spores. The spores are spread by the wind to healthy plants. The fungi sap the plant nutrients, causing discoloring and sometimes the death of the leaf. Certain powdery mildews also cause leaf or branch distortion. Since powdery mildew attacks many different kinds of plants, the fungi from a diseased plant may infect other plants in the garden.

SOLUTION: Several different fungicides—including those containing triforine, chlorothalonil, benomyl, and dinocap—control powdery mildew. For control suggestions, look under your specific plant in the alphabetical section beginning on page 157.

PROBLEM: Yellow, orange, red, or black powdery pustules appear on the topsides or undersides of leaves or, occasionally, on bark. The powdery material can be scraped or rubbed off. Leaves are discolored or mottled yellow to brown. Leaves may become twisted, distorted, and dry, then drop off. Infected stems may be swollen or blistered, or they may develop oblong or hornlike galls up to 2 inches long.

ANALYSIS: Leaf and stem rusts
Many different species of rust fungi infect trees and shrubs. Some rusts produce spore pustules on leaves or stems, and others produce galls or hornlike structures on various plant parts. Most rusts attack only one species or a few related species of plants. However, some rusts require two different plant species to complete their life cycles. In most cases, the symptoms produced on the two hosts are quite different. Rust spores are spread to healthy plants by wind and splashing water. When conditions are favorable (moist, with temperatures from 55° to 75° F), the spores germinate and infect the tissue.

SOLUTION: Use fungicides containing triforine or chlorothalonil to control rust. Look up your plant in the alphabetical section beginning on page 157 to determine which fungicide to use. Some rust fungi are fairly harmless and do not require control measures. Rake up and destroy leaves in the fall.

TREES, SHRUBS, AND VINES

Sooty mold on yew.

Leaf spots on catalpa.

Leaf spots on liquidambar.

PROBLEM: A black sooty mold grows on leaves and twigs. It can be completely wiped off the surfaces. Cool, moist weather hastens the growth of the mold.

ANALYSIS: Sooty mold
This common black mold is found on a wide variety of plants in the garden. It is caused by any of several fungi that grow on the sugary material left on plants by aphids, scales, mealybugs, whiteflies, and other insects that suck sap from plants. The insects are unable to digest all the sugar in the sap, so they excrete the excess in a fluid called honeydew, which drops onto the leaves below. The honeydew may also drop out of infested trees and shrubs onto plants growing beneath them. The sooty mold fungi develop on the honeydew, causing the leaves to appear black and dirty. Sooty molds are unsightly but are fairly harmless because they do not attack the foliage directly. Extremely heavy infestations prevent light from reaching leaves, however, so the foliage produces fewer nutrients and may turn yellow. The presence of sooty mold indicates that the plant or a nearby plant is infested with insects.

SOLUTION: Sooty mold can be wiped from the leaves with a wet rag, or it will eventually be washed off by rain. Prevent more sooty mold by controlling the insect that is producing the honeydew. Inspect the leaves and twigs above the sooty mold to find what type of insect is present.

PROBLEM: Spots and blotches appear on leaves and flowers.

ANALYSIS: Spots on leaves
Several diseases, insects, and environmental factors cause spots and blotches on leaves and flowers.

1. *Fungal leaf spot:* Spots caused by fungi are often small and circular and may be found on all the leaves. Sometimes only the older or younger leaves are affected. The spots range in size from barely visible to ¾ inch in diameter. They may be yellow, red, tan, gray, brown, or black, and they often have a definite edge. Spots sometimes join together to form blotches. Often the leaves turn yellow and die. Infection is usually most severe during moist, mild weather (50° to 85° F).

2. *Insects:* Several different types of insects—including lacebugs, leafhoppers, mites, plant bugs, and thrips—cause spotting of leaves. Leaf spots may be brownish, yellow, or white, or leaves may be completely discolored. Sometimes the insects are visible, feeding on the topsides or undersides of the leaves.

3. *Sun bleaching or sunburn:* On the leaves most directly exposed to the sun, shade-loving plants placed in a sunny location develop a whitish or yellowish bleached appearance between the veins. Or, in cases of sunburn, large, dark blotches form on the damaged tissue. Sun-loving plants may also develop these symptoms if they are allowed to dry out. Leaves not directly exposed to the sun remain green and uninjured.

SOLUTION: Take these measures to correct the condition or control the problem.

1. When new growth begins, spray plants with a fungicide containing benomyl, chlorothalonil, maneb, mancozeb, or zineb. Repeat at intervals of 2 weeks for as long as the weather remains favorable for infection. Make sure your plant is listed on the product label. Raking and destroying leaves in the fall may help control the fungus.

2. These insects can be controlled with various types of insecticides. Look up your plant in the alphabetical section beginning on page 157 to determine which insecticide to use.

3. Where practical, pick off the injured leaves and plant parts. Look up your plant in the alphabetical section beginning on page 157 to determine if it is adapted to sun or shade. Provide shade, or transplant shade-loving plants. Water plants regularly, especially on hot, sunny, or windy days.

GALLS OR GROWTHS

Gall rust on pine.

Leaf galls on willow.

A conk on the trunk of a bigleaf maple.

PROBLEM: Swellings, thickenings, and growths develop on leaves, shoots, branches, or trunk. Plants with numerous galls on branches or trunk may be weak with yellowing leaves. Branches may die.

ANALYSIS: Growths on leaves, branches, or trunk

These growths, or galls, result from three causes.

1. *Fungal leaf or stem gall:* Several different fungi, including rust fungi, cause enlargement and thickening of leaves and shoots. Affected plant parts are usually many times larger than normal and are often discolored and succulent. Some leaf or stem galls turn brown and hard with age. The galls are unsightly but rarely harmful to the plant. Fungal galls are most severe when spring weather is wet.

2. *Bacterial crown gall:* This plant disease is caused by a soil-inhabiting bacterium (*Agrobacterium tumefaciens*) that infects many ornamentals, fruits, and nuts in the garden. The bacteria enter the plant through wounds in the roots or the base of the trunk (the crown). The galls disrupt the flow of water and nutrients up the roots, stems, and trunk, weakening and stunting the top growth. Galls do not usually kill the plant.

3. *Insect galls:* Many different types of insects cause galls by feeding on plant tissue or by injecting a toxin into the tissue during feeding. As a result of this irritation, blisters or growths of various shapes form on leaves, swellings develop on roots or stems, and buds and flowers grow abnormally. Most gall-forming insects cause only minor damage to the plant, but the galls may be unsightly.

SOLUTION: Take these measures to correct the condition or control the problem.

1. Pick off and destroy affected parts as soon as they appear. If galls are a problem this year, spray next spring, just before the buds open, with a fungicide containing ferbam, zineb, mancozeb, or maneb. Add a spreader-sticker to the spray. Respray 2 weeks later.

2. Infected plants cannot be cured. However, they often survive for many years. To improve the appearance of shrubs with stem galls, prune out and destroy affected stems below the galled area. Sterilize pruning shears with rubbing alcohol after each cut. Destroy severely infected shrubs. Consult a professional horticulturist to remove galls from valued trees. The bacteria will remain in the soil for at least 2 years.

3. Many gall-forming insects require no control. However, if you feel the galls are unsightly or if the galls are causing dieback, control measures may be necessary. For recommended control measures, look up your plant in the alphabetical section beginning on page 157.

PROBLEM: White, yellow, gray, or brownish growths that are usually hard and woody protrude from the trunk, or mushrooms appear around the base of the tree. The plant may appear unhealthy.

ANALYSIS: Mushrooms and conks

Mushrooms and conks are the reproductive bodies of fungi. Most mushroom fungi live on decaying matter. When conditions are favorable, the fungi produce mushrooms and conks (hard, woody growths that protrude from tree trunks) containing spores that are spread by the wind. A number of different mushroom fungi decay the heartwood of living trees. Most of these organisms grow only in older wood, which they enter through wounds. Mushrooms or conks usually appear annually in the dead portions of trees. Some conks may remain attached to the wood for years. *Armillaria mella*, a fungus that causes a plant disease called armillaria root rot, mushroom root rot, oak root fungus, or shoestring root rot, invades healthy roots. In the fall or winter, mushrooms appear around the base of the plant, growing on the infected roots.

SOLUTION: By the time conks or mushrooms appear on the trunk, it is too late to do anything about the wood rot. Inspect the tree to determine the extent of decay (consult a professional arborist if necessary). Remove trees or branches with extensive decay. Keep plants vigorous by adding fertilizer and watering regularly. The spread of armillaria root rot may be inhibited if it is found in only part of the roots.

PROBLEMS COMMON TO MANY TREES, SHRUBS, AND VINES — GALLS OR GROWTHS

Lichen.

Leafy mistletoe.

Dwarf mistletoe. *Insert: Seeds.*

PROBLEM: Brown, gray, green, or yellow, crusty, soft, or leaflike growths develop on trees in moist forested areas. The growths are usually found on the lower or shaded part of trunks and branches.

ANALYSIS: Algae, lichens, and mosses

These organisms are sometimes mistaken for plant diseases, especially if the tree they are attached to appears unhealthy. However, they do not harm the plant. Most algae grow where moisture is abundant, on the lower, shady side of the trunk. They appear only as an inconspicuous green on the bark. Lichens are a combination of green algae and fungi. They range in color from brown to green and appear crusty or leaflike. They are sensitive to air pollution and are found only in areas where the air is clean. True mosses are small green plants with tiny leaves and stems growing in a mat. They are abundant in moist areas and are much more apparent than algae. Spanish moss is an extremely noticeable flowering plant (in the pineapple family) that hangs from branches of trees in the southern and western United States.

SOLUTION: Algae, lichens, and mosses do not harm trees, but they may be unsightly. Control algae, lichens, and mosses by pruning away surrounding vegetation to increase light and air flow, which will reduce the moisture in the soil and air around the plant.

PROBLEM: Leafy olive-green plants up to 4 feet across are attached to branches. The tufts are most noticeable during the winter, on trees without their leaves. Affected branches are often swollen. Some may break from the weight of the plants. Branches beyond the growth occasionally die.

ANALYSIS: Leafy mistletoe

(*Phoradendron* species)
Leafy mistletoe is a semiparasitic plant that manufactures its own food but depends on its host plant for water and minerals. The plant produces sticky seeds that are spread from one tree to another by birds or by falling from higher to lower branches. The seeds germinate almost anywhere but penetrate only young, thin bark. The rootlike attachment organs of the plant penetrate the water-conducting vessels of the tree, which are tapped for mineral nutrients and water. At the point of attachment, the host branch or trunk swells, sometimes to 2 or 3 times its normal size. Growth of mistletoe is slow at first, but after 6 to 8 years plants may be 3 feet across. Trees heavily infested with mistletoe may be weakened, and sometimes they die.

SOLUTION: Prune off limbs 18 inches below the point of mistletoe attachment. The rootlike attachment organs may spread through host tissue up to 1½ feet from the swollen area. They must be removed or the mistletoe will resprout. If it is impractical to prune the tree limbs, prevent the spread of seeds by removing tufts before seeds form in the spring. Wrap the infected areas with black plastic to prevent the mistletoe from resprouting.

PROBLEM: Twigs and small branches of conifers are swollen and have cankers (discolored lesions). Witches'-brooms (many small tufts of branches) usually form on infested branches. As swellings or witches'-brooms increase in size, the tree loses vigor. Foliage becomes sparse and yellowish, and over a period of years the portion of the tree above the mistletoe may die. Short, succulent, leafless, yellow, brown, or olive-green shoots develop in the bark of affected branches.

ANALYSIS: Dwarf mistletoe

(*Arceuthobium* species)
This parasitic plant infests many conifers. Dwarf mistletoe lacks a normal root system and true leaves. It relies on its host plant to supply most of the nutrients it requires. In this respect it is different from leafy mistletoe (see at left), which depends on its host plant only for water and minerals. In midsummer, dwarf mistletoe spreads by explosively discharging sticky seeds for distances up to 50 feet. Seeds land on needles and then slide down to the bark when the needles are moistened. When seeds germinate, usually the following spring, rootlike structures penetrate the bark. The structures form a network in the branches, causing swellings and the formation of cankers. Dwarf mistletoe weakens the tree as it saps nutrients and water, and it distorts the growth of branches. Within 1 to 3 years after infestation, the mistletoe produces aerial shoots from ½ to 4 inches long, depending on the species.

SOLUTION: Remove dying trees. Prune off branches of less severely infested trees, making the cuts at the trunk. Remove new infestations as they appear.

■ **HOLES OR TRAILS IN LEAVES**

Witches'-broom on hackberry.

Leafroller on linden.

Leafminer damage to holly.

PROBLEM: A dense tuft of small, weak twigs develops on a branch. Leaves on the tuft may be smaller than normal and off-color. The branches are weak and unhealthy.

ANALYSIS: Witches'-broom
A witches'-broom is a dense proliferation of twig growth. It is usually caused by an insect, plant disease, or mistletoe (see page 140). The witches'-broom looks messy but is not harmful to the plant. The insect or disease that caused it, however, may be.

SOLUTION: If the witches'-broom affects the appearance of the plant, prune it off. The home gardener may have difficulty identifying the cause of brooming. If witches'-brooms continue to develop, consult a professional arborist or the local cooperative extension office.

PROBLEM: Leaves are rolled, usually lengthwise, and held together with cobweb. The rolled leaves are chewed. When a rolled leaf is opened, a green caterpillar, ½ to ¾ inch long, may be found feeding inside. Flower buds may also be chewed.

ANALYSIS: Leafrollers
Several different leafrollers feed on the leaves and buds of woody ornamentals. Some species feed on only one plant; others feed on many plants. Leafrollers are the larvae of small (up to ¾ inch) brownish moths. The insects spend the winter as eggs or larvae on a plant. In the spring the larvae feed on the young foliage, sometimes tunneling into and mining the leaf first. They roll one or more leaves around themselves, tying the leaves together with a silken webbing, then feed within the rolled leaves. This provides protection from weather, parasites, and chemical sprays. Some leafroller species mature in summer and produce several generations each year; other leafrollers produce only one generation yearly. In the fall, the larvae either mature into moths and lay the overwintering eggs or spend the winter inside the rolled leaves.

SOLUTION: In the spring, when leaf damage is first noticed, spray with an insecticide containing acephate (ORTHENE®) or carbaryl (SEVIN®). For the insecticide to be most effective, apply it before the larvae are protected inside the rolled leaves. In the spring, check the plant periodically for the first sign of infestation.

PROBLEM: Green or whitish translucent winding trails, blisters, or blotches develop on leaves. The trails, blisters, or blotches later turn brown. Tearing open an infested leaf reveals one to several small green, yellowish, or whitish insects.

ANALYSIS: Leafminers
Leafminers are the larvae of flies, moths, beetles, or sawflies. The adult female moths lay their eggs on or inside the leaves, usually in early to late spring. The emerging larvae feed between the leaf surfaces, producing blisters, blotches, or trails. The infested tissue turns whitish or light green to brown, so it stands out prominently against normal green foliage. The insects pupate inside the leaves or in the soil and emerge as adults. Some adults also feed on the leaves, chewing holes or notches in them.

SOLUTION: Control of leafminers is difficult because they spend most of their lives protected inside the leaves. Insecticides are usually aimed at the adults. Once leafminer larvae are noticed in the leaves, inspect the foliage periodically to determine when adults are emerging. Or ask the local cooperative extension office about the emergence period in your area. Spray adult leafminers with an insecticide containing acephate (ORTHENE®), carbaryl (SEVIN®), malathion, or diazinon. Make sure your plant is listed on the product label.

HOLES OR TRAILS IN LEAVES

Root weevil notches in rhododendron leaves.

PROBLEM: Holes or notches appear in leaves and flowers. Some of the leaves, stems, and flowers may be sheared off. Severely infested plants may be stripped of foliage. No insects are visible on the plants during the day. When the affected plants are inspected at night with a flashlight, insects may be seen feeding on the foliage and flowers.

ANALYSIS: Nocturnal insects
Several types of insect feed on plants only at night, including beetles, weevils, and caterpillars. Beetles are hard-bodied insects with tough, leathery wing covers. The wing covers meet in the middle of the back, forming a straight line. Weevils look like beetles with elongated snouts. Caterpillars are smooth or hairy soft-bodied worms. Nocturnal insects usually hide in the soil, debris, or other protected places during the day.

SOLUTION: Control these insects with an insecticide such as acephate (ORTH-ENE®). Follow the directions on the product label.

Snail damage to aucuba.

PROBLEM: Irregular holes with smooth edges are chewed in leaves. Leaves may be sheared off entirely. Silvery trails wind around the plants and soil nearby. Snails and slugs move around or feed on the leaves, especially at night; check for them by inspecting the garden at night by flashlight.

ANALYSIS: Snails and slugs
These pests are mollusks and are related to clams, oysters, and other shellfish. They feed on a wide variety of plants, including ornamentals and vegetables. Like other mollusks, snails and slugs need to be moist all the time. For this reason they avoid direct sun and dry places and hide during the day in damp places such as under flowerpots or in thick ground covers. They emerge at night or on rainy days to feed. Snails and slugs are similar, except that the snail has a hard shell, into which it withdraws when disturbed. In protected places female slugs lay masses of white eggs encased in slime. Female snails bury their eggs in the soil, also in a slimy mass. The young look like miniature versions of their parents.

SOLUTION: Apply a bait containing metaldehyde or methiocarb around the trees and shrubs you wish to protect. Also apply the bait in areas where snails or slugs might be hiding, such as in dense ground covers, weedy areas, compost piles, or pot storage areas. Before spreading the bait, wet down the area to be treated to encourage snail and slug activity that night. Repeat the application every 2 weeks as long as snails and slugs are active.

■ WILTING

Wilting philadelphus.

PROBLEM: The plant wilts often, and the soil is frequently or always dry. The leaves or leaf edges may turn brown and shrivel.

ANALYSIS: Lack of water
Water in the soil is taken up by the plant roots. It moves up into the stems and leaves and evaporates into the air through tiny breathing pores in the surfaces of the foliage. Water pressure within plant cells keeps the cell walls rigid and prevents the leaves and stems from collapsing. When the soil is dry, the roots are unable to furnish the leaves and stems with water, the water pressure in the cells drops, and the plant wilts. Most plants will recover if they have not wilted severely; however, frequent or severe wilting curbs plant growth and may eventually kill the plant.

SOLUTION: Water immediately. To prevent future wilting, follow the cultural instructions for your plant in the alphabetical section beginning on page 157.

Leaf drop due to borer infestation of dogwood.

Wilting rhododendron.

Wilting dogwood.

PROBLEM: All or part of a plant is wilting, and the leaves may turn yellow, brown, and then die. There are wounds or sunken lesions (cankers) on the plant or holes, surrounded by sap or sawdust, in the branches or trunk.

ANALYSIS: Damaged trunk or stem
Damage to the wood or bark disrupts water and nutrient movement through the plant, causing wilting.

1. *Wounds:* Any kind of mechanical injury that breaks roots, stems, or bark causes a plant to wilt. Plants may be accidentally wounded by motor vehicles, animals, or foot traffic; their roots may be damaged by cultivation, construction, or other soil disturbance. In severe cases, the plants die.

2. *Cankers:* Cankers are sunken, dark-colored lesions that develop as a result of infection by fungi or bacteria. Cankers on small or young plants often cause the portion of the plant above the canker to wilt. Branches or the entire plant may eventually die.

3. *Borers:* Most borers are the larvae of beetles or moths. Many kinds of borers infest stems, branches, or trunks. The larvae feed by tunneling through the bark, sapwood, and heartwood, stopping the flow of nutrients and water in that area. Large trees and shrubs usually turn yellow and brown rather than wilt.

SOLUTION: Take these measures to correct the condition or control the problem.

1. Thin out some of the branches and keep the plant well watered. During hot weather provide shade to reduce evaporation from the leaves. Prevent mechanical injuries to plants by being careful when working around the roots and stems. If necessary, place barriers around plants to prevent damage from vehicles, animals, and foot traffic.

2. Prune dying branches below the canker. Avoid wounding plants. For more information about cankers and their control, see page 147.

3. Prune out stems containing borers. Keep the plant well watered and apply fertilizer if needed. For more information about borers and their control, see page 147.

PROBLEM: The plant is wilting, but the foliage usually looks healthy. There are no signs of insects or disease, and the soil is moist. Wilting is most common on shrubs or plants with limited root systems.

ANALYSIS: Extreme heat or wind
During hot, windy periods small or young plants may wilt, even though the soil is wet. Wind and heat cause water to evaporate quickly from the leaves. If the roots can't absorb and convey water fast enough to replenish this loss, the leaves wilt. For information about scorched leaves due to extreme heat and wind, see page 152.

SOLUTION: Keep the plant well watered during hot spells, and sprinkle it with water to cool off the foliage. The plant will usually recover when the temperature drops or the wind dies down. Provide shade during hot weather; supply temporary windbreaks for protection from wind. Plant shrubs adapted to the area.

TREES, SHRUBS, AND VINES

Arborvitae planted too shallow.

Dry rootball.

Leaf drop on linden due to transplant shock.

PROBLEM: A recently planted tree or shrub wilts frequently. Roots or the rootball may be exposed.

ANALYSIS: Planted too shallow

Newly planted trees and shrubs may wilt frequently if they are planted too shallow. Plants that have been set in the ground at a higher level than they were originally growing wilt because the exposed soil ball dries out quickly. This may kill the surface roots, especially if the soil washes away and exposes them.

SOLUTION: Replant the soil ball deeper. Whether currently growing in a pot or in the ground, the plant should be set at the same level as it was before being transplanted. Be careful not to plant too deep, since this can create an equally serious problem that may not show up for a few years. Water the plant thoroughly so the entire soil ball is moistened. Keep the plant well watered until it becomes established. In poor-drainage areas, plants may be set slightly high with a small amount of soil covering the rootball, as long as the soil is covered by a generous portion of mulch. If you plant with the burlap bag still around the rootball, be sure to trim off any burlap showing above the ground, or it will act as a wick and pull moisture away from the roots.

PROBLEM: The entire plant is wilting. The soil surrounding the plant is moist, but the rootball is dry.

ANALYSIS: Dry rootball

Nursery plants that are sold balled and burlapped are grown in fields. When the plants reach a size suitable for selling, they are dug up with a ball of soil around their roots. If the soil is extremely heavy, it sometimes shrinks as it dries and becomes impermeable to water. After planting, water runs off the outside of the ball causing the roots to dry out. If the soil in which these plants are set is much lighter or heavier than the soil in the rootball, the water may run into the lighter soil instead of moistening the soil around the roots; or the surrounding heavy clay soil may draw the water from the light soil in the rootball, causing the rootball to dry out.

SOLUTION: To wet a planted rootball, create a basin by building up a dirt wall around the plant the diameter of the rootball. Fill it with water. Add a wetting agent, which can be purchased at a local nursery. Keep the basin filled for 3 hours. For 6 weeks water whenever the rootball (not the surrounding soil) is moist but not wet 1 inch below the surface. Before planting examine the soil around the rootball. If the soil texture in the rootball is significantly different from that of the surrounding soil, provide a transition zone, using a mix of rootball and native soil. After positioning the rootball in the soil, provide a 3-hour basin watering. As described, provide basin waterings for 6 weeks. Covering the soil with a generous portion of mulch will also help conserve moisture. If you plant with the burlap bag around the rootball, trim off any burlap showing above the ground, or it will pull moisture away from the roots.

PROBLEM: The plant is wilting, but the foliage usually looks healthy. There are no signs of insects or disease, and the soil is moist. The plant was recently transplanted.

ANALYSIS: Transplant shock

Frequently, plants wilt or stop growing for a while after being transplanted. Transplant shock is not related to shock in humans; it is the result of roots being cut or injured during transplanting. Wilting occurs when the roots are unable to supply the plant with enough water, even when the soil is wet.

SOLUTION: To reduce the water requirement of the plant, prune off one fourth to one third of the branches. Water the plant well until it becomes established. If necessary, provide shade during hot weather. If possible in the future, transplant trees and shrubs when they are dormant and when the weather is cool—in early morning, late afternoon, or on a cloudy day.

144

FLUID ON BARK OR LEAVES

Slime flux on poplar.

Oozing sap on cherry.

Oozing sap on Coulter pine.

PROBLEM: Sour-smelling sap oozes from wounds, cracks, and branch crotches, mainly during the growing season. The sap drips down the bark and dries, causing unsightly gray streaks. Leaves on affected branches may wilt. Insects are attracted to the sour-smelling ooze.

ANALYSIS: Slime flux
Slime flux, also called wetwood, is a plant disease caused by a bacterium (*Erwinia nimipressuralis*). The bacteria infect the heartwood and ferment the sap, producing abnormally high sap pressure. This pressure forces the fermented sap, or flux, out of wounds, cracks, or crotches in the tree. Flux is especially copious when the tree is growing rapidly. Large areas of the bark may be coated with the smelly, bacteria-laden sap, which dries to a grayish white. Also, wounds do not heal and the bark is unsightly. A tree with this problem is often stressed by drought, which may cause wilting and scorched leaves. The problem may persist for years.

SOLUTION: There are no chemical controls for this condition. Bore a slightly upward-slanting drainage hole into the wet wood below each oozing wound. Insert a ½-inch-diameter plastic tube just until it stays firmly in place. Do not insert so far that the tube becomes plugged with wood; this will interfere with drainage rather than assisting it. The tube should carry the dripping sap away from the trunk. Disinfect tools with rubbing alcohol after pruning infected trees.

PROBLEM: Beads of amber-colored or whitish, sticky sap appear on healthy bark. Sap may ooze from patches of bark, cankers, wounds, or pruning cuts.

ANALYSIS: Oozing sap
To some degree oozing sap, also called gummosis, occurs in all trees and shrubs. It is caused by one or a combination of factors.

1. *Natural tendency:* Certain plant species have a tendency to ooze sap. Frequently, small beads of sap form on the healthy bark of these plants.

2. *Environmental stress:* Plants that are stressed because they are growing in wet soil may produce large quantities of sap, even though they are not diseased. Also, many plants respond to changes in weather conditions or soil moisture by oozing profusely.

3. *Mechanical injury:* Almost all plants ooze sap when the bark is wounded. This is especially noticeable on maple and birch. If these trees are injured during the fall, they will ooze a large amount of sap the following spring.

4. *Disease:* Plants respond to certain fungal and bacterial infections by forming cankers, dark, sunken areas that gum profusely. Gummosis is one of the initial signs of infection.

5. *Borer damage:* Many different insects bore holes into bark. Sap oozes from these holes. The tunnels insects bore often become infected by decay organisms.

SOLUTION: Take these measures to correct the condition or control the problem.

1. As long as the bark appears healthy, there is nothing to worry about.

2. If your plant is growing in wet, poorly drained soil, allow the soil to dry out between waterings. Make sure water can drain away from trunks and roots. If oozing sap occurs as a result of rapid changes in weather and soil moisture, reduce the effects of stress on the plant by keeping it healthy. Maintain plant health and vigor by watering regularly and applying fertilizer when needed.

3. Avoid mechanical injuries to the plant. Stake, tie, and prune plants properly.

4. Remove badly infected branches and cut out cankers. Keep the plant vigorous by watering regularly and applying fertilizer when needed.

5. Borers are difficult to control once they have burrowed into the wood. For more information about borers and their control, see page 147.

Honeydew on maple.

Rodent damage to crab apple.

Porcupine damage to elm.

PROBLEM: A shiny or sticky substance coats leaves and, sometimes, twigs. Insects may be found on the leaves directly above coated foliage, and ants, flies, or bees may be present. In many cases, a black sooty mold often grows on the sticky substance.

ANALYSIS: Honeydew
Honeydew is a sweet, sticky substance secreted by aphids, mealybugs, psyllids, whiteflies, and certain scales. These sucking insects cannot fully digest all the sugar in the plant sap, so they excrete the excess in a fluid called honeydew, which drops onto the leaves below or onto anything beneath the tree or shrub. Lawn furniture or cars under infested plants may be stained. Ants and certain flies and bees feed on honeydew, and they may be found around the plant. Often, a sooty mold develops on the sticky substance, causing the leaves and twigs to appear black and dirty. The mold does not infect the leaf; it grows superficially on the honeydew. Extremely heavy mold may prevent light from reaching the leaf, reducing food production.

SOLUTION: Honeydew can be wiped off the leaves with a wet rag or hosed off, or it will eventually be washed off by rain. Prevent honeydew by controlling the insects that produce it. Inspect the leaves and twigs above the honeydew to find what type of insect is present.

PROBLEM: Bark has been chewed or gnawed from the trunk and lower branches. In some cases, the trunk is entirely girdled. The tracks of deer, rabbits, mice, or squirrels may be evident, or the animals may be seen. Damage is usually most severe during the winter, when other food sources are scarce.

ANALYSIS: Bark-feeding animals
Several animals chew on tree bark.
1. *Deer:* These animals feed on leaves, shoots, buds, and bark. They feed by pulling and twisting the bark or twig tissue, leaving ragged or twisted twig ends or patches of bark. Generally deer feed on the lower branches and trunk. The males may cause damage by rubbing their antlers on the trunk and branches.
2. *Rabbits:* These animals chew on the bark at the base of the trunk. They chew bark and twigs off cleanly, leaving a sharp break. The damaged trunk is often scarred with paired gouges left by the rabbit's front teeth. Rabbits generally feed no more than 2 feet above the ground or snow level. They damage small or young plants most severely.
3. *Field mice or voles:* These animals damage trees by chewing off the bark at the bases of the trunks, just at or slightly above or below ground or snow level. They may girdle the trunk, often killing the plant. Mice leave tiny scratches in the exposed wood. Some mouse species feed on plant roots, causing the slow decline and death of the plant.
4. *Squirrels:* These animals damage trees and shrubs by wounding the bark. Red squirrels feed on maple sap in the spring. The resulting bark wounds are V-shaped. Canker disease fungi sometimes invade the wounds, weakening or killing the tree. Some squirrels feed on bark when food is scarce in the winter. Other species of squirrel use bark and twigs for building nests.

SOLUTION: Various methods may be used to exclude or control deer, rabbits, mice or voles, and squirrels in the garden. These methods usually involve protecting the plants with fencing and tree guards or controlling the animals by using traps. In some states trapping or killing these animals is illegal; consult the local Department of Fish and Game to determine regulations in your area.

Sapsucker holes.

Borer emergence holes.

Canker on ceanothus.

PROBLEM: Rows of parallel holes, ¼ inch in diameter, appear on a trunk. Sap often oozes from the holes, and portions of the surrounding bark may fall off. When damage is severe, part or all of the tree is killed. Yellow-bellied or red-breasted sapsuckers may be seen pecking on the tree.

ANALYSIS: Sapsuckers
Two different species of sapsuckers, members of the woodpecker family, feed on tree bark and sap. The red-breasted sapsucker is found in the Pacific Northwest. The yellow-bellied sapsucker is common throughout much of the United States. Sapsuckers peck into many trees before finding a suitable one that has sap with a high sugar content. Once the birds find a favorite tree, they visit it many times a day and feed on it year after year. Portions of the bark often fall off after sapsuckers have pecked many holes. If the trunk is girdled, the tree above the damaged area dies. Sometimes disease organisms enter the holes and damage or kill the tree.

SOLUTION: It is difficult to prevent sapsucker damage to trees. Wrapping the damaged trunk with burlap or smearing a sticky material, such as the latex used for ant control, above and below the holes may inhibit new pecking damage.

PROBLEM: Foliage on a branch or at the top of the tree is sparse; eventually the twigs and branches die. Holes are in the trunk or branches. Sap or sawdust usually surrounds the holes. In some areas, bark may die and slough off, revealing tunnels. Or there may be knotlike swellings on the trunk and limbs. Weak, young, or newly transplanted trees may be killed. Weakened branches break during wind- or snowstorms.

ANALYSIS: Borers
Borers are the larvae of beetles or moths. Many kinds of borer attack trees and shrubs. Females lay their eggs in bark crevices throughout the summer. The larvae feed by tunneling through the bark, sapwood, and heartwood. This stops the flow of nutrients and water in an area by damaging the conducting vessels; branch and twig dieback result. Sap flow acts as a defense against borers if the plant is healthy. When the insect burrows into the wood, tree sap fills the hole and drowns the insect. A tree weakened by mechanical injuries, transplanting, damage by leaf-feeding insects, and poor growing conditions is especially attractive to egg-laying females.

SOLUTION: Cut out and destroy all dead and dying branches. Remove severely infested young plants. Spray or paint the trunks and branches of remaining trees with an insecticide containing lindane. Contact the local cooperative extension office to learn the best time to spray in your area. Repeat the treatment 3 more times at intervals of 2 weeks. Maintain plant health and vigor by watering and applying fertilizer regularly.

PROBLEM: Sunken, oval, or elongated dark lesions (cankers) develop on the trunk or branches. The bark at the edge of the canker may thicken and roll inward. In some cases, sticky, amber-colored sap oozes from the canker. Foliage on infected plants may be stunted and yellowing; some of the leaves may turn brown and drop off. Twigs and branches may gradually die, and the plant may eventually be killed.

ANALYSIS: Canker
Many different species of fungi and bacteria cause canker. Infection usually occurs through injured or wounded tissue. Bark that has been damaged by sunscald, cold, pruning wounds, or mechanical injury is especially susceptible. Some decay organisms infect the leaves first, then spread down into healthy twigs. Cankers form as the decay progresses. Some plants produce a sticky sap that oozes from the cankers. The sap may clog the water- and nutrient-conducting vessels, and the portion of the branch or stem above the canker may die as a result. Cankers that form on the trunk are the most serious; they may kill the tree. The plant may halt a canker by producing callus tissue, a growth of barklike cells, to wall off the decay.

SOLUTION: Remove badly infected branches and cut out cankers. Avoid wounding the plant. Keep the plant vigorous by watering and applying fertilizer as needed.

TREES, SHRUBS, AND VINES

Bark shedding on madrone.

Sunscald.

Sunscald on dogwood.

PROBLEM: Bark is cracking or peeling, usually on the older branches and trunk.

ANALYSIS: Bark shedding

The shedding or cracking of bark is often noticeable and may be of concern to people not familiar with this natural process. The bark of young trees is live tissue, usually smooth and relatively soft. As the trees mature, the bark dies and hardens, sometimes becoming rough. Trunks and branches increase in diameter with age. The increase in girth causes the outer bark of many plants to crack in a variety of patterns. With some tree species, such as white birch, cracking develops to such an extent that the bark peels and falls off. Newly exposed bark is often smooth and lighter in color than the bark that was shed. Some trees, such as sycamore and shagbark hickory, characteristically have loose outer bark. The bark is constantly in the process of peeling and shedding.

SOLUTION: This process is normal. No controls are necessary.

PROBLEM: Patches of bark die, crack, and later develop into cankers. The dead bark eventually sloughs off, exposing undamaged wood. The affected bark area is always on the southwest side of the tree. Trees with dark bark may be more severely affected. The cracks and cankers develop in either summer or winter.

ANALYSIS: Sunscald

When a tree growing in a deeply shaded location is suddenly exposed to intense sunlight or when a tree is heavily pruned, the southwest side of newly exposed bark is injured by the rapid change in temperature that results. This may develop when a forested area is excessively thinned or when a tree is moved from a shaded nursery to an open area, such as a lawn.

1. *Summer sunscald:* With intense summer heat, exposed bark is killed and a canker develops, usually revealing the undamaged wood beneath the bark. Within several seasons, the tree may break at the cankered area and topple. Summer sunscald is most severe when the soil is dry.

2. *Winter sunscald:* Bark injury develops with rapid changes in bark temperature between cold nights and sunny winter days. Exposed bark, usually on the southwest side of the tree, becomes much warmer than the air during the day but cools rapidly after sunset. This rapid temperature change often results in bark cracking and, later, cankering. Trees with thin, dark bark are most severely affected.

SOLUTION: Once the bark is injured, there is nothing you can do. Wrap the trunks of recently exposed or newly transplanted trees with tree-wrap paper, available in nurseries. Coating trunks with white interior latex paint or whitewash is also effective. Leave the wrap or paint in place for at least 2 winters; remove the wrap for the spring and summer months to prevent it from harboring plant diseases and insects. Reapply the paint the second season if it has washed off. Trees will eventually adapt to increased exposure by producing thicker bark. Give trees, especially recently transplanted trees, adequate water in the summer and, if necessary, in the fall. Water transplants when the top 2 inches of the rootball are dry.

■ **TWIGS OR BRANCHES BREAK**

Lightning-damaged tree.

Frost cracks.

Twig girdler (2 times life size).

PROBLEM: Part or all of the tree suddenly turns brown and dies. There may be no external signs of damage, or a strip of bark may be burned or stripped from the entire length of the trunk. In less severe cases, trees survive for several years or recover completely. Sometimes tops of trees or branches explode, leaving a jagged stub. There has been a lightning storm recently.

ANALYSIS: Lightning damage
Tall trees, trees growing in open locations, and trees growing in moist soil or along riverbanks are susceptible to damage by lightning. Lightning damage is variable. Without any external sign that lightning has struck, some trees die suddenly from internal damage or burned roots. Other trees burst into flames or explode when struck. Sometimes only a strip of bark is burned or stripped from the trunk, and the tree recovers. Some scientists believe that trees high in starch, deep-rooted species, and decaying trees are more susceptible to damage than trees high in oils, shallow-rooted species, or healthy trees.

SOLUTION: Remove all loose and injured bark. To reduce or prevent damage, water trees during dry spells. Remove severely damaged trees. Valuable old trees can be protected with lightning conductors; consult a professional arborist about installation.

PROBLEM: Longitudinal cracks develop on a trunk, usually on the south and southeast but sometimes on the west side. The cracks generally close during the growing season.

ANALYSIS: Frost cracks
Frost cracks develop from the expansion and shrinkage of bark and wood during periods of wide temperature fluctuations. This causes internal mechanical stress, which causes already weakened or decayed areas of the bark and outer wood to split open. The sudden break is often accompanied by a loud noise. Cracks usually heal during the growing season, but they may remain partially open after the weather warms or reopen during the next winter.

SOLUTION: If a large crack fails to heal, a rod or bolt may be installed to hold it together; consult a professional arborist. Plant trees adapted to the climate. Protect young trees with tree-wrap paper in late fall or by whitewashing the trunk.

The following trees are most susceptible to frost cracks.

Botanical Name	Common Name
Acer	Maple
Aesculus	Horsechestnut
Liriodendron tulipifera	Tuliptree
Malus	Crab apple
Platanus × acerifolia	London plane tree
Prunus	Flowering peach and cherry
Quercus	Oak
Salix	Willow
Tilia	Linden
Ulmus	Elm

PROBLEM: Small, cleanly cut twigs, ¼ to 2 inches in diameter, lie under the tree in the fall. The tree is often abnormally bushy. Small (up to 1 inch), whitish larvae may be found inside the fallen twigs.

ANALYSIS: Twig pruners and twig girdlers
Several species of wood-boring beetles cause unsightly damage to trees by altering their natural form. In midsummer to fall, female wood-boring beetles lay their eggs in the wood of small twigs. The twig pruner larvae tunnel toward the base of the twigs, eating all but the outer bark. In the fall, they back into the hollowed-out twigs. High winds cause the nearly severed twigs containing the larvae to break and drop to the ground. Adult female twig girdlers lay eggs in twigs, then chew a circle around the outside of the twigs. The girdled twigs die and break off. The eggs in the fallen twig are able to develop without being hindered by the flow of sap through the twig. Both twig pruner and twig girdler larvae mature in the twigs on the ground. The damage to the tree is the result of the insects' excessive pruning of the branch tips. Several new side shoots develop where the twigs break off, causing abnormal bushiness and an unnatural shape.

SOLUTION: After the first leaves are fully expanded in spring, spray with an insecticide containing lindane. Respray 30 days later. Gather and destroy all severed twigs in the late fall, when the insects are inside them.

Limb breakage caused by weak fork.

Limb breakage caused by snow load.

Heart rot.

PROBLEM: Healthy branches break and fall, usually during storms or high winds. Some may drop in the middle of the day during a hot spell.

ANALYSIS: Limb breakage

Several different environmental factors cause limb breakage.

1. *Weak fork:* The angle between a branch and the trunk, called a fork, is normally greater than 45 degrees in most species. If the angle is much smaller than this, bark is sometimes trapped between the branch and the trunk, preventing the wood from growing together at that point. This weakens the branch. As the branch and trunk increase in length, the additional weight causes the fork to split at the weak junction. A large portion of the tree may fall. Some trees that develop weak forks break more readily than others because of their growth habits and brittle wood.

2. *Wind:* Branches may fall during high winds, especially in areas where there are tornadoes, hurricanes, and the like. Moderate winds often hasten the dropping of limbs weakened by injury, insects, or plant disease.

3. *Sudden limb drop:* Large limbs sometimes drop during the middle of the day for no apparent reason. This usually occurs on hot, calm days. The cause is not known.

4. *Snow and ice:* Plants heavily coated with snow or ice may lose large limbs because of the additional weight. Evergreen trees and deciduous trees with leaves still attached are most susceptible because of the greater surface to which the snow or ice can adhere.

SOLUTION: If the break is a split or if a third of the bark at the break is intact, the fracture can be bolted back together. If less than a third of the bark is intact or if the branch has fallen off the tree, prune off the remaining branch stub. To prevent further damage, brace or cable trees. Knock off snow and ice continually to prevent buildup. In areas with high winds, prune back some of the branches to reduce the wind load. In the future, do not plant trees with brittle wood that breaks easily.

PROBLEM: Branches break and fall, usually during storms. The wood in the area of breakage is discolored and often spongy. Soft or woody mushroom-like growths may be found on the wood.

ANALYSIS: Heart rot

Heart rot is caused mainly by fungi. Decay organisms rot dead wood (such as fallen trees) as part of nature's recycling process. A number may also invade live trees through wounds. Healthy, vigorous trees may stop the spread of decay by producing cells that wall off the invaded area. Old trees with many wounds often have little resistance to microorganisms, however, and decay spreads through the wood. The decay does not usually kill the living tissue of the tree, so branches and leaves remain alive. But internal decay reduces the strength of affected limbs. During a storm, weakened branches fall. Some of the decay organisms develop yellowish to brown, mushroomlike growths, called conks, on the outside wood in areas where decay is present. For more information about mushrooms and conks, see page 139.

SOLUTION: Cut off the remaining branch stub flush against the larger branch or tree trunk. Inspect the rest of the tree to determine the extent of decay; consult a professional arborist if necessary. Branches or the entire plant should be removed if decay is extensive. As much as possible, avoid wounding plants. Keep them vigorous by watering regularly and applying fertilizer as needed.

INVADING ROOTS

Roots cracking pavement.

Surface roots in a lawn.

PROBLEM: Roots are exposed on the surface of the soil or are making bumps by growing just beneath it. The roots may be cracking and raising pavement. Exposed roots may be lumpy and galled.

ANALYSIS: Surface roots
Several factors can cause roots near the surface to expand.

1. *Surface roots in lawns:* If plants receive only light irrigations on the soil surface, roots in the upper zone will expand, pushing above the surface. Plants growing in lawns that receive light irrigations often have shallow roots.

2. *Waterlogged soil:* Roots need oxygen to grow and develop. Waterlogged soil offers little oxygen for root growth, because the soil pores are filled with water. The only available oxygen is near the soil surface, so the surface roots develop most.

3. *Natural tendency:* Some plant species are more likely than others to develop surface roots.

4. *Compacted soil:* Trees and shrubs growing in compacted soil develop surface roots.

5. *Confined roots:* Plants growing in areas with limited root space, such as in containers, often have roots on the soil surface.

6. *Planting strips:* Trees growing in planting strips adjacent to lawns frequently crack the sidewalks that separate them from the lawns. All the available water and food is beyond the walk, in the lawns. The roots that extend into the lawn expand rapidly, cracking the walk.

SOLUTION: Take these measures to correct the condition or control the problem.

1. In addition to lawn watering, every 2 weeks water trees to a depth of 3 to 4 feet. Cover the roots with soil topdressing, slowly raising the level of the lawn 1 inch per year.

2. If the soil is waterlogged from overwatering, cut back on watering. If necessary, improve drainage around the plant. Cover exposed roots with 2 to 4 inches of soil. Before planting new trees and shrubs, make sure drainage is adequate.

3. Consult a plant book for a list of plants likely to develop surface roots.

4. Loosen compacted soil with a crowbar. Before planting in compacted earth, loosen the soil.

5. Plant shrubs or small trees that are adapted to growing in confined root areas.

6. Sever small roots that are pushing up pavement. If possible, avoid cutting large roots. In the future, plant large trees on the lawn side of the sidewalk, and use shrubs in planting strips.

DISCOLORED LEAVES

Salt burn on mock orange.

PROBLEM: Edges of older leaves turn brown or black, then die. The rest of the leaf may be a lighter green than normal. The browning or blackening develops in dry or wet soil, but it is more severe in dry soil. In the worst cases, leaves drop from the plant.

ANALYSIS: Salt burn
This problem is common in areas of low rainfall. It also occurs in soils with poor drainage, in areas where salt has been used to melt snow and ice, and where too much fertilizer has been applied. Excess salts dissolved in soil water accumulate in the leaf edges, where they kill the tissue. These salts also interfere with water uptake by the plant. This problem is rare in areas of high rainfall, where the soluble salts are leached from most soils. Poorly drained soils accumulate salts because they do not leach well; much of the applied water runs off instead of washing through. Fertilizers, most of which are soluble salts, also cause salt burn if too much is applied or if they are not diluted with a thorough watering after application.

SOLUTION: In areas with low rainfall, leach accumulated salts from the soil with an occasional heavy watering (about once a month). If possible, improve the drainage around the plants. If plants are severely damaged, replace them with healthy plants. Follow label directions when using fertilizers; several light applications are better than one heavy application. Water thoroughly afterward. Avoid the use of bagged steer manure, which may contain large amounts of salts.

PROBLEMS COMMON TO MANY TREES, SHRUBS, AND VINES — DISCOLORED LEAVES

Leaf scorch on maple.

Leaf scorch on birch.

Cedar-apple rust on hawthorn.

PROBLEM: Leaf edges and the tissues between the veins turn tan or brown. Leaves are scorched and have a dry appearance. Brown areas often increase in size until little green is left except around the center vein. Dead leaves may remain attached to the plant, or they may drop. Leaf scorch is most severe in the upper branches and when the soil is dry.

ANALYSIS: Leaf scorch
This condition is caused by a lack of water resulting from any of several factors.

1. *Extreme heat and wind:* Leaf scorch is caused by excessive evaporation of moisture from the leaves. In hot or windy weather, water evaporates rapidly from the foliage. If the roots can't absorb and convey water fast enough to replenish this loss, the leaves turn brown and wither. This usually occurs in dry soil, but leaves can also scorch when the soil is moist and temperatures are near 100° F for extended periods. Young plants with limited root systems are most susceptible.

2. *Winter burn:* Winter burn is similar to scorch from intense heat or wind except that it occurs during warm, windy days in late winter. In cold climates, water cannot be replaced by the roots because the soil is frozen; the result is leaf desiccation. Conifers are most susceptible, especially those planted in exposed areas. The symptoms may not appear until spring.

3. *Damaged roots:* After roots have been injured, trees and shrubs may develop scorched and yellow leaves, early fall color, and dieback.

4. *Underwatering:* Many plants that are regularly underwatered survive. They do not function normally, however, and the leaves frequently burn and wilt over the entire plant.

SOLUTION: Take these measures to correct the condition or control the problem.

1. To prevent further scorch, water plants deeply during periods of hot weather; wet down the entire root space. Because of their limited root systems, recently transplanted trees and shrubs need more frequent irrigation than established plants. Water transplants when the rootball is dry 2 inches below the surface. If the leaves scorched when the soil was moist, provide shade during periods of hot weather and add screens for protection from wind. Or move the plants to a protected area.

2. Provide windbreaks and shelter for plants growing in cold, windy regions. Covering smaller plants with burlap helps prevent leaf drying. If necessary, water in late fall or winter to ensure adequate soil moisture. Mulch plants after they are dormant to reduce the depth of frost penetration into the soil.

3. For more information about damaged roots, see pages 155 and 156.

4. Do not let the soil dry out to the point where leaves scorch. Learn the needs of your plant.

PROBLEM: Leaves are discolored or mottled yellow to brown. Yellow, orange, red, or blackish powdery pustules appear on the leaves. The powdery material can be scraped off. Leaves may become twisted, distorted, and dry, and then drop off. Twigs may also be infected. Plants are often stunted.

ANALYSIS: Leaf rusts
Many different species of leaf-rust fungi infect trees and shrubs. Some rusts require two different plant species to complete their life cycles. Part of the life cycle is spent on the tree or shrub and part is spent on various weeds, flowers, or other woody trees or shrubs. Rust fungi survive the winter as spores on or in living plant tissue or in plant debris. The spores are spread to healthy plants by wind and splashing water. When leaves are moist from rain, dew, or fog and temperatures range from 54° to 74° F, the spores germinate and infect the tissue. Leaf discoloration and mottling develop as the fungi sap the plant nutrients. Some rust fungi produce spores in spots or patches; others develop into hornlike structures.

SOLUTION: Several fungicides—including those containing triforine, chlorothalonil, ferbam, maneb, zineb, and cycloheximide—may be used to control rust. Look up your plant in the alphabetical section beginning on page 157 to determine which fungicide is appropriate. Some rust fungi are fairly harmless to the plant and do not require control measures. Where practical, remove and destroy infected leaves as they appear. Rake up and destroy leaves in the fall.

Leafhopper damage to dogwood.

Spider mite damage to holly.

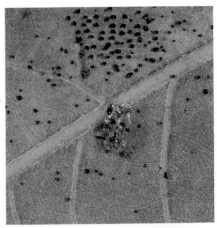
Lacebug and droppings (4 times life size).

PROBLEM: Leaves are stippled white, yellow, or light green, and leaves and stems may be distorted. Sometimes the plant has a burned appearance. Infested leaves may drop prematurely. When infestations are severe, twigs and small branches may die. Whitish or green wedge-shaped insects, up to ½ inch long, hop and fly away quickly when the plant is touched.

ANALYSIS: Leafhoppers

Many species of leafhopper infest ornamental trees and shrubs. Some leafhoppers cause only minor damage to the leaves; other species severely retard plant growth. Leafhoppers usually spend the winter as eggs in bark slits made by the females, although some may overwinter in the southern United States and migrate north in the spring. Injury to the bark from egg laying may kill twigs. When the weather warms in the spring, the young leafhoppers emerge and settle on the undersides of leaves, where they suck out plant sap, causing stippling and distortion. Severely infested leaves often drop in midsummer. Some leafhoppers cause a condition known as hopperburn, in which insect feeding causes distortion and gives leaves a burned appearance. There may be several generations of leafhoppers each year.

SOLUTION: When damage is first noticed, spray with an insecticide containing acephate (ORTHENE®) or diazinon. Cover the undersides of the leaves thoroughly.

PROBLEM: Leaves are stippled yellow, white, or bronze-colored and dirty. Sometimes there is a silken webbing on the leaves or stems. New growth may be distorted, and the plant may be weak and stunted. To determine if the plant is infested with spider mites, hold a sheet of white paper underneath an affected leaf or branch and tap it sharply. If mites are present, green, red, or yellow specks the size of pepper grains will drop to the paper and begin to crawl around.

ANALYSIS: Spider mites

Spider mites, related to spiders, are major pests of many plants. They cause damage by sucking sap from the leaves and buds. As a result of feeding, the green leaf pigment (chlorophyll) disappears, producing the stippled appearance. While they feed, many mites produce a fine cobwebbing over the foliage; the cobwebs collect dust and dirt. Some mites are active throughout the growing season and are especially favored by dry weather with temperatures above 70° F. Other mites, especially those infesting conifers, are most prolific in cooler weather. Cool-weather mites are most active in the spring and sometimes fall and during warm periods in winter in mild climates. At the onset of hot weather, these mites have usually caused their maximum damage.

SOLUTION: When damage is first noticed, spray with a miticide containing hexakis. Respray 2 more times at intervals of 7 to 10 days. Make sure your plant is listed on the product label.

PROBLEM: The topsides of leaves are mottled or speckled yellow, gray, or white and green. The mottling is distinguished from other insect damage—such as that caused by mites or leafhoppers—by the shiny, hard, black droplets on the undersides of damaged leaves. Small (⅛-inch), light or dark, spiny, wingless insects may be visible around the droplets; or the insects may be brown and have lacy wings. The plant is usually stunted. Damage occurs in spring and summer.

ANALYSIS: Lacebugs

Many species of lacebug feed on trees and shrubs. Each species usually infests only one type of plant. Some lacebug species spend the winter as adults in protected areas on the plant; others overwinter as eggs in leaf veins or cemented in the black droplets on the undersides of leaves. Both the spiny, wingless, immature insects and the lacewing adults suck sap from the undersides of the leaves. The green leaf pigment (chlorophyll) disappears, resulting in the characteristic speckling or mottling. As the lacebugs feed, droplets of brown excrement accumulate around them. Damage is unsightly and food production by the leaf is reduced, resulting in loss of plant vigor.

SOLUTION: When damage first appears in the spring, spray with an insecticide containing acephate (ORTHENE®). Cover the undersides of the leaves thoroughly. Respray 7 to 10 days later. A third application may be necessary if the plant becomes reinfested in midsummer.

PROBLEMS COMMON TO MANY TREES, SHRUBS, AND VINES — DISCOLORED LEAVES

Greenhouse thrips damage to coffee.

Overwatering damage to viburnums.

Nitrogen-deficient fuchsia.

PROBLEM: Young leaves may be severely curled and distorted. Parts of leaves may die and turn black, or entire leaves may drop from the plant. Instead, foliage may be flecked and bleached or silvery, often becoming papery and wilted. In some cases, shiny black spots cover the surfaces. Either buds fail to open properly or flowers are brown and distorted. Minute (1/25-inch), white or yellow, spindle-shaped insects and black or brown winged insects are barely visible inside the distorted leaves and flowers or on the undersides of the leaves. Heavily infested plants may be stunted.

ANALYSIS: Thrips
Thrips are common pests of many garden and greenhouse plants. Some species cause leaf or flower distortion; others cause flecked leaves, producing a bleached appearance. Thrips feed by rasping the soft plant tissue, then sucking the released plant sap. Some leaf thrips leave unsightly, black, varnishlike spots of excrement around the areas where they feed. The black or brown adults have wings. They can spread rapidly by flying to new plants, or they may be blown long distances by the wind. Females lay their eggs either on the plant or in surrounding weeds. The young are yellow or white and spindle-shaped.

SOLUTION: Spray the leaves or buds and flowers with an insecticide containing acephate (ORTHENE®) or malathion; follow label directions. Make sure your plant is listed on the product label. Remove and destroy infested buds and flowers.

PROBLEM: Leaves turn light green to yellow and may drop. The edges of the leaves may be brown. In many cases, the plant grows only a little. It may pull out of the ground easily because the roots are soft and rotted. The soil is frequently or constantly wet.

ANALYSIS: Overwatering or poor drainage
Overwatering and poor drainage are serious common problems that often kill plants. Roots require air to function. Air is contained in tiny pores in the soil. When the soil is watered, air is forced out of the soil pores and replaced with water. If the water cannot drain or if water is constantly reapplied, the soil pores remain filled with water. The roots cannot absorb the oxygen they need, and they die. As the roots rot, the root system is less able to supply the plant with nutrients and water, resulting in starvation and the eventual death of the plant.

SOLUTION: Do not apply water so frequently that the soil is constantly wet. Depending on the particular requirements of the tree or shrub, allow the soil to dry partially or completely between waterings. Look up your plant in the alphabetical section beginning on page 157 to determine the watering schedule. If the soil drains poorly, improve drainage.

PROBLEM: Beginning with the older foliage, leaves turn yellow and may drop. New leaves are small, and growth is slow.

ANALYSIS: Lack of nitrogen
Nitrogen, one of the most important nutrients for plant growth, is deficient in most soils. This nutrient is essential in the formation of green leaf pigment (chlorophyll) and in many other compounds necessary for plant growth. When plants are short on nitrogen, they take it from their older leaves for new growth. Plants grown in poorly drained, overwatered, compacted, and cold soils often show symptoms of nitrogen deficiency. Various soil problems and other nutrient deficiencies also cause leaf discoloration; study the symptoms carefully.

SOLUTION: For a quick response, spray the leaves and the soil beneath the plant with a liquid nutrient rated 23-19-17. Regularly apply a general-purpose plant food rated 10-10-10 or a fertilizer for a specific type of plant, such as rose food or azalea and rhododendron food. Blood meal containing nitrogen in a long-lasting, slow-release form can be used to supplement regular feeding. Add organic amendments to compacted soils and those low in organic matter, and improve drainage in poorly drained soils. Do not keep the soil constantly wet.

■ **WEAK OR DYING PLANT**

Iron-deficient azalea.

Lawn-mower blight on oak.

Root nematode damage.

PROBLEM: Leaves turn pale green or yellow. The newest leaves (those at the tips of the stems) are most severely affected. Except in extreme cases, the veins of affected leaves remain green. Older leaves may remain green. The plant may be stunted.

ANALYSIS: Iron deficiency

Plants frequently suffer from deficiencies of iron and other trace nutrients, such as manganese and zinc, that are essential to normal plant growth and development. Deficiencies can occur when one or more of these elements are lacking in the soil. Often these nutrients are present, but alkaline (pH 7.5 or higher) or wet soil conditions cause them to form compounds that cannot be used by plants. An alkaline condition can result from overliming or from lime leached from cement or brick. Alkaline soil usually exists in regions where soil is derived from limestone and in those with low rainfall.

SOLUTION: To correct the iron deficiency, spray the foliage with liquid iron and also apply it to the soil around the plants. Apply aluminum sulfate or lime-sulfur spray to correct the pH. A treatment of ferrous sulfate may also correct the pH of the soil. Place the ferrous sulfate in holes (6 inches deep for shrubs and 2 feet deep for trees) around the plant under the branches, and water it in well. Maintain an acidic pH by fertilizing with an azalea, camellia, and rhododendron food rated 10-7-7. When planting in an area with alkaline soil, add a handful of soil sulfur, or add enough peat moss to make up 50 percent of the amended soil and mix it in well.

PROBLEM: Leaves are small and discolored and often drop prematurely. Twigs may die. The plant is stunted and in a general state of decline. Bark at the base of the trunk is wounded. The tree is planted in a lawn.

ANALYSIS: Lawn-mower blight

Trees growing in lawns may be severely injured by slight but repeated bark injuries caused by lawn mowers. Lawn-mower blades may also slice through the bark into the wood. Nutrients and water cannot pass through the damaged part of the trunk to reach the top of the tree. In severe cases, young trees are killed. Lawn-mower wounds are often entry points for disease-producing organisms that may also kill the tree.

SOLUTION: Prune off dying twigs and branches, and apply a general-purpose plant food rated 10-10-10 or a tree and shrub food rated 14-7-7. To prevent additional damage to the trunk, kill all grass around the base of the tree by applying an edger containing oxyfluorfen and glyphosate. Or install a tree guard to eliminate the need for edging and trimming grass around the trunk.

PROBLEM: Leaves are small and discolored and often drop prematurely. Eventually twigs and then larger branches die. The plant is stunted and in a general state of decline.

ANALYSIS: Root nematodes

Root nematodes are microscopic worms that live in the soil. There are many varieties, some highly beneficial and some highly destructive. The destructive types feed on plant roots, damaging, stunting, or causing them to become enlarged. Such roots can't supply sufficient water and nutrients to the aboveground plant parts, and the plant is stunted or slowly dies. Nematodes are found throughout the United States, especially in southern areas with moist, sandy loam soil. The worms can move only a few inches each year on their own, but they may be carried long distances by soil, water, tools, or infested plants. Laboratory testing of roots and soil is the only method for confirming the presence of nematodes. Contact the local cooperative extension office for sampling instructions and addresses of testing laboratories. Soil and root problems—such as poor soil structure, drought stress, overwatering, nutrient deficiency, and root rot—can produce symptoms of decline similar to those caused by nematodes. Eliminate these problems as causes before sending soil and root samples for testing.

SOLUTION: Chemicals to kill nematodes in planted soil are not available to homeowners. However, nematodes can be controlled by soil fumigation with metam-sodium (VAPAM®) before planting. Mulch, water, and add fertilizer to plants to minimize stress.

PROBLEMS COMMON TO MANY TREES, SHRUBS, AND VINES — WEAK OR DYING PLANT

Tree death caused by grade change.

Tree decline due to construction and grade change.

Root weevil damage to azalea.

PROBLEM: Leaves turn yellow and may drop. Branches die. The tree declines, usually over a period of several years, and may die. The soil level under the tree was recently changed, either raised or lowered.

ANALYSIS: Grade change

Raising or lowering the level of the soil (the grade) around trees can be extremely damaging. If the grade has been raised, the tree emerges from the soil in a straight line, without flaring at the base of the trunk. If the grade has been lowered, roots are exposed.

1. *Grade raised:* A large quantity of soil dumped around a tree usually suffocates the roots by cutting off their supply of air and water. The extent of damage depends on the kind of tree, its age and condition, the type and depth of fill, and how much of the root system is covered. Young, healthy trees are much more tolerant than old trees, and soil containing gravel or sand causes less injury than heavy clay soil. If only a portion of the root system is covered or if the fill is relatively shallow (less than 3 inches of porous soil or less than 1 inch of clay soil), the tree will be weakened, but it does not usually die. Severe symptoms of decline (progressive dieback from the top down) often do not occur for several years. Insects or diseases may kill the weakened plant sooner than it would have been killed otherwise.

2. *Grade lowered:* Many roots may be severed when soil is removed from around a tree, and exposed roots will dry out. The number and size of the roots severed determine the extent of damage. Cutting large roots close to the trunk is more likely to kill the tree than cutting the ends of roots. The plant is often unstable and may blow down in a strong wind.

SOLUTION: Once symptoms of decline develop, considerable damage has already occurred. Take these measures to correct the condition or control the problem.

1. By the time symptoms caused by raising the grade are noticed, it is usually too late to do anything. If possible, remove the fill if no symptoms exist and it has been around the tree for less than one growing season. If the tree is in a severe state of decline, remove it. If decline is not severe and fill is less than 12 inches deep, therapeutic treatments may save the tree. Remove all dead and dying branches and remove the soil from around the base of the trunk. Dig holes to the original soil level every few feet over the entire root area (under the branches) and place 6-inch bell tiles in the holes. In the future, valuable trees to be filled over should be protected by installing tile pipes in a thick bed of gravel covered with a minimum amount of fill.

2. Remove the tree if it is in a severe state of decline caused by lowering the grade. Unstable trees should be cabled to a stable object or removed. For trees with symptoms, prune off damaged roots and torn bark. Cut back the top growth so it is in balance with the remaining roots (if 20 percent of the roots are damaged, cut off 20 percent of the branches). Water trees during dry periods.

PROBLEM: Leaves are small and discolored and often drop prematurely. Eventually twigs and then larger branches die. The plant is stunted and in a general state of decline. Leaves from last year are notched around the edges. Removing soil from around the base of the plant, exposing some roots, reveals undersized rootlets or chewed root bark. White grubs may be found in the soil around the roots.

ANALYSIS: Root weevil larvae

Root weevil larvae, called grubs, infest the roots of many ornamental plants. The damage caused by the white, legless grubs is often so gradual that the insects are well established before injury is apparent. If the grubs remain undetected, the plant may die abruptly with the onset of hot, dry weather. During the summer months, female weevils lay eggs at the soil line near the stem. The emerging grubs burrow into the soil. They feed on the roots in the fall and then spend the winter in the soil. Most root weevils cause their major damage in the spring. Their feeding girdles roots and stems, disrupting the flow of nutrients and water through the plant and causing the roots and the top of the plant to die.

SOLUTION: Discard dying plants. To prevent the next generation of weevils from causing damage, eliminate the adults. Spray the foliage and the ground under the plant with an insecticide containing acephate (ORTHENE®). Contact the cooperative extension office to learn the time of weevil emergence in your area. Respray 2 more times at 3-week intervals.

BRANCHES DIE ■ **ABIES (FIR)**

Fireblight on crab apple.

PROBLEM: Blossoms
and leaves of some twigs
suddenly wilt and turn
black as if scorched by fire. Leaves curl
and hang downward. The bark at the base
of a blighted twig becomes water-soaked,
then dark, sunken, and dry; cracks may
develop at the edge of the sunken area. In
warm, moist spring weather drops of
brown ooze appear on the sunken bark.

ANALYSIS: Fireblight
This plant disease is caused by a bacterium (*Erwinia amylovora*) that is extremely
destructive to many trees and shrubs. Bacteria of this species spend the winter in
the sunken areas (cankers) on the
branches. In the spring, the bacteria ooze
out of the cankers and are carried by insects to the plant blossoms. Flies and other insects are attracted to the sweet, sticky
ooze and become smeared with it. When
the insects visit a flower for nectar, they
infect it with the bacteria. Bees visiting
these infected blossoms carry bacteria-
laden nectar to healthy blossoms. Rain,
wind, and tools may also spread the bacteria. Fireblight spreads rapidly through
plant tissue in humid weather above
65° F.

SOLUTION: During spring and summer,
prune out infected branches about 12
inches beyond any visible discoloration;
destroy the branches. Sterilize the pruning tools with rubbing alcohol after each
cut. Before bud break in the spring, spray
with a pesticide containing basic copper
sulfate or streptomycin; this will help prevent infection. Respray at intervals of 5 to
7 days until the end of bloom. In summer
or fall, after the disease stops spreading,
prune out infected branches.

PROBLEMS OF INDIVIDUAL TREES, SHRUBS, AND VINES

This section is arranged alphabetically by
the botanical name of each plant.

ABIES (FIR)

ADAPTATION: Zones 4 through 7.
To determine your zone, see the map on
page 348. Not adapted to hot, dry areas.

LIGHT: Full sun.

SOIL: Grows best in well-drained, non-
alkaline (below pH 7.0) soil.

FERTILIZER: According to label directions, apply a fertilizer higher in nitrogen (14-7-7, for example).

WATER:
How much: Apply enough water to wet
the soil 3 to 4 feet deep.
How often: Firs grow best in moist soil.
Water when soil is moist but not wet 4
inches below the surface.

PRUNING: Plant firs in open areas
where the trees have room to spread. Do
not prune off branches unless necessary.
New side growth can be sheared to develop a dense, bushy tree. New growth
does not usually develop on the lower
trunk if a limb is removed. To avoid altering the pyramidal growth of the tree,
do not prune off the top.

ABIES (FIR)

Spruce budworm (2 times life size).

Balsam twig aphid damage.

Tussock moth damage. *Insert:* Larva (life size).

PROBLEM: Needles on the ends of branches are chewed and webbed together. In mid-July the branch ends often turn reddish brown. Branches or the entire tree may die after three to five years of defoliation. Reddish brown caterpillars, 1¼ inches long, with yellow or white raised spots, feed on the needles.

ANALYSIS: Spruce budworms

(*Choristoneura* species)
Spruce budworms are extremely destructive to ornamental spruce, fir, and Douglas fir and may infest pine, larch, and hemlock. Budworm populations are cyclical. They come in epidemics 10 or more years apart. The moths are small (½ inch long) and grayish, with bands and spots of brown. The females lay pale green eggs in clusters on the needles in late July and August. The larvae that hatch from these eggs crawl to hiding places in the bark or in lichen mats, or they are blown by the wind to other trees, where they hide. The tiny larvae spin silken cases and hibernate until spring. In May, when the weather warms, the caterpillars tunnel into needles. As the worms grow, they feed on opening buds; later they chew off needles and web them together. The larvae feed for about five weeks, pupate on twigs, and emerge as adults.

SOLUTION: When the buds begin to grow in late May, spray with an insecticide containing acephate (ORTHENE®).

PROBLEM: The youngest needles are curled and twisted, with their lighter undersides turned upward. These needles drop from the plant prematurely. Some needles are killed. Young twigs are twisted and bark is roughened. Shoots may become saturated with a shiny, sticky secretion, so needles adhere to one another. A black sooty mold may grow on this sticky substance. Tiny (⅛-inch) waxy bluish gray adult or pale green immature, soft-bodied insects cluster on the shoots.

ANALYSIS: Balsam twig aphids

(*Mindarus abietinus*)
In small numbers twig aphids do little damage. However, aphids are extremely prolific and populations can rapidly build up to damaging numbers during the growing season. Damage occurs when the aphid injects its saliva into a plant as it sucks the juices from the fir shoots. The aphid is unable to digest fully all the sugar in the sap and excretes the excess in a fluid called honeydew. The honeydew often drops onto the shoots or other plants below. A sooty mold fungus may develop on the honeydew, causing the fir leaves to appear black and dirty. In bark crevices late in the summer, females lay several small (¹⁄₁₀-inch) eggs covered with tiny rods of white wax. The eggs are conspicuous and are a useful index of the amount of injury that may occur during the next year.

SOLUTION: Kill aphids at bud break in late April or early May by spraying with an insecticide containing acephate (ORTHENE®) or malathion. Respray in 2 weeks if the tree becomes reinfested.

PROBLEM: Much of the foliage is eaten, starting at the top of the tree and progressing downward. The entire tree may be defoliated in one season. Trees that lose most of their needles the second year are usually killed. Inch-long, hairy, gray or light brown caterpillars with tufts of orange hairs on their backs may be feeding on the needles.

ANALYSIS: Douglas-fir tussock moth

(*Orgyia pseudotsugata*)
Douglas-fir tussock moth populations in forests are cyclical. Every 7 to 10 years populations build up to epidemic proportions. When this occurs, true firs, Douglas firs, spruces, pines, and larches may be completely defoliated. In cities, damaging numbers may be found every year. In mid- to late summer the hairy, wingless female moths lay their eggs in a frothy substance covered with a layer of hairlike scales. When the eggs hatch the following spring, the caterpillars begin feeding on the new needles at the top of the tree. As the younger foliage is devoured, the caterpillars move downward, feeding on older needles. Large numbers of tan excrement pellets accumulate around the base of the tree. Since conifers do not replace their old needles, defoliated trees are often killed after two seasons. Less severely damaged trees may be killed later by bark beetles. In August, the caterpillars pupate to emerge as adults.

SOLUTION: When damage or caterpillars are first noticed in May or early June, spray with an insecticide containing acephate (ORTHENE®). Respray 2 weeks later if damage continues.

ACER (MAPLE, BOX ELDER) ─────────────────────────────────────

Pear thrips damage on sugar maple.

Cottonycushion scales on maple (¼ life size).

ACER
(MAPLE, BOX ELDER) _____

ADAPTATION: Throughout the United States.

LIGHT: Full sun to part shade.

SOIL AND PLANTING: Any good, deep, well-drained garden soil. When choosing a planting site, pick an area that can accommodate the ultimate spread and height of the tree.

FERTILIZER: According to label directions, apply a fertilizer higher in nitrogen (14-7-7, for example).

WATER:
How much: Apply enough water to wet the soil 3 to 4 feet deep.
How often: Maples prefer moist soil. Water when soil is moist but no longer wet 4 inches below the surface.

PROBLEM: Leaves are small, mottled yellow and brown, and distorted. Blisterlike scars may be found on the veins. In moderate infestations, the leaves in the crown are yellow and sparse, a condition resembling the damage caused by late frost. When damage is severe, the tree is defoliated in spring but produces new leaves in June or July.

ANALYSIS: Pear thrips
(*Taeniothrips inconsequens*)
Pear thrips infest a variety of forest trees but have recently become a serious pest of sugar maples. The insects damage the foliage by piercing the leaves and sucking the plant juices. Pear thrips have slender, brownish bodies less than ¹⁄₁₆ inch long. They emerge from the soil in April or May and migrate to the expanding buds of the trees, where the females lay eggs in the buds and feed on the young foliage. Larvae hatch from the eggs within two weeks, feed until early June, then drop to the soil to pupate.

SOLUTION: There is presently no control available for this pest. Researchers are studying the problem. Contact the local cooperative extension office for advice.

PROBLEM: The undersides of leaves amd stems or branch crotches are covered with white, cottony, cushionlike masses. Leaves turn yellow and may drop prematurely. In some cases, a shiny or sticky substance coats the leaves. A black sooty mold often grows on the sticky substance. Sometimes, numerous side shoots grow out of an infested crotch area. Twigs and branches may die back.

ANALYSIS: Cottonycushion scales or mealybugs
Cottonycushion scales and mealybugs are common on maples throughout the United States. The similar appearances of these insects make separate identification difficult. They are conspicuous in late spring and summer because the adult females are covered with a white, cottony egg sac containing up to 2,500 eggs. The insects that hatch from these eggs are yellowish brown to green. They feed throughout the summer on the stems and undersides of the leaves. Damage is caused by the withdrawal of plant sap from leaves and branches. The insects are unable to digest fully all the sugar in the sap, and they excrete the excess in a fluid called honeydew. The honeydew often drops onto leaves or plants below. A sooty mold fungus may develop in the honeydew, causing whatever it covers to appear black and dirty. If the insects are not controlled, heavily infested branches may die after several seasons.

SOLUTION: In midsummer, when the young are active, apply an insecticide containing acephate (ORTHENE®) or diazinon. The following spring, when trees are dormant, spray with lime sulfur to control insects on the bark.

ACER (MAPLE, BOX ELDER)

Galls caused by bladder gall mites.

Anthracnose on Norway maple.

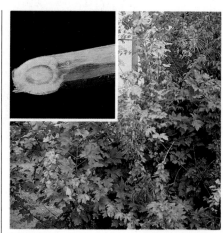

Verticillium wilt. *Insert:* Infected stem.

PROBLEM: In early spring, maple leaf tissue develops irregular, spherical, or bladderlike growths, known as galls, on the upper surfaces of the leaves. Leaves next to the trunk and on large branches are most affected. The galls are yellowish green at first but later turn pinkish to red and finally black. If the galls are numerous, leaves become deformed, and some turn yellow and drop prematurely.

ANALYSIS: Bladder gall mites or spindle gall mites
(*Vasates quadripedes* or *Vasates aceriscrumena*)
These galls are caused by tiny mites too small to be seen with the naked eye. Each gall contains one mite. The mites congregate on buds just before they open in the spring. As the buds open, each mite punctures and enters a leaf on the underside, injecting a growth-promoting substance that causes abnormal tissue formation. A gall encloses the mite, with an opening remaining on the underside. The mites feed, and females lay eggs inside their galls. Sometime after the eggs hatch, the young mites crawl out through the opening and infest new leaves. In July, mite activity stops and the insects migrate to the bark to spend the winter.

SOLUTION: Control measures are not necessary because galls generally cause no serious injury. However, if you wish to prevent unsightly leaves next year, spray before the buds start to open in spring; treat buds, branches, and trunk with a dormant oil spray or a miticide containing hexakis.

PROBLEM: Irregular, light brown spots of dead tissue appear on leaves from late May to August. The spots develop during or just following wet, humid weather. Many occur along the veins. The spots may enlarge and run together, causing the death of entire leaves. Foliage partially killed appears as if sunscorched. This disease is distinguished from sunscorch by the presence of dark dots (spore-producing structures) barely visible on the undersides of leaves. The spore-producing structures develop while the leaves are still on the tree. Sunken reddish oval areas often develop on the infected twigs.

ANALYSIS: Maple anthracnose
This plant disease is caused by a fungus (*Gloeosporium apocryptum*) that spends the winter on fallen leaves or in sunken cankers on twigs in the tree. During rainy weather, spores are blown and splashed onto young leaves. Dead spots develop on the leaves where the fungi enter the tissue. The spots expand and the fung can kill a leaf in rainy seasons, causing defoliation. The tree will grow new leaves if defoliation takes place in spring or early summer. When the tree is severely affected for successive years, the fungi will enter and kill branches.

SOLUTION: Trees affected by this disease for a single year do not require a chemical control. Rake and destroy old leaves and prune out dead twigs below the canker on the bark. This reduces the amount of disease next year. If the following spring is wet and humid, treat valuable specimens; when the leaves uncurl, spray them with a fungicide containing maneb. Repeat the treatment 2 more times at 2-week intervals.

PROBLEM: The leaves on a branch turn yellow at the edges, then brown and dry. During hot weather, the leaves may wilt. New leaves may be stunted and yellowish. The infected tree may die slowly, branch by branch, over several seasons. Or the whole tree may wilt and die within a few months. Some trees may recover. The tissue under the bark on the dying side contains dark streaks that may be quite apparent or barely visible when exposed. To examine for streaks, peel back the bark at the bottom of the dying branch.

ANALYSIS: Verticillium wilt
This plant disease affects many ornamental trees and shrubs. It is caused by one of several soil-inhabiting fungi (*Verticillium* species) that persist indefinitely on plant debris or in the soil. The disease is spread by contaminated seeds, plants, soil, equipment, and ground water. The fungi enter the tree through the roots and spread up into the branches through the water-conducting vessels in the trunk. The vessels become plugged and discolored. This plugging cuts off the flow of water and nutrients to the branches, causing leaf discoloration and wilting.

SOLUTION: No chemical control is available. Add fertilizer and water the infected tree to stimulate vigorous growth. Remove all dead wood. Do not remove branches on which leaves have recently wilted; these branches may produce new leaves in 3 to 4 weeks or next spring. Remove dead trees. If replanting in the same area, plant trees and shrubs that are resistant to verticillium.

AESCULUS (HORSECHESTNUT) ▪ BETULA (BIRCH) ▪ BUXUS (BOXWOOD)

Summer leaf scorch.

Dieback. *Insert:* Adult borer (½ life size).

PROBLEM: During hot weather, usually in July or August, leaves turn brown around the edges and between the veins. Sometimes the whole leaf dies. Many leaves may drop during late summer. This problem is most severe on the youngest branches. Trees do not usually die.

ANALYSIS: Summer leaf scorch
In hot weather water evaporates rapidly from leaves. If the roots can't absorb and convey water fast enough to replenish this loss, the leaves turn brown and wither. This usually occurs in dry soil, but leaves can also scorch when the soil is moist. Horsechestnut trees vary in their susceptibility; one may be very susceptible while the tree next to it may show no sign of scorch. Drying winds, severed roots, limited soil area, or low temperatures can also cause scorch.

SOLUTION: To prevent further scorch, water trees deeply during periods of hot weather; wet down the entire root space. Add mulch over the root system; water newly transplanted trees whenever the rootball is dry 1 inch below the surface. There is no control for scorch on trees in moist soil. Plant trees adapted to your climate.

The California buckeye (*Aesculus californica*) is summer-deciduous. Every spring, about May or June, its leaves begin to show scorch symptoms that progress until all the leaves have dropped. This is normal and cannot be prevented.

PROBLEM: Leaves are yellowing, and foliage at the top of the tree is sparse. There is increased side growth on the lower branches. Twigs and branches may die. The leaves on these branches turn brown but don't drop. D-shaped holes and ridges are on the trunk and branches. Swollen ridges are packed with sawdust. Weak, young, or newly transplanted trees may be killed.

ANALYSIS: Bronze birch borers
(*Agrilus anxius*)
The birch borer is the larva of an olive-brown beetle about ½ inch long. For about six weeks in summer, adult female beetles lay eggs in bark crevices, usually around a wound. They feed on leaves during egg laying. The larvae that hatch from these eggs are white and have flat heads. They bore into the wood just beneath the bark. The feeding and tunneling of the larvae stop the flow of nutrients and water in that area by cutting the conducting vessels; branch and twig dieback result. If the tree is healthy, sap flow acts as a defense against borers; when the insect burrows into the wood, tree sap fills the hole and drowns the borer. Factors that weaken the tree—such as poor growing conditions, transplanting, and mechanical injuries—make it more attractive to female beetles.

SOLUTION: Cut out and destroy all dead and dying branches. Remove severely infested young trees. In spring, spray or paint the trunk and branches with an insecticide containing lindane, which kills young larvae before they burrow into the wood. At 2-week intervals, repeat the treatment 3 more times. Maintain tree vigor by watering regularly and applying fertilizer as needed.

BUXUS (BOXWOOD)

ADAPTATION: Zones 5 through 10. To determine your zone, see the map on page 348. Protect from drying winds.

LIGHT: Full sun or partial shade (shade is especially important in hot climates).

SOIL: Well drained, rich in organic matter.

FERTILIZER: Apply a fertilizer higher in nitrogen (14-7-7, for example); follow label directions.

WATER:
  How much: Apply enough water to wet the soil 1 to 2 feet deep.
  How often: Boxwood does not tolerate drought. Water when soil is moist but not wet 2 inches below the surface.

BUXUS (BOXWOOD)

Boxwood psyllid damage.

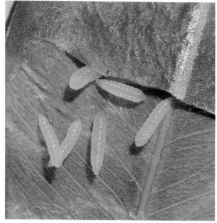

Boxwood leafminer larvae (5 times life size).

Volutella leaf and stem blight.

PROBLEM: Terminal leaves are cupped and yellowing. Buds inside the cupped leaves are often dead. There is no new growth on branch tips with damaged leaves. Peeling open cupped leaves reveals a tiny (1/16-inch), grayish green, immature insect. It is usually covered with a white, waxy material. Damage begins in early spring when buds first open. Small (1/8-inch) flies with transparent wings are sometimes seen jumping on leaves or flying around the plant in late May.

ANALYSIS: Boxwood psyllid
(*Psylla buxi*)
The boxwood psyllid is prevalent in temperate regions of the United States where boxwood is grown. American boxwood is more severely attacked than English boxwood. The immature psyllid feeds by sucking the juices from growing leaves, resulting in yellowing and cupping. As it feeds it secretes a white, waxy material that protects it from parasites and chemical sprays. The insect matures in early summer, and the female fly lays her eggs in the base of buds, where they remain until the following spring.

SOLUTION: When damage is first noticed in early spring, control psyllids by using an insecticide containing acephate (ORTHENE®). Spray plants thoroughly to penetrate the waxy secretions and leaf buds. Respray 2 weeks later.

PROBLEM: Leaves are puckered or blistered. The undersides are spotted yellow; the topsides become flecked with brown and yellow. Leaves may drop prematurely. Growth is poor and the plant is rangy. Twigs may die back if the plant is infested more than one year. Tearing open an affected leaf reveals two or more small (1/8-inch), yellowish maggots or brownish pupae.

ANALYSIS: Boxwood leafminer
(*Monarthropalpus buxi*)
The boxwood leafminer is one of the most serious pests of boxwood. The larvae spend the winter in leaves. When the weather warms in spring, they feed on the tissue between the leaf surfaces. In late April or May, a tiny (1/10-inch), gnat-like, orange fly emerges from each pupal case inside a leaf. The emerging flies swarm around the plant in early morning, mating and laying eggs in the leaves. New blisters develop in midsummer from feeding by this generation of larvae. When the weather turns cold, the larvae become inactive until the following spring.

SOLUTION: Leafminer control is most effective when insecticides are applied just before egg laying in late April or early May. Spray with an insecticide containing acephate (ORTHENE®). If eggs are laid before a control is applied, applying an insecticide containing dimethoate in late June may kill young miners.

PROBLEM: In the spring, before new growth appears, leaves on the tips of affected branches turn pale green; then red; tan; and, finally, yellow. The bark loosens and peels off at the base of infected stems and branches, revealing areas of darkened, discolored wood; the entire twig or stem eventually dies. Cream-pink pustules appear on the undersides of infected leaves that have survived the winter. Later in the season, new growth may turn yellow and develop pustules, especially if the weather is wet.

ANALYSIS: Volutella canker and blight
This plant disease is caused by a fungus (*Volutella buxi*) that attacks both American and English boxwood. Plants are more susceptible to the disease if they have been weakened by winter injury, poor growing conditions, or insect infestation. Fungi of this species survive the winter on infected stems, leaves, and plant debris. Wind and splashing water spread the spores to healthy leaves and twigs. In the early spring, cankers form in twigs and branches, resulting in dieback. The fungi can continue to blight new growth throughout the growing season as long as conditions remain moist.

SOLUTION: Remove dying shrubs. Prune out and destroy infected twigs and branches. Clean up accumulated plant debris. Just before growth begins in the spring or whenever the disease is first noticed, spray shrubs with a fungicide containing benomyl or basic copper sulfate. Respray 3 more times at intervals of 10 days. Maintain the health of plants.

CAMELLIA ■ **CATALPA**

Virus.

Sooty mold.

Catalpa sphinx caterpillars (½ life size).

PROBLEM: Irregular yellow splotches of various sizes and shapes appear on leaves. Some leaves may be entirely yellow. The uninfected portions remain dark green. Colored flowers may have irregular white blotches. White flowers show no symptoms. Some camellia varieties with extensive leaf yellowing may be weak and stunted.

ANALYSIS: Camellia yellow mottle-leaf virus
The virus is transmitted by propagating from an infected plant or by grafting from an infected plant to a healthy one. This generally occurs in the nursery where the plant was grown. Sometimes the virus disease is intentionally transmitted to get variegated flowers. The disease is usually fairly harmless unless there is extensive leaf yellowing. Yellowing results from suppression of the development of green pigment (chlorophyll). The leaves produce less food, weakening the plant.

SOLUTION: Once the plant is infected, no chemical can control the virus. Remove excessively weak camellias. Buy only healthy plants.

___

Camellia cultural information
Light: Protect from hot sun
Water: When soil is moist below mulch
Soil: Rich, well drained, mulched
Fertilizer: Acidic

PROBLEM: A black sooty mold grows on leaves and twigs. It can be completely wiped off the surfaces.

ANALYSIS: Sooty mold
This common black mold is caused by any of several species of fungi that grow on the sugary material left on plants by aphids, scales, mealybugs, whiteflies, and other insects that suck sap from plants. The insects are unable to digest all the sugar in the sap, so they excrete the excess in a fluid called honeydew, which drops onto the leaves below. The honeydew may also drop out of infested trees and shrubs onto camellias growing beneath them. Sooty mold is unsightly but it is fairly harmless because it does not attack foliage directly. Extremely heavy infestations prevent light from reaching leaves, however, so the foliage produces fewer nutrients and may turn yellow. The presence of sooty mold indicates that the camellia or another plant near it is infested with insects.

SOLUTION: Sooty mold can be wiped from the leaves with a wet rag or hosed off, or it will eventually be washed off by rain. Prevent more sooty mold by controlling the insect that is producing the honeydew. Inspect the leaves and twigs above the sooty mold to find out what type of insect is present.

PROBLEM: Small holes are chewed in the topsides of leaves. Large yellow-and-black–striped caterpillars, each with a sharp "horn" at the tail end, feed in groups on young leaves. As the caterpillars develop (to a length of 1 to 3 inches), they spread throughout the tree and feed singly on leaf edges. The tree may be completely defoliated. Damage occurs from May to August.

ANALYSIS: Catalpa sphinxes
(Ceratomia catalpae)
The catalpa sphinx caterpillar is the larval stage of a large night-flying moth that is seldom seen. The moth passes the winter as a pupa in the ground. In spring, the moth emerges and the female lays her eggs on young catalpa leaves. The eggs hatch, and the larvae feed for several weeks. If the larvae are uncontrolled, they develop into the second generation of caterpillars in the year. These caterpillars may completely defoliate the tree by mid- to late summer.

SOLUTION: When damage is first noticed in spring, spray with an insecticide containing acephate (ORTHENE®). Repeat in midsummer if the tree becomes reinfested. In fall, clean up debris beneath the tree to reduce the number of overwintering pupae.

___

The catalpa sphinx caterpillar is good fishing bait. Control the insects by hand-picking them off the tree, and then go fishing.

163

CELASTRUS (BITTERSWEET) ■ **CORNUS (DOGWOOD)**

Euonymus scale (4 times life size).

Summer leaf scorch.

Dogwood borer. *Insert:* Adult (life size).

PROBLEM: Yellow or whitish spots appear on the topsides of leaves. The leaves may drop, and the plant may be bare by midsummer. In severe cases, stems die back. The stems and the undersides of the leaves are covered with dark brown, oyster shell–shaped, crusty bumps or soft, white, elongated scales. The bumps and scales can be scraped off.

ANALYSIS: Euonymus scales
(*Unaspis euonymi*)
These scales, serious pests of bittersweet and other ornamental shrubs, are found throughout the United States. The scales spend the winter on the twigs and branches of bittersweet. Adult females lay their eggs in spring. In late spring to early summer, the young scales, called crawlers, settle on leaves or stems. These small ($\frac{1}{10}$-inch), soft-bodied pests feed by inserting their mouthparts and sucking sap. Their legs atrophy, and a crusty or waxy shell develops over their bodies. The males are white and quite noticeable on leaves and stems. The mature female scales are brown and shaped like oyster shells. They lay their eggs underneath their hard body coverings. A population may produce up to three generations during the growing season. An uncontrolled infestation may kill the plant after two or three years.

SOLUTION: In early summer (late spring in the South), when the young are active, spray with an insecticide containing acephate (ORTHENE®). The following spring, before new growth begins, spray the trunk and branches with a dormant oil spray to control overwintering insects.

PROBLEM: During hot weather, usually in July or August, leaves turn brown at the edges and between the veins. Sometimes the whole leaf dies. Many leaves may drop during late summer. This problem is most severe on the youngest branches. Trees do not generally die. Browning and withering can develop whether the soil around the roots is moist or dry.

ANALYSIS: Summer leaf scorch
Leaf scorch is caused by excessive evaporation of moisture from the leaves. In hot weather, water evaporates rapidly from foliage. If the roots can't absorb and convey water fast enough to replenish this loss, the leaves turn brown and wither. For optimum growth, dogwoods require moist soil. Leaf scorch is most severe when water is unavailable because the soil is dry. However, if the weather is extremely hot, scorch may also develop when the soil is moist. Drying winds, severed roots, and limited soil area can also cause scorch.

SOLUTION: To prevent further scorch, water trees deeply during periods of hot weather; wet down the entire root space. Water newly transplanted trees whenever the rootball is dry 2 inches below the surface. There is no control for scorch on trees in moist soil. Plant trees adapted to your climate. In hot-summer areas, plant dogwoods in partial shade.

PROBLEM: In mid-summer, leaves turn red and drop prematurely; eventually, twigs or branches die back. Bark sloughs off around holes in a swollen area on the trunk or at the base of branches. Late in the summer, fine sawdust may drop from the holes. Young trees are usually killed.

ANALYSIS: Dogwood borers
(*Synanthedon scitula*)
The dogwood borer, also known as the pecan borer, is the larva of a brownish, clear-wing moth, $\frac{1}{2}$ inch long. The borer infects flowering dogwood, pecan, and many other ornamental and fruit trees. The moths are active from May until September. They may be seen flying around trees during the summer. The female moth lays her eggs on the bark, usually near a wound or old borer injury. After the eggs hatch, the $\frac{1}{2}$-inch-long white larvae with brown heads find an opening in the bark. They feed in the wood just under the bark, girdling the branches and causing dieback. The larvae spend the winter inside the tree. Several other borers also infest dogwood.

SOLUTION: Beginning in April or May, spray or paint the trunk and branches with an insecticide containing lindane. Repeat 4 more times at monthly intervals. Water regularly and apply fertilizer as needed to maintain tree vigor. To prevent borer entrance, avoid pruning during the summer months when the moths are present and avoid wounding the trunks and branches. Reduce damage by inserting a fine wire up the entry hole to kill the larva.

COTONEASTER ■ **CRATAEGUS (HAWTHORN)**

Blister mite damage.

Fireblight.

Leaf spot.

PROBLEM: Reddish or brownish blisters, ⅛ inch across, develop on the undersides of foliage. The blisters may be massed together to almost cover a leaf. The topside is mottled brown or blackish. Berries may be deformed.

ANALYSIS: Pearleaf blister mites
(*Phytoptus pyri*)
This microscopic pinkish or white mite is found wherever cotoneaster is grown. It also infests pear, apple, mountain ash, and serviceberry. Adults spend the winter in bud scales, often hundreds in a single bud. As the buds swell in spring, the mites lay their eggs; the young feed and burrow into the undersides of unfolding leaves. New generations of mites are produced inside the blisters throughout the summer. As cold weather approaches, the mites migrate back to the bud scales to overwinter.

SOLUTION: Once the mite has entered the underside of the leaf, it is difficult to control. When damage is first noticed, spray the undersides of leaves with a miticide containing hexakis. Repeat 10 days later. The following early spring, just before growth starts, spray with an oil spray or with a lime-sulfur spray. As the leaves emerge, spray with a miticide containing hexakis. Repeat 10 days later.

PROBLEM: Blossoms and leaves of some twigs suddenly wilt and turn black as if scorched by fire. Brown or blackened leaves cling to the branches. The bark at the base of a blighted twig becomes water-soaked, then dark, sunken, and dry; cracks may develop at the edge of the sunken area. In warm, moist spring weather, drops of brown ooze appear on the sunken bark. Young trees may die.

ANALYSIS: Fireblight
This plant disease is caused by a bacterium (*Erwinia amylovora*) that is extremely destructive to hawthorn and many other related plants. Bacteria of this species spend the winter in the sunken cankers on the branches. In spring, the bacteria ooze out of the cankers and attract bees and other insects. When the insects visit a hawthorn flower for nectar, they infect it with the bacteria. Insects visiting these infected blossoms later carry bacteria-laden nectar to healthy blossoms. Rain, wind, and tools may also spread the bacteria. Fireblight spreads rapidly through plant tissue in humid weather above 65° F.

SOLUTION: During spring and summer, prune out infected branches 12 to 15 inches beyond any visible discoloration; destroy the branches. A protective spray of a pesticide containing basic copper sulfate or streptomycin, applied before bud break in spring, will help prevent infection. Respray at intervals of 5 to 7 days until the end of bloom. In the fall, prune out infected branches. Sterilize pruning shears with rubbing alcohol after each cut. When planting new trees, use resistant varieties.

PROBLEM: Spots and blotches appear on leaves. The spots may be red, purple, yellow, brown, or black. They range in size from barely visible to ¼ inch in diameter. Several spots may join to form blotches. Infected leaves may die and drop. If spotting is severe, the tree may defoliate prematurely. Leaf spotting is most severe in moist, humid weather.

ANALYSIS: Leaf spot
Several different fungi, including *Fabraea thuemenii*, cause leaf spot on hawthorn. The spots are unsightly but rarely harmful to the plant. However, severe, recurrent infection can cause repeated defoliation that may weaken the tree and reduce its flowering potential. Leaf-spot fungi are spread by wind and splashing water. Spots develop where the fungi enter the leaf tissue. The fungi survive the winter on twigs and in fallen leaves and plant debris. Most leaf-spot fungi do their greatest damage in moist weather between 50° and 85° F.

SOLUTION: There is no way to get rid of spots once leaves are infected. To help prevent spotting next year, clean up and destroy fallen leaves and other plant debris. In the spring, when the leaves emerge, spray trees with a fungicide containing captan or chlorothalonil. Respray when the leaves are half grown and again when they are fully grown. Continue spraying at intervals of 10 to 14 days as long as wet weather continues.

CYPRESS FAMILY (ARBORVITAE, CHAMAECYPARIS, INCENSE CEDAR)

CYPRESS FAMILY (ARBORVITAE, CHAMAECYPARIS, INCENSE CEDAR)

ADAPTATION:
Chamaecyparis species: Zones 4 through 9. Protect plants from hot, dry winds.
Cupressocyparis and *Cupressus* species: Zones 5 through 10.
Thuja species: Zones 2 through 9.
To determine your climate zone, see the map on page 348.

LIGHT: Full sun.

SOIL:
Chamaecyparis species: Needs good drainage.
Cupressocyparis and *Cupressus* species: Tolerate a wide variety of soils.
Thuja species: Any good garden soil.

FERTILIZER: Apply a fertilizer rated higher in nitrogen (for example, 14-7-7); follow label directions.

WATER:
How much: Apply enough water to wet the soil 6 to 12 inches deep.
How often:
Chamaecyparis species: Grows best in moist soil but can tolerate some drought. Water when soil is moist, but no longer wet, 4 inches below the surface.
Cupressocyparis species: Water when soil is barely moist 4 inches below the surface.
Cupressus species: Grows best if kept on the dry side. Water when soil is dry 4 inches below the surface.
Thuja species: Tolerates wet soil but does best in moist soil. Water when soil is moist, but not wet, 4 inches below the surface.

Twig and needle blight damage on western red cedar.

PROBLEM: Needles, twigs, and branches turn brown. In some cases, the upper branches die from the tips back; in other cases, the lower two thirds of the plant dies. The needles often drop in late summer, starting at the branch tips and leaving affected branches bare. Sometimes minute black dots appear on the dead needles and stems. This disease is most serious in wet weather or in shady locations. Diseased plants may die.

ANALYSIS: Twig and needle blight
A number of different fungi cause twig and needle blight on plants in the cypress family. During wet weather, spores germinate on twigs and spread into the needles and twigs above and below the point of entrance, killing them. Reinfection may continue until the whole plant dies. Or the plant may live for many years, becoming more unsightly over time. With some fungi, black spore-producing bodies develop and spend the winter on dead needles.

SOLUTION: Prune out and destroy infected branches below the line between diseased and healthy tissue, making each cut into live tissue. At weekly intervals spray valuable specimens with a fungicide containing basic copper sulfate. Continue the weekly treatments throughout the growing season. Plant trees in areas with adequate air circulation and full sun.

Leaf browning on cedar.

PROBLEM: The older leaves, on the inside of the tree nearest the trunk, turn brown and drop. This condition may develop in a few days or over several weeks, in either spring or fall.

ANALYSIS: Leaf browning and shedding
Leaf browning and shedding is a natural process similar to the dropping of leaves of deciduous trees. It is usually more pronounced on arborvitae (*Thuja*) than on other plants in the cypress family. Sometimes shedding takes place every year; in other cases, it occurs every second or third year. When growing conditions have been favorable the previous season, leaf shedding occurs over several weeks and is only slightly noticeable. However, if during the growing season the plant has been exposed to unfavorable conditions, such as drying or an insect infestation, leaf drop occurs within a few days. Leaf drop is also caused by new growth shading older interior growth.

SOLUTION: No chemical controls are necessary. Water plants regularly and apply fertilizer as needed. Provide full sun. Check plants for mites and other insects during the growing season.

Leafminer damage to arborvitae.

Winter injury to arborvitae.

Powdery mildew.

PROBLEM: Leaftips turn yellow, then brown and dry, contrasting sharply with the healthy green foliage. Damage is most severe in plants growing in shady areas. Tearing open a yellow leaf reveals a small (⅕-inch-long) greenish caterpillar with a dark head. Gray or brownish moths with a ⅕-inch wingspread may be seen flying around the plant in April, May, or June.

ANALYSIS: Leafminers, or tip moths
(*Argyresthia* species)
Several insect species, known as leafminers in the eastern United States and tip moths on the West Coast, infest arborvitae, cypress, and juniper. Damage is unsightly, but plants may lose over half their foliage and still survive. The larvae spend the winter inside the leaftips. When the weather warms in late spring, adult moths emerge. The females lay eggs on the leaves. The eggs hatch and the larvae tunnel into the leaftips, devouring the green tissue. The tips above the point of entry yellow and die. The larvae feed until late fall or through the winter until early spring.

SOLUTION: When eggs are hatching in June or July (mid-August in the far northeastern states), spray with an insecticide containing acephate (ORTHENE®). Trim and destroy infested leaves in fall and spring.

PROBLEM: Leaves turn yellow at first, then rusty brown and dry. Twigs and branches may die back. The tree is growing in a climate where cold, dry, windy days are common or where plants may be exposed to late fall or early spring freezes. The soil may be frozen.

ANALYSIS: Winter injury
Arborvitae are damaged by cold, drying winter winds, especially if temperatures are below freezing. These trees are commonly planted as windbreaks and in exposed areas where growing conditions may be unfavorable. As a result the leaves lose moisture more rapidly than the root system can replace it. Cells in the leaves dry out and die. This condition is most pronounced when water is unavailable because the soil is dry or frozen. Leaves, along with twigs and branches, also die during early fall or late spring freezes when the plant is growing. Young succulent growth cannot withstand freezing temperatures.

SOLUTION: Prune out dead twigs and branches. Provide shelter for plants growing in extremely cold areas. To avoid succulent growth in fall, do not apply fertilizer late in the season. During a dry fall, irrigate plants thoroughly to reduce winter injury.

PROBLEM: The surfaces of leaves are covered with a thin layer or irregular patches of a grayish white powdery growth. Infected leaves are yellow and may drop prematurely. In late summer, tiny black dots (spore-producing bodies) are scattered over the white patches like ground pepper.

ANALYSIS: Powdery mildew
This plant disease is caused by one of two species of fungi (*Oidium euonymi japonici* or *Microsphaera alni*) that thrive in both humid and dry weather. The powdery patches or thin powdery layer consists of fungal strands and spores. The spores are spread by wind to healthy plants. The fungi sap plant nutrients, causing leaf yellowing and sometimes the death of the leaf. In late summer and fall, the fungi form small black spore-producing bodies that are dormant during the winter but produce spores to reinfect new plants the following spring. The fungi can be especially devastating in shady areas and are generally most severe in late summer and fall. Since *Microsphaera alni* attacks many different kinds of plants, fungi of this species from a diseased plant may infect other types of plants in the garden.

SOLUTION: When mildew is first noticed, spray with a fungicide containing triforine. Respray in 7 to 10 days if fungus reappears. Clean up plant debris in late summer.

Euonymus cultural information
Light: Full sun to part shade
Water: When soil is moist or dry
Soil: Tolerates many types
Fertilizer: Light

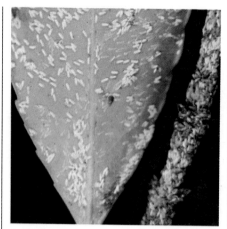

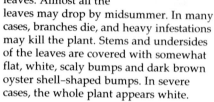

Euonymus scale (2 times life size).

Crown gall.

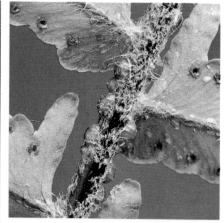

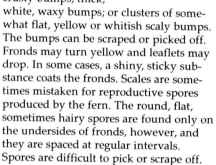

Brown scale (2 times life size).

PROBLEM: Yellow or whitish spots appear on leaves. Almost all the leaves may drop by midsummer. In many cases, branches die, and heavy infestations may kill the plant. Stems and undersides of the leaves are covered with somewhat flat, white, scaly bumps and dark brown oyster shell–shaped bumps. In severe cases, the whole plant appears white.

ANALYSIS: Euonymus scales
(*Unaspis euonymi*)
Many species of scale infest euonymus, but the most common and destructive are euonymus scales. They are especially damaging to evergreen euonymus. The dark brown females spend the winter on the plant and lay their eggs in the spring. In late spring to early summer, the young scales, called crawlers, settle on the leaves and twigs or are blown by the wind to other susceptible plants. These small ($\frac{1}{10}$-inch), soft-bodied pests suck sap from the plant. Their legs atrophy and a shell develops, brown for females and white for males. The females lay their eggs underneath their shells.

SOLUTION: Euonymus scale may be hard to detect until after it has caused serious damage. Check the plant periodically for yellow spotting and scales. In early June and mid-July, spray with an insecticide containing acephate (ORTHENE®) or an oil spray. In the South, a third application may be necessary in early September. To control scales during the dormant season, spray with an oil spray. For extremely heavy infestations, cut plants to the ground and spray new growth in June.

PROBLEM: Large, corky galls up to several inches in diameter appear at the base of the plant and on the stems and roots. The galls are rounded, with rough, irregular surfaces. Plants with numerous galls are weak; growth is slowed and leaves turn yellow. Branches may die back.

ANALYSIS: Crown gall
This plant disease is caused by a soil-inhabiting bacterium (*Agrobacterium tumefaciens*) that infects many ornamentals, fruit trees, and vegetables in the garden. Bacteria of this species are often brought into a garden initially on the roots of an infected plant and are spread with the soil and by contaminated pruning tools. The infection enters a shrub through wounds in the roots or at the base of the stem (the crown). The bacteria produce a substance that stimulates rapid cell growth in the plant, causing gall formation on roots; crown; and, sometimes, branches. The galls disrupt the flow of water and nutrients up the roots and stems, weakening and stunting the top of the plant. Galls do not usually cause the shrub to die.

SOLUTION: Crown gall cannot be eliminated from the shrub. However, an infected plant may survive many years. To improve its appearance, prune out and destroy infected stems below the galled area. Sterilize pruning shears with rubbing alcohol after each cut. Destroy severely infected shrubs. The bacteria will remain in the soil for 2 to 3 years. If you replace the shrub, plant only a resistant species.

PROBLEM: Fronds are covered with brown crusty bumps; thick, white, waxy bumps; or clusters of somewhat flat, yellow or whitish scaly bumps. The bumps can be scraped or picked off. Fronds may turn yellow and leaflets may drop. In some cases, a shiny, sticky substance coats the fronds. Scales are sometimes mistaken for reproductive spores produced by the fern. The round, flat, sometimes hairy spores are found only on the undersides of fronds, however, and they are spaced at regular intervals. Spores are difficult to pick or scrape off.

ANALYSIS: Scales
Many different types of scale infest ferns. The females lay their eggs on the fronds. In spring to midsummer, the young scales, called crawlers, settle down to feed. These small ($\frac{1}{10}$-inch), soft-bodied young feed by sucking sap from the plant. Their legs usually atrophy, and a hard crusty or waxy shell develops over their bodies. The mature female scales lay their eggs underneath their shells. Some species of scale are unable to digest fully all the sugar in the sap, so they excrete the excess in a fluid called honeydew, which coats the fronds.

SOLUTION: When the young are active, spray with an insecticide containing malathion, carbaryl (SEVIN®), or acephate (ORTHENE®). Some ferns may be damaged by these chemicals, however; test the spray on a frond before covering the entire plant. Wait a few days to see if the area turns brown. Contact the local cooperative extension office to determine the best time to spray for scales in your area. Cut off infested fronds on plants that are sensitive to insecticides. Discard severely infested plants. To treat 1 or 2 small plants, use a spray containing resmethrin.

Mealybugs (⅓ life size).

Scorch.

Mimosa webworm damage on honeylocust.

PROBLEM: Leaflets or stems are covered with white, cottony, cushion-like masses. Leaflets turn yellow and may drop; fronds may die.

ANALYSIS: Cottonycushion scales or mealybugs

Cottonycushion scales and mealybugs infest many plants in the garden. Mealybugs are usually found outdoors only in the warmer climates. The similar appearances of these insects make separate identification difficult. They are conspicuous in late spring and summer because the adult females are covered with a white, cottony egg sac containing up to 2,500 eggs. Females lay their egg masses on leaves and stems. The young insects that hatch from these eggs are yellowish brown to green. They feed throughout the summer, causing damage by withdrawing plant sap from the ferns. Some species of scale and mealybug are unable to digest fully all the sugar in the plant sap, and they excrete the excess in a fluid called honeydew.

SOLUTION: When insects are first noticed, spray with an insecticide containing malathion or acephate (ORTHENE®). Some ferns may be damaged by this chemical. Test the spray on a small portion before using it on the whole fern. Wait a few days to see if the area turns brown. Cut off infested stems on plants that are sensitive to sprays. Discard severely infested plants. To treat 1 or 2 small plants, use a spray containing resmethrin.

Fern cultural information
Light: Partial shade to shade
Water: Keep soil moist
Soil: Loose, rich, well drained
Fertilizer: Medium

PROBLEM: The tips and edges of fronds turn brown or black and die. Entire fronds may wilt, turn yellow or brown, and die. The problem usually occurs first on the youngest fronds. This condition usually develops when the soil is dry but may also occur when it is moist.

ANALYSIS: Scorch

Scorch is caused by excessive evaporation of moisture from the fronds. In hot weather, water evaporates rapidly from them. Water loss is especially heavy when the weather is dry and windy. If the roots can't absorb and convey water fast enough to replenish this loss, the fronds turn brown or black and wither. Scorch usually occurs when the soil is allowed to dry out, but ferns can also suffer from scorch if the soil is moist if the weather is exceptionally hot and dry. Winds, severed roots, limited soil area, and low temperatures can also cause scorch.

SOLUTION: To prevent further scorch, water plants thoroughly. Ferns need to be kept moist. They must be watered frequently and deeply enough so that the soil doesn't dry out. During periods of exceptionally hot, dry weather, keep ferns wet by gently hosing down or sprinkling the fronds several times a day to reduce scorch damage. Grow ferns in shady areas that are protected from strong winds. Keep beds mulched.

PROBLEM: Small clumps of leaves lashed together with silken threads are scattered over the tree. The topsides of the leaves are skeletonized. The leaves turn brown and die, causing infested trees to look as if they have been scorched by fire. Small (up to 1-inch), pale gray or brown caterpillars with five white stripes feed inside the leaf clumps. Small trees or the Sunburst variety of thornless honeylocust may be completely defoliated by late summer. Trees are not killed, but repeated defoliations can seriously weaken them.

ANALYSIS: Mimosa webworms
(*Homadaula anisocentra*)
The mimosa webworm is the larval stage of a small moth. It feeds only on honeylocust and mimosa trees. Webworms pass the winter as pupae in white silken cocoons in sheltered places, such as in crevices in the bark of the infested tree or in soil and plant refuse beneath the tree. The moths emerge in the spring, when the females lay eggs. When the eggs hatch, the larvae crawl to the leaflets and feed on them for several weeks. A second generation of webworms hatches in August. The larvae of this generation are the most damaging because they are usually so numerous. In warmer areas, a third generation hatches in September.

SOLUTION: When cobwebs first appear, spray with an insecticide containing acephate (ORTHENE®). Repeat in August. Use high pressure to penetrate the cobwebs, and cover the tree thoroughly. In the fall, rake up and burn debris under infested trees, or turn over the soil and bury the leaves.

Pod gall midge damage.

Flowerless plant.

Sunburn.

PROBLEM: Green, globular, podlike galls, ⅛ inch in diameter, develop on new leaflets in spring and early summer. The galls turn reddish, then brown, and many of the infested leaflets drop. Twigs or branches sometimes die back after several years of infestation. Up to several whitish larvae, ¼ inch long, feed inside each gall.

ANALYSIS: Honeylocust pod gall midges
(*Dasineura gleditschiae*)
The larvae of this tiny black fly cause unsightly galls on honeylocust trees, especially the thornless varieties. The adult female midge begins laying eggs on new leaflets in the spring. When the eggs hatch, the larvae feed on the leaf tissue, causing the leaflet to fold over them and form a pod gall. As the young midges develop inside, the galls turn brown. The larvae emerge as flies, and the females lay more eggs. Honeylocusts produce new leaves over a long period, so the cycle may repeat itself up to seven times annually. The galls are not usually damaging to the tree. However, its ornamental value is reduced when the galled leaflets dry up and drop prematurely. Twigs sometimes die back after repeated attack, but new shoots usually form at the base of the dead twigs.

SOLUTION: Prune off dead twigs. In late May and again in late July, spray with an insecticide containing malathion or carbaryl (SEVIN®).

PROBLEM: Hydrangeas fail to produce blooms in the spring.

ANALYSIS: Failure to bloom
Hydrangeas may fail to bloom for several reasons.
1. *Cold injury:* Extreme winter temperatures or late spring cold snaps kill hydrangea flower buds, which form during the late summer or fall.
2. *Improper pruning:* Because some hydrangea species produce flower buds in the late summer or fall, pruning in the winter or spring removes these potential flowers.
3. *Too much shade:* Hydrangeas growing in deep shade may fail to form flower buds.

SOLUTION: Take these measures to correct the condition or control the problem.
1. Plant hydrangeas in a sheltered spot in the garden. Protect them by placing a wire cylinder around each plant and then filling it with loosely packed straw, or cover the cylinder with burlap. Protect hydrangeas in containers by moving them to a cool basement during the winter.
2. Prune hydrangeas after they have finished blooming by cutting back the longer branches.
3. Provide more light by pruning away some of the surrounding vegetation. Or transplant hydrangeas to a location that receives filtered or half-day sun or, in cool-winter areas, full sun.

PROBLEM: During warm, sunny weather, leaves on the outside of the plant turn yellowish or brown in the center of the leaf tissue. Some leaves may drop.

ANALYSIS: Sunburn
Hydrangeas are shade plants; their leaves are sensitive to the heat of the sun. The outside leaves facing the light turn yellow or brown when the shrub is planted in full sun. The injury is unsightly but is not damaging to the plant. Plants are more susceptible to sunburn when the soil in which they are planted is dry. Hydrangea leaves may also scorch (die and turn brown at the edges) during hot weather. For more information about sunburn, see page 152.

SOLUTION: Move the injured plant to a shaded location, or provide some shade where it is now growing.

Hydrangea cultural information
Light: Partial shade to full sun in cool coastal areas
Water: When soil is moist 4 inches below surface
Soil: Rich, well drained
Fertilizer: Acidic; for blue flowers apply aluminum sulphate

JUNIPERUS (JUNIPER)

Drought damage.

Root rot damage.

JUNIPERUS (JUNIPER)

ADAPTATION: Throughout the United States.

LIGHT: Full sun or, in hot climates, partial shade.

SOIL: Junipers prefer sandy, well-drained soil but they can thrive in almost any type of garden soil.

FERTILIZER: Apply a general-purpose fertilizer rated 10-10-10; follow label directions.

WATER:
How much: Apply enough water to wet the soil 1 to 3 feet deep, depending on the size of the juniper.
How often: Water young junipers when soil 4 inches below the surface is just barely moist. Established plants are drought resistant and require summer watering in the hottest climates only. In hot climates, water when soil 4 inches below the surface is dry. Do not plant junipers where they will receive water meant for a lawn.

PRUNING: Some junipers grow tall (to 90 feet) or spread up to 15 feet. The best course is to plant a variety that will fit the area rather than to depend on pruning to keep a tree within its confines. Older junipers do not sprout new growth from older wood, so never remove all the foliage from a branch. If a shrub is to be sheared, begin when the plant is young and shear lightly and on a regular schedule.

PROBLEM: Needles turn yellow and then brown and dry on the outer, lower branches; on the inside of the plant, nearest the trunk; from the top of the plant down; or from the tips back. Sometimes only a branch or one side of the plant is affected. In other cases, the whole plant turns brown.

ANALYSIS: Needle browning
A number of different conditions may cause the needles to turn brown on junipers.

1. *Dog urine:* When dogs urinate on junipers, the foliage on the outer, lower branches turns yellow, then brown, as if scorched. The salts in the urine burn the foliage.

2. *Natural leaf browning and shedding:* The older needles, on the inside of the plant nearest the trunk, turn brown and drop off in spring or fall. This is a natural process similar to the dropping of leaves of deciduous plants.

3. *Drought or winter injury:* When the plant is damaged by drought or winter injury, needles gradually turn yellow, then brown or reddish from the top of the plant down and from the tips of the branches back. This may happen when the soil is dry and the plant is not getting enough water or when the soil is frozen in the winter.

4. *Salt burn:* Needles turn brown from the tips back. This condition may develop on one side of the plant only or on the whole plant. Salt burn is common in alkaline soils, in areas where water has a high salt content, in soils with poor drainage, in overfertilized soils, or along roadsides where winter runoff contains road salts. The salts in the soil inhibit water and nutrient uptake, causing the needles to turn brown. Similar symptoms can occur in oceanfront plantings from wind-borne salt mist.

SOLUTION: Take these measures to correct the condition or control the problem.

1. Wash the foliage and thoroughly soak the ground around the plant to dilute the salts in the urine.

2. No controls are necessary.

3. Prune out dead twigs and branches. Provide adequate water during periods of extended drought, and shelter plants growing in windy locations. Water in late fall or early winter, if necessary, to ensure adequate soil moisture during the winter. Mulch plants after they are dormant to reduce the depth of frost penetration into the soil. Do not plant junipers in areas for which they are not adapted.

4. Prune off badly damaged areas. Avoid new injury by giving plants a heavy irrigation once during the growing season. If you suspect that your water contains salts, have it analyzed through the cooperative extension office or local water department. Do not overfertilize plants; follow package directions. Avoid planting in areas where road or sea salt may be a problem. Occasionally hose down oceanfront plantings to remove salt accumulations on the foliage.

JUNIPERUS (JUNIPER)

Dieback caused by phytophthora root rot.

Stem browning.

Spider mite damage (on left).

PROBLEM: Normal foliage color dulls, and the plant loses vigor. The foliage may wilt, or it may turn yellow or light brown. Major branches or the entire plant may die. The plant sometimes lives for many months in a weakened condition, or it may die quickly. The roots and lower stems are brownish, and the roots are often decayed. There may be fine woolly brown strands on the roots and white powdery spores on the soil surface; or there may be fan-shaped plaques of white strands between the bark and wood of the roots and lower stems. Mushrooms may appear at the base of the plant in the fall.

ANALYSIS: Root and crown rot

On junipers this condition is caused by several different fungi. The fungi live in the soil and on living roots.

1. *Phytophthora* species: These fungi cause browning and decay on the roots and browning on the lower stems. Infected plants usually die slowly, but young plants may wilt and die rapidly. The disease is most prevalent in heavy, water-logged soils.

2. *Phymatotrichum omnivorum:* This fungus, also known as cotton root rot or Texas root rot, is a severe problem on many plants in the Southwest. The plant often wilts and dies suddenly. Older plants may die more slowly, showing general decline and dieback symptoms. Brown strands form on the roots and white powdery spores form on the soil. The disease is most severe in heavy, alkaline soils.

3. *Armillaria mellea:* This disease—also known as shoestring root rot, mushroom root rot, or oak root fungus—is identified by the presence of fan-shaped plaques of white fungal strands between the bark and the wood of the roots and lower stems. These fungi grow rapidly under wet conditions. Honey-colored mushrooms appear at the base of the plant in the fall.

SOLUTION: Take these measures to correct the condition or control the problem.

1. Remove dead and dying plants. When replanting, use plants that are resistant to *Phytophthora*. Improve soil drainage. Avoid overwatering junipers.

2. Remove dead and dying plants. When replanting, buy only resistant varieties. Before planting, increase the soil acidity by adding 1 pound of ammonium sulfate to every 10 square feet of soil. With soil, make a circular ridge around the planting area and fill the resulting basin with 4 inches of water. In 5 to 10 days, reapply the ammonium sulfate and refill the basin. Improve drainage.

3. Remove dead plants. The life of a newly infected plant may be prolonged if the disease has not reached the lower stems. Expose the base of the plant to air for several months by removing several inches of soil. Prune off diseased roots. When replanting, use only resistant varieties.

PROBLEM: Needles are stippled yellow or grayish and dirty. Cobweb may cover the twigs. Needles may turn brown and fall off. To determine if the plant is infested with mites, hold a sheet of white paper underneath some stippled needles and tap the foliage sharply. If mites are present, minute green, red, yellow, or black specks the size of pepper grains will drop to the paper and crawl around. The pests are easily seen against the white background.

ANALYSIS: Spruce spider mites or two-spotted spider mites

(*Oligonychus ununguis* or *Tetranychus urticae*)
Spider mites, related to spiders, are among the most significant pests of junipers and other evergreen trees and shrubs. They cause damage by sucking sap from the needles. As a result of feeding, the green leaf pigment (chlorophyll) disappears, producing the stippled appearance. Spruce spider mites are prolific in cool weather. They feed and reproduce primarily during spring and, in some cases, fall. Spruce spider mites cause most of their damage when the temperature is below 70° F. Two-spotted mites, on the other hand, develop rapidly in dry temperatures above 70° F, so by midsummer populations build up to tremendous numbers.

SOLUTION: When damage is first noticed, spray with a miticide containing hexakis. Repeat the application 3 more times at intervals of 7 days. Hose down plants frequently to knock off cobwebs and mites.

Juniper scale (4 times life size).

Cedar-apple rust.

Privet rust-mite damage.

PROBLEM: The tree or shrub looks gray and off-color, and there is no new growth. Eventually the needles turn yellow. Branches and possibly the whole plant may die back. The foliage is covered with clusters of tiny (⅛-inch), somewhat flat, yellow and white scaly bumps. In many cases, a shiny, sticky substance may coat the needles. A black sooty mold may grow on the sticky substance.

ANALYSIS: Juniper scales
(*Carulaspis juniperi*)
These pests are found throughout the United States on many types of junipers and also on cypress (*Cupressus* species only) and incense cedar. The female scales spend the winter on the plant. They lay their eggs in spring. In midsummer (late spring in the South), the new generation, called crawlers, settles on the needles. These small (⅒-inch), soft-bodied young feed by sucking sap from the plant. Their legs atrophy, and a crusty shell develops over their bodies. The mature female scale lays her eggs underneath her shell. Juniper scales are unable to digest fully all the sugar in the plant sap, so they excrete the excess in a fluid called honeydew. A sooty mold fungus may develop on the honeydew. An uncontrolled infestation of scales may kill the plant in two or three seasons.

SOLUTION: In midsummer (late spring in the South), when the young are active, spray with an insecticide containing acephate (ORTHENE®) or carbaryl (SEVIN®). Early the following spring, before new growth begins, spray the trunk and branches with a dormant oil spray to control overwintering insects.

PROBLEM: In spring or early summer, brownish green swellings, or galls, appear on the topsides of needles. The galls enlarge until, by fall, they range in size from 1 to 2 inches in diameter. The galls turn chocolate brown and become covered with small circular depressions. The following spring, during warm, rainy weather, the depressions swell and produce orange, jellylike "horns" up to ¾ inch long. The galls eventually die, but they remain attached to the tree for a year or more. Infected twigs usually die.

ANALYSIS: Cedar-apple rust
This plant disease is caused by a fungus (*Gymnosporangium juniperi-virginianae*) that infects both juniper and apple trees. It cannot spread from juniper to juniper or apple to apple, but alternates between the two. Wind-borne spores from apple leaves infect juniper needles in the summer. The fungi grow little until the following spring, when the galls begin to form. The second spring, spores from the orange "horns" are carried by the wind to infect apple trees. By midsummer, orange spots appear on the apples and topsides of the leaves. (For more information about cedar-apple rust on apples, see page 217.) In August, spores are released and carried by the wind back to junipers. The entire cycle takes 18 to 20 months on juniper plus 4 to 6 months on apple.

SOLUTION: Remove galls and destroy them. When possible, do not plant junipers and apple trees within several hundred yards of one another. Spraying junipers with ferbam in August may help prevent new infections from apple trees.

PROBLEM: Leaves are dull green and severely cupped. They may turn bronze, brown, or yellow, then drop; or they may drop off the plant while still green. The plant is weak and often stunted.

ANALYSIS: Privet rust mites or privet mites
(*Aculus ligustri* or *Brevipalpus obovatus*)
Both of these mites are extremely small and generally cannot be seen without magnification. They cause damage by sucking sap from the leaf tissue. As a result of feeding, the leaf cups, or curls under, and often drops from the plant. The privet rust mite may feed only on the cells in the surface of the leaf, causing a bronze russeting or browning; the green leaf pigment (chlorophyll) is unaffected. Or the rust mite may feed deeper in the tissue, resulting in leaf yellowing caused by the disappearance of the green pigment. Some types of privet drop their leaves before discoloration develops. The rust mite is most prolific during cool weather. It feeds and reproduces primarily during spring and fall. The privet mite is usually active throughout the growing season. By midsummer populations may build up to tremendous numbers.

SOLUTION: When damage is first noticed, spray with a miticide containing hexakis. Spray the foliage thoroughly, being sure to cover both the topsides and undersides of the leaves. Repeat the application 3 more times at intervals of 7 days.

LIGUSTRUM (PRIVET) ——— ■ **MALUS (CRAB APPLE)** ———————————

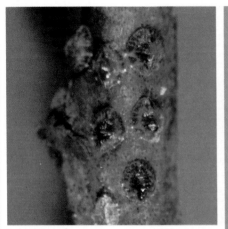

Scales (life size).

PROBLEM: The undersides of leaves, trunk, or branches are covered with brownish crusty bumps or clusters of somewhat flat, yellowish, brown, reddish, gray, or white scaly bumps. The bumps can be scraped or picked off. Leaves turn yellow and may drop, and twigs or branches may die back. A shiny, sticky substance often coats the leaves. A black sooty mold may grow on the sticky substance.

ANALYSIS: Scales
Many different types of scale infest privet. Females lay their eggs on the leaves or bark. In spring to midsummer, the young scales, called crawlers, settle on leaves, twigs, or trunk. These small ($\frac{1}{10}$-inch), soft-bodied young feed by sucking sap from the plant. Their legs usually atrophy, and a hard crusty shell develops over their bodies. Mature female scales lay their eggs underneath their shells. Some species of scale that infest privet are unable to digest fully all the sugar in the plant sap, so they excrete the excess in a fluid called honeydew. A sooty mold fungus may develop on the honeydew, causing the privet leaves to appear black and dirty. An uncontrolled infestation of scales may kill twigs or branches after two or three seasons.

SOLUTION: When the young are active, spray with an insecticide containing acephate (ORTHENE®) or carbaryl (SEVIN®). Contact the local cooperative extension office to determine the best time to spray for scales in your area. The following early spring, before new growth begins, spray the trunk and branches with an oil spray to control overwintering insects.

MALUS (CRAB APPLE) ———

ADAPTATION: Zones 2 through 10. To determine your zone, see the map on page 348. Most crab apples are not adapted to mild winter or desert areas.

FLOWERING TIME: Spring.

LIGHT: Full sun.

SOIL: Adapted to a wide variety of soils, but grows best in rich, well-drained garden soil.

FERTILIZER: Apply a fertilizer rated higher in nitrogen (14-7-7, for example); follow label directions.

WATER:
How much: Apply enough water to wet the soil 3 to 4 feet deep.
How often: Water when soil is barely moist 4 inches below the surface.

INSECTS AND DISEASES: Problems of crab apple trees are very similar to those of apple trees. For further information about the problems of crab apple, read about the insects and diseases that affect apple trees; see the section starting on page 214.

Fireblight.

PROBLEM: Blossoms and leaves of some twigs suddenly wilt and turn black as if scorched by fire. The leaves curl and hang downward. The bark at the base of a blighted twig becomes water-soaked, then dark, sunken, and dry; cracks may develop at the edge of the sunken area. In warm, moist spring weather, drops of brown ooze appear on the sunken bark. Young trees may die.

ANALYSIS: Fireblight
This plant disease is caused by a bacterium (*Erwinia amylovora*) that is extremely destructive to many trees and shrubs. Bacteria of this species spend the winter in the sunken areas (cankers) on the branches. In the spring, the bacteria ooze out of the cankers. Insects attracted to this ooze become smeared with it. When the insects visit a flower for nectar, they infect it with the bacteria. Insects visiting these infected blossoms later carry bacteria-laden nectar to healthy blossoms. Rain, wind, and tools may also spread the bacteria. Fireblight spreads rapidly through plant tissue in humid weather above 65° F. Tender or damaged leaves may be infected in midsummer.

SOLUTION: Prune out infected branches 12 to 15 inches beyond any visible discoloration; destroy the branches. Sterilize pruning shears with rubbing alcohol after each cut. A protective spray of a pesticide containing fixed copper or streptomycin, applied before bud break in spring, will help prevent infection. Respray at intervals of 5 to 7 days until the end of bloom.

Scab.

Cedar-apple rust.

Tent caterpillars ($\frac{1}{10}$ life size).

PROBLEM: Velvety olive-green spots, ¼ inch or more in diameter, appear on leaves. The tissue around the spots may be puckered. The leaves often turn yellow and drop. In a wet year, the tree may lose all its leaves by midsummer. The fruit and twigs develop circular, rough-surfaced, olive-green spots that eventually turn corky and black. The fruit is usually deformed.

ANALYSIS: Apple scab

This plant disease is caused by a fungus (*Venturia inaequalis*). It is a serious problem on crab apples and apples in areas where spring weather is humid with temperatures from 60° to 70° F. This fungus species spends the winter in infected fallen leaves. In the spring, spore-producing structures in the dead leaves continually discharge spores into the air. The spores are blown by the wind to new leaves and flower buds. If there is water on the tissue surface, the fungi infect the tissue and a spot develops. More spores are produced from these spots and from twig infections from the previous year. The spores are splashed by the rain to infect new leaf and fruit surfaces. As temperatures increase during the summer, the fungi become less active.

SOLUTION: To obtain adequate control of scab, apply protective sprays as soon as bud growth begins in spring. Spray with an insecticide containing chlorothalonil. Repeat 5 to 8 times at intervals of 7 to 10 days. Rake up and destroy infected leaves and fruit in the fall. When planting new trees, use resistant varieties.

PROBLEM: Pale yellow spots appear on leaves and fruit in mid- to late spring. These spots gradually enlarge, turn orange, and develop minute black dots. Small ($\frac{1}{16}$-inch) cups with fringed edges form on the undersides of the leaves. Infected leaves and fruit may drop prematurely; the fruit is often deformed.

ANALYSIS: Cedar-apple rust

This disease is caused by a fungus called *Gymnosporangium juniperi-virginianae*, which infects both crab apples and certain species of juniper and red cedar. This disease cannot spread from crab apple to crab apple or from juniper to juniper, but must alternate between the two. In the spring, spores from brown and orange galls on juniper or cedar are blown up to 3 miles to crab apple trees. During mild, wet weather, the spores germinate and infect the leaves and fruit, causing spotting and premature leaf and fruit drop. During the summer, spores are produced in small cups on the undersides of the leaves. These spores are blown back to junipers and cedars, causing new infections. For more information about cedar-apple rust on juniper, see page 173.

SOLUTION: Cedar-apple rust cannot be controlled on this season's foliage and fruit. Next spring, when the flower buds turn pink, spray trees with an insecticide containing chlorothalonil. Spray again when 75 percent of the petals have fallen from the blossoms, and treat once more 10 days later. If possible, do not plant crab apples within several hundred yards of junipers or red cedar.

PROBLEM: In spring, silken nets appear in the crotches of trees or on the ends of branches. The leaves are chewed, and the tree may become completely defoliated. Groups of hairy bluish or black caterpillars with yellow or white stripes and blue or white spots feed in or around the nets.

ANALYSIS: Tent caterpillars

(*Malacosoma* species)
Tent caterpillars feed on many ornamental and fruit trees. The insects are found in nearly all parts of the United States. In summer, female tent caterpillars lay masses of 150 to 300 eggs in bands around twigs. The eggs hatch in early spring, when leaves are beginning to unfold; the young caterpillars immediately begin to construct nets. On warm, sunny days they devour the surrounding foliage and may strip trees in just a few days. The caterpillars feed for four to six weeks and then pupate. In mid- to late summer, brownish or reddish moths emerge and the females lay the overwintering eggs.

SOLUTION: Cut out and destroy large nets. Or, when nets are first noticed, spray with an insecticide containing carbaryl (SEVIN®) or acephate (ORTHENE®), or treat with a bacterial insecticide containing Bt (*Bacillus thuringiensis*). Bacterial insecticide is most effective against small caterpillars, so spray before nets are large. Use a high-pressure sprayer to penetrate the nets. To prevent damage next year, destroy the brown egg masses that encircle the twigs during the winter.

PICEA (SPRUCE)

PICEA (SPRUCE)

ADAPTATION: Zones 2 through 8. To determine your zone, see the map on page 348. Not adapted to desert areas.

LIGHT: Full sun to partial shade.

SOIL: Tolerates a wide variety of soils.

FERTILIZER: Apply fertilizer higher in nitrogen (14-7-7, for example); follow label directions.

WATER:
How much: Apply enough water to wet the soil 3 to 4 feet deep.
How often: Water when soil is just barely moist 4 inches below the surface.

PRUNING: Prune to maintain the shape of the tree. If two leaders (tops) develop, remove one. For dense, bushy growth, remove a third of each year's new growth. When planting, allow enough room for spread and height—some spruce grow to 150 feet.

Spruce budworm larva (2 times life size).

PROBLEM: Needles on the ends of branches are chewed and webbed together. In mid-July the branch ends often turn reddish brown. Branches or the entire tree may die after three to five years of defoliation. Reddish brown caterpillars, 1¼ inches long, with yellow or white raised spots, feed on the needles.

ANALYSIS: Spruce budworms
(*Choristoneura* species)
Spruce budworms are extremely destructive to ornamental spruce, fir, and Douglas fir and may infest pine, larch, and hemlock. Budworm populations are cyclical. They come in epidemics 10 or more years apart. The moths are small (½ inch long) and grayish, with bands and spots of brown. The females lay pale green eggs in clusters on the needles in late July and August. The larvae that hatch from these eggs crawl to hiding places in the bark or in lichen mats, or they are blown by the wind to other trees, where they hide. The tiny larvae spin silken cases and hibernate there until spring. In May, when the weather warms, the caterpillars tunnel into needles. As the worms grow, they feed on opening buds; later they chew off needles and web them together. The larvae feed for about five weeks, pupate on twigs, and emerge as adults.

SOLUTION: When the buds begin to grow in late May, spray with an insecticide containing acephate (ORTHENE®).

Galls.

PROBLEM: The ends of branches develop green, pineapple-shaped galls in the spring; in late summer, the galls turn brown and dry. Growth continues beyond the galls, but the branch may be severely stunted. Galled stems are weak and may break during storms. Large numbers of galls may lessen the vigor of the tree.

ANALYSIS: Eastern spruce gall aphids (adelgids)
(*Adelges abietis*)
These gall aphids are most damaging to Norway spruce but may occasionally infest white, black, and red spruce. The insects spend the winter at the bases of terminal buds. When buds begin to grow in the spring, the females lay clusters of several hundred eggs that are covered with white, waxy threads. The young that hatch from these eggs feed on developing needles. They suck the juices, inducing the formation of galls that enclose the insects. The aphids live and feed in chambers inside the galls. In mid- to late summer, the galls turn brown and crack open. Mature aphids emerge, and the females lay eggs near the tips of the needles. The young that hatch from these eggs spend the winter at the bases of the buds.

SOLUTION: In the spring, just before growth begins, spray with an insecticide containing malathion or diazinon. Spray again around late September, after the galls turn brown and crack open.

Damaged needles. *Insert:* Larva (life size).

Spruce aphid damage to blue spruce.

Pine needle scale (4 times life size).

PROBLEM: Groups of brown needles are cob-webbed together, usually near the inside of the lower branches. There is a sawdustlike material around the webbing. The entire tree may be severely infested, giving it an unsightly appearance. Breaking open a partially brown needle reveals a small (up to ¼-inch), greenish brown larva feeding inside.

ANALYSIS: Spruce needleminers

(*Taniva albolineana*)
The spruce needleminer is the larva of a small (½-inch) dark brown moth. The female moth lays eggs on the undersides of old needles in late spring to early summer. The larvae that hatch from these eggs bore into the bases of the needles, feeding on the interiors. When the interiors are consumed, each caterpillar cuts off a few needle bases and webs the needles together, forming a nest. Needleminers feed until the first frost and then enter a hollow needle, where they spend the winter. When the weather warms in spring, the larvae continue feeding until April or May. They pupate inside the webbed nests of needles and emerge as adults to lay more eggs. Several other types of needleminers cause similar damage to spruce trees.

SOLUTION: Before treatment, wash out infested needles with a strong stream of water; destroy them. In late June spray with an insecticide containing acephate (ORTHENE®). Respray in 7 to 10 days.

PROBLEM: Many older needles turn brown and drop; only the newest needles remain green. The tree looks bare and sickly. Tiny (⅛-inch) green soft-bodied insects feed on the needles.

ANALYSIS: Spruce aphids or green spruce aphids

(*Elatobium abietinum* or *Cinara fornacula*)
These aphids can be extremely destructive to spruce in the northern United States. The aphids appear in early spring, around February. They are prolific and populations can rapidly build up to damaging numbers during March and April. Damage occurs when the aphids suck the juices from the spruce needles. The insects usually remain on a single needle until it is almost ready to drop. By the time the needles turn brown and the damage is noticeable, the insect population has declined. A heavily damaged tree may take several years to recover and replace its lost foliage.

SOLUTION: By the time the damage is noticed, it is usually too late in the year to treat the tree. The following February or March, spray with an insecticide containing acephate (ORTHENE®) or diazinon. Respray 10 days later.

PROBLEM: Needles are covered with clusters of somewhat flat, white, scaly bumps. When heavily infested, the foliage may appear completely white. The bumps can be scraped or picked off; their undersides are usually soft. Needles turn brown and eventually drop. Repeated severe infestations may kill young trees or weaken older trees.

ANALYSIS: Pine needle scales

(*Chionaspis pinifoliae*)
These scale insects may seriously damage spruce and pine trees and may infest fir, hemlock, and cedar. The scales survive the winter on spruce needles, as eggs beneath dead mother scales. The eggs hatch in late spring, and the young scales, called crawlers, move to new green needles. The small (⅒-inch) soft-bodied young feed by inserting their mouthparts and sucking sap from the plant. The crawlers' legs atrophy, and a crusty white shell develops over their bodies. Mature female scales lay their eggs underneath their shells in June or July. This next generation feeds throughout late summer and matures in fall. Females of this generation lay the overwintering eggs.

SOLUTION: In late spring, when the young are active, spray young trees with an insecticide containing acephate (ORTHENE®) or diazinon. Early the following spring, before new growth begins and when the danger of frost is past, spray with a pesticide containing lime sulfur to kill the overwintering eggs. Inspect ornamental spruce in early and late spring for evidence of infestation. Older trees seldom require controls.

PICEA (SPRUCE)

Spruce spider mite damage.

PROBLEM: Needles are  stippled yellow and dirty. There may be a silken webbing on the twigs and needles. Needles usually turn brown and fall off. To determine if the tree is infested with mites, hold a sheet of white paper underneath some stippled needles and tap the foliage sharply. If mites are present, minute dark green to black specks about the size of pepper grains will drop to the paper and begin to crawl around. The pests are easily seen against the white background.

ANALYSIS: Spruce spider mites
(*Oligonychus ununguis*)
These mites are among the most damaging pests of spruces and many other conifers. Spruce spider mites suck sap from the undersides of the needles. As a result of this feeding, the green pigment (chlorophyll) disappears, causing a stippled appearance. This symptom may be mistaken for certain types of air pollution damage. Spider mites first appear between April and June. In subtropical areas, mites may be active during warm periods in winter. A complete generation may be produced in only 17 days, so mites can rapidly build up to tremendous numbers during the growing season. Young spruce trees may die the first season. If left uncontrolled for several years, older trees may die, with symptoms progressing from the lower branches upward. Several other kinds of mite may infest spruce trees.

SOLUTION: As soon as damage is noticed, control with a miticide containing hexakis. Respray 2 more times, 7 to 10 days apart. Additional sprays may be needed in early fall or spring if the tree becomes reinfested.

Dieback. *Insert:* White pitch on bark.

PROBLEM: The needles on the branches nearest the ground turn brown and dry. Occasionally this condition develops first in the upper branches. The needles may drop immediately, or they may remain attached for a year. Eventually the entire branch dies back. Amber-colored pitch usually oozes from the infected area, becoming white as it dries. The infection may spread to the higher branches. To determine if the tree is infected, slice off the bark on a dead branch in the area where the diseased tissue and healthy tissue meet. Small black spore-producing bodies are beneath the bark of an infected tree.

ANALYSIS: Canker and dieback
This plant disease is caused by a fungus (*Cytospora kunzei*) that is extremely destructive to Norway and Colorado blue spruce. Fungi of this species enter the tree at a wound, killing the surrounding healthy tissue. A canker develops and expands through the wood in all directions. When the canker encircles a branch, the branch dies and the needles turn brown. Sap oozes from the dying branch. Eventually small black spore-producing bodies develop in the bark. Trees more than fifteen years old and weak or injured trees are most susceptible to the disease.

SOLUTION: Prune off and destroy dead or dying branches well below the infected area or where the branch meets the trunk. After each cut, sterilize the pruning shears with rubbing alcohol. Do not prune during wet weather. Avoid wounding trees with lawn mowers, tools, and other equipment. Keep trees vigorous by watering during dry spells and applying fertilizer every few years.

PINUS (PINE)

PINUS (PINE)

ADAPTATION: Throughout the United States.

LIGHT: Full sun.

SOIL: Tolerates a wide variety of soils, but soil should be well drained.

FERTILIZER: To avoid excessive growth, do not overfertilize. Apply a fertilizer higher in nitrogen (14-7-7, for example); follows label directions.

WATER: Once established, pines require little supplemental watering. Water young plants and potted plants when soil is barely moist 2 inches below the surface. Established plants usually require irrigation during periods of extended drought only, especially when growing in areas that normally receive water.

PRUNING: Prune to maintain the shape of each plant. To slow growth or increase bushiness, cut back the candles (new growth before needles begin to emerge) at least halfway. When planting, allow large species enough room for growth. Pines often drop many needles annually. This is a natural process of growth, not a cause for concern.

Needle cast. *Insert:* Fruiting structures.

Pitch mass on damaged tree.

Nematode damage to Japanese black pine.

PROBLEM: The tips of the needles of last year's growth turn brown in winter. By spring, these needles are completely discolored, giving the tree a scorched appearance. Many needles may drop from the tree, leaving only the new green growth. Tiny, black, elongated structures develop on the midribs of dead needles. The black structures may be swollen, with cracks down the middle. In severe cases, branch tips die back. Shaded parts of the tree are more frequently affected.

ANALYSIS: Needle cast
This plant disease is caused by one of two species of fungi (*Hypoderma lethale* and *Lophodermium pinastri*). It is most severe on young pine trees, but older trees may be infected on the lower branches. In the summer, during wet weather, spores are released from the elongated black fruiting structures on infected needles. Splashing rain and wind can carry the spores several hundred feet. The fungi enter needle tissue at this time, but the symptoms do not appear until early the following spring. In March or April brown spots with yellow edges develop on the foliage. The fungi grow through the tissue, and by late April or May the needles are completely brown. The needles drop, and the spores they carry continue the cycle.

SOLUTION: If needle cast was serious in the spring, spray valuable specimens in late July with a fungicide containing chlorothalonil. Repeat the treatment through September, at intervals of 10 to 14 days. If trees are shaded, remove as many shade-producing structures or plants as possible.

PROBLEM: Needles in the crown of the tree turn yellow at first, then turn brownish orange to reddish brown. Small holes appear in the trunk. Tubelike masses of pitch may also be present. Cutting away the bark near the holes or pitch tubes reveals legless grubs with brown heads in tunnels under the bark.

ANALYSIS: Bark beetles
(*Dendroctonus* species)
Pine bark beetles feed primarily on pine and occasionally on spruce and larch. Injured, weak, and dying trees are most susceptible to attack. Some bark beetles, the turpentine beetles, create tubes of pitch on the lower bark of trees. The pine bark beetle, a species from another group, attacks the middle and upper trunk and does not create pitch tubes. Adult beetles of all species burrow under the bark, where the females lay eggs. The larvae that hatch feed by tunneling through the bark. They form pupae in their tunnels and emerge as adults. A few beetles in a tree will not kill it; however, many pitch tubes indicate that enough beetles are present to kill or seriously weaken it.

SOLUTION: As soon as possible, remove and destroy severely infested trees. If pitch tubes are present on moderately infested trees, smash the tubes with a heavy rubber mallet to close the tunnels and squash the insects in the galleries beneath. Spray the trunk with an insecticide containing lindane. Keep the tree healthy by watering it thoroughly every 4 to 6 weeks during dry months. Apply fertilizer around weakened trees. Avoid injuring tree roots and trunk. Do not pile freshly cut pine wood or trimmings near trees; these attract beetles.

PROBLEM: The tree is yellowing and growing poorly. Branches die, or the entire tree turns brown and dies.

ANALYSIS: Root nematodes
Many different types of root nematode infect pines. Nematodes are microscopic worms that live in the soil. They are not related to earthworms. Root nematodes feed on plant roots, damaging and stunting them. The damaged roots can't supply sufficient water and nutrients to the aboveground parts, and the plant is stunted or slowly dies. Root nematodes prefer moist, sandy loam soils. These microscopic worms can move only a few inches each year on their own, but they may be carried long distances by soil, water, tools, or infested plants. Testing roots and soil is the only method for confirming the presence of nematodes. Contact the local cooperative extension office for sampling instructions and addresses of testing laboratories. Soil and root problems such as poor soil structure, drought stress, nutrient deficiency, and root rots can produce symptoms of decline similar to those caused by nematodes. Eliminate these problems as causes before sending soil and root samples for testing. Another type of nematode that lives inside the conducting vessels causes similar aboveground symptoms.

SOLUTION: There are no chemicals available to homeowners to kill nematodes in planted soil. However, they can be controlled before planting by soil fumigation.

PINUS (PINE)

Monterey pine damaged by spruce spider mite.

Woolly aphids on Austrian pine (life size).

Pine needle scale (life size).

PROBLEM: Needles are stippled yellow and are dirty. Sometimes there is a silken webbing on the twigs and needles. To determine if the tree is infested with mites, hold a sheet of white paper underneath some stippled needles and tap the foliage sharply. If mites are present, tiny dark red, green, or black specks the size of pepper grains will drop to the paper and begin to crawl around. The pests are easily seen against the white background.

ANALYSIS: Spruce spider mites
(*Oligonychus ununguis*)
These mites are among the most damaging pests of evergreen trees. Spruce spider mites suck sap from the undersides of the needles. As a result of this feeding, the green leaf pigment (chlorophyll) disappears, producing a stippled appearance. This symptom may be mistaken for certain types of air pollution damage. Spider mites first appear between April and June, hatching from eggs laid at the base of pine needles the previous fall. Mites can rapidly build up to tremendous numbers during the growing season. Young pine trees may die the first season. If left uncontrolled for several years, older trees sometimes die, with symptoms progressing from the lower branches upward. Several other species of mite also infest pines on the West Coast. Some of these mites are most numerous in the spring; others are found throughout the summer and fall.

SOLUTION: Spray with an insecticide containing hexakis. Repeat the application 2 more times at intervals of 7 to 10 days. Additional sprays may be needed later in the season or in spring if the tree becomes reinfested.

PROBLEM: The foliage or trunk is covered with white, woolly masses. If the infestation is heavy, the tree appears to be covered with snow. Infested shoots may droop; the needles turn yellow and may die. Trees heavily infested for several years are usually stunted.

ANALYSIS: Woolly aphids
(*Eriosomatinae* subfamily)
These small (⅛-inch), soft-bodied insects are not true aphids, but they are closely related to aphids. The adults are always covered with dense white filaments of wax. When this substance is removed, the insects appear purplish or green. Some species of these woolly "aphids" spend part of their lives on evergreens other than pines (usually spruce), often producing galls on the branches. In early summer, the insects migrate to pines and suck sap from the needles. Other species spend their entire lives on pines, feeding and reproducing on the trunks. Those species that spend the winter on other plants produce a generation in the fall that flies to the winter host.

SOLUTION: Spray pines with infested trunks in late April; spray pines with infested needles in late June. Use an insecticide containing acephate (ORTHENE®) or malathion. Cover the tree thoroughly. Respray if the plant becomes reinfested.

PROBLEM: Needles are covered with clusters of somewhat flat, white, scaly bumps. When heavily infested, the foliage may appear completely white. The bumps can be scraped or picked off; their undersides are usually soft. Needles turn brown and eventually drop. Repeated severe infestations may kill young trees or weaken older trees.

ANALYSIS: Pine needle scales
(*Chionaspis pinifoliae*)
These scale insects may seriously damage pine and spruce trees and may infest fir, hemlock, and cedar. The scales survive the winter on pine needles, as eggs beneath dead mother scales. The eggs hatch in late spring, and the young scales, called crawlers, move to new green needles. The small (1/10-inch) soft-bodied young feed by inserting their mouthparts and sucking sap from the plant. The crawlers' legs atrophy, and a crusty white shell develops over their bodies. Mature female scales lay their eggs underneath their shells in July. This next generation feeds throughout late summer and matures in fall. Females of this generation lay the overwintering eggs.

SOLUTION: In late spring, when the young are active, spray young trees with an insecticide containing acephate (ORTHENE®). Early the following spring, before new growth begins and when the danger of frost is past, spray with a pesticide containing lime sulfur to kill the overwintering eggs. Inspect ornamental pines in early and late spring for evidence of infestation. Older trees seldom require controls.

Needle rust.

Aphids on white pine (life size).

Pine spittlebug (3 times life size).

PROBLEM: Cream-colored, baglike pustules (blisters), 1/16 to 1/8 inch long, develop on needles in the spring. The pustules rupture, releasing bright orange spores. Trees with heavy infestations often drop many needles. Young trees may be stunted.

ANALYSIS: Needle rust

This plant disease is caused by any of several different fungi (*Coleosporium* species) that infect pine, goldenrod, and aster. The fungi cannot spread from pine tree to pine tree, but must alternate between pine and goldenrod or aster. Wind-borne spores from goldenrod or aster infect pine needles in summer and fall. The following spring, cream-colored pustules develop and needles may drop. The pustules rupture, and orange spores are blown to goldenrod and aster, where bright orange-yellow pustules develop on the under-sides of the leaves.

SOLUTION: During the summer and fall, spray young or valuable pine trees with a fungicide containing ferbam or zineb. Where practical, remove goldenrod and aster around pine trees.

PROBLEM: Needles are discolored and may be deformed; many may drop from the tree. New growth is often slow, and twigs may die. In many cases, a shiny, sticky substance coats the needles and branches. A black sooty mold may grow on the sticky substance. Small (up to 1/8-inch), green, brown, or black soft-bodied insects cluster on the needles, twigs, or main stems of small trees. An uncontrolled infestation may kill young trees.

ANALYSIS: Aphids

(*Cinara* species or *Eulachnus* species) Several different types of aphid infest the needles or bark of pines. Aphids do little damage in small numbers. However, they are extremely prolific and populations can rapidly build up to damaging numbers during the growing season. Damage occurs when the aphid sucks the juices from the pine needles, growing tips, or bark. The aphid is unable to digest fully all the sugar in the sap and excretes the excess in a fluid called honeydew, which often drops onto the needles and bark below. Plants or objects beneath the tree may also be coated with honeydew. Ants feed on this sticky substance and are often present where there is an aphid infestation. A sooty mold fungus may develop on the honeydew, causing the pine needles, bark, or other coated objects to appear black and dirty.

SOLUTION: When aphids first appear, control with an insecticide containing acephate (ORTHENE®) or malathion. Respray if the tree becomes reinfested. Be sure to check the tree in the fall as well.

PROBLEM: A frothy mass of bubbles appears on the twigs at the base of needles. A small (1/4-inch) tan or green wingless insect may be found inside the mass. Needles may turn yellow and drop off; black sooty mold may grow on surrounding branches. Continuous heavy infestations of insects kill branches or cause the death of young or weak trees.

ANALYSIS: Pine spittlebugs or Saratoga spittlebugs

(*Aphrophora parallela* or *A. saratogensis*) The pine spittlebug may cause serious injury to Scotch and white pines. The Saratoga spittlebug kills branches of jack and red pines. The pine spittlebug adults are grayish brown, wedge-shaped insects, 1/2 inch long. The females lay their eggs at the bases of buds in late summer. The eggs hatch the following May, and the young insects suck the sap from twigs and the main trunk. Drops of undigested sap mixed with air are excreted by the bug, producing the frothy "spittle" that surrounds its body. Some of the excreted sap drops onto lower branches, which may be colonized by a black sooty mold fungus. The life cycle of the Saratoga spittlebug is similar, but the tan females lay their eggs on plants beneath the tree. The adults migrate to trees in late June; feed until late fall; and then return to the low-growing plants, where the females lay their eggs.

SOLUTION: When insects are first noticed, spray with an insecticide containing acephate (ORTHENE®) in late May and again in July for the pine spittlebug and in late June or early July for the Saratoga spittlebug. Use a high-pressure sprayer.

PINUS (PINE)

Sawfly larvae (life size).

European pine-shoot moth damage.

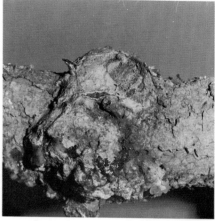

Pitch-moth damage.

PROBLEM: Needles are partially chewed, or the entire branch may be defoliated. In some cases, only the younger needles are eaten. Usually, however, the insects prefer the older needles. Gray-green, tan, or black caterpillarlike larvae, up to an inch long, are clustered on the needles. The larvae have many legs (prolegs) on their abdomens.

ANALYSIS: Sawflies
(*Neodiprion* species and *Diprion* species) Many species of sawflies infest pines. The dark, clear-winged adults are nonstinging wasps. With sawlike egg-laying organs, the female wasps insert rows of eggs in the needles. The larvae that hatch from these eggs feed in groups on the outer part of the foliage. As the larvae grow, they feed on a larger portion; eventually, entire needles are devoured. Small trees may be completely defoliated. The larvae then move to adjacent trees to feed. Some sawfly species feed only in the spring or summer. Others are present throughout the growing season, producing five or six generations each year. When the larvae mature, they drop to the ground and spin cocoons. Most sawflies spend the winter in the soil, although several species overwinter as eggs on the needles.

SOLUTION: When damage or insects are first noticed, spray the needles with an insecticide containing acephate (ORTHENE®). Inspect trees periodically during the growing season to detect infestations before severe defoliation occurs.

PROBLEM: Branch tips turn yellow, then brown and dry. The dead branches contrast sharply with healthy green foliage. In the summer, pitch accumulates around the dead needles. Trees may appear bushier than normal, or they may be crooked and distorted. At the bases of needles or inside a brown, resin-coated tip, cream-colored to reddish brown worms up to ¾ inch long feed on the tissue. Young trees may die.

ANALYSIS: Pine tip moths
(*Rhyacionia* species)
Seven species of pine tip, or pine shoot, moth infest various pines in different parts of the country. The adult is a reddish brown and gray moth, up to an inch long. The moths fly at night, but they may be seen during the day if a branch is disturbed. In mid- to late spring, female moths lay their eggs at the ends of branches. The larvae that hatch from these eggs bore into needles and buds, where they feed and mature. Depending on the species, pupation occurs in the mined-out area or in the soil around the base of the tree. Most species of tip moth produce one generation each year. In warm climates populations of Nantucket pine tip moths, *Rhyacionia frustrana*, produce as many as four or five generations yearly.

SOLUTION: If practical, prune out and destroy infested twigs in May or early June. In mid-April or early May, spray with an insecticide containing acephate (ORTHENE®). Respray in mid-May. If reinfestation occurs the same year, the Nantucket pine tip moth is probably involved. In this case, spraying every 4 weeks from early May to August may be necessary.

PROBLEM: One or more masses of sticky cream-colored, yellow, or pinkish pitch appear on the trunk. These masses may be 2 to 3 inches wide and protrude 1 to 2 inches. The pitch masses are usually found in wounds or in branch crotches. Scraping away the pitch mass reveals a larva up to 1 inch long.

ANALYSIS: Pitch moths
(*Vespamima* species)
Pitch moths attack pine, spruce, and Douglas fir. The adults are clear-winged moths that resemble yellowjackets. During the spring and summer, the females lay eggs in the trunks and larger limbs, particularly at sites of recent trunk injury or where old pitch masses exist. Usually there is one larva per pitch mass. The larva feeds on the inner bark for one to two years, pupates, and finally emerges as an adult moth during the summer. Although pitch masses are unsightly, pitch moths do not usually threaten the life of the tree. However, tree limbs may be weakened enough to break under the weight of snow.

SOLUTION: Scrape away fresh pitch masses and kill the larvae. The larvae can be found in the bark under the pitch mass or in the pitch mass itself. Avoid mechanical injury to trees. Confine pruning of larger limbs to fall and early winter months.

■ **PLATANUS (SYCAMORE, PLANE TREE)** —

White pine weevil damage.

Western gall rust on Monterey pine.

Sycamore lacebug damage.

PROBLEM: The main shoot at the top of the tree stops growing and turns yellow in midsummer. The shoot tip usually droops, producing a "shepherd's crook." Several new shoots may develop from below the dying shoot so that the top of the tree is forked. In fall and winter, the drooping shoot appears brown and dry. There is white resin on the bark, and the dead shoot contains small holes.

ANALYSIS: White pine weevils
(*Pissodes strobi*)
The white pine weevil attacks the main shoot, or leader, of both pine and spruce. This small (⅕-inch), brown, snouted beetle with white patches spends the winter in dead plant material at the base of the tree. In the spring, just before new growth begins, it moves to the top of the tree to feed on the inner bark tissue. The female lays eggs in small punctures in the bark. Resin droplets that ooze from the punctures later dry and turn white. The ¼-inch larvae that hatch from the eggs bore into the wood. The feeding cuts off the flow of water and nutrients through the stem, causing the shoot to droop and die. Several new shoots often develop from below the dead shoot, destroying the natural shape of the tree. In late summer, the larvae mature and return to the ground.

SOLUTION: In spring, when the buds begin to swell, control the adults by using an insecticide containing lindane. Spray the top of the tree thoroughly. (Spraying large trees is usually impractical for the home gardener. Hire a professional arborist.) In early summer, before the beetles emerge, prune out and destroy infested twigs. Select one side branch to replace the dead leader. Prune back all the other side branches to half the length of the newly selected leader.

PROBLEM: Rough, spherical swellings develop on branches or on the main trunk. In the spring, the swellings appear orange or yellow. Growth beyond the galls is often stunted, distorted, and off-color.

ANALYSIS: Western gall rust or eastern gall rust
These plant diseases are caused by one of two species of fungi (*Cronartium harknessii* or *C. quercuum*). Western gall rust requires only one host to complete its life cycle; spores from one pine can infect another. Eastern gall rust requires both pine and oak to complete its life cycle. In early spring, orange or yellow spores are produced over the ruptured surfaces of the swellings (galls). The spores are blown and carried by wind and insects to susceptible trees. When moisture and temperatures are optimum, western gall-rust spores infect pine tissue, causing an increase in the number and size of plant cells. Within six months to a year, swellings develop. The galls enlarge and produce spores after one to two years. Eastern gall-rust spores infect only oak. Spores produced on the oak trees reinfect pines. The galls caused by both fungi interrupt the sap movement in the tree. They also stimulate witches'-brooms, dense stunted growth beyond the galls. If many of these develop, the tree becomes unsightly and weak and limbs may break during storms.

SOLUTION: Where practical, prune off galled branches before the galls produce spores in early spring.

PROBLEM: The topsides of leaves are mottled or speckled white and green. The mottling may be confused with mite or leafhopper damage. Unlike mottling caused by mites and leafhoppers, however, this discoloration is accompanied by shiny, hard, brown droplets that adhere to the undersides of damaged leaves. Small (⅛-inch), light or dark, spiny, wingless insects or brownish insects with clear lacy wings may be visible around the droplets. Foliage on severely infested trees may be completely white, then turn brown by mid-August.

ANALYSIS: Sycamore lacebugs
(*Corythucha* species)
Two species of lacebug infest sycamores and London plane trees. The insects survive the winter as adults in bark crevices or in other protected areas on the tree. When the buds begin to open in the spring, adult females use a brown sticky substance to attach their eggs to the undersides of the leaves. The eggs hatch and the spiny, wingless, immature insects—and later the brown lacy-winged adults—suck sap from the undersurfaces of the foliage. The green leaf pigment (chlorophyll) disappears, resulting in the characteristic white and green mottling. As the lacebugs feed, droplets of brown excrement accumulate around them.

SOLUTION: When damage first appears in spring, spray young trees with an insecticide containing acephate (ORTHENE®). Cover the undersurfaces of the leaves thoroughly. Repeat 7 to 10 days later. Early spraying is essential to damage prevention. Spraying large trees is usually impractical for the home gardener; hire a professional.

183

PLATANUS (SYCAMORE, PLANE TREE) ■ POPULUS (ASPEN, COTTONWOOD, POPLAR)

Anthracnose. *Insert:* Spore-producing bodies.

PROBLEM: In the spring, buds or expanding shoots turn brown and die. Dead areas appear along the veins of young leaves. As the leaves mature, the spots may expand and cover them entirely. Most infected leaves drop from the tree. Later in the season, twigs and older leaves may be infected. Infected twigs hang on the tree or drop to the ground with the leaves. Larger limbs may die. Dark brown spore-producing bodies appear on the bark and dead leaves. The tree is often stunted and bushy.

ANALYSIS: Sycamore anthracnose
This plant disease is caused by a fungus (*Gnomonia platani*) that is the most serious problem of sycamore and causes minor damage to the London plane tree. Fungi of this species survive the winter on fallen leaves and twigs and in swollen cankers in the tree. During wet weather below 55° F, spores are blown and splashed onto buds, expanding shoots, and young leaves. The fungi enter the tissue and kill it, causing the buds and shoots to die back. The fungi move down onto the twigs, and spores develop. The spores may infect mature leaves or any new growth on the tree, causing a sunscorched appearance. Swollen, cracked cankers develop on infected twigs and branches. When the cankers encircle the wood, the limbs die.

SOLUTION: Prune off and destroy infected twigs and dead branches. In areas where spring is cool and moist, spray trees when buds begin to grow in the spring; use a fungicide containing chlorothalonil. Respray when leaves reach full size and again 2 weeks later.

POPULUS (ASPEN, COTTONWOOD, POPLAR)

ADAPTATION: Throughout the United States.

LIGHT: Full sun.

SOIL: Tolerates a wide variety of soils. Roots are invasive.

FERTILIZER: Apply a fertilizer rated higher in nitrogen (14-7-7, for example); follow label directions.

WATER:
How much: Apply enough water to wet the soil 3 to 4 feet deep.
How often: Some poplars are drought tolerant once established. However, most poplars prefer moist soil, and some even tolerate soil that is soggy or flooded.

PRUNING: Prune off suckers and broken branches, and prune the tree to maintain its shape.

Satin moth caterpillars (life size).

PROBLEM: The surfaces of leaves are eaten, giving the remaining tissue a lacy appearance, or leaves are chewed all the way through. Sometimes cobwebs appear on foliage and branches. The tree may be completely defoliated. Damage appears any time between spring and fall. Caterpillars feed on the leaves. Repeated heavy infestations may weaken or kill trees.

ANALYSIS: Leaf-feeding caterpillars
Many different species of caterpillar feed on poplar leaves wherever the trees are grown. From early spring to midsummer, female moths lay the eggs from which the caterpillars hatch; the time depends on the species. The larvae that hatch from these eggs feed singly or in groups on buds, on one leaf surface or the other, or on entire leaves. Certain caterpillars web leaves together or web a branch as they feed. In some years, damage is minimal due to environmental conditions unfavorable to the pest or control by predators and parasites. However, when conditions are favorable, entire trees may be defoliated by late summer. Defoliation weakens trees because no leaves remain to produce food. When heavy infestations occur several years in a row, branches or entire trees may be killed.

SOLUTION: When damage is first noticed, spray with an insecticide containing acephate (ORTHENE®) or carbaryl (SEVIN®) or apply a bacterial insecticide containing *Bacillus thuringiensis*. Cover the leaves thoroughly. Respray if the tree becomes reinfested.

Oystershell scales (¼ life size).

Poplar willow borer (½ life size).

Dieback. *Insert:* Canker.

PROBLEM: The trunk, stems, or undersides of leaves are covered with brown, black, or red-orange crusty bumps or somewhat flat, brownish, white, or grayish scaly bumps. The bumps can be scraped or picked off; their undersides are usually soft. Leaves turn yellow and may drop. In some cases, a shiny, sticky substance coats them. A black sooty mold often grows on the sticky substance. Large portions of the tree may be killed if infestations are heavy.

ANALYSIS: Scales
Many different types of scale infest poplar. The females lay their eggs on leaves or bark. In spring to midsummer, the young scales, called crawlers, settle on leaves, twigs, and trunk. The small (¹⁄₁₀-inch), soft-bodied young feed by sucking sap from the plant. Their legs usually atrophy, and a hard crusty shell develops over their bodies. Mature female scales lay their eggs underneath their shells. Some species of scale that infest poplar are unable to digest fully all the sugar in the plant sap, so they excrete the excess in a fluid called honeydew. A sooty mold fungus may develop on the honeydew, causing the poplar leaves to appear black and dirty. An uncontrolled infestation of scales may kill the tree after two or three seasons.

SOLUTION: When the young are active, spray with an insecticide containing acephate (ORTHENE®) or carbaryl (SEVIN®). Contact the local cooperative extension office to determine the best time to spray for scales in your area. To control overwintering insects, spray with an oil spray before growth begins in the spring.

PROBLEM: Swollen areas with holes in the centers develop on twigs, branches, or the trunk. Many side shoots may grow from below the swellings, destroying the natural form of the tree. The leaves on infested twigs and branches turn yellow and may be chewed on the edges. A sawdustlike material and many broken twigs lie beneath the tree.

ANALYSIS: Poplar borers
(*Saperda* species)
At least five species of beetle feed on poplars, causing galls to form. The inch-long, striped and spotted, brownish or gray beetles with long antennae appear in late spring or early summer. The females lay eggs in small holes gnawed in the bark of twigs and branches more than ½ inch in diameter. As the legless, whitish grubs hatch from these eggs, they tunnel into the wood. Excess tissue grows around the wound, resulting in a swollen area, or gall. When infestations are severe, nearly all twigs and branches more than ½ inch in diameter have one or more galls. The galls weaken the twigs and branches, causing them to break and litter the ground during stormy weather. The grubs remain in the wood for one or two years.

SOLUTION: Remove and destroy severely damaged trees. In late May or early June, spray the bark of less severely damaged trees with an insecticide containing lindane. Repeat the treatment 2 weeks later.

PROBLEM: Dark sunken areas appear on the twigs, branches, or trunk. Leaves on infected branches may be spotted, or they may be stunted and a lighter green than normal. Twigs and branches are often killed. Young or weakened trees are most susceptible.

ANALYSIS: Canker and dieback
Several different fungi cause canker and dieback on poplars. Lombardy poplars are especially vulnerable. The fungi enter the tree through a wound or, in some cases, through the leaves, killing surrounding healthy tissue. A dark sunken canker develops in the wood and expands through it in all directions. If the fungi infect the leaves first, the infection spreads down through the leaf stems and forms cankers on the twigs. The canker cuts off the flow of nutrients and water, causing the leaves to turn yellow. Twig or branch dieback follow if the canker girdles the wood. The tree may wall off the spreading fungi by producing callus tissue, a rapid growth of barklike cells. If the expanding canker is stopped before it covers half the diameter of the trunk, the tree usually survives. However, the fungi may grow faster than the callus, or the tree may not produce a callus; the death of the branch or the whole tree results.

SOLUTION: Prune off dead twigs and small cankered branches, cutting well below the canker. Remove and destroy severely infected trees. To prevent the development of new cankers, avoid wounding trees. Keep trees vigorous by applying fertilizer and watering when necessary.

PYRACANTHA ■ QUERCUS (OAK)

Fireblight.

PROBLEM: Blossoms and leaves of some twigs suddenly wilt and turn black as if scorched by fire. The leaves curl and hang downward. The bark at the base of a blighted twig becomes water-soaked, then dark, sunken, and dry; cracks may develop at the edge of the sunken area. In warm, moist spring weather, drops of brown ooze appear on the sunken bark. Young plants may die.

ANALYSIS: Fireblight
This plant disease is caused by a bacterium (*Erwinia amylovora*) that is extremely destructive to many trees and shrubs. Bacteria of this species spend the winter in sunken areas (cankers) on the branches. In the spring, the bacteria ooze out of the cankers. Bees, flies, and other insects are attracted to the sweet, sticky ooze and become smeared with it. When the insects visit a flower for nectar, they infect it with the bacteria. Insects visiting these infected blossoms later carry bacteria-laden nectar to healthy blossoms. Fireblight spreads rapidly through plant tissue in humid weather above 65° F. Tender or damaged leaves may be infected in midsummer.

SOLUTION: During spring and mid- to late summer, prune out infected branches 12 to 15 inches beyond any visible discoloration; destroy the branches. A protective spray of a bactericide containing basic copper sulfate or streptomycin, applied before bud break in spring, will help prevent infection. Respray at intervals of 5 to 7 days until the end of bloom. In the fall, prune out infected branches. Sterilize pruning shears with rubbing alcohol after each cut.

QUERCUS (OAK)

ADAPTATION: Throughout the United States. There are oaks for all climates and conditions, including salt air, heat, wind, and moisture.

LIGHT: Full sun.

SOIL: Any good, deep, well-drained garden soil. Some oaks do not tolerate alkaline soil (pH 7.0 and above).

FERTILIZER: Some oaks benefit from periodic feedings under the outer branches. Apply a fertilizer higher in nitrogen (14-7-7, for example); follow label directions.

WATER: Some oaks grow best with ample water and can thrive in lawns. Others, such as the western native oaks, prefer drier conditions. These oaks decline and eventually die if overwatered.
  How much: Apply enough water to wet the soil 4 to 5 feet deep.
  How often: Water young trees when soil is barely moist 4 inches below the surface. *Oaks requiring ample water:* Water established trees when soil is barely moist 4 inches below the surface. *Oaks preferring dry conditions:* Never water a dry-climate oak around the trunk. Most of these oaks need no supplemental water once established.

PRUNING: Prune to maintain the shape of the oak and to remove dead wood. When planting, allow room for growth.

Oak leaf blister.

PROBLEM: Puckered, circular areas up to ½ inch in diameter appear on leaves in the spring. The blisterlike spots are yellowish green at first; they later die and turn brown. The leaves usually remain attached to the tree.

ANALYSIS: Oak leaf blister
This tree disease is caused by a fungus (*Taphrina caerulescens*) that is unsightly but rarely harmful to the tree. Fungi of this species infect various species of oak, particularly red, black, scarlet, and live oaks. The fungi spend the winter in the bud scales on the tree. During cool, wet spring weather, it enters the developing leaves. Green blisters form where the fungi enter the tissue. The infected tissue eventually dies and turns brown. In the fall, the organisms produce overwintering spores. If the following spring is cool and wet, the cycle begins again.

SOLUTION: If leaf blister was a problem the previous year and the weather this spring is cool and wet, spray the tree one or two weeks before the leaves appear; use a fungicide containing chlorothalonil. Cover the entire tree thoroughly with the spray.

Borer hole.

Gypsy moth caterpillars (½ life size).

Oak pit scales (3 times life size).

PROBLEM: Foliage on a branch or at the top of the tree is sparse; eventually the twigs and branches die. Holes are in the trunk or branches. Sap or a sawdustlike material sometimes surrounds the holes. In some areas, bark may die and slough off, revealing tunnels. Weak, young, or newly transplanted trees may be killed. Weakened branches may break during wind- or snowstorms.

ANALYSIS: Borers

Borers are the larvae of beetles or moths. Several kinds of borer attack oaks. Throughout the summer, females lay their eggs in bark crevices. The larvae feed on the bark, sapwood, and heartwood. This stops the flow of nutrients and water in that area by damaging the conducting vessels; branch and twig dieback result. Sap flow acts as a defense against borers if the tree is healthy. When the borer burrows into the wood, tree sap fills the hole and kills the insect. A tree weakened by mechanical injuries, transplanting, damage by leaf-feeding insects, and poor growing conditions is especially attractive to egg-laying females.

SOLUTION: Borers are difficult to control once they have burrowed into the wood. Cut out and destroy all dead and dying branches. Remove severely infected young trees. In May, spray the trunks and branches of remaining trees with an insecticide containing lindane. Respray 2 weeks later and again in July and August. Maintain plant vigor by watering during periods of drought and applying fertilizer regularly.

PROBLEM: The surfaces of leaves are eaten, giving the remaining tissue a lacy appearance, or leaves are chewed all the way through. Sometimes the leaves are webbed together. The tree may be completely defoliated. Damage appears any time between spring and fall. Caterpillars feed on the leaves. Repeated heavy infestations may weaken or kill trees.

ANALYSIS: Leaf-feeding caterpillars

Many different species of caterpillar feed on oak leaves wherever the trees are grown. From early spring to midsummer, female moths lay the eggs from which the caterpillars hatch; the time depends on the species. The larvae that hatch from these eggs feed singly or in groups on buds, on one leaf surface or the other, or on entire leaves. Certain caterpillars web the leaves together as they feed. In some years, damage is minimal due to environmental conditions unfavorable to the pest or control by predators and parasites. However, when conditions are favorable, entire trees may be defoliated by late summer. Defoliation weakens trees because no leaves remain to produce food. When heavy infestations occur several years in a row, branches or entire trees may be killed.

SOLUTION: When damage is first noticed, spray with an insecticide containing acephate (ORTHENE®) or carbaryl (SEVIN®) or apply a bacterial insecticide containing *Bacillus thuringiensis*. Spray the leaves thoroughly. Respray if the tree becomes reinfested.

PROBLEM: During the summer or early fall, leaves turn brown and twigs or branches die back. Dead leaves usually remain attached to the branches throughout the winter. In the spring, new leaves on infested deciduous oaks may appear three weeks late. Repeated heavy infestations often kill young trees. Small (1/12-inch); somewhat flat; green, golden, or brown scaly bumps cluster on the twigs and branches. The bumps, which are insects, cluster in pitted bark.

ANALYSIS: Pit scales

(*Asterolecanium* species)
Several species of pit scale may seriously damage oaks. The female scales lay their eggs in spring and summer. The young scales, called crawlers, that hatch from these eggs settle on new growth and last year's branches, not far from the parent. The small (1/16-inch), soft-bodied young feed by inserting their mouthparts and sucking sap from the plant. Pits develop where the scales feed. The crawlers' legs atrophy, and a hard, crusty shell develops over their bodies. The mature female scales lay eggs underneath their shells. Several other types of scales also infest oak.

SOLUTION: In mid-May to June, when the young are active, spray with an insecticide containing acephate (ORTHENE®). To control overwintering insects, spray with an oil spray in winter or spring. Cover the tree thoroughly with the spray.

QUERCUS (OAK)

Cankers.

Fungal mats.

PROBLEM: Leaves are stunted and yellow, and the foliage throughout the tree may be sparse. Branches eventually die. Weakened trees are most severely infected. Occasionally trees die suddenly, without showing symptoms; but, in most cases, trees die slowly over a period of several years. During fall or winter, honey-colored mushrooms, 2 to 5 inches in diameter, may grow singly or in clusters on the lower trunk or on the ground near infected roots. Removing soil around the base of the tree reveals black rootlike strands, about the diameter of pencil lead, attached to the larger roots. A white fan-shaped growth occurs between the bark and wood of these larger roots and on the trunk just below the soil surface. The infected tissue has a mushroom odor.

ANALYSIS: Armillaria root rot

This plant disease, also called oak root fungus or shoestring root rot, is caused by a fungus (*Armillaria mellea*) that rots the roots of many woody and nonwoody plants. Oaks are often lightly infected with this species for years and show no damage. However, when the trees are under stress from drought, overwatering, physical injuries, insects, or diseases, they often succumb to *Armillaria*. The infection is spread short distances (under 12 inches) through the soil by the rootlike fungal strands. When they touch susceptible plant roots, the strands penetrate the host if conditions are favorable. Once the fungi enter the bark tissue, they produce a white fan-shaped mat of fungal strands that invade and decay the tissue of the roots and lower trunk. The fungi spread rapidly if the oak tree is in a weakened state. Infection inhibits water and nutrient uptake by the roots, causing the foliage and branches to die. In the fall, mushrooms—the reproductive bodies of fungi—often appear around infected trees. A closely related fungus (*Clitocybe tabescens*) that infects oak in the southeastern United States produces symptoms similar to armillaria root rot.

SOLUTION: Remove and destroy infected trees, including the stumps and the root systems. The fungi can live on the stumps and roots for many years, infecting susceptible plants nearby. Healthy-looking plants growing adjacent to diseased trees may already be infected. Check around the roots and lower stems for signs of fungi. The life of a tree may be prolonged if it is not severely infected. Remove the soil from around the rotted parts of the roots and trunk. Cut out the diseased tissue, exposing healthy wood. Allow it to air-dry through the summer. Do not water the tree. Cover the exposed parts before temperatures drop below freezing. Replace infected trees with armillaria-resistant plants. Avoid planting susceptible species in recently cleared forest lands where armillaria root rot is common. To inhibit disease development in an established oak tree, provide optimum growing conditions, avoid injuring the tree, and control pests and diseases.

■ RHODODENDRON (AZALEA)

RHODODENDRON (AZALEA)

ADAPTATION: Zones 4 through 10 except in desert areas. To determine your zone, see the map on page 348. Azaleas are more tolerant of warm, dry climates than rhododendrons.

FLOWERING TIME: Late winter to early summer. A few bloom in mid- to late summer.

LIGHT: Partial shade (full sun in cool-summer areas). Plants don't bloom well in deep shade.

SOIL: Rich, well-drained, acidic (pH 4.5 to 6.0) soil, high in organic matter and low in salts. When planting, add at least 50 percent peat moss to the soil, and keep 2 inches of mulch around the base of each plant.

FERTILIZER: Apply a fertilizer slightly higher in nitrogen (10-7-7, for example); follow label directions.

WATER:
How much: Apply enough water to wet the soil 1 to 2½ feet deep.
How often: Water when soil under the mulch is moist but not wet.

PRUNING: Prune just after flowering.
Azaleas: For bushier plants, pinch off growing tips.
Rhododendrons: Remove dead flower trusses; be careful not to break the new buds. To renew old, lanky plants, reduce the height of the plant by a third for 3 successive years.

Salt burn.

Sunburn on azalea.

Phytophthora root rot.

PROBLEM: Leaf edges are brown and dead. Browning usually occurs on older leaves first. This distinguishes the problem from windburn, which develops on young, exposed leaves first. Leaves may be a lighter green than normal. In a severe case, leaves drop off.

ANALYSIS: Salt burn
This problem is most common in areas of low rainfall. It also occurs in soils with poor drainage and where too much fertilizer has been applied. Excess salts dissolved in the soil water accumulate in the leaf edges, where they kill the tissue. These salts also interfere with water uptake by the plant. This problem is rare in areas of high rainfall, where the soluble salts are leached from most soils. Poorly drained soils do not leach well; much of the applied water runs off the surface instead of washing through. Fertilizers, most of which are soluble salts, also cause salt burn if too much is applied or if they are not diluted with a thorough watering after application.

SOLUTION: Salt burn damage does not disappear from the leaves, but injury can be avoided in the future. In areas of low rainfall, leach accumulated salts from the soil with an occasional heavy irrigation (about once a month). If possible, improve the drainage around the plants by removing them and adding soil amendments before replanting. If plants are severely damaged, replace them with healthy plants. Follow label directions when using commercial fertilizers; water thoroughly after application. Avoid the use of bagged steer manure, which contains large amounts of salt.

PROBLEM: During warm, sunny weather the center portion of the leaf bleaches to a tan or off-white color. Once the initial damage has occurred, the spot does not usually increase in size. Injury is generally more severe on plants with light-colored flowers.

ANALYSIS: Sunburn
Rhododendrons and azaleas are generally classified as shade plants. Their leaves are sensitive to the heat of direct sun, which kills the leaf tissue. Sunburn occurs when the shrub is planted in full sun. The intense reflection from a light-colored, south-facing wall can also burn leaves. It takes only one hot summer day for damage to appear. The injury is unsightly but is not damaging to the plant. However, weakened leaves are more susceptible to invasion by fungi and bacteria. Plants that do not receive enough water are more susceptible to sunburn.

SOLUTION: Move the injured plant to a shaded location, or provide some shade where it is now planted. Once leaves are sunburned, they will not recover. Where practical, remove affected leaves. Don't let plants dry out during hot weather.

PROBLEM: Young leaves are yellowish and wilting. Eventually the whole plant wilts and dies, even though the soil is moist. Dead leaves remain attached to the plant and are rolled along the midrib. The symptoms may develop over a few weeks, or they may take many months. The tissue under the bark close to ground level is darkly discolored; to check for discoloration, peel back the bark at the bottom of the plant. A distinct boundary exists between white healthy wood and dark diseased wood.

ANALYSIS: Wilt and root rot
This plant disease is caused by one of several different soil-inhabiting fungi (*Phytophthora* species or *Pythium* species), also known as water molds. These fungi attack a wide variety of ornamental plants. The fungi destroy the roots and may work their way up the stem. If they girdle the stem, the plant wilts and dies. Extremely wet conditions favor the fungi, which are most common in heavy, poorly drained soils. Although azaleas and rhododendrons need constant moisture, they must also have adequate drainage.

SOLUTION: No chemical control is available. Dry the soil out. If plants have died, improve the drainage of the soil before replanting azaleas or rhododendrons in the same location. If drainage cannot be improved, plant in beds raised 12 inches or more above grade or plant shrubs that are resistant to wilt and root rot.

RHODODENDRON (AZALEA) ■ **ROSA (ROSE)**

Azalea bark scale (life size).

Flower thrips damage.

RHODODENDRON (AZALEA)

PROBLEM: Clusters of somewhat flat white, yellowish, brown, reddish, or gray scaly bumps cover the undersides of the leaves and young branches or the branch crotches. The bumps can be scraped or picked off; their undersides are usually soft. Leaves may turn yellow and drop off, and branches may die back. The plant is killed when infestations are heavy.

ANALYSIS: Scales
Many species of scale infest rhododendrons and azaleas throughout the country. Scales spend the winter on the trunk and twigs of the plant. Females lay eggs in spring and in midsummer. The young scales, called crawlers, settle on the various parts of the shrub. The small ($\frac{1}{10}$-inch), soft-bodied young feed by inserting their mouthparts and sucking sap from the plant. Their legs usually atrophy, and a scaly or crusty shell develops over their bodies. Mature female scales lay their eggs underneath their shells. Leaf drop and twig dieback occur when scales completely cover the leaves and branches. An uncontrolled infestation may kill a plant after two or three seasons.

SOLUTION: In midsummer (late spring in the southern United States), when the young are active, spray with an insecticide containing acephate (ORTHENE®), carbaryl (SEVIN®), malathion, or diazinon. The following early spring, before new growth begins, spray the branches and trunk with a dormant oil spray to control overwintering insects.

ROSA (ROSE)

ADAPTATION: Throughout the United States.

FLOWERING TIME: Spring and summer (through fall in the South).

LIGHT: Full sun. Plant in areas with ample air circulation.

SOIL: Any good, well-drained garden soil.

FERTILIZER: Apply a fertilizer higher in phosphorus (8-12-4, for example); follow label directions.

WATER:
How much: Apply enough water to wet the soil 1½ to 2 feet deep.
How often: Roses need plenty of water. Water when soil 4 inches deep is moist but not wet.

PRUNING: Remove dead or unhealthy wood. Remove branches that cross through the center of the plant. Prune off at least a third to half of last year's growth. For more information about pruning and care of roses, see ORTHO's book *All About Roses*.

ROSA (ROSE)

PROBLEM: Young leaves are distorted, and foliage may be flecked with yellow. Flower buds are deformed and usually fail to open. The petals of open blossoms, especially those of white or light-colored varieties, are often covered with brown streaks and spots. If a deformed or streaked flower is pulled apart and shaken over white paper, tiny yellow or brown insects fall out and are easily seen against the white background.

ANALYSIS: Flower thrips
(*Frankliniella tritici*)
Flower thrips are the most abundant and widely distributed thrips in the United States. They live inside the buds and flowers of many garden plants. Both the immature and the adult thrips feed on plant sap by rasping the tissue. The injured petal tissue turns brown, and the young expanding leaves become deformed. Injured flower buds usually fail to open. Thrips initially breed on grasses and weeds. When these plants begin to dry up or are harvested, the insects migrate to succulent green ornamental plants. The adult females lay their eggs by inserting them into the plant tissue. A complete life cycle may occur in two weeks, so populations can build up rapidly. Most damage to roses occurs in early summer.

SOLUTION: Thrips are difficult to control because they continually migrate to roses from other plants. Immediately remove and destroy infested buds and blooms. At intervals of 7 to 10 days, spray 3 times with an insecticide containing acephate (ORTHENE®).

Failure to bloom.

Lack of flowering caused by poor pruning.

Black spot.

PROBLEM: Plants fail to bloom or bloom only sparsely.

ANALYSIS: Few or no blooms

Roses produce few or no buds or flowers for any of several reasons.

1. *Too much shade:* Roses grow and bloom best in full sun. They need at least 4 hours of direct sunlight each day for normal blooming.

2. *Improper dormant pruning:* Most rose varieties are grafted onto rootstock. Tree roses and some climbing roses are grafted onto intermediate trunkstock. If the hybrid canes are pruned off below the bud union, the rootstock or trunkstock will produce suckers that are flowerless or that produce flowers different from the desired variety. Some climbing roses and many old garden roses bloom from flower buds formed the previous season. Heavy pruning of such plants will remove all these buds.

3. *Excessive or improper pruning during the growing season:* If roses are excessively trimmed and pruned during the growing season, many or all of the developing flower buds may be removed.

4. *Old flowers left on plant:* Roses do not produce as many new flowers when the old blooms are allowed to fade and form seeds.

5. *Flushes of bloom:* Many roses bloom in flushes. The first flush usually occurs in late spring, and the second flush occurs in late summer or early fall.

6. *Diseased or infested plants:* Roses that have been attacked by diseases or insects do not flower well.

SOLUTION: Take these measures to correct the condition or control the problem.

1. Thin out shading trees and shrubs, or transplant roses to a sunnier location. Replace them with shade-loving plants.

2. Do not prune roses below the bud union. Take special care when pruning climbing roses and standard tree roses, since the bud union between the trunkstock and the grafted variety may be several feet from the ground. Prune old garden roses lightly during the dormant season. If heavy pruning is needed, wait until after the plants have bloomed in spring. For more information about pruning roses, see Ortho's book *All About Roses.*

3. During the growing season, prune roses only to shape them or to remove suckers and dead or dying growth. When cutting flowers or removing faded flowers, leave at least two 5-leaflet leaves on the cane to ensure continued flower production.

4. Remove flowers as they begin to fade.

5. There is nothing you can do; this is a natural plant cycle.

6. Look up the symptoms beginning on page 190 to determine the cause. Treat accordingly.

PROBLEM: Circular black spots with irregular edges appear on the topsides of leaves in the spring. The tissue around the spots or the entire leaf may turn yellow, and the infected leaves may drop prematurely. Severely infected plants may lose all their leaves by midsummer. Flower production is often reduced and quality is poor.

ANALYSIS: Black spot

This plant disease is caused by a fungus (*Diplocarpon rosae*) that is a severe problem in areas where high humidity or rain is common in spring and summer. Fungi of this species spend the winter on infected leaves and canes. Spores are spread from plant to plant by splashing water. The fungi enter the tissue, forming spots the size of a pinhead. The black spots enlarge, up to ¾ inch in diameter, as the fungi spread; spots may join to form blotches. Twigs may also be infected. Plants are often killed by repeated infection.

SOLUTION: Spray with a fungicide containing chlorothalonil or triforine. Repeat the treatment at intervals of 7 to 10 days for as long as the weather remains wet. Spraying may be omitted during hot, dry spells in summer. Cut off infected canes. Avoid overhead watering. In the fall, rake up and destroy fallen leaves. After pruning plants during the dormant season, spray with a lime-sulfur spray. The following spring, when new growth starts, begin the spraying program again. Plant resistant varieties.

ROSA (ROSE)

Powdery mildew.

Rust.

Spider mite damage.

PROBLEM: Young leaves, young twigs, and flower buds are covered with a thin layer of grayish white powdery material. Infected leaves may be distorted and curled, and many may turn yellow or purplish and drop off. New growth is often stunted, and young canes may be killed. Badly infected flower buds do not open properly. In late summer, tiny black dots (spore-producing bodies) may be scattered over the powdery covering like ground pepper.

ANALYSIS: Powdery mildew
This common plant disease is caused by a fungus (*Sphaerotheca pannosa* var. *rosae*) and is one of the most widespread and serious diseases of roses. The powdery covering consists of fungal strands and spores. The spores are spread by the wind to healthy plants. The fungi sap the plant nutrients, causing distortion, discoloring, and often the death of the leaves and canes. Powdery mildew may occur on roses any time during the growing season when rainfall is low or absent, temperatures are between 70° and 80° F, nighttime relative humidity is high, and daytime relative humidity is low. In areas of high spring and summer rainfall, control may not be needed until the drier months of late summer. Rose varieties differ in their susceptibility to powdery mildew.

SOLUTION: At the first sign of mildew, apply a fungicide containing triforine. Respray at intervals of 7 to 10 days if mildew reappears. Rake up and destroy leaves in the fall.

PROBLEM: Yellow to brown spots, up to ¼ inch in diameter, appear on the topsides of the leaves, starting in the spring or late fall. The lower leaves are affected first. On the undersides of the leaves are spots or blotches containing a red, orange, or black powdery material that can be scraped off. Infected leaves may become twisted and dry. In some cases they drop off the plant; in others they remain attached. Twigs may also be infected. Severely infected plants lack vigor.

ANALYSIS: Rust
Rose rust is caused by any of several species of fungi (*Phragmidium* species) that infest only rose plants. Rose varieties differ in their susceptibility to rust. The orange fungal spores are spread by wind to rose leaves. With moisture (rain, dew, or fog) and temperatures from 55° to 75° F, the spores enter the tissue on the undersides of the leaves. Spots develop directly above, on the topsides. In the fall, black spores develop in the spots. These spores can survive the winter on dead leaves. In spring, the fungi produce the spores that cause new infections. Rust may also infect and damage young twigs.

SOLUTION: At the first sign of rust, pick off and destroy the infected leaves and spray with a fungicide containing triforine or a lime-sulfur spray. Repeat the treatment at intervals of 7 to 14 days for as long as conditions remain favorable for infection. Rake up and destroy infected leaves in the fall. Prune off and destroy infected twigs. Apply a lime-sulfur spray during the dormant season. Plant resistant varieties.

PROBLEM: Leaves are stippled, bronze-colored, and dirty. There may be a silken webbing on the undersides of the leaves or on the new growth. Infested leaves often turn brown, curl, and drop off. New leaves may be distorted. Plants are usually weak and appear unhealthy. To determine if the plant is infested with mites, hold a sheet of white paper underneath an affected leaf and tap the leaf sharply. If mites are present, minute green, red, or yellow specks the size of pepper grains will drop to the paper and begin to crawl around. The pests are easily seen against the white background.

ANALYSIS: Spider mites
These mites, related to spiders, are major pests of many garden and greenhouse plants. They cause damage by sucking sap from the undersides of the leaves. As a result of feeding, the green leaf pigment (chlorophyll) disappears, producing a stippled appearance. Many leaves may drop off. Severely infested plants produce few flowers. Mites are active throughout the growing season, but most are favored by dry weather above 70° F. By midsummer, they build up to tremendous numbers.

SOLUTION: When damage is first noticed, spray with a miticide containing hexakis. Cover the undersides of the leaves thoroughly. Repeat the application 2 more times at intervals of 7 to 10 days.

Virus disease.

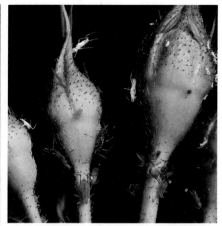
Rose aphids (life size).

Japanese beetle (life size).

PROBLEM: Yellow or brown rings or yellow splotches of various sizes appear on leaves. The uninfected portions remain dark green. New leaves may be puckered and curling; flower buds may be malformed. Sometimes, brown rings appear on the canes. The plants are usually stunted.

ANALYSIS: Mosaic and streak viruses

A number of viruses infect roses. The viruses are transmitted when an infected plant is grafted or budded to a healthy one. This generally occurs in the nursery where the plant was grown. Some plants may show symptoms in only a few leaves. However, the whole plant is infected, and further symptoms may appear later. Most rose viruses are fairly harmless unless there is extensive yellowing or browning. The virus suppresses the development of the green pigment (chlorophyll), causing the splotches or rings. Food production is reduced, which may result in stunted plant growth.

SOLUTION: No cure is available for virus-infected plants. There is little natural spread of rose viruses; therefore, only weak plants need to be removed. When purchasing rosebushes, buy only healthy plants from a reputable dealer.

PROBLEM: Tiny (⅛-inch) green or pink soft-bodied insects cluster on leaves, stems, and developing buds. When insects are numerous, flower buds are usually deformed and may fail to open properly. In some cases, a shiny, sticky substance coats the leaves. A black sooty mold may grow on the sticky substance. Ants may be present.

ANALYSIS: Rose aphids
(*Macrosiphum rosae*)

These insect pests do little damage in small numbers; plants can tolerate fairly high populations without much effect. However, rose aphids are extremely prolific, and populations can rapidly build up to damaging numbers during the growing season. Damage occurs when aphids suck the juices from the rose stems and buds. Aphids are unable to digest fully all the sugar in the plant sap. They excrete the excess in a fluid called honeydew, which often drops onto the leaves below. A sooty mold fungus may develop on the honeydew, causing the rose plants to appear black and dirty. Ants feed on the sticky substance and are often present where there is an aphid infestation. When aphid populations are high, flower quality and quantity are reduced.

SOLUTION: When clusters of aphids are noticed, spray with an insecticide containing acephate (ORTHENE®), malathion, insecticidal soap, or pyrethrins. Repeat the treatment if the plant becomes reinfested.

PROBLEM: Holes appear in flowers and flower buds; open flowers may be entirely eaten. Affected buds often fail to open, or they are deformed. Stem tips may be chewed, or the leaves may be notched or riddled with holes. Red, green-spotted, brownish, or metallic green beetles up to ½ inch long are sometimes seen on the flowers or foliage.

ANALYSIS: Beetles

A number of different beetles infest roses. They may destroy the ornamental value of a plant by seriously damaging the flowers and foliage. The insects usually spend the winter as larvae in the soil or as adults in plant debris on the ground. In late spring or summer, mature beetles fly to roses and feed on the flowers; buds; and, sometimes, the leaves. Punctured flower buds usually fail to open, and flowers that do open are often devoured. Many beetles feed at night, so their damage may be all that is noticed. Female beetles lay their eggs in the soil or in the flowers in late summer or fall. The emerging larvae crawl down into the soil to spend the winter, or they mature and pass the winter as adults. The larvae of some beetles feed on plant roots before maturing in fall or spring.

SOLUTION: Spray with an insecticide containing acephate (ORTHENE®) or carbaryl (SEVIN®). Follow label directions.

ROSA (ROSE) ▪

Crown gall.

PROBLEM: Large, corky galls up to several inches in diameter appear at the base of the plant and on the stems and roots. The galls are rounded, with rough, irregular surfaces, and they may be dark and cracked. Plants with numerous galls are weak; growth is slowed and leaves turn yellow. Branches or the entire plant may die back.

ANALYSIS: Crown gall
This plant disease is caused by a soil-inhabiting bacterium (*Agrobacterium tumefaciens*) that infects many ornamentals and fruit trees in the garden. Bacteria of this species are spread with the soil and contaminated pruning tools, and are often brought into a garden initially on the stems or roots of an infected plant. The infection enters a plant through wounds in the roots or the stem. The bacteria produce a compound that stimulates rapid cell growth in the plant, causing gall formation on roots; crown; and, sometimes, branches. The galls disrupt the flow of water and nutrients up the roots and stems, weakening and stunting the top of the plant. Galls do not usually cause the death of the plant.

SOLUTION: Crown gall cannot be eliminated from a plant. However, an infected plant may survive for many years. To improve its appearance, prune out and destroy galled stems. Sterilize pruning shears with rubbing alcohol after each cut. Destroy severely infected plants. The bacteria will remain in the soil for 2 to 3 years. If you wish to replace the infected roses, select other plants that are resistant to crown gall.

SALIX (WILLOW) ▪

Mottled willow borer (life size).

PROBLEM: Leaves turn yellow, and holes appear in the twigs. Large quantities of sawdust cling to the bark just below the holes. Sap often oozes from the holes. Young trees may be killed, and older trees may lose their natural form because of the growth of numerous side shoots. Small (⅜-inch) black or dark brown weevils with pale yellow spots and long snouts may be seen around the tree from midsummer until fall.

ANALYSIS: Mottled willow borers
(*Cryptorhynchus lapathi*)
All willows and most species of poplars may be attacked by this weevil, which is also called the poplar-and-willow borer. The adult weevils cause minor injury by chewing holes in the bark of twigs. The major damage is caused by the C-shaped larvae, which are white with brown heads. During mid- to late summer, the larvae hatch from eggs laid in holes chewed by the female weevils. The larvae burrow into and feed on the inner bark. In the spring, large quantities of frass (sawdust and excrement) are expelled from the holes as the larvae tunnel into the center of the twigs to pupate. The feeding and tunneling cause branches to break easily and disrupt nutrient and water movement through the tree. The leaves turn yellow, and the tree often becomes bushy from the growth of numerous side shoots. The larvae pupate in June and emerge as adults in midsummer. Several other borers may also infest the trunk and branches of willows.

SOLUTION: Before early summer, remove and destroy severely infested trees or branches. In late July or early August, spray the bark of remaining trees with an insecticide containing lindane.

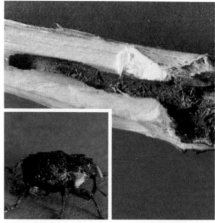

Damaged stem. *Insert:* Adult (3 times life size).

PROBLEM: Swollen areas with holes in their centers develop on twigs, branches, or the trunk. Many side shoots may grow from below the swellings, destroying the natural form of the tree. The leaves on infested twigs and branches turn yellow and may be chewed on the edges. Sawdust and many broken twigs are often found beneath the tree.

ANALYSIS: Willow borers
(*Saperda* species)
At least five species of this beetle feed on willows, causing galls, or swollen areas, to form. The 1-inch, striped and spotted, brownish or gray beetles with long antennae appear in late spring or early summer. The females lay their eggs in small holes that they gnaw in the bark of twigs and branches that are more than ½ inch in diameter. The emerging legless, whitish grubs tunnel into the wood. Excess tissue accumulates around the wound, resulting in a gall. When infestations are severe, nearly all twigs and branches more than ½ inch in diameter have one or more galls. The galls weaken the twigs, causing them to break and litter the ground during stormy weather. The grubs remain in the wood one to two years before maturing into adults.

SOLUTION: Remove and destroy severely damaged trees. In late May or early June, spray the bark of less severely damaged trees with an insecticide containing lindane. Respray 2 weeks later.

SORBUS (MOUNTAIN ASH) ——— ■ SYRINGA (LILAC) ———

Fireblight.

Powdery mildew.

Borer damage.

PROBLEM: Blossoms and leaves of some twigs suddenly wilt and turn black as if scorched by fire. The leaves curl and hang downward. The bark at the base of a blighted twig becomes water-soaked, then dark, sunken, and dry; cracks may develop at the edge of the sunken area. In warm, moist spring weather, drops of brown ooze appear on the sunken bark. Young trees may die.

ANALYSIS: Fireblight
This plant disease is caused by a bacterium (*Erwinia amylovora*) that is extremely destructive to many trees and shrubs. Bacteria of this species spend the winter in the sunken cankers on the branches. In the spring, the bacteria ooze out of the cankers. Bees, flies, and other insects are attracted to the sticky ooze and become smeared with it. When the insects visit a mountain ash flower for nectar, they infect it with the bacteria. Insects visiting these infected blossoms later carry bacteria-laden nectar to healthy blossoms. Rain, wind, and tools may also spread the bacteria. Fireblight spreads rapidly through plant tissue in humid weather above 65° F. Tender or damaged leaves may be infected in midsummer.

SOLUTION: Prune out infected branches 12 to 15 inches beyond any visible discoloration; destroy the branches. Sterilize pruning shears with rubbing alcohol after each cut. A protective spray of a pesticide containing basic copper sulfate or streptomycin, applied before bud break in the spring, will help prevent infection. Respray at intervals of 5 to 7 days until the end of bloom.

PROBLEM: Leaves are covered with a thin layer or irregular patches of a grayish white powdery material. Infected leaves may turn yellow and drop off. New growth is often stunted. In late summer, tiny black dots (spore-producing bodies) are scattered over the white patches like ground pepper.

ANALYSIS: Powdery mildew
This common plant disease is caused by a fungus (*Microsphaera alni*) that thrives in both humid and dry weather. The powdery patches consist of fungal strands and spores. The fungi sap plant nutrients, causing yellowing and sometimes the death of the leaves. Since this mildew attacks many different kinds of trees and shrubs, the fungi from a diseased plant may infect other plants in the garden.

SOLUTION: When the plant shows the first sign of mildew, spray plants with a fungicide containing triforine. Cover both surfaces of each leaf thoroughly. Repeat the treatment at intervals of 7 to 10 days until mildew disappears.

Syringa cultural information
Light: Full sun
Water: When soil 4 inches below surface is barely moist
Soil: High in organic content
Fertilizer: Medium

PROBLEM: Branch tips wilt in late summer, especially during warm, dry periods. Affected branches may die or break off. The stems near the ground are swollen and cracked. Sawdust is often found around holes in the stems and on the ground below infested stems.

ANALYSIS: Lilac borers
(*Podosesia syringae*)
The lilac borer is the larva of a brownish, clear-winged moth that resembles a wasp. The moths may be seen flying around the plant in late spring. The females lay their eggs in cracks or bark wounds at the bases of the stems. The cream-colored larvae bore into the wood and feed on the sap-wood and heartwood. The stems become swollen and may break where the larvae are feeding. Their feeding cuts off the flow of nutrients and water through the stems, causing the shoots to wilt and die. The larvae spend the winter in the stems. In the spring, they feed for a few weeks before maturing into moths. Several other borers may infest lilac.

SOLUTION: Before the moths emerge in the spring (April to May), cut out infested stems to ground level and destroy them. In late April, spray or paint the trunks and stems with an insecticide containin lindane. Repeat the treatment 2 more times at intervals of 7 to 10 days. Bo can also be destroyed by using an c to inject liquid insecticides into th Then plug the holes with putty c Or kill borers by inserting a fle into the borer hole in early sur Avoid pruning during the sp when moths are present.

TAXUS (YEW) ━━━━━━━━━━ ■ ULMUS (ELM) ━━━━━━━━━

Yew in poorly drained soil.

PROBLEM: Young leaves turn yellow. Eventually the entire plant may turn yellow, wilt, and die. The plant is growing in heavy, poorly drained, acidic or alkaline soil.

ANALYSIS: Poor soil
Yews are particularly sensitive to improper growing conditions. When they are planted in soil that is heavy, poorly drained, extremely acid (between pH 4.5 and 5.5) or extremely alkaline (above pH 7.5), the plants do not usually survive. The bark on the roots decays and sloughs off, and the roots die. The roots can no longer supply sufficient amounts of nutrients and water to the leaves, resulting in leaf yellowing and wilting. The plant usually dies within several months.

SOLUTION: Improve soil drainage or, if the plant is small, move it to an area with better drainage. Check the acidity of the soil. If the pH is below 6.0, add ground limestone around the base of the plant. Add aluminum sulfate to the soil if the ⁱ is above 7.0. The optimum pH for ⁱs between 6.0 and 6.5. Do not water ⁱvily.

ⁱnformation

ⁱes below surface
ⁱe during driest

ULMUS (ELM) ━━━━━━━━━━

ADAPTATION: Zones 3 through 10. To determine your zone, see the map on page 348. Not adapted to desert areas.

LIGHT: Full sun.

SOIL: Tolerates a wide variety of soils.

FERTILIZER: Apply a fertilizer higher in nitrogen (14-7-7, for example); follow label directions.

WATER: Water during periods of extended drought.

PRUNING: Prune off dead wood and destroy or strip off the bark to eliminate breeding sites for elm bark beetles, which transmit Dutch elm disease.

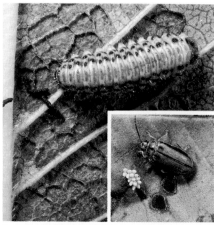

Larva. *Insert:* Beetle (3 times life size).

PROBLEM: The undersides of leaves are eaten between the veins, giving the leaves a lacy appearance. There may also be small holes in the leaves. Severely infested leaves turn brown; the entire tree may appear scorched. Many leaves drop off by midsummer. Small (½-inch) yellow and black insects or ¼-inch yellow beetles with green and black stripes may be found on the undersides of the leaves.

ANALYSIS: Elm leaf beetles
(*Pyrrhalta luteola*)
All species of elm are susceptible to attack by leaf beetles, but local beetles may prefer one species over another. The beetles spend the winter as adults in buildings or in protected places outside. In the fall, when the beetles are looking for shelter, they often become a nuisance inside homes. The adults fly back to elm trees in the spring. They eat small holes in the developing leaves and mate; the females lay their eggs. The emerging black larvae feed on the undersides of leaves, between the veins. As the larvae mature, they turn a dull yellow with black stripes. After feeding for several weeks, the larvae pupate. Bright yellow pupae may be seen around the base of the tree in late June or early July; adults emerge later. There may be one or two more generations in the same year. Trees that lose many of their leaves early in the season may grow new ones, which may also be eaten.

SOLUTION: When damage is first noticed, spray with an insecticide containing acephate (ORTHENE®) or carbaryl (SEVIN®). To prevent severe leaf damage, apply the spray just as the leaves grow to full size. Respray if the tree becomes reinfested.

■ **WISTERIA** ■

Dutch elm disease.

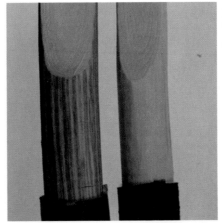
Diseased stem on left.

Failure to bloom.

PROBLEM: Leaves wilt, curl, and turn yellow on one or more branches in the top of the tree; many leaves drop off. Trees may die slowly over a period of a year or longer, or they may wilt and die within a few weeks, often in the spring soon after they have leafed out. Cross sections of infected branches may show a ring of brown dots in the wood, just underneath the bark. Small holes may be found in the bark of infected branches.

ANALYSIS: Dutch elm disease

Dutch elm disease is caused by a fungus (*Ceratocystis ulmi*) that invades and plugs the water-conducting vessels in the tree. The infection is spread primarily by elm bark beetles. In the spring, the adult beetles emerge from holes in the bark of elm trees where they have spent the winter. If the trees are infected with the Dutch elm fungi, the beetles have sticky fungal spores on and inside their bodies. The beetles disperse to healthy elms, where they feed in crotches of small twigs, usually high in the trees, and deposit the spores in feeding wounds. The fungi then spread through the tree. The infected elm usually develops the disease that summer. The fungi produce a toxin that interferes with the water-conducting vessels in the wood, reducing the amount of water available to the leaves. The foliage on the infected branch wilts, turns yellow, and drops. Surrounding branches, and eventually the entire tree, become infected; the tree dies. When elms are closely planted (50 feet or less between trees), the fungi may spread through natural root grafts between trees. Trees infected through the roots generally wilt and die rapidly, often when growth begins in spring. These trees do not show browning in the wood when the branches are cut.

SOLUTION: Curing a tree of Dutch elm disease is usually impossible. Disease development may be delayed on lightly infected trees (where less than 5 percent of the foliage and branches show evidence of the disease) that were initially infected by bark beetles rather than by root grafts. Using tree surgery to remove early-stage infections may save a tree for a number of years. Remove yellowing branches at least 10 feet below the point where brown streaks are visible in the wood. Sterilize pruning tools with rubbing alcohol after each cut. Spray the wound with an insecticide containing methoxychlor. Systemic fungicides (fungicides that are carried throughout the tree) injected into the tree by a trained arborist may increase the life span of a lightly infected tree. Consult an arborist when yellowing is first noticed. Prevention involves 3 different measures that should be carried out on a communitywide basis.
1. An effective sanitation program will slow the spread of the fungus species. Since bark beetles carrying the fungi breed in dead or dying elm wood, all dead or dying trees, damaged limbs, and prunings should be removed and burned or buried. The bark of all stumps should be peeled to just below ground level.
2. Controlling bark beetles by using an insecticide is practical only on valuable specimens and when the insecticide is used in conjunction with a sanitation program. In early spring, before leaves come out, treat with a spray containing methoxychlor. Use a high-pressure sprayer, and cover the entire tree thoroughly.
3. To prevent transmission of the disease through the roots of closely planted trees, sever grafted roots by mechanical trenching or by injection of a chemical into the soil. Consult a professional arborist to complete this important step.

PROBLEM: No flowers appear in the spring, but the vine is healthy and vigorous.

ANALYSIS: Not blooming

Most wisteria purchased from nurseries bloom well after two or three years. These plants are usually asexually propagated (started from cuttings or by some method other than from seeds). Often, vines started from seeds do not bloom for 10 to 15 years or longer. Wisteria may also fail to bloom because of improper growing conditions, poor pruning practices, or freeze damage. Young plants should be well fed and watered; plants old enough to bloom flower best with less food and water. Too much nitrogen fertilizer during the growing season causes lush, overly vigorous green growth and poor flower bud production (flower buds for next season's bloom are produced in early summer). Heavy pruning may also produce lush, overly vigorous growth, or flower buds may be mistakenly removed.

SOLUTION: Do not grow wisteria from seeds; buy nursery-grown vines. If your old wisteria did not bloom in spring and is lush and growing vigorously, do not use nitrogen fertilizer for an entire season. In early summer add a fertilizer rated 19-24-18, to promote flower bud formation for next season. Prune back vigorous shoots in summer. In winter, cut back or thin out side shoots from the main stems. Spurs (short fat stems bearing flower buds) develop on these side shoots. Cut back spurs to 2 or 3 buds. Do not drastically prune the side shoots—drastic pruning will eliminate all the spurs, so no flowers will be produced.

FRUIT AND NUT TREES

The desire for old-fashioned fruit flavor has led rural gardeners to experiment with antique varieties and suburban gardeners to plant their first dwarf apple or apricot trees. The piquancy of a handful of home-grown walnuts has inspired many gardeners to raise their own nut crops. A fresh ripe peach, plum, or pear is one of the delights of summer. Growing healthy trees and a satisfying crop requires consideration throughout the plants' life cycle and in all seasons.

PRODUCING A CROP

To tend your fruit and nut trees well, you must be aware of natural production cycles; take an interest in the mysteries of pollination; learn the practical art of thinning; and, as always, remain alert for problems. Most gardeners agree unhesitatingly that the reward of a bumper harvest is worth the trouble.

Pollination

If your fruit tree is festooned with blossoms, but yields pea-sized fruit that drops off instead of growing, poor pollination may be the cause. Some fruit trees, such as apricots, nectarines, peaches, pomegranates, persimmons, sour cherries, and most citrus, are self-fruitful. They can be successfully fertilized by their own pollen. But most sweet cherries, plums, apples, papayas, pears, and nut trees must be grown within 100 feet of a different variety of the same fruit or nut tree that flowers at the same time.

An early-blooming tree cannot cross-pollinate a late-blooming tree. If your garden lacks space for cross pollinating trees and there are none in the immediate vicinity, talk to your local nursery or a friend with fruit trees. Sometimes setting a bucket of compatible blossom-filled branches under your target tree will do the trick.

You may see labels declaring plums to be self-fruitful. Some are, to a limited extent. But fruiting will be markedly better if pollen comes from another plum tree. Plums are quite fussy about which plum tree variety provides this pollen, so read specifics when you purchase to prevent problems.

Apples and pears have some of the same fussiness about their mates. If the nearby variety blossoms irregularly or has

a different genetic base, fruit may not set. If trees were present when you moved onto the property, or the label has been misplaced, you may have to do some investigation to find out which varieties you have in order to improve fruiting.

Your local nursery, county agricultural extension service, or old-time apple association can usually help here.

Insect pollinators Insect pollinators are necessary to transfer pollen within a tree, or from one fruit or nut tree to another. Though birds, animals, and breezes transfer some pollen, insects move most of the pollen within a tree or from one tree to another. In its search for food, an insect may land on the male part of a flower, or anther. The anther contains pollen, which sticks to the insect's body. Later, if the insect visits the female part of a flower, the stigma, pollen may brush off. If it does, pollination occurs. Pollination is the necessary first step to producing a crop.

But bad weather limits insect movements. If there is continued heavy rain, unseasonal cold, or heavy wind during prime flowering season, not only are some of the blossoms knocked off, but pollinators don't get out to do their job.

Honeybees do most fruit and nut tree pollination. Experts have estimated that they are crucial to over $20 billion in food crops each year. Honeybees move from flower to flower, collecting both nectar and pollen. Nectar is the sweet juice from inside a flower; bees transform it into honey. Bees need both nectar and pollen to multiply and survive.

In today's world of rapid construction and decreasing open space the bee population seems to be declining. If you want bees for fruit and nut tree pollination, you should take steps to encourage their presence. Provide them with a continuous supply of clean water. A water supply for bees must be shallow, as they will drown in the attempt to drink. Place some gravel in a bucket, then fill the bucket with just enough water to cover the stones. The gravel provides a place for the bees to sit as they refresh themselves.

Bees are extremely sensitive to controls for other insects. The best course is not to use pesticides on any plant in an area where bees are feeding. If you must use a pesticide, however, do so in the late afternoon, when fewer bees are visiting flowers. If possible, keep pesticides away from fruit and nut trees.

Insects known as syrphids, hover flies, or flower flies are second only to bees as pollinators. These ¼- to ½-inch-long insects are often confused with honeybees or yellowjacket wasps. Unlike bees and wasps, however, syrphids do not sting. They hover in the air, seemingly motionless, over blossoms, occasionally dipping down to feed on both nectar and pollen. In addition to their work as pollinators, syrphids perform an important pest-control service.

Young syrphids, ⅛- to ½-inch-long green or brown worms, eat an average of one aphid per minute and also feed on mealybugs, leafhoppers, and the like.

Wasps do a share of pollination and pest control. Wasps destroy flies, beetle larvae, and caterpillars. Treat wasps as

Opposite: Picking an overflowing basket of fruit is surely one of the most satisfying gardening tasks.
Right: That yellowish mass on the bee's rear leg is pollen. Some shakes loose at each stop the bee makes.

A simple light bulb inside a plastic tent raises the temperature enough to protect this citrus.

This citrus was not protected and has sustained frost damage.

beneficial insects unless their presence is potentially harmful to people. Some wasp species, most notably the yellowjacket, can be irritated by swatting and other disturbances. The result could be a series of painful stings.

Hand pollination   What do you do if rain, wind, cold, or other environmental factors keep insect pollinators from doing their job? You must—literally—put your hand to the task. The best time to pollinate by hand is when the weather has been warm and dry for at least 2 days. Shaking blossoms of one variety over those of another is usually a reasonably effective means of cross-pollination. To be more precise, move your fingertip over an anther. If yellow grains come off on your finger, pollen is available. Use a small natural-hair artist's brush or a cotton swab to transfer pollen from anthers of one variety to stigmas of another. Whichever method you use, transfer pollen every day until the trees are finished flowering. Hand-pollination may not result in a bumper crop, but in the absence of insect pollinators it is the only alternative if you want fruit or nuts.

Other Crop Problems
Fruit and nut yields are subject to natural cycles as well as weather conditions and the vicissitudes of pollination.

Failure to Bear
Before worrying about a tree that is not bearing fruit or nuts, make sure it is mature enough to produce a crop. Peaches bear after three years, dwarf apples at two to three years, and plum trees at

about four years. Sweet-cherry trees bear at five to seven years.

If your tree is mature yet produces little or no fruit despite adequate pollinators, again you may have no cause for concern. Some tree varieties, particularly apple, pear and citrus, tend toward light crops in alternate years, even when plants are extremely healthy. Heavy fruiting takes energy away from flower production for the following year. If the number of flowers is low, the yield is small. Thorough thinning helps trees produce yields of consistent size from year to year.

Poor Weather
Poor fruiting and premature fruit drop occur if temperatures are too low or if hot and cold weather alternate in late fall and early spring. In either case the fruit or nut tree is fooled into thinking spring has arrived. It sets new leaves and blossoms, which are particularly susceptible to damage from temperature extremes.

Alternate freezing and thawing can cause soil movement that damages roots. If the damage is severe, the nutrient flow to the trunk is disrupted.

To protect fruit and nut trees from extreme weather, mulch them with a 6-inch layer of straw, evergreen branches, chopped leaves, wood chips, or pine needles. If you expect the temperature to drop below freezing during the night, temporarily cover trees with fabric or plastic sheets. Make sure the covers are loose and remove them in the morning; left in place they block sunlight and impede air circulation. For prized fruit or nut trees, consider installing a heat source. Sometimes the heat from a simple

60-watt bulb turned on and set under a tree draped with clear plastic is enough to prevent freezing. Ask local nursery professionals or the cooperative extension agent what heat source works best in your microclimate.

Thinning
Trees normally do some of their own thinning so the remaining fruit will receive the nutrients to reach proper size. It takes 30 healthy leaves to ripen one full-size orange or apple. If all the fruit a tree set stayed on the branches, each fruit would probably be undersize because of nutrient shortage.

Even so, in most cases you must take an active role in ensuring large fruit or nuts by removing some immature crop yourself. This process is known as thinning. In addition to providing each remaining fruit or nut with a bigger share of nutrients, thinning affords more sun and air to each fruit; therefore, it is less susceptible to disease.

Each type of fruit or nut tree has its own thinning requirements. For example, thin apples and pears by cutting the stems with sharp scissors or pinching the stems between thumb and forefinger. Leave the stem behind when you cut. Thin pears after natural spring fruit drop, when the fruits turn downward. Leave 2 pears per cluster. With apples, leave one per cluster. When thinning, you may notice that the "crown" fruit in the middle of an apple cluster is malformed. If so, be certain to remove it. But if not, leave it, as it can be larger and quite good. The clusters should be about 6 inches apart.

CORRECTING GENERAL PROBLEMS

In addition to solving problems relative to crops, gardeners must often solve problems such as drought, wind stress, and sucker and seedling growth.

Drought

A lack of water can be caused by a lack of rainfall, of course, but it can also result from inadequate saturation.

Make the most of rain and irrigation by digging a shallow basin around your fruit or nut tree. Extend the basin about a foot beyond the branch tips, and keep enlarging it as the tree grows. Construct an earth barrier about a foot from the trunk; it should be high enough to keep the water in the basin from touching the trunk.

Lawn watering does not suit fruit or nut trees. In most cases, lawn watering only soaks the top 2 inches of soil. Sprinkler systems keep trunk and top roots wet, encouraging plant diseases. Trees suffering from lawn watering grow slowly and usually have small yellowing leaves that drop early.

To lessen the problems of lawn watering, aim sprinklers so they do not reach the tree trunk or crown. If possible, leave a 2-foot space between tree trunk and grass. To ensure soil saturation, use root irrigation to deliver water 2 to 3 feet below the surface.

Wind Stress

Constant wind causes rapid water evaporation. If the roots cannot take in and move as much water as the leaves are losing, the result is wilted leaves. Wilting is most common in young trees, which usually do not have root systems substantial enough to counter the evaporation. Constant wind stress slows growth.

Keeping the stressed plant well watered at all times can mitigate wind damage. Another solution is a windbreak, wall, or shrub that blocks the wind. If you plant a living windbreak, make certain it does not compete with the stressed tree for water or sun. In serious cases of wind stress, consider moving the plant to another location.

Suckers

A sucker is a shoot that grows from the roots or the lower part of the trunk. Sucker leaves may look different than those on higher branches. If suckers appear at the base of a new tree and there is no tree top growth, the cause may be root injury during planting or cultivation around the trunk. Cut suckers at the base as soon as they emerge from the ground. Suckers weaken a tree by using nutrients that should go into tree growth. Provide sufficient water and wind protection to prevent stress while roots recover.

Seedlings

Fruits and nuts often fall from the trees that bore them; seedlings often sprout from the fallen crop. Though the seedlings may bear edible fruit, this second generation is usually inferior. In many cases, the seedlings do not develop true to type. If you want to experiment, move the seedling to another site. Otherwise, it may grow larger than the parent tree and shade it out.

PURCHASING A NEW TREE

A tree buyer has two goals: selecting a healthy tree and buying it at the right time of year.

The area of a tree just under the bark is called the cambium. This is the area in which the tree creates new cells; therefore, an assessment of the health of the cambium provides a test of whether the tree you are thinking about buying has the potential to grow, given supportive conditions. The cambium should be bright green. The bark that covers it should not be shriveled.

Check containerized trees for girdling, or roots that circle around inside or outside the container. As girdling roots grow, they wrap ever more tightly around each other, cutting off nutrient flow. The result can be the death of the tree. To check for girdling roots inside the container, poke your finger 2 to 3 inches into the soil near the trunk. Brush away a bit of topsoil. If you see or feel a root that is damaged or constricted by another root, select a different tree.

To ease transplant shock, purchase your tree as soon as the weather is warm enough to permit safe planting. In early spring the tree is still dormant; it has no leaves or buds to support. After you plant it, the tree can devote its energy to repairing the damage that even the most careful installation causes. By the time the tree is ready to produce spring growth, it has recovered from the trauma of planting.

PLANTING THE TREE

To get a new tree off to the best possible start, provide trunk support and take care to minimize transplant shock.

Trunk Support

A swaying trunk prevents roots from getting a good grip into the soil. If not anchored solidly by roots, the tree trunk may snap in a strong wind. To prevent this, install support posts before installing the tree. A standard-sized tree requires 8-foot posts, semi-dwarfs 6-foot posts, and dwarf trees 4-foot posts. Oak stakes stand up well to all types of weather. To avoid damage to the roots of the new tree, place the post in the hole before lowering the tree into the hole. Place the stake on the side of incoming winds. Use rubber ties, plastic tape, wire shielded with lengths of garden hose to connect the tree to the stake. Provide enough slack to allow the trunk to sway slightly. There must be some leeway for this encourages a strong trunk. Check the ties regularly and loosen or replace them as necessary to prevent constriction and damage to the trunk.

This peach tree has been properly thinned so that fruit will develop to full size.

Transplant Shock

In a nursery, a bare-root, burlapped, or container tree is carefully watered, shaded, and nurtured. Newly arrived in the garden, the same tree may be propped against a heat-reflecting wall, causing it to bake. If the tree is unwrapped or removed from its container, the plant is even more susceptible to hot sun and drying wind. Left unprotected for even a few hours, a fruit or nut tree can be in shock and dying even before being placed in the planting hole. If possible, plant the tree immediately and water it well. When transplanting a tree from a container to the ground, soak the rootball in water while it is still in the container; then place the tree into the planting hole.

If you must wait a few days before planting the tree, place it in a shallow holding trench you have dug in a shady location before purchasing the plant. Lean the trunk and rootball against one side of the trench. Thoroughly cover the roots with soil and water. Place the tree into the planting hole as soon as possible.

Containerizing

If you want a fruit crop but have limited space or poor drainage, a dwarf tree in a container may be a solution. A dwarf tree also tends to bear fruit earlier in its life than a standard-sized tree, so a dwarf may also be the answer if you want a quick crop. Unfortunately, containerized dwarf trees are quickly affected by poor care. The results are yellowing, drooping, curling leaves, and poor fruit production.

Purchase only healthy plants. Leaves should be large and green. Choose a tree with few flowers or fruit rather than one full of blossoms or fruit. The less orna-mented tree may not be as appealing now, but will put more energy into valu-able first-year root development. Avoid root-bound plants. Circling or matted roots must be cut back to encourage them to grow outward, and cutting encourages transplant shock.

Top: The suckers should be pruned away from this apple tree and, because they may indicate root damage, the tree should be tended diligently.
Bottom: When you bring home a bare-root tree from the nursery, plant it immediately to help prevent shock.

The container for a dwarf tree should be about 3 inches wider than the roots when they are spread out. Do not use soil directly from the garden unless you have good loam. Avoid clay; it holds water and fruit trees do not like soggy soil.

Fruit trees in containers cannot expand out into surrounding soil to obtain moisture or nutrients. What you provide in the container is what they attempt to live with. Lack of water is a major problem.

Water when the top of the soil feels dry to the touch. Do not allow the leaves to dry to the point of wilting; repeated wilting can cause death. Do not overwater. Containerized soil that stays soggy invites crown and root rot.

Apply fruit-tree fertilizer once a month to correct or prevent iron chlorosis or zinc deficiencies. If leaf edges turn brown and dry, excess fertilizer may be accumulating in the container. To leach out the fertilizer, put a garden hose into the container and turn the water on low. Let water run through the container for about 20 minutes.

HARVESTING

Picking fruit at just the right time ensures peak flavor. But it's often difficult to tell exactly when a fruit is ready to be taken off the tree. Color is a good indicator on some trees such as pears. Citrus fruit, however, can have a ripe coloration for several months before being edible. Your only course is to learn the harvest time for each type of fruit you pick. The list that follows presents guidelines for harvesting a few common trees.

• Taste citrus fruit to determine their picking time. Leaving them on too long will do no harm; ripe citrus can remain on a tree for over 2 months.

• Harvest pears when they reach full size and are starting to lose their green color. Do not allow them to soften or turn yellow on the tree. Overripe pears are mealy, mushy, or gritty.

• Pick plums, astringent persimmons, figs, and apricots when they are fully colored and slightly soft.

• Remove cherries from the tree when they are fully colored and soft or firm. Soft cherries tend to be sweeter, but the birds will probably get to them first.

DISEASES OF FRUIT AND NUT TREES

Anthracnose	Serious fungus disease affecting mango, papaya, and walnut trees. Brown spots appear on leaves and fruit. Infected areas decay rapidly. Fruit or nuts drop prematurely. Clear and destroy debris regularly. At 2-week intervals, spray with fungicide containing benomyl, maneb, or zineb.
Bacterial canker	Affects mainly cherry, fig, nectarine, peach, plum, and almond trees. Fruit is not usually infected, but entire branches may die back. Difficult to control; spraying in fall with basic copper sulfate may help. Resistant tree varieties are available. See pages 207, 220, and 222.
Bacterial leaf spot	One of the more destructive diseases of stone-fruit trees, infecting apricot, nectarine, peach, and plum. Fruit may be ruined. Spraying with basic copper sulfate when buds open may help combat disease, but no total control exists. Resistant tree varieties are available. See pages 218, 228, and 236.
Black rot	Infects mainly apple and pear trees. Fruit may be ruined. Remove all rotted fruit from tree and ground. Prune as advised (see page 217). Spray with captan as soon as disease is noticed; respray the following spring, when growth begins.
Brown rot	Fungus disease destructive to stone-fruit trees—mainly apricot, cherry, nectarine, peach, and plum—but also sometimes infecting citrus. Fruit is often ruined. Spray uninfected blossoms and maturing fruit with captan or benomyl. Resistant tree varieties are available. See pages 219, 229, and 235.
Crown and root rot	May infect nearly any fruit or nut tree. The whole tree generally loses vigor and appears ill. Only the upper branches may bloom and fruit. No controls are available. Infected trees usually die; replace them with resistant varieties. See page 213.
Fireblight	Severe on pear trees but can also infect apple. Fruit may be ruined. Spraying with basic copper sulfate at intervals before and throughout blooming helps combat the disease. Resistant tree varieties are available. See page 231.
Leaf curl	Infects peach and nectarine trees. Fruit crop is decreased, but fruit is edible. Leaf curl cannot be treated once it appears, but spraying in fall and spring with lime sulfur or a dormant disease control may prevent recurrence. See page 228.
Powdery mildew	Affects apple, cherry, papaya, and almond trees. Infected apples and papaya may be edible if peeled, but infected cherries are generally ruined. Spray at 2-week intervals with benomyl, dinocap, or sulfur. See page 210.
Scab	Serious problem on apple trees but can also affect apricot, avocado, citrus, mango, nectarine, peach, pear, and pecan. Infected fruit is edible if peeled. Scab cannot be treated once it appears, but spraying with captan in spring, after blossoms drop, may prevent recurrence. Resistant tree varieties are available. See page 216.
Shothole fungus	Infects apple, apricot, nectarine, peach, and almond trees. Yield is reduced, but fruit is edible if peeled. Shothole fungus cannot be treated once it appears, but spraying in spring with captan, lime sulfur, or a dormant disease control should help prevent recurrence. See pages 214 and 227.

PROBLEMS COMMON TO MANY FRUIT AND NUT TREES

Poor-quality pear.

Poor-quality apples.

PROBLEM: Fruits and nuts are not flavorful. Fruits may be dry, watery, pulpy, or grainy and may taste sour or tart.

ANALYSIS: Poor-tasting fruits and nuts

Fruits and nuts may be poor in flavor for a number of reasons.

1. *Lack of nutrients:* Trees planted in infertile soil grow poorly and often produce small crops of inferior-tasting fruits and nuts.

2. *Environmental stress:* Trees may be stressed by too much or too little soil moisture; excessively high or low temperatures; or rapid, unseasonable weather changes. Under environmental stress, many types of fruits or nuts may fail to ripen properly, resulting in a dry, pulpy, or otherwise poor-tasting harvest.

3. *Disease or insect damage:* Diseases and pests often slow root, shoot, and leaf growth and prevent fruits and nuts from ripening properly. Fruits and nuts themselves may also be infected or infested, resulting in poor flavor.

4. *Untimely harvest:* When fruits are prematurely harvested, they may taste tart, flavorless, dry, or starchy. Pears seem gritty or mealy if they are allowed to ripen on the tree.

5. *Fruit naturally unflavorful:* Tree varieties vary considerably in the quality of their fruits and nuts. No matter how healthy and vigorous the tree, the variety may just naturally produce a flavorless crop. Seedling trees often produce insipid fruit.

SOLUTION: Take these measures to correct the condition or control the problem.

1. Use a fertilizer rated 14-7-7 regularly according to label directions.

2. To reduce stress caused by too much or too little soil moisture, avoid overwatering or underwatering. Minimize tree stress resulting from weather and temperature fluctuations by maintaining the overall health of the tree. For specific cultural information, look up your tree in the alphabetical section beginning on page 214.

3. To help ensure high-quality fruit and nut crops, keep trees as free of insect pests and diseases as possible. To determine what is affecting your tree, look up your tree in the alphabetical section.

4. As a general rule, fruits are ripe when they are fully colored; slightly soft; and, when gently lifted, easy to separate from the branch. For details on harvesting, look up your specific tree in the alphabetical section.

5. If the tree appears to be healthy but has continued to produce a poor-quality crop over several years, plant a variety that bears a more flavorful yield. Ask the local cooperative extension office for a list of flavorful-crop producers that are adapted to your area.

■ ANIMAL DAMAGE

Small cherries.

Bird-damaged apple.

Squirrel eating green cherry.

PROBLEM: The tree is healthy and produces many small fruit. There are no signs of pests or diseases.

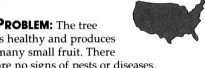

ANALYSIS: Fruit too small

Certain fruit trees—including peach, nectarine, Japanese plum, and apple—tend to produce large quantities of small fruit when not pruned or thinned adequately. If the fruit-bearing wood is not pruned during the dormant season, the tree will set many more fruit than can grow to full size. Even when properly pruned, certain fruit trees have a tendency to overbear. A tree has only a limited amount of nutrients that can be supplied to the fruit. When a tree overbears, it distributes smaller quantities of nutrients to each maturing fruit, resulting in large numbers of small fruit.

SOLUTION: Prune the tree properly during the dormant season, and thin the young fruit when they are thumbnail-sized (4 to 8 weeks after bloom). For pruning and thinning details, look up your fruit tree in the alphabetical section beginning on page 214.

PROBLEM: Ripened fruits and nuts have holes in them and may be partially eaten. Fruits and nuts may disappear from the tree or may be knocked to the ground. Birds, tree squirrels, or raccoons may be seen feeding nearby.

ANALYSIS: Animals eating fruits and nuts

Some birds and animals, especially tree squirrels and raccoons, feed on tree fruits and nuts.

1. Birds are notorious pests of many tree fruits—especially cherries; figs; persimmons; and other soft, sweet fruits. They peck at the ripening fruits, leaving holes in the flesh. The wounded fruits may decay, becoming inedible. Some birds also feed on the fruit blossoms and tiny developing fruits, greatly reducing the overall fruit yield.

2. Tree squirrels feed on a large variety of foods, including bark, leaves, insects, and eggs. However, they prefer maturing nuts and fruits. They can strip entire trees of nuts, many of which they store for later use. These squirrels often leave partially eaten nuts on the ground around the tree. Tree squirrels are especially fond of filberts.

3. Raccoons are usually found in wooded areas near a source of water. They feed on a wide variety of foods, including ripening fruits and nuts. Raccoons may strip off fruits and nuts and carry them away or feed on them in the tree. In the process of feeding, they often knock many fruits and nuts to the ground.

SOLUTION: Take these measures to correct the condition or control the problem.

1. The most effective way of controlling birds is to cover trees with nets, securing the nets tightly around the trunks. Birds are most likely to damage ripened fruits. Check the trees every morning, and harvest fruits and nuts that have ripened. Bright, shiny objects hung in trees frighten birds and will repel them for a while.

2. Prevent tree squirrels from climbing fruit and nut trees by wrapping 2-foot-wide bands of metal (made from materials like aluminum roof flashing) snugly around tree trunks at least 6 feet above ground level. Prune the trees so that all branches are at least 6 feet above the ground and 6 feet away from other trees and structures. If necessary, enclose dwarf trees or shrubs in a chicken-wire cage. If permissible in your area, you can trap tree squirrels.

3. Raccoons are intelligent, inquisitive animals that can be difficult to control. To discourage raccoons from climbing between trees or from a building to a tree, keep the limbs pruned so that they do not touch each other and do not make contact with the roof. Wrap metal guards at least 18 inches wide around tree trunks, at least 3 feet above the ground.

ANIMAL DAMAGE ———— ■ **BARK OR WOOD PROBLEMS** ————

Ground squirrel damage to almond trees.

Gummosis on peach.

Gummosis on apricot.

PROBLEM: Leaves and buds or shoots are chewed from the trees. Bark may be chewed or gnawed from the trunk or lower branches. In some cases, the trunk is entirely girdled. The tracks of deer, rabbits, or mice may be evident, or the animals may be seen. Damage is usually most severe during the winter months.

ANALYSIS: Bark-feeding animals
Several animals chew on tree bark.
1. *Deer:* These animals damage trees by feeding on leaves, shoots, buds, and bark. They feed by pulling or twisting the bark or twigs, leaving ragged or twisted twig ends or patches of bark. The males may cause damage by rubbing their antlers on the trunk and branches.
2. *Rabbits:* These animals damage fruit trees by chewing on the bark at the bases of the trunks and by clipping off tender shoots. They chew bark and twigs off cleanly, leaving a sharp break. The trunk is often marked with paired gouges left by the rabbit's front teeth. Rabbits generally feed no more than 2 feet above ground or snow level. They damage young or dwarf trees most severely.
3. *Field or meadow mice:* These creatures damage fruit trees by chewing off the bark at the bases of the trunks, just at or slightly above or below ground or snow level. They may girdle the trunk, killing the tree. Mice leave tiny scratches in the exposed wood.

SOLUTION: Various methods may be used to control deer, rabbits, and mice. These usually involve protecting the trees with fencing or tree guards, or controlling the smaller animals by using traps. In some areas, trapping or killing these animals is illegal; consult the local Department of Fish and Game to determine regulations in your area.

PROBLEM: Beads of sticky, amber-colored sap appear on healthy bark, cankers (sunken lesions), wounds, or pruning cuts.

ANALYSIS: Gummosis
Oozing sap (gummosis), which occurs to some degree in all trees, is caused by one or several of the following factors.

1. *Natural tendency:* Certain species of fruit tree—especially cherries, apricots, peaches, and plums—have a natural tendency to ooze sap. Small beads of sap often form on the bark of these trees.

2. *Environmental stress:* Trees that are under stress because they are growing in wet, poorly drained, or extremely dry soil may produce large quantities of sap, even though they are not diseased. Also, many fruit trees respond to rapid changes in weather conditions or soil moisture by gumming profusely.

3. *Mechanical injury:* Almost all trees ooze sap when the bark or wood is wounded. Wounding results from limb breakage; lawn-mower injury; pruning; improper staking, tying, or guying techniques; and other practices that damage the bark and wood.

4. *Disease:* Fruit trees respond to certain fungal and bacterial infections by forming cankers that gum profusely. Gummosis is often one of the initial signs of infection.

5. *Insect damage:* Several species of insects bore into tree bark, causing sap to ooze from the damaged areas. The larvae of certain beetles and moths are the most damaging types of boring insects. The tunnels they form in the wood often become infected with decay organisms.

SOLUTION: Take these measures to correct the condition or control the problem.

1. As long as the bark appears healthy, there is nothing to worry about.

2. If the tree is growing in wet, poorly drained soil, allow the soil to dry out between waterings. Make sure water can drain away from tree trunks and roots. To help prevent crown rot, carefully remove enough soil around the base of the trunk to expose the first major roots.

3. Avoid unnecessary mechanical injuries to the tree. Stake, tie, guy, and prune properly. For more information, see Ortho's book *All About Pruning*.

4. Remove badly infected branches and cut out cankers. Keep the tree healthy. For cultural information, look up your tree in the alphabetical section beginning on page 214.

5. Borers are difficult to control once they have burrowed into the wood (see page 208).

Fruit overload on apple branch.

Cytospora canker on peach.

Sunscald.

PROBLEM: Branches laden with large quantities of ripening fruit break off.

ANALYSIS: Limb breakage

Branches of trees that produce large fruit—such as peaches, nectarines, apples, and pears—sometimes break as the fruit reaches full size. Branches that have not been pruned or thinned properly are the most likely to snap. Those with narrow crotch angles are subject to breakage at the point of attachment to the tree. Trees that produce fruit on thin, year-old wood—for example, peach and nectarine trees—are most susceptible to limb breakage.

SOLUTION: Prune off stubs where branches have broken. To prop up branches that are bent or appear ready to break, cut a notch at one end of a board. Place the board about a third of the way in from the tip of the sagging branch. Set the branch into the notch, and then push the board into the ground. If the soil is not soft, you may need to dig a hole in the ground first. The board should be pushed in at a slight angle (20 degrees), leaning toward the center of the tree. During the dormant season, prune the tree properly and thin young fruit. For pruning and thinning details, look up your fruit tree in the alphabetical section beginning on page 214.

PROBLEM: Sunken, oval, or elongated dark lesions (cankers) develop on the trunk or branches. The bark at the edge of the canker may thicken and roll inward. In some cases, sticky, amber-colored sap oozes from the canker. The foliage on infected branches may be stunted and yellowing; some of the leaves may turn brown and drop off. Twigs and branches may die back, and the tree may eventually die.

ANALYSIS: Canker

Several different species of fungi and bacteria cause canker on fruit and nut trees. These organisms are spread by wind, splashing water, or contaminated tools. Infection usually occurs through injured or wounded tissue. Bark that has been damaged by sunscald, cold, pruning wounds, or mechanical injury is especially susceptible. The decay organisms sometimes infect the leaves directly, then spread down into healthy twigs. Cankers form as the decay progresses. Many fruit trees produce a sticky sap that oozes from the cankers. The sap may clog the water- and nutrient-conducting vessels, killing the portion of the branch or stem above the canker. Cankers that form on the trunk are the most serious; they may kill the tree. The tree may halt a canker by producing callus tissue, a growth of bark-like cells, to wall off the infection.

SOLUTION: Remove badly infected branches and cut out cankers. Avoid wounding the tree, and keep it healthy. For cultural information, see the alphabetical section beginning on page 214.

PROBLEM: Patches of bark on the trunk or branches darken and die. Often, these patches appear on the southwest side of the tree. Cracks and sunken lesions (cankers) may eventually develop in the dead bark. Damaged trees have been recently transplanted or heavily pruned.

ANALYSIS: Sunscald

When a tree is shaded by other trees or structures or is covered with dense foliage, the bark on the trunk and branches remains relatively thin. If the tree is suddenly exposed to intense sunlight, the newly exposed bark and the wood just beneath the bark may be injured by the heat. This frequently happens when young trees are moved from a shaded nursery to an open area or when trees are heavily pruned during periods of intense sunlight. The problem also occurs on cold, clear days in winter, as cold bark is quickly warmed by the sun. The damaged bark usually splits open, forming long cracks or cankers. Fungi may invade the exposed wood. Sunscald is most severe when the soil is dry. Young trees may die from sunscald.

SOLUTION: Unless the tree is very young or extremely damaged, it will usually recover with proper care. Water and add fertilizer to stimulate new growth. To prevent further damage, wrap the trunks and main branches of recently pruned or newly transplanted trees with tree-wrap paper or coat the exposed bark with a white interior latex paint or whitewash. The tree will eventually adapt to increased exposure by growing more foliage and producing thicker bark.

FRUIT AND NUT TREES

Borer holes.

Cherry scale. *Insert:* Lecanium scale (life size).

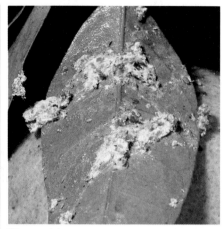

Citrus mealybugs.

PROBLEM: Foliage on a branch or at the top of the tree is sparse; eventually the twigs and branches die. Holes are in the trunk or branches. Sap or sawdust may be present near the holes. In some areas, the bark may die and slough off, revealing tunnels. Or there may be knotlike swellings on the trunk and limbs. Weak, young, or newly transplanted trees may be killed. Weakened branches break during wind- or snowstorms.

ANALYSIS: Borers
Borers are the larvae of beetles or moths. Many kinds of borer attack fruit and nut trees. Females lay their eggs in bark crevices throughout the summer. The larvae feed by tunneling through the bark or wood. Borer tunnels stop the flow of nutrients and water in an area by damaging the conducting vessels; branch and twig dieback result. Sap flow may act as a defense against borers if the tree is healthy. When the borer burrows into the wood, tree sap fills the hole and drowns the insect. Trees weakened by mechanical injuries, disease, poor growing conditions, or insect infestation are susceptible to borer attack.

SOLUTION: Cut out and destroy all dead and dying branches. Remove severely infested young trees. Spray or paint the trunk and branches of remaining trees with an insecticide containing lindane to kill young larvae before they burrow into the wood. Contact the local cooperative extension office to determine the appropriate time to apply the insecticide in your area. Make sure your tree is listed on the product label. Maintain tree health and vigor by watering and applying fertilizer regularly.

PROBLEM: The stems or undersides of leaves are covered with crusty bumps or thick, white, waxy bumps or clusters of somewhat flat, scaly bumps. The bumps can be scraped or picked off; their undersides are usually soft. Leaves turn yellow and may drop. In some cases, a shiny or sticky substance coats them.

ANALYSIS: Scales
Several different types of scale infest fruit trees. They lay their eggs on leaves or bark. In spring to midsummer, the young scales, called crawlers, settle on leaves and twigs. The small ($\frac{1}{10}$-inch), soft-bodied young feed by sucking sap from the plant. Their legs usually atrophy, and a hard crusty or waxy shell develops over their bodies. Mature female scales lay their eggs underneath their shells. Some species of scale are unable to digest fully all the sugar in the plant sap, so they excrete the excess in a fluid called honeydew. An uncontrolled infestation of scales may kill the plant after two or three seasons.

SOLUTION: When the young are active, spray with an insecticide containing carbaryl (SEVIN®), diazinon, or malathion. Make sure your fruit tree is listed on the product label. Contact the local cooperative extension office to determine the best time to spray for scales in your area. Early the following spring, before new growth begins, spray the trunk and branches with a dormant oil spray to control overwintering insects.

PROBLEM: Branch crotches, the trunk, or stems and the undersides of leaves are covered with white, cottony masses. Leaves may be curled, distorted, and yellowing, and knotlike galls may form on the stems or trunk. In some cases, a shiny or sticky substance coats the leaves. Twigs and branches may die.

ANALYSIS: Cottonycushion scales, mealybugs, or woolly aphids
The similar appearances of cottonycushion scales, mealybugs, and woolly aphids make separate identification difficult. All produce white, waxy secretions that cover their bodies. When the insects are young, they are usually inconspicuous on the host plant. Their bodies range in color from yellowish green to brown, blending in with the leaves or bark. As the insects mature, they exude filaments of white wax, giving them a cottony appearance. Mealybugs and scales generally deposit their eggs in white, fluffy masses. All three insect types feed on plant sap, damaging the leaves, branches, or trunk. The pests are unable to digest fully all the sugar in the plant sap, so they excrete the excess in a fluid called honeydew, which often drops onto the leaves or plants below.

SOLUTION: Spray the branches, trunk, and foliage with an insecticide containing diazinon or malathion. Make sure that the fruit tree is listed on the product label. During the dormant season, spray the trunk and branches with an oil spray.

Aphids (life size).

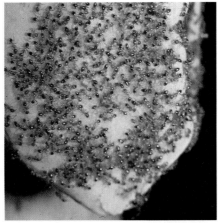

Ants feeding on papaya (½ life size).

Tent caterpillar nest (life size).

PROBLEM: The youngest leaves are curled, twisted, discolored, and stunted. Leaves may drop, and in severe cases the trees may defoliate. The developing fruit may be small and misshapen. A shiny or sticky substance may coat the leaves. A black sooty mold often grows on the sticky substance. Tiny (⅛-inch) yellow, green, purplish, or black soft-bodied insects cluster on the young shoots and undersides of leaves.

ANALYSIS: Aphids
Many species of aphid infest fruit trees. Aphids do little damage in small numbers. However, they are extremely prolific and populations can rapidly build up during the growing season. Damage occurs when the aphid sucks the juices from the leaves and immature fruits. The aphid is unable to digest fully all the sugar in the sap and excretes the excess in a fluid called honeydew, which often drops onto the leaves below. Ants feed on this sticky substance and are often present where there is an aphid infestation. A sooty mold fungus may develop on the honeydew, causing the leaves to appear black and dirty. At harvest time, fruits may be small, misshapen, and pitted because of aphid damage earlier in the season.

SOLUTION: Spray with an insecticide containing diazinon or methoxychlor. Make sure your tree is listed on the product label. Respray if the tree becomes reinfested.

PROBLEM: Ants crawl on the trunk, branches, and fruit. In many cases, the trees are also infested with aphids, scales, and leafhoppers.

ANALYSIS: Ants
Most ants do not directly damage plants. They may be present for any of several reasons. Many ants feed on honeydew, a sweet, sticky substance excreted by several species of insects, including aphids, scales, mealybugs, whiteflies, and leafhoppers. Ants are attracted to plants infested with these pests. To ensure an ample supply of honeydew, ants may carry aphids to an uninfested tree. Ants may also feed on flower nectar, fruit, or tree exudate, or on rotting fruit or fruit with broken skin. Ants usually live in underground nests. Some species make colonies in trees and building foundations.

SOLUTION: Destroy ant nests by treating anthills with diazinon granules or by spraying the nest and surrounding soil with a diazinon solution. Control aphids, scales, mealybugs, and whiteflies by spraying infested plants with an insecticide containing carbaryl (SEVIN®), malathion, or diazinon. Make sure your fruit tree is listed on the product label. To prevent ants from crawling up the trunk, apply a ring of sticky latex ant deterrent to the trunk.

PROBLEM: In the spring or summer, silken nests appear in the branch crotches or on the ends of branches. The leaves are chewed; branches or the entire tree may be defoliated. Groups of bluish, black, tan, or greenish hairy caterpillars, with spots or stripes feed in or around the nests.

ANALYSIS: Tent caterpillars or fall webworms
(*Malacosoma* species or *Hyphantria cunea*) These insects feed on many fruit and ornamental trees. Several species of tent caterpillar and the fall webworm are distributed throughout the United States. In the summer, adult female tent caterpillar moths lay masses of eggs in a cementing substance around twigs. The eggs hatch in early spring as the leaves unfold, and the young caterpillars immediately begin to construct their nests. On warm, sunny days, they devour the surrounding foliage. In mid- to late summer, brownish or reddish adult moths appear. Adult female fall webworm moths lay many eggs on the undersides of leaves in the spring. In early summer, the young webworms begin feeding and surrounding themselves with silken nests. The webworms drop to the soil to pupate. Up to four generations occur between June and September.

SOLUTION: Spray with an insecticide containing diazinon, acephate (ORTHENE®), or methoxychlor or with a compound containing the bacterial insecticide *Bacillus thuringiensis*. For best results, use *Bacillus thuringiensis* while the caterpillars are small. Remove egg masses found in the winter. Prune out branches with tents and destroy them.

INSECTS

Yellowjacket feeding on honeydew.

PROBLEM: A shiny or sticky substance coats leaves, fruit, and sometimes twigs. In many cases, a black sooty mold grows on the sticky substance. Insects may be found on the leaves, and ants, flies, or bees may be present.

ANALYSIS: Honeydew

Honeydew is a sweet, sticky substance secreted by aphids, mealybugs, whiteflies, and some scales. These sucking insects cannot digest all the sugar in the plant sap, so they excrete the excess in a sticky fluid called honeydew, which drops onto the leaves below or onto anything beneath the tree. Ants, flies, and bees feed on honeydew, and they may be found around the plant. Often, a sooty mold develops on the sticky substance, causing the leaves, fruit, and twigs to appear black and dirty. The mold does not infect the leaf; it grows on the honeydew. Extremely heavy mold may prevent light from reaching the leaf, reducing food production.

SOLUTION: Honeydew will eventually be washed off by rain, or it can be hosed off. Prevent honeydew by controlling the insects that produce it. Inspect the foliage to determine what type of insect is present.

POWDERY MATERIAL ON LEAVES

Powdery mildew.

PROBLEM: Gray-white powdery patches appear on leaves. New growth is often stunted, curled, and distorted. Infected buds may be shriveled and open later than usual, and infected leaves often turn brittle and die. The fruit is sometimes small and misshapen and may be russet-colored or covered with white powdery patches.

ANALYSIS: Powdery mildew

This common plant disease is caused by one of several fungi that thrive in both humid and dry weather. These fungi spend the winter in leaf and flower buds. In the spring, spores are blown to the new leaves, which are extremely susceptible to infection. The fungi sap plant nutrients, causing distortion and often the death of the tender foliage. Fruit yield may be greatly reduced. Warm days and cool nights favor powdery mildew.

SOLUTION: Spray infected trees with a fungicide containing benomyl, dinocap, or sulfur (do not use sulfur on apricots). Make sure your fruit tree is listed on the product label. Most fruit trees should be sprayed at regular intervals of 10 to 14 days until 3 to 4 weeks after the petals have fallen from the blossoms. Resume spraying whenever the mildew recurs. For more details about spraying, check the listing for your fruit tree in the alphabetical section beginning on page 214.

LEAVES DISCOLORED OR MOTTLED

Sooty mold on citrus.

PROBLEM: A black sooty mold grows on leaves, fruit, and twigs. It can be completely wiped off the surfaces. Cool, moist weather hastens the growth of this substance.

ANALYSIS: Sooty mold

This common black mold is found on a wide variety of plants in the garden. It is caused by any of several species of fungi that grow on the sugary material left on plants by aphids, scales, mealybugs, whiteflies, and other insects that suck sap from plants. The insects are unable to digest fully all the sugar in the sap, so they excrete the excess in a fluid called honeydew, which drops onto the leaves and fruit below. The sooty mold fungus develops on the honeydew, causing the leaves to appear black and dirty. Sooty mold is unsightly but it is fairly harmless because it does not attack foliage directly. Extremely heavy infestations prevent light from reaching leaves, however, so the foliage produces fewer nutrients and may turn yellow. The presence of sooty mold indicates that the tree is infested with insects.

SOLUTION: Sooty mold will eventually be washed off by rain. Prevent more sooty mold by controlling the insect that is producing the honeydew. Inspect the foliage to determine what type of insect is present.

Leaf scorch on hickory.

Iron-deficient apple leaves.

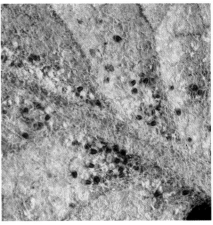
Spider mites (6 times life size).

PROBLEM: During hot weather, leaves turn brown around the edges and between the veins. Sometimes the whole leaf dies. Many leaves may drop during late summer. This problem is most severe on the youngest branches. In general, trees do not die.

ANALYSIS: Leaf scorch

Leaf scorch is caused when water evaporates from the leaves faster than it can be replenished. In hot weather, water evaporates rapidly from the leaves. If the roots can't absorb and convey water fast enough to replenish this loss, the leaves turn brown and wither. This usually occurs in dry soil, but leaves can also become scorched when the soil is moist and temperatures are extremely high for extended periods. Drying winds, severed roots, limited soil area, salt buildup, low temperatures, or weed killers can also cause scorch.

SOLUTION: To prevent further scorch, water trees deeply during periods of hot weather; wet the entire root space. Water newly transplanted trees whenever the rootball is dry 2 inches below the surface. There are no controls for scorch on trees in moist soil; the best prevention is to plant trees adapted to your climate.

PROBLEM: Leaves turn pale green or yellow. The newest leaves (those at the tips of the branches) are most severely affected. Except in extreme cases, the veins of affected leaves remain green. Older leaves may remain green. Fruit production may be reduced, and fruit flavor may be poor.

ANALYSIS: Iron deficiency

Plants frequently suffer from deficiencies of iron and other trace nutrients, such as manganese and zinc, that are essential to normal tree growth and development. Deficiencies can occur when one or more of these elements are lacking in the soil. Often these nutrients are present, but alkaline (pH 7.5 or higher) or wet soil conditions cause them to form compounds that cannot be used by trees. An alkaline condition can result from overliming or from lime leached from cement or brick. Alkaline soil usually exists in regions where soil is derived from limestone and in those with low rainfall.

SOLUTION: To correct the iron deficiency, apply a liquid iron solution to foliage and soil or apply a plant food rated 12-6-6 to the soil around the plants. Check the soil pH. If necessary, correct it by treating the soil with ferrous sulfate and watering well.

PROBLEM: Leaves are stippled, yellowing, silvered, or bronzed. There may be cobwebbing over flower buds, between leaves, or on the undersides of leaves. The fruit may be roughened or russet-colored. To check for mites large enough to be seen, hold a sheet of white paper underneath an affected leaf and tap the leaf sharply. If visible mites are present, minute green, red, or yellow specks the size of pepper grains will drop to the paper and begin to crawl around.

ANALYSIS: Mites

These pests, related to spiders, commonly attack fruit trees and other garden plants. Certain mites, like the two-spotted spider mite, are large enough to be detected against a white background. Smaller mites, like plum and pear rust mites, are microscopic and cannot be seen without the aid of a strong hand lens or microscope. Mites cause damage by sucking sap from fruit surfaces and the undersides of leaves. As a result of feeding, the green leaf pigment (chlorophyll) disappears, producing the stippled or silvered appearance. Mites are active throughout the growing season but are favored by dry weather above 70° F. By midsummer, they build up to tremendous numbers.

SOLUTION: Spray infested trees with a miticide containing hexakis. Respray at least 2 more times at intervals of 7 to 10 days. Make sure your tree is listed on the product label. If you are not sure whether your tree is infested with microscopic mites, take an infested shoot or twig to the local cooperative extension office for examination.

LEAVES DISCOLORED OR MOTTLED

Nitrogen-deficient peach.

Nitrogen-deficient citrus.

■ TREE STUNTED OR DECLINING

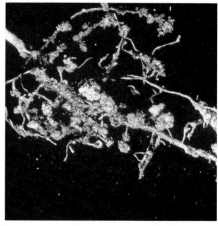

Root knot nematode damage.

PROBLEM: Older leaves turn yellow. Eventually, the rest of the leaves turn yellow-green, and then yellow. Yellow leaves usually die and drop off. New leaves are small, and growth is slow. Fruit production is poor.

ANALYSIS: Nitrogen deficiency

Nitrogen, the most important nutrient for plant growth and development, is deficient or unavailable in almost all soils. Nitrogen is essential in the formation of plant tissue, green leaf pigment (chlorophyll), and many other compounds. When a tree cannot obtain enough nitrogen from the soil, it utilizes nitrogen from its older leaves for new growth. The older leaves become deficient in nitrogen and turn yellow. A continuing shortage of nitrogen causes overall yellowing, stunting, and death of the older leaves; it also reduces fruit yield. Fast-growing, young fruit trees usually require large amounts of nitrogen. If it is not supplied, the foliage turns yellow and grows poorly. Nitrogen naturally present in the soil is made available to trees as organic matter decomposes. Soils that are low in organic matter, such as sandy and readily leached soils, are often infertile. Also, nitrogen is leached from the soil more quickly when rainfall or irrigation is heavy. Poorly drained, overwatered, and compacted soils lack oxygen, which is necessary for the utilization of nitrogen. Trees growing in these soils often exhibit symptoms of nitrogen deficiency. In addition, trees growing in temperatures below 50° F and above 90° F, in acidic (pH 5.5 and lower) soil, or in alkaline (pH 7.8 and higher) soil are often low in nitrogen.

SOLUTION: Regularly apply a fertilizer rated 14-7-7 (follow label directions for fruit and nut trees) or 10-10-10, or a soluble plant food rated 23-19-17. A blood-meal fertilizer rated 12-0-0, which contains nitrogen in a long-lasting, slow-release form, can be used to supplement a regular feeding program. Add organic matter to compacted soils and those low in organic substances. Improve soil drainage in poorly drained soils. Do not keep the soil constantly wet. Raise or lower soil pH in soils that are acidic or alkaline.

PROBLEM: Leaves are bronzed and yellowing. They may wilt on hot, dry days but recover at night. The tree is generally weak. After several years, the tree is noticeably stunted; branches may die.

ANALYSIS: Nematodes

Nematodes are microscopic worms that live in the soil. There are various types, some highly beneficial and some highly destructive. They are not related to earthworms. Destructive nematodes feed on tree roots. The damaged roots can't supply sufficient water and nutrients to the branches and leaves, and the tree is stunted or slowly dies. Nematodes are found throughout the United States but are most severe in the South. They prefer moist, sandy loam soils. Nematodes can move only a few inches each year on their own, but they may be carried long distances by soil, water, tools, or infested plants. Testing roots and soil is the only method for confirming the presence of nematodes. Contact the local cooperative extension office for sampling instructions and addresses of testing laboratories. Soil and root problems—such as poor soil structure, drought stress, nutrient deficiency, and root rots—can produce symptoms of decline similar to those caused by nematodes. Eliminate these problems as causes before sending soil and root samples for testing.

SOLUTION: Chemicals to kill nematodes in planted soil are not available to homeowners. However, nematodes can be controlled by soil fumigation before planting.

Crown rot on cherry.

Phytophthora rot on apple.

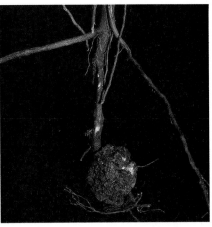

Crown gall on cherry.

PROBLEM: Normal leaf color dulls, and the plant loses vigor. Leaves may wilt or turn yellow or light brown. Major branches or the entire tree may die. The tree sometimes lives for many months in a weakened condition, or it may die quickly. Fruit growing only on the upper branches is a common sign of decline. The roots and cambium (the thin layer of tissue just beneath the bark) of the lower trunk are brownish, and the roots may be decayed. Fine woolly brown strands may form on the roots and white powdery spores on the soil surface. Or fan-shaped plaques of white strands may grow between the bark and wood of the roots and lower stems. Mushrooms may grow at the base of the plant in the fall.

ANALYSIS: Root and crown rot
This condition is caused by any of several different fungi that live in the soil and on roots. They are spread by water, soil, and transplants.

1. *Phytophthora* species: These fungi cause browning and decay of the roots and browning of the cambium and wood of the lower trunk. The tree usually dies slowly, but young trees may wilt and die rapidly. The disease is most prevalent in heavy, waterlogged soils.

2. *Phymatotrichum omnivorum:* This fungus, commonly known as cotton root rot or Texas root rot, is a serious problem on many plants in the Southwest. Young trees may suddenly wilt and die. Brown strands form on the roots, and white powdery spores form on the soil. The disease is most severe in heavy, alkaline soils.

3. *Armillaria mellea:* This disease is commonly known as shoestring root rot, mushroom root rot, or oak root fungus. It is identified by the presence of fan-shaped plaques of white fungal strands between the bark and the wood of the roots and lower trunk. Honey-colored mushrooms may appear at the base of the plant.

SOLUTION: Take these measures to correct the condition or control the problem.

1. Remove dead and dying trees. When replanting, use plants that are resistant to *Phytophthora.* Improve soil drainage. Avoid overwatering plants.

2. Remove dead and dying trees. When replanting, use only resistant varieties. Before planting, increase the soil acidity by adding 1 pound of ammonium sulfate to every 10 square feet of soil. With soil make a circular ridge around the planting area, and fill the resulting basin with 4 inches of water. In 5 to 10 days, reapply the ammonium sulfate and refill the basin. Improve soil drainage.

3. Remove dead trees and as much of the root system as possible. Newly infected plants may be saved if the disease has not reached the lower trunk. Expose the base of the plant to air for several months by removing 3 to 4 inches of soil. Prune off diseased roots. Use a fertilizer to stimulate growth. When replanting, use only resistant plants.

PROBLEM: Large corky galls up to several inches in diameter appear at the base of the tree and on the roots. The galls are rounded, with rough, irregular surfaces. Trees with numerous galls are weak; growth may be slowed and the foliage may turn yellow.

ANALYSIS: Crown gall
This plant disease is caused by a soil-inhabiting bacterium (*Agrobacterium tumefaciens*) that infects many ornamentals, fruit trees, and vegetables in the garden. Bacteria of this species are spread in the soil and are often brought into a garden initially on the roots of an infected plant. The infection enters a tree through wounds in the roots or the base of the trunk (the crown). The bacteria produce a substance that stimulates rapid cell growth in the plant, causing gall formation. The galls disrupt the flow of water and nutrients up the roots and trunk, weakening and stunting the top growth. They do not usually cause the tree to die.

SOLUTION: An infected tree cannot be cured; however, it can often survive for many years. To improve the appearance of a valued tree, hire a professional horticulturist or landscape contractor to remove the galls. The bacteria will remain in the soil for as long as 3 years after an infected tree has been removed. If you replace the infected tree, select a resistant variety.

ALMOND ——————— ▪ APPLE ——————

PROBLEMS OF INDIVIDUAL FRUIT AND NUT TREES

This section is arranged alphabetically by the name of each plant.

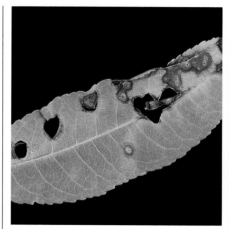

Shothole fungus.

PROBLEM: Small purplish spots appear on leaves in early spring. The spots turn brown and enlarge to ¼ inch in diameter. The centers of the spots die and drop out, leaving a small round hole. The blossoms may turn brown and have a gummy exudate at the base. The almond yield may be reduced, and corky spots may appear on the hulls. In severe cases, the tree drops all its leaves.

ANALYSIS: Shothole fungus
This plant disease is also called coryneum blight and peach blight. It is caused by a fungus (*Coryneum carpophilum*) that attacks almond and other stone fruit trees. Fungi of this species spend the winter in lesions on the twigs and buds. The spores are spread by spring rains and infect the new leaves. Infection causes the leaf tissue to produce a layer of cells that walls off the damaged area. The center of the spot then drops out. Severe infection may defoliate the tree, produce smaller almonds, and cause some almonds to drop. Wet spring weather favors the disease.

SOLUTION: There is no adequate control during the growing season. Next spring, when the petals have emerged from the buds but before the buds are fully open, spray the tree with a fungicide containing calcium polysulfide or chlorothalonil or with a lime-sulfur spray. Spray again when the petals have fallen from the flowers.

APPLE _____

ADAPTATION AND POLLINATION: Zones 2 through 10, depending on variety.

SOIL: Any good, deep, well-drained soil. pH 5.5 to 7.5.

FERTILIZER: Apply a fertilizer higher in nitrogen (14-7-7, for example); follow label directions.

WATER:
  How much: Apply enough water to wet the soil 3 to 4 feet deep.
  How often: Water when soil 6 inches below the surface is just barely moist.

PRUNING: Apples are borne on short fruiting branches (spurs) that grow on 2-year-old wood. The spurs continue to fruit for about 10 years. Prune lightly, since the removal of many spurs will reduce the apple yield. Thin out weak, crossing, or dead twigs and branches. When apples are thumbnail-sized, thin them to 6 inches apart, with 1 fruit per spur.

HARVEST: Apples are ripe when their seeds turn dark brown to black, the flesh turns creamy white, and the apple stem separates easily from the spur when the fruit is gently lifted. Harvest earlier if you prefer tart apples.

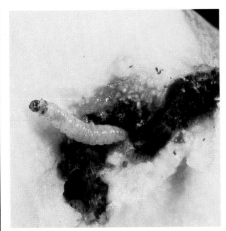

Codling moth larva (life size).

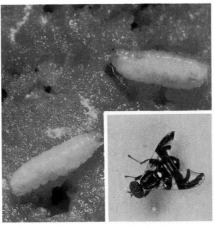

Apple maggots (4 times life size). *Insert:* Adult.

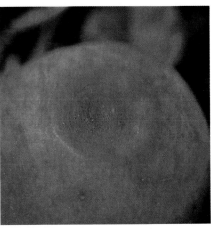

Bitter rot.

PROBLEM: Fruit is blemished by small holes surrounded by dead tissue. A brown, crumbly material resembling sawdust may surround the holes. Brownheaded, pinkish white worms up to 1 inch long may be found in the fruit. In most cases, the interior of the fruit is dark and rotted. Affected apples drop prematurely.

ANALYSIS: Codling moths
(*Carpocapsa pomonella*)
These worms, the larvae of small gray-brown moths, are among the most serious apple pests in the United States. These insects attack pear, quince, and several other fruit and nut trees in addition to apple. The moths appear in the spring, when the apple trees are blooming. Adult females lay their eggs on the leaves, twigs, and developing fruit. When the eggs hatch, the larvae tunnel into the fruit. They feed for several weeks, then emerge from the fruit, often leaving a mass of dark excrement on the skin and in the flesh. After pupating in sheltered locations on or around the tree, another generation of moths emerges in midsummer. Apples may be damaged by worms throughout the summer. In the fall, mature larvae spin cocoons in protected places, such as under loose bark or in tree crevices. They spend the winter in these cocoons, emerging as moths in the spring.

SOLUTION: Once the worms have penetrated the apples, spraying will not control the pests. To protect uninfested apples, spray with an insecticide containing carbaryl (SEVIN®), malathion, or diazinon at intervals of 10 days. Remove and destroy all fallen apples, and clean up debris. Next spring, spray according to label directions when the new growth appears.

PROBLEM: Fruit may be dimpled and pitted, with brown trails winding through the flesh. White, tapered, maggots about ⅜ inch long may be present in the fruit. Severely infested apples are brown and pulpy inside. In many cases, apples drop prematurely.

ANALYSIS: Apple maggot
(*Rhagoletis pomonella*)
These worms, also known as railroad worms and apple fruit flies, are the larvae of flies that resemble the common housefly. Apple maggots infest plums, cherries, and pears in addition to apples. The adult flies emerge from pupae between late June and the beginning of September. The females lay eggs in the fruit through holes they puncture in the skin. The maggots that emerge from the eggs make brown trails through the flesh as they feed. Infested apples usually drop to the ground. The mature maggots emerge from the apple and burrow in the soil to pupate. They remain in the soil throughout the winter and emerge as adult flies the following June.

SOLUTION: There is no way to kill the maggots after apples are infested. Protect healthy apples from the adult flies by spraying at intervals of 7 to 10 days from the end of June until the beginning of September; use an insecticide containing carbaryl (SEVIN®). Pick up and destroy fallen apples every week throughout the summer.

PROBLEM: Sunken, light brown, circular spots appear on half-grown fruit. These spots gradually enlarge to 1 inch in diameter. Concentric rings and sticky pink masses of spores may appear on the spotted areas during moist weather. The rotted apple flesh tastes bitter. Sunken lesions may form on the branches.

ANALYSIS: Bitter rot
This plant disease, which also affects pears, is caused by a fungus (*Glomerella cingulata*). Fungi of this species spend the winter in rotted apples left on the tree and on the ground and in sunken lesions on the branches. Splashing rain spreads spores to healthy apples in the spring. Infection can occur throughout the fruiting season. In areas where hot, humid conditions last for long periods, bitter rot can quickly destroy an entire apple crop. This disease primarily attacks the fruit; it does not severely damage the health of the tree.

SOLUTION: Spray infected trees with a fungicide labeled for that use. To prevent recurrence next year, prune out and destroy branches with lesions and remove and destroy rotted apples. Next spring, just before the blossoms start to open, spray the trees with an appropriate fungicide. Continue spraying according to label directions. Plant resistant varieties.

APPLE

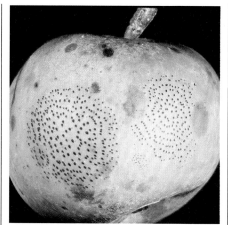

Sooty blotch and fly speck.

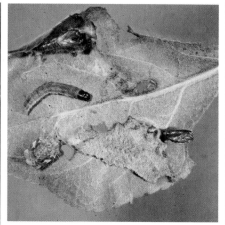

Fruit tree leafrollers (life size).

Scab.

PROBLEM: Clusters of 10 to 30 or more raised, shiny, black specks appear on apple skins. Indefinite dark brown to olive-green smudges are on the surface of the fruit.

ANALYSIS: Sooty blotch and fly speck

Although these two plant diseases are not caused by the same fungus, they are so commonly found in association that they are usually described together. Sooty blotch is caused by the fungus *Gloeodoes pomigena*, and fly speck is caused by the fungus *Microthyriella rubi*. These fungi spend the winter on the twigs of apples and many other woody plants. During mild, wet weather in spring, the fungi produce spores that are blown to and infect the developing apples. About a month after the initial infection, specks and blotches appear on the maturing fruit. Although these diseases are unsightly, they are external and do not generally affect the taste of the apples. Spores are not produced when temperatures rise above 85° F, so infection generally occurs during the spring and late summer or fall but rarely in midsummer.

SOLUTION: To prevent the possible infection of healthy fruit, spray during fruit growth with a fungicide labeled for this use. Infected apples are edible; rub them vigorously to remove the specks and blotches. Next spring, when the new growth appears, respray with an appropriate fungicide. Follow label directions.

PROBLEM: Irregular holes appear in leaves and fruit. Some leaves are rolled and held together with cobweb. Inside these rolled leaves are brown-headed, pale green worms up to ¾ inch long. The maturing apples are scarred and misshapen.

ANALYSIS: Fruit tree leafrollers
(*Archips argyrospilus*)
These worms, the larvae of brown moths, are common pests of many fruit and ornamental trees. The female moths lay their eggs on branches or twigs in June or July. The eggs hatch the following spring, and the emerging larvae feed on the blossoms and developing fruit and foliage. Leafrollers often wrap leaves around ripening fruit, then feed on the fruit inside. After about a month, the mature larvae pupate within rolled leaves, to emerge as moths in June or July.

SOLUTION: If practical, pick off and destroy rolled leaves to reduce the numbers of moths that will emerge later in the season. Next spring, when 75 percent of the petals have fallen from the blossoms, spray the tree with an insecticide containing diazinon. Respray according to the directions on the label.

PROBLEM: Olive-brown velvety spots, ¼ inch or more in diameter, appear on leaves and young fruit. As the infected apples mature, the spots develop into light to dark brown corky lesions. The fruit is often cracked and malformed and may drop prematurely. Severely infected trees may completely defoliate.

ANALYSIS: Scab

This plant disease is caused by a fungus (*Venturia inaequalis*). It is one of the most serious diseases of apples in areas where spring weather is wet and ranges from 60° to 70° F. Fungi of this scab species spend the winter in infected leaf debris. In the spring, spores are produced and blown by the wind. If there is adequate moisture on foliage and fruit, the fungi infect them and spots develop. The infected tissues produce more spores, which infect other leaf and fruit surfaces, and further spotting and decay occur. As the temperature increases, the fungi becomes less active. However, late summer rains initiate additional spore production, and apples that are infected when they are almost ready to be harvested will develop scab lesions after being picked.

SOLUTION: Unless severely infected, the apples are edible. To prevent recurrence of the disease next year, remove and destroy leaf debris and infected fruit in the fall. Next spring, spray with a fungicide containing captan.

Apple varieties resistant to scab: Prima, Priscilla, Sir Prize.

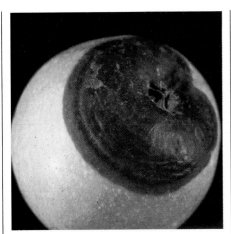

Black rot.

Cedar-apple rust.

Pacific flatheaded borer (2 times life size).

PROBLEM: A firm spot composed of concentric light and dark brown rings appears on the apples. This spot gradually turns dark brown or black and enlarges, rotting part or all of the fruit. Spots on the leaves are also formed of light and dark concentric rings. Reddish brown, slightly sunken lesions up to several feet in length may be on the branches or trunk of the tree.

ANALYSIS: Black rot

This plant disease, also known as frog-eye leaf spot, is caused by a fungus (*Physalospora* species) that also attacks pears. Fungi of this species spend the winter in rotted apples and in cankers. When temperatures reach 60° F and higher in the spring, spores are produced on infected tissues and splashed by water to the foliage and fruit. Branches and trunks are susceptible to black rot when the bark has been weakened by sunscald, cold, or heavy shading. Pruning cuts also encourage fungal infection. As the fungi decay the wood, cankers form, weakening the branches and reducing the overall vigor of the tree. Fruit infection is generally more severe in warm, moist areas, and canker formation is more prevalent in cool climates.

SOLUTION: As soon as infection is noticed, spray with a fungicide registered for this use (contact the cooperative extension office); follow label directions. Next spring, respray when the new growth appears. Each year remove all rotted apples from the tree and ground; destroy rotted fruit. Prune out infected branches at least 12 inches below visible cankers. Thin densely branched trees to provide adequate light and air circulation.

PROBLEM: Pale yellow spots appear on leaves and fruit in mid- to late spring. These spots gradually enlarge, turn orange, and develop minute black dots. Small ($\frac{1}{16}$-inch) cups with fringed edges form on the undersides of the leaves. Infected leaves and fruit may drop prematurely; the fruit is often small and deformed.

ANALYSIS: Cedar-apple rust

This plant disease is caused by a fungus (*Gymnosporangium juniperi-virginianae*) that infects both apples and certain species of juniper and red cedar. This disease cannot spread from apple to apple, or juniper to juniper, but must alternate between the two. In the spring, spores from brown and orange galls on juniper or cedar are blown up to 3 miles to apple trees. During mild, wet weather, the spores germinate and infect the leaves and fruit, causing spotting and premature leaf and apple drop. During the summer, spores are produced in the small cups on the undersides of the leaves. These spores are blown back to junipers and cedars, causing new infections. For more information about cedar-apple rust on junipers, see page 173.

SOLUTION: Cedar-apple rust cannot be controlled on this season's apples and leaves. Next spring, when the flower buds turn pink, spray apple trees with a fungicide containing zineb or ferbam. Spray again when 75 percent of the petals have fallen from the blossoms, and treat once more 10 days later. If possible, do not plant apples within several hundred yards of junipers or red cedar.

PROBLEM: Leaves wilt and turn brown. Patches of bark on the trunk are sunken, discolored, and may be soaked with sap. There may be holes about $\frac{3}{8}$ inch in diameter in the affected bark. Sawdust-filled tunnels in the wood may contain yellowish white flat-headed grubs about $\frac{3}{4}$ inch long. In late spring to midsummer, bronze- or copper-colored beetles $\frac{1}{2}$ to $\frac{3}{4}$ inch long feed on the foliage. Newly planted or weak trees are most severely affected.

ANALYSIS: Flatheaded borers

(*Chrysobothris* species)
In addition to damaging apples, these insects attack many other trees and shrubs. In late spring to midsummer, the females begin to lay eggs in crevices in the bark. The emerging larvae bore through the bark into the outer layer of wood, creating winding tunnels. These tunnels damage the nutrient- and water-conducting vessels in the tree, causing twig and branch dieback and sometimes killing the tree. The mature larvae bore deep into the heartwood to pupate; adult beetles emerge the following spring. Newly transplanted, weakened, and diseased trees are most susceptible to borer infestation.

SOLUTION: Apply an insecticide containing lindane according to label directions. Keep the tree healthy and vigorous by watering and pruning it properly; apply fertilizer as needed. For cultural information, see page 214. Discourage borer infestation by wrapping the trunk soon after bloom with tree-wrap paper or burlap. Prune out and destroy infested branches.

APRICOT

APRICOT

ADAPTATION AND POLLINATION:
Zones 5 through 9, depending on
variety.

SOIL: Any good, deep, well-drained
garden soil. pH 5.5 to 8.0.

FERTILIZER: Apply a fertilizer higher in
nitrogen (14-7-7, for example); follow
label directions.

WATER:
How much: Apply enough water to
wet the soil 3 to 4 feet deep.
How often: Water when soil 6 inches
below the surface is just barely moist.

PRUNING: Apricots are borne on short
fruiting branches (spurs), which grow
on 2-year-old wood. The spurs continue
to fruit for 2 to 4 years. Prune back last
year's growth to half its length, and thin
out spurred branches that have stopped
fruiting (4 years or older). Thin out
weak, crossing, or dead twigs and
branches. For large apricots, thin the
fruit when they are large enough to
handle so the space between them is 3 to
5 inches, with no more than 2 fruits
per spur.

HARVEST: Harvest when the fruit is
fully colored and slightly soft. When
apricots are ripe, the stems separate easily
from the spurs when the fruit is gently lifted.

Plum curculio (5 times life size).

PROBLEM: Ripening fruit
is misshapen and rotten; it
often drops prematurely.
The crop contains holes about ⅛ inch in
diameter and deep, crescent-shaped scars.
Cutting open damaged fruit may reveal
crescent-shaped yellow-gray grubs with
brown heads.

ANALYSIS: Plum curculios
(*Conotrachelus nenuphar*)
These insects, found east of the Rockies,
attack other stone fruits, apples, and
pears, as well as apricots. The adult insects are brown beetles with long curved
snouts. They hibernate in debris and other protected places during the winter. The
beetles emerge in the spring, when new
growth starts, and begin feeding on
young leaves, blossoms, and developing
fruit. After five to six weeks, the female
beetles start to lay eggs in the young fruit.
The grubs that hatch from the eggs feed
for several weeks in the fruit. Usually the
infested apricots drop to the ground. The
grubs eventually leave the fruit and bore
into the soil, where they pupate. The
emerging beetles feed on fruit for a few
weeks, then go into hibernation. Or, in
southern areas, they lay eggs, producing
a second generation of grubs in the late
summer.

SOLUTION: Once grubs are inside the
fruit, sprays cannot reach them. Spray
with a product containing carbaryl (SE-
VIN®) or malathion to kill beetles that
may be feeding on fruit or laying eggs;
follow label directions. Pick up and destroy all fallen fruit. Next spring, spray
the trees when the petals are falling from
the blossoms; repeat applications according to directions on the label.

Bacterial leaf spot.

PROBLEM: Water-soaked
spots on the undersides of
leaves turn brown or
black; in many cases, the centers of the
spots fall out. The tips of the leaves may
die, and eventually the leaves drop. The
surfaces of newly set fruit may be dotted
with spots that later turn into deep sunk-
en brown pits, which are often surrounded by yellow rings. Sunken lesions often
develop at the joints of the twigs.

ANALYSIS: Bacterial leaf spot
This plant disease is caused by a bacterium (*Xanthomonas pruni*) that also attacks
peach, nectarine, and plum trees. The infection is common east of the Rocky
Mountains and is one of the more destructive diseases of stone fruits. The bacteria spend the winter in the lesions on
the twigs, oozing out in the spring to be
carried by splashing raindrops to the
young leaves and shoots, which they infect and decay. Periods of frequent rainfall
favor the infection.

SOLUTION: There is no adequate control
for this disease. Spraying with basic copper sulfate when the buds open may help
suppress bacterial leaf spot, but the treatment will not eliminate it.

Blossom and twig blight.

Brown rot.

Scab.

PROBLEM: Blossoms and young leaves wilt, decay, and turn brown during the first two weeks of the bloom period. The decayed blossoms may fail to drop and may hang on the tree throughout the growing season. In humid conditions, masses of gray spores may appear on the infected flower parts. There is often extensive twig dieback. Sunken lesions (cankers) may develop on the twigs and branches as the season progresses; in many cases a thick gummy material oozes from these cankers.

PROBLEM: Many twigs die. Small circular brown spots appear on the young apricots. Later in the season, as the apricots start to mature, these spots may enlarge to rot part or all of the fruit. During moist weather, the rotted apricots are covered with tufts of gray spores. Slicing open infected fruit reveals brown, firm, and fairly dry flesh. Infected apricots either drop prematurely or dry, turn dark brown, and remain on the tree past the normal harvest period. Healthy fruit may rot when it touches infected fruit in storage.

PROBLEM: Small, olive-green spots appear on half-grown fruit. These spots are usually clustered near the stem end of the apricot. The spots eventually turn brown and velvety. The fruit is often dwarfed, deformed, or cracked. There may be small brown spots and holes in the leaves, and many twigs die back.

ANALYSIS: Brown rot
This plant disease, caused by either of two closely related fungi (*Monilinia laxa* or *M. fructicola*), is destructive to apricots and all other stone fruits. The fungi spend the winter in twig cankers or in rotted apricots (mummies) in the tree or on the ground. In the spring, spores are blown or splashed from cankers or mummies to the healthy flower buds. After penetrating and decaying the flowers, the fungi grow down into the twigs, producing brown, sunken cankers. During moist weather a thick, gummy sap oozes from the lesions, and tufts of gray spores may form on the infected areas. Spores from cankers and infected blossoms or mummies are splashed and blown to the maturing fruit. Young apricots are fairly resistant to infection, but maturing apricots are vulnerable. Brown rot develops most rapidly in mild, moist conditions.

ANALYSIS: Scab
This plant disease is caused by a fungus (*Cladosporium carpophilum*) that attacks peaches, nectarines, cherries, and plums, as well as apricots. Fungi of this species spend the winter on twig lesions. In the spring, spores are splashed and blown to the developing foliage and fruit. The young fruit does not show scab lesions for at least a month after it is initially infected. Spores produced on the infected leaves, twigs, and fruit will continue to infect healthy apricots throughout the growing season.

SOLUTION: If uninfected blossoms remain on the tree, spray with a fungicide containing chlorothalonil or triforine to protect them from infection. Respray 10 days later. Next spring, spray trees when the first flowers begin to open; continue treatment according to label directions. To protect maturing apricots from infection, spray about 3 weeks before they are harvested; use a fungicide containing triforine. Each year remove and destroy all infected apricots and mummies as they appear. Prune out cankers and blighted twigs. Clean up and destroy all debris around the tree. Plant resistant varieties.

SOLUTION: It's too late to do anything about the spots on this year's fruit, but it is edible if peeled. Next year, when the petals have fallen from the blossoms, spray with a fungicide containing captan or chlorothalonil. If scab is serious in your area, continue to spray at intervals of 10 to 14 days until about a month before the apricots are harvested.

Apricot resistance to brown rot:
  Most susceptible: Blenheim, Derby Royal, Royal.
  Fairly resistant: Tilton.

APRICOT

Cytospora canker.

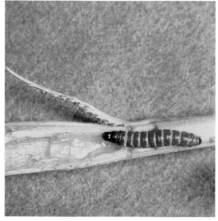

Peach twig borer (2 times life size).

San Jose scales (4 times life size).

PROBLEM: Oval or oblong sunken lesions on the bark enlarge gradually. A sticky gum may ooze from the lesion, sometimes followed by the emergence of curly orange threads. Later, small black freckles appear on the bark along the edges of the lesions. Leaves on the affected branches may turn brown and die, or the entire branch may die.

ANALYSIS: Cytospora canker
This plant disease, also known as perennial canker, is caused by one of two related fungi (*Valsa cincta* or *Cytospora leucostoma*) that also attack peach, plum, and cherry. The fungi spend the winter in sunken lesions (cankers) or on dead wood. In the spring, black fungal bodies develop in the bark, and curly orange fungal chains form. These chains release spores that are spread by wind and splashing rain to healthy trees. Infection usually occurs through injured tissues. Bark that is damaged by sunscald, cold, pruning wounds, or mechanical injury is especially susceptible. Fungal decay causes the formation of depressed lesions (cankers). A sticky gum may ooze from the cankers. The branch or stem above the canker may die because of decay or clogging of the water-conducting tissue in the branch. Wet weather from 70° to 85° F enhances the development of this disease.

SOLUTION: No fully adequate control is available; a combination of procedures must be used. Remove badly infected branches and cut out cankers. Avoid mechanical injuries to the tree, and paint the trunk with white latex paint to protect against cold injury and sunburn.

PROBLEM: New growth at the tips of the twigs wilts and dies. Slicing affected twigs lengthwise reveals worms about ½ inch long. The reddish brown color of these worms distinguishes them from worms of the oriental fruit moth, which cause similar damage. Later in the season, some of the maturing fruit also contain reddish worms. During the summer, there may be cocoons attached to the branches or tree crotches.

ANALYSIS: Peach twig borers
(*Anarsia lineatella*)
This borer attacks all the stone fruits and is particularly damaging along the Pacific Coast. The young larvae hibernate during the winter in burrows under loose bark or in other protected places on the tree. When the tree blooms in the spring, the larvae emerge and bore into the young buds, shoots, and tender twigs, causing twig and leaf death. When mature, they leave the twigs and pupate in cocoons attached to branches. After several weeks, gray moths emerge. The females lay eggs on the twigs, leaves, and fruit. Egg laying and larval damage can occur all through the growing season. Later in the summer, larvae feed almost exclusively on maturing fruit. In addition to ruining the fruit, these pests may cause abnormal branching patterns in young trees.

SOLUTION: Worms in the twigs and fruit cannot be reached with pesticides. To prevent future worm damage, kill the moths by spraying infested trees with a chemical containing methoxychlor; follow label directions. Next spring, spray again just before the blossoms open. Repeat the treatment 2 more times at intervals of 10 to 14 days.

PROBLEM: Leaves are pale green to yellow and may drop prematurely from weakened limbs. The bark is encrusted with small (1/10-inch or smaller) hard, circular, slightly raised bumps with dull yellow centers. Scraping off a hard bump reveals a yellow or olive-colored insect. Limb dieback may be severe, and entire branches may be killed. Fruit may be marred by red-purple specks.

ANALYSIS: San Jose scales
(*Quadraspidiotus perniciosus*)
These insects infest the bark, leaves, and fruits of many fruit trees. Female scales bear live young in the spring. In late spring to midsummer, the young scales, called crawlers, settle on leaves and twigs. The small (1/16-inch), soft-bodied young feed by inserting their mouthparts and sucking sap from the plant. Their legs atrophy, and a hard, crusty shell develops over their bodies. An uncontrolled infestation of San Jose scales may kill large branches after two or three seasons.

SOLUTION: During the dormant season, just prior to growth in early spring, spray the trunk and branches with an oil spray. In late spring, kill the crawlers by applying an insecticide containing diazinon or malathion.

CHERRY ⎯⎯⎯⎯⎯⎯⎯⎯⎯⎯⎯⎯⎯⎯⎯⎯⎯⎯⎯⎯⎯⎯⎯⎯⎯⎯⎯⎯⎯⎯⎯⎯

Cherry fruit fly maggots (3 times life size).

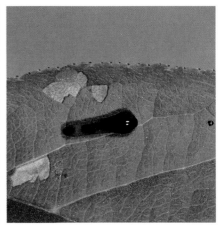

Pearslug larva (2 times life size).

CHERRY

ADAPTATION AND POLLINATION:
Zones 4 through 9, depending on
variety.

SOIL: Any good, deep, well-drained
garden soil. pH 5.5 to 8.0.

FERTILIZER: Apply a fertilizer higher in
nitrogen (14-7-7, for example); follow
label directions.

WATER:
   How much: Apply enough water to
wet the soil 3 to 4 feet deep.
   How often: Water when soil 6 inches
below the surface is just barely moist.

PRUNING: Cherries are borne on short
fruiting branches (spurs) that grow on 2-
year-old wood. The spurs are very long-
lived and often continue to bear for 10
years or more. Prune lightly, thinning
out weak, crossing, or dead twigs and
branches.

HARVEST: Harvest when the cherries
are fully colored. When cherries are ripe,
the stems separate easily from the spurs
when the fruit is gently lifted or pulled.
When picking cherries, avoid damaging
the spurs.

PROBLEM: The fruit
is malformed, shrunken,
or shriveled. Often the
cherries are rotten and pulpy; there may
be holes in the fruit. Tapered, yellow-
white, legless worms up to ¼ inch long
may be found in the cherries. Many
cherries drop prematurely.

ANALYSIS: Cherry fruit flies
(*Rhagoletis* species)
These worms are the larvae of several
closely related flies. The adult flies, about
half the size of the common housefly, appear in the late spring for about a month.
They lay eggs in the cherries through
holes they puncture in the skins. After
several days the eggs hatch into maggots
that tunnel through the cherry flesh. Infested cherries usually drop to the
ground, and the mature maggots burrow
into the soil to pupate. They remain in
the soil throughout the winter and
emerge as adults next spring.

SOLUTION: You cannot control the
worms in this year's fruit, but you can
probably prevent the recurrence of the
problem next year. Look for the adult flies
in late spring as the fruit is forming. As
soon as fruit flies appear, spray with an
insecticide containing diazinon. Repeat
the application 2 more times at intervals
of 14 days.

PROBLEM: The upper
surfaces of leaves
are chewed between the
veins, leaving a lacy, translucent layer of
tissue that turns brown. Dark green to
orange, wet, sluglike worms up to ½ inch
long may be feeding on the leaves. Severely infested trees may be defoliated.

ANALYSIS: Pearslugs
(*Caliroa cerasi*)
Although pearslugs closely resemble
slugs, they are actually the larvae of
black-and-yellow sawflies that infest pear,
plum, and some ornamental trees in addition to cherry. The adult flies appear in
the late spring. The females lay their eggs
in the leaves. The young larvae that hatch
from these eggs exude a slimy, olive-green
substance, giving them a sluglike appearance. They feed on the foliage for about a
month, then drop to the ground, burrow
into the soil, and pupate. Young trees that
are severely infested by pearslugs may be
greatly weakened. Fruit yield may be low
and cherries may be of poor quality.

SOLUTION: As soon as damage is observed, spray the infested tree with an insecticide labeled for pearslug (or sawflies).
Respray if infestation recurs.

CHERRY

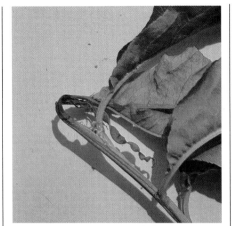

Oriental fruit moth damage.

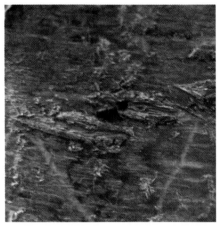

Shothole borer beetle.

Bacterial canker.

PROBLEM: New growth at the tips of the twigs wilts and dies. Slicing an affected twig lengthwise reveals pinkish white worms up to ½ inch long. Later in the season, some of the maturing fruit may also contain these worms.

ANALYSIS: Oriental fruit moths
(*Grapholita molesta*)
The larvae of these night-flying moths damage stone fruits, apples, and pears. The pests hibernate in cocoons on the tree bark or in branch crotches. In the spring, they pupate and emerge as brown adult moths. The females lay eggs on the young cherry twigs and leaves. The larvae bore into the young buds, shoots, and tender twigs, causing twig and leaf death. When the worms mature they leave the twigs, spin cocoons, and pupate in the tree or in debris on the ground. After several weeks, moths emerge and the females lay their eggs. Egg laying and larval damage can occur all through the growing season. Later in the summer, larvae feed almost exclusively on the maturing cherries. The larvae leave gum-filled holes in the fruit when they exit to pupate. In addition to ruining the fruit, these pests may cause abnormal branching patterns on young trees when large numbers of twigs are infested.

SOLUTION: Worms in the twigs and fruit cannot be reached with pesticides. To prevent future worm damage, kill the moths by spraying infested trees with an insecticide containing carbaryl (SEVIN®) or diazinon. Apply as directed on the label.

PROBLEM: Many small holes (⅟₁₆ to ⅛ inch in diameter) are bored in the twigs, branches, and sometimes trunk of the tree. A sticky gum may ooze from the holes. The holes may be plugged with the bodies of dead insects. Slicing open the branches reveals sawdust-filled tunnels in the wood. Pinkish white, slightly curved grubs may be found in the tunnels. Brownish black beetles ⅟₁₀ inch long are often present on the bark. The foliage on damaged branches sometimes wilts and turns brown. Twigs and buds may be killed, and entire branches may die.

ANALYSIS: Shothole borers
(*Scolytus rugulosus*)
This beetle, sometimes known as the fruit tree bark beetle, also attacks other stone fruits and many ornamental trees. The adult beetles that emerge in the late spring or early summer feed at the bases of buds and small twigs, often killing them. The female beetles bore into the wood, creating tunnels in which they lay their eggs. The grubs that hatch from the eggs bore into the inner wood, creating sawdust-filled burrows 2 to 4 inches long. The grubs pupate just under the bark, then emerge as adult beetles. The last generation of grubs spends the winter in the tunnels, emerging the following spring. Weakened, diseased, and dying trees and branches are most susceptible to borer infestation.

SOLUTION: Apply a spray containing lindane to the lower part of the trunk, wetting the bark thoroughly. Avoid spraying the fruit and foliage. During the dormant season, remove and destroy infested branches. Keep the tree healthy by watering properly and applying fertilizer when necessary. For cultural information, see page 221.

PROBLEM: Sunken, elliptical lesions appear on the trunk or branches. Throughout the fall, winter, and spring, thick, amber-colored, sour-smelling gum oozes from these lesions. In the spring, especially when the weather is wet and cold, blossoms may turn brown and wither. Individual branches may fail to produce foliage, or, as the season progresses, entire branches may die back. There may be angular holes in the leaves. Sometimes, dark and sunken lesions appear in the fruit.

ANALYSIS: Bacterial canker
This plant disease, also known as bacterial gummosis or bacterial blast, attacks various fruit and nut trees but is most severe on cherry trees. This disease is caused by a bacterium (*Pseudomonas syringae*). During the fall, winter, and early spring, large quantities of bacteria-containing gum oozes from the cankers. Splashing rain spreads the bacteria to dormant buds, twigs, and branches. Infection occurs through wounds in the twigs and branches, and bacterial decay causes cankers to form. Bacterial activity decreases in summer, but slowly developing cankers may continue to grow until they encircle branches. By midsummer, the affected branches and limbs start to die back. With the onset of cool, wet fall weather, bacterial activity increases again. This disease is most serious on young trees.

SOLUTION: Bacterial canker is difficult to control. Prune out diseased branches. After each cut, sterilize pruning shears with rubbing alcohol. In the fall, spray with a fungicide containing basic copper sulfate. Keep the tree healthy. For care of cherry trees, see page 221.

CHERRY ——————————————————— ■ **CITRUS** ———————————————

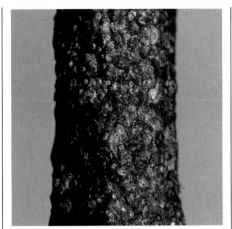

San Jose scales.

Cherry leaf spot.

CITRUS ————————————

PROBLEM: Some leaves are pale green to yellow and may drop prematurely from weakened limbs. Or they may turn brown and wither and remain attached to the tree into the winter. The bark is encrusted with small (¹⁄₁₀-inch), hard, circular, slightly raised bumps with dull yellow centers. Scraping off a hard bump reveals a yellow or olive-colored insect. Limb dieback may be severe, and entire branches may be killed. The fruit may be marred by specks.

ANALYSIS: San Jose scales
(*Quadraspidiotus perniciosus*)
These insects infest the bark, leaves, and fruits of many fruit trees. Female scales bear live young in the spring. In late spring to midsummer, the young scales, called crawlers, settle on leaves and twigs. The small (¹⁄₁₆-inch), soft-bodied young feed by inserting their mouthparts and sucking sap from the plant. Their legs atrophy and a hard, crusty shell develops over their bodies. An uncontrolled infestation of San Jose scales may kill large branches after two or three seasons.

SOLUTION: During the dormant season, just prior to bud break, spray the trunk and branches with an oil spray. In late spring, kill the crawlers by applying an insecticide containing diazinon or malathion.

PROBLEM: Purple spots appear on the topsides of leaves. The centers of the spots may fall out, leaving holes. Many of the spotted leaves are yellow and dying. The undersides of the leaves may be dotted with cream-colored masses of spores. In severe cases, the fruit is also spotted. The tree defoliates prematurely, and the cherry yield is reduced and of poor quality. The fruit is often soft and watery.

ANALYSIS: Cherry leaf spot
This plant disease, also known as yellow leaf spot, is caused by a fungus (*Coccomyces hiemalis*). Fungi of this species spend the winter in fallen leaves. By the time the cherry trees are finished blooming, large numbers of spores have been splashed and blown from the ground to the emerging leaves. The infection and premature death of the leaves greatly reduces the amount of food the tree can make and store. This results in weakened trees and reduced, poor-quality fruit yields. Infected trees are much more susceptible to cold injury during the following winter. Cherry leaf spot is most severe during wet weather from 60° to 70° F.

SOLUTION: Spray with a fungicide containing captan or chlorothalonil. In the fall, remove and destroy all leaf debris around the tree. Next spring, spray when the petals fall; respray at least 2 more times at intervals of 10 to 14 days. If the problem is severe, continue spraying until 7 days before harvest. 'Meteor' and 'Northstar' cherries are resistant to cherry leaf spot.

ADAPTATION: Zones 8 through 10.

SOIL: Any good, well-drained soil. pH 5.5 to 8.0.

FERTILIZER: Apply a fertilizer higher in nitrogen and lower in phosphorus (14-7-10, for example); follow label directions.

WATER:
How much: Apply enough water to wet the soil 3 to 4 feet deep. To avoid wetting the trunk and crown of the plant, water into a basin that keeps the water at least 12 inches out from the trunk.
How often: Water when soil 6 to 12 inches below the surface is just barely moist.

PRUNING: Prune only to shape the tree and to remove suckers and dead twigs and branches. Lightly thin the inside of the tree if the growth is dense.

HARVEST: When the fruit is fully colored, taste one to determine if it is ripe. If the flavor is not yet sweet enough for the variety, allow the fruit to ripen for another few weeks, then try again. To harvest, clip fruit off with pruning shears rather than pulling it off.

CITRUS

Citrus thrips damage.

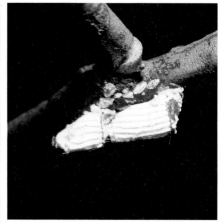

Cottonycushion scale (2 times life size).

Damaged leaves. *Insert:* Mite (12 times life size).

PROBLEM: Leaf buds shrivel and turn brown. Some of the leaves are silvery gray, leathery, curled, and distorted. The fruit may be silvery, scabbed, streaked, and deformed. To determine if the plant is infested with insects, hold a sheet of white paper underneath an affected shoot and tap the stem sharply. If citrus thrips are present, minute yellow-brown insects, resembling wood slivers, will drop to the paper and begin to crawl around.

ANALYSIS: Citrus thrips
(*Scirtothrips citri*)
These insects are pests of citrus and various ornamental trees. Thrips cause their damage by rasping the tissue of young leaves and immature fruits. They feed on the plant sap that exudes from the injured tissue. The female adult thrips lay their eggs in leaves and stems in the fall. The following spring, the young thrips that emerge from these eggs begin feeding on the new growth. These pests are often found in protected areas such as the insides of leaf buds. Thrips damage occurs throughout the growing season and is especially severe during hot, dry weather.

SOLUTION: As soon as damage is observed, spray infested plants with an insecticide containing diazinon or malathion. Follow directions carefully, and repeat at regular intervals of 7 to 10 days as long as new damage appears.

PROBLEM: White, cottony masses cluster on the leaves, stems, branches, and possibly the trunk. Some of the foliage may wither and turn yellow; leaves and fruit may drop. In many cases, a shiny or sticky substance coats the leaves. A black, sooty mold may grow on the sticky substance.

ANALYSIS: Mealybugs and cottonycushion scales
(*Planococcus citri* and *Icerya purchasi*)
These insects, frequently found together on citrus plants, look so much alike that separate identification is difficult. In late spring and summer, the females are covered with white, cottony masses containing up to 2,500 eggs. Females lay their conspicuous egg masses on leaves, twigs, and branches. The inconspicuous young insects that hatch from these eggs are yellowish brown to green. They feed by sucking sap from the plant tissues. They are unable to digest fully all the sugar in the plant sap, and they excrete the excess in a fluid called honeydew. A sooty mold fungus may develop on the honeydew, causing the citrus leaves to appear black and dirty. Mealybugs and scales can be spread in any of several ways: The wind can blow egg masses and insects from plant to plant, ants can carry them to new locations on the plant, or the active young insects can crawl to new locations by themselves.

SOLUTION: Spray infested trees with an insecticide containing malathion or diazinon, covering both surfaces of the leaves. Respray 5 to 7 days later. Use a spreader-sticker when spraying. Do not spray when the plant is in full bloom. Do not apply within 7 days of harvest.

PROBLEM: Leaves are stippled, yellowing, or scratched in appearance. There may be cobwebbing over flower buds, between leaves, or on the undersides of the leaves. The fruit is often brown or russet-colored, leathery, or silvery, and it may drop prematurely. To determine if the plant is infested with mites large enough to be seen, hold a sheet of white paper underneath an affected branch and tap the branch sharply. If visible mites are present, minute green, red, or yellow specks will drop to the paper and begin to crawl around. Some mite species are so small that, to see them, you must inspect the leaves with a 10-power magnifying glass.

ANALYSIS: Mites
These pests, related to spiders, are extremely damaging to all types of citrus. There are several mite species that attack citrus, including citrus red mites, citrus bud mites, purple mites, and citrus rust mites. Mites cause damage by sucking sap from the leaves and young fruit. As a result of feeding, the green leaf pigment (chlorophyll) disappears, producing a yellowed, stippled appearance. Feeding damage also causes tissue death, resulting in the browning and silvering of the fruit and foliage. Mites are active throughout the growing season but are favored by dry weather above 70° F. By midsummer, they build up to tremendous numbers. A severe mite infestation weakens the plant and can seriously reduce the size and quality of the fruit.

SOLUTION: Spray infested trees with a miticide containing hexakis. Be sure to cover both surfaces of the leaves. Respray at least 2 more times at intervals of 7 days.

Nitrogen-deficient citrus leaves.

Cold-damaged Valencia oranges.

Cold damage.

PROBLEM: Newer foliage turns pale green. Older leaves gradually turn yellow and may fall off. Overall growth is stunted. The tree may flower profusely but usually fails to set much fruit.

ANALYSIS: Lack of nitrogen

Nitrogen, the most important nutrient for plant growth and development, is deficient in almost all soils. Nitrogen is essential in the formation of plant protein, fiber, enzymes, chlorophyll (green leaf pigment), and many other compounds. When a plant becomes deficient in nitrogen, it breaks down chlorophyll and other compounds in its older leaves to recover nitrogen, which it reuses for new growth. This loss of chlorophyll causes the older leaves to turn yellow. Soils that are low in organic matter, and sandy, readily leached soils are frequently deficient in nitrogen. These kinds of soils, in particular, need to be supplemented with fertilizers. Poor drainage, temperatures below 50° F, and acidity or alkalinity can also cause soil nitrogen to become less available for plant use.

SOLUTION: For a quick response, spray the foliage with a soluble plant food rated 23-19-17. Apply a food rated 14-7-10 as directed on the label.

PROBLEM: The tree has been exposed to freezing temperatures. Tender shoots may blacken and die; older foliage often turns yellowish brown, leathery, and eventually withers and falls. The fruit rind may be scarred with brown or green sunken lesions. Or, even though the fruit rind appears normal, cutting the fruit reveals dry flesh. Severely damaged trees suffer twig and branch dieback. The bark along the branches or trunk may split open.

ANALYSIS: Cold damage

Citrus plants are frost-tender and are easily damaged by temperatures below 32° F. Although many citrus plants can recover from a light frost, they cannot tolerate long periods of freezing weather. Damage to fruit occurs when the juice-filled cells freeze and rupture. The released fluid evaporates through the rind, leaving the flesh dry and pulpy. In addition to causing leaf and twig dieback, temperatures of 20° F and lower promote bark splitting, which may not become apparent for several weeks or months.

SOLUTION: Don't prune back damaged branches immediately. If danger of frost remains, drive 4 stakes into the ground around the tree; cover the tree with fabric, cardboard, or plastic; and stake down the cover. Remove covers when the weather warms up. The trunks and main limbs of young trees may be protected by wrapping them with corn stalks, palm fronds, or fiberglass building insulation. Do not shade the foliage. Keep the soil moist during a freeze, but be careful not to overwater. Limit fertilizer to a minimum. Damaged fruit can be removed immediately following the freeze; always wait for new growth to appear before pruning. As soon as the danger of frost has passed, prune blackened shoots and withered foliage. If the tree has suffered serious injury, it may take as long as 6 months before you can determine the extent of the damage to the trunk and main limbs. You can then prune out the dead wood. For more information on pruning, see Ortho's book *All About Pruning*.

CITRUS ■   FIG ■   PEACH AND NECTARINE

Iron deficiency on orange leaves.

Bird damage to mission fig.

PROBLEM: Some leaves turn pale green or yellow. The newest leaves (those at the tips of the branches) are most severely affected. Except in extreme cases, the veins of affected leaves remain green. In extreme cases, the newest leaves are small and completely white or yellow. Older leaves may remain green.

ANALYSIS: Iron deficiency
Citrus trees frequently suffer from deficiencies of iron and other trace nutrients, such as manganese and zinc, that are essential to normal plant growth and development. Deficiencies can occur when one or more of these elements are lacking in the soil. Often these nutrients are present, but alkaline (pH 7.5 and higher) or wet soil conditions cause them to form compounds that cannot be used by trees. An alkaline condition can result from over-liming or from lime leached from cement or brick. Alkaline soil usually exists in regions where soil is derived from limestone and in those with low rainfall. Some citrus trees turn yellow naturally in cold weather; however, if iron is available, the foliage will turn green again when the weather warms.

SOLUTION: Apply a liquid iron solution to the foliage at 2-week intervals during the new- or rapid-growth period. Repeat the treatment whenever new growth appears, but do not apply the solution if the temperature is expected to exceed 90° F within 24 hours of application. Or apply a plant food rated 14-7-10 to the soil around the plants. Improve soil drainage.

PROBLEM: Ripened figs have holes in them and may be partially eaten. They may have been knocked to the ground. Birds may be seen feeding on ripening figs.

ANALYSIS: Bird damage
Some birds feed heavily on ripening figs. When the fruit is fully ripe, birds peck at the soft flesh, leaving holes. The wounded figs may decay, becoming inedible.

SOLUTION: Harvest figs daily. Nets thrown over the tree are also effective in reducing bird damage. Nets may be purchased at a local nursery or hardware store.

Fig cultural information
Water: When soil 6 inches below surface is barely moist.
Fertilizer: Medium.
Pruning: Lightly thin out branches and head back long shoots.
Harvest: When fruit bends over at the neck and flesh is soft. Remove with stem still attached. Wear gloves if you find sap irritating.

PEACH AND NECTARINE

ADAPTATION AND POLLINATION: Zones 5 through 10, depending on variety.

SOIL: Any good, deep, well-drained soil. pH 5.5 to 7.5.

FERTILIZER: Apply a fertilizer higher in nitrogen (14-7-7, for example); follow label directions.

WATER:
  How much: Apply enough water to wet the soil 3 to 4 feet deep.
  How often: Water when soil 6 inches below the surface is just barely moist.

PRUNING: Peach and nectarine trees bear on 1-year-old wood. Prune half of last year's growth annually. Thin out weak, crossing, or dead twigs and branches. When fruit is thumbnail-sized, thin so fruits are 6 inches apart.

HARVEST: Harvest when fruit is fully colored and slightly soft. The stem of a ripe peach or nectarine separates easily from the branch when the fruit is gently lifted.

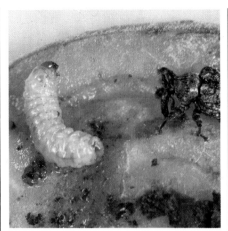

Plum curculio and larva (4 times life size).

Scab.

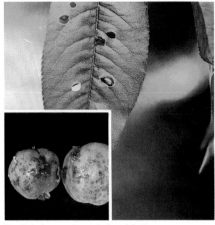

Shothole fungus. *Insert: Infected fruit.*

PROBLEM: Ripening fruit is misshapen and rotten; it often drops prematurely. Holes about ⅛ inch in diameter and deep, crescent-shaped scars appear on the fruit. Cutting open damaged fruit may reveal crescent-shaped yellow-gray grubs with brown heads.

ANALYSIS: Plum curculios
(*Conotrachelus nenuphar*)
These insects, found east of the Rocky Mountains, attack stone fruits, apples, and pears. The adults are brown beetles with long, curved snouts. They hibernate in debris and other protected places during the winter. The beetles emerge in the spring, when new growth starts, and begin feeding on young leaves, blossoms, and developing fruit. After five to six weeks, the female beetles start to lay their eggs in the young fruit, cutting distinctive, crescent-shaped slits into peaches or nectarines. The grubs that hatch from the eggs feed for several weeks in the fruit. Infested fruit usually drops to the ground. The grubs eventually leave the fruit and bore into the soil, where they pupate. The emerging beetles feed on fruit for a few weeks, and then go into hibernation. In southern areas, they lay eggs, producing a second generation of grubs in late summer.

SOLUTION: Once grubs are inside the fruit, sprays cannot reach them. Spray with an insecticide containing carbaryl ((SEVIN®) or malathion to kill beetles that are feeding on fruit or laying eggs; follow label instructions. Pick up and destroy all fallen fruit. Next spring, spray the trees when the petals are falling from the blossoms. Repeat applications according to directions on the label.

PROBLEM: Small, olive-green spots appear on half-grown fruit. These spots are usually clustered near the stem end of the peach or nectarine. The spots eventually turn brown and velvety. The fruit is often dwarfed, deformed, or cracked. There are usually small brown spots and holes in the leaves, and many twigs die.

ANALYSIS: Scab
This plant disease is caused by a fungus (*Cladosporium carpophilum*) that attacks all the stone fruits. In the spring, spores are splashed and blown from lesions on the twigs to the developing foliage and fruit. The young fruit does not show scab lesions for at least a month after it is initially infected. Spores that are produced on the infected leaves, twigs, and fruit will continue to infect healthy peaches or nectarines throughout the growing season.

SOLUTION: It's too late to do anything about the spots on this year's fruit, but it is edible if peeled. Next year, when the petals have fallen from the blossoms, spray with a fungicide containing captan or chlorothalonil. If scab is a serious problem in your area, continue to spray at intervals of 10 to 14 days until about a month before the fruit is harvested.

PROBLEM: Small purplish spots appear on young twigs, leaves, and developing fruit in early spring; foliage and fruit eventually turn brown. The leaf spots often drop out, leaving shotholes in the leaves. Infected buds, shoots, and foliage may die. The spots on the maturing peaches or nectarines turn scablike; drop off; and leave rough, corky lesions.

ANALYSIS: Shothole fungus
This plant disease, also called coryneum blight and peach blight, is caused by a fungus (*Coryneum carpophilum*) that attacks peach, nectarine, apricot, plum, and almond trees. Fungi of this species spend the winter in lesions on the twigs and buds. In the spring, the spores are splashed by rain to the developing buds, leaves, and fruit, causing spotting and tissue death. Infection causes the leaf tissue to produce a layer of cells that walls off the damaged area. The center of the spot then drops out. Severe infection may cause extensive twig and bud blighting and, possibly, premature defoliation, which reduces the peach or nectarine yield. The disease is favored by wet spring weather.

SOLUTION: To prevent twig and leaf bud infection, prune out infected twigs and branches as soon as they are discovered. In the fall, immediately after the leaves have dropped, spray the tree with a lime-sulfur spray or a fungicide containing chlorothalonil. To reduce or prevent fruit infection, apply a fungicide containing chlorothalonil 1 to 2 weeks after petals have fallen.

PEACH AND NECTARINE

Bacterial leaf spot.

Leaf curl on peach.

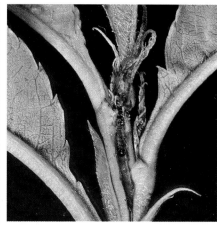

Peach twig borer (life size).

PROBLEM: Brown or black angular spots appear on leaves. In many cases, the centers of the spots fall out. The tips of the leaves may die, and eventually the leaves turn yellow and drop. The surface of the fruit may be dotted with brown to black spots and become pitted and cracked. Sunken lesions may form on the twigs. Severely infected trees may drop all their leaves.

ANALYSIS: Bacterial leaf spot
This plant disease is caused by a bacterium (*Xanthomonas pruni*) that also attacks apricots and plums. This is one of the more destructive diseases of stone fruits east of the Rocky Mountains. In the spring, bacteria ooze from lesions on the twigs and are carried by splashing rain to the young leaves, shoots, and developing fruit. Frequent rainfall favors the infection. Trees that defoliate early in the summer are weakened and produce small crops of poor quality.

SOLUTION: There is no adequate control for this disease. Spraying with basic copper sulfate when the flower buds open in the spring may help suppress bacterial leaf spot, but the treatment will not eliminate it. When planting new trees, use resistant varieties.

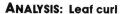

Peach varieties and resistance to bacterial leaf spot:
   Susceptible: Blake, Elberta, Rio Oso Gem.
   Fairly resistant: Lizzie, Redhaven, Redskin, Sunhaven.
   Resistant: Belle of Georgia, Early-Free-Red, Hiley.

PROBLEM: Leaves are puckered, thickened, and curled from the time they first appear in the spring. Emerging shoots are swollen and stunted. Initially the infected foliage is red or orange, but it later turns pale green to yellow. As the season progresses, a grayish white powdery material develops on the leaves. Eventually these leaves shrivel and drop. Fruiting is poor, and the fruit that is present may be covered with raised, wrinkled, irregular lesions.

ANALYSIS: Leaf curl
This plant disease is caused by a fungus (*Taphrina deformans*) that attacks peaches and nectarines wherever they are grown. Infection occurs as soon as the buds begin to swell in early spring. Rain splashes fungal spores from the bark to the buds. Later in the season, the infected leaves develop a grayish white covering of spores that are blown onto the bark. Infected trees are greatly weakened by the premature loss of foliage in early summer. Leaf curl is most severe when spring weather is cool and wet.

SOLUTION: Infected leaves cannot be cured. To prevent the recurrence of the disease next year, spray in the fall, immediately after the leaves have dropped, or in the spring, after the buds begin to swell but before they open. Use a lime-sulfur spray or a fungicide containing chlorothalonil. If the disease has been severe in past years, spray in both fall and spring.

PROBLEM: New growth at the tips of the twigs wilts and dies. Slicing affected twigs lengthwise reveals worms about ½ inch long. The reddish brown color of these worms distinguishes them from worms of the oriental fruit moth, which cause similar damage. Later in the season, some of the maturing fruits also contain reddish worms. During the summer, there may be cocoons attached to the branches or tree crotches.

ANALYSIS: Peach twig borers
(*Anarsia lineatella*)
This borer attacks all the stone fruits and is particularly damaging on the Pacific Coast. The young larvae hibernate during the winter in silk-lined burrows under loose bark or in other protected places on the tree. When the tree starts to bloom in the spring, the larvae bore into young buds and shoots. They feed on the tender twigs, killing twigs and leaves. When mature, they leave the twigs and pupate in cocoons attached to branches. After several weeks, gray moths emerge. The females lay their eggs on the twigs, leaves, and fruit. Egg laying and larval damage can occur all through the growing season. Later in the summer, larvae feed almost exclusively on the maturing fruit. In addition to ruining the fruit, peach twig borers may cause abnormal branching patterns in young trees when large numbers of twigs are infested.

SOLUTION: Worms in the twigs and fruit cannot be reached with pesticides. To prevent future worm damage, kill the moths by spraying infested trees with a chemical containing methoxychlor; follow label directions. Next spring, spray again just before the blossoms open. Repeat the treatment 2 more times at intervals of 10 to 14 days.

Blighted shoots.

Fruit rot.

Catfacing on peach.

PROBLEM: Blossoms and young leaves wilt, decay, and turn brown during the first two weeks of the bloom period. The decayed blossoms may fail to drop and may hang on the tree throughout the growing season. In humid conditions, masses of gray spores may appear on the infected flower parts. There is often extensive twig dieback. Sunken lesions (cankers) may develop on the twigs and branches as the season progresses; in many cases, these lesions exude a sticky ooze. Many twigs die. Canker growth usually stops with the onset of warm dry weather.

ANALYSIS: Brown rot

This plant disease, caused by either of two closely related fungi (*Monilinia laxa* or *M. fructicola*), is destructive to all stone fruits. The fungi spend the winter in twig cankers or in rotted fruit (mummies) in the tree or on the ground. In the spring, spores are blown or splashed from cankers or mummies to the healthy flower buds. After penetrating and decaying the flowers, the fungi grow down into the twigs, producing brown, sunken cankers. During moist weather, a thick, gummy sap oozes from the lesions, and tufts of gray spores may form on the infected areas. Spores from cankers and infected blossoms or mummies are splashed and blown to the maturing fruit. Young peaches or nectarines are fairly resistant to infection, but maturing fruit is vulnerable. Brown rot develops most rapidly in mild, moist conditions.

SOLUTION: If uninfected blossoms remain on the tree, spray with a fungicide containing chlorothalonil or triforine to protect them from infection. Respray 10 days later. To protect maturing peaches or nectarines from infection, spray about 3 weeks before they are harvested; use a fungicide containing triforine. Each year remove and destroy all infected fruit and mummies as they appear. Prune out cankers and blighted twigs. Clean up and destroy all debris around the tree. Next spring, spray trees as the first flowers begin to open, and continue to spray according to label directions.

PROBLEM: Small circular brown spots appear on the young fruit. Later in the season, as the peaches or nectarines start to mature, these spots may enlarge to rot part or all of the fruit. During moist weather, the rotted fruit is covered with tufts of gray spores. Slicing open the infected peaches or nectarines reveals brown, firm, and fairly dry flesh. Infected fruit either drops prematurely or dries, turns dark brown, and remains on the tree past the normal harvest period. Healthy fruit may rot when it touches infected fruit in storage.

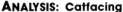

PROBLEM: Sunken, corky areas mar the fruit surfaces. Blossoms may drop without setting fruit. Many of the young fruit drop prematurely. Some of the developing leaves and twigs are deformed. Brown, green, or rust-colored bugs ¼ to ½ inch long may be seen feeding on the buds and fruit.

ANALYSIS: Catfacing

The sunken, corky "catface" disfigurations that appear on the fruit are usually caused by the tarnished plant bug (*Lygus lineolaris*) and various species of stinkbugs. The insects hibernate in vetch or other broadleafed weeds during the winter. When the trees start to bloom in the spring, these bugs feed on the young buds, blooms, and fruits, causing bud and fruit drop, twig malformation, and catfacing. Most of the damage occurs early in the season, although the bugs may occasionally feed on the fruits up until harvest. Hail or cold weather may also cause catface injuries by damaging the tender blooms and fruit surfaces.

SOLUTION: To control plant bugs, spray when the buds turn pink; use an insecticide containing captan or malathion. Respray when the petals have dropped from most of the blossoms and whenever bugs are seen in the trees. Next fall, clean up weeds and plant debris to eliminate hibernating locations for the overwintering bugs.

Aphid damage.

PROBLEM: New leaves are curled and twisted. Leaves may turn yellow and drop. The developing fruit may be small and misshapen. In many cases, a shiny or sticky substance coats the leaves. A black sooty mold often grows on the sticky substance. Tiny (⅛-inch) yellow, light green, or black soft-bodied insects cluster on the young shoots and undersides of the leaves. Ants may be present.

ANALYSIS: Aphids
Several species of aphid, including the green peach aphid (*Myzus persicae*), infest peaches or nectarines. Aphids do little damage in small numbers. However, they are extremely prolific and populations can rapidly build up to damaging numbers during the growing season. Damage occurs when the aphid sucks the juices from young peach or nectarine leaves. The aphid is unable to digest fully all the sugar in the sap and excretes the excess in a fluid called honeydew, which often drops onto the leaves below. Ants feed on this sticky substance and are often present where there is an aphid infestation. A sooty mold fungus may develop on the honeydew, causing the leaves to appear black and dirty.

SOLUTION: As soon as the insects appear, spray with an insecticide containing diazinon or malathion. Respray if the tree becomes reinfested. To avoid killing bees, do not spray during bloom.

PEAR

ADAPTATION AND POLLINATION: Zones 4 through 9, depending on variety.

SOIL: Any good, deep, well-drained soil. pH 5.5 to 8.0.

FERTILIZER: Apply a fertilizer higher in nitrogen (14-7-7, for example); follow label directions.

WATER:
How much: Apply enough water to wet the soil 3 to 4 feet deep.
How often: Water when soil 6 inches below the surface is barely moist.

PRUNING: Pears are borne on short fruiting branches (spurs) that grow on 2-year-old wood. The spurs continue to fruit for 5 to 8 years. Prune lightly, because removal of many spurs will reduce the pear yield. Thin out weak, crossing, or dead twigs and branches.

HARVEST: Unlike most other fruits, pears should not be allowed to ripen on the tree. Pick them when they have reached their mature size and are starting to lose their green color; don't let them soften or turn entirely yellow before harvesting. Most pears may be safely harvested during late summer. Contact the local cooperative extension office for specific harvest dates for your location. After harvesting, place the pears in a plastic bag and refrigerate them for at least 2 weeks. To ripen them, remove them from the refrigerator and keep at room temperature. After 5 to 10 days, they should be fully ripe.

Scab.

PROBLEM: Olive-brown velvety spots, ¼ inch or more in diameter, appear on leaves and young fruit. As the infected pears mature, the spots develop into light to dark brown corky lesions. The fruit is often cracked and malformed and may drop prematurely. There are small, blisterlike pustules on many of the twigs.

ANALYSIS: Scab
This plant disease is caused by a fungus (*Venturia pyrina*) that commonly infects pears. Fungi of this species spend the winter in infected plant debris and twig lesions. In the spring, spores are produced and discharged into the air. They are blown to the developing leaves, flowers, twigs, and young pears. If the surfaces are wet, the fungi infect them and spots develop. The infected tissues produce more spores, which further spread the disease. As temperatures increase in the summer, the fungi become less active.

SOLUTION: Unless they are severely infected, the pears are edible if the scabby areas are removed. To prevent recurrence of the disease next year, remove and destroy leaf debris and infected fruit in the fall. Next spring, spray with a fungicide containing captan.

Infected blossoms.

Blighted twig.

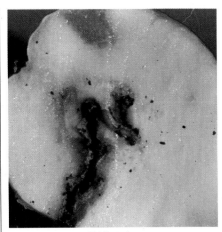

Codling moth larva (¾ life size).

PROBLEM: Blossoms turn black and die. Young leafy twigs wilt from the tips down, turn black, and die. A bend often develops at the tip of an affected twig. On the branches and at the bases of blighted twigs, the bark becomes water-soaked, then dark, sunken, and dry. Cracks may develop at the edge of a sunken area. In warm, moist spring weather, drops of brown ooze appear on the surfaces of these lesions. During the summer, shoots or branches may wilt and turn dark brown to black. Infected fruit shrivels, turns black, and remains on the tree.

ANALYSIS: Fireblight

This plant disease is caused by a bacterium (*Erwinia amylovora*) that is severe on pears and also infects apples and several ornamental plants in the rose family. Bacteria of this species spend the winter in sunken lesions (cankers) on the branches and twigs. In the spring, the bacteria ooze out of the cankers and are carried by insects to the pear blossoms. Once a few of the blossoms have been contaminated, splashing rain, honeybees, and other insects continue to spread the bacteria to healthy blossoms. The bacteria spread down through the flowers into the twigs and branches, where cankers develop. In many cases, developing cankers encircle a shoot or branch by midsummer, causing conspicuous branch and twig dieback. Although fireblight is spread primarily through flower infection, leaves and twigs damaged by hail or wounded in some other manner are also susceptible. Tender, succulent shoots and sprouts are also vulnerable to infection. Although severely diseased trees may be killed, usually only the fruiting stems die. The result is greatly reduced fruit yield. Fireblight is most severe during wet weather from 65° to 85° F.

SOLUTION: After the infection has stopped spreading in the summer or fall, prune out and destroy infected twigs and branches at least 12 inches beyond visible decay. Sterilize pruning shears with rubbing alcohol after each cut. A protective spray of basic copper sulfate or streptomycin, applied before the blossoms open next spring, will help prevent infection. Respray at intervals of 5 to 7 days until the end of the blooming period. To prevent excess growth of shoots and suckers, avoid high-nitrogen fertilizers. Plant fireblight-resistant varieties.

Pear varieties resistant and susceptible to fireblight:
   Susceptible: Barlett, Bosc, Clapp.
   Fairly resistant: Baldwin, Dutchess, Garber, Moonglow, Orient, Seckel, Starking Delicious.

PROBLEM: Fruit is blemished by small holes surrounded by dead tissue. A brown, crumbly material that resembles sawdust may surround the holes. Brown-headed, pinkish worms up to 1 inch long may be found in the fruit. In most cases, the interior of the fruit is dark and rotted. Many pears drop prematurely.

ANALYSIS: Codling moths

(*Laspeyresia pomonella*)
These worms, the larvae of small gray-brown moths, attack apple, quince, and several other fruit and nut trees in addition to pears. The moths appear in the spring, and the adult females lay their eggs on the leaves, twigs, and developing fruit. The eggs soon hatch, and the larvae that emerge tunnel into the fruit. They feed for several weeks, then emerge from the pears, often leaving a mass of dark excrement on the skin and inside the flesh. After pupating in sheltered locations on or around the tree, another generation of moths emerges at midsummer. Pears may be damaged by worms throughout the summer. In the fall, the mature larvae spin cocoons in protected places, such as under loose bark or in tree crevices. They spend the winter in these cocoons and, with the warming temperatures of spring, pupate and emerge as moths.

SOLUTION: Once the worms have penetrated the pears, spraying will not control the pests. To protect uninfested pears, spray with an insecticide containing carbaryl (SEVIN®), malathion, or diazinon at intervals of 10 to 14 days; follow label directions. Remove and destroy all fallen pears, and clean up debris. Next spring, spray 10 to 14 days after petals have fallen, according to label directions.

PEAR

Spider mite damage.

PROBLEM: Leaves are stippled, yellowing, or bronzed. There may be cobwebbing over flower buds, between leaves, or on the undersides of the leaves. Fruit may be russeted. To determine if the tree is infested with mites large enough to be seen, hold a sheet of white paper underneath an affected leaf and tap the leaf sharply. If visible mites are present, minute green, red, or yellow specks the size of pepper grains will drop to the paper and begin to crawl around.

ANALYSIS: Mites
Several species of mite, including the two-spotted spider mite (*Tetranychus urticae*) and the pear rust mite (*Epitrimerus pyri*), attack pears. Two-spotted spider mites, which cause leaf stippling and cobwebbing, may be detected against a white background. Pear rust mites—which cause fruit russeting, leaf stippling, and bronzing—cannot be seen without the aid of a microscope or strong hand lens. These pests, related to spiders, cause damage by sucking plant sap. As a result of feeding, the green leaf pigment (chlorophyll) disappears, producing the stippled or bronzed appearance. Mites are active throughout the growing season but are favored by hot, dry weather above 70° F.

SOLUTION: Spray infested trees with a miticide containing diazinon or malathion. Respray 2 more times at intervals of 7 to 10 days. After the leaves have dropped next fall, spray the tree with a lime-sulfur solution and a dormant oil. If you are not sure whether your tree is infested with pear rust mites, take an infested fruit spur to the local cooperative extension office for examination.

San Jose scales (life size).

PROBLEM: Some leaves are pale green to yellow and may drop prematurely from weakened limbs. The bark is encrusted with small ($\frac{1}{16}$-inch), hard, circular, slightly raised bumps with dull yellow centers. Scraping off a hard bump reveals a yellow or olive-colored insect. Entire branches may be killed. Red-purple spots mar some of the infested fruit and shoots.

ANALYSIS: San Jose scales
(*Quadraspidiotus perniciosus*)
These insects infest the bark, leaves, and fruits of many fruit trees. Female scales bear live young in the spring. In late spring to midsummer, the young scales, called crawlers, settle on leaves, twigs, and fruit. The small ($\frac{1}{16}$-inch), soft-bodied young feed by inserting their mouthparts and sucking sap from the plant. Their legs atrophy and a hard, crusty shell develops over their bodies. An uncontrolled infestation of San Jose scales may kill large branches after two or three seasons.

SOLUTION: During the dormant season, just prior to bud break, spray the trunk and branches with an oil spray. In late spring, after the petals have fallen, kill the crawlers by applying an insecticide containing diazinon or malathion.

PECAN

Pecan weevil (2 times life size).

PROBLEM: Immature pecans that drop to the ground during August are marked with dark patches and tobaccolike stains. Later in the season, $\frac{1}{8}$-inch holes appear in some of the ripe nuts. When cut open, the kernels are found to be destroyed, and they may contain creamy-white curved grubs up to $\frac{1}{2}$ inch long. Reddish brown to gray long-beaked beetles, $\frac{1}{2}$ inch long, are in the tree. If the limbs are shaken, these beetles drop to the ground.

ANALYSIS: Pecan weevils
(*Curculio caryae*)
In both its immature and adult stages, this insect is extremely damaging to pecans and hickories. The adult weevils appear in late summer and feed on the immature pecans. The injured nuts drop from the tree. As soon as the kernels harden, the female weevils drill holes through the shucks and shells and lay their eggs in the kernels. The grubs that hatch from these eggs feed on the kernels for several weeks, then leave the nut, drop to the ground, and burrow into the soil. They will emerge after two to three years as adult weevils.

SOLUTION: Spray severely infested trees with an insecticide containing carbaryl (SEVIN®). Respray at intervals of 10 to 14 days until the shucks split from the shells. Weevils may also be partially controlled by shaking them from lightly infested trees. Place sheets under a tree, then lightly jar the limbs. Collect and kill the dislodged weevils that fall onto the sheet. Repeat every 2 weeks until the weevils are no longer present.

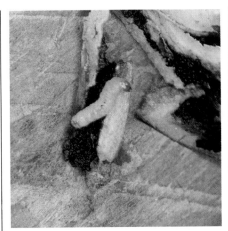

Hickory shuckworm (2 times life size).

Pecan nut casebearer damage.

Sunburn.

PROBLEM: Cream-colored worms up to ⅜ inch long feed in the immature nuts, many of which fall to the ground prematurely. Later in the season, after the shells have hardened, the worms may be found in the green shucks.

ANALYSIS: Hickory shuckworms
(*Laspeyresia caryana*)
These worms, the larvae of small brown moths, are also known as pecan shuckworms. They are pests of pecan and hickory wherever the trees are grown. The larvae spend the winter in shucks on the ground or in the tree. The shuckworms pupate and emerge as adult moths in the spring. The females lay their eggs on pecan leaves and nuts. The young larvae that hatch from these eggs tunnel into the soft green pecan shells and feed on the developing kernels. Infested nuts usually drop. Later in the season, after the nutshells have hardened, the larvae tunnel into the shucks. Their feeding damage interferes with the development of the kernels. Shuckworm damage may occur throughout the spring and summer.

SOLUTION: Chemical controls are not practical for the home gardener. Clean up and destroy all dropped nuts and shucks to eliminate many of the overwintering larvae.

Pecan cultural information
Water: When soil 6 inches below soil is barely moist
Fertilizer: Medium
Pruning: Light, to remove weak or dead twigs or branches
Harvest: In fall when shucks have split and nuts are exposed

PROBLEM: Olive-green worms up to ½ inch long, with yellow-brown heads, feed on the twigs, foliage, and developing nuts. Some of the young shoots are wilting. Nut clusters may be webbed together. There are holes in some of the nuts, and many of the kernels have been destroyed. Many nuts drop prematurely. Nuts may contain worms or pupae, either in the kernel or in the shuck.

ANALYSIS: Pecan nut casebearers
(*Acrobasis nuxvorella*)
These worms, the larvae of small, dark gray moths, are extremely damaging to pecans. The larvae come out of hibernation when the buds open in the spring. They feed on the developing buds for a short time, then tunnel into the new shoots to pupate. The adult moths emerge just as the nuts start to form, and the females lay their eggs on the young pecans. This second generation of worms webs clusters of nuts together, then bores into and feeds on them. This generation of casebearers usually damages many pecans because each worm eats three or four of the immature nuts during its larval stage. After reaching their mature size, the larvae pupate inside the nuts and become moths. Larval damage continues throughout the summer but lessens in severity as the nuts enlarge.

SOLUTION: Next spring, contact the local county extension office to determine when moths are laying eggs in your area. During the egg-laying period spray with an insecticide containing diazinon. Respray 6 weeks later. Destroy all infested nuts that fall to the ground.

PROBLEM: During hot weather, usually in August or September, dark brown or black patches appear on developing fruit. Leaves may turn brown around the edges and between the veins.

ANALYSIS: Sunburn
This condition is caused by excessive evaporation of moisture from the leaves and fruit. In hot weather, water evaporates rapidly from the fruit and foliage. If the roots can't absorb and convey water fast enough to replenish this loss, the fruit surfaces exposed to the sun overheat and burn; in severe cases, the leaves turn brown and wither. Sunburn usually occurs in dry soil, but fruit and leaves can also burn when the soil is moist and temperatures are around 100° F. Drying winds, severed roots, and limited soil area can also cause sunburn.

SOLUTION: There is nothing you can do once the fruit has been damaged, but it is still edible. To help prevent further sunburn, water plants deeply during periods of hot weather; wet down the entire root space. Water newly transplanted trees whenever the rootball is dry 2 inches below the surface.

233

PERSIMMON ━━━━━━━━━━━ ■ **PLUM** ━━━━━━━━━━━━━━━━━━

Fruit drop.

PROBLEM: Fruit drops prematurely. The tree appears to be healthy; there are no signs of pests or diseases.

ANALYSIS: Fruit drop
Persimmon trees have a natural tendency to drop their fruit prematurely. Large quantities of fruit may drop when the tree is under stress. Stress may be caused by excessive heat, drought, cold, or overwatering. Fruit drop may also occur on trees that are growing vigorously because of overuse of nitrogen fertilizer.

SOLUTION: Although fruit drop cannot be eliminated, it can be reduced. Avoid overfertilizing, overwatering, or underwatering the tree.

Persimmon cultural information
Water: When soil 6 inches below surface is barely moist
Fertilizer: Use a fertilizer rated 14-7-7
Pruning: Remove weak or lank growth and crossing or broken limbs
Harvest: When fully covered and soft; clip fruit off rather than pulling

---

PLUM ━━━━━━━━━━━━━━━━━

ADAPTATION AND POLLINATION: Zones 4 through 9, depending on variety.

SOIL: Any good, deep, well-drained soil. pH 5.5 to 8.0.

FERTILIZER: Apply a fertilizer higher in nitrogen (14-7-7, for example); follow label directions.

WATER:
How much: Apply enough water to wet the soil 3 to 4 feet deep.
How often: Water when soil 6 inches below the surface is just barely moist.

PRUNING: European and American plums are borne on short fruiting branches (spurs) that continue to fruit for many years. Prune lightly, because removal of many spurs will reduce the plum yield. Thin out weak, crossing, and dead twigs and branches. Japanese plums are borne on 1-year-old wood and on spurs that grow on 2-year-old wood. The spurs continue to fruit for 2 to 4 years. Prune back last year's growth to half its length, and thin out spurred branches that have stopped fruiting. Thin out weak, crossing, or dead twigs and branches. For large plums, thin fruit to 4 to 6 inches apart.

HARVEST: Harvest when the fruit is fully colored and slightly soft. When plums are ripe, the stems separate easily from the spur or branch when the fruit is gently lifted.

Plum curculio damage.

PROBLEM: Ripening fruit is misshapen and rotten; it often drops prematurely. Holes about ⅛ inch in diameter and deep, crescent-shaped scars appear on the fruit. Cutting open such fruit may reveal crescent-shaped, yellow-gray grubs with brown heads.

ANALYSIS: Plum curculios
(*Conotrachelus nenuphar*)
These insects, found east of the Rocky Mountains, commonly attack other stone fruits, apples, and pears, as well as plums. The adult insects are brown beetles with long curved snouts. They hibernate in debris and other protected places during the winter. The beetles emerge in the spring, when new growth starts, and begin feeding on young leaves, blossoms, and developing fruit. After five to six weeks, the female beetles start to lay eggs in the young fruit. During this process they cut distinctive crescent-shaped slits into the plums. The grubs that hatch from the eggs feed for several weeks in the fruit. Infested plums usually drop to the ground. The grubs eventually leave the fruit and bore into the soil, where they pupate. The emerging beetles feed on fruit for a few weeks, then go into hibernation. In southern areas, they lay eggs, producing a second generation of grubs in the late summer.

SOLUTION: Once grubs are inside the fruit, sprays cannot reach them. Spray with an insecticide containing carbaryl (SEVIN®) or malathion to kill beetles that may be feeding on fruit or laying eggs; follow label instructions. Pick up and destroy all fallen fruit. Next spring, spray the trees when the petals are falling from the blossoms; repeat applications according to the directions on the label.

Black knot.

Blossom blight.

Fruit rot.

PROBLEM: Soft greenish knots or elongated swellings form on twigs and branches. These knots develop into black, corky, cylindrical galls from ½ to 1½ inches in diameter and up to more than 12 inches in length. Twigs and branches beyond the galls are usually stunted and eventually die.

ANALYSIS: Black knot

This plant disease is caused by a fungus (*Dibotryon morbosum*) that is severe on plum trees and occasionally attacks cherry trees. Fungal spores form during wet weather in the spring. Galls appear six months to a year after infection. The galls slowly enlarge and elongate. They eventually cut off the flow of water and nutrients to the branches, causing stunting, wilting, and dieback. Black knot spreads most rapidly during warm wet spring weather 55° to 75° F.

SOLUTION: Prune out and destroy infected twigs and branches during the fall and winter. When pruning, cut at least 4 inches below visible signs of infection. Remove knots on the trunk or large limbs, cutting down to the wood and at least ½ inch outward past the diseased tissue. Next spring, just before the buds open, spray the tree with a fungicide containing benomyl. Respray 2 more times at intervals of 7 to 10 days. Plant resistant varieties.

Plum resistance to black knot:
   Very susceptible: Bluefre, Damson, Shropshire, Stanley.
   Moderately resistant: Bradshaw, Early Italian, Fellenberg, Formosa, Methley, Milton, Santa Rosa, Shiro.
   Resistant: President.

PROBLEM: Blossoms and young leaves wilt, decay, and turn brown during the first two weeks of the bloom period. The decayed blossoms may fail to drop and may hang on the tree through the growing season. In humid conditions, masses of gray spores may appear on the infected flower parts. There is often extensive twig dieback. Sunken lesions (cankers) sometimes develop on the twigs and branches as the season progresses; in many cases these lesions exude a sticky ooze. Many twigs die.

ANALYSIS: Brown rot

This plant disease, caused by either of two closely related fungi (*Monilinia laxa* or *M. fructicola*), is destructive to all the stone fruits. The fungi spend the winter in twig cankers or in rotted fruit (mummies) in the tree or on the ground. In the spring, spores are blown or splashed from cankers or mummies to the healthy flower buds. After penetrating and decaying the flowers, the fungi grow down into the twigs, producing brown, sunken cankers. During moist weather a thick, gummy sap oozes from the lesions, and tufts of gray spores may form on the infected areas. Spores from cankers and infected blossoms or mummies are splashed and blown to the maturing fruit. Young fruit is fairly resistant to infection, but maturing fruit is vulnerable. Brown rot develops most rapidly in mild, moist conditions.

SOLUTION: If uninfected blossoms remain on the tree, protect them from infection by spraying with a fungicide containing benomyl, chlorothalonil, or triforine. Respray 10 days later. To protect maturing plums from infection, spray about 3 weeks before they are harvested; use a fungicide containing benomyl. Each year remove and destroy all infected fruit and mummies as they appear. Prune out cankers and blighted twigs. Clean up and destroy all debris around the tree. Next spring, spray trees when the first flowers begin to bloom. Continue to spray according to label directions.

PROBLEM: Small circular brown spots appear on the young fruit. Later in the season, as the plums start to mature, these spots may enlarge to rot part or all of the fruit. During moist weather, the rotted fruit is covered with tufts of gray spores. Slicing open the infected plums reveals brown, firm, and fairly dry flesh. Infected plums either drop prematurely or dry, turn dark brown, and remain on the tree past the normal harvest period.

PLUM

Bacterial leaf spot on Stanley prunes.

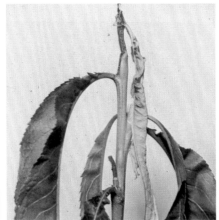

Oriental fruit moth damage.

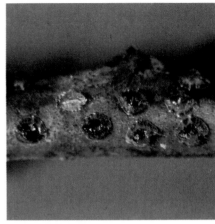

Terrapin scale (2 times life size).

PROBLEM: Brown or black angular spots develop on leaves. In many cases, the centers of the spots fall out. The tips of the leaves may die, and severely infected leaves turn yellow and drop. The surfaces of newly set fruit may be dotted with brown to black spots. As the fruit matures, the surfaces become pitted and cracked. Sunken lesions may form on the twigs. Severely infected trees may defoliate.

ANALYSIS: Bacterial leaf spot
This plant disease, caused by a bacterium (*Xanthomonas pruni*), also attacks apricots and peaches. The disease is common east of the Rocky Mountains. The bacteria spend the winter in lesions on the twigs, oozing out in the spring to be carried by splashing rain to young leaves, shoots, and developing fruit. Frequent rainfall favors the infection. Trees that defoliate early in the summer become weakened and produce a small, poor-quality crop.

SOLUTION: There is no adequate control for this disease. Spraying with basic copper sulfate when the flower buds open in the spring may help suppress bacterial leaf spot, but the treatment will not eliminate it.

PROBLEM: New growth at the tips of the twigs wilts and dies. Slicing an affected twig lengthwise reveals worms about ½ inch long. The pinkish white color of these worms distinguishes them from peach twig borers, which cause similar damage. Later in the season, some of the maturing fruit also contains pinkish worms. Plums may contain holes filled with a sticky gum.

ANALYSIS: Oriental fruit moths
(*Grapholita molesta*)
The larvae of these night-flying moths damage stone fruits, apples, and pears. The pests hibernate in cocoons on the tree bark or buried in branch crotches. In the spring, they pupate and emerge as brown adult moths. The females lay eggs on the young plum twigs and leaves. The larvae bore into the young buds, shoots, and tender twigs, causing twig and leaf death. When the worms mature they leave the twigs, spin cocoons, and pupate in the tree or in debris on the ground. After several weeks, moths emerge and the females lay eggs. Egg laying and larval damage continue throughout the growing season. Later in the summer, the larvae feed mainly on the maturing fruit. They leave gum-filled holes in the plums when they exit to pupate. In addition to ruining the fruit, these pests may cause abnormal branching on young trees.

SOLUTION: Worms in the twigs and fruit cannot be reached with pesticides. To prevent future worm damage, kill the moths by spraying infested trees with an insecticide containing methoxychlor. Next spring, spray again when the petals have fallen from the blossoms. Repeat the treatment 2 more times at intervals of 10 to 14 days.

PROBLEM: Stems, small branches, or the undersides of leaves are covered with brownish crusty bumps; thick, white, waxy bumps; or clusters of flat, yellowish, gray, or brownish scaly bumps. The bumps can be scraped or picked off; their undersides are usually soft. Leaves turn yellow and may drop. In some cases, a shiny or sticky substance coats them. A black sooty mold often grows on the substance.

ANALYSIS: Scales
Several different types of scale infest plum trees. Females lay their eggs on leaves or bark. In spring to midsummer, the young scales, called crawlers, settle on leaves and twigs. The small (⅒-inch), soft-bodied young feed by inserting their mouthparts and sucking sap from the plant. Their legs usually atrophy and a hard crusty or waxy shell develops over their bodies. Mature female scales bear live young or lay their eggs underneath their shells. Some species of scale are unable to digest fully all the sugar in the plant sap, so they excrete the excess in a fluid called honeydew, which often drops onto the leaves below. A sooty mold fungus may develop on the honeydew, causing the plum leaves to appear black and dirty.

SOLUTION: In midsummer, when the crawlers are active, spray with an insecticide containing diazinon or carbaryl (SEVIN®). The following early spring, while the tree is still dormant, spray the trunk and branches with an oil spray to control overwintering insects.

WALNUT

Walnut husk-fly damage.

Walnut blight.

Crown rot.

PROBLEM: Soft, black-ened, decayed areas cover part or all of the walnut husk. Cream- to yellow-colored maggots up to ⅞ inch long feed inside the husk. The walnut shells are stained dirty black; sometimes the husks stick to the shells. The kernels are often stained and may be shriveled.

ANALYSIS: Walnut husk flies
(*Rhagoletis* species)
These maggots are the larvae of several closely related flies. An adult walnut husk fly, slightly smaller than a housefly, is yel-low-brown with banded wings. The fe-male husk flies begin laying their eggs in the developing walnut husks in late July and early August. The maggots that hatch from these eggs feed in the husks for about a month, then drop to the ground and pupate in the soil until the following summer. As a result of maggot feeding, the husks become black and decayed, and the shells and kernels are stained. The maggots never feed on the kernels so, al-though the walnut meats may be shriv-eled or discolored, they usually taste normal.

SOLUTION: Walnut husk flies are diffi-cult to control. Obtain partial control by killing the adult flies before the females lay their eggs. Contact the local county ex-tension office for information regarding husk-fly emergence dates in your area. Spray with an insecticide containing mal-athion, covering all the foliage thorough-ly. Respray 2 weeks later.

PROBLEM: Buds turn dark brown to black, then die. There are brown spots on leaves and dead, sunken lesions on shoots. Some of the leaves may be de-formed. Black, sunken, hard areas develop on the nuts. A shiny black fluid may ex-ude from these lesions. Infected nuts have stained shells or shriveled kernels. Nut yield may be reduced.

ANALYSIS: Walnut blight
This plant disease is caused by a bacteri-um (*Xanthomonas juglandis*) that is com-mon on walnuts. The bacteria spend the winter in diseased buds, twig lesions, and old infected nuts attached to the tree. A thick, shiny fluid containing millions of bacteria exudes from the infected plant parts in the spring. Spring rains splash the bacteria to the buds, shoots, flowers, and developing nuts, starting new infec-tions. Bacterial infection reduces nut set and can continue to spread to healthy nuts and foliage throughout the summer during periods of wet weather. If the nuts are infected before their shells harden (when the nuts are three-quarters grown), the bacteria may spread into and decay the kernels. Because the wet, rainy condi-tions of spring favor the rapid spread of walnut blight, early-blooming walnut varieties are the most susceptible to this disease.

SOLUTION: Next spring, when catkins (flower spikes resembling cats' tails) start to shed pollen, spray with a fungicide containing basic copper sulfate. Spray again when the nutlets start to appear. If the weather remains wet, spray once more after 2 weeks. Plant late-blooming varieties such as Vina and Hartley.

PROBLEM: The bark on part or all of the trunk just above or below the soil line is darkened. Sap may ooze from the affected bark. Scraping away the diseased bark reveals discolored sapwood that is tan to black. Foliage may be sparse and yellowing. There is little new growth, and the tree may be stunted.

ANALYSIS: Crown rot
This plant disease is caused by one of sev-eral soil-inhabiting fungi (*Phytophthora* species) that infect many trees and shrubs. These fungi penetrate the bark of the lower trunk or upper roots, forming lesions. As the fungi progress inward, they decay the nutrient-conducting tissue under the bark, interfering with the flow of nutrients to the roots. If left unchecked, the fungi will encircle and decay the en-tire trunk, eventually causing the death of the tree. Wet soil encourages crown rot; trees planted in lawns, flower beds, or other moist areas are highly susceptible.

SOLUTION: If the rot has not completely encircled the tree, saving it may be possi-ble. To let the crown (where stem and roots meet) dry out, remove the soil with-in 4 feet of the base of the tree, exposing the major roots. Keep this area dry. Dur-ing the rainy season, slope the remaining soil away from the hole to keep it from filling with water. After the tree shows signs of recovering (look for healthy new growth), replace the soil around the base of the tree. Or, if possible, fill the hole with stones instead of soil to help keep the roots dry. Avoid planting flowers, shrubs, or other vegetation close to the tree.

VEGETABLES, BERRIES, AND GRAPES

Raising your own vegetables can be a source of enormous satisfaction. It can also be an extremely frustrating enterprise, as your crop is attacked by insects, overrun by weeds, eaten by birds and other animals, or just simply dies. Planning and regular maintenance should ensure a bumper crop.

MINIMIZING TRAFFIC DAMAGE

Pathways between vegetable rows are a way to reach produce without trampling on anything tasty. A narrow cracked path or a muddy one takes much of the pleasure from picking, however.

Gardeners usually make paths wide enough to allow easy foot traffic, but problems occur when the access is too narrow for wheelbarrows, carts, or other large equipment. What looks like a sufficient path in spring can become annoyingly tight by summer, when vegetable foliage spreads over furrows and into the passageways. In gardens in which space is at a premium, plan 12- to 18-inch-wide pathways—the minimum width for comfort. If possible, it is preferable to make pathways 2 feet wide.

Some gardeners like to establish grass pathways, which are appealing to the eye and comfortable to walk on. These pathways require mowing, however, and grass may escape into the vegetable beds if path edges aren't controlled faithfully.

Permanent pathways can be created from brick, concrete, or stones. They have the advantage of absorbing sunlight during the day, then sharing it with the surrounding soil at night.

Mulches make effective pathways too, and many varieties of mulch are available. Possible path mulches include leaves, sawdust, wood chips, grass clippings, and aged hay. Unfortunately, these materials provide shelter for snails, slugs, sowbugs, rodents, and earwigs, among others. And, since organic mulch materials decompose, you will have to renew them regularly. Try to keep path mulches at least 3 inches thick—a layer of organic mulch less than 3 inches thick can permit weeds to emerge. However, the disadvantages of mulch pathways are balanced by the benefits the soil receives from mulch decomposition.

Few gardeners realize that the list of path mulches also includes newspapers. Being lightweight, they must be held down by stones or other material. Try putting a layer of organic mulch over a layer of newspaper to create a solid renewable walkway. Black plastic or weed block rolled out along pathways does the job, too. Though not the most attractive path material, plastic coverings do not need the constant renewal that degradable mulches do. In addition, black plastic prevents almost all weeds in the covered area. Clear plastic can be used as a covering, but it does not control weeds.

After two to three years, plastic becomes brittle and may crack. Though still usable as a walkway, cracked plastic allows weed emergence. Weeds that spread into vegetable beds can prove an enormous problem because applying an herbicide in already planted areas requires much care. Check plastic mulches at the beginning of each planting season, and replace them when they begin to show signs of wear.

CONTROLLING WEEDS

Weeds in the vegetable garden compete for water, nutrients, and sunlight. If prolific, weeds post a fire hazard, give shelter to furry as well as insect pests, and make harvesting difficult.

Some crops—onions, carrots, strawberries, lettuce, spinach, and celery—need intensive weeding because their tops don't grow large enough to shade sunlight-reaching weeds. Brussels sprouts, pole tomatoes, and corn require comparatively minimal weeding once past the seedling stage. They provide enough shade to reduce weed competition.

Methods of weed control in the vegetable garden include hand-weeding, cultivation, mulching, solarization, and herbicide use. These methods are often used in combination, depending on the garden crop and land.

Annual weeds germinate, flower, and die back in one season. However, their seeds are extremely plentiful and are spread by gardeners, mulches, manure, compost, birds, animals, wind, and rain.

Common annual vegetable-garden weeds are chickweed, cheeseweed, wild oats, wild barley, mustards, shepherds-purse, sowthistle, annual bluegrass, bur clover, groundsel, nettle, crabgrass, nightshade, horseweed, purslane, fleabane, lamb's-quarters, prickly lettuce, milkthistle, sweet clovers, bristly oxtongue,

and barnyardgrass. A single barnyardgrass weed can produce over 1 million seeds in its short life.

Perennial weeds live on through winter, although they may die back. They reproduce from underground bulbs, rhizomes, or crowns on taproots. Common perennial weeds interfering with crop growth include nutsedge, witchgrass, bermudagrass, dallisgrass, milkweed, field bindweed, Johnsongrass, and oxalis. If some of these names seem familiar, it is because what's considered a weed in the vegetable garden may be considered grass in the front yard.

Unfortunately, grass seeds germinate as well in a strawberry bed or tomato patch as they do in a lawn. Sometimes better, if you keep garden soil in top condition. All that open space provides much less competition than that offered by a crowded front yard.

The cardinal precept of weed control is keep weeds out. Hand-pull all weeds as soon as they appear. Never let them go to seed in the vegetable garden or in a surrounding area. Weeding a thriving berry patch is difficult but necessary; consider the size of the weed crop of tomorrow if berry-eating birds spread the weed seeds through your garden today.

Make certain all commercially purchased soil additives, manures, or mulches are certified as weed-free. Even then, be vigilant—weed seeds may survive sterilization procedures. Fresh manure is loaded with weed seeds because most animals feed outdoors. Compost fresh manure, and make certain the compost pile is hot enough to kill weed seeds (see Ortho's book *Environmentally Friendly Gardening: Easy Composting* for details on composting).

Another weed source is seed set out for wild birds. Keep it in containers and away from planting areas. Weeds may also be spread by dumping leftover food of caged birds, guinea pigs, and hamsters, as well as the animals' waste products, outdoors.

Living Sunlight Blockers

Some vegetable plants can be a definite help in weed control. For example, tall corn shades out weeds. It is also easy to cultivate between the rows. Other weed shaders include cauliflower, broccoli, and tomato plants. Potato plants also shade the ground, but don't use them in any area infested with nutsedge—this particular weed encourages potato rot by piercing tubers. After two successive years of weed-shading vegetables, plant garlic,

Opposite: The vegetable garden can be a delight to the eye as well as the palate. Here, broadleaf endive, giant Japanese red mustard, and purple broccoli form an attractive display.

To be fully effective, the area receiving solarization should be at least 6 feet by 9 feet.

lettuce, carrots, strawberries, and other minimal-shade plants to reinvigorate the soil.

Soil Solarization

An increasingly popular way to decrease weeds as well as insect pests that overwinter or pupate in the ground is through soil solarization. Solarization involves using the rays of the sun to bake out problems. You need steady sun to accomplish this, because the temperature of the treated soil should stay at 80° F or above. Therefore, solarization works best in the hottest months of summer or fall.

Before beginning solarization, level and smooth the soil to be treated. Then wet the soil to encourage maximal heat penetration. Cover the entire area with a sheet of clear polyethylene plastic. Plastic that is 1 mil thick will do for most areas. If your garden receives a lot of wind, however, 2-mil-thick plastic has greater resistance to tearing. Smooth out the plastic as you place it; close contact with the wet soil encourages transmission of sunlight into the earth. Leave the plastic in place for 4 to 6 weeks. After that, unless you are using plastic that contains an ultraviolet inhibitor, you will have to remove the solarization covering. Left on too long, it may shred and be difficult to remove completely.

Not all weeds and weed seeds are destroyed by soil solarization. Nutsedge, sweet clover, purslane, crabgrass, and field bindweed are particularly resistant.

Hand-weeding

Pulling weeds manually doesn't always do the trick, since even a portion of some weeds, such as dandelion, will quickly regrow into an entire plant. Various implements are available to make weeding more effective, including hand tines, weeding hoes, chopping hoes, and push-pull hoes. You must remove all tuber and rhizome segments, and this may mean digging deep. Some gardeners use rotary tilling as a means of weed control. Although this benefits soil by aerating it,

Keep seedlings weeded, or overcrowding and competition will weaken them.

this kind of tilling may make a weed problem worse by chopping and spreading the still-viable weed roots.

Do not leave chopped or dug-out weed parts in the garden; put them in the compost heap or in a closed container. Weed seeds can spread from your gleanings, and weeds such as purslane can actually reroot where thrown if water is available.

Mulches

Weeds tend to be opportunists. They come up earlier than vegetables and grow much faster, crowding out desirable crops. By applying weed-blocking mulch early, you can give vegetable seedlings a head start on the weeds. Mulch keeps soil cool and may deter weed sprouting as well as early growth. Remove all weed parts before applying the covering. If weeds sprout through the mulch, dig them out immediately by hand. Be careful not to damage adjacent vegetable roots when hand-pulling or hoeing.

New synthetic weed-blocking fabrics appear on the market continually. They avoid many of the disadvantages of organic mulches, such as pest shelter and insufficient coverage. Your local garden center may offer photodegradable plastic film, nonwoven polypropylene fabric, or heavy pressed fibrous paper. Each has advantages you may want to investigate.

Herbicides

Using herbicides is an option if weeds cannot be satisfactorily controlled by other means. Preemergent herbicides eliminate annual weeds as they sprout. They

may be used among perennial crops such as cane berries and asparagus. Preemergent herbicides are not always selective about which annual seeds they eliminate, however. Check container instructions for a list of seeds that will not be killed by the herbicide. Be sure the seeds you intend to sow are included in that list, or do not use the herbicide.

Herbicide use in the vegetable garden always requires caution. Some weeds have susceptible crop cousins, so read the list of herbicide-resistant vegetables and berries carefully. Follow label instructions about when to apply the control, and learn what weeds are present, so you can select a postemergent herbicide with the appropriate ingredients. Avoid long-life herbicides. They might protect your summer crop but remain in soil past harvest and harm the winter crop.

Weeder Geese

Some gardeners use Chinese geese to control weeds in the vegetable and berry garden. The birds eat slugs, also. If you wish to try this option, read several books on goose care before beginning. Geese must be kept in a fenced area away from domestic and wild animals. Use 3-foot-high stakes and chicken wire of similar height to create a movable fence line. Like any other animal, geese must be provided with clean water and protection from rain, heat, and cold. In the vegetable garden, some supplemental food will be necessary.

Geese eat young tender weeds. If there is not a sufficient supply of weeds, they also eat crop seedlings. Move the fence to varying sites to provide an ongoing food supply. All geese feed primarily in the early morning and late evening. If you must set them out in the garden at specific times, work according to their schedule. Never use pesticides or herbicides in any area immediately before introducing weeder geese or when they are present. The herbicide label will cite the length of time that must pass before you can reintroduce animals in the treated area; follow the instructions.

CONTROLLING EROSION

If your vegetable garden is on a sloping hillside, erosion may present a problem. With water and wind action, soil tends to move from high areas to low ones. If the topsoil disappearance has gone on unimpeded for quite a while, bolster the soil

Top: Mulching around vegetables helps to deter weed growth by keeping sun from reaching the soil.
Bottom: A terraced hillside planted with vegetables can provide a feast for the eye and for the table.

with fresh topsoil and fertilizer before attempting to plant anything.

Also develop some type of erosion control. You may get ideas by looking at examples of terracing and retaining structures in pictures of hillside gardening in South America, Japan, India, Asia, and Italy, among many other countries where agricultural space is at a premium.

The basic concept of terracing is to provide a retaining structure that prevents soil loss to the beds beneath it. Heavy rain can wash soil past even the most effective retainers, however, so a sturdy wall of some type must be at the bottom of the terraced garden to hold the topsoil that makes it down the hill.

Construct retaining walls from railroad ties, concrete blocks, tires held with concrete and wire mesh, logs, bricks, or stones. You can terrace the entire area or separate sections, depending on need. Always follow land contour, rather than altering it.

PROVIDING FERTILIZER

Lack of available soil nutrients can ruin a vegetable or berry crop. Plants may grow but be stunted, distorted, or produce a limited yield. Since plants in poor health tend to suffer more from insect attack than healthy plants, other problems may follow nutrient deficiency.

A soil pH over 8.0 may make certain nutrients, such as manganese and iron, unavailable to plants. If symptoms of nutrient deficiency continue after the correct fertilizer is applied, pH imbalance may be the cause.

Treatments for Deficiencies

Nutrients required in soil for plant growth include phosphorus (see page 251), nitrogen (see page 254), iron, boron, potassium, magnesium, calcium, molybdenum, and zinc. The sections that follow describe how various deficiencies affect specific plants.

Boron deficiency   Most common in dry weather and in alkaline sandy soil, boron deficiency in beets causes a condition

known as heart rot. Black areas appear on the skin of the beet and inside the root. The root may be wrinkled and cracked. Most leaves die, leaving only a few deformed leaves. Plant growth slows markedly. Boron deficiency in celery causes brown horizontal cracks to appear across stalks. Leaves turn yellow and may die. Growth slows.

As soon as you identify boron deficiency in your garden soil, add borax, which is available in several forms. Before sowing, rake sodium tetraborate into the soil at the rate of 1 ounce for every 20 square yards of soil; mix in enough light sand to provide even distribution. Or, if plants are already growing, use 1 tablespoon of household borax dissolved in 12 quarts of water. This solution is sufficient for a 100-foot row. Repeat the treatment in 2 to 3 weeks. If necessary, correct soil pH to bring it between 6.0 and 7.0. Water as needed to prevent the soil from drying out.

Iron deficiency   Also called lime-induced chlorosis, iron deficiency causes leaves to turn pale green or yellow. New leaves are most severely affected, and they may be small. Leaf edges and leaftips may scorch. In severe cases, new leaves are all yellow or all white, though leaf veins may remain green. Iron deficiency almost always occurs when soil pH is above 7.5. (The condition affects raspberries at pH 8.0.) Reduce soil pH by adding acidic materials such as peat, or use an aluminum sulfate or ferrous sulfate

additive. After treatment, wait until the pH reaches at least 7.0 before planting.

Magnesium deficiency   A shortage of magnesium shows up as yellowing (chlorosis) of older leaves and upward curling of leaf edges. The edges may yellow, leaving a green area in the center of the leaf. Symptoms begin in the lower plant and proceed upward. Magnesium deficiency is common in all types of berries and vegetables because magnesium is easily washed out of soil during heavy rains. In addition, magnesium becomes unavailable to plants in the presence of potassium.

Magnesium deficiency of potato plants appears as yellowing of leaf areas between veins. The leaf then browns and becomes brittle. Plant growth slows. Magnesium deficiency of beets causes older leaves to turn pale between veins, then brown. Some beet varieties may develop bright red leaf tints. Magnesium deficiency of tomato plants is common in plants receiving high-potassium fertilizers. Yellow-orange bands appear between leaves. A similar coloring may appear on raspberry leaves. Lower leaves are affected first. Symptoms spread upward, turning older leaves brown. In grapevines, magnesium deficiency may appear as purple blotches rather than the typical yellow-orange discoloration between veins.

To treat magnesium deficiency, spray with a product containing magnesium sulfate; apply it at 7- to 10-day intervals throughout the growing season. Some leaf yellowing may persist on tomato plants, but the crop will be unaffected.

These pole beans are severely lacking in iron and may fail to produce a crop.

These beets show varying degrees of heart rot, with the worst cases on the right.

Manganese deficiency   The symptoms of manganese deficiency resemble those of magnesium deficiency and often occur in conjunction with iron deficiency. In general, leaf yellowing occurs. In beet and spinach plants, leaves also roll inward. Beet leaves may assume a triangular appearance. Yellow blotches appear between leaf veins. In severe cases, entire leaves may turn pale yellow.

Manganese deficiency in peas, which is called marsh spot, causes a dark rust-red spot or cavity in pea centers. Pods appear normal, but leaves may be slightly yellow between veins. Manganese deficiency usually occurs in sand, alluvial silt, and clay soils. It is more common where pH is over 7.5. Symptoms may appear suddenly after a heavy rainfall, since soggy soil may impede manganese release to plants. Prevention includes adding manganese to soil before planting, or spraying with a solution of 2 ounces of manganese sulfate in 3 gallons of water. Add an agent to help the solution stick to the plants. Repeat 2 or 3 times at 2-week intervals.

Molybdenum deficiency   Called whiptail, molybdenum deficiency is a problem only on brassicas such as broccoli and cauliflower. Heads of affected plants fail to develop. Leaf blades become thin, straplike, and rippled. Molybdenum deficiency occurs in acidic soils only. Add lime before sowing or planting.

Potassium deficiency   Also known as potash deficiency, a lack of potassium causes small brown spots to appear along leaf edges. Leaf edges turn yellow, then gradually turn brown, curl downward, and die. Vegetable and berry yields are small. The crops that do appear may be distorted and ripen poorly. Vegetables and berries with potassium deficiency are susceptible to fungus and virus diseases.

Potassium aids in moving food supplies from leaves to roots and stems. Without it, crops cannot grow properly. Light, sandy soil and peat and chalk soil are often low in potassium, as are soils in high-rainfall areas. Some crops, notably tomatoes, beans, and raspberries, demand more potassium than others. To remedy potassium deficiency, spray plant foliage with a liquid plant food, or water with a liquid plant-food additive. Apply a general-purpose fertilizer formulated for tomato plants—such fertilizers are usually high in potassium. For raspberries apply a fertilizer that contains sulfate of potash.

Fertilizer Burn

The condition called fertilizer burn may occur when gardeners use too much fertilizer or too strong a concentration, do not water fertilizer in properly, or allow undissolved granules to remain on leaves. In these cases, the accumulation of salts from both spray and granular fertilizers interferes with water use by the plant. Salts may accumulate in leaf edges, causing a burnt or scorched appearance. In strawberries, leaf edges and areas between veins turn dark brown and die. After fertilizer burn occurs in any plant, no amount of watering will restore the green to browned edges. The burned leaves may drop. Plant growth may slow or stop. In severe cases of fertilizer burn, plants die.

To prevent fertilizer burn, follow application instructions carefully. In areas with poor drainage, be especially careful because fertilizer will remain in the standing water. If possible, improve drainage before applying the treatment. Add fertilizer to moist soil only. Water fertilizer well; do not permit it to rest on leaves or on the soil surface. If you apply excess fertilizer by mistake, water the area thoroughly to leach salts out.

If you plan to add a dry fertilizer at seeding time, make furrows for fertilizer 3 inches from the empty seed rows and 2 inches deeper than seed depth. Put fertilizer in the furrows, and refill them with soil. Then plant the seeds.

Seedlings are especially sensitive to fertilizer burn. Excess fertilizer can cause seedling root damage or prevent seedlings from emerging. The key to correct application is following label directions.

Like commercial fertilizers, fresh manure from cattle and poultry can cause fertilizer burn because the manure is high in salts. Do not use fresh manure of any kind. In addition to causing fertilizer burn, fresh manure may contain large numbers of weed seeds, depending on what the animal ingested. Fresh manure may also contain insect eggs and larvae, if these were on the grasses eaten. Though fresh manure is often touted for its high nitrogen content, the amount of nitrogen manure actually contains varies considerably—again, according to the producer's diet. Before applying fresh manure to the soil or using manure as a mulch, thoroughly compost it. Add just a bit to the compost heap at a time or the pile may overheat, destroying beneficial microorganisms and earthworms.

PREVENTING COMPETITION

Competition from trees can prove fatal to many vegetables. Feeder roots, which reach out underneath the soil at least as far as the branches reach overhead, can divert nutrients and water from crops. If possible, establish your garden far from shallow-rooted trees, such as elms, maples, poplars, and willows. If limited space makes proximity to shallow-rooted trees unavoidable, dig a 3-foot-deep trench around the garden. If feeder roots are visible, cut them; limited root pruning will not harm the trees. Line the dividing trench with heavy-duty plastic or sheet metal, then backfill with soil. The feeder roots will take a while to penetrate this barrier.

Black walnut trees present special problems for tomato plants. Black walnut roots give off a substance that causes wilting and dwarfing of many tomato varieties. (Falling walnut leaves will not cause problems.) Digging a dividing trench may not be sufficient to save the plants. If you have no other growing space, plant tomatoes in containers.

WATERING

Without water to soften and break seed coats, seeds will not germinate. Once germinated, seedlings are especially sensitive to water stress. Their delicate roots may reach only into the top inch of soil. If this dries out, the seedling may die despite diligent rescue efforts. In hot weather in which soil becomes dry to the touch, seedlings may need water once a day. Even mature plants may not have a root system deep enough to allow them to survive temporary dry periods.

Effects of Drought

Plant wilting, followed by recovery after watering, is usually the first sign of water stress. Reliance on a plant's recuperative powers during drought is seldom wise. Repeated wilting results in poor plant growth. Fruit on stressed plants may not mature properly. It may crack open and have poor flavor. Cucumbers without sufficient water grow in odd shapes and have a bitter taste. Overcompensating for water stress by overwatering can also be harmful. Under these conditions, sweet-potato tubers may develop cracks and black spots within the roots.

Berry bushes can tolerate water stress better than other garden plants. Once berry bushes are established, they have an extensive root system. Unfortunately, their outstretched feeder roots are also pathways for fungi. The natural susceptibility of berry bushes to fungus diseases is enhanced by overwatering and high humidity.

Irrigation Schedules and Methods

When establishing a watering schedule for your garden, plan on including one thorough soaking per week during the growing season. Remember that most common vegetables are almost 90 percent water and must retain this amount to mature into tasty table food.

The amount of watering you need to do depends greatly on what type of soil you have. Sandy soil can hold less water than clay, and requires more frequent irrigation. Use water effectively by adding organic materials, such as compost, to the soil. Compost greatly improves the moisture retention and water distribution in any soil.

Drip irrigation   When watering vegetables, avoid overhead sprinkling if possible. Leaves that do not dry quickly are supportive habitats for fungi and water-transmitted viruses. Some form of drip irrigation—whether a drip, trickle, or soaker system—provides water without encouraging runoff. Drip system are becoming increasingly popular because they are highly economical as well as highly effective. They provide water at a slow rate, allowing it to seep to where it is most needed, at the root zone. If you want to give your tomato seedlings an even bigger boost than a drip system alone can provide, make shallow watering basins around each plant and fill them at each watering.

Water conservation through mulching   Using mulch helps slow water evaporation, cutting watering needs by as much as one third. Mulching may be a necessity for gardeners in warm climates where water is scarce. Put mulch down early for weed control, but do not apply it around crops until late spring, giving soil around crops a chance to warm up. Use mulch around transplants and any seedling that is at least 6 inches tall.

Effective organic mulches include peat moss, seaweed, sawdust, dry composted manure, bark chips, and straw. Do not use fresh hay as a mulch. If you have an ample hay supply, let it rot outdoors for a year before applying in the garden.

Mulch depth should be about 3 inches. Since mulch does hold moisture, avoid overmulching; piled up too high, mulch may encourage rot.

Black plastic mulch discourages weed growth and lessens evaporation caused by wind. Unfortunately, however, black plastic allows water to reach the ground only through whatever planting holes you make in it. During and after rain, puddles may form and stay on top of the covering. A new development, weed-blocking fabric, avoids this disadvantage. This fabric effectively prevents weeds but allows sunlight and water to pass through to the ground.

Application instructions vary slightly with each product. Basically, however, installation involves covering the vegetable patch with the plastic or fabric, then cutting holes for areas to be seeded or for transplanted seedlings. Seed holes will be slightly larger than seedling holes but, to prevent weed infiltration, make openings only as large as necessary. Hold the material in place with piles of earth, wood chips, or rocks at the edges. Black plastic or woven plastic mulch is particularly

Sturdy runner beans form a windbreak protecting delicate celery and leeks.

valuable for vine crops, such as squash and melon. The vines are free to spread without competition from weeds, and the crop is kept off of damp earth.

Clear plastic is not effective for water conservation or weed prevention. Sunlight goes through clear plastic, warming soil rather than cooling it. This added warmth can encourage heat-loving seeds, but it can also aid weed germination or produce enough heat to kill everything.

WEATHERPROOFING

The two most common weather problems for home gardeners are wind and extremes in temperature.

Windbreaks

If wind is a constant or intermittent problem, create a windbreak for the vegetable garden. Windbreaks serve multiple purposes. Not only do they cut the effect of drying summer winds and destructive winter winds, but they help retain heat—of special importance to spring seedlings. Also, windbreaks encourage bees to visit and pollinate—bees don't like strong winds any more than plants do.

Placing the garden where natural features or buildings shield it from the wind is the first step toward solving a wind problem. Building a low fence around the garden is another solution.

Hedges that do not block sunlight work well as living windbreaks. Protective hedges that also attract birds include barberry, yew, euonymus, and arborvitae. Trees can also be effective windbreaks if their branches are not allowed to grow dense and shade the garden. Trees or large shrubs may be inappropriate, however, if space is limited, because in a small area they compete with garden plants for nutrients, water, and light. Plan living windbreaks carefully, with growth patterns in mind, and prune hedge or tree foliage as necessary.

Since it takes time and labor to establish a fence or hedge windbreak, consider planting a flower windbreak. Some annuals grow high enough in a season to block a light breeze, although they are ineffective against strong winds. To protect garden seedlings against strong winds, shield the plants by placing topless and bottomless cans around the stems.

Protection From Heat and Cold

If you have access to old tires and do not mind their appearance, they make fine windbreaks for warmth-loving vegetables such as tomatoes and eggplant. Tires hold heat, particularly if you put stones where the inner tube used to be. Some gardeners create raised beds

Using a fingernail to pierce a kernel and check the juice is the best way to test corn for ripeness.

throughout their gardens from tires of various sizes that are filled with fertile soil. The elevation of the plants in the tires alleviates drainage problems. However, just as a tire holds heat during cold spells, it can produce a warmer environment during hot weather. Plants inside tires may need extra watering.

During extremely hot weather, drape newspaper tents or cheesecloth over susceptible crops. Anchor the covering with stones or dirt.

Frost is a continual concern in some areas and an intermittent concern in others. Among the possible solutions is covering the garden with plastic, blankets, or sheets on nights when frost is expected. Another emergency measure is covering plants with temporary terrariums made from clear plastic milk containers, bottoms removed. If frost threatens frequently, you may want to place heat-absorbing objects in the garden—objects that, after sunset, release stored heat and protect the vegetables from frost.

If you must plant warmth-loving vegetables in frost pockets, keep in mind that cold air tends to collect in low places. Block cold air with a hedge, stone fence, or embankment. However, since cold air, like water collecting behind a dam, can overflow, provide an outlet. Make a pathway through the embankment, allowing the air to flow harmlessly away from susceptible plants.

Since cold air and the frost that accompanies it settles in ditches and ground hollows, you might want to go one step further and dig a low-lying area at a site of your choosing. Raising the vegetable beds is another means of frost protection.

PROVIDING SUPPORT

Staking vegetable and berry plants can be a nuisance. The alternative, however—leaving plants to trail on the ground—can produce as much rot as food. Some plants, such as cane berries, turn into impenetrable thickets unless controlled by staking.

Always use rot-resistant wood when staking vegetables. A metal stake or uninsulated wire will heat up in summer, possibly burning any plant that touches it.

To stake red and yellow raspberries, use sturdy 3-foot-high posts that are 3 inches thick. Anchor the posts well into the ground; superficially anchored posts will topple in the wind or fall over from the weight of the canes or shifting wet soil. String two smooth 10- or 11-gauge wires between the posts, one wire near the tops and the other halfway up from the ground.

Climbing vegetables, such as beans and peas, do best off the ground, away from insects. One type of support structure for climbers consists of wood supports tilted in an inverted V shape. To create this structure, place 8-foot-high supports in 2 rows. Place the rows 24 inches apart, and set the stakes within each row 12 inches apart. Tilt the tops inward and secure them. Make certain that supports are extremely well anchored. If they fall over while supporting a heavy crop, they will be difficult to replace without doing crop damage.

This is a small but highly effective blueberry cage that keeps birds out.

Mesh netting with large openings is a space-effective support alternative for pea and bean vines. To avoid wind damage to the support system, encourage the vines to grow through the netting.

Cucumbers left to lie on the ground can take up quite a bit of space in a small garden. An easy way to let them climb is to provide nylon netting, which can be hooked over a sunny fence. Garden-supply stores and catalogs often offer green nylon netting, which is easily camouflaged by growing foliage.

For tomato plants, staking continues to be controversial. Some gardeners prefer to let them sprawl, keeping foliage open and fruit exposed to the sun. You will need at least 15 square feet per plant if you choose this option. Both slugs and hornworms go after lower tomatoes first, and ground rot may occur. Watch low-lying plants carefully for damage, and take corrective action if necessary.

One compromise between staking tomato plants and letting them sprawl is placing them on a 6-inch-thick mulch. Setting plants through slits in protective black plastic is another alternative. Tomatoes also receive ground protection from multiple layers of newspaper.

Gardeners sometimes underestimate the growth potential of plants. If you decide to stake them, provide 8-foot-high stakes at planting time rather than trying to lash stakes together to rig a higher support late in the season. Lashed stakes do not balance properly and are prone to toppling. Dig stakes 1 foot into the soil to anchor them against plant weight and wind. Keep stakes about 4 inches away from plants.

Cages to support tomato plants are available at most garden-supply stores. Place a cage around a plant when it is small. Placing a cage over a maturing bush or vine often damages foliage. Anchor the cage securely into the ground.

Tomato vines damage easily. Tie them to stakes or supports with soft cloth strips, bits of old nylon stocking, or commercially available tomato ties. Never bend vines at a sharp angle when handling. If you do accidentally angle a stem and it breaks partially, you may be able to do some garden doctoring. Join, then tape, the edges together. If the leaves do not wilt in a few days, the vine will survive.

HARVESTING
• Asparagus should not be harvested the first year. The second year, take no more than 2 spears from each plant, and remove them from mid-April to mid-June only. After this, the spears become spindly. Allow them to form feathery foliage to help build plant strength for the following season.
• Harvest all beets before severe frost. Beets are especially delicious when small, about the 1-inch size. They become less tender as they get larger.
• Pick broad beans when the seeds are about fingernail size. Left overlong on the vine, the pods develop black streaks, which indicate that the seeds have ripened and their skins have become tough.
• Harvest brussels sprouts from the bottom of the plant upward. Snap or cut them off cleanly and as close to the stem as possible.
• Dig up carrots when they reach baby length, about 3 inches long. Although they can remain in soil for quite a while

when mature, carrots longer than 3 inches tend toward woodiness. Remove all carrots before winter. Left in damp ground they are easy targets for wireworms and slugs, and heavy rains may cause split roots.

• Inspect corn carefully to determine picking time. Turn back the corn sheath until just a few kernels are visible. Pierce a kernel with your fingernail. If the juice is watery, the corn isn't ready yet. Test again a few days later. If the juice is milky white, the corn is ready. Remove the ear by giving it a quick twist. Cook corn as soon as possible.

• Harvest the cucumber crop regularly, and do not allow the cucumbers to get too large. Pickling size is 2 inches long; slicing cucumbers range from 6 to 8 inches long. If the vine is overburdened, production will be limited.

• Butterhead lettuce is ready for the table when a loose head forms. Tight-growing crisp lettuce varieties are best when heads are firm.

• Pick melons when they pass the smell test—that is, when the stem end exudes a strong pleasant aroma. The exception is cantaloupe, which is ready when fruit comes off the stem easily.

• Harvest onions when leaftips turn yellow and start bending over. Be sure that these are indeed signs of maturity, not of damage by thrips. Don't jerk the onions from the ground; ease them out with a hand spade. Let bulbs dry in the sun. If you have many onions and limited drying space, make an onion rope from heavy twine. Attach onions to the dangling cord, beginning at the bottom of the twine.

• Harvest summer squash when the skin is not yet firm. The converse is true of winter squash, which should have firm skin when harvested.

• Pick tomatoes at their peak, which comes about 6 days after first color appears. At their ripest, they are brightly colored, full fleshed, and shiny. Three days after ripening, they begin to lose flavor. Even refrigerator storage does not maintain prime taste. If you must pick full-sized tomatoes while they are still green, ripen them indoors between 60° and 70° F. Shield them from direct sunlight. Keep fruit from touching in the ripening container.

ANIMALPROOFING

As housing moves into former forests and fields, many native animals become garden pests. Birds, rabbits, gophers and moles, raccoons, and others can do a lot of damage. So can birds, both exotic species and common city and suburban residents.

Birds

Starlings, cowbirds, grackles, blackbirds, and crows are particularly voracious feeders. They and other species are as fond of berries as people and insects are. Like you, birds are attracted to the high sugar level in ripe fruit and often get to a juicy berry right before you're ready to pick it. Many gardeners like birds so much that they place a few extra berry plants in the yard to provide enough fruit for all. But if birds are eating into the family food supply, several remedies are available.

For raspberry protection, create a wood or metal frame around plants. Over this, drape netting with ¾-inch mesh. This size lets in air, water, and sunlight. Secure netting at the bottom so berry predators cannot slip underneath.

As clusters ripen, more fruit will be bagged. Remember to check to see if grapes are ready to be picked.

To protect blueberries, set 8-foot posts around the growing area to form a frame; keep the frame at least a foot away from the blueberry bushes. Nail ¾-inch mesh around sides and tops of posts. In large growing areas, place the screening and posts in rows. This prevents birds that have somehow gotten into one area from feeding in all areas.

For strawberry protection, cover plants with wire cages or ¾-inch mesh stretched over a frame.

To protect grapes, loosely tie paper bags over ripening fruit clusters. Allow just enough space around the vine to permit air circulation. Cut off the bottom corners of bags for additional necessary circulation. Provide bagged clusters with some afternoon shade, or grapes within may cook.

To protect vegetable seedlings from bird feeding, use floating row covers. Sold in rolls at most local garden centers, these plastic coverings resemble fabric and were created especially for the vegetable garden. They are lightweight and permit sun, water, and air to pass through.

Cover the seedling rows with the plastic. Secure the edges by weighting them down or burying them so animal pests cannot crawl underneath. Hefty rocks are effective weights, as are 2 by 4s. If you bury the edges, add weights at corners and at intervals along the sides. The drawback to row covers is that they can create temperatures underneath that are up to 30° F higher than the air temperature. Remove row covers in summer to avoid baked plants.

In some areas, crows are a particular problem. With great skill these large noisy birds pick up coverings, shred material, and find their way around obstacles. Ordinary row covers or nylon netting may not keep them away. Try using removable chicken wire cages over vegetable seedlings. Anchor the cages.

Many gardeners are tempted to create a scarecrow at one time or another. Scarecrows seldom work. Birds become accustomed to them quickly and learn that they are harmless. Shiny aluminum foil streamers fluttering from rope placed across the garden may discourage bird feeding. However, birds soon get accustomed to this, too. If netting or row covering is not an option, an active cat may do the job. A cat may be too effective, however, in that birds will flee the garden entirely, leaving insect pests unchecked.

Rabbits

In small numbers, rabbits just nibble on row ends; large populations go after the greenery as it comes from the ground. Dogs can sometimes keep them away. Some rabbits, however, just seem to run circles around canine protectors.

The first thing to do if you see signs of rabbit feeding is get rid of potential hiding places. These might include a woodpile or tall grass and weeds.

One method to deter rabbit feeding is to create a 24-inch fence. Around the garden periphery, pound in green plastic stakes of the appropriate height. Use metal clips to attach green plastic-coated wire fencing with 1- by 2-inch mesh to the stakes. The green mesh will blend with garden foliage, and the clips will allow you to adjust the fence when necessary.

Since rabbits can burrow underneath fences, you may want to extend the wire mesh at least 6 inches below ground. Determined rabbits will eventually tunnel underneath, but the below-ground shield may delay them long enough to allow crops to mature and be harvested. An alternative, particularly if you want mobile fencing, is to buy 36-inch-high wire mesh and fold out the bottom 12 inches around the entire periphery. Securely

By using cans to protect seedlings, you give them a chance to attain some growth before being exposed.

staked or weighted down, this horizontal portion will make it more difficult for rabbits to dig under the fence edge.

If fencing your garden is impractical, try protecting seedlings from rabbits by shielding the plants with large tin cans from which the metal tops and bottoms have been removed. In early spring, when the temperature needs a boost anyhow, leave on the plastic top that comes with many cans. It allows sunlight to come through and provides protection from wind and cold. Make certain that sufficient water condenses inside the container to provide moisture. If necessary, remove the cans to water the seedlings, then replace the cans. Using cans as protection becomes ineffective when the plant tops peek over the metal edges.

Gophers and Moles

Signs of gopher or mole invasion include wilted plants that have no roots and mounds of fresh pulverized earth. These animals eat underground vegetable parts, often eliminating them altogether in just one evening. They also pull entire plants down into their burrows.

Although gophers and moles are not communal animals, there can be as many as 20 per acre, each with a separate series of tunnels. If your garden is severely infested, you may have to dig the entire vegetable bed to a depth of 2 feet, line it with ½-inch–mesh chicken wire, and replace the soil.

If you cannot line the entire bed, consider making or purchasing individual wire mesh baskets for each plant. Again, mesh must be ½ inch or less and protect all below-ground portions of the plant.

Trapping is the most thorough method of gopher and mole control. One trap works only if there is only one hole. Gophers and moles make many exit and entry holes so they have many escape routes. Purchase at least 2 traps. Box traps are easier to use than Maccabee traps, but both are effective when employed according to directions.

Dig down to the main horizontal runway that connects with the surface hole. The runway can be as deep as 18 inches. Place traps on either side of your excavation. Since commercial traps vary, read and follow instructions. Bait the area with carrot tops or other fresh greens. Cover your excavation with a board to block out all light. Check the traps frequently.

Many gardeners do not consider poison an option because of the potential danger to cats, dogs, and even curious youngsters. Though poisoning is rare, it can happen. If you do choose to use poison, place bait in the deep tunnels close

to living quarters rather than in surface tunnel runways, which may be used intermittently. Make certain to close your digging hole with boards or earth after placing the bait.

Gopher and mole elimination may require persistence as well as multiple methodologies.

Raccoons

Raccoons are becoming much more common in urban and suburban vegetable gardens as home construction cuts a swath into their natural habitats. Raccoons are adaptable creatures, handy at removing garbage-can lids in search of food and curious enough to crawl down the chimney. Cute as they may be, raccoons are wild animals and may bite. Never handle a raccoon under any circumstances. If a raccoon is trapped under the house or by a dog, call animal control for help.

Because raccoons feed on pest insects as well as fruit and seeds, many homeowners tolerate their presence. Once raccoons have discovered a food source, however, they keep returning. In the process, they may discover your vegetable garden and berry patch. Therefore, protecting your garden means keeping the whole area free of raccoon-attracting food. Secure garbage-can lids thoroughly; locking devices are available. A spotlight on the garbage-can area is another raccoon deterrent. Bring pet food inside at night. Keep your compost pile turned, and hot enough to decompose fruit and other kitchen remainders.

Traps are most effective before your crop ripens. A ripe crop provides foods that compete successfully with baits. Raccoons like sweets, so peanut butter, marshmallows, or bread and honey are effective attractants. Raccoons may be protected by law in your vicinity. Ask at the county extension office or local animal control agency about regulations.

Deer

Like raccoons, deer are becoming increasingly problematic as suburbia intrudes into forested areas. Deer can easily jump 5-foot fences to get at vegetable greens. They tend to feed in the early morning or late evening, when few gardeners are around to chase them off the premises. A large watchdog may scare them away, although barking can annoy neighbors.

Fencing is perhaps the best deerproofing. To exclude deer, a traditional fence must be at least 8 feet high. In some areas a fence of this height is prohibited by building codes or is infeasible. Since deer jump high or wide, but usually not both at the same time, a special deer fence may be the answer. This is 6 feet high with a 3-foot-wide section across the top, parallel with the ground.

Some gardeners in deer areas have tried electrical fencing. The strands of such a fence should be 10 inches apart and the bottom one not more than 8 inches from the ground. Consult the county extension office for rules concerning electrified fencing in your area.

Rats and Mice

Rodents usually take up residence where the food pickings are easy, such as in a garden with a lot of debris or in an inefficient compost heap. Organic mulches provide rats and mice with hiding places. To keep the animals' winter homes away from your food supply, thin out strawberry plants in early fall and wait until the first frost to mulch.

In all seasons, keep your yard clear of debris. This includes trash piles, leaves, firewood, newspapers, boxes, pipes, logs, old doghouses, and tree cuttings. Clean out and close off the area under steps. If you must store construction materials outdoors, put them on platforms 12 to 18 inches off the ground.

Despite what you do, rats and mice may enter your garden from a neighboring property. If the problem is severe, you may have to press local officials to enforce trash abatement rules. This procedure can take a while. In the meantime, a pair of feisty cats may persuade rodents that living is easier elsewhere.

Ground Squirrels

Vegetable gardens that abut fields or open space are often plagued by ground squirrels. They feed on roots and tubers as well as aboveground plants. These squirrels store excess food in burrows, which may be as deep as 4 feet below the surface.

In some areas, regulations protect ground squirrels, so consult the county extension office before using traps or poison. Place baited box traps outside burrows. Do not use any type of poison bait if pets or children are present. Peanut butter is an effective bait for a live trap. Be sure to release squirrels in more appropriate surroundings, where they will not do more damage.

PROBLEMS COMMON TO MANY VEGETABLES, BERRIES, AND GRAPES

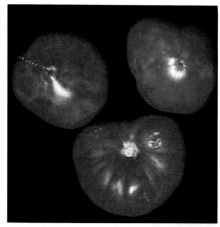

Poor-quality tomatoes.

Slow growth caused by insufficient light.

PROBLEM: Fruits and vegetables have a poor or strong flavor and are smaller than normal. Fruit yield is low.

ANALYSIS: Poor-quality produce
Vegetables and berries may yield poor-quality produce for many reasons.
1. *Hot weather:* High temperatures affect the flavor of some produce, especially cool-season crops such as lettuce and members of the cabbage family. Their taste becomes strong and bitter.
2. *Fluctuations in soil moisture:* Alternatively wet then dry soil results in erratic growth with poor-quality crops and reduced yields. The flavor of cucumbers is particularly sensitive to moisture fluctuation. Sweet-and-white potato tubers crack and appear unappetizing.
3. *Lack of soil nutrients:* Insufficient nutrition causes plants to grow poorly and yield few if any crops. The produce frequently has off-flavors, and the crops may not develop fully.
4. *Overmature fruit:* Once past their prime, crops deteriorate rapidly and lose flavor. Overripening on the plant reduces future yields by using energy the plant could use to produce more crops.

SOLUTION: Follow these guidelines for better-quality produce. (For more information on each of these recommendations, see the entry for your specific plant in the alphabetical section beginning on page 261.)
1. Plant vegetables and small fruits at the times of year suggested for your area.
2. Follow the irrigation guidelines for your plant.
3. Apply fertilizer to plants as instructed.
4. Pick crops as they mature, so more will be produced. Follow the harvesting guidelines specific to your plant.

PROBLEM: Plants grow slowly or not at all. Leaves are light green, and few or no flowers or fruit are produced. Plants are shaded for much of the day. Lower leaves may turn yellow and drop.

ANALYSIS: Insufficient light
Plants need sunlight to manufacture food and produce fruit. Without adequate sunlight they grow slowly. Vegetable and berry plants that yield fruit—such as tomato, bramble, strawberry, bean, and pepper plants—require at least 6 hours of sunlight a day. Some leafy and root vegetable plants, however, tolerate light shade. These include beet, cabbage, carrot, chive, kale, leek, lettuce, mustard, green onion, parsley, radish, Swiss chard, and turnip plants.

SOLUTION: Prune surrounding trees to allow more sunlight. Plant vegetables that require less sunlight in somewhat shady areas of the garden. If possible, move your garden site or grow vegetables in containers on a sunny patio or porch.

Phosphorus deficiency on corn.

Slow growth from too acidic soil.

Damping-off on radish seedlings.

PROBLEM: Plants grow slowly. Leaves are pale green to yellow, or darker than normal and dull. Few flowers and fruit are produced. Fruit that is produced matures slowly. Plants pulled from the soil may have small, black, and rotted root systems. Plants may die.

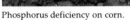

ANALYSIS: Slow growth
Plants may grow slowly and produce a small yield for any of several reasons.

1. *Excess water:* If the soil is constantly wet, either from frequent watering or poor drainage, lack of oxygen causes the roots to become shallow, stunting and sometimes killing plants. Also, wet soil encourages root-rotting fungi that destroy root systems and kill plants.

2. *Phosphorus deficiency:* Phosphorus is a major nutrient needed by plants for root formation, flower and fruit production, and overall cell growth. Phosphorus-deficient plants grow slowly and have dark leaves that may be tinted with purple or have purple veins. This nutrient may be lacking either because it is not present in the soil or because it is in a form that is unavailable to plants.

3. *Incorrect pH:* Soil pH limits the amounts and kinds of nutrients available to plants. Vegetables grow best with a pH of 6.0 to 7.0. Required nutrients are usually available in adequate amounts at this range.

4. *Cool weather:* Warm-season vegetables—such as tomatoes, beans, and okra—require temperatures over 70° F for best growth. If they are planted too early in the season, the cool weather slows their growth. Affected plants may take several months to recover from this setback and still may not produce abundantly.

SOLUTION: Take these measures to correct the condition or control the problem.

1. Allow the soil around plants to dry out. Remove and destroy any plants with rotting roots. Avoid future root-rot problems by planting in well-drained soil.

2. For a quick response, spray the leaves with a plant food rated 23-19-17. Apply a balanced fertilizer rated 8-10-8 or 10-10-10. Follow the instructions on the label or those given in the alphabetical section beginning on page 261.

3. Test the soil pH and, if necessary, correct it to 6.0 to 7.0.

4. Plant vegetables at the correct time of year. Discard warm-season vegetable plants that have been set back by cool temperatures. Replace the discards with healthy transplants.

PROBLEM: Seeds rot. Seedlings fail to emerge or fall over soon after they emerge. At the soil line stems are water-soaked and discolored. The base of an affected stem is soft and thin.

ANALYSIS: Damping-off
Damping-off is a common problem caused by one of several fungi and aggravated by wet soil with a high nitrogen level. Wet, rich soil promotes damping-off in two ways: The fungi that cause it are more active under these conditions, and the seedlings are more susceptible to attack. Damping-off is often a problem when weather remains cloudy and wet and when seedlings are heavily shaded or crowded. Seedlings started indoors in a wet, unsterilized medium are also susceptible.

SOLUTION: To prevent fungi from attacking seedlings, take the precautions that follow.
1. Allow the surface of the soil to dry slightly between waterings.
2. Do not start seeds in soil that has a high nitrogen level. Add nitrogen fertilizer only after the seedlings have produced their first true leaves.
3. Protect seeds during germination with a fungicide containing captan or thiram. Add a pinch of fungicide to a packet of seeds (or ½ teaspoon per pound) and shake well to coat the seeds.
4. Use a sterilized medium—such as a sterilized potting soil or a mixture of peat moss, perlite, and vermiculite—for starting seeds indoors.
5. Thin seedlings to allow adequate air circulation between plants.

PROBLEMS COMMON TO MANY VEGETABLES, BERRIES, AND GRAPES — SEEDLING PROBLEMS

Pea seedlings eaten by rabbits.

Bean seedlings eaten by slugs.

Root rot on broccoli.

PROBLEM: Seedling leaves are chewed ragged. Seedlings may completely disappear, or short stubs of the stems may remain.

ANALYSIS: Seedlings eaten
Several animal and insect pests feed on seedlings.

1. *Birds:* Many kinds of birds—especially grackles, blackbirds, and crows—eat entire seedlings. The plants are most susceptible to bird attack when they have just emerged.

2. *Snails and slugs:* These pests feed at night and on cloudy days, chewing holes in leaves or devouring entire seedlings. Silvery winding trails are evidence of their presence. During the day they hide in damp places, such as under rocks and flowerpots or in debris.

3. *Earwigs:* These are dark brown insects with pincers on their tail ends. They feed at night, and chew holes in leaves and stems.

4. *Rabbits:* These animals may eat entire seedlings or leave only short stubs of the stems standing in the soil.

5. *Grasshoppers:* As they deplete their food supply, these insects migrate from area to area throughout the growing season. They eat entire seedlings. Grasshoppers are prevalent in hot, dry weather.

SOLUTION: Take these measures to correct the condition or control the problem.

1. Cover seedlings with a tent made of cheesecloth or netting stretched over a wooden frame. Scarecrows and dangling aluminum pie plates may help to deter birds.

2. Control snails and slugs with pellets containing methaldehyde. Lightly wet the area before application to activate the pellets; the moisture will also attract snails and slugs. Treat along the seeded rows and in hiding places, such as under rocks, boards, and flowerpots or around compost piles. For more information on snails and slugs, see page 257.

3. To control earwigs, place granules containing carbaryl (SEVIN®) along the seeded rows and in hiding places, such as under rocks and in debris. For more information on earwigs, see page 260.

4. Keep rabbits out of the garden by enclosing it with a 2-foot-high fence of small-gauge fencing. To prevent the rabbits from digging underneath, anchor the bottom of the fence with boards 1 to 2 inches deep in the soil.

5. Control grasshoppers and protect uneaten seedlings with granules containing carbaryl (SEVIN®). Reapply the granules at weekly intervals as long as grasshoppers are present. For more information on grasshoppers, see page 259.

PROBLEM: Leaves wilt and turn yellow. Lower leaves are affected first, then upper ones. Few or no fruit are produced. Plants do not recover when watered, and they usually die.

ANALYSIS: Root and stem rot
This plant disease is caused by any of a number of different fungi, also known as water molds. These fungi live in the soil. They thrive in waterlogged, heavy earth. The fungi attack the plant roots or the stems at the soil level. Infection causes the roots and stems to decay, resulting in wilting, then yellowing, leaves and the eventual death of the plant. Many of these fungi also cause damping-off of seedlings. For more information about damping-off, see page 251.

SOLUTION: Allow the soil around the plants to dry out. Remove and discard severely infected plants. Avoid future root rot by planting in well-drained soil. Avoid overwatering by following the watering guidelines for your plant; look in the alphabetical section beginning on page 261.

■ **WILTING**

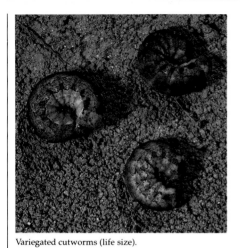

Variegated cutworms (life size).

Cutworms on celery (life size).

Fusarium wilt on tomato.

PROBLEM: Stems of young plants are chewed or cut off near the ground. Gray, brown, or black worms, up to 2 inches long, may be found in the top 2 inches of the soil near the bases of damaged plants. The worms coil when disturbed.

ANALYSIS: Cutworms

Several species of cutworm attack plants in the vegetable garden. Surface-feeding cutworms are common pests of young vegetables planted early in the season. A single surface-feeding cutworm can sever the stems of many young plants in one night; it eats through the stems just above ground level. Tomato, pepper, pea, and bean plants and members of the cabbage family are particularly susceptible. Some cutworms can climb up the stems or trunks of grapevines and blueberry, bramble, tomato, and other garden plants to feed on young leaves, buds, and fruits. Cutworms hide in the soil during the day and feed only after sundown. Adult cutworms are dark, night-flying moths with bands or stripes on their forewings.

SOLUTION: Apply an insecticide containing diazinon, chlorpyrifos, or methoxychlor, or a bait containing carbaryl (SEVIN®) around the bases of undamaged plants in areas where cutworm damage is observed. Make sure your plant is listed on the product label. Since cutworms are difficult to control, weekly reapplications will probably be necessary. Before transplanting new plants into the area, apply a preventive treatment of a diazinon product and work it into the soil. In late summer and fall, cultivate the soil thoroughly to expose and destroy eggs, larvae, and pupae. Further reduce damage by setting a "cutworm collar" around the stem of each plant. Make collars from stiff material: cottage cheese or milk cartons, tin cans, aluminum foil, or the like. Collars should be at least 2 inches high and pressed firmly into the soil. To reduce injury from climbing cutworms, inspect plants at night with a flashlight and pick off and destroy the pests.

PROBLEM: Leaves wilt, turn yellow, and may turn brown. Little or no fruit is produced. Growth slows and plants may be stunted. Slicing open a stem may reveal brown tissue just under the bark.

ANALYSIS: Wilt diseases

This disease infects many vegetables and berries. It is caused by any of several fungi that live in the soil. The fungi are spread by contaminated plants, soil, and equipment. They enter the plant through the roots and spread through the water-conducting vessels in the stems. The vessels become plugged and discolored. This plugging cuts off the flow of water and nutrients to the leaves, resulting in leaf yellowing and wilting. The plugging also results in a reduced yield and poor-quality fruit. Severely infected plants die.

SOLUTION: No available chemicals can cure infected plants. Wilt fungi can be removed from the soil by fumigation techniques only. The best prevention is usually to avoid plants that are susceptible to wilt disease. Don't put a plant where a wilt-infected plant of the same kind grew.

Nematode damage on bean.

Nitrogen-deficient tomato.

Root rot on bush bean.

PROBLEM: Plants wilt in hot, dry weather and recover at night. They are stunted and yellow. Round and elongated nodules may occur on the roots. Plants may die.

ANALYSIS: Nematodes

Nematodes are microscopic worms that live in the soil. There are various types, some highly beneficial and some highly destructive. They are not related to earthworms. Destructive nematodes feed on plant roots. The damaged roots can't supply sufficient water and nutrients to the aboveground plant parts, and the plant is stunted or slowly dies. Nematodes may also transmit viruses. Nematodes are found throughout the United States but are most severe in southern areas. The pests prefer moist, sandy loam soil. Nematodes can move only a few inches each year on their own, but they may be carried long distances by soil, water, tools, or infested plants. Testing roots and soil is the only positive method for confirming the presence of nematodes. Contact the local cooperative extension office for sampling instructions and addresses of testing laboratories. Soil and root problems—such as poor soil structure, drought stress, nutrient deficiency, and root rots—can also produce symptoms of decline similar to those caused by nematodes. Eliminate these problems as causes before sending soil and root samples for testing.

SOLUTION: Chemicals to kill nematodes in planted soil are not available to homeowners. However, nematodes can be controlled by soil fumigation before planting.

PROBLEM: The bottom leaves, including the veins, turn light green to pale yellow and may die or drop. Growth slows, and new leaves are small. Flowers turn yellow and drop. Fruit is small and may be distorted and discolored.

ANALYSIS: Nitrogen deficiency

Plants need nitrogen for making chlorophyll, the essential green pigment in their leaves, and for overall healthy growth and high-quality fruit. When plants lack nitrogen, growth slows, blossoms drop, and fruit yield declines. Nitrogen may either be lacking in the soil or be present in a form that is not available to plants. In cool, rainy, early spring weather, little or no nitrogen is available. Later in the season, as vegetables are growing rapidly and maturing, the plants may deplete the supply of nitrogen. During a drought, nitrogen is carried to the soil surface as the water it is dissolved in evaporates. Once the nitrogen is above the root zone, the roots are unable to absorb it. Rain or irrigation water carries the nitrogen back to the root zone where it is available to the plant. Soils high in organic matter or heavily mulched soils may require more nitrogen, since the organisms that break down the organic matter use it.

SOLUTION: For a quick response, spray the foliage with a liquid plant food rated 12-6-6 or 23-19-17. Water the plant with the same solution. Remove any fruit from severely affected plants to allow them time to resume normal growth. Apply fertilizer according to the recommendations for your plant in the alphabetical section beginning on page 261.

PROBLEM: Leaves turn yellow, starting with the older, lower leaves and progressing to the younger ones. Plants show little growth. Flowers yellow and drop. Fruit shrivels and does not ripen. When the plant is pulled up, the roots are black, soft, and rotted. The soil has frequently been quite moist.

ANALYSIS: Root rot

This plant disease is caused by any of a number of different fungi that are present in most soils. Some of these fungi normally do little damage, but they can cause root rot in wet or waterlogged soil. Waterlogged soil may result from overwatering or poor soil drainage. Infection causes the roots to decay, resulting in wilting, yellowing leaves, flower and fruit drop, reduced fruit yield, and the eventual death of the plant.

SOLUTION: To avoid root rot, do not overwater. Follow the watering guidelines under the entry for your plant in the alphabetical section beginning on page 261. Remove and destroy severely infected plants. Avoid future root rot by planting in well-drained soil. Do not plant the same crop where root rot was a problem in the past 3 to 5 years.

Spider mite damage on string bean.

Salt damage on radishes.

Grape with spray injury.

PROBLEM: Leaves are stippled, yellowing, and dirty. Leaves may dry out and drop. There may be cobwebbing over flower buds, between leaves, or on the undersides of the leaves. To determine if the plant is infested with mites, hold a sheet of white paper underneath an affected leaf or stem and tap the leaf or stem sharply. If mites are present, minute green, red, or yellow specks the size of pepper grains will drop to the paper and begin to crawl around. The pests are easily seen against the white background.

ANALYSIS: Spider mites
Mites, related to spiders, are major pests of many garden and greenhouse plants. They cause damage by sucking sap from the undersides of the leaves. As a result of feeding, the green leaf pigment (chlorophyll) disappears, producing a stippled appearance. Although mites do not attack the fruit directly, they do cause leaf drop, which weakens the plant and reduces fruit yield. If the plants are severely infected, flowers do not form or do not bloom, resulting in no fruit. Mites are active throughout the growing season, but most are favored by dry weather with temperatures above 70° F. By midsummer (or as early as March in Florida), they may build up to tremendous numbers.

SOLUTION: At the first sign of damage, treat infested plants with a miticide containing hexakis. Repeat the treatment at weekly intervals until no further damage occurs. Make sure your vegetable or berry is listed on the product label. Hose plants frequently with a strong stream of water to wash off mites and cobwebs.

PROBLEM: Leaf edges and areas between the veins turn dark brown and die. Burned leaves may drop. Growth slows or stops. A white or dark crust may be on the soil.

ANALYSIS: Salt damage
Salt damage occurs when salt accumulates to damaging levels in the soil. This can happen in either of two ways: The garden does not receive enough water from rainfall or irrigation to wash the salts from the soil, or the drainage is so poor that water does not pass through the soil. In either case, as water evaporates from the soil and plant leaves, the salts that were dissolved in the water accumulate near the soil surface. A white or dark brown crust of salts may form. Salts can originate in the soil, in the irrigation water, or in applied fertilizers.

SOLUTION: The only way to eliminate excess salt is to wash it through the soil with water. If the damage is only at a low spot in the garden, fill in the spot to level the area. If the soil drains well, increase the amount of water applied at each watering by 50 percent or more, so excess water will leach salts below the root zone of the plants. Apply fertilizer according to instructions for your plant in the alphabetical section beginning on page 261.

PROBLEM: Irregular spots occur on leaves. Young leaves and blossoms may be distorted and brown. Plants may have been recently sprayed with a pesticide.

ANALYSIS: Pesticide burn
Insecticides, fungicides, and herbicides damage plants when used improperly. Damage usually occurs within 24 hours of the time the plants are sprayed. However, in some crops, such as grapes, damage may not be apparent for several days after spraying. On windy days pesticides may drift from other areas on windy days and damage plants. Pesticides may burn plants when the temperature is above 90° F at the time of spraying or if it rises above 90° F within a few hours of spraying. Damage is also common during damp, humid weather when spray is slow to dry on the plant. Pesticides not mixed and applied according to label directions can also burn plants. Pesticides used in tanks that were once used for plant killers may be herbicide-contaminated, since traces of herbicides are difficult to remove from sprayers.

SOLUTION: Once plants are damaged, there is nothing to do except try to keep the plants healthy with regular watering and fertilizer applications. Do not spray when temperatures are above 90° F. Avoid spraying on windy days, when sprays may drift. Mix solutions according to label directions. Do not increase the dosage. When mixing 2 or more chemicals, be sure they are compatible. Always keep the solution well mixed by shaking the tank periodically while spraying; this is especially important when using wettable powder formulations. Purchase fresh pesticides each year. Keep a separate sprayer for herbicides.

VEGETABLES, BERRIES, AND GRAPES

Leaf spot on strawberry.

Powdery mildew on cucumber.

Leafminer trails on tomato.

PROBLEM: Spots and blotches appear on leaves. The spots may be yellow, red, tan, gray, or brown. They range in size from barely visible to ¼ inch in diameter. Several spots may join to form blotches. Leaves may be yellow and dying. Leaf spotting is most severe in warm, humid weather. Fruit may be spotted like the leaves or be discolored brown or yellow. A fine gray or white mold sometimes covers the infected leaf or fruit tissue in damp conditions.

ANALYSIS: Leaf spot
Several different fungi cause leaf spot. Some of these fungi may eventually kill the plant or weaken it so that it becomes susceptible to attack by other organisms; other fungi merely cause spotting that is unsightly but not harmful. Fruit yield is reduced. Fruit infected only slightly is still edible if the discolored tissue is cut away; severely infected fruit is inedible. Leaf-spot fungi are spread by wind or splashing water. They generally survive the winter in diseased plant debris. Most of the fungi do their greatest damage in mild weather from 50° to 85° F.

SOLUTION: At the first sign of the disease, treat infected plants with a fungicide containing chlorothalonil or captan. Repeat the treatment at intervals of 7 to 10 days until weather conditions are no longer favorable to the spread of the disease. Make sure your plant is listed on the product label. Remove all plant debris from the garden after harvest to reduce the number of overwintering spores.

PROBLEM: The topsides of the leaves and sometimes the stems are covered with a white powdery growth. Areas of the leaves turn brown and dry. Older leaves are affected first, then younger leaves. Leaves may become cupped, showing silvery undersides. Fruit may also be covered with the white powdery growth.

ANALYSIS: Powdery mildew
This common plant disease is caused by one of several fungi that thrive in both humid and dry weather. The powdery patches consist of fungal strands and spores. The spores are spread by the wind to healthy plants. The fungi sap the plant nutrients, causing yellowing and sometimes the death of leaves. Fruit yield may also be reduced. A severe infection may kill the plant. Since powdery mildew attacks many different kinds of plants, the fungi from a diseased plant may infect other types of plants in the garden. Under conditions favorable to powdery mildew, infection can spread through a closely spaced planting in a matter of days or weeks.

SOLUTION: At the first sign of the disease, control powdery mildew on vegetable and berry plants with a fungicide containing chlorothalonil. Continue spraying at intervals of 7 days as long as the disease is a problem. Make sure your plant is listed on the product label. Clean up and destroy plant debris after harvest. When available, grow varieties that are resistant to powdery mildew.

PROBLEM: Light-colored, irregular blotches, blisters, or tunnels appear on or in leaves. The tan areas peel apart easily, like facial tissue. Inside the tunnels are tiny black specks.

ANALYSIS: Leafminers
These insect pests belong to the family of leaf-mining flies. The tiny black or yellow adult females lay white eggs on the undersides of leaves or inside leaves. The maggots that hatch from these eggs tunnel between the leaf surfaces, feeding on the inner tissue. The tunnels and blotches are called mines. The black specks inside them are the maggots' droppings. Damaged portions of leaves are no longer edible. Leafmining damage does not usually affect the yield of fruit-producing vegetables and berries unless many leaves are damaged. Several overlapping generations occur during the growing season, so larvae are present from spring until fall.

SOLUTION: When the egg clusters are first seen under the leaves, control leafminers with an insecticide containing malathion or diazinon. Repeat 2 more times at weekly intervals to control succeeding generations. Once the leafminers enter the leaves, sprays are largely ineffective, controlling only those leafminers that attack after the application. Make sure your plant is listed on the insecticide label. Clean all plant debris from the garden after harvest to reduce overwintering spots for the pupae.

INSECTS ON THE PLANT

Cabbage plants damaged by nocturnal pests.

Slug damage.

Cabbage looper (2 times life size).

PROBLEM: Young plants are chewed or cut off near the ground. Some of the leaves, stems, flowers, and fruit are chewed. When the affected plants are inspected at night with a flashlight, insects may be seen feeding on the plants.

ANALYSIS: Nocturnal pests

Several kinds of insects—including some beetles, weevils, caterpillars, and all earwigs and cutworms—feed on plants only at night. Beetles are hard-bodied insects with tough, leathery wing covers. Weevils look like beetles, except they have elongated snouts. Earwigs are reddish brown, flat, elongated insects up to 1 inch long; pincers project from the rear of their bodies. Caterpillars and cutworms are smooth or hairy, soft-bodied worms. All these nocturnal pests usually hide in the soil, in debris, or in other protected locations during the day.

SOLUTION: Control nocturnal pests by treating with a bait containing carbaryl (SEVIN®).

PROBLEM: Irregular holes with smooth edges are chewed in leaves. Some leaves may be sheared off entirely. Silvery trails wind around the plant and soil nearby. At night, check with a flashlight for slimy leaf-feeding creatures with or without hard brown shells.

ANALYSIS: Snails and slugs

These pests are mollusks and are related to clams, oysters, and other shellfish. They feed on the leaves of a wide variety of garden plants and may completely devour a young seedling. Ripe and unripe fruit lying on the ground may be attacked by snails and slugs. This is especially true if the fruit is shaded by the foliage, as with strawberries and unstaked tomatoes. Like other mollusks, snails and slugs need to be moist all the time. For this reason they avoid direct sun and dry places and hide during the day in damp places, such as under flowerpots or in thick ground covers. They emerge at night or on cloudy days to feed. In protected places female slugs lay masses of white eggs encased in slime. Female snails bury their eggs in the soil, also in a slimy mass. The young look like miniature versions of their parents.

SOLUTION: Apply a bait containing metaldehyde or methiocarb in the areas you wish to protect. Also apply it in areas where snails and slugs might be hiding, such as in dense ground covers, weedy areas, compost piles, or pot storage areas. Wet down the areas to be treated, to encourage snail and slug activity that night. Repeat every 2 weeks as needed.

PROBLEM: Irregular or round holes appear in leaves and buds. Leaves, buds, and flowers may be entirely chewed off. Worms or caterpillars feed on the plants.

ANALYSIS: Caterpillars

Several species of these moth or butterfly larvae feed on many vegetable and berry plants. Some common caterpillars are budworms, hornworms, and loopers. Most adult female moths or butterflies start to lay their eggs on garden plants with the onset of warm weather in the spring. The larvae that emerge from these eggs feed on the leaves, flowers, and buds for two to six weeks, depending on weather and species. Mature caterpillars pupate in cocoons attached to leaves or structures or buried in the soil. There may be one generation each year or overlapping generations during the growing season. The last generation of caterpillars in the fall survives the winter as pupae. Moths and butterflies emerge from the pupae the following spring.

SOLUTION: Spray infested plants with an insecticide containing carbaryl (SEVIN®), diazinon, methoxychlor, or pyrethrins. A bacterial insecticide containing *Bacillus thuringiensis* is effective against the early stages of some caterpillars. Make sure your plant is listed on the product label. Repeat the treatment if reinfestation occurs, allowing at least 7 days to pass between applications.

PROBLEMS COMMON TO MANY VEGETABLES, BERRIES, AND GRAPES — INSECTS ON THE PLANT

Japanese beetles on grape (⅓ life size).

Spotted cucumber beetle (½ life size).

Flea beetles on turnip leaf (2 times life size).

PROBLEM: Leaf
tissue is chewed between the veins, giving the leaf a lacy appearance. Winged metallic green and bronze beetles, ½ inch long, feed in clusters on the foliage, especially on the tender new leaves.

ANALYSIS: Japanese beetles
(*Popillia japonica*)
As their name suggests, these beetles are native to Japan. They were first seen in New Jersey in 1916 and have since become a major pest in the eastern United States. They feed on hundreds of different plant species. The adult beetles are present from the beginning of summer to early fall. They feed only in the daytime, rapidly defoliating plants. Leaves exposed to direct sun are the most severely attacked. Badly damaged leaves drop. Any reduction in leaf tissue ultimately affects the overall vigor and production of fruit. The larva of the Japanese beetle, a white grub, feeds on grass roots, frequently killing entire lawns.

SOLUTION: Treat infested plants with an
insecticide containing carbaryl (SEVIN®), malathion, or pyrethrins; follow label directions. Japanese beetles can fly up to 5 miles and travel from garden to garden. Consequently, repeated treatments are necessary to control them. Make sure your plants are listed on the product label. Treat for grubs in the lawn as outlined on page 51. Use resistant plants.

PROBLEM: Yellow-green
beetles with black spots or stripes chew holes in leaves, leafstalks, and stems. Plants may be stunted; they may die prematurely.

ANALYSIS: Cucumber beetles
Both striped cucumber beetles (*Acalymma* species) and spotted cucumber beetles (*Diabrotica* species) are common pests of vegetable plants. Controlling these beetles is important because they may infect plants with two potentially fatal cucurbit diseases: mosaic virus (see page 283) and bacterial wilt (see page 282). Adult beetles survive the winter in plant debris and weeds. As soon as vegetable plants are set in the garden in the spring, the beetles attack the leaves and stems and may totally destroy the plants. Mature females lay their yellow-orange eggs in the soil at the bases of plants. The grubs that hatch from these eggs eat the roots and stems below the soil line, causing stunting or premature death. Severely infested plants produce few fruit. The slender white grubs feed for several weeks, pupate in the soil, and emerge as adults to repeat the cycle. There is one generation per year in northern parts of the United States but two or more in southern areas.

SOLUTION: At the first sign of the bee-
tles, treat the plants with an insecticide containing carbaryl (SEVIN®), diazinon, or pyrethrins. Make sure your plant is listed on the product label.

PROBLEM: Leaves are
riddled with shot holes about ⅛ inch in diameter. Tiny (¹⁄₁₆-inch) black beetles jump like fleas when disturbed. Leaves of seedlings and, eventually, whole plants may wilt and die.

ANALYSIS: Flea beetles
These beetles jump like fleas but are not related to them. Both adult and immature flea beetles feed on a wide variety of garden vegetable and berry plants. Immature beetles, legless gray grubs, injure plants by feeding on the roots and undersides of leaves. Adults chew holes in leaves. Flea beetles are most damaging to seedlings and young plants. Seedling leaves riddled with holes dry out quickly and die. Adult beetles survive the winter in soil and garden debris. They emerge in early spring to feed on weeds until vegetables sprout or plants are set in the garden. Grubs hatch from eggs laid in the soil, and these pests feed for two to three weeks. After pupating in the soil, they emerge as adults to repeat the cycle. There are one to four generations each year. Adults may feed for up to two months.

SOLUTION: When the leaves first show
damage, control flea beetles on vegetable and berry plants with an insecticide containing carbaryl (SEVIN®), diazinon, or pyrethrins. Watch new growth for evidence of further damage, and repeat the treatment at weekly intervals as needed. Make sure your plant is listed on the product label. Clean up and destroy plant debris after harvest to reduce the number of overwintering spots for adult beetles.

Grasshopper on blueberry.

Leafhopper (3 times life size).

Whiteflies (life size).

PROBLEM: Large holes are chewed in the edges of leaves. Greenish yellow to brown jumping insects, ½ to 1½ inches long, with long hind legs are eating the plants. Fruits and corn ears may be chewed.

ANALYSIS: Grasshoppers

Grasshoppers attack a wide variety of plants. They eat leaves and occasionally fruits, migrating as they deplete their food sources. In vegetable gardens, they are most numerous in the rows near weedy areas. In late summer, adult female grasshoppers lay their eggs in pods in the soil. The adults continue feeding until cold weather kills them. The eggs hatch the following spring. Grasshopper infestations are most severe during hot, dry weather. The insects migrate into green gardens and yards as surrounding areas dry up in the summer heat. Periods of cool, wet weather help keep these insect populations under control.

SOLUTION: As soon as grasshoppers appear, treat plants with an insecticide containing diazinon or use a bait containing carbaryl (SEVIN®). Repeat at weekly intervals if the plants become reinfested. Make sure your plant is listed on the product label.

PROBLEM: Spotted, pale green insects up to ⅛ inch long hop, move sideways, or fly away quickly when a plant is touched. The leaves are stippled. Cast-off skins may be found on undersides of leaves.

ANALYSIS: Leafhoppers

Leafhoppers feed on many vegetables and small fruits. They generally feed on the undersides of leaves, sucking the sap, which causes stippling. Severely infested vegetable and small fruit plants may become weak and produce little edible fruit. One leafhopper, the aster leafhopper (*Macrosteles fascifrons*), transmits aster yellows, a plant disease that can be quite damaging. Leafhoppers at all stages of maturity are active during the growing season. They hatch in the spring from eggs laid on perennial weeds and ornamental plants. Even areas where the winters are so cold that the eggs cannot survive are not free from infestation because leafhoppers migrate in the spring from warmer regions.

SOLUTION: Spray infested plants with an insecticide containing diazinon or pyrethrins. Be sure to cover the undersides of the leaves. Respray as often as necessary to keep the insects under control. Allow at least 10 days between applications. Make sure your plants are listed on the product label. Eradicate nearby weeds—especially thistles, plantains, and dandelions—that may harbor leafhopper eggs.

PROBLEM: Tiny, winged insects ⅟₁₂ inch long feed on the undersides of leaves. The insects are covered with white waxy powder. When the plant is touched, insects flutter rapidly around it. Leaves may be mottled and yellowing. Black mold may cover the leaves.

ANALYSIS: Whiteflies

These insects are common pests of many garden and greenhouse plants. The four-winged adult females lay eggs on the undersides of leaves. Each larva is the size of a pinhead. White waxy filaments radiate from its body. It feeds for about a month before changing to the adult form. The larval and adult forms suck sap from the leaves. The larvae are more damaging because they feed more heavily. Whiteflies cannot fully digest all the sugar in the plant sap. They excrete the excess in a fluid called honeydew, which often drops onto the lower leaves. A sooty mold fungus may develop on the honeydew, causing the leaves to appear black and dirty. In warm-winter areas whiteflies can be active the year around, with eggs, larvae, and adults present at the same time. Whiteflies are unable to live through freezing winters. Spring reinfestations in freezing-winter areas come from migrating whiteflies and infested greenhouse-grown plants placed in the garden.

SOLUTION: Control whiteflies by treating with an insecticide containing diazinon, malathion, or pyrethrins. Spray every 7 to 10 days, as necessary. Spray the foliage thoroughly, being sure to cover both surfaces of the leaves. Make sure your plant is listed on the product label. Sticky whitefly traps are also an effective control.

VEGETABLES, BERRIES, AND GRAPES

Aphids on spinach (½ life size).

Earwig (2 times life size).

Mole.

PROBLEM: Pale green, yellow, purple, or black soft-bodied insects cluster on the undersides of leaves. Leaves turn yellow and may be curled, distorted, and puckered. Plants may be stunted and produce few fruit.

ANALYSIS: Aphids

Aphids are one of the most common pests in the garden. They do little damage in small numbers, but they are extremely prolific and populations can rapidly build up to damaging numbers during the growing season. Damage occurs when the aphids suck the juices from vegetable or fruit leaves and flower buds. Aphids usually prefer young tender leaves. Severely infested plants may be stunted and weak, producing few fruit. Fruit yield is also reduced when the aphids spread plant virus diseases. Aphids feed on nearly every plant in the garden and are spread from plant to plant by wind, water, and people. Aphids are unable to digest fully all the sugar in the plant sap and excrete the excess in a fluid called honeydew, which often drops onto lower leaves. Ants feed on this sticky substance and are often present where there is an aphid infestation.

SOLUTION: As soon as the insects appear, control aphids on vegetables and berries; use an insecticide containing diazinon, malathion, or pyrethrins. Respray if the plants become reinfested. Make sure your plants are listed on the product label.

PROBLEM: Dark, reddish brown insects, up to an inch long, with rear pincers are under objects in the garden. They scurry for cover when disturbed. Holes may be chewed in leaves and blossoms.

ANALYSIS: Earwigs

Earwigs are present in most gardens and, usually, are only minor pests of vegetables and berries. They can become major pests, however, if their numbers are high. These insects feed predominantly on decaying plant material and other insects. Earwigs feed at night; in the daytime they hide under stones, debris, and bark chips. They have wings but seldom fly, preferring to run instead. Adult female earwigs lay eggs in the soil in late winter to early spring. The young that hatch from these eggs may feed on green shoots and eat holes in leaves. As the earwigs mature, they feed occasionally on blossoms and ripening fruit. Earwigs are beneficial when they feed on other insect larvae and on snails. They sometimes invade homes.

SOLUTION: Because earwigs typically cause only minor damage, control is seldom needed in the vegetable garden. However, if they are numerous and troublesome, treat the soil with an insecticide containing diazinon or use a bait containing carbaryl (SEVIN®). Since earwigs are most active at night, treat in the late afternoon or evening. Make sure your plant is listed on the product label. Pick fruit as it ripens. For information on controlling earwigs indoors, see page 312.

PROBLEM: Raised ridges, 3 to 5 inches wide, crisscross the garden. Plants may be disturbed. Mounds of soil with no holes appear in the garden.

ANALYSIS: Moles

Moles are small animals that live underground and feed on earthworms and insects. They are 4 to 6 inches long, with velvety fur and tiny, hidden eyes. They use their strong forelegs with broad, trowellike claws to dig and push the soil as they move through the ground. Although they do not feed on plants or roots, they often loosen the soil around plant roots as they search for earthworms and grubs. This loosened soil dries out quickly, causing the plants to wilt. Their tunnels are often used by other rodents that may damage plant roots.

SOLUTION: Tamp down the soil around wilted plants, water them thoroughly, and shade them until they recover. Because moles seldom eat the roots, the damage is usually temporary. In the eastern United States, trap moles by setting spear-type traps over active surface runs. Locate active runs by tamping down the ridges in a few spots. Spots that are raised again the next day are active. Western moles are not easily caught in surface traps. Locate a main run, usually 6 to 10 inches deep, by probing around a fresh pile of soil. Dig down to the run and set a scissors-type trap according to package directions. Poison baits are usually ineffective on moles. Poison gas is dangerous and difficult to use properly.

Raccoon.

Snapbeans eaten by rabbits.

PROBLEMS OF INDIVIDUAL VEGETABLES, BERRIES, AND GRAPES

This section is arranged alphabetically by the name of each plant.

PROBLEM: Plants are chewed or completely eaten. Ripening fruit, pods, and ears are partially or completely eaten. Deer, raccoons, squirrels, rabbits, woodchucks, or mice may be seen in the garden.

ANALYSIS: Wildlife
Various forms of wildlife feed in the garden.

1. *Deer:* Most active at dawn and dusk, deer feed on leaves and fruit.

2. *Raccoons:* To feed on maturing ears, raccoons knock over corn stalks. They may also feed on other ripening fruit. Raccoons feed at night.

3. *Squirrels:* These rodents feed on ripening fruit and climb corn stalks to feed on maturing ears.

4. *Rabbits:* These animals feed on young bean, pea, lettuce, and cabbage plants, eating the young leaves and frequently leaving short stubs of the stems standing in the soil.

5. *Woodchucks:* Also called groundhogs, woodchucks feed in the afternoons and avoid tomatoes, eggplants, red and green peppers, chives, and onions.

6. *Mice:* To eat the seeds, mice may bite into ripening tomatoes, cucumbers, and beans that are close to the ground. Mice frequently travel underground in mole tunnels.

SOLUTION: There are several ways to exclude or repel wildlife.

1. The only sure way to exclude deer is with a woven wire fence 8 feet tall. Cotton drawstring bags filled with bloodmeal fertilizer or human hair and suspended on stakes in the garden sometimes repel them.

2. Exclude raccoons with a 6-foot-tall fence. Electric fencing above the fence may also be needed. Protect corn by interplanting with members of the cucurbit family; raccoons will not walk on the prickly vines. Sprinkle ripening corn with cayenne pepper.

3. Protect ears of corn from squirrels by sprinkling corn silks with cayenne pepper.

4. To exclude rabbits, erect a fence 18 inches tall and anchor it by burying it 5 to 6 inches deep in the soil.

5. Deter woodchucks with a wire fence that is buried 1 foot deep and extends horizontally underground 10 to 12 inches.

6. Stake, trellis, or cage plants to keep fruit off the ground and away from mice.

ASPARAGUS

ASPARAGUS

ADAPTATION: Throughout the United States, except in the Southeast.

PLANTING TIME: Varies from February through April, depending on date of last frost in your region.

PLANTING METHOD: Set crowns, buds upward, 12 inches apart in a trench 6 to 8 inches deep. As the plants grow, gradually fill the trench with soil until even with surrounding soil. Or sow seeds 1 inch deep and 3 inches apart.

SOIL: Any good garden soil. pH 6.5 to 8.0.

FERTILIZER: At planting time, apply a fertilizer slightly higher in phosphorus (8-10-8, for example); use 4 pounds of fertilizer per 100 square feet. Side-dress with the same fertilizer in late July to early August; use 1½ pounds per 100-foot row. After the first year, apply fertilizer once in the spring before the shoots emerge and again just after harvest.

WATER:
How much: Apply enough water at each irrigation to wet the soil 1 to 1½ feet deep.
How often: Water when soil is just barely moist.

HARVEST: Asparagus must grow for 2 years before harvesting. In the spring of the third year, pick when the spears are 7 to 10 inches tall with tight heads. To avoid wounding the crown, snap the spears; do not tear or cut them. Harvest for 2 weeks. The fourth year, pick for 4 weeks; the fifth and following years, for 8 weeks. In California, harvest for 4, 8, and 12 weeks, respectively.

Small spears.

PROBLEM: Spears are small and skinny.

ANALYSIS: Small spears
Asparagus spears may be small for any of several reasons.
1. *Insufficient nutrients:* Undernourished plants cannot produce adequate fern growth and food for next year's crop.
2. *Immature plants:* Asparagus crowns produce small spears for the first two or three years following planting.
3. *Poor drainage:* Asparagus plants do not produce well in poorly drained soil.
4. *Overharvested plants:* When harvest continues late in the season, the plants are unable to produce enough foliage and do not store enough food for next year's crop.

SOLUTION: Follow the growing and harvesting guidelines.

Crooked spears.

PROBLEM: Spears are crooked or misshapen.

ANALYSIS: Crooked spears
Asparagus spears grow crooked when the growing shoot is damaged by insects (especially the asparagus beetle—see page 263), cultivation wounds on the crown, or windblown sand that pelts the tender shoots. The injured side grows more slowly than the uninjured side, causing the stem to curve. Although the spears are misshapen, they are still edible.

SOLUTION: Control asparagus beetles. To avoid wounding the crown, do not cultivate closer to it than 2 inches. Use tall plants or fencing as a windbreak to prevent "sandblasting."

For gourmet white asparagus spears, blanch the emerging shoots in the spring by mounding 10 to 12 inches of soil over the plants as the first shoots appear. When the spear tips emerge through the hill of soil, harvest by carefully digging down about 8 inches and cutting the spear with a sharp knife. Use the spears fresh or cooked.

Damaged spear.

Fusarium wilt.

Larvae. *Insert:* Adults (2 times life size).

PROBLEM: Spears turn brown and may be soft, or they may dry and wither.

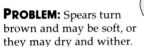

ANALYSIS: Freeze injury

Asparagus is the earliest vegetable in the spring garden and is sometimes damaged by spring frosts. The damage may not be noticed in the early morning following the frost, but as the temperature warms through the day the tissue discolors and softens. Damaged spears then dry rapidly as temperatures rise and humidity drops. A slight freeze injury may result in a crooked spear or slightly damaged spear tip. For information on other causes of crooked spears, see page 262.

SOLUTION:
Harvest and discard frost-damaged spears. When night temperatures below 32° F are predicted, protect the spears with a mulch of straw, newspaper, or leaves. Remove the mulch in the morning.

PROBLEM: The growing shoot turns yellow to dingy brown and wilts.

During wet weather, white or pink cottonlike strands often appear under the leaf scales. Wilting is most severe among full-grown plants during the months of July and August. Digging up an affected plant reveals a root system that is partially or totally reddish. The plant eventually dies.

ANALYSIS: Fusarium wilt

This wilt disease is caused by one of several fungi (*Fusarium* species). Asparagus plants under stress from poor growing conditions (such as drought, poor drainage, or insect or disease injury) are more severely affected than healthy plants. Fusarium-wilt fungi live on organic matter in the soil. The disease is spread by contaminated seeds, plants, soil, and equipment; it often enters a garden on the roots of a transplant. The fungi enter a plant through the roots and spread up into the stems and leaves through the water-conducting vessels. The vessels become plugged and discolored, and water flow to the leaves is blocked. Wet weather and temperatures from 70° to 85° F favor fusarium wilt.

SOLUTION:
No chemical control is available. The best course is to destroy infected plants. Next year, plant healthy crowns where asparagus has not been planted for two to four years. If you plant in infected soil, fumigate the soil with metam-sodium (VAPAM®) about three weeks before planting.

PROBLEM: The tips of young asparagus spears are chewed and scarred.

Chewing continues as and after the spears develop into asparagus ferns. Small (¼-inch) metallic blue or black beetles with yellow markings and a narrow red head feed on the tips of the spears and on the ferns and stems. Reddish orange beetles with black spots may be present. Shiny black specks are found on the spear tips. Humpbacked orange or slate-gray grubs may also be seen.

ANALYSIS: Asparagus beetles or spotted asparagus beetles
(*Crioceris asparagi* or *Crioceris duodecimpunctata*)

These two beetles injure asparagus plants all through the growing season. The blue-black asparagus beetle is found throughout the United States. The orange and black spotted asparagus beetle is found east of the Mississippi River. The beetles are a particular problem when young asparagus shoots emerge in the spring. Both adults and grubs injure the plants by feeding on shoots, ferns, and stems. This feeding robs the root system of food manufactured in the foliage and necessary for healthy growth next year.

SOLUTION:
When the beetles are first noticed, apply an insecticide containing pyrethrins or rotenone. Repeat the application every 2 to 3 days as long as the beetles or grubs are feeding. Also treat the fern growth in late summer or early fall to prevent adults from overwintering on the ferns and reinfesting next year's crop.

ASPARAGUS ■ **BEANS**

Rust.

PROBLEM: Tops turn yellow, then brown; they die back in early summer to midsummer. Reddish brown, orange, or black blisters appear on the ferns and stems. Spears mature earlier than usual.

ANALYSIS: Rust

This plant disease is caused by a fungus (*Puccinia asparagi*). This year's rust weakens the plant by reducing the amount of food manufactured in the leaves to be stored in the roots. Since this stored food supplies the energy for next year's crop, fewer shoots are produced the following year. Damage is most severe when the tops are attacked several years in a row. In severe cases, the plants die. Warm temperatures and high humidity from fog, heavy dew, or overhead watering favor rust infection. Rust spores from diseased tops that have been left in the garden infect new shoots as they emerge in the spring. The wind spreads the spores from plant to plant.

SOLUTION: After the harvest, spray the ferns and stems with a fungicide containing captan. Repeat the treatment at intervals of 10 days when weather conditions favor rust infection. Do not spray while spears are still being harvested. Cut the tops down close to the ground after they die in the fall; destroy them. Don't add them to the compost pile or leave them lying around the garden. If you plant more asparagus, select rust-resistant varieties.

Asparagus varieties resistant to rust: California 500, Martha Washington, Mary Washington, and Waltham Washington.

BEANS

ADAPTATION: Throughout the United States.

PLANTING TIME: Varies from February through May, depending on date of last frost in your area.

PLANTING METHOD: Sow seeds 1 to 1½ inches deep and 1 to 2 inches apart. Thin to 2 to 4 inches apart when the seedlings have their first set of leaves.

SOIL: Any good garden soil, somewhat friable for easy seedling emergence. pH 6.0 to 8.0.

FERTILIZER: At planting time, apply a fertilizer slightly higher in phosphorus (8-10-8, for example); use 3 pounds per 100 square feet or 1 pound per 25-foot row. Side-dress every 3 to 4 weeks with 1 pound per 25-foot row.

WATER:
How much: Apply enough water to wet the soil 8 to 10 inches deep.
How often: Water when soil is just barely moist.

HARVEST: Pick beans when they are ready. If overmature beans remain on the plants, production is greatly reduced. Break beans from the vines, being careful not to jerk or tear the vines. Refrigerate beans until using them.
Harvesting times:
Snap (green) beans: When the seed in the pod begins to swell.
Lima beans: When the pods are well filled but still bright green.

Mexican bean beetle (2 times life size).

PROBLEM: The tissue between leaf veins is eaten, giving the leaves a lacelike appearance. Copper-colored beetles about ¼ inch long feed on the undersides of the skeletonized leaves. The beetles have 16 black spots on their backs. Orange to yellow soft-bodied grubs about ⅓ inch long, with black-tipped spines on their backs, may also be present. Leaves dry up, and the plant may die.

ANALYSIS: Mexican bean beetles
(*Epilachna varivestis*)
Beetles of this species are found throughout the United States. They prefer lima beans but also feed on pole and bush beans and cowpeas. Feeding damage by both adults and larvae can reduce pod production. The adult beetles spend the winter in plant debris in the garden and emerge in late spring and early summer. The females lay yellow eggs on the undersides of the leaves. Larvae that hatch from these eggs, in early to midsummer, are green at first, then gradually turn yellow. There are one to four generations per year. Frequently, beetles at all stages of maturity appear at the same time throughout the season. Hot, dry summers and cold winters reduce beetle populations.

SOLUTION: When the adults first appear, apply an insecticide containing carbaryl (SEVIN®) or diazinon. Be sure to spray the undersides of the leaves, where the insects feed. Early treatment to control the adults may save applications later to control the larvae, which are more damaging and harder to kill. After the harvest remove and destroy all plant debris to reduce overwintering spots for adults.

Bean leaf beetle (5 times life size).

Anthracnose spots.

Halo blight.

PROBLEM: Holes are chewed in leaves. Yellow to red beetles with black spots and a black band around the outer edge of the body feed on the undersides of foliage. The plant may later turn yellow and wilt. Pulling the plant up may reveal slender white grubs, up to ⅓ inch long, feeding on the roots and stem.

ANALYSIS: Bean leaf beetles
(*Cerotoma trifurcata*)
This widely distributed insect species attacks all beans, as well as peas. Throughout the growing season, adult beetles feed on the undersides of leaves, blossoms, and pods. Grubs feed on the roots and stems below the soil line. Female beetles lay clusters of orange eggs on the soil at the bases of plants. The grubs that hatch from these eggs attack the plant below the soil, feeding on the roots and sometimes girdling the stem at soil level. This feeding can kill the plant. Both adults and grubs cause serious damage to young plants. There are one to three generations per year.

SOLUTION: At the first sign of damage, apply an insecticide containing carbaryl (SEVIN®) or diazinon. Be sure to spray the undersides of the leaves, where the beetles feed. Respray at intervals of 7 to 10 days whenever damage occurs. At the end of the season, clean all debris from the garden to eliminate overwintering spots for adults.

PROBLEM: Small brown specks on pods enlarge to black, circular, sunken spots. In wet weather, a salmon-colored ooze appears in the infected spots. Elongated dark reddish brown spots appear on the stems and veins on the undersides of the leaves. If seedlings are attacked, the stems may rot or the first young leaves may be spotted. In either case, the seedlings die.

ANALYSIS: Bean anthracnose
This plant disease is caused by a fungus (*Colletotrichum lindemuthianum*) that affects all kinds of beans but is most destructive on lima beans. It occurs in the eastern and central states, rarely west of the Rocky Mountains. Fungi of this species thrive in cool, wet weather. The salmon-colored ooze that often appears in the infected spots during wet weather consists of slime spores. The spores are carried to healthy plants by animals, people, tools, or splashing water. The fungi live on diseased bean seeds and on plant debris that has been left in the garden.

SOLUTION: When the beans flower, apply a fungicide containing chlorothalonil. Repeat 3 more times at intervals of 7 to 10 days. Continue treatments whenever wet weather occurs. Remove and destroy any diseased plants. The disease spreads rapidly on moist foliage, so do not work in the garden when the plants are wet. To avoid reintroducing bean anthracnose into your garden, purchase seeds from a reputable seed company. Do not plant beans in the infected area for 2 or 3 years. Plant beans in a different site every year.

PROBLEM: Small, water-soaked spots appear on leaves. These spots enlarge, turn brown, and may kill the foliage. In cool weather, narrow greenish yellow halos may border the infected spots. The leaves either turn yellow and die slowly or turn brown rapidly and drop off. Long reddish lesions may girdle the stem. In moist conditions, a tan or yellow ooze is produced in spots on pods.

ANALYSIS: Bacterial blights
Two widespread bacterial blights on beans are common blight (caused by *Xanthomonas phaseoli*) and halo blight (caused by *Pseudomonas phaseolicola*). These bacteria attack all kinds of beans. Common blight is more severe in warm, moist weather; halo blight is favored by cool temperatures. The bacteria are usually introduced into a garden on infected seeds, and can live on infected plant debris in the soil for as long as two years. They are spread by rain, splashing water, and contaminated tools. The bacteria multiply rapidly in humid weather. If the water-conducting tissue is invaded, bacteria and dead cells eventually clog the veins, causing leaf discoloration. Bacteria, in the form of a yellow or cream-colored mass, often ooze from infected spots.

SOLUTION: There are no chemical controls for bacterial blights. Avoid overhead watering. Do not work with the beans when the plants are wet. Do not plant beans in the same area more often than every third year. Purchase new seeds each year from a reputable company.

BEANS

Rust.

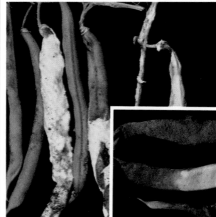

White mold. *Insert:* Gray mold.

Hopperburn. *Insert:* Leafhopper (3 times life size).

PROBLEM: Rust-colored spots form, mostly on the undersides of leaves. Severely infected leaves turn yellow, wilt, dry, and fall off. Stems and pods may also have spots.

ANALYSIS: Bean rust

This plant disease is caused by a fungus (*Uromyces phaseoli*) that infects bean plants only. It is most common on mature plants and most damaging to pole beans and lima beans. Scarlet runner beans are sometimes mildly affected. Each rust spot develops thousands of spores that are spread by wind and splashing water. The disease develops rapidly during periods of cool nights and warm days. High humidity from rain, dew, or watering also encourages rust. Heavy vine growth that shades the ground and prevents air circulation produces ideal conditions for the disease. At the end of the summer, when the nights are long, the bean-rust fungi produce another type of spore. These thick-walled black spores spend the winter on infected bean-plant debris.

SOLUTION: At the first sign of the disease, apply a fungicide containing chlorothalonil. Weekly applications may be necessary if conditions favorable to the disease continue. Avoid overhead irrigation. Water in the morning rather than the evening to allow wet foliage to dry quickly. Thin seedlings and space plants far enough apart to allow air to circulate freely. In the fall, remove and destroy all infected plants to prevent the fungi from surviving and reinfecting in the spring. Do not plant beans in the same area more often than every third year unless you plant resistant varieties.

PROBLEM: Soft, watery spots appear on stems, leaves, or pods. Under moist conditions, these spots enlarge rapidly. A fuzzy gray, gray-brown, or white mold forms on the infected tissue. Small, hard, black, seedlike structures may be embedded in the white mold. Bean plants may yellow, wilt, and die. Rotted pods are soft and mushy.

ANALYSIS: Mold

Mold on beans is caused by one of two related fungi. One fungus, *Sclerotinia sclerotiorum*, is responsible for white mold, also known as watery soft rot. White-mold fungi form dark, seedlike structures that can drop to the soil and survive through adverse conditions to infect bean crops for the next few years. The fungus *Botrytis cinerea* is responsible for gray mold. Gray-mold fungi produce tan to gray-brown fungal strands. Both fungi often attack weak or dead plant parts, such as old blossoms. Once established on a plant, these diseases can be spread to healthy plants by wind or splashing water or by contact between infected plants and healthy ones. Mold spreads quickly in cool, wet weather.

SOLUTION: Remove and destroy all diseased plants as soon as symptoms appear. Then spray healthy foliage with a fungicide containing benomyl or chlorothalonil. Water plants early in the day. Avoid wetting plant foliage. Do not plant beans in the affected area for 3 to 4 years. Until then, plant unsusceptible vegetables, such as corn, beets, Swiss chard, or spinach. Always plant beans in well-drained soil. To improve air flow, avoid overcrowding.

PROBLEM: Leaves are stippled. Some are scorched, with a green midrib and brown edges curled under. Spotted, pale green, winged insects up to ⅛ inch long hop, run, or fly away quickly when the plant is touched.

ANALYSIS: Hopperburn

Hopperburn is a plant disease caused by the potato leafhopper (*Empoasca fabae*), which injects a toxin into leaves as it feeds. Bean yields may be drastically reduced from hopperburn. Leafhoppers are active throughout the growing season. They hatch in the spring from eggs laid on perennial weeds and ornamental plants. Even areas that have winters so cold that the eggs cannot survive are not free from infestation, because leafhoppers migrate in the spring from warmer regions.

SOLUTION: At the first sign of damage, treat infested plants with an insecticide containing carbaryl (SEVIN®), diazinon, insecticidal soap, malathion, or pyrethrins. Be sure to cover the undersides of the leaves, where the leafhoppers feed. Respray as necessary to keep the insects under control. Allow at least 10 days between applications.

Fusarium root rot.

Bean yellow mosaic.

Flea beetle (5 times life size).

PROBLEM: Leaves turn yellow. Overall growth is slow, and the plant may be dwarfed. In hot, dry weather the plant suddenly wilts and sometimes dies. Few pods are produced. Red spots or streaks may be seen on stems and roots. Underground stems may be streaked dark brown or black.

ANALYSIS: Root rot
This plant disease is caused by any of several soil-inhabiting fungi (*Fusarium* species, *Pythium* species, and *Rhizoctonia solani*) that attack bean plants and many other vegetables. The fungi live in the soil, invading the plant through the roots and underground stem. As the disease progresses, the roots decay and shrivel. The leaves turn yellow, and growth slows. The plant becomes dwarfed, wilts, and sometimes dies. Under favorable growing conditions, the bean plants may grow new side roots to replace the rotted ones. These plants will survive, but the yield will be reduced. Root rots develop most rapidly at soil temperatures between 60° and 85° F.

SOLUTION: There is no completely effective chemical control for this problem. Pull out and discard wilted plants. Change the bean site yearly. If this is not practical, use a fungicide containing captan or PCNB at planting time; in each row sprinkle 1 teaspoon of fungicide for each 20 feet. Plant in well-drained soil and let the soil surface dry out between waterings.

PROBLEM: Leaves are mottled yellow and green. They may be puckered and longer and narrower than usual. Raised dark areas develop along the central vein, and the leaf edges curl downward. The whole plant is stunted. Pods on affected plants may be faded, rough, and few in number. The seeds inside are shriveled and small. The damage is most severe when the temperature is between 60° and 75° F.

ANALYSIS: Bean common mosaic and bean yellow mosaic
Both these widespread plant diseases are caused by viruses. Common mosaic virus affects only French and snap beans; yellow mosaic virus affects lima beans, peas, summer squash, clover, gladiolus, and some other perennial flowers. Both diseases are spread by aphids, which transmit the virus as they feed. In warmer parts of the United States, where aphid populations are large, the diseases spread rapidly. Common bean mosaic is also spread in infected seeds. If the infection occurs early in the season, when the plants are young, the plants may not bear pods. Infection later in the season does not affect pod production as severely.

SOLUTION: There are no chemical controls for plant viruses. To reduce the aphid population and the spread of disease, treat the plants as soon as the insects appear; use an insecticide containing diazinon or malathion. Remove all infected plants and all clover plants in the vicinity of the garden. Plant virus-resistant varieties of beans.

PROBLEM: Leaves are riddled with shot holes about ⅛ inch in diameter. Tiny (¹⁄₁₆-inch) black beetles jump like fleas when disturbed. Leaves of seedlings and, eventually, whole plants may wilt and die.

ANALYSIS: Flea beetles
These beetles jump like fleas but are not related to them. Both adult and immature flea beetles feed on a wide variety of garden vegetables. Immature beetles, legless gray grubs, injure plants by feeding on the roots and the undersides of leaves. Adults chew holes in leaves. Flea beetles are most damaging to seedlings and young plants. Seedling leaves riddled with holes dry out quickly and die. Adult beetles spend the winter in soil and garden debris. They emerge in early spring to feed on weeds until vegetables sprout or plants are set in the garden. Grubs hatch from eggs laid in the soil, and these pests feed for two to three weeks. After pupating in the soil, they emerge as adults to repeat the cycle. There are one to four generations each year. Adults may feed for up to two months.

SOLUTION: When the leaves first show damage, control flea beetles with an insecticide containing carbaryl (SEVIN®) or methoxychlor. Watch new growth for further evidence of feeding, and repeat the treatment at weekly intervals as needed. Remove all plant debris from the garden after the harvest to eliminate overwintering areas for the adult beetle.

BEETS ▪

Leafminer damage.

Cercospora leaf spot.

Curly top.

PROBLEM: Light-colored, irregular blotches, blisters, or tunnels appear in leaves. Brown areas peel apart easily, like facial tissue. Tiny black specks are found inside the tunnels.

ANALYSIS: Beet leafminers
(*Pegomya hyoscyami*)
These insect pests belong to a family of leafmining flies. The tiny black or yellow adult female fly lays her white eggs on the underside of a leaf. When the eggs hatch, the cream-colored maggots bore into the leaf. They tunnel between its surfaces, feeding on the inner tissue. The tunnels and blotches are called mines. The black specks inside are the maggot's droppings. The beet leaves are no longer edible, but the root is. Several generations occur during the growing season, so larvae are present continually from spring until fall.

SOLUTION: When the white egg clusters are first seen under the leaves, spray with an insecticide containing malathion or diazinon. Repeat 2 more times at weekly intervals to control succeeding generations. Once the miners enter the leaves, the sprays are ineffective; spraying after the miners appear controls only those leafminers that attack after the application. Leafminers are not active in the fall and winter. So, if beets grow in your area in the colder seasons, avoid leafminer damage by raising the plants at these times.

PROBLEM: Leaves have small, circular, distinct spots with dark borders. These spots may run together to form blotches or dead areas. The leaves often turn yellow and die. Spotting is most severe in warm, humid weather, when a fine gray mold may cover the infected tissue. Older leaves are more severely affected than younger ones.

ANALYSIS: Leaf spot
This disease is caused by a common, destructive fungus (*Cercospora beticola*) that attacks beet, spinach, and Swiss chard plants. Fungi of this species invade the leaves but not the beet root. However, severe infection damages many leaves and hinders root development. The spotting makes the leaves unappetizing. Infection is spread by wind, contaminated tools, and splashing water and is favored by moist conditions and high temperatures. Leaf spot is most common during the summer months and in warm areas. These fungi survive the winter on plant debris not cleaned out of the garden.

SOLUTION: Picking off and destroying the first spotted leaves retards the spread of leaf spot. Leaf spot on beets seldom causes enough damage to warrant fungicide sprays. If your planting is large or the disease becomes severe, however, spray weekly with a fungicide containing captan or chlorothalonil. Do not work among wet plants. If possible, avoid overhead watering; use drip or furrow irrigation instead. Use a mulch to reduce the need for watering. Clean all plant debris from the garden after the harvest to reduce the number of overwintering spores.

PROBLEM: Leaf edges roll upward and feel brittle. The undersides of the leaves are rough, with puckering along the veins. The leaves and roots are stunted; the plant may die. Insect swarms may be seen hovering around plants.

ANALYSIS: Curly top
This plant disease is caused by a virus that infects many vegetable plants, including beets, beans, tomatoes, squash, and melons. The virus is transmitted from plant to plant by the beet leafhopper (*Circulifer tenellus*) and is common only in the West, where this insect lives. The beet leafhopper, a pale greenish yellow insect about ⅛ inch long, feeds from early May through June. It sucks the sap and virus from infected leaves and then injects the virus into healthy plants at its next feeding stop. Curly-top symptoms vary in severity, depending on the variety and the age of the plant. Young infected plants usually die; older plants may turn yellow and die.

SOLUTION: There is no direct control for curly top. To reduce the chance of infection, control the beet leafhopper; when the insect swarms first appear, spray with an insecticide containing insecticidal soap or malathion. Destroy infected plants. Cheesecloth over the plants keeps leafhoppers from landing on them.

BLUEBERRIES

BRAMBLES

Cranberry fruitworms (¾ life size).

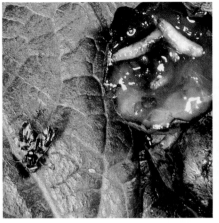

Blueberry maggots and adult (2 times life size).

BRAMBLES (BLACKBERRIES, RASPBERRIES)

PROBLEM: Clusters of berries are webbed together with silk. Berries may be shriveled and full of sawdustlike material. Inside the berries are smooth pink-red or pale yellow-green caterpillars about ⅜ to 1 inch long.

ANALYSIS: Cherry fruitworms or cranberry fruitworms

(*Grapholitha packardii* or *Acrobasis vaccinii*) These two fruitworms are serious pests of blueberries and cranberries. They also attack cherries and apples. Each caterpillar destroys two to six berries. They do not damage the leaves. In midspring, the adult female moths lay eggs on developing berries and leaves. The caterpillars that hatch from these eggs bore into the berries at the junction of the stem and berry. When they are about half grown, the fruitworms move to another berry, usually one touching the infested berry. In this way the fruitworm moves to a new food source without exposing itself. About mid-June, when the caterpillar is full grown, it crawls to the soil, garden debris, or a pruning stub, where it remains through the remainder of the growing season and the winter. Adult moths emerge in midspring to start the cycle again.

SOLUTION: Once the fruit is infested there is no way to kill the worms inside. Hand-pick and destroy all infested fruit. If your planting is large or if the fruitworm infestation is severe, spray the plants immediately after bloom, before the berries are ¼ inch in diameter, with an insecticide containing diazinon. Respray 10 days later.

PROBLEM: Ripening blueberries leak juice and are soft and mushy. White, tapered maggots about ⅜ inch long are feeding inside the berries.

ANALYSIS: Blueberry maggots

(*Rhagoletis mendax*) These insects, also called blueberry fruitflies, are the most significant pest of blueberries in the Midwest and on the East Coast. Maggots attack both green and ripe fruit and often ruin an entire crop. They are most severe after unusually cold winters and when the weather is quite wet at harvest time, making frequent pickings impossible. The maggots spend the winter as pupae in the soil. From late June through August, the adult female flies lay eggs just under the skin of the fruit. The maggots that hatch from the eggs feed in the berry for about 20 days, then drop to the soil where they pupate for one to two years. The insects produce only one generation each year.

SOLUTION: Harvest frequently, destroying any infested berries. Next year, beginning in early July, treat the plants with an insecticide containing diazinon. Repeat the treatment, at intervals of 10 days, through the harvest. Treatments the following year may be necessary to control any pupae that mature after 2 years.

Blueberry cultural information

Planting method: Plant 3 or more varieties. Prune plants back to 3 or 4 strong shoots. Set so top of rootball is 1 to 2 inches deeper than surrounding soil. Mulch.
Water: When soil is barely moist.
Harvest: When berries are solid blue with a whitish glow.

ADAPTATION: Throughout the United States.

PLANTING TIME: Late fall or early spring.

PLANTING METHOD: Select 1-year-old dormant plants that are 12 to 24 inches tall. Set plants 3 to 6 feet apart and deep enough so that the top of the rootball is 1 inch deeper than the surrounding garden soil. Prune canes back to 6- to 12-inch stubs.

SOIL: Any good garden soil that is high in organic matter. pH 5.5 to 6.8. Select a well-drained site.

FERTILIZER: At planting time, apply a general-purpose fertilizer (10-10-10, for example); use 1 pound per 20-foot row. Thereafter, apply 2 pounds per 20-foot row once a year in early spring, before new growth begins.

WATER:
How much: Apply enough water at each irrigation to wet the soil 1 to 2 feet deep.
How often: Water when soil 2 inches deep is barely moist.

HARVEST: Berries are ripe when they are a deep, rich color and slightly soft. Ripe fruit is easily removed when pulled gently. When picked, only raspberries pull free of their central core. All other bramble fruits have a central core. Pick every 2 to 3 days. Protect ripening fruit from birds by using netting available in your garden center or through mail-order garden-supply companies. Store berries in the refrigerator until use.

BRAMBLES (BLACKBERRIES, RASPBERRIES)

Cane blight on raspberry.

Crown gall on blackberry.

Powdery mildew on raspberry.

PROBLEM: Branches wilt and die in mid-summer. Brownish purple areas occur on pruned ends or wounded areas of canes and extend downward, sometimes encircling the stem. Infected canes turn gray in late summer.

ANALYSIS: Cane blight
This plant disease is caused by a fungus (*Leptosphaeria coniothyrium*). It is more prevalent on black raspberries than on red and purple raspberries and blackberries. Fungi of this species spend the winter on diseased canes. The spores are spread from plant to plant by the wind. In wet weather in late spring and early summer, the spores enter canes through cracks in the bark, broken fruit stems, and wounds from pruning and insects. The spores don't infect young tissue directly. Canes weakened from cane blight are susceptible to winter injury.

SOLUTION: In late fall and early spring, apply a dormant disease control containing calcium polysulfide. Follow with 2 applications of a fungicide containing ferbam: one just before bloom, when the new canes are 1½ to 2 feet tall, and the other just after harvest. Remove infected canes before growth starts in the spring. Prune just above a bud in dry weather at least 3 days before rain, so the wounds have time to dry.

PROBLEM: Plants are stunted; break and fall over easily; and produce dry, seedy berries. Irregular, wartlike growths (galls) may appear on canes. The canes may dry out and crack. Galls also occur just below the soil level on roots and crown. The galls range from pinhead-sized to several inches in diameter, and they are white or grayish brown.

ANALYSIS: Cane gall or crown gall
These plant diseases are caused by one of two bacteria (*Agrobacterium rubi* or *A. tumefaciens*) that occur on blackberries, raspberries, boysenberries, loganberries, and youngberries throughout the United States. The plants become weak and produce fewer berries. The bacteria are often brought into a garden on the roots of an infected plant, and they are spread with the soil and by contaminated pruning tools. The bacteria enter the plant through wounds in the roots or the base of the stem (the crown). They produce a substance that stimulates rapid cell growth in the plant, causing gall formation on the roots, crown, and canes. The galls disrupt the flow of water and nutrients up the roots and stems, weakening and stunting the top of the plant. Galls do not usually cause the plant to die.

SOLUTION: Crown gall cannot be eliminated from the plant. Although infected plants may survive for many years, they will produce few berries. Dig up the soil within 6 inches of a gall and discard it along with the diseased plants. Wait at least 3 years before replanting brambles in areas where the disease has occurred. Plant gall-free plants in clean soil. Prune and cultivate carefully to avoid wounding plants.

PROBLEM: A whitish gray powder covers the leaves, fruit, and young growing tips of the canes. Canes may be dwarfed or distorted. Fruit may wither and die.

ANALYSIS: Powdery mildew
This common plant disease seriously affects red raspberries and occasionally attacks purple and black raspberries and blackberries. It is caused by a fungus (*Sphaerotheca humuli*) that thrives in both humid and dry weather. The powdery patches consist of fungal strands and spores. The spores are spread by the wind to healthy plants. The fungi sap plant nutrients, causing yellowing and sometimes the death of leaves. A severe infection may kill the plant. Since this powdery mildew attacks many different kinds of plants, the fungi from a diseased plant may infect other types of plants in the garden. Under conditions favorable to powdery mildew, infection can spread through a closely spaced planting of berries in a matter of days or weeks.

SOLUTION: When the blossoms first open, spray the plants with a fungicide containing benomyl or with a lime-sulfur spray. Respray at weekly intervals if the plants become reinfected. Next fall and again in spring as the buds begin to swell, spray the plants with a lime-sulfur spray. Space the plants far enough apart to allow adequate air circulation; they should dry rapidly after rain or watering.

Red raspberry varieties resistant to powdery mildew: Chilcotin, Heritage, Meeker, Sumner, Willamette.

■ **CABBAGE FAMILY**

Orange rust on blackberry.

PROBLEM: Leaves are dwarfed, misshapen, and yellowish. Blisterlike pustules and bright orange dust cover the undersides of the foliage.

ANALYSIS: Orange rust
This plant disease is caused by a fungus (*Gymnoconia peckiana*). Its effect on wild and cultivated blackberries and dewberries is severe. It sometimes attacks black raspberries but doesn't affect red and purple raspberries. The disease spreads throughout the entire plant. Infected plants never recover and never bloom. Orange spores are produced on the plant each year after it is infected. The spores spread on the wind from plant to plant. In the spring, the fungi spread throughout the plant into the canes, crown, and roots. The disease spreads into new shoots as the plant grows.

SOLUTION: Fungicide sprays and pruning are not effective. Remove and destroy infected plants as soon as they are noticed. Remove any wild blackberries growing nearby. Thin the plants to provide adequate air circulation. Pull out all weeds. Grow rust-resistant varieties.

Blackberry varieties resistant to orange rust: Boysenberry, Ebony King, Eldorado, Lawton, Orange Evergreen, Youngberry. Leucretia is a rust-resistant dewberry.

CABBAGE FAMILY (BROCCOLI, BRUSSELS SPROUTS, CABBAGE, CAULIFLOWER, CHINESE CABBAGE, COLLARDS, KALE, KOHLRABI)

ADAPTATION: Throughout the United States.

PLANTING TIME: Varies from January to mid-May, depending on date of last frost in your region.

PLANTING METHOD: Set transplants so the tops of their rootballs are even with the garden soil.
   Spacing: Cabbage, cauliflower, and broccoli—15 to 24 inches apart; brussels sprouts—30 to 36 inches apart; kohlrabi—4 to 6 inches apart; kale and collards—8 to 12 inches apart. Or sow seeds ½ to 1 inch deep and 1 inch apart, then thin according to the preceding spacings when the seedlings have 2 or 3 leaves.

SOIL: Any good garden soil. pH 6.0 to 7.0.

FERTILIZER: At planting time, apply a fertilizer slightly higher in phosphorus (8-10-8, for example); use 2 to 4 pounds per 100 square feet or 1 pound per 25-foot row. Side-dress every 3 to 4 weeks with 1 pound per 25-foot row or 1 to 2 tablespoons per plant.

WATER:
   How much: Apply enough water at each irrigation to wet the soil 8 to 10 inches deep.
   How often: Water when soil 1 inch deep is barely moist.

HARVEST:
   Broccoli: When the buds are still tight, before they open into yellow flowers. Smaller heads will grow along the stem after the first head is harvested.
   Brussels sprouts: Pick sprouts from the bottom up when they are about 1 inch in diameter and still tight. Remove the leaves as you pick.
   Cabbage: Cut just below the head when it is firm and before it cracks.
   Cauliflower: Cut when the head is 6 to 8 inches in diameter with tight curds.
   Chinese cabbage: Cut the entire head when it is 12 to 16 inches tall.
   Collards and kale: Pick the leaves when the plant is 1 foot tall. Or the entire plant may be harvested. Kale flavor improves after a freeze.
   Kohlrabi: Harvest when the bulb is 2 to 3 inches in diameter.

CABBAGE FAMILY

Bolting broccoli.

Imported cabbageworm. *Insert:* Adult (life size).

Diamondback moth larvae (life size).

PROBLEM: In hot weather, an elongated stalk with flowers (a seed stalk) grows from the main stem of broccoli, cauliflower, or brussels sprouts plants. On cabbage, the head splits open, and the stalk emerges from within.

ANALYSIS: Bolting
Bolting, or seed stalk formation, results from exposure of the plants to cold temperatures early in their lives. Once a plant has matured to the point where its leaves are about 2 inches wide, exposure to temperatures from 40° to 50° F for several days in a row causes flower buds to form within the growing point. These buds remain dormant until hot weather arrives. With the arrival of hot weather, the buds develop into tall flower stalks. As the plant bolts, its flavor deteriorates and bitterness develops.

SOLUTION: Discard plants that have bolted. Avoid setting out plants too early in the winter or spring. If cabbage plants are set out in the fall or winter, harvest them before hot weather causes them to bolt. Cutting the flower stalk will not prevent poor flavor from developing.

PROBLEM: Round or irregular holes appear in leaves. Green worms up to 1½ inches long, with light stripes down their backs, feed on the leaves or heads. Masses of green or brown pellets may be found between the leaves. Cabbage and cauliflower heads may be tunnelled.

ANALYSIS: Cabbageworms
These destructive worms are either cabbage loopers (*Trichoplusia ni*) or imported cabbageworms (*Pieris rapae*). Both attack all members of the cabbage family, as well as lettuce. Adult females lay eggs throughout the growing season. The brownish cabbage looper moths lay pale green eggs on the topsides of leaves in the evening. Mature imported cabbageworms are white butterflies that are frequently seen around cabbage plants in the daytime. The females attach yellow, bullet-shaped eggs to the undersides of leaves. Cabbageworms may be present from early spring until late fall; in the southern United States, they may be present all year. Worms spend the winter as pupae attached to a plant or nearby object.

SOLUTION: As soon as damage is seen, control cabbageworms with an insecticide containing carbaryl (SEVIN®), diazinon, pyrethrins, insecticidal soap, or rotenone. Cabbageworms can also be killed with *Bacillus thuringiensis*, a biological control, while the worms are small. Repeat treatments weekly as long as worms are found, but stop 3 days before harvest. To destroy the pupae, remove plant debris after harvest.

PROBLEM: Small holes and transparent patches appear in leaves. Small (¼-inch) green worms feed on the undersides of the foliage. When disturbed, the worms wriggle rapidly and often drop from the plant on a silken thread.

ANALYSIS: Diamondback moths
(*Plutella xylostella*)
These worms are the larvae of gray or brown moths that fly in the evening. The adults don't damage plants. The larvae, however, feed on the undersides of leaves of members of the cabbage family, chewing holes and eating. After feeding for about two weeks, the larvae pupate in transparent silken cocoons attached to the undersides of leaves. Adult moths spend the winter under plant debris. Each year a population produces two to seven generations, so diamondback moths damage both spring and fall plantings.

SOLUTION: When the young worms first appear or when the leaves show feeding damage, apply an insecticide containing insecticidal soap, Bt (*Bacillus thuringiensis*), diazinon, or pyrethrins to the foliage. The insecticide must reach the undersides of the leaves to be most effective. Repeat the treatment each week as long as the caterpillars are found. Clean up plant debris in the fall, and cultivate the soil thoroughly to expose and destroy overwintering moths.

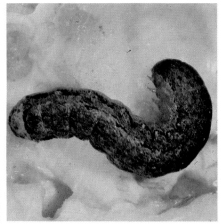

Cutworm (2 times life size).

Cabbage maggot (life size).

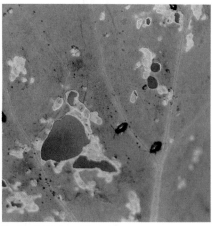

Flea beetles (2 times life size).

PROBLEM: Seedlings and young transplants are chewed or cut off near the ground. Digging near the freshly damaged plant about 2 inches down may reveal dull gray, brown, or black worms. They have spots or stripes on their smooth bodies, are about 1½ to 2 inches long, and coil when they are disturbed.

ANALYSIS: Cutworms
Several species of these moth larvae are pests in the vegetable garden. The most likely pests of young cabbage plants early in the season are surface-feeding cutworms. They spend the days hidden in the soil and feed after dark. A cutworm can sever the stems of several young plants in a single night. Adult cutworms are dark, night-flying moths with stripes on their forewings.

SOLUTION: Apply an insecticide containing diazinon, chlorpyrifos, or methoxychlor or a bait containing carbaryl (SEVIN®) around the bases of undamaged plants in areas where stem cutting is observed. Since cutworms are difficult to control, weekly reapplications will probably be necessary. Before transplanting in an area previously full of weeds, apply a preventive treatment of diazinon or methoxychlor and work it into the soil. Further reduce damage by setting a "cutworm collar" around the stem of each plant. Make collars from stiff paper, milk cartons, tin cans, or aluminum foil. Collars should be at least 2 inches high and pressed firmly into the soil. Cultivate the soil in late summer and fall to expose and destroy eggs, pupae, and larvae.

PROBLEM: Young plants wilt in the heat of the day. They may later turn yellow and die. Soft-bodied, white maggots about ⅓ inch long feed in the roots. The roots are honeycombed with slimy channels and scarred by brown grooves. Damage is particularly severe during cool, moist weather in spring, early summer, and fall.

ANALYSIS: Cabbage maggots
(*Hylemya brassicae*)
The cabbage maggot is a significant pest in the northern United States. Early maggots attack the roots and stems of cabbage, cauliflower, broccoli, radishes, and turnips in the spring and early summer. Later insects injure late cabbage, turnips, and radishes in the fall. The adult is a gray fly, somewhat smaller than a housefly, with black stripes and bristles down its back. The female lays eggs on stems and nearby soil. The maggots hatch in two to three days and tunnel into the stems and roots of plants, sometimes to a depth of 6 inches. The cabbage maggot causes feeding damage and also spreads black-rot bacteria (see page 274).

SOLUTION: Once the growing plant wilts and turns yellow, nothing can be done. To control maggots in the next planting, mix a chemical containing diazinon or chlorpyrifos 4 to 6 inches into the soil before seeding or transplanting. Control lasts about one month. Since control depends on the maggots coming into direct contact with the insecticide, correct timing and thorough mixing are important. To prevent egg laying, screen flies from the seedbed by covering it with cheesecloth.

PROBLEM: Leaves are riddled with shot holes, about ⅛ inch in diameter. Tiny (¹⁄₁₆-inch) black beetles jump like fleas when disturbed. Leaves of seedlings and, eventually, whole plants may wilt and die.

ANALYSIS: Flea beetles
These beetles jump like fleas but are not related to them. Both adult and immature flea beetles feed on a wide variety of garden vegetables. Immature beetles, legless gray grubs, injure plants by feeding on the roots and the undersides of leaves. Adults chew holes in leaves. Flea beetles are most damaging to seedlings and young plants. Seedling leaves riddled with holes dry out quickly and die. Adult beetles spend the winter in soil and garden debris. They emerge in early spring to feed on weeds until vegetables sprout or plants are set in the garden. Grubs hatch from eggs laid in the soil, and these pests feed for two to three weeks. After pupating in the soil, they emerge as adults to repeat the cycle. There are one to four generations each year. Adults may feed up to two months.

SOLUTION: When the leaves first show damage, control flea beetles with an insecticide containing carbaryl (SEVIN®), diazinon, pyrethrins, or rotenone. Watch new growth for evidence of further damage, and repeat the treatment at weekly intervals as needed. Clean all debris from the garden after harvest to eliminate overwintering spots for adult beetles.

Aphids on cabbage (2 times life size).

Black rot.

Clubroot on kohlrabi.

PROBLEM: Some leaves are yellowed and cupped downward. Tiny (⅛-inch) pale green or gray soft-bodied insects cluster under leaves, on stems, and on heads. A shiny, sticky substance may coat the leaves. Ants may be present.

ANALYSIS: Aphids

Aphids do little damage in small numbers. However, they are extremely prolific and populations can rapidly build up to damaging numbers during the growing season. Damage occurs when the aphid sucks the juice from the plant. The aphid is unable to digest fully all the sugar in the plant sap and excretes the excess in a fluid called honeydew. The honeydew often drops onto the leaves below. Ants feed on the sticky substance and are often present where there is an aphid infestation. The most common aphid attacking the cabbage family is the cabbage aphid (*Brevicoryne brassicae*). Cabbage aphid eggs overwinter on plant debris in the garden. In the southern United States, cabbage aphids are active the year around.

SOLUTION: As soon as the insects appear, treat with an insecticide containing diazinon, malathion, insecticidal soap, or pyrethrins. Repeat at intervals of 7 days if the plant becomes reinfected. Clean all plant debris from the garden after harvest to reduce the number of overwintering eggs.

PROBLEM: Young plants turn yellow, then brown, and then die. On older plants, yellow areas develop along the leaf edges, then progress into the leaf in a V-shape; these areas later turn brown and die. Lower (older) leaves wilt and drop off. The veins running from the infected leaf edges to the center stem are black. Cutting the stem to form a cross-section reveals a black ring and, sometimes, yellow ooze.

ANALYSIS: Black rot

This plant disease is caused by a bacterium (*Xanthomonas campestris*) that affects all members of the cabbage family at any stage in their growth. Black-rot bacteria live in or on seeds or in infected plant debris for as long as two years. Insects, splashing water, and garden tools carry the infection to other leaves and plants. The bacteria enter the plant through natural openings or wounds and spread through the water- and nutrient-conducting vessels of the plant. The infected tissue may form pockets where dead cells and bacteria accumulate as a yellow ooze. Warm, humid weather favors the spread and development of the bacteria. Black rot can kill seedlings rapidly. The diseased heads are edible but unappetizing.

SOLUTION: There are no chemical controls for black rot. Discard infected plants. To avoid further infection, plant only disease-free seeds and healthy plants. Place plants far enough apart to allow adequate air circulation. Avoid overhead irrigation. Plant in soil that has not grown cabbage for at least 2 years.

PROBLEM: The plant wilts on hot, sunny days and recovers at night. The older, outer leaves turn yellow and drop. The roots are swollen and misshapen. The largest swellings are just below the soil surface. Growth slows, and the plant eventually dies.

ANALYSIS: Clubroot

This plant disease is caused by a soil-inhabiting fungus (*Plasmodiophora brassicae*) that persists in the soil for many years. Warm, moist weather, together with acidic soil, favor the infection. Clubroot fungi cause cells to grow and divide within the root tissue. This causes swelling and a general weakening of the plant, allowing other fungi and bacteria to invade the roots and cause root rot. As the roots decompose, they liberate millions of spores into the soil, where they are spread by shoes or tools or in drainage water. Most rutabaga varieties and many turnip varieties are resistant to clubroot; most members of the cabbage family are susceptible. Weeds in this family—such as mustard, pennycress, and shepherd's-purse—can also harbor the disease.

SOLUTION: Once a plant is infected, it cannot be cured. To reduce the severity of the disease next year, do not grow susceptible plants where any members of the cabbage family have grown for the past 7 years. If you must plant in infected soil, pour ¾ cup of a solution of 3 tablespoons of PCNB fungicide per gallon of water in the soil around the roots of each transplant. To discourage infection, apply garden lime to the soil until soil pH is 7.2.

CARROTS

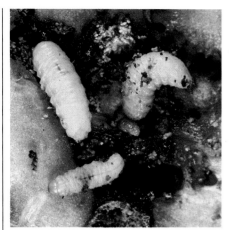

Carrot weevil larvae damage (3 times life size).

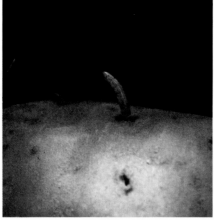

Wireworm (2 times life size).

Aster yellows. *Insert:* Infected root.

PROBLEM: The upper part of the root is scarred with zigzag tunnels. White, curved, legless grubs, about ⅓ inch long, may be found in the root and soil.

ANALYSIS: Carrot weevils
(*Listronotus oregonensis*)
These insects feed on carrots, dill, celery, parsley, and parsnips. The adult females are dark brown beetles that lay eggs in the carrot tops. In May and June the eggs hatch into white grubs, which travel down to the developing root. Here the grubs tunnel into and feed on the upper tissue, scarring the root. After a short resting period in the soil, the pests emerge as adults. A second generation hatches in August. The adults of this generation spend the winter in debris in and around the garden.

SOLUTION: No insecticides are currently registered for use on this insect pest. Some control may be obtained when spraying for leafhoppers (see page 281). Clean up garden debris in the fall to eliminate overwintering spots for the adults. Do not add infested debris to the compost pile.

Carrot cultural information
Planting method: Sow seeds ¼ inch deep and thin to 1 to 3 inches apart
Water: When soil is barely moist
Fertilizer: Vegetable food, 2 pounds per 100-foot row, every 3 to 4 weeks
Harvest: Pull any time from finger-sized until they reach size stated on seed packet

PROBLEM: Plants are stunted and grow slowly. Roots are poorly formed. Tunnels wind through the roots. Shiny, hard, jointed, creamy yellow, dark brown, or gray worms up to ⅞ inch long are in the roots and soil.

ANALYSIS: Wireworms
Wireworms attack carrot, corn, potato, beet, pea, bean, lettuce, and many other plants. They feed on underground plant parts only, devouring seeds, underground stems, tubers, and roots. Infestations are most extensive in soil where lawn grass was previously grown. The adult is known as a click beetle because it makes a clicking sound when turning from its back to its feet. The female lays eggs in the spring. After the eggs hatch, the wireworms feed for two to six years before maturing into adult beetles. All sizes and ages of wireworm may be found in soil at the same time.

SOLUTION: Just before planting, treat the soil with an insecticide containing diazinon, chlorpyrifos, or methoxychlor. Work the insecticide into the top 6 to 8 inches of soil.

PROBLEM: Inner leaves are yellow, stunted, and grow in tight bunches. Outer leaves turn rusty red to reddish purple. The roots are stunted, deformed, and have a bitter taste. Tiny hairlike roots grow in great profusion out of the main root. Numerous tiny leaves grow from the top of the root.

ANALYSIS: Aster yellows
This plant disease is caused by mycoplasmas, microscopic organisms similar to bacteria. The mycoplasmas are transmitted from plant to plant primarily by leafhoppers. The symptoms of aster yellows are more severe and appear more quickly in warm weather. Even when the disease is present in the plant, aster yellows may not manifest its symptoms in temperatures below 55° F. The disease also infects many other vegetables, ornamental plants, and weeds.

SOLUTION: Aster yellows cannot be eliminated entirely, but it can be kept under control. Remove and destroy infected plants. To remove sources of infection, eradicate nearby weeds that may harbor aster yellows and leafhopper eggs. Treat leafhopper-infested plants with a chemical containing carbaryl (SEVIN®) or malathion. Repeat the treatment whenever leafhoppers are seen.

CORN

CORN

ADAPTATION: Throughout the United States.

PLANTING TIME: Mid- to late spring.

PLANTING METHOD: Sow seeds 1 to 2 inches deep and 12 to 16 inches apart. Or set transplants so that the tops of their rootballs are even with the garden soil. Space 12 to 16 inches apart.

SOIL: Any good garden soil that is high in organic matter. pH 6.0 to 7.5.

FERTILIZER: At planting time, apply a fertilizer slightly higher in phosphorus (8-10-8, for example); use 3 pounds per 100-foot row. Side-dress with the same amount when the plants are 8 inches tall, and side-dress again when they are 18 inches tall.

WATER:
How much: Apply enough water at each irrigation to wet the soil 8 to 10 inches deep.
How often: Keep soil moist, never allowing it to dry out. Corn needs constant moisture all season, especially from tasseling to picking time.

HARVEST: Corn is generally ready to be picked 3 weeks after the silks appear. When ready, the silks become dark brown and dry. Test ripeness by pressing a kernel with your finger. If it spurts milky juice, it is ready. To pick, grab the ear at its base, bend it downward, and twist. Do not damage the main stalk. Pick corn just before cooking, because flavor deteriorates rapidly when stored.

Corn earworm (¾ life size).

PROBLEM: Striped yellow, brown, or green worms feed on the tip of the ear inside the husk. The worms range in size from ¼ to 2 inches long. Leaves may be chewed and ragged.

ANALYSIS: Corn earworms
(Heliothis zea)
These worms are the most serious pests of corn. The insects attack many other garden vegetables and flowers as well and are also known as tomato fruitworms and cotton bollworms. Corn earworms are the larvae of light gray-brown moths with dark lines on their wings. In the spring, female moths lay yellow eggs singly on corn silks and the undersides of leaves. The worms that hatch from these eggs feed on the new leaves in the whorls. This feeding doesn't reduce the corn yield, but the leaves that develop are ragged and the plant may be stunted. More serious damage is caused when the worms feed on the silks, causing poor pollination, and when they feed on the developing kernels. Worms enter the ear at the silk end, or they may bore through the husk. There are several generations a year. In the southern United States, where these pests survive the winter, early and late plantings suffer the most damage. Adult moths migrate into northern areas, where late plantings are severely damaged. Undamaged parts of infested ears are edible.

SOLUTION: Once the worms are in the ears, insecticides are ineffective. In the future, treat plants with a garden dust containing carbaryl (SEVIN®) when 10 percent of the ears show silk. Repeat the treatment 3 to 4 times at intervals of 3 days. If the infestation continues, repeat as necessary until harvest.

Armyworm (¼ life size).

PROBLEM: Leaf edges are chewed, and some leaves may be completely eaten. Light tan to dark brown caterpillars 1½ to 2 inches long—with yellow, orange, or dark brown stripes—are feeding on the leaves and may be boring into the ears.

ANALYSIS: Armyworms
Armyworms attack corn, grains, grasses, and other garden crops. These pests do not overwinter in cold-winter areas, but the moths migrate great distances in the spring as the females search for places to lay their eggs. The tan to gray adult females lay eggs on the blades of grasses and grains. The caterpillars that hatch from these eggs feed on corn leaves, ears, and ear stalks. The worms get their name from their feeding habits. After they have eaten everything in one area, they crawl in a drove to another area in search of more food. After several weeks of feeding, they pupate in the soil, then emerge as adult moths to repeat the cycle. There are several generations each year, beginning in mid-May. These pests are most numerous after cold, wet spring weather that slows the development of the natural parasites and diseases that help keep armyworm populations in check.

SOLUTION: When the worms are first seen, spray or dust with an insecticide containing carbaryl (SEVIN®) or diazinon. Four or five days may pass before results are noticeable. Repeat the treatment at weekly intervals if the plants become reinfested. To control worms that bore into the ears, spray when 10 percent of the ears show silk and repeat 3 or 4 more times at intervals of 3 days.

Poor pollination.

Corn smut.

Flea beetle (12 times life size).

PROBLEM: Corn ears are not completely filled with kernels. Plants are healthy.

ANALYSIS: Poor pollination
Poorly filled ears result from ineffective or incomplete pollination. Pollen grains produced on the tassels must fall on the sticky silks for complete pollination. Each strand of silk is attached to a kernel, so for each pollinated silk, one kernel develops. Corn pollen is spread by the wind; if the wind is blowing across a single row of corn, the pollen on the tassels is carried away from the silks, resulting in poorly filled ears. Poor pollination can also result from dry soil during pollination and from hot, dry winds. Prolonged periods of rain reduce the amount of pollen shed from the tassels. Damage to the silks from corn earworms (see page 276), rootworm adults (see page 278), armyworms (see page 276), and grasshoppers (see page 278) may also result in incomplete ears.

SOLUTION: To help ensure pollination, grow corn in blocks of at least 3 or 4 short rows rather than in 1 long row. Plant seeds 12 to 16 inches apart in rows 30 to 36 inches apart. Keep the soil moist, letting the surface dry slightly between waterings. Control insect pests. Corn can be hand-pollinated by shaking the tassels onto the silks.

PROBLEM: Galls, or puffballs, appear on the stalk, leaves, ears, or tassels. Galls are white and may be smooth, or they may be covered with a black greasy or powdery material. They range from pea-sized to 5 inches in diameter.

ANALYSIS: Corn smut
This plant disease is caused by a fungus (*Ustilago maydis*) that attacks any above-ground part of corn. Germinating seedlings are not affected. Galls are full of black powdery spores that survive the winter on or in soil, corn debris, and manure. They are spread from plant to plant by wind, water, and manure. A gall forms only where a spore lands. The disease does not spread throughout the plant. Young plants are susceptible; most plants are infected when they are from 1 to 3 feet tall. Corn is less susceptible after the ears have formed. Corn smut is most prevalent in temperatures from 80° to 95° F and when dry weather early in the season is followed by moderate rainfall as the corn matures. Stem and leaf smut doesn't reduce the corn yield directly; rather, it saps energy from the plant, reducing ear development.

SOLUTION: There are no chemical controls for this disease. Cut off galls before they release the black powdery spores. Grow corn varieties tolerant to smut. Clean all plant debris from the garden after harvest. Avoid using manure in the soil if corn smut is a problem in your garden.

PROBLEM: Leaves are riddled with shot holes about ⅛ inch in diameter. Tiny (1/16-inch) black beetles jump like fleas when disturbed. Leaves of seedlings and, eventually, whole plants may wilt and die.

ANALYSIS: Flea beetles
These beetles jump like fleas but are not related to them. Both adult and immature flea beetles feed on a wide variety of garden vegetables. Some flea beetles are responsible for spreading the bacterial wilt that kills corn plants. Immature beetles, legless gray grubs, injure plants by feeding on the roots and the undersides of leaves. Adults chew holes in leaves. Flea beetles are most damaging to seedlings and young plants. Seedling leaves riddled with holes dry out quickly and die. Adult beetles survive the winter in soil and garden debris. They emerge in early spring to feed on weeds until vegetables sprout or plants are set in the garden. Grubs hatch from eggs laid in the soil, and these pests feed for two to three weeks. After pupating in the soil, they emerge as adults to repeat the cycle. There are one to four generations each year. Adults may feed for up to two months.

SOLUTION: When the leaves first show damage, control flea beetles on corn with an insecticide containing carbaryl (SEVIN®), diazinon, or pyrethrins. Watch new growth for evidence of further damage, and repeat the treatment at weekly intervals as needed. Remove all plant debris from the garden after harvest to eliminate overwintering spots for adult beetles.

CORN

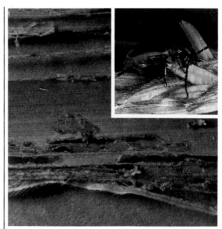

Rootworm damage. *Insert:* Adult (3 times life size).

Grasshoppers (½ life size).

European corn borer (2 times life size).

PROBLEM: Yellow, pale green, or brownish red beetles with very long antennae crawl on the plants. Some beetles may have black spots or stripes. Corn ears are malformed, with undeveloped or partially developed kernels; leaves may be chewed.

ANALYSIS: Corn rootworms
(*Diabrotica* species)
As young worms and adult beetles, these pests attack corn. For information on the larvae, see page 279. The adult beetles feed on the pollen, silks, and tassels. This interferes with pollination and results in malformed ears and undeveloped kernels. Beetles may also feed on the leaves. The adult females lay yellow-orange eggs in the soil at the bases of the corn plants. The young worms that hatch from these eggs feed on the corn roots for several weeks, then pupate in the soil to emerge as beetles in late July and August. These pests are most common where corn has grown consecutively for two or more years. Late-planted corn and corn under drought stress are the most susceptible.

SOLUTION: When the beetles first appear on the plants, treat them with a garden dust containing carbaryl (SEVIN®). Repeat at weekly intervals if the plants become reinfested. Control the rootworm larvae as suggested on page 279.

PROBLEM: Large holes are chewed in the edges of leaves. Greenish yellow to brown jumping insects, ½ to 1½ inches long, with long hind legs infest corn plants. Kernels on ears may be chewed or undeveloped.

ANALYSIS: Grasshoppers
Grasshoppers attack a wide variety of plants including corn, grains, and grasses. They eat corn leaves and silk, migrating as they mature and as they deplete their food sources. They are most numerous in the rows adjacent to weedy areas. In the late summer adult females lay eggs in pods in the soil. The adults continue feeding until cold weather kills them. The eggs hatch the following spring. Grasshopper infestations are most severe during hot, dry weather. The insects migrate into green gardens and yards as surrounding areas dry up in the summer heat. Periods of cool, wet weather help keep these insect populations under control. The loss of a small amount of leaf tissue to a small population of grasshoppers doesn't reduce the corn yield significantly.

SOLUTION: As soon as grasshoppers appear, treat plants with an insecticide containing diazinon or use a bait containing carbaryl (SEVIN®). Repeat at weekly intervals if the plants become reinfested. Clean up weedy areas near the garden and destroy plant debris after harvest.

PROBLEM: Leaves are riddled with tiny shot holes. Tassels may be broken and ear stalks bent. Holes filled with sawdustlike material are bored into the main stalks. Pinkish caterpillars with dark brown heads and two rows of brown dots are inside the stalks.

ANALYSIS: European corn borers
(*Ostrinia nubilalis*)
These insects are among the most destructive pests of corn. They also feed on tomato, potato, and pepper plants. Early plantings are the most severely affected. The borers survive the winter in corn plants, pupate in the spring, and emerge as adult moths in early summer. The adults are tan with dark wavy lines on the wings. Mature females lay clusters of about 20 white eggs on the undersides of the lower corn leaves. The borers that hatch from these eggs feed first in the whorl of leaves, riddling the leaves with shot holes. Later they bore into stalks and the bases of ears. This feeding results in broken stalks and tassels, poor ear development, and dropped ears. The borers continue feeding for a month, pupate, and emerge as moths to repeat the cycle. Cool, rainy weather in the early summer inhibits egg laying and washes the hatching larvae from the plants, reducing borer populations. Extremely dry summers and cold winters also reduce borer populations.

SOLUTION: Treat ear shoots and centers of leaf whorls at the first sign of borers or when 10 percent of the ears show silk; use an insecticidal dust or spray containing carbaryl (SEVIN®) or rotenone. Repeat at weekly intervals until borers are no longer seen. Destroy the plants at the end of the season. Avoid early planting.

Stalk borer damage. *Insert:* Larva (life size).

Black cutworm (⅓ life size).

Corn rootworm larva (life size).

PROBLEM: Leaves are chewed and ragged. Stalks don't produce ears and may be distorted and curled. Dark brown to purple caterpillars, 1 inch long, with white stripes and bands, may be found inside the stalks.

ANALYSIS: Common stalk borers
(*Papaipema nebris*)
These insects are serious pests of corn east of the Rocky Mountains. They feed on a variety of plants but prefer corn. These borers spend the winter as eggs on grasses and weeds, especially giant ragweed. After hatching in the early spring, the worms feed in the leaf whorls and then bore into the sides of the stalks and burrow upward. After pupating in the soil, the grayish brown adult moths emerge in late summer and early fall. The female moths lay eggs on grasses. Common stalk borers produce only one generation per year.

SOLUTION: Once the damage is noticed, it is too late for any controls. Destroy all infested plants. Clean all plant debris from the garden after harvest. Eliminate nearby grasses and weeds, especially giant ragweed. If stalk borers were serious this year, next year treat the plants in early to midspring; use an insecticide containing diazinon or carbaryl (SEVIN®).

PROBLEM: Young plants are chewed or cut off near the ground. Gray, brown, or black worms, 1½ to 2 inches long, may be found about 2 inches deep in the soil near the bases of damaged plants. The worms coil when disturbed.

ANALYSIS: Cutworms
Several species of cutworm attack plants in the vegetable garden. The most likely pests of corn seedlings are surface-feeding cutworms. The two most common on corn are the black cutworm (*Agrotis ipsilon*) and the dingy cutworm (*Feltia ducens*). A single surface-feeding cutworm can sever the stems of many young plants in one night. Cutworms hide in the soil during the day and feed only after sundown. All adult cutworms are dark night-flying moths with bands or stripes on their forewings.

SOLUTION: Apply an insecticide containing diazinon, chlorpyrifos, or methoxychlor or a bait containing carbaryl (SEVIN®) around the bases of undamaged plants in areas where stem cutting is observed. Since cutworms are difficult to control, weekly reapplications will probably be necessary. Before planting more corn in the same area, apply a preventive treatment of a methoxychlor product and work it into the soil. In late summer and fall, cultivate the soil thoroughly to expose and destroy eggs, larvae, and pupae. Further reduce damage by setting a "cutworm collar" around the stem of each plant or each plant grouping. Make collars from stiff paper, milk cartons, tin cans, or aluminum foil. Collars should be at least 2 inches high and pressed firmly into the soil.

PROBLEM: Corn plants are dwarfed, yellow, and fall over easily. The bases of the stalks may have a crook-necked shape. Brown-headed white worms, from ½ to ¾ inch long, eat the roots.

ANALYSIS: Corn rootworm larvae
(*Diabrotica* species)
Several species of this pest attack corn. The larvae, or worms, feed on corn roots, completely devouring small ones and tunneling into larger ones. The worms hatch from eggs in early summer to midsummer and migrate through the soil, feeding on corn roots. This feeding damage can be so serious to young plants that some gardens may need to be replanted. When populations are large, all the roots may be destroyed. The worms pupate in the soil and emerge as greenish yellow or light brown beetles, some with black spots or stripes. There are one to three generations per year. Adult beetles feed on larvae and silks. For information on adult corn rootworms, see page 278. Corn plants are affected most severely when they are growing in dry soil, where root regrowth is minimal. Rot diseases may enter the damaged roots, injuring them further. Several parasitic insects and diseases help keep beetle populations under control most years.

SOLUTION: Discard damaged plants and clean up weedy areas where the insects lay eggs and spend the winter. At planting time apply an insecticide containing diazinon or methoxychlor to the soil at planting time. Don't grow corn in the same soil for more than 2 consecutive years.

CORN ■ CUCURBIT FAMILY

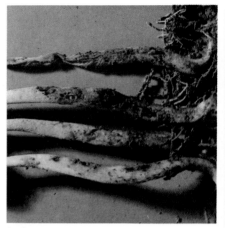

Seedcorn maggot damage.

PROBLEM: Seeds don't sprout, or the seedlings are weak and don't develop leaves. Pearly white worms, ¼ inch long, feed in the seeds. The seeds are hollow.

ANALYSIS: Seedcorn maggots
(*Hylemya platura*)
Seedcorn maggots feed on seeds and seedlings. They are attracted to large-seeded vegetables such as peas, beans, and corn. The maggots are most numerous in cool periods in the spring and fall and in cold soil that is high in organic matter. The black, hairy adult flies are attracted to the organic matter, and the females lay eggs in the soil. The maggots that hatch from these eggs burrow into the seeds and eat the inner tissue, leaving a hollow shell. Rot fungi may enter a damaged seed and further destroy it. After one to two weeks, the maggots burrow deep into the soil and pupate. The adult flies that emerge feed on nectar and plant juices before the females lay more eggs. There are several generations each year. In warm-winter areas, these pests are active all year. In cold-winter areas, they survive the winter as pupae, emerging as adults in the early spring.

SOLUTION: Treat seeds with an insecticide powder that contains diazinon; mix ¼ teaspoon of insecticide with each packet. Shake off the excess, and plant the seeds 1 to 2 inches deep. Since adult flies are attracted to organic matter, don't add manure to the soil in the spring when planting beans, peas, or corn.

CUCURBIT FAMILY (CUCUMBERS, GOURDS, MUSKMELONS, PUMPKINS, SUMMER SQUASH, WATERMELON, AND WINTER SQUASH)

ADAPTATION: Throughout the United States.

PLANTING TIME: Varies from mid-February through May, depending on date of last frost in your region.

PLANTING METHOD: Start seeds indoors or directly in the garden. Plant cucumber, muskmelon, and watermelon seeds 1 to 2 inches deep. Plant squash and pumpkin seeds 2 to 3 inches deep. Set transplants in the garden so that the tops of their rootballs are even with the surrounding garden soil. Space transplants or thin seedlings as follows: Cucumbers and muskmelons—12 inches apart or, if planted in hills, 24 to 36 inches apart. Pumpkins and vining squash—36 to 40 inches apart. Bush squash and watermelon—24 to 36 inches apart.

SOIL: Any good garden soil high in organic matter. pH 5.5 to 8.0.

FERTILIZER: At planting time, apply a fertilizer slightly higher in phosphorus (8-10-8, for example). Use 2 pounds per 50-foot row or 1 to 2 tablespoons per plant. Side-dress when the runners are 12 to 18 inches long and again when the first fruit has set.

WATER:
How much: Apply enough water at each irrigation to wet the soil 1 to 1½ feet deep.
How often: Water when soil 2 inches deep is barely moist.

HARVEST: When netting becomes pronounced and skin color turns yellow-tan; stem should separate or slip easily from the fruit.
Gourds and pumpkins: After the vines die in the fall but before a hard frost.
Summer squash: Continuous picking ensures a steady supply. Zucchini and crookneck: 1½ to 2 inches in diameter. Bush scallop: 3 to 4 inches.
Watermelon: When the spot where the melon touches the ground turns from white to creamy yellow; green skin is dull, not shiny; the melon makes a dull thud when hit with the palm of the hand.
Winter squash: After the vines die in the fall, but before a hard frost; when a fingernail doesn't scratch the hardened skin.

STORING: Most cucurbits are used soon after harvesting. Refrigerate them until use. Winter squash and pumpkins can be stored over the winter. Pick these two cucurbits only when they are mature, and cure them at temperatures between 80° and 85° F for 10 days. Then move the squash or pumpkins to a well-ventilated place with temperatures between 50° and 60° F. Store in a single layer; they rot easily if stored in piles.

Blossom-end rot on melon.

Beet leafhopper damage to zucchini.

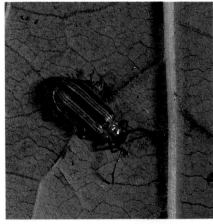

Striped cucumber beetle (4 times life size).

PROBLEM: A water-soaked, sunken spot develops on the blossom ends (opposite the stem ends) of squash and watermelons. The spot enlarges and turns brown to black. Mold may grow on the spot.

ANALYSIS: Blossom-end rot
This disorder of squash, watermelons, tomatoes, and peppers is caused by a lack of calcium in the developing fruits. This lack is the result of slowed growth and damaged roots caused by any of several factors.
1. Extreme fluctuations in soil moisture.
2. Rapid early-season plant growth followed by extended dry weather.
3. Excessive rain that smothers root hairs.
4. Excess soil salts.
5. Cultivating too close to the plant.
The first fruits of the season are the most severely affected. As the name implies, the disorder always starts at the blossom end, though the rot may enlarge to affect half of the fruit. Moldy growths on the rotted area are caused by fungi or bacteria that invade the damaged tissue.

SOLUTION: Take these measures to correct the condition or control the problem.
1. Maintain uniform soil moisture by mulching and proper watering.
2. Avoid high-ammonia fertilizers and large quantities of fresh manure. Water regularly during dry periods.
3. Plant in well-drained soil.
4. If the soil or water is salty, provide more water at each watering to help leach salts through the soil. Avoid using high-ammonia fertilizers and fresh manure.
5. Within 1 foot of the plant, do not cultivate deeper than 1 inch.

PROBLEM: Spotted, pale green, winged insects up to ⅛ inch long hop and fly away quickly when a plant is touched. The leaves are stippled and may be curled, puckered, and brittle.

ANALYSIS: Beet leafhoppers
(*Circulifer tenellus*)
Leafhopper is a western insect that is found only as far east as Missouri and Illinois. It attacks all members of the cucurbit family and frequently infects them with the virus that causes curly top. Plants infected with curly top are stunted, brittle, and sometimes die. The beet leafhopper feeds from early May through June. It sucks the sap and virus from infected leaves, and then injects the virus into healthy plants at its next feeding stop.

SOLUTION: At the first sign of damage, treat infested plants with an insecticide containing carbaryl (SEVIN®), diazinon, insecticidal soap, or pyrethrins. Be sure to cover the undersides of the leaves. Repeat the treatment at intervals of 7 to 10 days if the plants become reinfested.

PROBLEM: Yellow-green beetles with black stripes or spots chew holes in leaves, leafstalks, and stems. Plants may be stunted or wilted; they may die prematurely.

ANALYSIS: Cucumber beetles
Cucumber beetles, both *striped* (*Acalymma* species) and *spotted* (*Diabrotica* species), are common pests of cucumbers, melons, squash, and pumpkins. Controlling these beetles is important because they carry two serious diseases that damage and may kill cucurbits: mosaic virus (page 283) and bacterial wilt (page 282). Adult beetles survive the winter in plant debris and weeds. They emerge in the early spring and feed on a variety of plants. As soon as cucurbits are planted in the garden, the beetles attack the leaves and stems and may totally destroy the plants. Mature females lay their yellow-orange eggs in the soil at the bases of plants. The grubs that hatch from these eggs eat the roots and stems below the soil line, causing stunting, wilting, or premature death. The slender white grubs feed for several weeks, pupate in the soil, and emerge as adults to repeat the cycle. There is one generation per year in the northern United States but two or more in southern areas.

SOLUTION: At the first sign of the beetles, treat the plants with an insecticide containing carbaryl (SEVIN®), diazinon, or pyrethrins. Repeat at weekly intervals as the plants become reinfested. Control early in the season helps prevent susceptible young seedlings and plants from becoming infected with bacterial wilt.

CUCURBIT FAMILY

Squash bugs (life size).

PROBLEM: Squash and pumpkin leaves wilt and may become black and crisp. Bright green to dark gray or brown flat-backed bugs, about ½ inch long, cluster on the plants.

ANALYSIS: Squash bugs

(*Anasa tristis*)
Both the young (nymphs) and the adult squash bugs attack cucurbits, but infestations are most serious on squash and pumpkins. Squash bugs injure and kill the plants by sucking the sap from the leaves and stems. The dark brown adults, which are sometimes incorrectly called stink bugs, emit a disagreeable odor when crushed. The females lay brick-red egg clusters on the leaves in the spring. Although there is only one generation each year, all stages are found throughout the summer.

SOLUTION: Squash bugs are elusive and difficult to control. When the bugs first appear, treat the plants and the soil around them with an insecticide containing carbaryl (SEVIN®), insecticidal soap, or pyrethrins. Repeat the treatment every 7 days until the bugs are controlled. Plant varieties that are resistant to attack by squash bugs.

Squash varieties resistant to squash bugs: Butternut, Royal Acorn, Sweet Cheese.

Borer damage. *Insert:* Borer in stem (¾ life size).

PROBLEM: Squash vines suddenly wilt. Holes in the stems are filled with a tan sawdustlike material. Slitting infested stems lengthwise with a knife reveals fat white worms up to 1 inch long.

ANALYSIS: Squash vine borers

(*Melittia cucurbitae*)
These insect pests primarily attack squash and gourds and only rarely attack cucumbers and melons. Hubbard squash is especially susceptible. The larvae damage and kill the plants by tunneling in the stems, preventing the rest of the vine from receiving the water and nutrients it needs. The metallic green adult female moths lay eggs on the vines. Egg laying occurs in April and May in the southern United States and in June and July in northern areas. When the eggs hatch, the white larvae bore into the stems and feed for four to five weeks. They then crawl out of the stems and into the soil to pupate.

SOLUTION: Insecticides applied after the borer is inside the stem are not effective. Instead, slit the infested stems with a knife and destroy the borer. If the plant has not already died from the tunneling, cover the damaged portion of the stem with soil. Keep the soil moist to encourage new roots to grow. The vine may recover. Next year, during the egg-laying period, dust the plant with an insecticide containing methoxychlor.

Bacterial wilt. *Insert:* Bacterial ooze.

PROBLEM: A few leaves wilt and dry and may be chewed. Wilted leaves often recover at night, but they wilt again on sunny days and finally die. Fruit shrivels. Cutting a wilted stem near the base of the plant and squeezing out the sap produces a milky white substance. Touch a knife to the sap and withdraw it slowly. If the plant is infected with bacterial wilt, white ooze will string out in a fine thread.

ANALYSIS: Bacterial wilt

This plant disease is caused by a bacterium (*Erwinia tracheiphila*) and is more prevalent on cucumbers and muskmelons than on pumpkins and squash. Watermelons are not affected. The bacteria spend the winter in striped or spotted cucumber beetles and are spread to plants when the beetles feed. (For more information on cucumber beetles, see page 281.) An entire plant may become infected within 15 days. The disease is most prevalent in cool weather in areas with moderate rainfall.

SOLUTION: There are no chemical controls for bacterial wilt. Remove and discard all infected plants promptly. Control cucumber beetles with a chemical containing carbaryl (SEVIN®) or diazinon. Repeat the treatment every 7 days if the plants become reinfected. Grow varieties resistant to this disease. There are no resistant muskmelon varieties.

Cucumber variety resistant to bacterial wilt: Saladin.

Anthracnose on melon.

Mosaic on squash. *Insert:* Mosaic on cucumbers.

Powdery mildew on cucumber.

PROBLEM: Yellow, water-soaked areas spot melon and cucumber leaves, enlarge rapidly, and turn brown and dry. These spots then shatter, leaving a ragged hole. On watermelon leaves, the spots turn black. Elongated dark spots with light centers may appear on the stems. Whole leaves and vines die. Large fruit is spotted with sunken, dark brown, circular spots. Pinkish ooze may emerge from the spots. Young fruit darkens, shrivels, and dies.

ANALYSIS: Anthracnose
This plant disease is caused by a fungus (*Colletotrichum lagenarium*) and is the most destructive disease of melons and cucumbers in the eastern United States. It rarely attacks squash and pumpkins. The disease affects all aboveground parts of the plants, and is most prevalent in humid weather with frequent rain and temperatures from 70° to 80° F. The spores overwinter in seeds and plant debris not removed from the garden. Spores are spread by splashing water, cucumber beetles, and tools.

SOLUTION: At the first appearance of the disease, treat plants with a fungicide containing chlorothalonil. Repeat every 7 days or more frequently if warm, humid weather occurs. Grow varieties resistant to this disease.

PROBLEM: Leaves are mottled yellow and green and are distorted, stunted, and curled. Cucumber fruits are mottled with dark green and pale green-to-white blotches and covered with warts. Or the skins may be smooth and completely white. Summer squash may also be covered with warts.

ANALYSIS: Mosaic virus
This plant disease is caused by several viruses that attack cucumber, muskmelon, and summer squash plants. The viruses overwinter in perennial plants and weeds, including catnip, pokeweed, wild cucumber, motherwort, and milkweed. The viruses are spread from plant to plant by aphids and cucumber beetles, and they can infect plants at any time from the seedling stage to maturity. Infection early in the season is more damaging. Infected fruits taste bitter. Fruits that are more than half grown at the time of infection are immune to attack. Roots are not affected.

SOLUTION: There are no chemical controls for virus diseases. Remove and destroy all infected plants immediately. Control aphids and cucumber beetles by using an insecticide containing diazinon. Repeat at intervals of 7 to 10 days if the plants become reinfested. Remove weeds in and near the garden. Grow resistant cucumber varieties. There are not yet any resistant varieties of summer squash or muskmelon.

PROBLEM: The topsides of leaves are covered with a white powdery growth. Areas of the leaves and stems turn brown, wither, and dry. Fruit may be covered with the growth.

ANALYSIS: Powdery mildew
This common plant disease is caused by either of two fungi (*Erysiphe cichoracearum* or *Sphaerotheca fuliginea*) that thrive in both humid and dry weather. The powdery patches consist of fungal strands and spores. The spores are spread by the wind to healthy plants. The fungi sap the plant nutrients, causing yellowing and sometimes the death of leaves. A severe infection may kill the plant. Since powdery mildew attacks several different kinds of plants, the fungi from a diseased plant may infect other types of plants in the garden. Under conditions favorable to powdery mildew, infection can spread through a closely spaced planting in a matter of days or weeks.

SOLUTION: At the first sign of the disease, treat the plants with a fungicide containing chlorothalonil. Continue treatment at intervals of 7 days for as long as the disease is a problem. Grow varieties resistant to powdery mildew.

Flea beetle (2 times life size).

Tomato hornworm (⅓ life size).

GRAPES

PROBLEM: Leaves are riddled with shot holes about ⅛ inch in diameter. Tiny (⅟₁₆-inch) black beetles jump like fleas when disturbed. Leaves of seedlings and, eventually, whole plants may wilt and die.

ANALYSIS: Flea beetles
These beetles jump like fleas but are not related to them. Both adult and immature flea beetles feed on a wide variety of garden vegetable plants, including eggplants. Immature beetles, legless gray grubs, injure plants by feeding on the roots and the undersides of leaves. Adults chew holes in leaves. Flea beetles are most damaging to seedlings and young plants. Seedling leaves riddled with holes dry out quickly and die. Adult beetles survive the winter in soil and garden debris. They emerge in early spring to feed on weeds until vegetable seeds sprout or plants are set in the garden. Grubs hatch from eggs laid in the soil, and these pests feed for two to three weeks. After pupating in the soil, they emerge as adults to repeat the cycle. There are one to four generations each year. Adults may feed for up to two months.

SOLUTION: When the leaves first show damage, control flea beetles on eggplants with an insecticide containing carbaryl (SEVIN®), methoxychlor, or pyrethrins. Watch new growth for evidence of further damage, and repeat the treatment at weekly intervals as needed. Clean all plant debris from the garden after harvest to eliminate overwintering spots for adult beetles.

PROBLEM: Fat green or brown worms, up to 5 inches long, with white diagonal side stripes, chew on leaves. A red or black "horn" projects from each worm's rear end. Black droppings soil the leaves.

ANALYSIS: Tomato hornworms or tobacco hornworms
(*Manduca quinquemaculata* or *M. sexta*) Hornworms feed on eggplant, pepper, or tomato fruits and foliage. Although only a few worms may be present, each consumes large quantities of foliage and causes extensive damage. The adult hornworm moth, a large gray or brown creature with yellow and white markings, emerges from hibernation in late spring and drinks nectar from petunias and other garden flowers. The worms hatch from eggs laid on the undersides of the leaves, and these young feed for three to four weeks. Then they crawl into the soil, pupate, and later emerge as adults to repeat the cycle. There is one generation each year in the northern United States and two to four in southern areas. Some worms may have white sacs that look like puffed rice on their bodies. These sacs are the cocoons of parasitic wasps that feed on and eventually kill the hornworms.

SOLUTION: Treat the plants with an insecticide containing carbaryl (SEVIN®) or pyrethrins or with a bacterial insecticide containing *Bacillus thuringiensis*. Follow label directions. Don't destroy worms covered with white sacs; let the wasps inside the worms mature, emerge, and infest other hornworms. If practical, hand-pick unaffected worms.

ADAPTATION: Throughout the United States.

PLANTING TIME: Spring.

PLANTING METHOD: Purchase 1-year-old rooted vines, either bare-root or containerized plants. Plant them 6 to 10 feet apart and with the tops of their rootballs well below the level of the surrounding soil. Cut the tops back, leaving only 2 or 3 buds.

SOIL: Any good garden soil that is high in organic matter. pH 6.0 to 8.0.

FERTILIZER: At planting time, apply a general-purpose fertilizer (10-10-10, for example); use 1 pound per 100 square feet or 1 tablespoon per plant. For the first year, side-dress with the same amount in midspring and midsummer. In subsequent years, apply fertilizer each spring, before new growth begins; use ½ to 1 pound of fertilizer per plant.

WATER:
How much: Apply enough water at each irrigation to wet the soil 1½ to 3 feet deep.
How often: Water when soil 6 to 12 inches deep is almost dry.

HARVEST: Table grapes should taste sweet and be plump with even color. Wine grapes may be slightly tart but should be plump and slightly soft with even color.

Black rot.

Grapes damaged by grape berry moth larvae.

Grape leaf skeletonizers (life size).

PROBLEM: Light brown spots surrounded by a dark brown line appear on grapes. The grapes turn black, shrivel, and dry up like raisins. They remain attached to the stems. Reddish brown circular spots appear on leaves. The leaves may wilt. Sunken purple to black elongated lesions spot the canes, leaf stems, and tendrils.

ANALYSIS: Black rot

This plant disease is caused by a fungus (*Guignardia bidwelli*). It is the most destructive disease that attacks grapes, often destroying all the fruit. Black-rot fungi spend the winter in infected dormant canes, tendrils on the support wires, and mummified fruit. In warm, moist spring weather, spores infect new shoots, leaves, and tendrils. Eventually the spores spread to the developing fruit. The fruit is affected in all stages of development, but damage is most severe when the grapes are one-half to two-thirds grown. Spores for future infections are produced on infected leaves, canes, and fruit. The severity of the disease depends on the amount of diseased material that survives the winter and on the spring and early summer weather.

SOLUTION: Destroy all infected fruit and prune out infected canes and tendrils. Once the fruit has begun to shrivel, fungicide sprays are ineffective. Next year, spray the plants with a chemical containing captan. Treat when new shoots are 6 to 10 inches long and just before and immediately after bloom. Continue spraying at intervals of 10 to 14 days until the grapes are full-sized. Treat more frequently if leaf symptoms develop or if the weather is wet.

PROBLEM: Grapes are webbed together and to leaves. Dark green to purple worms, up to ⅜ inch long, with dark brown heads are inside the grapes. White cocoons cling to the leaves between flaps of leaf tissue.

ANALYSIS: Grape berry moths
(*Endopiza viteana*)
The grape berry moth is the most serious insect pest of grapes in the eastern United States. The worms damage both green and ripening fruit by feeding on the inner pulp and seeds. They web the grapes together and to leaves with silken threads as they feed and move from cluster to cluster of grapes. One worm can injure several berries. The worms spend the winter as pupae on leaves and on the ground. The purplish brown moths emerge in late spring, when the females lay eggs on blossom stems and small fruit. The larvae that hatch from these eggs feed on the buds, blossoms, and fruit. After three to four weeks of feeding, they cut a small bit of leaf, fold it over, and make a cocoon inside, where they pupate. Within a few weeks, adult moths emerge to repeat the cycle, this time laying eggs on ripening fruit. This second generation feeds for three to four weeks, then pupates for the winter.

SOLUTION: Destroy infested grapes. Discontinue cultivation in late summer so that the cocoons remain on top of the ground and are removed with fallen grape leaves at the end of the season. This will reduce the number of overwintering pupae. Next year, immediately after bloom, treat the plants with a spray containing diazinon. Repeat the application 7 to 10 days later. To control the second generation, spray again in midsummer.

PROBLEM: Yellow caterpillars with purple or black stripes feed in rows on the leaves. The caterpillars may be covered with black spines. They chew on the topsides and undersides of the leaves, eating everything but the leaf veins.

ANALYSIS: Grape leaf skeletonizers
(*Harrisina* species)
These pests frequently attack grapes in home gardens and abandoned vineyards. The young caterpillars characteristically feed side by side in a row on the leaves. They feed heartily and may defoliate a vine in several days. The loss of leaf tissue slows the growth of the vine and fruit and reduces production. These pests survive the winter as pupae in cocoons on leaves and in debris on the ground. In late spring the metallic green or smoky black adult moths emerge. The females lay their eggs on the undersides of the leaves. The yellow caterpillars that hatch from these eggs feed on the leaves, usually chewing on the surface layer of tissue on topsides and undersides; as they mature, however, they sometimes eat all the tissue between the veins. There are two or three generations each year, so damage continues from mid-May to August. If touched with bare skin, the black spines on the western grape skeletonizer may cause welts.

SOLUTION: As soon as the caterpillars appear, treat the infested plants with an insecticide containing carbaryl (SEVIN®). Spray both surfaces of the leaves. Repeat the treatment if the plants become reinfested.

GRAPES

Grape leafhopper (15 times life size).

Eutypa dieback.

Anthracnose.

PROBLEM: Areas on the leaves are stippled and turn pale yellow, white, then brown. Some of the leaves may fall. Black spots may be evident on berries. On the undersides of the leaves are pale yellow or white, ⅛-inch, flying or jumping insects with red or yellow body markings.

ANALYSIS: Grape leafhoppers
(*Erythroneura* species)
Both young and adult grape leafhoppers suck the juices from grape leaves, causing white spots that later turn brown. This damage reduces normal vine growth, resulting in delayed maturity of fruit and poor vine growth the following year. The insects' black droppings may also mar the fruit, making it unappetizing. Leafhoppers survive the winter as adults in protected places. When new growth begins in the spring, these adults emerge and begin feeding. The adult females lay their eggs in the leaves, causing blisterlike swellings. There are two or three generations each season, so leafhoppers of all stages of maturity can be found feeding from the time of new growth in the spring until the leaves drop in the fall.

SOLUTION: As soon as leafhoppers are noticed, treat infested grapevines with an insecticide containing diazinon or malathion. Spray both surfaces of the leaves. Repeat the treatment at intervals of 10 to 14 days if the plants become reinfested. To reduce the number of overwintering leafhoppers, clean up and destroy plant debris after harvest.

PROBLEM: Dark, irregular spots develop on young leaves. These spots may drop out, leaving holes in the foliage. Elongated, sunken spots develop on the current season's canes. Shoot growth may be weak and stunted, and the leaves, which have crinkled edges, are small, yellowish, and cupped. Later in the season, the leaves may become scorched and tattered. Sunken lesions (cankers) may develop on the woody canes and trunk. Entire branches may die.

ANALYSIS: Eutypa dieback
This plant disease is caused by a fungus (*Eutypa armeniacae*). Fungi of this species survive the winter in trunk and branch cankers. Fungal spores that form in the cankers are carried by splashing water to pruning wounds, where they infect the plant. Infection causes the formation of cankers that reduce the flow of water and nutrients through the trunk and branches. The portion of the plant above the canker weakens and may eventually die.

SOLUTION: Prune out and destroy infected branches and canes. Late winter pruning reduces the probability of infection. Make each pruning cut at least 6 inches below the canker and any discolored wood. If cankers are present on the trunk, remove and destroy the entire plant, cutting the trunk below the lowest canker but above the bud union. Maintain 2 to 4 suckers on the trunk. Treat fresh pruning wounds with a fungicide containing benomyl. The plant will not produce grapes this year but will yield a normal crop next year.

PROBLEM: Circular, sunken spots with light gray centers and dark borders appear on shoots, fruit, tendrils, and leafstalks. The fruit remains firm. The leaves may curl downward and the brown areas drop out.

ANALYSIS: Anthracnose
This plant disease is caused by a fungus (*Elsinoe ampelina*) that may do considerable damage a few years in a row and then disappear. It is often called bird's-eye rot because of the similarity of the spots to a bird's eye. It is seldom severe on 'Concord' or muscadine grapevines. The disease first attacks the new growth. The spots on the stems often merge, girdling the stem and killing the vine tips. Anthracnose is prevalent during wet periods in the spring and in poorly maintained vineyards. Anthracnose fungi survive the winter on old lesions on the canes. Although this disease doesn't kill the grapevines, the infected fruit are often misshapen and unappetizing. Several years of attack from anthracnose sufficiently weakens the vines and makes them more susceptible to other problems.

SOLUTION: Discard infected fruit, and prune out diseased canes. Sprays applied after spotting occurs are ineffective. Next spring, before the buds open, spray the vines with a fungicide containing lime sulfur. Treat the plants with a fungicide containing ferbam when the shoots are 1 to 2 inches long, when they are 6 to 10 inches long, just before bloom, just after the blossoms fall, and 2 to 3 more times at intervals of 2 weeks. Spray all canes and leaves thoroughly.

■ LETTUCE

Downy mildew.

Bibb lettuce bolting.

Cabbage looper damage and droppings.

PROBLEM: Small yellow spots appear on the topsides of the leaves. The lowersides are covered with a white cottony growth. Older leaves are affected first. Leaves, shoots, and tendrils turn brown and brittle and are often distorted. Grapes may be covered with the white growth, or they may be shriveled and brown, yellow, or red.

ANALYSIS: Downy mildew
This plant disease is caused by a fungus (*Plasmopara viticola*) that attacks grape foliage and fruit from before bloom to the end of harvest. Downy mildew causes leaf defoliation and prevents proper ripening. When the disease is severe, entire grape clusters may be killed. Reduced vine vigor results in poor growth the following season. This disease is favored by cool, moist weather and is always more serious in rainy growing seasons. This species survives the winter in diseased leaves on the ground.

SOLUTION: Destroy severely infected leaves and fruit. At the first sign of the disease, spray the vines with a fungicide labeled for this use. Repeat every 10 days until 7 days before harvest. Remove and destroy plant debris at the end of the season to reduce the number of overwintering spores. The following year, spray immediately before bloom, just after the petals fall, when the grapes are about the size of peas. Respray every 10 days thereafter until 7 days before harvest.

'Concord' grape is resistant, but not immune, to downy mildew.

PROBLEM: A seed stalk emerges from the center of the lettuce plant. The lettuce tastes bitter.

ANALYSIS: Bolting
Lettuce is a cool-weather crop; it grows best between 55° and 60° F. When temperatures rise above 60° F for several days in a row, mature plants form flower stalks, or seed stalks. As a stalk grows, sugars and nutrients are withdrawn from the leaves for the growth of the stalk, making the foliage bitter and tough. The formation of a flower stalk in vegetables that are grown for their leaves is known as bolting. Once bolting begins, it cannot be stopped; cutting off the stalk does not help.

SOLUTION: If it is harvested as soon as bolting begins, the lettuce may still be edible; quality deteriorates rapidly as the stalk forms, however. In the future, plant lettuce so that it matures during cool weather or grow varieties that are slow to bolt.

Lettuce varieties resistant to bolting:
  Head: Great Lakes 659.
  Loose Leaf: Oak Leaf, Royal Oak Leaf, Salad Bowl, Slo-Bolt.
  Butterhead: Augusta, Buttercrunch, Butter King, Green Lake, Hot Weather.

PROBLEM: Leaves have round or irregular holes. Green worms up to 1½ inches long, with light stripes down their backs, feed on the leaves or heads. Masses of green or brown pellets may be found between the leaves.

ANALYSIS: Cabbage loopers
(*Trichoplusia ni*)
Several worms attack lettuce, the most damaging of which is the cabbage looper. The looper attacks all varieties of lettuce, as well as members of the cabbage family. The brownish adult female moths lay pale green eggs on the topsides of leaves in the evening. Egg laying occurs throughout the growing season. After hatching, the worms eat lettuce leaves and heads. Their greenish brown excrement makes the plants unappetizing. Worms may be present from early spring until late fall. In the southern United States, they may be present all year. Worms spend the winter as pupae attached to plants or objects near plants.

SOLUTION: Control cabbage loopers with an insecticide containing carbaryl (SEVIN®), diazinon, or pyrethrins or with a bacterial spray containing *Bacillus thuringiensis*, a biological control. *Bacillus thuringiensis* is more effective while the caterpillars are small. Repeat treatments at weekly intervals if the plants become reinfested. Clean all plant debris from the garden to reduce the number of overwintering pupae.

LETTUCE

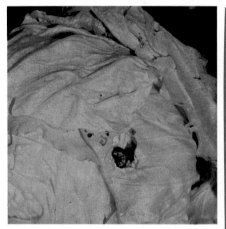

Cutworm (⅓ life size).

PROBLEM: Young plants are chewed or cut off near the ground. Gray, brown, or black worms, 1½ to 2 inches long, may be found about 2 inches deep in the soil near the bases of damaged plants. The worms coil when disturbed.

ANALYSIS: Cutworms
Several species of cutworm attack plants in the vegetable garden. The most likely pests of lettuce plants in the spring are surface-feeding cutworms. A single surface-feeding cutworm can sever the stems of many young plants in one night. Cutworms hide in the soil during the day and feed only after sundown. Adult cutworms are dark, night-flying moths with bands or stripes on their forewings. In southern parts of the United States, cutworms may also attack fall-planted lettuce.

SOLUTION: Apply an insecticide containing diazinon, chlorpyrifos, or methoxychlor or bait containing carbaryl (SEVIN®) around the bases of undamaged plants in areas where stem cutting is observed. Since cutworms are difficult to control, weekly reapplications will probably be necessary. Before transplanting in the area, apply a preventive treatment of a diazinon or methoxychlor product and work it into the soil. In late summer and fall, cultivate the soil thoroughly to expose and destroy eggs, larvae, and pupae. Further reduce damage by setting a "cutworm collar" around the stem of each plant. Make collars from stiff paper, milk cartons, tin cans, or aluminum foil. Collars should be at least 2 inches high and pressed firmly into the soil.

■ ONION FAMILY

ONION FAMILY
(CHIVES, GARLIC, LEEKS, ONIONS, AND SHALLOTS)

ADAPTATION: Throughout the United States.

PLANTING TIME: Varies from January through April, depending on date of last frost in your region.

PLANTING METHOD:
Chives: Sow seeds ½ inch deep. Thin seedlings or set transplants to grow 8 inches apart. Place transplants so that the tops of their rootballs are even with the surrounding garden soil.
Garlic: Plant individual cloves 1 to 2 inches deep and 5 to 6 inches apart.
Leeks: Plant like onion transplants or seeds.
Onions: Sow onion seeds ½ inch deep and thin plants to stand ¾ to 3 inches apart. Plant sets 1 to 2 inches deep, side by side, or up to 3 inches apart. Set transplants 2 to 3 inches deep and 3 to 5 inches apart. When planting green onions, place bulbs closer than when planting dry onions. For a continual harvest, plant every couple of weeks.
Shallots: Plant individual sections 1 to 1½ inches apart and 3 to 5 inches apart.

SOIL: Loose, crumbly soil that is rich in organic matter. pH 6.0 to 7.0.

FERTILIZER: At planting time, apply a general-purpose fertilizer (10-10-10, for example); use 2 pounds per 100 square feet or 1½ pounds per 50-foot row. Every 3 to 4 weeks, side-dress with 1 pound per 25-foot row.

WATER:
How much: Apply enough water at each watering to wet the soil 8 to 10 inches deep.
How often: Water when soil 2 inches deep is barely moist.

HARVEST:
Chives: Snip with sharp shears any time there are young, fresh leaves. Use fresh, or dry or freeze leaves for later use.
Dry onions: Harvest when half or more of the tops have turned yellow and fallen over. Dry in a warm, airy spot for 4 to 5 days. Shake off loose soil and skins. Place bulbs in a slatted crate or mesh bag, and continue drying in a well-ventilated, dry area for 2 to 4 weeks. After drying, store in a dry area between 35° and 40° F.
Garlic: Harvest when the tops dry; cure like dry onions.
Green onions: Pull the largest as needed, when about pencil-sized.
Leeks: For white stems, gradually hill soil around the plants through the growing season. Pick when the stems are ¾ to 1 inch in diameter. Store in a root cellar or refrigerator until used.
Shallots: Treat like dry onions.

Onion maggot damage.

Fusarium basal rot.

Pink root.

PROBLEM: Plants grow slowly, turn yellow, wilt, and die. Bulbs may rot in storage. White maggots, up to ⅓ inch long, burrow inside the bulb.

ANALYSIS: Onion maggots

(*Hylemya antiqua*)

These larvae are the most serious pest of onions. They burrow into the onion bulb, causing the plant to wilt and die. Once the bulb is damaged by the maggot's feeding, it is susceptible to attack by bacterial soft rot. Early plantings are the most severely injured. When the onions are young and growing close together, the maggots move easily from one bulb to another, destroying several plants. Cool, wet weather favors serious infestations. Maggots spend the winter as pupae in plant debris or in the soil. The brownish gray adult female flies emerge in the spring to lay clusters of white eggs at the bases of plants. The maggots that hatch from these eggs burrow into the soil and bulbs. After feeding, they pupate in the soil and emerge as adults to repeat the cycle. There are two or three generations a year, the last one attacking onions shortly before they are harvested. When maggot-infested bulbs are placed in storage, the maggots continue to feed and damage the bulbs.

SOLUTION: Discard and destroy maggot-infested onions. Remove all debris from the garden at the end of the season to reduce the number of overwintering pupae. At planting time, treat the soil in the row with a chemical containing diazinon or chlorpyrifos.

PROBLEM: Leaftips wilt and die back. The neck of the bulb is soft. A white fungal growth may appear on the base of the bulb. The bulb is soft and brown inside. Bulbs may also be affected in storage.

ANALYSIS: Fusarium basal rot

This plant disease is caused by a soil-inhabiting fungus (*Fusarium* species) that attacks onions, shallots, garlic, and chives. Fungi of this species persist indefinitely in the soil. The disease is spread by contaminated bulbs, soil, and equipment. The fungi enter the bulb through wounds from maggots and old root scars. The infection spreads up into the leaves, resulting in leaf yellowing and dieback. Bulbs approaching maturity are the most susceptible to attack. If infection occurs during or after harvest, the rot may not show until the bulbs are in storage. Fusarium basal rot is most serious when bulbs are stored in a moist area at temperatures above 70° F.

SOLUTION: No chemical controls are available. Destroy infected plants and bulbs. Harvest and dry healthy bulbs promptly at maturity. Fusarium can be removed from the soil only by fumigation techniques. Control onion maggots to reduce chances of infection. Store bulbs in a dry area at 35° to 40° F. If possible, do not plant fusarium-susceptible crops in the same site 2 years in a row.

PROBLEM: Plants grow slowly, and their tops may be stunted. Roots turn light pink and shrivel, then they turn a darker pink and die. Leaves may turn yellow or white, then die.

ANALYSIS: Pink root

This plant disease is caused by a fungus (*Pyrenochaeta terrestris*) that attacks onions, garlic, shallots, leeks, and chives. The species persists indefinitely in the soil and infects plants at all stages of growth. Mature and weakened bulbs are the most susceptible to attack. Plants infected early in their lives seldom produce large bulbs. Pink root is favored by temperatures from 60° to 85° F.

SOLUTION: No chemical control is available. Discard all infected plants. Pink-root fungus can be removed from the soil only by fumigation techniques. Weak plants are the most susceptible to attack, so keep plants healthy by providing adequate water and nutrients. Grow varieties that are resistant to pink root.

ONION FAMILY ■ **PEAS**

Onion thrips damage (life size).

Powdery mildew.

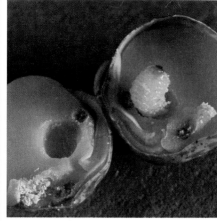

Pea weevil (5 times life size).

PROBLEM: White streaks or blotches appear on onion leaves. Tips may be distorted. Plants may wilt, wither, turn brown, and die. Bulbs may be distorted and small. Small pale green to white insects are observed at the bases of the leaves.

ANALYSIS: Onion thrips
(*Thrips tabaci*)
Onion thrips attack many vegetables, including onions, peas, and cabbage. Thrips are barely visible insects, less than ½₅ inch long, and dark brown to black. They reduce the quality and yield of onion bulbs by rasping holes in the leaves and sucking out the plant sap. This rasping causes the white streaks. Plants often die when thrips populations are high. Damage is most severe in the leaf sheath at the base of the plant. Thrips favor this protected area where the elements and pesticides have difficulty reaching them. Onion thrips survive the winter in grass stems, plant debris, and bulbs in storage. Thrips are active throughout the growing season; in warm climates they are active all year.

SOLUTION: At the first sign of thrips damage, treat infested onion plants with an insecticide containing diazinon or methoxychlor. Repeat at weekly intervals until new growth is no longer damaged.

PROBLEM: A white powdery coating develops first on the topsides of the lower leaves. Stems, pods, and other leaves may then become infected. Foliage may turn yellow and be malformed. Pods may be distorted, with dark streaks or spots.

ANALYSIS: Powdery mildew
This common plant disease is caused by a fungus (*Erysiphe polygoni*) that thrives in both humid and dry weather. The powdery coating consists of fungal strands and spores. The spores are spread by the wind to healthy plants. The fungi sap plant nutrients, causing yellowing and sometimes the death of leaves. A severe infection reduces pea yield considerably and may kill the plant. Fall crops are most susceptible to serious damage; spring crops are attacked late in the season. Since powdery mildew attacks many vegetables, the fungi from a diseased plant may infect other plants in the garden. Under conditions favorable to powdery mildew, infection can spread through a planting in a matter of days or weeks.

SOLUTION: Treat plants with a garden sulfur. Repeat at intervals of 7 to 10 days as needed. This fungicide does not cure infected leaves, but it does protect healthy ones from infection.

PROBLEM: Peas have small round holes. The peas are partially or completely hollow, and fat white grubs with brown heads may be found inside. When the pea plants are blooming, ⅕-inch-long dark brown beetles with light markings may be seen crawling or flying about the plants.

ANALYSIS: Pea weevils
(*Bruchus pisorum*)
These insect pests attack all varieties of edible peas. Weevils emerge from hibernation as peas are beginning to bloom. The adults feed on pea nectar and pollen. This feeding does not harm the plant. Adults can migrate up to 3 miles in search of food. Females lay orange to white eggs on the developing pods. The white grubs that hatch from these eggs eat through the pod and into peas. They continue feeding for six to eight weeks, then pupate inside the hollow peas. Adult weevils emerge in one to three weeks and hibernate to repeat the cycle the following year. There is only one generation each year. Infested peas are inedible.

SOLUTION: Insecticides must be applied to kill the adults before the female weevils lay eggs. Once the eggs are laid on the pods, it is too late to prevent plant injury. Soon after the first blooms appear and before pods start to form, treat the plants with a dust or spray containing rotenone. Additional sprays may be needed to control migrating weevils.

PEPPERS

ADAPTATION: Throughout the United States.

PLANTING TIME: Varies from February through May, depending on date of last frost in your region.

PLANTING METHOD: Sow seeds ¼ inch deep. Thin seedlings or set transplants to grow 18 to 24 inches apart. Plant transplants so tops of rootballs are even with the surrounding garden soil.

SOIL: Any good garden soil that is rich in organic matter. pH 5.5 to 7.5.

FERTILIZER: At planting time, use 3 to 4 pounds of general-purpose fertilizer per 100 square feet or 1 pound per 25-foot row. Every 3 to 4 weeks, side-dress with 1 pound per 25-foot row or 1 to 2 tablespoons per plant.

WATER:
  How much: Apply enough water to wet the soil 10 to 12 inches deep.
  Containers: About 10 percent of the applied water should drain out the bottom of each pot.
  How often: Water when soil 2 inches deep is barely moist.

HARVEST: Cut peppers from plant with pruning shears or a sharp knife, leaving ½ to 1 inch of stem attached. Refrigerate until use.
  Green or yellow peppers: Pick when fruit is of usable size and has a rich color. Peppers should be slightly soft.
  Red peppers: Red peppers are green peppers that have remained on the plants and matured. Pick when they have a rich red color.

Blossom drop.

PROBLEM: Few or no fruit develop. Those that do develop may have rough skin or be misshapen. Plants remain vigorous, with lush foliage.

ANALYSIS: Blossom drop
Pepper blossoms are sensitive to temperature fluctuations during pollination. Normal pollination and fruit set don't occur when night temperatures fall below 58° F and daytime temperatures rise above 85° F. If temperatures remain outside the pollination range, the blossoms fall off, often before pollination. If pollination has occurred and the fruit has begun to set but isn't completely fertilized at the time the blossoms drop, rough and misshapen fruit result.

SOLUTION: Blossom drop delays fruit production. When the temperatures are less extreme, a full crop of fruit will set, and the plants will be productive the rest of the season. Discard rough or misshapen fruit; they will never develop fully. Irrigation for cooling during hot periods can help to reduce losses.

Sunscald.

PROBLEM: An area on the pepper fruit becomes soft, wrinkled, and light in color. Later this area dries and becomes slightly sunken, with a white, paperlike appearance. An entire side of the fruit may be affected. Black mold may grow in the affected areas.

ANALYSIS: Sunscald
Pepper fruit exposed directly to sunlight may be burned by the heat. The fruit may be exposed to the sun as a result of leaf diseases that cause leaf drop or early fruit on small plants without enough protective foliage may be burned. Also, some varieties do not produce enough foliage to shade the fruit. Rot organisms sometimes enter the fruit through the damaged area, making the fruit unappetizing or inedible. Sunscalded fruit without rot is still edible if the discolored tissue is removed.

SOLUTION: Control leaf diseases that may defoliate the plants. Keep plants healthy with lush foliage by applying appropriate fertilizer. Select pepper varieties that form a protective canopy of leaves.

PEPPERS

Blossom-end rot.

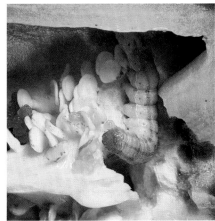

Corn earworm larva (life size).

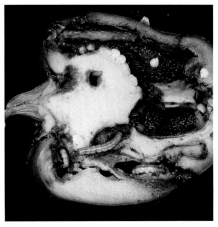

European corn borers (½ life size).

PROBLEM: A round, sunken, water-soaked spot develops on the blossom end (opposite the stem end) of fruit. The spot enlarges, turns brown to black, and feels leathery. Mold may grow on the rotted surface.

ANALYSIS: Blossom-end rot

Blossom-end rot occurs on peppers, tomatoes, squash, and watermelons from a lack of calcium in the developing fruits. This lack results from slowed growth and damaged roots caused by any of several factors.
1. Extreme fluctuations in soil moisture.
2. Rapid early-season plant growth followed by extended dry periods.
3. Excessive rain that smothers root hairs.
4. Excess soil salts.
5. Cultivating too close to the plant.
The first fruits of the season are the most severely affected. As the name implies, the disorder always starts at the blossom end, though the rot may enlarge to affect up to half of the fruit. Moldy growths on the rotted area are caused by fungi or bacteria that invade the damaged tissue. This rotted area is unsightly, but the rest of the fruit is edible.

SOLUTION: Blossom-end rot is difficult to eliminate, but it can be controlled by following these guidelines.
1. Maintain uniform soil moisture by mulching and proper watering.
2. Avoid overuse of high-nitrogen fertilizers and large quantities of fresh manure.
3. Plant in well-drained soil.
4. If the soil or water is salty, provide more water at each watering to help leach salts through the soil.
5. Within 1 foot of the plant, do not cultivate deeper than 1 inch.

PROBLEM: Holes are chewed in the fruit. Inside the fruit are striped yellow, green, or brown worms from ½ to 2 inches long. These worms may also feed on the leaves.

ANALYSIS: Corn earworms
(*Heliothis zea*)
These pests attack many vegetables and flowers. They are also known as tomato fruitworms and cotton bollworms. Corn earworms feed on the foliage and also chew holes in the fruit, making them worthless. The worms are the larvae of light gray-brown moths with dark lines on their wings. In the spring, female moths lay yellow eggs on the leaves and stems. The worms that hatch from these eggs feed on the new leaves. When they are about ½ inch long, the worms move to the fruit and bore inside. After feeding for two to four weeks, they drop to the ground and pupate 2 to 6 inches deep in the soil. After several weeks, they emerge as adults to repeat the cycle. There are several generations each year. In the southern United States, where earworms survive the winter, early and late plantings suffer the most damage. Adult moths migrate into northern areas, where they do not survive the winter.

SOLUTION: Once the worms are inside the fruit, sprays are ineffective. Pick and destroy infested fruit. Clean all plant debris from the garden after harvest to reduce the number of overwintering adults. Next year, treat the plants when the worms are feeding on the foliage or when the fruit are 1 to 2 inches in diameter; use a dust or spray containing carbaryl (SEVIN®). Repeat the treatment at intervals of 10 to 14 days if the plants become reinfested.

PROBLEM: Pink or tan worms, up to 1 inch long, with dark brown heads and two rows of brown dots, feed inside the pepper. The fruit is decayed inside.

ANALYSIS: European corn borers
(*Ostrinia nubilalis*)
Larvae of this moth species are destructive pests of pepper, eggplant, corn, tomato, and bean plantings. The worms feed and promote decay inside the fruits. The borers spend the winter in plant debris, pupate in the spring, and emerge as adults in early summer. The adults are tan moths with dark wavy lines on their wings. The females lay clusters of 15 to 30 white eggs on the undersides of the leaves. In midsummer, the eggs hatch and young borers enter the fruit where it attaches to the cap. After feeding for one month inside the fruit, the borers pupate and later emerge as adults to repeat the cycle. There are two to three generations each year. Cool, rainy weather in early summer inhibits egg laying and washes the hatching larvae from the plants, reducing borer populations. Extremely dry summers and cold winters also reduce borer populations. Peppers are edible if the damaged part is cut away.

SOLUTION: Remove infested fruit. When remaining fruit is 1 to 1½ inches in diameter, treat the plants with an insecticide containing carbaryl (SEVIN®). Repeat the treatment 2 more times, 7 days apart. Clean all debris from the garden after harvest to reduce overwintering sites for the larvae.

■ **POTATOES**

Tomato hornworm (⅓ life size).

PROBLEM: Fat green or brown worms, up to 5 inches long, with white diagonal side stripes, chew on leaves. A red or black "horn" projects from each worm's rear end. Black droppings are on the leaves and the soil surface beneath the damaged foliage.

ANALYSIS: Tomato hornworms or tobacco hornworms
(*Manduca quinquemaculata* or *M. sexta*)
Hornworms feed on pepper, eggplant, or tomato fruits and foliage. Although only a few worms may be present, each consumes large quantities of foliage and causes extensive damage. The adult hornworm moth, a large gray or brown creature with yellow and white markings, emerges from hibernation in late spring and drinks nectar from petunias and other garden flowers. The worms hatch from eggs laid on the undersides of the leaves, and these young feed for three to four weeks. Then they crawl into the soil, pupate, and later emerge as adults to repeat the cycle. There is one generation each year in northern parts of the United States and two to four in southern areas. Some worms may have white sacs that look like puffed rice on their bodies. These sacs are the cocoons of parasitic wasps that feed on and eventually kill the hornworms.

SOLUTION: Treat the plants with carbaryl (SEVIN®) or pyrethrins or with a bacterial insecticide containing *Bacillus thuringiensis*. Don't destroy worms covered with white sacs; let the wasps inside the worms mature, emerge, and infest other hornworms. If practical, hand-pick unaffected worms.

POTATOES

ADAPTATION: Throughout the United States.

PLANTING TIME: Varies from January through April, depending on date of last frost in your region.

PLANTING METHOD: Plant 1½- to 2-ounce seed pieces (about the size of a medium egg) with at least one eye on each piece, in trenches 3 to 4 inches deep. Allow 12 to 18 inches between pieces. Certified potato seed pieces are confirmed by the State Department of Agriculture as being free of viruses. Purchase new seed pieces each year.

SOIL: Any good garden soil that is rich in organic matter. pH 4.8 to 6.8.

FERTILIZER: At planting time, use 1 to 2 pounds of a fertilizer slightly higher in phosphorus per 100 square feet, or ½ pound per 25-foot row. Side-dress when plants are 4 to 6 inches tall.

WATER:
How much: Apply enough water to wet the soil 8 to 12 inches deep.
How often: Water when soil 2 inches deep is barely moist.

HARVEST: Dig potatoes as needed, 2 to 3 weeks after flowering. Dig those to be stored after the tops naturally turn yellow and die. Carefully loosen them by using a spade or pitchfork, being careful not to wound the tubers. Discard any diseased tubers.
To store: Cure potatoes in the dark for 1 week at 70° F and high humidity. Then store them in a humid area between 40° and 45° F until used. Check stored tubers periodically for rot.

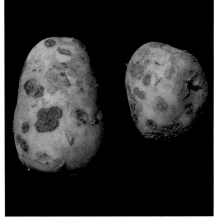
Scab.

PROBLEM: Brown corky scabs or pits occur on potato tubers. Spots enlarge and merge together, sometimes covering most of a tuber. Leaves and stems are not affected.

ANALYSIS: Common scab
This plant disease is caused by a fungus (*Streptomyces scabies*) that persists in the soil for long periods. Besides potatoes, scab infects beets, carrots, and parsnips. Scab affects only the tubers, not the leaves and stems. The fungi that cause common scab spend the winter in the soil and in infected tubers left in the garden. Infection occurs through wounds and through the breathing pores in the tuber skins when the tubers are young and growing rapidly. Scab is most severe in dry soil from 75° to 85° F in which the pH is 5.7 to 8.0. The severity of scab often increases when the pH is raised with lime or wood ashes. Scab is not a problem in acidic soils with a pH of 5.5 or less. A soil low in nutrients also encourages scab. The fungal spores can withstand temperature and moisture extremes. Because the spores can pass intact through the digestive tracts of animals, manure can spread the disease. Tubers infected with scab are edible; however, since blemishes are removed, much may be wasted.

SOLUTION: No chemical control is available. Test soil pH; if necessary, correct it to 5.0 to 5.5 with aluminum sulfate. Avoid alkaline materials such as wood ashes and lime. Do not use manure on potatoes. Plant potatoes in the same area only once every 3 to 4 years. Use certified seed pieces that are resistant to scab.

POTATOES

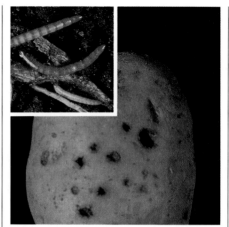

Damaged potato. *Insert:* Wireworms (2 times life size).

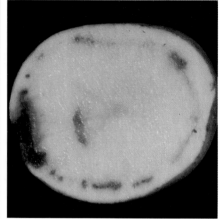

Bacterial ring rot.

Adult (½ life size). *Insert:* Larva (life size).

PROBLEM: Plants are stunted and grow slowly. Tunnels wind through stems, roots, and in and on the surface of tubers. Shiny, hard, jointed, cream to yellow worms up to ⅞ inch long are in the tubers and in the soil.

ANALYSIS: Wireworms

Wireworms feed on potato, corn, carrot, beet, pea, bean, lettuce, and many other plants. Wireworms feed entirely on underground plant parts, devouring seed potatoes, underground stems, tubers, and roots. Infestations are most extensive in soil where lawn grass was recently grown. Adults are known as click beetles because they make a clicking sound when turning from their backs to their feet. Wireworm larvae feed for two to six years before maturing into adult beetles, so all sizes and ages of wireworm may be found in the soil at the same time. Undamaged portions of the tubers are edible.

SOLUTION: At the first sign of damage, control wireworms with an insecticide containing diazinon, chlorpyrifos, or methoxychlor. Work the insecticide into the top 6 to 8 inches of soil. Do not store damaged tubers. Repeat the soil treatment next year, just before planting.

PROBLEM: Shoot tips are stunted, forming rosettes. Between the veins, leaves turn yellow, then brown. Leaf edges curl upward, and stems may wilt. Stems cut at ground level exude a creamy white ooze. Only a few stems on a plant may show symptoms. Tubers may be cracked and, when cut near the stem end, reveal a yellow to light brown ring of crumbly decay.

ANALYSIS: Ring rot

This disease is caused by a bacterium (*Corynebacterium sepedonicum*) that attacks both tubers and stems. Infected tubers are inedible. Tuber decay may be evident at harvest, or it may not develop until after several months in storage. Other rot organisms frequently invade and completely rot the tubers. Ring-rot bacteria enter plants through wounds, especially those caused by cutting seed pieces before planting. They do not spread from plant to plant in the field. The bacteria survive between seasons in infected tubers and storage containers.

SOLUTION: At the first sign of the disease, discard all infected tubers and plants. Next year, use only certified seed pieces for plants. Plant them whole; or, if you cut them, disinfect the knife between cuts by dipping it in rubbing alcohol. Disinfect storage containers with household bleach, rinsing and drying afterward. Wash storage bags in hot water.

PROBLEM: Black-striped yellow-orange beetles, about ⅜ inch long, eat the leaves. Fat, red, humpbacked larvae with two rows of black dots may also be present.

ANALYSIS: Colorado potato beetles
(*Leptinotarsa decemlineata*)
These insect pests, also known as potato bugs, often devastate potato, tomato, and pepper plantings. Both the adults and the larvae damage plants by devouring leaves and stems. Small plants are most severely damaged. The beetles, native to the Rocky Mountains, spread eastward in the late 1800s as potato plantings increased. In some areas of the nation, beetle populations may reach epidemic proportions. The female beetles lay their yellow-orange eggs on the undersides of the leaves as the first potato foliage emerges from the ground in the spring. The larvae that hatch from these eggs feed for two to three weeks, pupate in the soil, and emerge one to two weeks later as adults, which lay more eggs. One generation is completed in a month. There are one to three generations a year, depending on the area.

SOLUTION: When the insects are first noticed, apply an insecticide containing carbaryl (SEVIN®), diazinon, methoxychlor, or pyrethrins. Repeat every 7 days as long as the infestation continues.

Flea beetle damage.

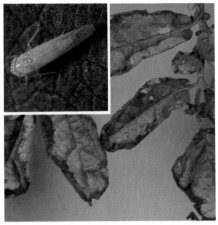

Damage. *Insert:* Potato leafhopper (4 times life size).

Early blight.

PROBLEM: Leaves are riddled with shot holes about ⅛ inch in diameter. Tiny (¹⁄₁₆-inch) black beetles jump like fleas when disturbed. Leaves of seedlings and, eventually, whole plants may wilt and die.

ANALYSIS: Flea beetles
These beetles jump like fleas but are not related to them. Both adult and immature flea beetles feed on a wide variety of garden vegetable plants, including potatoes. Immature beetles, legless gray grubs, injure plants by feeding on the roots and the undersides of leaves. Adults chew holes in leaves. Flea beetles are most damaging to young plants. Adult beetles survive the winter in soil and garden debris. They emerge in early spring to feed on weeds until vegetables sprout. The adults and the new grubs, which hatch from eggs laid in the soil, can be quite damaging to potato tubers. The grubs feed for two to three weeks and then pupate in the soil. They then emerge as adults to repeat the cycle. There are one to four generations each year. Adults may feed for up to two months.

SOLUTION: When the leaves first show damage, control flea beetles on potato plants with an insecticide containing carbaryl (SEVIN®), diazinon, methoxychlor, or pyrethrins. Spray or dust carefully at the bases of stems. Watch new growth for evidence of further damage, and repeat the treatment at weekly intervals as needed. Clean all plant debris from the garden after harvesting to eliminate overwintering spots for adult beetles.

PROBLEM: Spotted, pale green insects up to ⅛ inch long hop, run sideways, or fly away quickly when a plant is touched. The leaves are stippled or appear scorched, with green midribs and brown edges curled under.

ANALYSIS: Potato leafhoppers
(*Empoasca fabae*)
These insects feed on potato and bean plants and on some fruit and ornamental trees. It sucks plant sap from the undersides of the leaves, causing leaf stippling. This leafhopper is responsible for hopperburn, the browning and curling of the edges of potato leaves. The leafhopper injects toxic saliva into the nutrient-conducting tissue, interrupting the flow of food within the plant. Potato yields may be reduced drastically by hopperburn. Leafhoppers at all stages of maturity are active during the growing season. Both early and late varieties of potatoes are infested. Leafhoppers live the year around in the Gulf States and migrate northward on warm spring winds, so even areas that have winters so cold that the eggs cannot survive are not free from infestation.

SOLUTION: Spray infested plants with an insecticide containing carbaryl (SEVIN®), malathion, insecticidal soap, or pyrethrins. Be sure to cover the undersides of the leaves. Respray as often as necessary to keep the insects under control; allow at least 10 days between applications. Eradicate nearby weeds that may harbor leafhopper eggs.

PROBLEM: Irregular dark brown to black spots, ⅛ to ½ inch in diameter, appear on the lower leaves. Concentric rings develop in the spots. Spots may enlarge, causing the leaves to die and fall off. Tubers may be infected with brown, corky, dry spots.

ANALYSIS: Early blight
This plant disease is caused by a fungus (*Alternaria solani*) that attacks both vines and tubers. It is most severe toward the end of the growing season, when the vines approach maturity and after tubers are formed. Many leaves may be killed. The potato yield is reduced, but the plant seldom dies. Tubers are frequently infected through wounds inflicted during harvest. Early blight is favored by moisture and temperatures from 75° to 85° F. The fungal spores spend the winter in plant debris left in the garden. Infected tubers are inedible.

SOLUTION: As soon as leaf spotting occurs, spray plants with a fungicide containing chlorothalonil. Repeat the treatment every 7 to 10 days until the leaves die back naturally. Clean up and destroy plant debris after harvest. Do not store infected tubers. Next year, begin spraying the plants when they are 6 inches tall, and continue at intervals of 7 to 10 days until the tops die back. Avoid overhead watering by using drip or furrow irrigation. Maintain adequate nutrients. Use seed potatoes certified by state departments of agriculture to be free of diseases.

POTATOES ▪ RADISHES ▪

Late blight.

Flea beetle damage.

Root maggot (life size).

PROBLEM: Brownish water-soaked spots appear on leaves. Spots enlarge rapidly, turn black, and kill leaves; then the spots kill leaf stems and main stems. In moist weather a gray mildew grows on the undersides of the leaves. Tuber skins are infected in the ground or in storage with brownish purple spots that become a wet or dry rot.

ANALYSIS: Late blight
This plant disease is caused by a fungus (*Phytophthora infestans*) that seriously injures potatoes and tomatoes. This disease was responsible for the great famine in Ireland from 1845 to 1850. Fungi of this species spread rapidly, killing an entire planting in a few days. Infected tubers are inedible. The tubers are infected when the spores wash off the leaves and into the soil. Tubers may also be attacked during harvest and rot in storage. A soft rot often invades the damaged tubers. Late blight is prevalent in moist humid weather with cool nights and warm days. Foggy, misty weather and heavy dew provide enough moisture for infection. The spores survive the winter in infected tubers in the garden or compost pile.

SOLUTION: If late blight is an annual problem in your area, spray when the plants are 6 inches tall; use a fungicide containing chlorothalonil. Continue at intervals of 7 to 10 days until the plants naturally turn yellow and die. Avoid overhead watering; use drip or furrow irrigation. Wait at least a week after plants die naturally before digging the tubers. This allows time for the spores to die. Clean up and destroy plant debris after harvest.

PROBLEM: Leaves are riddled with shot holes about ⅛ inch in diameter. Tiny (1/16-inch) black beetles jump like fleas when disturbed.

ANALYSIS: Flea beetles
These beetles jump like fleas but are not related to them. Both adult and immature flea beetles feed on a wide variety of garden vegetable plants. Immature beetles, legless gray grubs, injure plants by feeding on the roots and the undersides of leaves. Adults chew holes in leaves. Adult beetles survive the winter in soil and garden debris. They emerge in early spring to feed on weeds until vegetable seeds sprout. Grubs hatch from eggs laid in the soil and feed for two to three weeks. After pupating in the soil, they emerge as adults to repeat the cycle. There are one to four generations each year. Adults may feed for up to two months.

SOLUTION: When the plants first emerge through the soil or at the first sign of damage, control flea beetles on radishes with an insecticide containing diazinon or pyrethrins. Watch new growth for evidence of further damage, and repeat the treatment at weekly intervals as needed. Clean up and destroy plant debris after harvest to eliminate overwintering spots for adult beetles.

PROBLEM: Young plants wilt in the heat of the day. They may later turn yellow and die. Soft-bodied, yellow-white maggots, about ¼ inch long, feed in the roots. The roots are honeycombed with slimy channels and scarred by brown grooves.

ANALYSIS: Root maggots
(*Hylemya* species)
Root maggots are most numerous during cool, wet weather in spring, early summer, and fall. Early maggots attack the roots, stems, and seeds of radishes, cabbage, broccoli, and turnips in the spring and early summer. Later insects damage fall crops. The adult is a gray fly slightly smaller than a housefly, with black stripes and bristles down its back. The female lays eggs on stems and nearby soil. The maggots hatch in two to five days and tunnel into radish roots, making them inedible.

SOLUTION: Once the growing plant wilts and turns yellow, nothing can be done. To control maggots in the next planting of radishes, mix an insecticide containing diazinon, chlorpyrifos, or methoxychlor 4 to 6 inches into the soil before seeding. Control lasts about one month. To prevent egg deposits, screen adult flies from the seedbed by using a cheesecloth cover.

RHUBARB ■

Crown rot.

PROBLEM: Leaves wilt. Brown, sunken, water-soaked spots appear on the bases of the leafstalks. Leaves yellow and stalks collapse and die. The whole plant eventually dies.

ANALYSIS: Crown rot

This plant disease—also called stem rot, foot rot, or root rot—is caused by one of several fungi (*Phytophthora* species) that live in the soil. These fungi thrive in waterlogged, heavy soils, and they attack plant crowns (where stems and roots meet) and the bases of stems. The stems and roots rot, resulting in wilting and eventual death of the plant. The fungi are most active in moist soils from 60° to 75° F in the late spring and early summer. The spores are spread to healthy plants in running or splashing water or by contaminated soil or infected plants.

SOLUTION: Remove and destroy dying leaves and plants. Apply a drench of fungicide containing captan or basic copper sulfate to the crown or base of the plant and to the surrounding soil. When replanting, purchase disease-free plants from a reputable company; plant them in well-drained soil. Avoid overwatering.

Small stalks.

PROBLEM: Rhubarb stalks are thin and small.

ANALYSIS: Small stalks

Rhubarb stalks may be small for any of several reasons.
1. *End of the harvest season:* Rhubarb stalks are produced from food stored in the roots. Toward the end of the harvest season, the food is used up and the stalks become smaller and smaller.
2. *Lack of nutrients:* Rhubarb plants are heavy feeders, requiring large amounts of fertilizer to encourage healthy growth so that an adequate food supply will be stored for the following year's harvest.
3. *Young plants:* Rhubarb stalks are small until the plants establish their roots and are able to store an adequate amount of food. This may take two years after planting.
4. *Overcrowding:* Rhubarb plants are vigorous growers with deep roots. The plants may compete with each other if not divided every five to seven years.
5. *Crown rot:* This disease reduces plant vigor and kills the roots. For more information, see first column.
6. *Poor soil drainage:* Rhubarb does not tolerate wet soil. The roots rot and the plants eventually die.

SOLUTION: To improve the harvest, fertilize each spring before new leaves begin to grow. Harvest second year for two weeks, subsequent year for 6 to 8 weeks. Pull only large stalks, never more than two thirds of those present on the plant. Discard leaf. Control crown rot, and improve soil drainage.

SPINACH ■

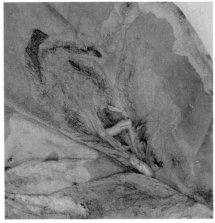

Leafminers (life size).

PROBLEM: Irregular tan blotches, blisters, or tunnels appear on or in leaves. The tan areas peel apart like facial tissue. Tiny black specks and white or yellow maggots are inside the tunnels.

ANALYSIS: Leafminers

These insect pests belong to the family of leaf-mining flies. The tiny black or yellow adult female flies lay white eggs on the undersides of leaves. The maggots that hatch from these eggs bore into the leaf and tunnel between the surfaces, feeding on the inner tissue. The tunnels and blotches are called mines. The black specks inside are the maggots' droppings. Several overlapping generations occur during the growing season, so larvae are present from spring until fall. Infested leaves are not edible.

SOLUTION: When the white egg clusters are first seen under the leaves, control leafminers on spinach with an insecticide containing diazinon or malathion. Repeat 2 more times at weekly intervals to control succeeding generations. Once the leafminers enter the leaves, spraying will control only those leafminers that attack after the application. Clean all plant debris from the garden after harvest to reduce overwintering spots for the pupae.

STRAWBERRIES ───────────────────────────

STRAWBERRIES ─────────

ADAPTATION: Throughout the United States.

PLANTING TIME: Early spring.

PLANTING METHOD: Select dormant or growing plants. Pick off all but 2 or 3 of the healthiest leaves. Prune away a third of the roots. Set the plants 18 inches apart, with the roots fanning outward. The crown should be just above the soil level. As runners develop, maintain the rows no wider than 18 to 24 inches. Runners can be removed throughout the season and established as separate plants.

SOIL: Any good, well-drained garden soil that is high in organic matter. pH 5.5 to 7.5.

FERTILIZER: At planting time, apply a general-purpose fertilizer (10-10-10, for example); add 2 pounds per 100 square feet or ½ pound per 25-foot row. After harvest each year, side-dress with ½ to 1 pound of fertilizer per 25-foot row.
   Containers: Water thoroughly every 3 to 4 weeks with a solution of a plant food rated 23-19-17.

WATER:
   How much: Apply enough water at each irrigation to wet the soil 8 to 10 inches deep.
   How often: Water when soil 1 inch deep is barely moist.

HARVEST: For maximum production the second year, remove blossoms and runners the first planting year. Plants are productive for 3 to 4 years.

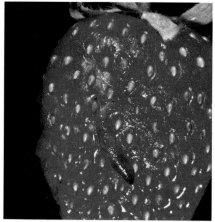

Slug (3 times life size).

PROBLEM: Stems and leaves are sheared off and eaten. Holes are often found in ripening berries, especially under the berry cap. Silvery trails wind around on the plants and soil nearby. Snails or slugs move around or feed on the plants, especially at night; inspect the garden for them at night by flashlight.

ANALYSIS: Snails and slugs
These pests are mollusks and are related to clams, oysters, and other shellfish. They feed on a wide variety of garden plants. Like other mollusks, snails and slugs need to be moist all the time. For this reason they avoid direct sun and dry places and hide during the day in damp places, such as under flowerpots or in thick ground covers. They emerge at night or on cloudy days to feed. Snails and slugs are similar except that the snail has a hard shell, into which it withdraws when disturbed. In protected places female slugs lay masses of white eggs encased in slime. Female snails bury their eggs in the soil, also in a slimy mass. The young look like miniature versions of their parents.

SOLUTION: Apply a bait containing metaldehyde in the areas you wish to protect. Also apply it in areas where snails or slugs might be hiding, such as in dense ground covers, weedy areas, compost piles, or pot storage areas. Before applying, wet down the areas to be treated, to encourage snail and slug activity that night. Repeat the application every 2 weeks as long as snails and slugs are active. Do not apply the bait to leaves.

Gray mold.

PROBLEM: A light tan spot appears on berries. Some berries are soft, mushy, and rotting. A fluffy gray mold may cover rotting berries.

ANALYSIS: Gray mold
Gray mold is caused by a fungus (*Botrytis cinerea*). It is the most damaging rot of strawberries and greatly reduces the amount of edible fruit. Gray-mold fungi attack both flowers and berries. The flowers are infected when in bloom and may not produce fruit. Berries are attacked at all stages of development. Healthy fruit is infected directly when it touches infected fruit, soil, or leaves. Infected berries are inedible. The fuzzy gray mold on the berries is composed of fungal strands and millions of microscopic spores. The fungi are most active in cool, humid weather and are spread by people and splashing water as well as infected fruit. Crowded plantings, rain, and overhead watering enhance the spread of gray mold.

SOLUTION: Destroy infected fruit. To reduce the spread of the fungi to uncontaminated fruit, treat fruit at the first sign of the disease; use a fungicide containing captan or chlorothalonil. Continue treating every 8 to 10 days. Pick berries as they ripen. Avoid overhead watering by using soaker or drip hoses. Mulch with straw, pine needles, or other material to keep fruit off the ground. To help prevent infection next year, remove and destroy plant debris in the fall and reinstate the 8- to 10-day treatment program when the plants bloom. When setting out new plants, provide enough space between plants to allow adequate air circulation and rapid drying after rain and irrigation.

Damaged buds. *Insert:* Adult (5 times life size).

Spider mite webbing.

Virus disease.

PROBLEM: Flower buds droop, turn brown and dry, and hang from the plant or fall to the ground. Small holes appear in the sides of the buds. Dark reddish brown, ⅛-inch weevils with curved snouts crawl on the plants.

ANALYSIS: Strawberry bud weevils
(*Anthonomus signatus*)
These insect pests of strawberries, dewberries, blueberries, and wild blackberries are also known as clippers because they clip the flower bud stems, causing buds to droop and fall to the ground. By destroying the flower buds, they reduce the berry crop. Adult weevils survive the winter in debris in and near the garden. In the spring, they puncture holes in the sides of unopened flower buds. The females lay an egg in each hole. Then the adults cut notches in the flower stems ⅛ to ¼ inch below the buds. The buds droop for a few days and then fall to the ground. Within a week the eggs hatch, and fat, white grubs feed on the pollen inside the buds. After feeding for about four weeks, the grubs pupate and emerge as adults in early summer to midsummer. These adults feed on blackberry and dewberry pollen, hibernate, and emerge in the spring to repeat the cycle. There is only one generation each year.

SOLUTION: When cut buds first appear, treat plants with an insecticide containing carbaryl (SEVIN®). Repeat through the closed-bud stage as long as damage occurs. At the end of the season, clean up and destroy plant debris in and near the garden to reduce overwintering locations for the adults.

PROBLEM: Leaves are stippled, yellowing, and dirty. Leaves may dry out and drop. There may be cobwebbing between leaves or on the undersides of leaves. Few berries are produced. To determine if the plant is infested with mites, hold a sheet of white paper underneath an affected leaf and tap the leaf sharply. If mites are present, minute green, red, or yellow specks the size of pepper grains will drop to the paper and begin to crawl around. These pests are easily seen against the white background.

ANALYSIS: Spider mites
Spider mites, related to spiders, are major pests of many garden and greenhouse plants. Spider mites are larger than cyclamen mites, which also attack strawberries. Spider mites attack the older leaves; cyclamen mites attack the younger leaves. Spider mites cause damage by sucking sap from the undersides of foliage. As a result of feeding, the green leaf pigment (chlorophyll) disappears, producing a stippled appearance. Berry production is also reduced. Mites are active throughout the growing season, but most are favored by dry weather above 70° F. By midsummer, they build up to tremendous numbers.

SOLUTION: When the damage first appears, treat infested strawberry plants with a miticide containing hexakis. Repeat the treatment at 7- to 10-day intervals until harvest or until damage no longer occurs. Be sure the pesticide touches the undersides of the leaves, where the mites live.

PROBLEM: Strawberry leaves are crinkled, yellowed, or distorted. Plants may be stunted, with cupped leaves, or leaves may grow in a tight rosette. Small, dull fruit or no fruit is produced. Plants produce few runners.

ANALYSIS: Viruses
Two types of viruses attack strawberries: killer viruses and latent viruses. Killer viruses have obvious symptoms, and they kill individual mother plants and the daughter plants attached to the ends of runners. Latent viruses cause few or no symptoms. A single latent virus may merely reduce the number of runners and fruit produced. However, plants infected with more than one kind of latent virus are so weakened that they are frequently attacked and killed by other diseases. Viruses are transmitted by aphids and nematodes through runners from mother to daughter plants. Aphids are most numerous in cool spring and fall weather.

SOLUTION: Remove and destroy all infected plants. If aphids are present, control them with a chemical containing diazinon or malathion; follow label directions. When replanting, buy certified plants from a reputable company. Certified plants are grown in special isolated conditions and are essentially virus-free. Or choose virus-tolerant varieties.

Strawberry varieties tolerant of viruses: Florida Belle, Florida Ninety, Klonmore, Shasta, Tennessee Beauty, Tioga, Totem, Sumas.

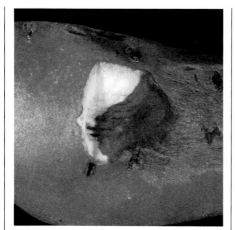

Black rot.

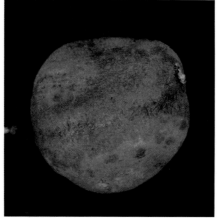

Scurf.

Flea beetle larva (½ life size).

PROBLEM: Black spots occur on roots in the ground and in storage. Tiny black specks appear in the center of blackened areas. Black lesions occur on stems at the soil line. Leaves are yellow and dwarfed.

ANALYSIS: Black rot

This plant disease is caused by a fungus (*Ceratocystis fimbriata*) that attacks all underground parts of sweet-potato plants. Black-rot fungi usually enter the plants through injuries, but uninjured parts may also be attacked under conditions favorable to the rot. Infections occur between 75° and 85° F during periods of high humidity. Infected roots may not show symptoms when dug up, but once in storage they develop blackened areas. Both discolored tissue and surrounding healthy tissue taste bitter. The fungi survive in sweet-potato debris, manure, and weeds for at least two years. Spores are spread by wind, water, and insects, including the sweet-potato weevil.

SOLUTION: There are no chemical controls for this disease. Remove and discard all infected plants and roots. Disinfect the storage area thoroughly with a solution of 1 part household bleach to 9 parts water. Rinse and let dry. Purchase certified slips or seed potatoes. Do not plant sweet potatoes in the same soil 2 years in a row.

PROBLEM: Dark brown to black spots or irregular patches stain sweet-potato skins. Discoloration affects only the skin, not the inside of the root.

ANALYSIS: Scurf

This plant disease, also called soil stain, is caused by a fungus (*Monilochaetes infuscans*) that attacks only sweet-potato roots. Although the appearance of infected tubers is somewhat unappetizing, their flavor is unaffected and they are still edible. Scurf is most severe in wet, poorly drained soils and those high in organic matter. It is favored by soils with a high pH and temperatures between 70° and 80° F. The disease appears more frequently when heavy rains occur just before harvest. Scurf spots may enlarge in storage. The scurf injury to the root surface allows rapid water loss, causing roots to shrivel. Scurf fungi are introduced into the garden on infected roots and slips. The spores persist from one crop to the next in infected vines rotting in the garden and in humus or partially decomposed organic matter.

SOLUTION: Use scurf-infected roots promptly, without storing them. Avoid planting in heavy soil. Improve soil drainage. If you add organic matter, till it into the soil a year before planting so it will decompose. Test the soil pH and make it more acidic if necessary. Purchase disease-free slips from a reputable company. If possible, change the sweet-potato planting site every 3 or 4 years.

PROBLEM: Yellow irregular channels are chewed in the surfaces of leaves. Tiny (7/16-inch) black beetles jump like fleas when disturbed. Shallow, dark tunnels scar the surface of the root.

ANALYSIS: Sweet-potato flea beetles

(*Chaetocnema confinis*)
These beetles jump like fleas but are not related to them. Both adults and immature flea beetles feed on sweet potatoes. The immature beetles, legless white grubs, feed on the surface tissue of the roots, making them unattractive but still edible. Adults chew channels in leaves. Flea beetles are present nearly everywhere sweet potatoes are grown and are most damaging to young plants. Adult beetles survive the winter in soil and garden debris. They emerge in early spring to feed on weeds until slips are set in the garden. Grubs hatch from eggs laid in the soil and feed for two to three weeks. After pupating in the soil, they emerge as adults to repeat the cycle. There are several generations each year.

SOLUTION: When the leaves first show damage, control flea beetles on sweet potatoes with an insecticidal spray containing methoxychlor. Watch new growth for evidence of further damage, and repeat the treatment at weekly intervals as needed. Remove all plant debris from the garden after harvest to eliminate overwintering spots for the adult beetles.

TOMATOES

TOMATOES

ADAPTATION: Throughout the United States.

PLANTING TIME: Varies from February through May, depending on date of last frost in your region.

PLANTING METHOD: Sow seeds ½ inch deep. Thin seedlings when they have 2 or 3 leaves, or set transplants 18 to 36 inches apart. Set transplants horizontally, with only the top third of the plant above the soil. Remove fruit and flowers from transplants before planting.

SOIL: Any good garden soil that is high in organic matter. pH 5.5 to 7.5.

FERTILIZER: At planting time, apply a fertilizer slightly higher in phosphorus (8-10-8, for example); use 3 to 4 pounds per 100 square feet or 1 pound per 25-foot row. In hot-summer areas, side-dress every 3 to 4 weeks with 1 pound per 25-foot row or 1 to 2 tablespoons per plant. In cool-summer areas, side-dressing may produce excess foliage and green fruit that doesn't ripen.

Containers: Water thoroughly every 2 to 4 weeks with a solution of a plant food rated 23-19-17.

WATER:
How much: Apply enough water to wet the soil 18 to 20 inches deep.
How often: Water when soil 2 inches deep is barely moist.

HARVEST: Harvest tomatoes when they have a deep, rich color. Store at room temperature until use. If your plants still have green fruit at the first frost, ripen it either by hanging the plants upside down in the garage, or storing green fruit in boxes at room temperature.

Poor fruit set.

PROBLEM: Little or no fruit develops. The plants are healthy and may even be extremely vigorous.

ANALYSIS: Poor fruit set
Poor fruit set occurs on tomatoes for any of several reasons.
1. *Extreme temperatures:* The blossoms drop off without setting fruit when night temperatures fall below 55° F or day temperatures rise above 90° F for extended periods.
2. *Dry soil:* Blossoms dry and fall when the plants don't receive enough water.
3. *Shading:* Few blossoms are produced when the plants receive less than six hours of sunlight a day.
4. *Excessive nitrogen:* High levels of nitrogen in the soil promote leaf growth at the expense of blossom and fruit formation.

SOLUTION: Take these measures to correct the condition or control the problem.
1. Plant early-, mid-, and late-season varieties at the appropriate time of year.
2. Water tomatoes regularly, never allowing the soil to dry out. Mulch with straw, black plastic, or other material to reduce the need for watering.
3. Plant tomatoes in an area that receives at least 6 hours of sunlight a day. If the yard is shady, grow tomatoes in containers on a sunny porch or patio.
4. Correct the nitrogen imbalance with a fertilizer rated 0-20-0 or 0-10-10. To prevent future problems, follow the fertilizer application recommendations.

Growth cracks.

PROBLEM: Circular or radial cracks mar the stem end (top) of ripening fruit. Cracks may extend deep into the fruit, causing it to rot.

ANALYSIS: Growth cracks
Tomatoes crack when environmental conditions encourage rapid growth during ripening. The rapid growth is frequently promoted by a drought followed by heavy rain or watering. Tomatoes are most susceptible to cracking after they have reached full size and begin to change color. Some varieties crack more easily than others. Cracking is more severe in hot weather. Some cracks may be deep, allowing decay organisms to enter the fruit and rot it. Shallow cracks frequently heal over but may rupture if the fruit is roughly handled when picked. Cracked tomatoes are edible.

SOLUTION: Maintain even soil moisture with regular watering. Grow varieties that are crack tolerant.

Tomato varieties that are crack tolerant: Avalanche, Bragger, Early Girl, Glamor, Heinz 1350, Heinz 1439, Jet Star, Marglobe Supreme F, Red Glow, Roma, Willamette.

TOMATOES

Sunscald on tomatoes.

Blossom-end rot.

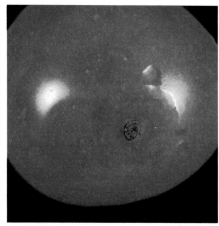

Anthracnose.

PROBLEM: On green and ripening fruit, a light patch develops on the side facing the sun. This area blisters and finally becomes slightly sunken and grayish white, with a paperlike surface. A black mold may grow on the affected area, causing the fruit to rot.

ANALYSIS: Sunscald
Sunscald occurs on tomatoes when they are exposed to the direct rays of the sun during hot weather. It is most common on green fruit, but ripening fruit is also susceptible. Sunscald is most prevalent on varieties with sparse foliage and on staked plants that have lost their foliage because of leaf diseases such as early blight, late blight, septoria leaf spot, fusarium or verticillium wilt (see page 304), or leaf roll. Fruit on plants that have been pruned to hasten ripening are also subject to sunscald. Tomatoes are still edible if the sun-scalded areas are removed. Fungi frequently invade the damaged tissue, resulting in moldy and inedible fruit.

SOLUTION: Cover exposed fruit with straw or other lightweight material to protect tomatoes from the rays of the sun. Do not prune leaves to hasten ripening. Control leaf diseases. Grow varieties that resist verticillium and fusarium wilt.

PROBLEM: A round, sunken, water-soaked spot develops on the blossom end (opposite the stem end) of fruit. The spot enlarges, turns brown to black, and feels leathery. Mold may grow on the rotted surface.

ANALYSIS: Blossom-end rot
Blossom-end rot occurs on tomatoes, peppers, squash, and watermelons from a lack of calcium in the developing fruits. This results from slowed growth and damaged roots caused by any of several factors.
1. Extreme fluctuations in soil moisture.
2. Rapid early-season plant growth followed by extended dry weather.
3. Excessive rain that smothers root hairs.
4. Excess soil salts.
5. Cultivating too close to the plant.
The first fruits of the season are the most severely affected. As the name implies, the disorder always starts at the blossom end, though the rot may enlarge to affect up to half of the fruit. Moldy growths on the rotted area are caused by fungi or bacteria that invade the damaged tissue. The rotted area is unsightly, but the rest of the fruit is edible.

SOLUTION: To prevent future blossom-end rot, follow these guidelines.
1. Maintain uniform soil moisture by mulching and proper watering.
2. Avoid using high-nitrogen fertilizers or large quantities of fresh manure.
3. Plant in well-drained soil.
4. If the soil or water is salty, provide more water at each watering to help leach salts through the soil.
5. Within 1 foot of the plant, do not cultivate deeper than 1 inch.

PROBLEM: Sunken spots up to ½ inch in diameter occur on ripe tomatoes. The centers of the spots darken and form concentric rings. Spots may merge, covering a large part of the tomato.

ANALYSIS: Anthracnose
This plant disease is caused by a fungus (*Glomerella phomoides*) that rots ripe tomatoes. Green tomato fruit is also attacked, but the spots don't appear until the fruit ripens. Infected fruit is inedible. Anthracnose is most common on overripe fruit and fruit close to the ground. Fruit on plants partially defoliated by leaf-spot diseases is also prone to infection. The leaves may be infected but are usually not severely damaged. Anthracnose fungi are most active in wet weather from 60° to 90° F, and when infection is severe fruit is damaged in a short time. Infections frequently become epidemic in hot, rainy weather. Water from heavy dew, overhead watering, and frequent abundant rain provides the moisture necessary for infection.

SOLUTION: At the first sign of the disease, spray tomato plants with a fungicide containing chlorothalonil. Repeat at intervals of 7 to 10 days until harvest. Destroy all infected fruit. Pick tomatoes as they mature, and use them promptly. To reduce the spread of the disease, do not work around wet plants. Clean up and destroy plant debris after harvest.

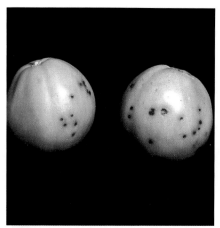

Bacterial spot.

Tomato (top) and tobacco hornworms (life size).

Flea beetle damage.

PROBLEM: Dark, raised, scablike spots, ⅛ to ¼ inch in diameter, appear on green tomatoes. The centers of the spots are slightly sunken. Dark, greasy, ⅛-inch spots occur on the older leaves, causing them to drop.

ANALYSIS: Bacterial spot
This plant disease is caused by a bacterium (*Xanthomonas vesicatoria*) that attacks green but not red tomatoes. It also attacks peppers. Bacteria that cause spot infect all aboveground parts of the plants at any stage of growth. Infected blossoms drop, reducing the fruit yield. Fruit is infected through skin wounds caused by insects, blowing sand, and mechanical injuries. Infected fruit does not ripen properly and is frequently invaded by rot organisms. The bacteria are most active after heavy rains and in temperatures from 75° to 85° F. They spread rapidly in the rain, often resulting in severe defoliation that weakens the plant and exposes the fruit to sunscald. The bacteria spend the winter in the soil and are carried on tomato seeds.

SOLUTION: Pick and destroy all infected green fruit. At the first sign of the disease, spray with a fungicide containing both maneb and basic copper sulfate. Repeat at intervals of 7 to 10 days as long as weather favorable to the spread of bacterial spot continues. To reduce the spread of the disease, do not work around wet plants. Avoid overhead watering by using drip or furrow irrigation. Purchase disease-free plants or seeds from a reputable dealer. Do not save seeds from infected fruit.

PROBLEM: Fat green or brown worms, up to 5 inches long, with white diagonal stripes chew on leaves. A red or black "horn" projects from each worm's rear end. Black droppings soil the leaves.

ANALYSIS: Tomato hornworms or tobacco hornworms
(*Manduca quinquemaculata* or *M. sexta*) Hornworms feed on tomato, pepper, or eggplant fruits and foliage. Although only a few worms may be present, each worm consumes large quantities of foliage and causes extensive damage. The adult hornworm moth, a large gray or brown creature with yellow and white markings, emerges from hibernation in late spring and drinks nectar from petunias and other garden flowers. The worms hatch from eggs laid on the undersides of the leaves, and these young feed for three to four weeks. Then they crawl into the soil, pupate, and later emerge as adults to repeat the cycle. There is one generation a year in the northern United States and two to four in southern areas. Some worms may have white sacs that look like puffed rice on their bodies. These sacs are the cocoons of parasitic wasps that feed on and eventually kill the hornworms.

SOLUTION: Treat the plants with an insecticide containing carbaryl (SEVIN®) or diazinon or with a bacterial insecticide containing *Bacillus thuringiensis*. Don't destroy worms covered with white sacs; let the wasps inside the worms mature, emerge, and infest other hornworms. If practical, hand-pick and destroy unaffected worms.

PROBLEM: Leaves are riddled with shot holes about ⅛ inch in diameter. Tiny 1/16-inch black beetles jump like fleas when disturbed. Leaves of seedlings may wilt and die.

ANALYSIS: Flea beetles
These beetles jump like fleas but are not related to them. Both adult and immature flea beetles feed on a wide variety of garden vegetable plants, including tomatoes. Immature beetles, legless gray grubs, injure plants by feeding on the roots and the undersides of the leaves. Adults chew holes in leaves. Flea beetles are most damaging to seedlings and young plants. Seedling leaves riddled with holes dry out quickly and die. Adult beetles survive the winter in soil and garden debris. They emerge in early spring to feed on weeds until vegetables sprout or plants are set in the garden. Grubs hatch from eggs laid in the soil and feed for two to three weeks. After pupating in the soil, they emerge as adults to repeat the cycle. There are one to four generations each year. Adults may feed for up to two months.

SOLUTION: When the leaves first show damage, control flea beetles on tomatoes with an insecticide containing carbaryl (SEVIN®), diazinon, methoxychlor, or pyrethrins. Watch new growth for evidence of further damage, and repeat the treatment at weekly intervals as needed. Clean all plant debris from the garden after harvest to eliminate overwintering spots for adult beetles.

TOMATOES

Fusarium wilt.

Nematode-infested roots.

Cutworm (life size).

PROBLEM: Lower leaves turn yellow, wilt, and die; then upper shoots wilt. Eventually the whole plant dies. Wilting usually occurs first on one side of the leaf or plant, then the other. Slicing the stem lengthwise near the soil line reveals dark brown tissue ⅛ inch under the bark.

ANALYSIS: Fusarium wilt
This wilt disease is caused by a soil-inhabiting fungus (*Fusarium oxysporum*) that infects only tomato plants. Fungi of this species persist indefinitely on plant debris or in the soil. Fusarium wilt is more prevalent in warm-weather areas. The disease is spread by contaminated soil, seeds, plants, and equipment. The fungi enter a plant through the roots and spread up into the stems and leaves through the water-conducting vessels. These vessels become plugged and discolored. This plugging cuts off the flow of water and nutrients to the leaves, causing leaf yellowing and wilting. Infected plants may or may not produce fruit. Fruit that is produced is usually deformed and tasteless. Many plants will die.

SOLUTION: No chemical control is available. Destroy infected plants promptly. Fusarium fungi can be removed from the soil only by fumigation with metam-sodium (VAPAM®). Use plants that are resistant to fusarium wilt. They are denoted by the letter *F* after the name of the tomato variety.

PROBLEM: Plants are stunted, yellow, and wilt in hot, dry weather. Round and elongated nodules occur on roots.

ANALYSIS: Nematodes
Nematodes are microscopic worms that live in the soil. There are various types, some highly beneficial and some highly destructive. They are not related to earthworms. Destructive nematodes feed on plant roots. The damaged roots can't supply sufficient water and nutrients to the aboveground plant parts, and the plant is stunted or slowly dies. Nematodes are found throughout the country but are most severe in the South. They prefer moist, sandy loam soils. Nematodes can move only a few inches each year on their own, but they may be carried long distances by soil, water, tools, or infested plants. Testing roots and soil is the only method for confirming the presence of nematodes. Contact the local cooperative extension office for sampling instructions and addresses of testing laboratories. Soil and root problems—such as poor soil structure, drought stress, nutrient deficiency, and root rots—can produce symptoms of decline similar to those caused by nematodes. Eliminate these problems as causes before sending soil and root samples for testing.

SOLUTION: Chemicals to kill nematodes in planted soil are not available to homeowners. However, nematodes can be controlled by soil fumigation before planting. Some varieties are resistant to nematodes. Resistance is indicated by an *N* after the variety name.

PROBLEM: Young plants are chewed or cut off near the ground. Gray, brown, or black worms, 1½ to 2 inches long, may be found about 2 inches deep in the soil near the bases of damaged plants. The worms coil when disturbed.

ANALYSIS: Cutworms
Several species of cutworm attack plants in the vegetable garden. The most likely pests of young tomato plants early in the season are surface-feeding cutworms. For information on climbing cutworms, see page 253. A single surface-feeding cutworm can sever the stems of many young plants in one night. Cutworms hide in the soil during the day, and feed only after sundown. Adult cutworms are dark, night-flying moths with bands or stripes on their forewings.

SOLUTION: Apply an insecticide containing diazinon, chlorpyrifos, or methoxychlor or a bait containing carbaryl (SEVIN®) around the bases of undamaged plants in areas where stem cutting is observed. Since cutworms are difficult to control, weekly reapplications will probably be necessary. Before transplanting into the area, apply a preventive treatment of a diazinon or methoxychlor product and work it into the soil. In late summer and fall, cultivate the soil thoroughly to expose and destroy eggs, larvae, and pupae. Further reduce damage by setting a "cutworm collar" around the stem of each plant. Make collars from stiff paper, milk cartons, tin cans, or aluminum foil. Collars should be at least 2 inches high and pressed firmly into the soil.

■ **TURNIPS** ■

Damping-off.

Root maggots (½ life size).

Cabbage looper (life size).

PROBLEM: Seeds don't sprout, or seedlings fall over soon after they emerge. At the soil line the stems are water-soaked and discolored. The base of an affected stem is soft and thin.

ANALYSIS: Damping-off

Damping-off is a common problem in wet soil with a high nitrogen level. Wet, rich soil promotes damping-off in two ways: The fungi that cause it are more active under these conditions, and the seedlings are more succulent and susceptible to attack. Damping-off is often a problem with crops that are planted too early in the spring, before the soil has had a chance to dry and warm sufficiently for quick seed germination. Damping-off can also be a problem when the weather remains cloudy and wet while seeds are germinating or when seedlings are too heavily shaded.

SOLUTION: To prevent damping-off, take the precautions that follow.
1. Allow the surface of the soil to dry slightly between waterings.
2. Do not start seeds in soil that has a high nitrogen level. Add nitrogen fertilizer only after the seedlings have produced their first true leaves.
3. Plant seeds after the soil has reached at least 70° F, or start seeds indoors in sterilized potting mix.
4. Protect seeds during germination by coating them with a fungicide containing captan. Add a pinch of fungicide to a packet of seeds and shake well to coat the seeds.

PROBLEM: Young plants wilt in the heat of the day. They may later turn yellow and die. Soft-bodied, yellow-white maggots, ¼ to ⅓ inch long, feed in the roots and on seeds. The roots are honeycombed with slimy channels and scarred by brown grooves.

ANALYSIS: Root maggots

(*Hylemya* species)
Root maggots are a damaging pest of turnip plants in the northern United States. They are most numerous during cool, wet weather in the spring, early summer, and fall. Early maggots attack the roots, stems, and seeds of turnip, cabbage, broccoli, and radish plants in the spring and early summer. Later insects damage crops in the fall. The adult is a gray fly somewhat smaller than a housefly, with black stripes and bristles down its back. The female lays eggs on stems and in nearby soil. The maggots hatch in two to five days to feed and tunnel into the roots, rendering them inedible.

SOLUTION: Once the maggots are in the roots, nothing can be done. To control maggots in the next planting of turnips, mix an insecticide containing diazinon, chlorpyrifos, or methoxychlor into the top 4 to 6 inches of soil before seeding. Control lasts about one month. To prevent egg deposits, screen adult flies from the seedbed by using a cheesecloth cover.

PROBLEM: Leaves have ragged, irregular, or round holes. Green caterpillars, up to 1½ inches long, feed on the leaves. Masses of greenish brown pellets may be found by parting the outer leaves.

ANALYSIS: Cabbage caterpillars

These destructive caterpillars are cabbage loopers (*Trichoplusia ni*), native to the United States, or the imported cabbageworms (*Pieris rapae*), introduced into North America from Europe around 1860. Both species attack all members of the cabbage family, including turnips. Adult females lay their eggs singly on leaves in the spring. The brownish cabbage looper moth lays its pale green eggs at night on the topsides of leaves; the white cabbageworm butterfly attaches its tiny, yellow, bullet-shaped eggs to the undersides of leaves. The larvae that hatch from these eggs feed on the foliage. The cabbageworms also cause damage by contaminating plants with its greenish brown excrement. Populations may produce as many as five generations in a season, so caterpillar damage can occur from early spring through late fall. The caterpillars spend the winter as pupae attached to plants or nearby objects.

SOLUTION: When the caterpillars first appear, treat the turnip leaves with an insecticide containing diazinon, Bt (*Bacillus thuringiensis*), or pyrethrins. Or, if practical, hand-pick and destroy caterpillars on the leaves. Clean all plant debris from the garden to reduce the number of overwintering pupae.

HOUSEHOLD PESTS

Improved living standards have markedly diminished parasite and fly problems. Yet the same buildings that shelter people also shelter household pests, which are often attracted to homes by conditions in the yard and garden.

INSPECTING THE OUTDOORS

Piles of grass clippings or other damp trash, along with weather conditions, can encourage sowbugs and pillbugs; windowsill dampness can lead them into your home. Caterpillars of all sorts may wander indoors, looking for warmth and shelter. Larvae may even be blown in by the wind. Spiders and termites can inhabit your woodpile or wainscoting. Because many indoor pest problems begin outdoors, begin your pest-control efforts outside your home. Is landscaping overgrown with weeds or plants that badly need thinning or trimming? Insects find such areas prime nesting habitat. If there is outdoor pet food or an open garbage can, you may be providing food and water, too. If you feed pets outdoors, remove food at night. Cover garbage cans tightly, so raccoons and stray dogs cannot invade and scatter contents. Sometimes the food you leave out for the birds becomes a pest attractant; remove excess if it is on the ground.

Wear protective gloves at all times when cleaning yard trash. If you live in an area possibly populated by brown recluse spiders, black widow spiders, poisonous snakes, biting ants, ground wasps, or scorpions, work with long sleeves and a long stick when turning over logs or construction remnants.

Put leaves and lawn clippings in a secure closable container or in a properly constructed compost pile. Be aware that a compost pile must be functioning properly to reach temperatures high enough to destroy pests among the clippings and debris. If your compost pile is not degrading adequately, destroy debris or haul it away promptly. Moving trash from one section of the yard to another merely moves the problem.

Uncirculating water in fishponds, decorative ponds, or currently unused above- or below-ground pools attracts all kinds of water-loving insects, from water beetles to mosquitoes. Bees and wasps like standing water too—they are attracted by both reflected light and moisture.

When inspecting the building exterior, pay particular attention to the area

Opposite: When using traps such as these, which are set out for rodents, keep children and pets out of the room.

where building meets earth. This is a favorite pest entrance. Outdoor wood invites termites, carpenter beetles, carpenter ants, and other cellulose chewers.

Discard excess construction materials or move them away from the house. If you are saving wood for fireplace use, stack it well away from the house, on an elevated platform. If firewood will not be used for some time, spray it with a pesticide such as diazinon to hold down pest populations. Follow label directions regarding time to allow between spraying and burning.

Keep shrubs that are close to the house trimmed back so they do not touch the walls. Use mulch sparingly on any plants near the foundation of the home. Consider treating areas around the foundation with long-acting pesticides such as chlorpyrifos or diazinon to prevent pest entry; heed warnings regarding pets and beneficial wildlife such as birds.

Are there cracks or holes around doors or windows, where insect pests can gain entry? Check all exterior doors, including garage doors and side entry doors. Check any areas where utility lines, such as power or phone lines, make entry. Use a quality caulk and a caulking gun to seal every crack you find. Weather-strip around doors and windows. This will not only help keep pests out, it will help keep heat in and thereby reduce your winter heating bills.

Inspect screens on doors, windows, and vents. Patch or replace them as necessary with screening small enough to keep tiny insects out. Buy or construct a spark arrester screen for your chimney, preferably of 1-inch mesh hardware cloth. Be sure your clothes dryer vent has a flap closure in proper working order.

You should be able to recognize whatever poisonous pests live in your area.

INSPECTING INDOORS

How you effectively eliminate indoor pests depends on many factors. These include the pest type, its life cycle, how it entered the home, how it moves about, and whether pets or children limit treatment options. A thorough periodic inspection indoors will help keep potential entries closed to pests and ensure that you spot problems before they become severe.

Once pests do enter your home, they require food, water, and appropriate hiding places. Eliminating these necessities will go a long way toward eliminating the pests.

Caulk cracks along baseboards and cabinets to destroy potential insect homes. Be aware that items stored for recycling can be attractive havens for pests. Piles of newspapers and bins of empty soft-drink cans offer both hiding places and food. If your community offers weekly curbside recycling, put out whatever materials you have collected each week. If you must take your efforts to a recycling center, add a trip there to your list of weekly chores—perhaps you can turn in recyclables on your way to do the food shopping. Do not allow recyclables to sit in your home for long periods.

Leaky pipes anywhere in the home provide the damp situation many insects seek. These pipes can become highly populated breeding grounds. Repair or replace faulty plumbing as soon as possible.

Drop ceilings, often used in converted basements or garages, seem to be particularly inviting homes for rodents. Push one of the sections aside and flash a light around the space above the ceiling; you may find it littered with mouse or rat droppings and chewed insulation. Since neither children nor pets can reach this

Standing water can be a breeding ground for mosquitoes. Their larvae live in stagnant pools of water.

Rats are capable of chewing through walls, electrical wiring, and this sewer pipe.

In warm-winter areas, termites are a constant problem.

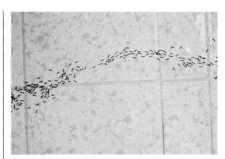

Top: Ants leave a scent trail so that hundreds more can follow.
Bottom: This is the caterpillar and pupa stage of a grain moth, the stages you are likely to find in infested grains.

area, it is a fairly safe place for setting out traps or bait. Handle either with care.

Specific rooms in the house present particular pestproofing problems. The sections that follow constitute a room-by-room tour and will alert you to potential pest attractants.

The Kitchen

A seemingly immaculate kitchen may still be host to a daunting number of ants, cockroaches, grain moths, and beetles. Pests can gain entrance in packages of food or even in the grocery bags themselves. Cockroaches and silverfish hide within the seams of cardboard cartons.

If bringing cartons into the house is unnecessary or if you suspect the cleanliness, leave them outdoors.

Grains are particularly prone to insect pests. Check all flours, cake mixes, and cereals for infestation when you bring them into the home. Destroy contaminated foods immediately. Or, if you intend to return them to the store, keep them in an animalproof container outdoors. If foods seem pest-free, seal each product in a separate lock-tight plastic container. Sealing these foods keeps insects out or, if the products are infested, keeps insects from spreading to other packages. Do not store grain products for long periods. Check them often so that any infestation that does occur can be stopped as quickly as possible. Store large bags of pet food in a metal or plastic garbage can with a tight-fitting lid. Plastic is usually effective, but desperate rodents may actually chew through it and force you to turn to metal.

Of course, crumbs littering the counter, fruit ripening in a bowl, vegetable trimmings in the sink, and cake or bread protected only by plastic wrap offer a free banquet to whatever pests may be present. Vigorous cleaning and a constant eye toward food protection will help starve invaders out of your home.

Pests need water as well as food. Presumably, you have already repaired

leaky pipes. The kitchen offers other water sources, however. Water in the dish rack or the soggy sponge at the sink can provide plenty of liquid refreshment. Water may be collecting in the drain pan of your frost-free refrigerator. If you have pets, the water you put out for them can be used by less desirable animals.

Make a thorough stove check, both back and sides. Foods tend to drop or spill here and act as household pest attractants. If possible without disturbing gas or other connections, pull the stove away from the wall. Clean walls and stove thoroughly and regularly.

Undersink areas often contain sweaty or leaky pipes, paper bags, and other items among which pests hide. Use a flashlight to inspect pipe and utility line entryways. Home centers sell caulk and other products with which to fill or cover the area between pipe and wall, so pest insects cannot enter from outdoors. Clean trash containers daily. Clean undersink areas thoroughly on a regular basis. Also clean the trash container often kept under the sink.

Every so often, clean behind kitchen drawers. Caulk around cupboards where they meet the wall. Purchase caulk that can be painted to match the surroundings.

As you can see, keeping a clean kitchen is not enough to prevent pests. You must also eliminate pest access, make regular sweeps through their hiding places, remove sources of food and water, and react quickly to pest incursions.

The Bathroom and Laundry Room

Although these rooms do not usually contain food for pests, they do provide an array of possible water sources. Repair leaky faucets as well as cracked toilet backs or bowls. A leak provides continual dampness for destructive insects and fungi attracted to water, and even a tiny long-term drip can cause severe damage to your home. Caulk cracks where pipes enter walls, and seal any open areas between toilet bowls and floor. Empty and clean bathtub and sink drain traps on a

weekly basis. Hair and other organic matter trapped here can provide a breeding ground for small pest flies of all kinds.

Check water connections to washing machines. Drips can occur anywhere along the lines. Clean filters in both washer and dryer regularly.

An often-neglected infestation source is laundry brought home from a vacation or by youngsters returning from camp or college. Wash such laundry immediately. Moths are the most common pest cargo in dirty clothing, though it may harbor other insects too.

The Living Room and Bedrooms

Unfortunately, garage sale finds, thrift store treasures, antiques, and donations from friends or relatives can be alive with pests. Inspect all used furniture carefully. Consider spraying newly acquired pieces with insecticide before bringing them indoors.

Vacuuming regularly is a good frontline pest preventive. Use a corner attachment to get into hard-to-reach areas, where carpet insects and fleas tend to hide. Get some assistance, and move heavy furniture occasionally so you can vacuum underneath it, including where furniture legs meet carpet. Vacuum under furniture cushions and into furniture folds. After each vacuuming, empty the vacuum-cleaner bag outdoors and place the contents in a sealed bag for disposal.

Top: This is the adult form of a grain moth, which you may see flying about your kitchen. Bottom: You can often find evidence of a rat infestation in the attic or in a drop ceiling.

Many insects find the vacuum-cleaner bag a lovely place to breed.

Regular dusting is also important. Scientists are giving the dust mite increasing attention as a source of human allergy. In sensitive individuals, dust mites may cause asthmatic symptoms. Wash bedclothes frequently to keep dust mites from accumulating in mattresses and pillows.

The Attic

Even if it is only a storage place, clean your attic regularly. Pest bugs frequently move into attics because they are dark, quiet, and often somewhat damp. Discard attic debris, and use a broom to sweep spiderwebs out of the corners. Consider using a high-powered indoor insect fogger on a regular basis to discourage problems. Seal all cracks, and put small-mesh screen on vents.

In addition to damaging items in your home and encouraging rot and other structural damage, roof and plumbing leaks can provide water for many unwanted attic residents. Trace a leak to its source—water tends to run along rafters or framing before it seeks an exit—and correct the problem as soon as possible.

One potential inhabitant of the attic should be encouraged to stay outside, but not driven away. Bats devour an immense number of insect pests, and can be highly beneficial. If one or more has taken up residence in your attic, wait until

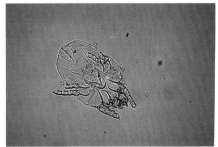

Visible only through an electron microscope, dust mites can be the source of allergy problems.

they have left on their nightly feeding flight and install screening to prevent re-entry. Purchase a bat roost and hang it in an appropriate site. Your insect-control program will get a welcome boost.

The Basement

Like attics, basements are dark, damp, quiet, and often full of stored materials. These provide ideal hiding and breeding places for pests. Use an indoor fogger in your basement if it appears to be harboring large numbers of insects.

Regularly inspect basement floors for damp areas and cracks. These can indicate overhead leakage from plumbing. Correct leaks and patch cracked areas so that insects do not crawl up from under the soil. Check all exposed wood, particularly in areas close to the ground. Decay organisms often enter a home at low points and move to the rest of the house.

CONTROLLING PESTS SAFELY

The improper use and disposal of insect and rodent control materials may cause more problems than the pest.

Control Preparation

Before using any control, read all the instructions thoroughly. If the instructions are unclear, ask a knowledgeable sales-clerk or an agent from the cooperative extension office to explain them to you. Follow instructions exactly. If you are physically unable to use the material as stated, call a licensed pest-control operator for assistance.

To avoid having to store mixed sprays, try to use up all sprays on the day you prepare them. Store mixed and unmixed controls where children cannot reach them by any means, including by climbing on something. Do not transfer control materials from one container to another—children and pets can easily spill pesticides or rodenticides in cups, glasses, or open bottles. Immediately return any undiluted excess to the original labeled container. Never leave control materials in an unlabeled container.

Drain flies can breed in the hair trapped in a drain and are known carriers of disease.

Safe Use

To avoid inhaling chemical vapors, have an ample fresh-air supply available when using controls. Open windows and doors for cross-ventilation. Make certain, before using an aerosol, that the spray opening is pointed away from your face. Do not use a spray near an open flame, and do not smoke while spraying—some controls are extremely flammable. Do not throw aerosol cans into fire, where heat may make them explode. If any chemical control gets on your body, wash it off immediately. After handling chemicals, wash your hands before handling food.

Safe Disposal

Pest control presents two disposal problems: disposal of chemicals and their containers and disposal of dead pests.

Disposal of chemicals In some communities throwing chemicals or their containers in the trash or sewer is illegal. Most of these communities have set aside special days for the collection of hazardous wastes; on these days you can dispose of your pest controls and pest-control containers along with used motor oil, empty paint cans, and the like. If such a service is unavailable in your area, take your controls and containers to a local collection site as soon as possible.

If pest-control containers can go into the regular trash, rinse them out thoroughly. Then wrap them in newspaper before putting them out for pickup with the rest of the rubbish.

Disposal of dead pests Don't forget that the end product of your efforts is a chemically destroyed insect or rodent. Sweep or vacuum up dead insects and seal them in a plastic bag. Keep dead rodents away from children and pets by sealing carcasses in bags and discarding them in a rubbish container with a tight-fitting lid. If this is not possible, or if rubbish pickup is infrequent, bury rodents deep in the soil so animals cannot dig them up.

PESTS AROUND THE HOME

Housefly (4 times life size).

Vinegar fly (10 times life size).

Spider (½ life size).

PROBLEM: Flies are present in the home and other living areas.

ANALYSIS: Houseflies
(*Musca domestica*)
These insect pests are common throughout the world. In addition to their annoying presence, they can spread a number of serious human diseases and parasites such as diarrhea, dysentery, typhoid, cholera, intestinal worms, and salmonella bacteria. Several other closely related fly species, including face flies (*M. autumnalis*) and little houseflies (*Fannia canicularis*), may also infest the home. Flies feed on and lay their eggs in decaying organic materials. The eggs hatch within several days, even within 12 hours if conditions are ideal. The creamy-white maggots (up to ⅓ inch long) burrow into and feed on the decaying material for several days, pupate, and then emerge as adult flies. Under warm conditions, the entire life cycle may be completed within 14 days. However, cooler conditions greatly extend this period. The adults usually live for 15 to 25 days.

SOLUTION: To reduce the fly population, maintain sanitary conditions in the home and garden. Keep garbage tightly covered, and dispose of it regularly. Maintain door and window screens. Kill flies indoors with a spray containing allethrin, chlorpyrifos, or pyrethrins. Kill flies outdoors with a spray or fogger containing malathion or resmethrin.

PROBLEM: Tiny (up to ⅒-inch), yellowish brown, clear-winged insects fly around rotting fruit and vegetables; garbage cans; and other wet, fermenting, or rotting materials. These insects fly in a slow, hovering manner.

ANALYSIS: Vinegar flies
(*Drosophila* species)
These insects, also known as fruit flies, do not constitute a serious health menace but can be annoying in locations where garbage, fruit, or vegetables are allowed to rot and ferment. The adult female flies lay their eggs in the decaying fruit or vegetables. The eggs hatch in a few days, and the tiny maggots feed on yeasts growing in the decaying food. The maggots pupate and become adults; the entire life cycle takes only 10 to 12 days.

SOLUTION: To reduce the fly population, maintain sanitary conditions. Keep garbage tightly covered, and dispose of it regularly. Wash garbage cans on a regular basis. Kill flies with a spray or fogger containing allethrin, chlorpyrifos, or pyrethrins.

PROBLEM: Spiderwebs and spiders are in secluded, rarely disturbed areas in and around the home.

ANALYSIS: Household spiders
Many kinds of spiders wander into the home. With only a few exceptions, these familiar creatures are harmless and cannot reproduce indoors. Spiders are often beneficial, feeding on other spiders and insects, including such household pests as flies and moths. The more insects there are inside the home, the more likely spiders are to be there. Most spiders spin silken webs. Some, such as tarantulas, are active hunting spiders that do not spin webs. When spiders bite humans, it is usually because they have been squeezed, lain on, or somehow provoked. Only a few spiders, particularly the black widow and brown recluse, are dangerous to people, but their bites are rarely fatal. (For more information about black widow and brown recluse spiders, see pages 327 and 328.)

SOLUTION: Knock down webs with a broom or duster. Kill spiders and the insects they feed on by spraying infested areas with a chemical containing boric acid, chlorpyrifos, or pyrethrins. To reduce the number of spiders entering the home, seal cracks, inspect and repair window screens, and clean up accumulations of debris outdoors that may harbor spiders or their prey. Spray with a chemical containing boric acid or chlorpyrifos around doors, windows, and foundations where spiders may enter.

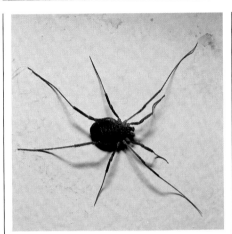

Daddy longlegs (2 times life size).

House cricket (life size).

Moth on door screen.

PROBLEM: Spiderlike creatures with a small body and long delicate legs are found in or around the home and garden. They are sometimes seen in large gatherings, standing with their legs interlaced.

ANALYSIS: Daddy longlegs

Daddy longlegs, also called harvestmen, are closely related to spiders but are not true spiders. They are not capable of producing silken webbing. Daddy longlegs are most common in areas near a source of water. In northern states, most daddy longlegs die in autumn after the females lay eggs. In southern states, females usually spend the winter under ground litter and lay eggs in the spring. They lay eggs in the soil under stones, wood, and other debris. Daddy longlegs feed mainly on small insects. They are most active at night and do not bite humans. Occasionally they wander indoors, but they do not cause any damage.

SOLUTION: Reduce the number of daddy longlegs coming indoors by cleaning up wood, trash, and other debris outside the home. Trim plant growth so it does not touch the house. Seal cracks and crevices around windows and doors, and repair broken screens.

PROBLEM: Crickets are chirping in the home. These insects, which look like grasshoppers, are light to dark brown, $\frac{1}{2}$ to $\frac{3}{4}$ inch long, and have long antennae that curve back along the sides of their bodies. Holes may be chewed in clothing, curtains, carpets, and upholstery in severely infested homes.

ANALYSIS: Crickets

(*Gryllus* species or *Acheta domesticus*)
The two types of crickets that may invade the home are field crickets and house crickets. Field crickets usually live outdoors, feeding on vegetation and plant debris. In the fall, when their natural food supply fails or during periods of heavy rainfall, they may invade buildings in search of food. Field crickets cannot reproduce in the home and usually die by winter. House crickets, however, can survive and reproduce indoors. During the day, both types of crickets hide in dark, warm locations, such as behind baseboards, in closets, and in attics. Male crickets make a chirping sound by rubbing the file and scraper on their forewings together. Crickets may chew fabrics and paper items, and large numbers of the insects may cause serious problems.

SOLUTION: To control crickets outdoors, apply a chemical containing diazinon or chlorpyrifos along the foundation of the house. To control crickets indoors, spray with a chemical containing diazinon or chlorpyrifos. Remove dense vegetation and debris around the building foundation, where crickets may hide. Seal openings around doors and windows.

PROBLEM: Numerous insects fly around indoor or outdoor lights at night. Their physical presence as well as their buzzing or droning is bothersome. Dead insects may accumulate below lights, attracting ants and other insects to the site.

ANALYSIS: Night-flying insects

Many night-flying insects use the moon and stars as points of orientation to help them discern direction. When they see a brighter source of light, such as a light bulb, they mistake it for one of these objects and orient to it, eventually colliding with the light. Lights attract a wide variety of night-flying insects, including most moths and certain beetles, mosquitoes, flies, gnats, and leafhoppers. When many insects become adults during a short period, large numbers may be attracted to lights.

SOLUTION: Spray a fogger containing resmethrin or burn citronella candles to temporarily eliminate outdoor flying insects. Spray with an insecticide containing tetramethrin to control flying insects indoors. Replace white light bulbs with yellow ones; yellow light is less visible to insects and therefore less attractive to them. Use light bulbs of lower wattage, and turn off lights when not needed. Place outdoor lights at least 25 feet from doors and behind shrubs or walls rather than where the lights are visible to insects from long distances. Install or repair screens to prevent insects from moving indoors. If entertaining outdoors, consider using candles for light; their lower intensity is less attractive to insects. For more information on insects and lighting, see Ortho's book *How to Design & Install Outdoor Lighting.*

PESTS AROUND THE HOME

Giant water bug (2 times life size).

Earwig (2 times life size).

Smoky brown cockroach (3 times life size).

PROBLEM: Insects are in the swimming pool. They swim actively, flounder, or are dead. Even well-maintained pools can have this problem. Some of these insects may inflict painful bites.

ANALYSIS: Swimming-pool pests
Many insects and related organisms become pests in swimming pools. Sowbugs, millipedes, springtails, and other insects that are living in nearby vegetation may crawl into the pool and drown. They are particularly common if there is an abundance of organic matter lying under shrubbery near the pool. Bees and wasps may fall into the pool as they search for water. Insects that can live even in chlorinated and clean pools include some beetles and backswimmers, giant water bugs, water boatmen, and water striders. Backswimmers and giant water bugs can inflict painful bites similar to beestings. These insects, as well as many moths, are attracted to pool lights. If a swimming pool is not kept chlorinated and clean, mosquitoes and midges may breed in the water.

SOLUTION: Skim insects off the surface of the water with a dip net. Use lights sparingly near the pool. Switch to yellow lights (which are less attractive to insects) if insects are a continual problem, or place a bright light a couple of hundred feet away to attract night fliers away from the pool. Keep the pool chlorinated and clean. Keep grass and shrubbery trimmed near the pool. Control insects in nearby shrubbery; do not spray the pool directly.

PROBLEM: Reddish brown, flat, elongated insects up to an inch long, with straight or curved rear pincers, are present in the home. They are often found in dark, secluded places such as in pantries, closets, and drawers, and even in bedding. They may be seen scurrying along baseboards or moving from room to room.

ANALYSIS: Earwigs
Several species of this nocturnal insect may infest the home, including the European earwig (*Forficula auricularia*), the ringlegged earwig (*Euborellia annulipes*), and the striped earwig (*Labidura riparia*). Earwigs are usually found in the garden, where they feed on mosses, decaying organic matter, vegetation, and other insects. However, large numbers of earwigs may invade homes—especially during hot, dry spells. They enter through cracks or openings in the foundation, doors, and window screens. Although they do not damage household furnishings, their presence is annoying, and they may feed on stored food items or hide in areas where food is kept. They may inflict painful pinches when provoked.

SOLUTION: Store food in sealed containers. Repair cracks or openings in window screens, doors, and the building foundation. Control earwigs indoors by using a bait containing propoxur, by spraying with an insecticide containing diazinon or chlorpyrifos, or by dusting with a chemical containing chlorpyrifos. Follow label directions. To prevent reinfestations, control earwigs outdoors.

PROBLEM: Cockroaches are found outdoors in woodpiles, ground covers, leaf litter, and other protected areas. Occasionally they wander indoors.

ANALYSIS: Outdoor-originating cockroaches
These cockroaches, often called wood roaches, live mainly outdoors; they occasionally wander inside but cannot reproduce there. The American cockroach (*Periplaneta americana*) and the smokybrown cockroach (*P. fuliginosa*) are two species that can live equally well indoors and outdoors in warm climates. The smokybrown cockroach, in particular, is a pest in many southern states. It moves indoors when weather conditions outside become adverse. Another recent arrival, the Asian cockroach (*Blattella asahinai*), reproduces outdoors only, is attracted to light, and looks similar to the German cockroach. Outdoor-living cockroaches are more likely to wander indoors if suitable places for them to live and breed are next to the house. Favorite habitats include plantings of ground covers and piles of wood, compost, and other debris. These cockroaches are general scavengers, eating decaying plant and animal material.

SOLUTION: To keep cockroaches from coming indoors, move compost and woodpiles away from the house. Clean up litter and debris near the home. Apply a spray containing diazinon or chlorpyrifos in a 5-foot band around the foundation and in nearby ground covers. Make sure the ground cover is listed on the product label. Repair windows, door screens, cracks, and crevices in the walls and foundation. Inspect firewood before bringing it indoors (see page 330).

Silverfish (3 times life size).

House centipede (life size).

Winged psocid (12 times life size).

PROBLEM: Paper and fabric products—especially those made with glue, paste, or sizing—are stained yellow, chewed, or notched and may be covered with excrement and silver or gray scales. When infested products are moved, flat, slender, wingless insects up to ½ inch long may scurry away. These insects have long, thin antennae and may be silvery and shiny or dull and mottled gray.

ANALYSIS: Silverfish and firebrats
(*Lepisma* and *Thermobia* species)
These common household pests are similar in size, shape, and feeding habits; their coloration and hiding places differ. Silverfish are silvery and prefer damp locations from 70° to 80° F, such as basements and wall voids. Firebrats are mottled gray and prefer damp locations from 90° to 105° F, such as hot-water pipes and areas near the oven or furnace. Both pests are active at night and hide during the day. They feed on a wide range of foods, especially products high in starches, including human food, paper, paste, and linen and other fabrics. Silverfish damage books by feeding on the bindings. Both pests crawl throughout the house along pipes and through holes or crevices in the walls or floor. The adult females lay eggs in cracks or openings behind baseboards and other protected areas.

SOLUTION: Treat with an insecticide containing chlorpyrifos or diazinon; follow label directions. Where practical, seal all cracks and crevices in the infested areas. Store valued papers and clothes in tightly sealed plastic bags.

PROBLEM: A thin centipedelike creature with long legs crawls on the floor or wall. The insect is up to 1½ inches long, with extremely long antennae and legs in comparison with its body size; the antennae and rear set of legs can be more than twice the length of the body. The creature runs quickly, with sudden stops.

ANALYSIS: House centipedes
(*Scutigera coleoptrata*)
House centipedes are found both indoors and outdoors in warm regions of the United States, but only indoors where winters are colder. Unlike other centipedes, which wander indoors but cannot reproduce there, house centipedes can live and reproduce indoors. They prey on other insects and become most numerous where there is an abundance of insects to feed on. They prefer dampness and thrive in typically moist areas such as cellars, closets, or bathrooms. Outdoors they are common in moist piles of compost and other debris. House centipedes are most active at night. They seldom bite humans; when they do, the bite is no more severe than a beesting.

SOLUTION: To control house centipedes and the insects they feed on, spray indoor areas with a chemical containing allethrin or tetramethrin, especially along baseboard cracks. Or fog the premises with a fogger containing pyrethrins. Eliminate moist areas in and around the home. Air out damp places. Outdoors, remove piles of compost and other materials that provide hiding places near the house.

PROBLEM: Numerous tiny insects, each the size of a pinhead, crawl in stored food products or around books. These insects may emerge from behind walls for several months after construction of a building. They run along surfaces in a hesitating, jerky manner.

ANALYSIS: Booklice
These insects, also known as psocids, thrive in warm, damp, undisturbed places. They feed mainly on microscopic molds that may develop on certain kinds of adhesives used in bookbinding and wallpaper. Booklice sometimes infest damp Spanish moss, straw, or other vegetable matter used in making upholstered furniture. They feed directly on cereals and other starchy materials (particularly if these products are stored for a long period in damp conditions) and on dead insects. Although booklice contaminate stored food with their body parts, they do not cause other damage. Insect damage seen on books is caused by other insects such as silverfish (see first column) or cockroaches (see page 330). Booklice do not bite or carry disease organisms.

SOLUTION: Dry out infested areas of the home. If booklice are in the food pantry, search for and throw out any infested food. Ventilation and artificial heat can aid in drying out cupboards. Booklice will disappear in new homes as the structure dries. Control infested furniture by thoroughly drying the item in sunlight for several days; having it fumigated by a pest-control operator; or, if practical, discarding the infested stuffing. Infested areas can also be treated with an insecticide containing pyrethrins. Make sure the site you spray is listed on the product label.

PESTS AROUND THE HOME

Carpet beetles and larvae (3 times life size).

Black ants (2 times life size).

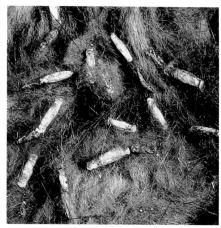

Clothes moths (life size).

PROBLEM: Irregular holes chewed in carpets, blankets, clothing, and other articles made of animal fur, hair, feathers, or hides. Light brown to black grubs up to ¼ inch long may be seen crawling on both damaged and undamaged items. The grubs are distinctly segmented and covered with circular rows of stiff, dark hairs.

ANALYSIS: Carpet beetles
(*Attagenus megatoma* or *Anthrenus* species)
The larvae of these beetles damage carpets, clothes, upholstery, and other products of animal origin. Some species also feed on stored foods. The adult beetles are about ⅛ inch long and may be black or mottled gray, brown, and white. They usually live outdoors, feeding on pollen and nectar. The beetles fly into homes during the late spring or early summer and lay their eggs in cracks or crevices or on clothes, carpets, or other materials. The emerging larvae seek out dark, undisturbed locations in which to feed. They shed their skins a number of times during their development. Most of the larvae hibernate during the winter and pupate in the spring.

SOLUTION: Shake out, brush, and air infested clothes and blankets. To kill remaining grubs, dry-clean infested items. Spray clean clothes with a chemical containing tetramethrin, and place them in airtight closets or containers. Clothes will be protected 6 months in storage. Vacuum infested rooms, particularly under furniture and in corners. Destroy the vacuum-cleaner bag immediately. Kill remaining insects with an insecticide containing chlorpyrifos, diazinon, or pyrethrins.

PROBLEM: Ants are present in the house. Trails of ants crawl in cupboards and on floors, walls, baseboards, and counters. The insects are generally most troublesome in the kitchen or pantry.

ANALYSIS: Ants
A number of species of ant invade households. Most ants are strongly attracted to sweets, starches, fats, and grains; they invade houses to carry these foods back to their nests. Adverse outdoor conditions, such as flooding or drought, may cause ants to move their nests or colonies into buildings. Ant colonies are often built underground in the garden, but they may also be found under flooring and in building foundations, wall partitions, attics, and other protected locations. These nests may contain from several hundred to several thousand individuals. Find an ant colony by following established ant trails to their source.

SOLUTION: Destroy ant colonies by treating them with a dust containing chlorpyrifos or spraying nests and ant trails with an insecticide containing chlorpyrifos or tetramethrin. Eliminate ant colonies from the garden by treating the anthills with granules containing diazinon or by spraying the nests and surrounding soil with a solution containing diazinon. Store food in sealed containers, and do not keep exposed food. Place a bait containing propoxur in areas where ants have been observed.

PROBLEM: Holes are chewed in clothing, blankets, carpets, pillows, upholstery, and other items. Infested articles may be covered with a webbing of silken tubes, cases, or strands. Shiny white caterpillars up to ½ inch long may be seen crawling on damaged items.

ANALYSIS: Clothes moths
(*Tineola bisselliella* or *Tinea pellionella*)
The larvae of these small, yellowish to tan moths damage clothes and other items made of fur, wool, feathers, and leather. The female moths attach their eggs to the fabric. Soon after the larvae emerge they spin silken tubes, strands, or cases. The larvae usually feed from within these protective casings, but they may crawl out to feed unprotected. The larvae pupate in cocoons attached by silken threads to the infested item and emerge as adult moths. New infestations occur when moths lay eggs on clothing, carpets, and other articles and when moth-, larva-, and egg-ridden items are stored with uninfested articles. Clothes moths are not attracted to light.

SOLUTION: Shake out, brush, and air infested clothes and blankets in a sunny location. To kill remaining moths, dry-clean infested items. Spray clean clothes with a chemical containing tetramethrin, and place them in airtight closets or containers. Clothes will be protected 6 months in storage. Vacuum or sweep infested rooms, and destroy the vacuum-cleaner bag immediately. Seek professional help to protect carpets and furs.

Boxelder bug (4 times life size).

Clover mite (30 times life size).

Pigeon.

PROBLEM: During the fall, hordes of brownish black bugs ½ inch long with red stripes on their wings swarm into the home and outdoor living areas. They congregate on walls, walks, furniture, drapes, and other objects. When crushed, they emit a strong, unpleasant odor.

ANALYSIS: Boxelder bugs
(*Leptocoris* species)
These insects are common in all parts of the United States. They are most numerous in areas where boxelder trees (*Acer negundo*) grow. In the spring, the female bugs lay their eggs in the bark of boxelders or sometimes of maples, ash, and fruit trees. The young feed on tender twigs, foliage, and seeds through the spring and summer. During the fall, especially on bright, sunny days, the bugs migrate in large numbers into tree trunks; homes; buildings; or other dry, protected locations to hibernate for the winter. Boxelder bugs do not feed on fabric or furniture but may stain household items with their excrement. Occasionally, boxelder bugs bite, and they may feed on houseplants.

SOLUTION: Vacuum boxelder bugs with a tank-type vacuum cleaner, and then destroy the bag. Or spray the bugs with an insecticide containing malathion, diazinon, or pyrethrins. Keep the doors and windows screened and the cracks around them well sealed.

PROBLEM: Reddish brown mites with long front legs, each mite smaller than a pinhead, are present in the home in the fall. They may be found on walls, windowsills, floors, and furniture, and even in bedding and clothes. When crushed, these mites leave a blood-red stain. They are often so numerous that they give infested surfaces a reddish appearance.

ANALYSIS: Clover mites
(*Bryobia praetiosa*)
These pests, related to spiders, are found throughout the United States. Clover mites feed and reproduce on clover, grasses, and other plants. They are most active in the spring and fall and on warm winter days. The mites lay eggs during the summer and fall. The young, which hatch from these eggs, feed on vegetation and then migrate into homes and other protected areas during the early autumn. Mites enter homes through cracks or openings in the foundation and around doors and windows. Mite activity usually decreases when temperatures rise above 85° F or fall below 40° F.

SOLUTION: Remove mites from household furnishings by vacuuming them from infested surfaces. Destroy the vacuum-cleaner bags. Do not crush the mites because they will leave a red stain. Kill mites indoors by spraying them directly with a miticide containing chlorpyrifos. Treat outdoor areas with a chemical containing chlorpyrifos, diazinon, or malathion. To reduce mite movement into the home, around the foundation keep a strip of soil 18 to 24 inches wide free of vegetation and debris.

PROBLEM: Birds roost or nest in wall voids, under eaves, and in other areas around the home.

ANALYSIS: Birds
Most birds are harmless and pleasant, but a few species—especially pigeons, starlings, and sparrows—may become a nuisance around the home. These birds are adapted to urban and suburban environments. They roost and build nests on chimneys, ledges, rafters, eaves, drainpipes, and similar locations, and they often return to the same nesting site year after year. In addition to their messy droppings and irritating chirping, birds may transmit to humans such diseases as pigeon ornithosis, aspergillosis, encephalitis, and histoplasmosis.

SOLUTION: Where possible, exclude birds with screens. Apply a bird-repellent adhesive or jelly to roosting and nesting areas. Clean up possible food or nest-building materials (such as dried weeds or vegetation) to discourage bird activity in the vicinity. Place flashings of wood, plastic, or metal at a 45-degree angle on nesting or roosting areas. Birds may also be trapped or poisoned. If you are considering poison, consult a licensed pest-control operator or the county agricultural commissioner's office for regulations pertaining to your city.

HOUSEHOLD PESTS

PESTS AROUND THE HOME

Raccoon.

House mouse.

House mouse.

PROBLEM: Raccoons are present around the home. They overturn garbage cans at night, scattering and feeding on the contents and causing a great commotion. They occasionally invade attics, crawl spaces under buildings, and other secluded locations.

ANALYSIS: Raccoons

(*Procyon lotor*)

Raccoons are a nuisance mainly in rural and suburban areas. They generally live near a source of natural water such as a stream, marsh, or pond. Raccoons are dextrous and inquisitive animals. They frequently turn over garbage cans in their search for food. They sometimes take up residence in attics, basements, barns, or similar locations. Although these animals carry fleas and ticks, they are not a serious health threat. Raccoons can be dangerous if cornered.

SOLUTION: Keep garbage cans securely anchored in racks or immovable frames. Lids should be tightly secured to the can. Screen or seal openings into buildings. Consult the regional office of the Department of Fish and Game to find out about local raccoon-control restrictions and regulations. Live traps baited with pieces of melon, prunes, honey-coated bread, or smoked fish are usually effective in controlling raccoons. Attach traps to a tree, stake, or fence post. If possible, push the trap back and forth in the ground until soil covers the wire mesh on the bottom of the trap. Wait a few days before setting the trap; this allows the animal a chance to become accustomed to it. Transport the trapped animal to a wooded area at least several miles away.

PROBLEM: Signs of mouse infestation—including droppings, tracks, or gnawed doors, baseboards, or kitchen cabinets—are found. Books, fabrics, furniture, and other objects may be chewed or shredded, and packages of food may be gnawed open and the contents eaten. Mice may be seen in the garage or home.

ANALYSIS: House mice

(*Mus musculus*)

These familiar pests often go unnoticed if only a few are present, but they may cause significant damage when their numbers are large. In addition to gnawing on clothing, furniture, and other items, mice contaminate food with their urine and droppings, and they may spread parasites and diseases. Mice are generally active at night. Under ideal conditions, the females produce up to 50 young in a year. Mice are agile: They can jump as high as 12 inches off the ground, run up almost any rough vertical surface, swim, and squeeze through openings slightly larger than ¼ inch. House mice feed primarily on cereal grains but eat many other kinds of food including butter, fat, meat, sweets, and nuts.

SOLUTION: Apply a bait consisting of cereal grains treated with cholecalciferol (vitamin D-3), a new-generation rodenticide. This bait is safer to use around pets and other domestic animals than anticoagulant baits. The bait is contained in packets that should be placed in the same areas traps would be placed and out of the reach of children and pets. Another way to eliminate mice in the home is to trap them. Mice are more likely to seek bait in traps if their normal source of food is scarce. Remove food from areas where mice can get to it, and store grains in sealed metal, glass, or heavy plastic containers. Place traps where mouse droppings, gnawings, and damage indicate the presence of mice. These include such areas as behind refrigerators and other protective objects, in dark corners, along baseboards, and in cupboards. Bait the traps with pieces of bacon, nutmeats, raisins, or peanut butter. Tie the bait to the trigger so the mouse won't be able to remove the bait without springing the trap. Check the traps daily to dispose of trapped mice. Wear gloves when handling dead mice, or use tongs to pick them up to avoid bites from mouse parasites. If you are unable to eliminate all the mice, contact a professional pest-control operator. After the mice have been eliminated, prevent them from returning by sealing holes or cracks larger than ¼ inch in walls, floors, windows, doors, and areas of the foundation that open to the outside. For details on mouseproofing your home, contact the local cooperative extension office.

Gray squirrel.

Roof rat.

Norway rat.

PROBLEM: Squirrels are seen or heard in the building. Nuts or other food remnants, droppings, gnawed holes, and nesting materials in the attic, garage, wall voids, and other areas indicate their presence.

ANALYSIS: Tree squirrels

Several species of tree squirrels invade houses, including the fox squirrel (*Sciurus niger*), eastern gray squirrel (*S. carolinensis*), and flying squirrels (*Glaucomys* species). Squirrels enter buildings through vents; broken windows; construction gaps under eaves and gables; and, occasionally, chimneys and fireplaces. They may build nests or store food in attics, wall voids, garages, and similar locations and damage items stored in attics or garages.

SOLUTION: Contact the regional office of the State Department of Fish and Game for regulations governing the control of tree squirrels in your area. Eliminate animals inside the building by placing traps in the areas they are inhabiting. Bait the traps with nutmeats, chunk-style peanut butter, sunflower seeds, or raisins. If tree squirrels are entering the building via trees or power lines, secure traps to tree limbs or the rooftop to intercept them. Once squirrels have been eliminated from the building, seal entry routes into the home with sheet metal or hardware cloth. Prune off tree limbs so they are at least 6 feet away from the roof or any other part of the building.

PROBLEM: Signs of rat infestation—including droppings, tracks, and loosely constructed nests made of rags, paper, and other scraps—are found. Pipes, beams, and wiring may be gnawed. Books, fabrics, furniture, and other objects may be chewed or shredded, and packages of food may be gnawed open and the contents eaten. Rats may be seen or heard in the attic, garage, basement, wall voids, or other areas of the home.

ANALYSIS: Rats (*Rattus* species)

Rats are distributed worldwide and infest well-maintained suburban residences as well as rundown urban houses and apartments. The species that most frequently infest houses are the Norway rat (also known as the brown, house, wharf, or sewer rat) and the roof rat. Rats enter buildings through almost any opening, including toilets, pipes, chimneys, and garbage chutes. They are excellent climbers and can gain access to homes from nearby trees. Young rats can squeeze through openings as small as ½ inch wide. These animals make their nests and breed in wall voids, attics, crawl spaces, basements, and other secluded locations. They also breed in heavy vegetation, such as ivy or juniper ground covers, near the home. Their long front teeth grow constantly. To keep them worn down, rats gnaw on almost anything, including clothing, furniture, and electrical wires. They can also gnaw through gas lines, causing gas leaks. Rats are notorious for contaminating food with their urine, droppings, and hair, spreading parasites and diseases. They occasionally bite people, especially sleeping infants. The bites are dangerous and must be treated by a doctor.

SOLUTION: Apply a bait consisting of cereal grains treated with cholecalciferol (vitamin D-3), a new-generation rodenticide. This bait is safer to use around pets and other domestic animals than anticoagulant baits. The bait is contained in packets that should be placed in the same areas traps would be placed and out of the reach of children and pets. It is especially effective against warfarin-resistant Norway rats. Another way to control rats in the home is by trapping them. Use rattraps because the smaller mouse traps will not be effective. Rats are more likely to seek bait in traps if their normal source of food is scarce. Remove food from areas where rats can get to it easily. Store food in glass or tin containers with screw-on or otherwise tightly sealed lids. Place traps along rat runways, anchoring the trap securely to a nearby object so the animal won't drag it away. Bait traps with pieces of beef, bacon, fish, nutmeats, or carrots. Tie the bait to the trigger so the rat won't remove the bait without springing the trap. Check the traps daily to dispose of captured rats. Wear gloves, or use tongs to pick them up to avoid bites from rat parasites such as fleas and mites. Poisoned baits may also be used. Place baits where children and pets cannot reach them. If you are unable to eliminate the rats, contact a professional pest-control operator. Ratproof the building. Clear landscape plantings to at least 18 inches from the structure. Identify ground burrows, place bait inside, and cover the holes. Ratproofing may involve much expense and work because it involves sealing all openings larger than ¼ inch leading into the building from the outside. Sealing such small openings also keeps out mice. For details, contact the local cooperative extension office.

Skunk.

Fleas.

Flea larvae (6 times life size).

PROBLEM: The tracks and strong scent of skunks are present around the home. The animals are observed living beneath the building.

ANALYSIS: Skunks
(*Mephitus* species)
Skunks become household pests when they take up residence under a house. They are most likely to make a den under a house when natural burrows or dens are not readily available. The strong scent they spray when threatened may cause nausea and even temporary blindness. Skunks can eject this potent fluid as far as 10 feet. Skunks carry a variety of diseases, including rabies. They may transmit rabies to humans and pets. Rabid skunks often show abnormal behavior such as listlessness, unprovoked aggressiveness, or a tendency to wander around during the day. Such animals will bite if handled.

SOLUTION: Contact the local Department of Fish and Game for skunk-control regulations. Eliminate skunks by placing mothballs, open pans of household ammonia, or several floodlights under the building to drive them out. Live-catch, box-type traps may also be used. When handling skunks, wear old clothing and goggles. After the animals have been eliminated, screen off or seal openings into the building. Skunk bites should be treated immediately by a physician or veterinarian. Skunk scent may be neutralized with tomato juice, vinegar, or neutroleum alpha, a compound that may be obtained through a hospital-supply outlet.

PROBLEM: Fleas infest pets, pet quarters, rooms, carpets, upholstered furniture, or the garden.

ANALYSIS: Fleas
These pests of humans, dogs, cats, and many other warm-blooded animals are found throughout the world. In addition to causing annoying bites, they can transmit several serious diseases such as bubonic plague, murine typhus, and tapeworms. The cat flea (*Ctenocephalides felis*), the dog flea (*C. canis*), and the human flea (*Pulex irritans*) are the most common species found around the home. These fleas have a wide host range, attacking humans, dogs and cats, and a number of other animals. The female fleas lay eggs shortly after feeding upon animal blood. The eggs are usually laid on the host's body or the host's bedding. The eggs often fall off the host's body into floor crevices, dog and cat quarters, carpets, and other areas where the infested animals spend time. Within 10 days the eggs hatch into tiny, wormlike larvae that feed on dried blood, lint, excrement, and other organic debris. Pupation occurs after one week to several months. The adult fleas may emerge after only a week if conditions are favorable, or emergence may be delayed up to a year. The adults often remain in their pupal cocoons until a host is present. A flea's life cycle may vary from two weeks up to two years. Because fleas have the ability to survive for many months in their cocoons, they can remain in vacated residences for long periods of time, waiting to emerge and bite returning pets and humans. Fleas are mainly spread by infested animals. Uninfested animals can easily pick up fleas when visiting flea-ridden areas. Fleas may also be spread by infested articles of clothing or furniture.

SOLUTION: Treat infested pets with a dust or spray containing pyrethrin. At the same time, destroy infested pet bedding, or wash it in hot, soapy water. Vacuum carpeting, chairs, sofas, and other areas or objects that may contain eggs and larvae-ridden lint or debris, and then dispose of the vacuum-cleaner bag. Kill remaining fleas in the house with an insecticide containing chlorpyrifos or pyrethrins. Kill fleas in the yard by spraying with an insecticide containing chlorpyrifos, diazinon, or malathion. To prevent fleas from returning, treat the house with a pesticide containing methoprene. This insect growth regulator prevents flea larvae from developing into adults. To prevent reinfestation, do not allow infested animals to enter the house and yard, and keep pets away from infested areas. Flea collars may help prevent reinfestation.

Chigger-infested field.

Pajaroello tick (2 times life size).

Pacific coast tick (4 times life size).

PROBLEM: Welts and hard, raised bumps (papules) appear on the skin, particularly on parts of the body where clothing is binding or where body parts come in contact, such as the belt line, the armpits, the backs of the knees, and under cuffs and collars. Itching is severe and may last as long as two weeks. Welts and itching often develop within several hours to a day after the affected person has been in a scrubby, thicket-covered, or otherwise heavily vegetated area.

ANALYSIS: Chiggers
(*Trombicula* species)
These parasites, also known as red bugs, are the larval forms of several closely related microscopic mites. Only the larvae are harmful. They hatch from eggs laid in the soil of uncultivated, scrubby woodland or marshy areas and attach themselves to people and other hosts as they pass by. Chiggers insert their mouthparts into the skin and feed on blood for several days until they become engorged and drop off. Chiggers are sometimes a problem in lawns around new home developments.

SOLUTION: To remove chiggers from skin, bathe it thoroughly in hot, soapy water. Ask a druggist for compounds to relieve the itching. When walking through chigger-infested areas, wear protective clothing and tightly button or tape sleeves, pant cuffs, and collars. Apply repellents such as diethyltoluamide or ethyl hexanediol to the skin and clothing, especially around the ankles, underarms, waist, sleeves, and cuffs. Treat infested areas around your home with an insecticide containing diazinon; follow label directions.

PROBLEM: Oval, leathery, reddish brown to dark brown ticks are attached to a person or pet. These ticks, which range in size from $\frac{1}{16}$ to $\frac{1}{8}$ inch before feeding, are usually found on the pet's ears and neck and between the toes. Engorged ticks are round, $\frac{1}{2}$ inch in diameter, and blue to olive-gray.

ANALYSIS: Ticks
These blood-sucking pests, which are related to spiders, attack humans, dogs, cats, and other animals. Most ticks are found in grassy or brushy areas. In addition, the brown dog tick may drop off infested dogs in households and establish itself in the home. Ticks attach themselves to passing people and pets and sink their heads and mouthparts into the flesh. If left undisturbed, they may continue to suck blood for as many as 15 days before dropping off. Tick-infested dogs become restless and often lose their vitality because of the irritating bites and loss of blood. Ticks transmit several human diseases, including Rocky Mountain spotted fever, tularemia, and Lyme disease. Lyme disease, carried by deer ticks, was first diagnosed in 1970 and has spread across the United States since then. Ticks can live for up to 18 months without food or water.

SOLUTION: When ticks are sharply pulled or brushed off the skin, their mouthparts usually break off, remaining embedded in the flesh. This may cause small ulcers or infections to develop in the wounded areas. There are no foolproof methods to make a tick withdraw its mouthparts, but the recommended way is to slowly and steadily pull the tick from the skin, then wash the area with soap and water.

If the wound becomes infected or illness ensues, contact a doctor or veterinarian. Treat infested pets lightly with an insecticide containing carbaryl (SEVIN®), pyrethrins, or tetramethrin. If the animal is severely infested, contact a veterinarian. Spray grassy or brushy areas around the home with a spray containing carbaryl (SEVIN®) or chlorpyrifos. Kill ticks in the home by fogging or dusting with an insecticide containing permethrin or pyrethrins. Destroy infested animal bedding, and spray animal quarters and other infested indoor areas with an insecticide containing carbaryl (SEVIN®), pyrethrins, or chlorpyrifos.

PET AND BODY PESTS ▬▬▬▬ ■ STRUCTURAL PESTS

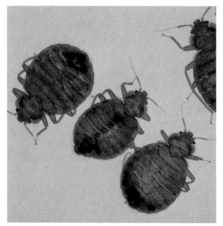

Bedbugs (6 times life size).

Subterranean termites (2 times life size).

Termite-damaged book.

PROBLEM: Painful swellings develop on the body. Dark brown to black spotted stains appear on pillows, sheets, and other bedding. When the lights are turned on at night, reddish brown, oval-shaped bugs about ¼ inch long may be seen crawling on the skin and bedclothes.

ANALYSIS: Bedbugs
(*Cimex lectularius*)
These distasteful bugs have become an infrequent problem in the United States. However, they still infest homes where living conditions are unsanitary and may be transported to well-maintained residences on infested clothing and furniture. Bedbugs hide during the day behind baseboards, in mattresses and upholstered furniture, in cracks and crevices in the floor, in bed frames, and in similar locations. These pests are nocturnal and become quite active at night. They crawl onto sleeping people, pierce their skins, and suck their blood for several minutes. Bedbugs usually deposit telltale masses of dark excrement on bedding after they feed. They may crawl from room to room during the night.

SOLUTION: Spray baseboards, wall crevices, and floor cracks with an insecticide registered for such use, or consult your local public health department for recommendations. Launder all bedding thoroughly. Keep the house clean.

PROBLEM: On warm, sunny spring or fall days, brown to brownish black winged insects, about ⅜ inch long, swarm in and around the house. These insects resemble flying ants but have thick rather than constricted waists. Their discarded wings may be found around the building. Earthen tubes extend from the soil up along the foundation and any other termiteproof surface to infested wooden structures. These tubes are commonly found in basements and crawl spaces under buildings. When broken off, they are rebuilt within several days. Dark or blistered areas may develop in the flooring.

ANALYSIS: Subterranean termites
These wood-feeding insects cause more structural damage to buildings than any other insect. Subterranean termites live in colonies as deep as 5 feet in the ground. They move up to infest wooden structures through tubes of soil they build over masonry or metal to bridge the gap from soil to wood. Except for the dark, winged swarmers, these termites are white, wingless, and extremely sensitive to moisture loss. They always remain within the nest, soil tubes, or infested wood, protected from desiccation and insect predators. Within their colony, termites maintain a complicated caste system that includes sterile workers and soldiers, winged reproducers, and an egg-laying queen. Colonies are formed when a pair of winged reproducers leaves the parent colony and excavates a nest in a piece of wood that is on top of or buried in the ground. As the new colony develops, galleries are formed deep in the soil. Termite colonies develop slowly—three or four years usually pass before the reproductive swarmers develop, and structural damage may not be noticed for several more years. However, when buildings are erected over established termite colonies, serious damage may occur within a year. Termites hollow out the inside of a wooden structure, leaving only an outer shell. Damage is most severe when they infest main supporting wooden beams and girders. One species of subterranean termite, the Formosan termite (*Coptotermes formosanus*), is not native to the United States but is present in areas of the Southeast and Southwest. This termite is more vigorous and aggressive than native North American species and is more difficult to control.

SOLUTION: Termite infestations can be treated most effectively only after a thorough and accurate diagnosis of the damage. Accurate diagnosis is usually difficult and requires the aid of a professional termite- or pest-control operator. Once the termite colony has been located and the damage revealed, a physical or chemical barrier is placed between the soil and the building to prevent the termites from reaching it. An insecticide containing chlorpyrifos is applied to the soil around and underneath the building. Discourage additional infestations by keeping the area under and around the house free of wood debris above and below the ground. If the soil around the foundation remains moist due to faulty plumbing or improper grade, repair the plumbing and alter the grade; termites prefer moist soil. For details on termite-resistant construction methods, contact a reliable building contractor or the local cooperative extension office.

Powderpost beetle and larva (3 times life size).

Emergence holes.

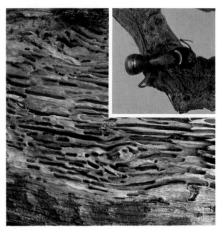

Slitlike holes. *Insert:* Carpenter ant (2 times life size).

PROBLEM: Wood flooring, structural timbers, cabinets, furniture, and other items are riddled with round holes that range in size from $\frac{1}{16}$ to $\frac{3}{8}$ inch in diameter. Wood powder or tiny pellets may be piled around the holes or on the floor below. When the infested item is tapped, additional pellets or wood powder is expelled from the holes. Tiny red, brown, or black beetles ranging in size from $\frac{1}{12}$ to $\frac{1}{3}$ inch long may be seen crawling around the infested wood or flying around windows and electric lights in the evening. Cutting open the damaged wood reveals that the inside is riddled with sawdust-filled tunnels or pulverized into a mass of wood powder or pellets.

ANALYSIS: Powderpost beetles

These wood-feeding beetles—including the powderpost, false powderpost, and death-watch beetles—damage wood houses and household furnishings throughout the United States. Powderpost beetles feed only on dead wood. They are brought into the home in infested timber or furnishings, or they may fly from infested lumber or woodpiles in the yard. The female beetles deposit their eggs in unfinished wood. The grubs, which hatch from the eggs, tunnel through the wood, leaving masses of sawdust or pellets behind them. They pupate just under the surface of the wood and emerge as adult beetles through the round holes they chew. Beetle larvae present in wood before it has been coated with paint, varnish, shellac, or other finishings can chew through the finished surface when they have matured, leaving round emergence holes. However, beetles do not lay eggs in coated wood, so reinfestation in it cannot occur.

SOLUTION: If infestation is localized in a building structure, remove and destroy badly infested timbers. Replace them with kiln-dried or insecticide-treated wood. Or treat unfinished exterior wood yourself by painting or spraying it with an insecticide containing chlorpyrifos. Wherever possible, apply paint, shellac, varnish, paraffin wax, or other wood coatings to unfinished wood around the home to prevent further infestation. Inspect woodpiles periodically for signs of powderpost beetle infestation. Infested wood may also be treated with an insecticide containing chlorpyrifos. If the infestation is widespread, contact a professional pest-control operator to fumigate the building. Individual pieces of furniture may also be fumigated to kill beetle eggs and larvae. Many pest-control operators maintain fumigation chambers for movable items. Eggs and larvae in small wooden items may be killed by placing the items in the freezer for 4 days. When purchasing furniture, ensure that all woodwork is made from kiln-dried stock.

PROBLEM: Black or reddish black, winged or wingless ants up to $\frac{1}{2}$ inch long are seen around the home. Piles of sawdust may be found in the basement or attic, under porches, or near supporting girders or joists. Slitlike holes are often present in woodwork. On warm spring days, swarms of winged ants may cluster around windows. Unlike termites, these pests have constricted waists.

ANALYSIS: Carpenter ants
(*Camponotus* species)
Many closely related species of these wood-damaging ants are found throughout the United States. Carpenter ants bore into moist, decaying wood, forming extensive galleries in which they make nests. They do not eat their sawdustlike wood borings, but feed on other insects, plant sap, pollen, and seeds. When ant colonies grow too large, part of the colony migrates, often invading nearby homes through windows and similar entry points. They will either colonize undisturbed hollow spaces such as walls or bore into structural timbers, ceilings, and floor areas. They require damp and rotted wood. In addition to weakening wood, carpenter ants may infest pantries and inflict painful bites.

SOLUTION: Dust baseboards, windowsills, door frames, and other places where ants crawl with ORTHO Ortho-Klor Ant Killer Dust. Dust into nests if possible. Remove nearby logs, stumps, and woodpiles. Seal openings in the foundation, windows, and other access areas into the home. Spray along the foundation and around the outside of door and window frames and sills with ORTHO Ortho-Klor Soil Insect & Termite Killer.

STRUCTURAL PESTS

Old house borer damage.

Old house borer (2 times life size).

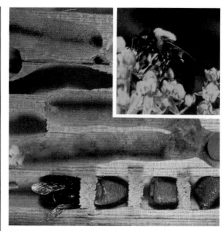

Galleries. *Insert:* Adult carpenter bee (life size).

PROBLEM: Oval holes ¼ to ⅓ inch wide appear in walls and flooring. Or holes appear in wallpaper, plaster, linoleum, and other coverings over wood. Sawdustlike borings may be piled around the holes. In some cases, rasping or ticking sounds may be heard before the holes appear, and the wood may be blistered or rippled. Grayish brown to black beetles, 1 inch long, with antennae may be seen around the house.

ANALYSIS: Roundheaded borers

The larvae of these beetles, including the new house borer (*Arhopalus productus*) and the old house borer (*Hylotrupes bajulus*), cause damage to fir, pine, and other softwood structural timbers. New house borers generally do not cause structural damage—the holes they make in wood or covered wood surfaces are of cosmetic concern only. Female new house borers lay their eggs in the bark of weak and dying forest trees; female old house borers lay their eggs in seasoned lumber. The yellow grubs tunnel into wood that is later incorporated into a building before the adult beetles emerge. New house borers may continue to emerge through holes in wood and wood coverings for up to a year after construction. They cannot reinfest the building. Old house borer beetles generally do not emerge from timbers until three to five years after the building has been constructed. It is the only species of roundheaded borers that reinfests wood, and old house borers may cause serious structural damage. Sometimes the grubs make rasping or clicking noises while they feed. If they are tunneling close to the surface, wood blistering or rippling may result.

SOLUTION: New house borers are the problem if damage occurs within a year after construction. To repair new house borer damage, seal or fill emergence holes. Localized areas may be painted with an insecticide containing chlorpyrifos, but because damage is only cosmetic and will stop within a year, this expensive procedure is seldom justified. Old house borers are the problem if damage occurs at least 3 years after construction. Buildings infested with old house borers must be fumigated; contact a professional pest-control operator. To prevent future infestations of old house borers when building new structures, purchase pressure-treated wood.

PROBLEM: Metallic blue or black buzzing bees fly around the home and yard. They may be seen entering and leaving 1-inch-wide holes in decks, posts, beams, rafters, and other wooden structures. Slicing damaged wood reveals partitioned galleries. The partitions may contain immature bees.

ANALYSIS: Carpenter bees

(*Xylocopa* species)
These insects do not usually cause serious damage; however, continued burrowing and gallery formation year after year eventually weakens wood structures. Carpenter bees burrow into wood to make their nests. The female bees partition the galleries into small cells in which the carpenter bee larvae mature. When bee nests are approached, the males hover around the head of the intruder. Although they are frightening because of their loud buzzing and large size, the male bees do not sting; the females sting only when handled.

SOLUTION: Paint wood surfaces once a year to discourage bee tunneling. Flood galleries in exposed wood with an insecticide containing chlorpyrifos. Close the holes with putty, caulk, dowel pins, or plastic wood to prevent bees from returning to the nest.

Woodwasp (life size).

Dry rot.

Infested firewood.

PROBLEM: Round holes about ¼ inch in diameter appear in wood floors, walls, doors, and other surfaces. Or holes appear in wallpaper, linoleum, carpeting, and other types of covering over wood. Metallic blue, black, or multicolored wasplike insects may be seen flying around the home. These buzzing insects are 1 to 2 inches long and may have hornlike "tails."

ANALYSIS: Woodwasps

These insects, also known as horntails, do not cause structural damage; the holes they make in wood or covered wood surfaces are of cosmetic concern only. Woodwasps lay their eggs in weak and dying forest trees. The adult insects can emerge from the wood up to five years later, often long after the tree has been used for construction. Most woodwasp holes, however, appear within the first two years after the cut wood has been used. These insects lay their eggs only in forest trees; they do not reinfest buildings.

SOLUTION: Seal or fill emergence holes. There is nothing you can do to prevent the woodwasps from emerging. For future construction, purchase lumber that has been kiln-dried or vacuum-fumigated. These processes kill woodwasp larvae embedded in the wood.

PROBLEM: Foundation timbers, paneling, flooring, and other wooden structures are damp and soft, or dry, cracked, brown, and crumbling. Often the wood is broken into small, cubical pieces. Thin mats of white fungal strands may be seen on the rotted wood. Thick white, brown, or black fungal cords up to 2 inches wide may extend across the rotted area. These cords often extend over impenetrable surfaces such as brick and concrete to reach wood surfaces beyond.

ANALYSIS: Dry rot

Dry rot is caused by fungi that live in the soil and grow into wood that is in direct contact with damp earth. The white fungal strands penetrate and decay the wood fibers, causing a soft rot. In some cases, the fungi draw water from the soil up through the thick fungal cords that extend across the rotted area. The water is used to moisten dry wood, providing the damp condition in which the fungi thrive. After the fungi die, badly rotted wood cracks and crumbles into chunks when handled.

SOLUTION: Remove any water-conducting fungal cords from the wood. As much as possible, eliminate moist soil conditions around wood structures by improving ventilation, changing soil grade and drainage, or fixing leaky plumbing. As soon as the soil and wood dry out, the fungi will become dormant. Replace badly rotted wood with wood that has been pressure-treated with preservatives. Remove all wood scraps around the building foundation. When building new structures, use pressure-treated wood in all areas where wood and soil make contact.

PROBLEM: Firewood is riddled with holes. Small piles of sawdust accumulate around the holes or on the ground around the firewood. If the wood has been stored indoors, insects may be crawling around the woodpile or flying around lights or windows.

ANALYSIS: Firewood insects

Many insects develop in and emerge from cut firewood. If infested wood is stored either indoors or outdoors so that it rests against the house, there is a chance that insects will invade the wooden structure of the home. Insects capable of moving from firewood into the structure include carpenter ants (see page 321), termites (see page 320), and powderpost beetles (see page 321). Some insects—such as bark beetles, most flatheaded and roundheaded borers (see page 322), and woodwasps (see first column)—emerge from firewood but attack only living or recently killed trees; these insects do not damage structural wood or household articles.

SOLUTION: Spray infested firewood outdoors with an insecticide containing chlorpyrifos or diazinon. Sprayed firewood should not be burned until at least 2 weeks have passed since treatment, to avoid creating noxious fumes. Store all firewood outdoors unless you plan to burn it within a couple of days. Do not lean an outdoor woodpile against the home; stack it so that at least 1 inch remains between the wood and the structure. If practical, place the woodpile at least 10 feet away from the house.

STRUCTURAL PESTS

BITING AND STINGING PESTS

Cliff swallow.

Yellowjackets (2 times life size).

Yellowjacket (2 times life size).

PROBLEM: Mud nests are found beneath eaves of the building. The nests are shaped like gourds, are about 6 inches in diameter, and have necklike entranceways with round holes. Nests are usually grouped together. Bird droppings and mud are scattered beneath the mud structures. In spring, birds fly in and out of the nests.

ANALYSIS: Cliff swallows
(*Hirundo pyrrhonota*)
These birds, also known as mud swallows, spend their winters in South America and annually migrate northward to the United States. From March through June they build their mud nests, usually against a vertical wall just beneath an overhang such as an eave. The same nesting sites are used year after year, and many of the birds return to the same area they nested in the year before. The birds abandon the nests by the end of June.

SOLUTION: Swallows are protected by state and federal regulations, so obtain a depredation permit from the U.S. Fish and Wildlife Service before removing swallow nests. Wash the nests from under the eaves with a strong stream of water. This must be done consistently over an extended period, or the birds will rebuild the mud colony. Or, after washing the nests away, string a wire across the nest area (usually that means stringing a wire along the junction of the wall and the roof overhang) and drape a 12-inch curtain of aluminum foil or polyethylene sheeting over it. This prevents cliff swallows from attaching their nests to the wall—the new surface is too smooth. If the problem continues, contact a licensed pest-control operator.

PROBLEM: Yellowjackets are present around the home. They hover around patios, picnic areas, garbage cans, and other areas where food or garbage is exposed. Yellowjackets may be seen flying into underground nests, wall voids, or heating ducts. Yellowjackets inflict painful stings when threatened or harmed or when their nests are approached.

ANALYSIS: Yellowjackets
(*Vespa* and *Vespula* species)
Unlike most other wasp species, yellowjackets live in large colonies, often numbering in the thousands. Some species of yellowjackets feed their young on insects and spiders; others scavenge scraps of meat from recreational areas or dump sites. These pests may also feed on nectar, sap, and other sugary fluids, and they may be seen hovering around soft drinks and cut fruit. Yellowjackets can inflict painful stings and are capable of repeated stinging. The venom injected along with the sting causes reddening, swelling, and itching of the affected area. Some people who are sensitive to the stings experience extreme swelling, dizziness, difficulty in breathing, and even death. Yellowjackets are protective of their nests, and large numbers may emerge to sting intruders. Some species build their nests underground; the only evidence of the nest is a raised mound of dirt surrounding a depression several inches deep. Other species build football-shaped nests in trees or shrubs or under eaves. Almost all yellowjackets die in the late fall. Overwintering queens start new nests in a different location the following spring.

SOLUTION: Keep food and garbage covered, and empty garbage frequently. To kill yellowjackets before picnicking, spray with an insecticide containing resmethrin or place a properly baited yellowjacket trap downwind from the picnic or barbecue area (the yellowjackets will be attracted to the bait and die within minutes after entering the trap). To permanently remove yellowjackets from the vicinity, you must eliminate their nests. After locating the nests, spray them at dusk or during the night with an insecticide containing methylcarbamate. Stay 8 feet away from the nest, and spray directly into the entrance hole. If you need to illuminate the area, cover a flashlight lens with red cellophane and use it for only short periods. Stop spraying when the yellowjackets begin to emerge; leave the nest area quickly by walking, not running, away. Respray every evening until insects fail to emerge, then quickly cover the hole with moistened soil. Contact a professional pest-control operator to remove yellowjacket nests in difficult locations or if the insects are inside the home. If you are stung, apply a cold compress or ice pack to the affected area. If a severe reaction develops, call a doctor.

Swarm (⅒ life size). *Insert:* Honeybee.

Paper wasps (life size).

Mud dauber nest.

PROBLEM: Bees are hovering around flowering plants in the garden.
The insects may sting when threatened or harmed. Large numbers of bees may cluster on shrubs or trees. Hives may be in attics, chimneys, and wall voids.

ANALYSIS: Honeybees
(*Apis mellifera*)
These familiar and often feared insects provide honey and wax and play a significant role as pollinators. On warm, sunny days bees forage for nectar among flowering garden plants, then return to their hives in the evening. When an established hive gets too crowded, thousands of bees leave in a swarm. Swarms fly for a mile or so before settling in a new location. En route, they often rest in a tight cluster on a tree branch or other object. Some people are allergic to beestings and when stung experience extreme swelling, dizziness, and difficulty in breathing. To an extremely sensitive person, a beesting can be fatal. A bee cannot sting more than once because its stinger and venom sac rip out of its body when it flies away. The injured bee soon dies.

SOLUTION: When stung, scrape the stinger off the skin with a knife or fingernail. Avoid squeezing the stinger; this forces more venom into the wound. Apply cold compresses or ice packs to the swollen area. If a severe reaction develops, call a doctor immediately. Avoid using plants that are attractive to bees, especially around pools, patios, and other recreation areas. Do not try to remove hives or swarms yourself; contact a professional beekeeper or pest-control operator for help.

PROBLEM: Single-layered paper nests are suspended from eaves, ceilings, or branches. These nests are composed of exposed, open cells and have a honeycomb appearance. They are often umbrella-shaped. Black or brown wasps with yellow or red stripes may be seen hovering around or crawling on the nests.

ANALYSIS: Paper wasps
(*Polistes* species)
Paper wasps, also known as umbrella wasps, usually live in small colonies consisting of 20 to 30 wasps. They build paper nests in which they raise their young. Paper wasps feed on insects, nectar, and pollen. They are not as aggressive and protective of their nests as yellowjackets. (For more information about yellowjackets, see page 324.) However, paper wasps will sting if threatened, causing swelling, itching, and more generalized symptoms in sensitive individuals.

SOLUTION: To remove paper wasps from the vicinity, you must eliminate their nests. Spray the nests at dusk or during the night with a fogger containing propoxur, diazinon, or resmethrin. Spray the nest from a distance of 8 feet. Stop spraying when wasps begin to emerge; leave the nest area quickly by walking, not running, away. Respray every evening until the insects fail to emerge. Remove the nest and dispose of it. If you are stung, apply a cold compress or ice pack to the swollen area. If a severe reaction develops, call a doctor.

PROBLEM: Wasps fly around the garden. Some of these insects are black with yellow, red, or white markings. Others are black, brown, blue, red, or yellow. Many wasps have thin elongated waists. Their mud nests may be found under eaves and on plants or rocks.

ANALYSIS: Solitary wasps
Unlike the social yellowjackets, many wasp species—including potter and mason wasps, mud daubers, and spider wasps—live alone. Most of them build nests of mud and sand in which they raise their young. Many of these wasps feed on insects; a few feed on pollen and nectar. These wasps are not as aggressive and protective of their nests as yellowjackets, and they do not sting as readily. (For more information about yellowjackets, see page 324.) If highly provoked, however, they can sting, causing swelling, itching, and more generalized symptoms in sensitive individuals.

SOLUTION: Eliminate mud nests by hosing or knocking them down. Kill wasps by spraying them with a fogger containing propoxur, diazinon, or resmethrin; follow label directions. Even though many of the solitary wasps are docile, they could be misidentified yellowjackets; avoid threatening or provoking them. If you are stung, apply a cold compress or ice pack to the swollen area. If a severe reaction develops, call a doctor.

BITING AND STINGING PESTS

Saddleback caterpillar (2 times life size).

Horsefly (3 times life size).

Blackflies (3 times life size).

PROBLEM: An irritating rash forms where a hairy or spiny caterpillar touched the skin. Reactions vary depending on the caterpillar and the individual. Symptoms can include mild itching, rash, swelling, local severe pain, local lesions, and fever.

ANALYSIS: Stinging caterpillars

There are about 25 species of stinging caterpillars. These insects have hollow hairs that contain a mild poison. The hairs release the irritating substance when people handle the caterpillars or accidentally brush against them. Most stinging caterpillars are capable of causing only a mild itching or skin rash. The caterpillar that causes one of the most severe reactions is the puss caterpillar (*Megalopyge opercularis*). It can cause intense itching, swelling, local numbness, nausea, and fever (especially in children). This caterpillar is widely distributed in the southeastern and south central United States and feeds on a variety of deciduous trees and shrubs. During some years it increases to unusually large numbers. The saddleback caterpillar (*Sibine stimulea*), the io moth caterpillar (*Automeris io*), and the flannel moth caterpillar (*Norape ovina*) are other caterpillars known for their stinging hairs.

SOLUTION: Avoid handling stinging caterpillars. Spray shrubs and trees on which these caterpillars are found with an insecticide containing carbaryl (SEVIN®). Make sure your plant is listed on the product label. Contact a doctor if a severe reaction develops.

PROBLEM: Black, brown, or black-and-white biting flies about ½ to 1 inch long are present around the home. They are especially bothersome in areas where horses and domestic animals are common.

ANALYSIS: Biting flies

These flies, including several species of horseflies and deerflies, attack humans and domestic animals in rural and suburban areas. The female flies deposit their eggs in still pools of water, in moist soil, or on vegetation. The larvae feed on other insects or decaying vegetation, and then pupate in damp plant debris. The adult flies inflict painful bites that often continue to bleed after the fly has left. Some people bitten by horseflies may suffer from fever and general illness.

SOLUTION: Keep doors and windows tightly screened. Spray outdoor living areas with a fogger containing resmethrin and tetramethrin. Kill biting flies indoors by spraying with an insecticide containing pyrethrins or tetramethrin. Apply an insect repellent, available at a drugstore, to the skin. Remove fly breeding areas by removing stagnant pools of water and wet, decaying vegetation around the yard.

PROBLEM: During the late spring and summer, many black or gray humpbacked flies ⅟₂₅ to ⅕ inch long are present around the home. They inflict painful bites.

ANALYSIS: Blackflies

These annoying flies, also known as buffalo gnats or turkey gnats, attack humans and domestic animals in rural and suburban areas throughout the United States. The female flies deposit their eggs in swiftly running water, including streams and irrigation ditches. The larvae develop in the water and emerge as adult flies during the spring and summer. Blackflies may be blown many miles from their breeding areas. They bite any exposed part of the body and may also bite under clothing, especially where clothes bind, such as around belts and collars. These irritating bites often swell and itch for several days. The victim may suffer headache, fever, and nausea.

SOLUTION: Keep windows and doors tightly screened. Spray outdoor living areas with an insecticide containing resmethrin and tetramethrin. Kill blackflies indoors by spraying with an insecticide containing tetramethrin or pyrethrins. Apply an insect repellent, available at a drugstore, to the skin.

Biting midge (15 times life size).

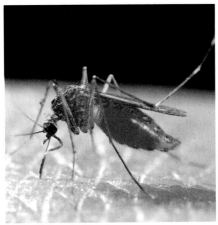

Mosquito (8 times life size).

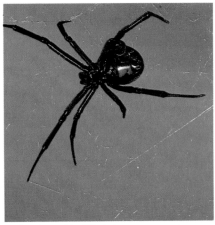

Black widow spider (life size).

PROBLEM: During the spring and summer, tiny black biting midges ½₅ to ⅛ inch long infest the yard. They are most common in coastal areas and near lakes, streams, marshlands, and swamps.

ANALYSIS: Biting midges

These annoying insects are also known as no-see-ums, sand flies, or black gnats. They feed on humans, many warm-blooded animals, and birds. Biting midges breed in wet sand or mud; damp, rotting vegetation; shallow stagnant or brackish water; and similar locations. They rarely infest a home but are bothersome outdoors, inflicting bites around the feet, legs, ears, and under clothing—especially in cuff, collar, and belt areas where clothes bind. The bites are not usually painful, but they produce tiny swellings or blisters that itch for several days.

SOLUTION: Spray infested areas of the yard with an insecticide containing resmethrin; follow label directions. Apply an insect repellent, available at a drugstore, to the skin.

PROBLEM: Biting mosquitoes are present in the home and yard. They are most bothersome at dusk and during the night.

ANALYSIS: Mosquitoes

Many different species of this insect pest occur throughout the world. In addition to their annoying bites, they transmit encephalitis within North America and, in other parts of the world, other serious diseases such as yellow fever and malaria. Adult mosquitoes emerge from hibernation in warm spring weather. The males feed on nectar, honeydew, and plant sap; the females require a blood meal to produce their eggs. Larval development takes place exclusively in water. Typically, eggs are laid in shallow accumulations of fresh, stagnant, or salty water. The larvae may mature within five days, or they may take months to mature.

SOLUTION: Maintain door and window screens. Kill mosquitoes indoors by fogging with an insecticide containing pyrethrins or tetramethrin. Kill mosquitoes outdoors by spraying the lawn and foundation of the house with a chemical containing chlorpyrifos, diazinon, or malathion. Spray under eaves with an insecticide containing pyrethrins, chlorpyrifos, or tetramethrin. Apply an insect repellent, available at a drugstore, to the skin. Drain unnecessary accumulations of water. Stock ornamental ponds with mosquito fish (*Gambusia affinis*), which eat mosquito larvae. Goldfish also eat mosquito larvae, but they are not as effective as mosquito fish.

PROBLEM: Black widow spiders are shiny, black, and about the size of a quarter, and they have a red hourglass marking on the underside of their abdomens. Outdoors, they live under rocks or clods of dirt or in wood- and rubbish piles. Indoors, they are found in garages, attics, cellars, and other dark secluded places, such as under boards or cluttered debris, in old clothing, or in crevices. Black widow webs are coarse and irregular, about 1 foot wide.

ANALYSIS: Black widow spiders

(*Latrodectus* species)
Several species of these poisonous spiders are found throughout the United States. Black widows live in secluded locations and feed on insects trapped in their webs. If the spiders are accidentally touched or their webs are disturbed, they bite the intruder. Their venom may cause serious illness and, on rare occasions, death. The females produce egg sacs that contain hundreds of eggs. The tiny spiderlings that emerge are also capable of inflicting poisonous bites. Spiderlings may be carried long distances by the wind.

SOLUTION: Kill spiders by spraying webs and infested areas with an insecticide containing chlorpyrifos, propoxur, or diazinon, or dust areas where spiders may hide with an insecticide containing chlorpyrifos. Remove loose wood, trash, and clutter from possible spider areas. Wear gloves and protective clothing when cleaning up infested sites. Vacuum infested areas indoors to remove egg sacs, then destroy the vacuum-cleaner bag. Put ice on black widow spider bites and call a doctor immediately.

BITING AND STINGING PESTS

Brown recluse spider (2 times life size).

Mound. *Insert:* Fire ant (4 times life size).

Harvester ant mound.

PROBLEM: The brown recluse spider is light to dark brown, ⅓ to ½ inch in length, and has a violin-shaped marking behind the head. Outdoors, brown recluse spiders are found under rocks. Indoors, they are found in old boxes, among papers and old clothes, behind baseboards, underneath tables and chairs, and in other secluded places. Grayish, irregular, sticky webs and round white egg sacs ¾ inch wide may be found in the infested areas.

ANALYSIS: Brown recluse spiders
(*Loxosceles reclusa*)
These poisonous spiders are found in the Midwest and Southeast. Other related but less poisonous spiders (*Loxosceles* species) are found throughout most of the United States. Brown recluse spiders live in secluded places and are extremely shy, moving away quickly when disturbed. If they are touched or trapped in shoes, clothing, or bedding, they may bite. Their venom is rarely fatal, but it causes a severe sore that is slow to heal and sometimes causes illness.

SOLUTION: Indoors, kill spiders by spraying webs and infested areas with an insecticide containing chlorpyrifos or diazinon. Spray outdoor areas where spiders may hide with an insecticide containing resmethrin. Remove loose wood, trash, or clutter from possible spider areas. Wear gloves and protective clothing when cleaning up infested sites. Indoors, vacuum infested areas to remove egg sacs, then destroy the vacuum-cleaner bag. Put ice on brown recluse spider bites and call a doctor immediately.

PROBLEM: Small (¼-inch) reddish to black ants crawl to and from large mounds of soil in the lawn and garden. These ants inflict painful stings to people or animals disturbing the mounds.

ANALYSIS: Fire ants
(*Solenopsis* species)
These ants are notorious for their large mounds and painful stings. The mounds, which are their nests, are usually found in lawns and gardens. Occasionally the ants move into or underneath homes during periods of rain or drought. They feed mainly on other insects but also feed on young succulent plants; seeds; fruit; household foods; and even small, weak animals such as newly hatched birds. Because fire ants feed on other insects, they are of some benefit in the yard. However, the threat of their painful stings can greatly limit use of the garden. The sting results in a pustule that develops within 24 hours. The bite heals within several weeks.

SOLUTION: Control fire ants in the lawn by sprinkling it with a powder containing acephate (ORTHENE®) or by drenching the mounds with an insecticide containing diazinon or chlorpyrifos. Also treat the area surrounding the mounds to a distance of 4 feet. Spray ants indoors with an insecticide containing chlorpyrifos. If a severe reaction to a fire ant sting develops, call a doctor.

PROBLEM: Large ants up to ½ inch long crawl on cleared areas on the ground and enter holes or large craters in the ground. The holes are surrounded by a cleared area from 3 to 35 feet in diameter. The cleared area may be strewn with small pebbles and seed husks. Ant trails radiate from the nest in all directions. If there is a mound, it is usually low. If disturbed, the ants may inflict painful stings.

ANALYSIS: Harvester ants
(*Pogonomyrmex* species)
Harvester ants do not invade the home, but they may be a problem in lawns and gardens. These ants eat all tender vegetation surrounding their nests, resulting in a large cleared area where they dump small pebbles removed from their nests, husks, and other inedible portions of seeds. They are primarily seed eaters. Harvester ants aggressively sting and bite anything that disturbs their nests; they have been known to kill very small animals that accidentally wander over the sites.

SOLUTION: Treat the entrances to the ant nests and the cleared area around them with an insecticide containing acephate (ORTHENE®), chlorpyrifos, or diazinon. If you are stung, apply a cold compress or ice pack to the swollen area. If a severe reaction develops, call a doctor.

■ **PANTRY PESTS**

Scorpion (2 times life size).

Tarantula (½ life size).

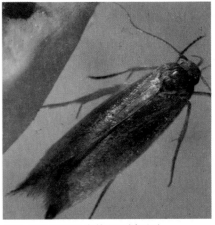

Angoumois grain moth (6 times life size).

PROBLEM: Scorpions are found in the garden under rocks, boards, and protective debris. Indoors, they may be found in attics or crawl spaces under the home. They may move down into living areas such as kitchens and bathrooms when attic temperatures rise above 100° F.

ANALYSIS: Scorpions

All scorpions are capable of inflicting stings; however, only a few species found in the Southwest are dangerous. Scorpions feed at night on insects and small animals. During the day, they hide in dark, protected locations. They are shy and sting only when touched, trapped, or provoked. Except for a few fatally poisonous scorpions (*Centruroides* species), most deliver stings that are no more serious than beestings. The venom varies in potency from season to season, however, and—like many insect stings—may cause severe illness in a sensitive individual. Although scorpions live mostly in the garden, they may crawl into the home through open or loose doors and windows.

SOLUTION: To eliminate scorpion hiding places, remove loose boards, rocks, clutter, and other debris around the yard and in the home. Wear gloves and protective clothing when cleaning up infested areas. Spray locations where scorpions might hide in the yard with an insecticide containing diazinon; spray in the home with a pesticide containing chlorpyrifos. Maintain window and door screens and weather stripping. Call a doctor if you are stung by a scorpion.

PROBLEM: A large, hairy spider, up to 5 inches across, crawls on the floor indoors or outside in the garden.

ANALYSIS: Tarantulas

These spiders are often feared because of their large size and hairy bodies. Although a few South American species can give a painful bite, the bite of all tarantulas native to the United States is little worse than a beesting. Their hairs, which easily rub off their bodies, can irritate human skin. When cornered, tarantulas may make a purring sound or rear up on their back legs. Usually, however, tarantulas are sluggish. They bite only rarely and can be handled with ease. In recent years, tarantulas have become more acceptable as pets and are often sold in pet stores. Female tarantulas may live 20 years or more in captivity. In comparison, males are short-lived. Tarantulas are nocturnal, living in dark cavities or burrows during the day and hunting at night.

SOLUTION: Capture the spider in a large jar or box and release it in a secluded area. Chances of being bitten while catching it are minimal, but be prudent by wearing long rubber gloves or other protective clothing and avoiding sudden, quick movement. If a severe reaction to a tarantula bite develops, call a doctor. To control spiders, spray a 5-foot band around the home with an insecticide containing diazinon or dust a 2-foot band around the foundation with a powder containing chlorpyrifos.

PROBLEM: Pinkish or greenish caterpillars up to ⅝ inch long are feeding inside silken webbing in stored grain, flour, cereals, and other grain products. Beige, gray, and coppery winged moths ⅓ inch long may be seen flying around in the home.

ANALYSIS: Flour moths

The larvae of Indian meal moths (*Plodia interpunctella*) and Mediterranean flour moths (*Anagasta kuehniella*) damage ground or broken grain products, dried fruits, powdered milk, and other pantry items. The larvae of angoumois grain moths infest whole wheat and corn kernels. Adult female moths lay eggs in stored grain products. The larvae that emerge spin silken webs, under which they feed. When mature, they usually leave the infested food to pupate in a corner or crack in the cupboard.

SOLUTION: Discard all infested food. Clean cupboards thoroughly before restocking. If infestation is widespread, remove all food and utensils and fog the infested area with an insecticide containing pyrethrins. Or, after removing food and utensils, spray cracks and crevices along shelves with an insecticide containing chlorpyrifos, diazinon, or tetramethrin. Do not treat countertops or other food-preparation areas. Line shelves with fresh paper and replace pantry items after the spray has dried. If you suspect that food is infested, kill the eggs, larvae, and pupae by deep-freezing food for 4 days or heating it in a shallow pan at 150° F for 30 minutes. Keep foods in airtight glass, plastic, or metal containers. Keep the pantry clean, and avoid buying broken packages—they are more likely to be infested.

PANTRY PESTS

German cockroaches (life size).

Oriental cockroach (2 times life size).

Mealworms (life size).

PROBLEM: Cockroaches infest the kitchen, bathroom, and other areas of the home. These flat, shiny insects range in size from ½ to 1¾ inches long. They may be light brown, golden tan, reddish brown, or black. In large numbers, they emit a fetid odor.

ANALYSIS: Cockroaches

These insect pests thrive in human habitations throughout the world. The most significant household species in the United States are the German cockroach (*Blattella germanica*); the brown-banded cockroach (*Supella longipalpa*); the Oriental cockroach (*Blatta orientalis*); the American cockroach (*Periplaneta americana*); and the Asian cockroach (*Blattella asahinai*), a recent arrival in North America and similar in appearance to the German cockroach. In addition to their annoying presence, cockroaches spread diseases, such as salmonella poisoning and parasitic toxoplasmosis, by contaminating food with their infected droppings. These pests proliferate in areas where food and water are available. Cockroaches prefer starchy foods but will feed on any human and pet food scraps, garbage, paper, or fabrics soiled with food. Unless infestations are heavy or their hiding places are disturbed, they are rarely seen in exposed locations during the day. These nocturnal insects seek out dark, protected areas in which to live and breed. Usually they congregate in kitchens and bathrooms. They may be found behind or under sinks, refrigerators, and water heaters; within the walls of household appliances; behind baseboards and molding; in wall voids; around pipes; in garbage cans; and in piles of cluttered paper or grocery bags. They may be present in cracks or crevices in cupboards, cabinets, desks, dressers, and closets. They may infest basements, crawl spaces, and sewers. Cockroaches move from one room to another through wall voids; through cracks in walls, floors, and ceilings; and along pipes and conduits. If their living conditions become too crowded, they may migrate. Infestations usually begin when stray insects or egg cases are brought into the home with shipped items; secondhand furniture; or appliances, grocery bags, or debris. They may also move into homes from sewers.

SOLUTION: Eliminate cockroach food sources by keeping the kitchen and other areas of the home free of food scraps. Clean up the kitchen after each meal, and store food in tightly sealed metal, glass, or plastic containers. Empty household garbage and pet litter regularly. Do not leave pet food out overnight. Fix leaking faucets and pipes. Clean up water puddles or moist areas around the kitchen, basement, and other infested areas. With a filling material such as putty or caulk, plug cracks around baseboards, shelves, cupboards, sinks, and pipes. Remove food and utensils, then apply an insecticide containing chlorpyrifos, diazinon, or boric acid in cracks in cupboards, surfaces underneath sinks, along moldings, behind appliances, and in other areas where insects are likely to congregate. Allow the spray to dry and then line the shelves with fresh paper before replacing food and utensils. Put out a bait containing propoxur in other hiding places. Nontoxic sticky traps are also effective in controlling small infestations.

PROBLEM: Shiny, yellow to brown grubs up to 1¼ inches long feed in damp or moldy flour or grain products. Flat, shiny, brown to black beetles ¼ to ¾ inch long may also be found.

ANALYSIS: Mealworms

(*Tenebrio* and *Alphitobius* species)
These insects prefer to feed on damp or moldy grain products stored in dark, rarely disturbed, dusty locations such as warehouses. However, if infested food items are brought into the pantry, the mealworms and beetles may migrate to infest and reproduce in poorly sealed bags of flour, bran, crackers, and other grain products.

SOLUTION: Discard infested food items. Clean cupboards thoroughly. Keep grain products in dry, tightly sealed glass, plastic, or metal containers. To prevent reinfestation treat cabinets with insecticides labeled for controlling pantry pests.

Red flour beetle (6 times life size).

Rice weevils (4 times life size).

Cigarette beetle, larva, and pupa (2 times life size).

PROBLEM: Reddish to dark brown, elongated beetles $\frac{1}{10}$ to $\frac{1}{7}$ inch long, and yellowish white, wiry grubs $\frac{1}{5}$ inch long are feeding in flour, cereals, cake mixes, macaroni, and other flour and grain products.

ANALYSIS: Flour beetles
(*Tribolium* species or *Oryzaephilus* species)
Several species of beetle—including the sawtoothed grain beetle, the red flour beetle, and the confused flour beetle—infest grain products in the pantry, grocery store, and packing plant. These pests feed on and reproduce in stored grain products. They can migrate to and infest nearby broken or poorly sealed containers and can also chew through and infest flimsy paper and cellophane packages. Even when infested packages are removed, the beetles can live on flour and cereals that sift into cracks in the cupboard.

SOLUTION: Discard all infested food. Clean cupboards thoroughly before restocking. If infestation is widespread, remove food and utensils from the pantry and treat cracks and the area behind shelves with an insecticide containing diazinon or tetramethrin or fog the infested area with an insecticide containing pyrethrins or diazinon. Let the spray dry before replacing food and utensils. Keep food in airtight glass, plastic, or metal containers. If you suspect food is contaminated, kill the beetles, grubs, and eggs by deep-freezing food for 4 days or heating it in a shallow pan at 150° F for 30 minutes. Keep the pantry clean, and avoid buying broken packages—they are more likely to be infested.

PROBLEM: Reddish brown to black beetles, $\frac{1}{8}$ to $\frac{1}{6}$ inch long, with elongated snouts are feeding in stored whole-grain rice, corn, wheat, and beans. The beetles may be seen crawling around the pantry. Yellow-white grubs may be inside infested kernels.

ANALYSIS: Grain weevils
(*Sitophilus* species)
These pantry pests include the granary weevil and the rice weevil. They usually damage whole grains but occasionally infest flour and other broken or processed grain products. Adult female weevils lay eggs inside grain kernels. Larvae that hatch from the eggs mature inside the kernels, pupate, and emerge as adults. The adults wander about and are often seen far from the site of infestation.

SOLUTION: Discard all infested food. Clean cupboards thoroughly before restocking. If the infestation is widespread, remove all food and utensils and fog the kitchen with an insecticide containing pyrethrins or spray shelves and cracks in pantry cupboards with an insecticide containing tetramethrin or diazinon. Do not spray countertops or other food-preparation areas. After the spray has dried, line shelves with fresh paper and replace food. Keep food in airtight glass, plastic, or metal containers, and avoid buying broken packages—they are more likely to be infested.

PROBLEM: Reddish or reddish brown, oval-shaped beetles, $\frac{1}{8}$ inch long, or yellowish white, curved grubs feed in stored tobacco, cigars, or cigarettes. They may also be found in spices, such as red pepper and paprika, coffee beans, and other stored foods derived from plants.

ANALYSIS: Cigarette and drugstore beetles
(*Lasioderma serricorne* or *Stegobium paniceum*)
These beetles are native to tropical parts of the world and can survive in the United States only in buildings above 65° F. These pests feed on and reproduce in foods and spices. They may also feed on wool, leather, paper, drugs, and other household items. When infested products are brought into the home, the beetles can invade nearby uncontaminated foods that are kept in unsealed, broken, or flimsy containers. They may also chew through sealed paper containers.

SOLUTION: Remove and destroy all infested foods. Clean cupboards thoroughly before restocking. If the infestation is widespread, remove food and utensils and spray shelves and cracks with an insecticide labeled for controlling pantry pests. Let the spray dry before replacing food. Keep foods and spices in airtight glass, metal, or plastic containers. Refrigerate food kept in paper packages. Do not purchase items in broken or unsealed packages—they are more likely to be infested.

APPENDIX

Some houseplants that tolerate low light:

Botanical name	Common name
Aglaonema	Chinese evergreen
Aspidistra	Cast-iron plant
Cissus	Grape ivy
Dieffenbachia	Dumbcane
Dracaena	
Palmae	
Chamaedorea	Parlor palm
Howea	Kentia palm
Rhapis	Lady palm
Philodendron	
Sansevieria	Mother-in-law's tongue
Scindapsus and	Pothos
Epipremnum	
Spathiphyllum	Spathe flower
Syngonium	Nephthytis

Some houseplants that produce easily rooted cuttings:

Botanical name	Common name
Aglaonema	Chinese evergreen
Begonia	
Chlorophytum	Spider plant
Chrysanthemum	
Cissus	Grape ivy
Coleus	
Crassula	Jade plant
Fittonia	Nerve plant
Gynura	Purple passion vine
Hedera	Ivy
Impatiens	
Maranta	Prayer plant
Pelargonium	Geranium
Philodendron	
Pilea	Aluminum plant
Plectranthus	Swedish ivy
Saintpaulia	African violet
Scindapsus	Pothos
Syngonium	Nephthytis
Tolmiea	Piggyback plant
Tradescantia	Wandering Jew

Some houseplants that are sensitive to salts in the soil:

Botanical name	Common name
Aphelandra and	Zebra plant
Calathea	
Aspidistra	Cast-iron plant
Avocado	
Chamaedorea	Parlor palm
Chlorophytum	Spider plant
Cissus	Grape ivy
Citrus	
Coffea	Coffee plant
Cordyline	Ti plant
Cycas	Sago palm
Dracaena	
× Fatshedera	Aralia ivy
Fatsia	Japanese aralia
Ficus	Ornamental fig, rubber plant
Haworthia	
Hedera	Ivy
Howea	Kentia palm
Maranta	Prayer plant
Monstera	Split-leaf philodendron
Pandanus	Screw pine
Philodendron	
Polypodiaceae	Fern family
Saxifraga	Strawberry geranium
Spathiphyllum	Spathe flower
Tolmiea	Piggyback plant

Some houseplants that tolerate full light:

Botanical name	Common name
Aeschynanthus	Lipstick plant
Asparagus	Asparagus fern
Begonia	Wax begonia
Brassaia	Schefflera
Cactaceae	Cactus family
Caladium	
Capsicum	Ornamental pepper
Chrysanthemum	
Citrus	
Codiaeum	Croton
Coffea	Coffee plant
Coleus	
Columnea	Column flower
Cycas	Sago palm
Dizygotheca	False aralia
Euphorbia	Poinsettia
Fatsia	Japanese aralia
Ficus	Ornamental fig, rubber plant
Gynura	Purple passion vine
Hedera	Ivy
Hippeastrum	Amaryllis
Hoya	Wax plant
Passiflora	Passion flower
Pelargonium	Geranium
Rosa	Miniature rose
Senecio	Parlor ivy, string-of-beads

Turfgrass climate zones:

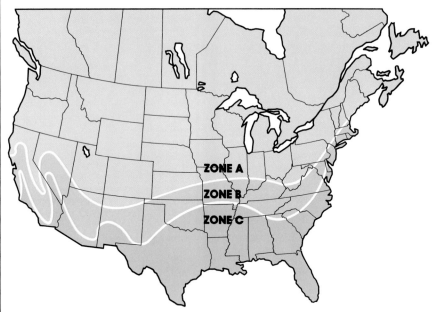

Zone A   Cool-season grasses.

Zone C   Warm-season grasses.

Zone B   This is a transition zone in which both warm-season and cool-season grasses are grown. Because warm-season grasses have long dormant periods in this zone, cool-season grasses are usually preferred. Tall fescue does particularly well in this zone.

From *Turf Managers Handbook,* W. H. Daniel and R. P. Freeborg.

Characteristics of some turfgrasses:

Grass	Zone	Drought Resistant	Shade Tolerant	Days to Germinate	Low Maintenance*
Bahiagrass	C			21–28	
Bentgrass	A		•	5–12	
Bermudagrass, common	C	•		14–20	•
Bermudagrass, improved	C	•		Sprigs	•
Carpetgrass	C			21	
Centipedegrass	C			14–20	
Fescue, red	A	•	•	5–12	•
Fescue, tall	A	•	•	5–12	•
Kentucky bluegrass	A			20–30	
St. Augustine grass	C		•	Sprigs	
Zoysiagrass	C	•	•	Sprigs	•

*Low maintenance turfgrasses are those that tolerate irregular fertilizing, watering, and mowing.

Some turfgrass varieties resistant to dollar spot:

BLUEGRASS
A-20
Adelphi
Bonnieblue
Bristol
Columbia
Majestic
Parade
Park
Touchdown
Vantage
Victa

FESCUE
Jamestown chewing
Pennlawn creeping

BENTGRASS
Arlington
Pennpar

Some bluegrass varieties resistant to fusarium blight:

RESISTANT
A-20
Adelphi
Bonnieblue
Columbia
Enmundi
Glade
Parade
Rugby
Sydsport
Trenton
Vantage
Windsor

MODERATELY RESISTANT
Majestic
Merit
Ram #2

SUSCEPTIBLE
Arboretum
Belturf
Brunswick
Campus
Cougar
Delft
Enita
Fylking
Geronimo
Merion
Modena
Newport
Nugget
Park
Pennstar
Pio-Cebaco
Plush
Ram #1
South Dakota Certified

Some bluegrass varieties resistant to stripe smut:

A-20
A-34
Adelphi
Aquila
Birka
Bonnieblue
Brunswick
Enmundi
Glade
Newport
Plush
Ram #1
Sydsport
Touchdown
Vantage

Some bluegrass varieties resistant to helminthosporium leaf spot:

RESISTANT
A-20
Adelphi
Birka
Bonnieblue
Bristol
Brunswick
Majestic
Merion
Newport
Nugget
Parade
Pennstar
Rugby
Sydsport
Touchdown
Vantage
Victa

MODERATELY RESISTANT
Baron
Cheri
Enmundi
Glade

SUSCEPTIBLE
Delta
Geary
Kenblue
Newport
Park

Some bluegrass varieties resistant to rust:

A-20
A-34
Bonnieblue
Fylking
Glade
Majestic
Park
Pennstar
Rugby

Some bluegrass varieties resistant to red thread:

A-34
Adelphi
Birka
Bonnieblue
Touchdown

Some bluegrass varieties resistant to fusarium patch:

Adelphi
Birka
Bonnieblue
Touchdown

Some drought-resistant ground covers:

Botanical name	Common name
Aegopodium podagraria	Goutweed
Arctostaphylos uva-ursi	Manzanita
Artemisia	Wormwood
Baccharis pilularis	Dwarf coyote bush
Carpobrotus, Lampranthus, and other genera	Ice plant
Cistus	Rockrose
Coronilla varia	Crown vetch
Cotoneaster adpressus	Creeping cotoneaster
C. dammeri	Bearberry cotoneaster
C. horizontalis	Rock cotoneaster
Festuca ovina var. *glauca*	Blue fescue
Helianthemum nummularium	Sunrose
Hypericum	St. John's wort
Juniperus	Juniper
Phalaris arundinacea var. *picta*	Ribbon grass
Phyla nodiflora	Lippia
Rosmarinus officinalis 'Prostratus'	Dwarf rosemary
Santolina	Lavender cotton
Sedum	Stonecrop
Thymus	Thyme
Verbena peruviana	Peruvian verbena

Some ground covers for shady areas:

Botanical name	Common name
Adiantum pedatum	Maidenhair fern
Ajuga	Carpet bugle
Asarum	Wild ginger
Asparagus densiflorus	Asparagus fern
Athyrium goeringianum	Japanese painted fern
Cyrtomium falcatum	Holly fern
Dryopteris	Wood fern
Duchesnea indica	Mock strawberry
Epimedium	Barrenwort
Euonymus fortunei	Winter creeper
Galium odoratum	Sweet woodruff
Hedera	Ivy
Hypericum	St. John's wort
Liriope	Lilyturf
Ophiopogon japonicus	Mondo grass
Pachysandra terminalis	Japanese spurge
Sarcococca hookerana var. *humilis*	Small Himalayan sarcococca
Soleirolia soleirolii	Baby's tears
Vinca	Periwinkle
Viola odorata	Sweet violet

Some ground covers for sunny areas:

Botanical name	Common name
Achillea tomentosa	Woolly yarrow
Arabis	Rockcress
Arctostaphylos uva-ursi	Manzanita
Artemisia	Wormwood
Baccharis pilularsis	Dwarf coyote bush
Carpobrotus, Lampranthus, and other genera	Ice plant
Ceanothus griseus var. *horizontalis*	Wild lilac
Cerastium tomentosum	Snow-in-summer
Cotoneaster adpressus	Creeping cotoneaster
C. dammeri	Bearberry cotoneaster
C. horizontalis	Rock cotoneaster
Helianthemum nummularium	Sunrose
Hypericum	St. John's wort
Juniperus	Juniper
Lantana	
Phlox subulata	Moss pink
Phyla nodiflora	Lippia
Pyracantha koidzumii 'Santa Cruz'	Santa Cruz firethorn
Rosmarinus officinalis 'Prostratus'	Dwarf rosemary
Santolina	Lavender cotton
Sedum	Stonecrop
Taxus × *media* 'Chadwicki'	Chadwick yew
Thymus	Creeping thyme
Trachelospermum	Star jasmine
Vaccinium angustifolium	Lowbush blueberry

Planting and blooming of some common flowers:

Flower	Plant	Planting season	Blooming season	Ideal soil temperature for germination (° F)	Days to germination
Ageratum	A	Sp*	Sp–Su	60–65	10
Amaranth	A	Sp	Sp–Su	60–70	12
Anemone	Tu	F or Sp	Sp	**	**
Aster	P	Sp	Sp–Su–F	70	12–14
Astilbe	P	Sp	Sp–Su	60–70	14–21
Begonia	Tp	Sp	Sp–Su	70–75	15–20
Bellflower	P	Sp	Sp–Su–F	68–86	10–14
Black-eyed Susan	A, P	Sp	Su–F	70–75	5–10
Blanket flower	A, P	Sp*	Su–F	70	15–20
Candytuft	A, P	Sp*	Sp–Su	70–85	7–15
Canna	Rh	Sp	Su–F	**	**
Cape marigold	A	Sp	Su	70–85	15–20
Chrysanthemum	A, P	Sp	Su–F	70	7–10
Cineraria	A	Sp*	W–Sp	45–60	20
Cockscomb	A	Sp	Su	70–85	7–14
Columbine	P	F or Sp	Sp–Su	70–85	21–28
Coral bells	P	F or Sp	Sp–Su	70–85	5–20
Coreopsis	A, P	F or Sp	Su–F	70	15–20
Cosmos	A	Sp	Su–F	70–85	10–15
Crocus	Corm	F	Sp	**	**
Dahlia	Tu	Sp	Su–F	70–85 (seed)	15–20
Daylily	Tu	Sp*	Su	**	**
Delphinium	A, P	Sp*	Su	55–60	15–30
Flowering onion	B	F or Sp	Sp–Su	**	**
Foxglove	Bi, P	Sp	Sp–Su	70–85	15–20
Freesia	Corm	Sp*	Sp	**	**
Geranium	P	Sp	Sp–Su–F	68–86	5–15
Gladiolus	Corm	Sp	Su–F	**	**
Hollyhock	Bi	Sp–Su	Sp–Su	68	7–21
Hyacinth	Bu	F	Sp	**	**
Impatiens	A, Tp	Sp	Su	70	15–20
Iris	Rh, B	F	Sp–Su	**	**
Lantana	Tp	Sp	Sp–F	70	40–50
Lily	Bu	Sp	Su	**	**
Lily-of-the-valley	P	F (from pips)	Sp	**	**
Lobelia	A	Sp*	Su–F	70–85	15–20
Marigold	A	Sp	Su–F	70–75	5–7
Ornamental pepper	A	Sp	Su	70	15–20
Painted tongue	A	Sp	Su	70–75	15–20
Phlox	A, P	Sp*	Su–F	55–65	8–20
Pink	A, P	Sp*	Sp–Su	70	15–30
Pot marigold	A	Sp*	W–Sp	70–85	7–14
Primrose	A, P	Sp*	W–Sp	55–65	20
Ranunculus	Tu	F or Sp	Sp–Su	**	**
Sage	A, P	Sp	Su	70	12–15
Snapdragon	A	Sp*	Sp–Su	70	15
Solanum	A, P	Sp	Su–F	70	15–30
Spider flower	A	Sp*	Su	55–85	10–14
Stock	A	Sp	Sp–Su	55–90	15
Sweet alyssum	A, P	Sp	Sp–Su–F	70	7–15
Sweet pea	A	W–Sp	Sp	70	15
Sunflower	A, P	Sp	Su–F	70–85	15–20
Sunrose	P	F or Sp	Su	70	15–20
Transvaal daisy	Tp	Sp	Su	70	15
Yarrow	P	Sp	Su–F	70	5–15

Florida gardeners may find differences in planting times and soil temperatures. Check with your local extension agent.

* Planted in the fall in zones 9 and 10. See page 348 for USDA zone map.

** Not usually planted from seed.

KEY: A — Annual; Bu — Bulb; Bi — Biennial; P — Perennial; Rh — Rhizome; Tp — Tender perennial, grown as annual in all but zones 9 and 10; Tu — Tuber; Sp — Spring; Su — Summer; F — Fall; W — Winter.

Some lily species resistant and susceptible to lily mosaic:

RESISTANT TO MODERATELY RESISTANT

Lilium amabile
L. brownii
L. davidii
L. hansonii
L. henryi
L. martagon
L. monadelphum
L. pardalinum
L. pumilum
L. regale

SUSCEPTIBLE

L. auratum
L. canadense
L. concolor
L. formosanum
L. lancifolium
L. × *maculatum*
L. pensylvanicum
L. superbum
*L. tigrimun**

*Easily infected, but not apparently injured; can become a carrier to other susceptible species.

Some chrysanthemum varieties resistant to chrysanthemum rust:

Achievement
Copper Bowl
Escapade
Helen Castle
Mandalay
Matador
Miss Atlanta
Orange Bowl
Powder Puff

Adapted from *Chrysanthemum Cultivars Resistant to Verticillium Wilt and Rust,* University of California Cooperative Extension leaflet 21057.

Some flowers susceptible to various fusarium wilts:

Botanical name	Common name
Antirrhinum	Snapdragon
Astilbe	
Browallia	
Callistephus	China aster
Campanula	Bellflower
Centaurea	Bachelor's-button
Chrysanthemum	Mum, daisy, marguerite
Cosmos	
Cyclamen	
Dahlia	
Delphinium	
Dianthus	Carnation, pink, sweet william
Digitalis	Foxglove
Dimorphotheca	Cape marigold
Lantana	
Lilium	Lily
Matthiola	Stock
Narcissus	Daffodil
Paeonia	Peony
Salpiglossis	Painted tongue
Senecio	Cineraria
Tagetes	Marigold
Tulipa	Tulip

Some plants susceptible to aster yellows:

Botanical name	Common name

FLOWERS

Anemone	
Antirrhinum	Snapdragon
Aster	
Calendula	Pot marigold
Callistephus	China aster
Celosia	Cockscomb
Centaurea	Bachelor's-button
Chrysanthemum	Mum, daisy, marguerite
Coreopsis	
Cosmos	
Delphinium	
Dianthus	Carnation, pink, sweet william
Dimorphotheca	Cape marigold
Gaillardia	Blanket-flower
Gladiolus	
Helichrysum	Strawflower
Lobelia	
Petunia	
Phlox	
Scabiosa	Pincushion flower
Tagetes	Marigold

VEGETABLES

Broccoli
Cabbage
Carrot
Cauliflower
Celery
Endive
Lettuce
New Zealand spinach
Onion
Parsley
Parsnip
Potato
Pumpkin
Radish
Spinach
Squash
Tomato

WEEDS

Ambrosia	Ragweed
Cirsium	Thistle
Conyza	Horseweed
Daucus	Wild carrot
Erigeron	Fleabane
Plantago	Plantain
Taraxacum	Dandelion

Some rose varieties resistant to black spot (BS), powdery mildew (PM), or rust (R):

HYBRID TEAS

Audie Murphy	R
Aztec	PM, R
Carrousel	PM
Charlotte Armstrong	BS
Chrysler Imperial	BS
Command Performance	BS, R
Coronado	BS
Ernest H. Morse	BS
Forty-niner	BS
Fred Howard	R
Garden Party	BS, R
Golden Rapture	PM
Grand Opera	BS
Jamaica	PM
John F. Kennedy	BS, R
Lowell Thomas	PM
Lucy Cramphorn	BS
Matterhorn	PM
Miss All-American Beauty	PM
Pascali	PM
Pink Favorite	R
Queen Charlotte	PM
Radiant	BS
Sante Fe	PM
Sierra Dawn	PM, R
Simon Bolivar	PM, R
Sphinx	BS
Sutter's Gold	BS, PM
Tiffany	BS
Trade Winds	R
Tropicana	BS
White Bouquet	R

FLORIBUNDAS

Alain	R
Burma	R
Donald Prior	R
Etiole de Hollande	R
Fashionette	R
Garden Party	R
Gold Cup	R
Red Gold	BS, R
Red Radiance	R
Sarabande	BS, PM, R
Simplicity	BS
Summer Snow	R
Tiara	BS
Wildfire	PM

CLIMBERS

Blaze	BS, PM
Bonfire	PM
Cécile Brünner	PM
Paul's Scarlet	BS, PM

Some plants resistant to verticillium wilt:

GENERAL CATEGORIES
Ferns
Conifers (cypress, fir, larch, juniper, pine, sequoia, spruce, and others)
Monocots (bamboo, corn, gladiolus, grasses, iris, onion, orchids, palms, and others)
Cacti

Botanical name	Common name
TREES AND SHRUBS	
Arctostaphylos	Manzanita
Betula	Birch
Buxus	Boxwood
Carpinus	Hornbeam
Ceanothus	Wild lilac
Cornus	Dogwood
Crataegus	Hawthorn
Eucalyptus	
Fagus	Beech
Gleditsia	Honey locust
Ilex	Holly
Juglans	Walnut
Liquidambar	Sweet gum
Malus	Apple, crab apple
Morus	Mulberry
Nerium	Oleander
Platanus	Plane tree, sycamore
Pyracantha	Firethorn
Quercus	Oak
Salix	Willow
Tilia	Linden
FLOWERS	
Ageratum	
Alcea	Hollyhock
Alyssum	
Anemone	
Aquilegia	Columbine
Begonia	
Calendula	Pot marigold
Dianthus	Carnation, pink, sweet william
Gaillardia	Blanket-flower
Gypsophila	Baby's breath
Helianthemum	Sunrose
Helleborus	Christmas rose
Heuchera	Coral bells
Iberis	Candytuft
Impatiens	
Lantana	
Mimulus	Monkey flower
Nemesia	
Nemophila	Baby-blue-eyes
Penstemon	
Platycodon	Balloon flower
Portulaca	Moss rose
Potentilla	Cinquefoil
Primula	Primrose
Ranunculus	
Scabiosa	Pincushion flower
Tropaeolum	Nasturtium
Verbena	
Vinca	Periwinkle
Viola	Pansy, viola, violet
Zinnia	
VEGETABLES	
Asparagus	Lettuce
Bean	Pea
Carrot	Sweet potato
Celery	

Adapted from *Plants Resistant or Susceptible to Verticillium Wilt,* University of California Cooperative Extension Service leaflet 2703.

Powdery mildews and some of the plants they infect:

Botanical name	Common name
Erysiphe cichoracearum:	
Achillea	Yarrow
Ajuga	Carpet bugle
Alcea	Hollyhock
Antirrhinum	Snapdragon
Aster	
Baccharis	Coyote bush
Begonia	
Calendula	Pot marigold
Centaurea	Bachelor's button
Chrysanthemum	Mum, daisy, marguerite
Citrullus	Watermelon
Cosmos	
Cotinus	Smoke tree
Dahlia	
Eucalyptus	
Gerbera	Transvaal daisy
Hebe	
Helianthus	Sunflower
Lactuca	Lettuce
Myosotis	Forget-me-not
Papaver	Poppy
Ranunculus	
Rhus	Sumac
Rudbeckia	Black-eyed Susan
Salpiglossis	Painted tongue.
Salvia	Sage
Senecio	Cineraria
Spiraea	
Verbena	
Zinnia	
Erysiphe polygoni:	
Amaranthus	Amaranth
Aquilegia	Columbine
Begonia	
Beta	Beet
Brassicaceae	Cabbage family
Delphinium	
Eschscholzia	California poppy
Iberis	Candytuft
Lathyrus	Sweet pea
Lobularia	Sweet alyssum
Phaseolus	Bean
Pisum	Pea
Raphanus	Radish
Vinca	Periwinkle
Viola	Pansy, viola, violet
Microsphaera alni:	
Alnus	Alder
Corylus	Hazelnut
Lonicera	Honeysuckle
Platanus	Plane tree, sycamore
Quercus	Oak
Symphoricarpos	Snowberry
Syringa	Lilac

Adapted from *A List of Powdery Mildews of California,* University of California Cooperative Extension Service leaflet 217.

Botanical name	Common name
***Microsphaera* species:**	
Acacia	
Catalpa	
Ceanothus	Wild lilac
Erica	Heath
Euonymus	
Hydrangea	
Juglans	Walnut
Lagerstroemia	Crape myrtle
Ligustrum	Privet
Liriodendron	Tulip tree
Lonicera	Honeysuckle
Magnolia	
Passiflora	Passion flower
Platanus	Plane tree, sycamore
Populus	Poplar
Raphiolepis	India hawthorn
Rhododendron	Rhododendron, azalea
Robinia	Locust
Vaccinium	Blueberry
Viburnum	
Phyllactinia corylea:	
Aesculus	Horsechestnut
Cornus	Dogwood
Philadelphus	Mock orange
Quercus	Oak
Rubus	Bramble
***Podosphaera* species:**	
Acer	Maple
Fraxinus	Ash
Malus	Apple, crab apple
Photinia	
Prunus	Plum, peach, apricot, cherry, laurel
Pyracantha	Firethorn
Pyrus	Pear
Spiraea	
Sphaerotheca fuliginea:	
Cucumis	Cantaloupe, cucumber
Cucurbita	Winter squash
***Sphaerotheca* species:**	
Cotoneaster	
Crataegus	Hawthorn
Dianthus	Carnation, pink, sweet william
Erica	Heath
Fragaria	Strawberry
Gaillardia	Blanket-flower
Heuchera	Coral bells
Kalanchoe	
Nicotiana	Flowering tobacco
Petunia	
Phlox	
Potentilla	Cinquefoil
Ribes	Currant, gooseberry
Rosa	Rose
Tolmiea	Piggyback plant

Some plants resistant to cotton root rot (*Phymatotrichum omnivorum*):

Botanical name	Common name
TREES AND SHRUBS	
Celtis	Hackberry
Deutzia	
Morus alba 'Pendula'	Weeping mulberry
Palmae	Palm family
Polypodiaceae	Fern family
Punica	Pomegranate
Quercus	Oak
FLOWERS	
Amaranthus	Amaranth
Antirrhinum	Snapdragon
Calceolaria	Slipper flower
Canna	
Cyclamen	
Digitalis	Foxglove
Eschscholzia	California poppy
Freesia	
Gypsophila	Baby's breath
Hyacinthus	Hyacinth
Iberis	Candytuft
Iris	
Lobularia	Sweet alyssum
Matthiola	Stock
Narcissus	Daffodil
Papaver	Poppy
Petunia	
Phlox	
Portulaca	Moss rose
Primula	Primrose
Tropaeolum	Nasturtium
Zantedeschia	Calla
Zinnia	

VEGETABLES AND FRUITS

Asparagus
Cabbage family
Cantaloupe
Celery
Cranberry
Cucumber
Currant
Dewberry
Garlic
Grape
Leek
Onion
Pumpkin
Spinach
Squash
Strawberry
Watermelon

Some plants susceptible to southern blight* (*Sclerotium rolfsii*):

Botanical name	Common name
SHRUBS	
Daphne	
Hydrangea	
Pittosporum	
Rosa	Rose
FLOWERS	
Alcea	Hollyhock
Anemone	
Calendula	Pot marigold
Callistephus	China aster
Campanula	Bellflower
Canna	
Chrysanthemum	Mum, daisy, marguerite
Cosmos	
Dahlia	
Delphinium	
Dianthus	Carnation, pink, sweet william
Gladiolus	
Iris	
Lathyrus	Sweet pea
Lilium	Lily
Lupinus	Lupine
Narcissus	Daffodil
Phlox	
Rudbeckia	Black-eyed Susan
Scabiosa	Pincushion flower
Sedum	Stonecrop
Tagetes	Marigold
Tulipa	Tulip
Viola	Pansy, viola, violet
Zinnia	

VEGETABLES AND FRUITS

Apple
Artichoke
Avocado
Bean
Beet
Cabbage
Cantaloupe
Carrot
Cucumber
Eggplant
Lettuce
Okra
Onion
Pea
Peanut
Pepper
Potato
Rhubarb
Squash
Strawberry
Tomato
Turnip
Watermelon

*Southern blight has been reported on hundreds of plants. This is a partial list of plants that are frequently infected by this disease.

Some plants attractive to bees:

Botanical name	Common name
TREES AND SHRUBS	
Abelia	
Acacia	
Arctostaphylos	Manzanita
Berberis	Barberry
Callistemon	Bottlebrush
Calluna	Heather
Ceanothus	Wild lilac
Cotoneaster	
Cytisus	Broom
Erica	Heath
Eriobotrya	Loquat
Escallonia	
Gleditsia	Honeylocust
Lantana	
Ligustrum	Privet
Lonicera	Honeysuckle
Myrtus	Myrtle
Nerium	Oleander
Pittosporum	
Pyracantha	Firethorn
Raphiolepis	India hawthorn
Rosmarinus	Rosemary
Thymus	Thyme
Trachelospermum	Star jasmine
Wisteria	
FLOWERS	
Achillea	Yarrow
Campanula	Bellflower
Helianthus	Sunflower
Lavandula	Lavender
Lobularia	Sweet alyssum
Myosotis	Forget-me-not
Nicotiana	Flowering tobacco
Salvia	Sage

A few small trees for areas with restricted root space:

Botanical name	Common name
Acer campestre	Hedge maple
A. ginnala	Amur maple
A. palmatum	Japanese maple
Albizia julibrissin	Silk tree
Carpinus	Hornbeam
Cercis	Redbud
Cornus	Dogwood
Crataegus	Hawthorn
Elaeagnus angustifolia	Russian olive
Ilex	Holly
Koelreuteria	Goldenrain tree
Magnolia × *soulangiana*	Saucer magnolia
M. stellata	Star magnolia
Malus	Crab apple
Pistacia chinensis	Chinese pistache
Prunus	Flowering cherry, peach, plum
Styrax	Snowbell
Viburnum prunifolium	Black haw
V. rufidulum	Southern black haw
V. sieboldii	Siebold viburnum

From *Trees for American Gardens,* Donald Wyman. Copyright 1951, 1965, Macmillan Publishing Co., Inc. Reprinted by permission.

APPENDIX

Some trees, shrubs, and perennials for wet soil:

Botanical name	Common name
TREES	
Acer rubrum	Red maple
A. saccharinum	Silver maple
Alnus	Alder
Amelanchier arborea	Serviceberry
Betula nigra	River birch
Casuarina equisetifolia	Horsetail tree
Ilex cassine	Dahoon holly
I. opaca	American holly
Larix laricina	American larch
Liquidambar styraciflua	Sweet gum
Magnolia virginiana	Sweet bay
Nyssa sylvatica	Sour gum
Platanus	Plane tree, sycamore
Populus	Poplar
Quercus bicolor	Swamp white oak
Q. palustris	Pin oak
Salix	Willow
Taxodium distichum	Bald cypress
Tristania laurina	Kanooka tristania
SHRUBS	
Aronia arbutifolia	Red chokeberry
Bambusa disticha	Fernleaf bamboo
Betula occidentalis	Water birch
Calycanthus	Sweet shrub
Cephalanthus occidentalis	Buttonbush
Cornus sericea	Red-osier dogwood
Ilex glabra	Gallberry
I. verticillata	Winterberry
Lindera benzoin	Spicebush
Myrica pensylvanica	Bayberry
Rhododendron arborescens	Smooth azalea
R. vaseyi	Pink-shell azalea
Rosa palustris	Swamp rose
Salix	Willow
Thuja	Arborvitae
Viburnum trilobum	Cranberry bush

Botanical name	Common name
PERENNIALS	
Aconitum	Monkshood
Acorus calamus	Sweet flag
Althaea officinalis	Marshmallow
Aster novae-angliae	New England aster
Astilbe	
Caltha palustris	Marshmarigold
Cimicifuga racemosa	Black snakeroot
Colocasia esculenta	Elephant's ear
Cyperus	Sedge
Eupatorium maculatum	Joe-pye-weed
Hydrophyllum virginianum	Virginia waterleaf
Iris kaempferi	Japanese iris
I. sibirica	Siberian iris
Lilium canadense	Canada lily
Lobelia cardinalis	Cardinal flower
L. siphilitica	Great lobelia
Lysimachia nummularia	Moneywort, creeping-charlie
Mentha	Mint
Mimulus	Monkey flower
Myosotis scorpioides	Forget-me-not
Phalaris arundinacea var. picta	Ribbon grass
Polypodiaceae	Fern family
Primula japonica	Japanese primrose
Ranunculus	
Sanguinaria canadensis	Bloodroot
Sisyrinchium californicum	Golden-eyed-grass
Tolmiea menziesii	Piggyback plant
Trollius	Globeflower
Typha latifolia	Common cattail
Viola blanda	Sweet white violet
V. lanceolata	Lance-leaved violet
Zantedeschia	Calla

Some oaks that need no water after the first two seasons in the ground:

Botanical name	Common name
Quercus agrifolia	Coast live oak
Q. chrysolepis	Canyon oak
Q. douglasii	Blue oak
Q. dumosa	California scrub oak
Q. engelmannii	Mesa oak
Q. garryana	Oregon white oak
Q. ilex	Holly oak
Q. kelloggii	California black oak
Q. lobata	Valley oak
Q. suber	Cork oak
Q. wislizenii	Interior live oak

Some oaks that need added water during periods of drought:

Botanical name	Common name
Quercus alba	White oak
Q. bicolor*	Swamp white oak
Q. coccinea	Scarlet oak
Q. macrocarpa	Bur oak
Q. palustris*	Pin oak
Q. phellos	Willow oak
Q. robur	English oak
Q. rubra	Red oak

*Will tolerate wet soil

Some trees and shrubs with shallow root systems:

Botanical name	Common name
Acacia	
Acer saccharinum	Silver maple
Ailanthus altissima	Tree-of-heaven
Alnus	Alder
Cornus nuttallii	Pacific dogwood
Eucalyptus	
Ficus	Fig
Fraxinus uhdei	Evergreen ash
Gleditsia	Honey locust
Morus	Mulberry
Platanus	Plane tree, sycamore
Populus	Poplar
Rhus	Sumac
Robinia	Black locust
Salix	Willow
Ulmus	Elm

Some trees, shrubs, vines, and ground covers for sandy soil:

Botanical name	Common name
TREES	
Crataegus phaenopyrum	Washington hawthorn
Elaeagnus angustifolia	Russian olive
Ilex opaca	American holly
Juniperus virginiana	Eastern red cedar
Malus	Crab apple
Nyssa sylvatica	Sour gum
Parkinsonia aculeata	Jerusalem thorn
Picea glauca	White spruce
Pinus banksiana	Jack pine
P. echinata	Yellow pine
P. elliottii	Slash pine
P. resinosa	Red pine
P. rigida	Pitch pine
P. strobus	Eastern white pine
P. thunbergiana	Japanese black pine
P. virginiana	Scrub pine
Platanus × acerifolia	London plane tree
Populus alba	White poplar
Quercus alba	White oak
Q. palustris	Pin oak
Q. stellata	Post oak
Sophora japonica	Japanese pagoda tree

Botanical name	Common name
SHRUBS	
Aronia arbutifolia	Red chokeberry
Berberis thunbergii	Japanese barberry
Buddleia davidii	Orange-eye butterfly bush
Chaenomeles speciosa	Flowering quince
Juniperus chinensis 'Pfitzerana'	Pfitzer's juniper
Kalmia angustifolia	Sheep laurel
K. latifolia	Mountain laurel
Kerria japonica	Japanese rose
Lespedeza thunbergii	Bush clover
Ligustrum amurense	Amur privet
Lonicera tatarica	Tatarian honeysuckle
Myrica cerifera	Wax myrtle
M. pensylvanica	Bayberry
Philadelphus coronarius	Mock orange
Potentilla fruticosa	Shrubby cinquefoil
Prunus maritima	Beach plum
Pyracantha coccinea	Firethorn
Rhamnus cathartica	Common buckthorn
Rhus glabra	Smooth sumac
Rosa rugosa	Japanese rose
Spiraea japonica	Japanese spirea
Tamarix parviflora	Tamarisk
Vaccinium corymbosum	Highbush blueberry
Weigela florida	Weigela

Botanical name	Common name
VINES AND GROUND COVERS	
Actinidia arguta	Hardy kiwi
Arctostaphylos uva-ursi	Manzanita
Campsis radicans	Trumpetcreeper
Celastrus scandens	American bittersweet
Juniperus chinensis var. procumbens	Japanese garden juniper
J. conferta	Shore juniper
J. horizontalis	Creeping juniper
Lantana montevidensis	Trailing lantana
Liriope spicata	Lilyturf
Lonicera japonica 'Halliana'	Hall's Japanese honeysuckle
Parthenocissus quinquefolia	Virginia creeper
Phyla nodiflora	Lippia
Pteridium aquilinum	Bracken
Rhus aromatica	Fragrant sumac
Rosa wichuraiana	Memorial rose
Sedum acre	Golden-carpet
Thymus vulgaris	Common thyme
Vitis	Grape
Wedelia trilobata	Wedelia

Some plants tolerant of saline soil:

Botanical name	Common name
Araucaria heterophylla	Norfolk Island pine
Arctotheca calendula	Cape weed
Baccharis pilularis	Coyotebrush
Bougainvillea	
Callistemon viminalis	Weeping bottlebrush
Carissa grandiflora	Natal plum
Chamaerops humilis	European fan palm
Coprosma repens	Mirror plant
Cordyline indivisa	Blue dracaena
Cortaderia selloana	Pampas grass
Delosperma 'Alba'	White ice plant
Drosanthemum	Rosea ice plant
Euonymus japonica	Spindle tree
Gazania	
Lampranthus	Trailing ice plant
Nerium oleander	Oleander
Phyla nodiflora	Lippia
Pinus halepensis	Aleppo pine
Pittosporum crassifolium	Karo
Pyracantha	Firethorn
Rosmarinus officinalis 'Lockwood de Forest'	Rosemary
Syzygium paniculatum	Brush cherry

Susceptibility of some trees to injury from fill:

Botanical name	Common name
MOST SUSCEPTIBLE	
Acer saccharum	Sugar maple
Cornus	Dogwood
Fagus	Beech
Liriodendron	Tulip tree
Picea	Spruce
Pinus	Pine
Quercus	Oak
MODERATELY SUSCEPTIBLE	
Betula	Birch
Carya	Hickory
Tsuga	Hemlock
LEAST SUSCEPTIBLE	
Platanus	Plane tree, sycamore
Populus	Poplar
Quercus palustris	Pin oak
Robinia	Locust
Salix	Willow
Ulmus	Elm

From *Tree Maintenance*, P. P. Pirone. Copyright 1978 Oxford University Press, Inc. Reprinted by permission.

Some trees with weak forks and brittle wood:

Botanical name	Common name
Acacia	
Acer saccharinum	Silver maple
Aesculus	Horsechestnut
Ailanthus	Tree-of-heaven
Callistemon citrinus	Bottlebrush
Casuarina stricta	She-oak
Eucalyptus	
Fraxinus velutina var. *glabra*	Modesto ash, Arizona ash
Liriodendron	Tulip tree
Magnolia grandiflora	Southern magnolia
Melaleuca	
Melia azedarach	Chinaberry
Morus alba	White mulberry
Populus	Poplar
Quercus prinus	Chestnut oak
Robinia	Locust
Salix	Willow
Sassafras	
Sequoia sempervirens	Coast redwood
Ulmus pumila	Siberian elm

Some low-growing trees suitable for planting under wires along streets:

Botanical name	Common name
Acer campestre	Hedge maple
A. ginnala	Amur maple
A. palmatum	Japanese maple
A. spicatum	Mountain maple
A. tataricum	Tatarian maple
Cercis	Redbud
Cotinus	Smoke tree
Koelreuteria paniculata	Golden-rain tree
Lagerstroemia indica	Crape myrtle
Malus	Crab apple
Prunus	Flowering cherry, peach, plum
Styrax japonicus	Snowbell

Some trees susceptible to lightning injury:

Botanical name	Common name
SUSCEPTIBLE	
Fraxinus	Ash
Liriodendron	Tulip tree
Picea	Spruce
Pinus	Pine
Populus	Poplar
Quercus	Oak
Ulmus	Elm
LESS SUSCEPTIBLE*	
Aesculus	Horsechestnut
Betula	Birch
Fagus	Beech

*No species is totally immune, and location and size of the tree are also factors influencing susceptibility.

From *Tree Maintenance*, P. P. Pirone. Copyright 1978 Oxford University Press, Inc. Reprinted by permission.

Some trees commonly damaged by sapsuckers:

Botanical name	Common name
Abies	Fir
Acacia	
Acer rubrum	Red maple
Acer saccharum	Sugar maple
Betula	Birch
Casuarina	Beefwood
Eriobotrya	Loquat
Fagus	Beech
Grevillea	Silk oak
Larix	Larch
Magnolia	
Malus	Apple, crab apple
Palmae	Palm family
Picea rubens	Red spruce
Pinus	Pine
Populus tremuloides	Quaking aspen
Pseudotsuga menziesii	Douglas fir
Salix	Willow
Tsuga	Hemlock

Some palms frequently attacked by the palm leaf skeletonizer (*Homaledra sabalella*):

Botanical name	Common name
Acoelorrhaphe wrightii	Paurotis palm
Butia capitata	Pindo palm
Cocos nucifera	Coconut palm
Livistona chinensis	Chinese fan palm
Phoenix	Date palm
Sabal palmetto	Cabbage palm
Washingtonia	Washington palm

Some trees and shrubs relatively free of insects and diseases:

Botanical name	Common name
Ailanthus	Tree-of-heaven
Brachychiton	Bottle tree
Calocedrus decurrens	Incense cedar
Carpinus	Hornbeam
Cedrus	Cedar
Celtis australis	European hackberry
Ceratonia siliqua	Carob
Cercidiphyllum japonicum	Katsura tree
Cornus mas	Cornelian cherry
C. officinalis	Japanese cornelian cherry
Corylus colurna	Turkish filbert
Cotinus	Smoke tree
Cytisus	Broom
Eucommia ulmoides	Hardy rubber tree
Ficus	Fig
Franklinia	Franklin tree
Ginkgo	Maidenhair tree
Grevillea robusta	Silk oak
Gymnocladus dioica	Kentucky coffee tree
Kalopanax pictus	Castor-aralia
Kerria	Japanese rose
Koelreuteria paniculata	Goldenrain tree
Laburnum	Goldenchain tree
Ligustrum lucidum	Glossy privet
Magnolia acuminata	Cucumber tree
M. kobus var. *borealis*	Kobus magnolia
M. salicifolia	Anise magnolia
M. stellata	Star magnolia
Metasequoia	Dawn redwood
Myrica	Bayberry
Myrtus	Myrtle
Nyssa	Sour gum
Ostrya	Hop hornbeam
Parrotia persica	Persian parrotia
Phellodendron	Cork tree
Pistacia chinensis	Chinese pistache
Podocarpus	
Potentilla	Cinquefoil
Rhamnus	Buckthorn
Sciadopitys verticillata	Umbrella pine
Sophora japonica	Japanese pagoda tree
Stewartia	
Styrax	Snowbell
Tamarix	Tamarisk
Taxodium	Bald cypress
Viburnum sieboldii	Siebold viburnum
Xylosma congestum	Shiny xylosma

Some trees and shrubs resistant to crown gall:

Botanical name	Common name
Abelia	
Ailanthus	Tree-of-heaven
Albizia	Silk tree
Amelanchier	Serviceberry
Berberis	Barberry
Betula	Birch
Buxus	Boxwood
Calluna	Heather
Carpinus	Hornbeam
Catalpa	
Cedrus	Cedar
Cercis	Redbud
Cladrastis	Yellowwood
Cotinus	Smoke tree
Cryptomeria	
Deutzia	
Fagus	Beech
Ginkgo	Maidenhair tree
Gymnocladus	Kentucky coffee tree
Ilex	Holly
Kalmia	Mountain laurel
Koelreuteria	Goldenrain tree
Laburnum	Goldenchain tree
Larix	Larch
Leucothoe	
Liquidambar	Sweet gum
Liriodendron	Tulip tree
Magnolia	
Mahonia	Oregon grape, holly grape
Nyssa	Sour gum
Picea	Spruce
Pieris	Andromeda
Pyracantha	Firethorn
Rhus	Sumac
Sambucus	Elderberry
Sassafras	
Tsuga	Hemlock
Zelkova	

Adapted from *Crown Gall*, W. A. Sinclair and W. T. Johnson. Cornell University Tree Pest leaflet A-5.

Some plants susceptible and resistant to *Phytophthora cinnamoni* and *P. lateralis:*

SUSCEPTIBLE TREES AND SHRUBS

Botanical name	Common name
Abelia	
Abies	Fir
Acacia	
Arctostaphylos	Manzanita
Calluna	Heather
Calocedrus	Incense cedar
Camellia japonica	Common camellia
Castanea	Chestnut
Casuarina	Beefwood
Ceanothus	Wild lilac
Cedrus	Cedar
Chamaecyparis	False cypress
Cinnamomum	Camphor tree
Cornus	Dogwood
Cupressus	Cypress
Daphne	
Erica	Heath
Eucalyptus	
Fatsia	Aralia
Hibiscus	
Hypericum	St. John's wort
Juglans	Walnut
Juniperus	Juniper
Larix	Larch
Laurus	Sweet bay
Myrtus	Myrtle
Olea	Olive
Picea	Spruce
Pieris	Andromeda
Pinus	Pine
Pittosporum	
Platanus	Plane tree, sycamore
Pseudotsuga	Douglas fir
Quercus	Oak
Rhododendron	Rhododendron, azalea
Salix	Willow
Sequoia sempervirens	Coast redwood
Taxodium	Bald cypress
Taxus	Yew
Thuja	Arborvitae
Viburnum	

RESISTANT TREES AND SHRUBS

Botanical name	Common name
Camellia sasanqua	Sansangua camellia
Chamaecyparis nootkatensis	Alaska cedar
C. pisifera var. *filifera*	Sawara cypress
C. thyoides	White cedar
Daphne cneorum	Rock daphne
Juniperus chinensis 'Pfitzerana'	Pfitzer's juniper
J. sabina	Savin juniper
J. squamata 'Meyeri'	Meyer juniper
Pinus mugo var. *mugo*	Dwarf mugho pine
Rhododendron obtusum	Hiryu azalea
Thuja occidentalis	American arborvitae

SUSCEPTIBLE FRUITS AND BERRIES

Apricot
Avocado
Blueberry (highbush)
Cherry
Citrus
Peach
Pear

RESISTANT BERRY

Blueberry (rabbiteye)

Some plants susceptible to bacterial blight (*Pseudomonas syringae*):

Almond
Apple
Avocado
Bean
Cherry
Citrus
Lilac
Oleander
Pea
Peach
Pear
Plum
Rose
Stock

Some junipers resistant to phomopsis twig blight:

Botanical name	Common name
Juniperus chinensis	Chinese juniper
'Foemina'	
'Keteleeri'	
var. *sargentii*	
'Pfitzerana Aurea'	
J. communis	Common juniper
'Aureospica'	
'Prostrata'	
'Repanda'	
'Suecica'	
var. *depressa*	
J. horizontalis	Creeping juniper
J. sabina	Savin juniper
'Broadmoor'	
'Campbelli'	
'Fargesi'	
'Pumila'	
'Skandia'	

Some junipers highly susceptible to and resistant to Kabatina twig blight:

Botanical name	Common name

HIGHLY SUSCEPTIBLE JUNIPERS

Juniperus chinensis	Chinese juniper
'Densaerecta	
Spartan'	
'Torulosa'	Hollywood juniper
('Kaizuka')	
Juniperus horizontalis	Creeping juniper
'Bar Harbor'	
'Blue Horizon'	
'Blue Rug'	
'Emerson's Creeper'	
'Plumosa Compacta'	
'Wiltonii'	
Juniperus virginiana	Eastern red cedar
'Skyrocket'	

RESISTANT JUNIPERS

Juniperus chinensis	Chinese juniper
'Aurea Gold Coast'	
'Glauca Hetzii'	
'Pfitzerana Aurea'	
var. *sargentii* 'Glauca'	
var. *sargentii* 'Viridis'	
Juniperus communis	Common juniper
'Hornibrookii'	
Juniperus horizontalis	Creeping juniper
'Marcella'	
Juniperus sabina	Savin juniper
'Tamariscifolia'	
Juniperus squamata	Single-seed juniper
'Expansa Parsonii'	
Juniperus virginiana	Eastern red cedar
'Prostrata Glauca'	

Some pines susceptible to and resistant to pine wilt:

Botanical name	Common name

SUSCEPTIBLE PINES

Pinus contorta var. *latifolia*	Lodgepole pine
P. densiflora	Japanese red pine
P. lambertiana	Sugar pine
P. monticola	Western white pine
P. mugo	Mugho pine
P. nigra	Austrian pine
P. pinaster	Cluster pine
P. radiata	Monterey pine
P. sylvestris	Scotch pine
P. taeda	Loblolly pine
P. thunbergiana	Japanese black pine
P. virginiana	Scrub pine

RESISTANT PINES

Pinus banksiana	Jack pine
P. caribaea	Cuban pine
P. echinata	Shortleaf pine
P. elliottii	Slash pine
P. jeffreyi	Jeffrey pine
P. palustris	Longleaf pine
P. pungens	Table mountain pine
P. rigida	Pitch pine
P. strobus	White pine

Some plants susceptible to quince rust (*Gymnosporangium clavipes* or *G. libocedri*):

Botanical name	Common name
Amelanchier	Serviceberry
Aronia	Chokeberry
Calocedrus decurrens	Incense cedar
Crataegus	Hawthorn
Juniperus communis and its varieties	Common juniper
Juniperus virginiana	Eastern red cedar
Sorbus	Mountain ash

Some plants resistant to and susceptible to cedar-apple rust (*Gymnosporangium juniperi-virginianae*):

Botanical name	Common name

RESISTANT

Juniperus chinensis	Chinese juniper
'Foemina'	
'Keteleeri'	
var. *sargentii*	
J. communis	Common juniper
'Aureospica'	
'Saxatilis'	
'Suecica'	
var. *depressa*	
J. sabina	Savin juniper
'Broadmoor'	
'Knap Hill'	
'Skandia'	
J. squamata	Single-seed juniper
J. virginiana	Eastern red cedar
'Tripartita'	

SUSCEPTIBLE

Juniperus scopulorum and its varieties	Rocky Mountain juniper
J. virginiana	Eastern red cedar
Malus	Apple, crab apple

PARTICULARLY SUSCEPTIBLE APPLE VARIETIES

Jonathan
Rome
Wealthy
York Imperial
Bechtel (crab apple)
Parkman (flowering crab apple)

Some varieties of pyracantha resistant to scab:

Mohave
Orange glow
Rogersiana
Shawnee
Watereri

Some plants resistant to armillaria root rot:

Botanical name	Common name
TREES AND SHRUBS	
Abies concolor	White fir
Acacia longifolia	Bush acacia
A. verticillata	Star acacia
Acer macrophyllum	Bigleaf maple
A. palmatum	Japanese maple
Ailanthus altissima	Tree-of-heaven
Arbutus menziesii	Madrone
Berberis polyantha	Barberry
Betula pumila	Swamp birch
Buxus sempervirens	Boxwood
Calocedrus decurrens	Incense cedar
Catalpa bignonioides	Common catalpa
Celtis	Hackberry
Ceratonia siliqua	Carob
Cercis occidentalis	Western redbud
C. siliquastrum	Judas tree
Chaenomeles speciosa	Flowering quince
Chamaecyparis lawsoniana 'Ellwoodii'	Elwood cypress
Cotinus coggygria	Smoke tree
Cryptomeria japonica	Japanese cedar
Cupaniopsis anacardioides	Carrotwood
× *Cupressocyparis leylandii*	Leyland cypress
Cupressus arizonica var. *glabra*	Smooth Arizona cypress
Elaeagnus angustifolia	Russian olive
Erica arborea	Tree heath
Eucalyptus camaldulensis	Red gum
E. cinerea	Silver-dollar tree
Eugenia	Eugenia
Fraxinus uhdei	Evergreen ash
F. velutina var. *glabra* 'Modesto'	Modesto ash
Ginkgo biloba	Maidenhair tree
Gleditsia triacanthos 'Shademaster'	Shademaster locust
Hibiscus syriacus	Rose-of-Sharon
Hypericum patulum	St. John's wort
Ilex aquifolium	English holly
Jacaranda acutifolia	Jacaranda
Liquidambar orientalis	Oriental sweet gum
L. styraciflua	Sweet gum
Liriodendron tulipifera	Tulip tree
Lonicera nitida	Box honeysuckle
Magnolia grandiflora	Southern magnolia
Mahonia aquifolium	Oregon grape, holly grape
Malus floribunda	Japanese flowering crab apple
Maytenus boaria	Mayten tree

Botanical name	Common name
Metasequoia glyptostroboides	Dawn redwood
Morus	Mulberry
Myrica pensylvanica	Bayberry
Nandina domestica	Heavenly bamboo
Palmae	Many genera of palms
Pinus canariensis	Canary Island pine
P. nigra	Austrian pine
P. radiata	Monterey pine
P. sylvestris	Scotch pine
P. torreyana	Torrey pine
Pistacia chinensis	Chinese pistache
Pittosporum rhombifolium	Queensland pittosporum
Platanus	Plane tree, sycamore
Prunus caroliniana	Cherry laurel
P. ilicifolia	Holly-leaf cherry
P. lyonii	Catalina cherry
Quercus ilex	Holly oak
Q. lobata	Valley oak
Raphiolepis umbellata	Yedda hawthorn
Rhus aromatica	Fragrant sumac
Sambucus canadensis	American elder
Sequoia sempervirens	Coast redwood
Sophora japonica	Japanese pagoda tree
Taxodium distichum	Bald cypress
Ternstroemia	
Ulmus parvifolia	Chinese elm
Vitex agnus-castus	Chaste tree
Wisteria sinensis	Chinese wisteria

FRUITS, NUTS, AND BERRIES

Botanical name	Common name
Carya illinoinensis	Pecan
Castanea dentata	American chestnut
Diospyros kaki	Japanese persimmon
D. virginiana	Common persimmon
Ficus carica 'Kadota'	Kadota fig
F. carica 'Mission'	Mission fig
Juglans hindsii	Black walnut
Malus	Apple, crab apple
Persea americana	Avocado
Prunus cerasifera	Cherry plum
P. serotina var. *salicifolia*	Black cherry
Pyrus calleryana	Callery pear
P. communis	Pear
Rubus ursinus var. *loganobaccus*	Loganberry
R. ursinus	Ollalie

Some plants susceptible to fireblight:

Botanical name	Common name
TREES AND SHRUBS	
Amelanchier	Serviceberry
Chaenomeles	Flowering quince
Cotoneaster	
Crataegus	Hawthorn
Eriobotrya	Loquat
Malus	Apple, crab apple
Photinia	
Prunus	Flowering almond, plum, and cherry
Rosa	Rose
Sorbus	Mountain ash
Spiraea	

FRUIT TREES AND BERRIES

Apple
Pear
Quince
Raspberry

Some species of pyracantha and hawthorn tolerant of fireblight:

Botanical name	Common name
PYRACANTHA	
P. coccinea 'Lalandei'	Laland's firethorn
P. fortuneana	
HAWTHORN	
Crataegus phaenopyrum	Washington hawthorn

These species are not immune to fireblight, but are not damaged by it as severely as are other species.

Some avocado varieties for California and Florida, from most hardy to least hardy:

For California	For Florida
Bacon	Brogdon
Zutano	Tonnage
Fuerte	Choquette
Hass	Pollock

Some plants that may be infested by the Mediterranean fruit fly:

Apple
Apricot
Avocado
Cantaloupe
Cherry
Citrus
Cucumber
Fig
Grape
Guava
Loquat
Olive
Peach
Pear
Pepper
Persimmon
Plum
Pumpkin
Pyracantha
Quince
Squash (hubbard)
Strawberry
Tomato
Walnut

Adapted from *California Agriculture*, March-April 1981.

Some plants susceptible to *Botryosphaeria ribis:*

Botanical name	Common name
TREES AND SHRUBS	
Acer	Maple
Castanea	Chestnut
Cercis	Redbud
Cornus	Dogwood
Forsythia	
Ilex	Holly
Liquidambar	Sweet gum
Nyssa	Sour gum
Populus	Poplar
Pyracantha	Firethorn
Rhododendron	Rhododendron, azalea
Rosa	Rose
Salix	Willow

FRUIT AND NUT TREES AND SMALL FRUITS

Apple
Avocado
Citrus
Currant
Fig
Hickory
Pear
Pecan

Regional adaptations of some blueberry varieties:

FOR THE SOUTH AND SOUTHERN CALIFORNIA:

Rabbiteye (*Vaccinium ashei*)

Bluebelle	Tifblue
Bluegem	Woodward
Climax	

Highbush (*Vaccimium corymbosum*)

Avonblue	Sharpblue
Floridablue	

FOR THE VERY COLDEST REGIONS:

Meader	Northland

WIDELY ADAPTED:

Berkeley	Collins
Bluecrop	Jersey
Blueray	Patriot
Bluetta	

Cold hardiness of citrus, from most hardy to least hardy:

Kumquat
Orangequat
Sour orange
'Meyer' lemon
'Rangpur' lime
Mandarin orange (tangerine)
Sweet orange
'Bearss' lime
Tangelo
Lemon
Grapefruit
Limequat
'Mexican' lime

Home gardeners in Florida and California can plant a wide variety of citrus in the milder areas of their states. In the warmest areas, you will have success with the more tender citrus such as grapefruit, lemons, and limes. South Texas gardeners can plant Meyer lemon, Satsuma mandarin, and Marr's early orange.

The pH Scale

	SOME FAMILIAR FOODS AND MATERIALS	Acid	SOILS

Grapefruit — 3

Grape — 4 } Peat moss

} Best for rhododendron, azalea, and other acid-loving plants

Bread — 5

Milk — 6 } Average eastern soils

Pure water—Neutral — 7

} Average western soils

Baking soda — 8

Soap — 9

Milk of magnesia — 10 } Alkali soils

— 11

Alkaline

Apply limestone to raise pH

Pounds of ground limestone needed per 100 square feet to raise pH to 6.5:

Present pH of soil	Pounds needed to raise sandy loam to pH 6.5	Pounds needed to raise loam to pH 6.5	Pounds needed to raise clay loam to pH 6.5
4.0	11.5	16	23
4.5	9.5	13.5	19.5
5.0	8	10.5	15
5.5	6	8	10.5
6.0	3	4	5.5

Dolomitic limestone is recommended because it adds magnesium as well as calcium to the soil. The limestone should be cultivated into the soil.

Adapted from *Soil Acidity Needs of Plants*, New York Cooperative Extension Service, publication D-2-25.

Some plants that will grow in alkaline soil (pH 7.5 to 8.4):

Botanical name	Common name

TREES AND SHRUBS

Botanical name	Common name
Acer negundo	Box elder
Albizia	Silk tree
Berberis thunbergii	Japanese barberry
Casuarina	Beefwood
Celtis	Hackberry
Cercocarpus	Mountain mahogany
Deutzia	
Elaeagnus angustifolia	Russian olive
Forsythia	
Fraxinus velutina	Velvet ash
Hibiscus syriacus	Rose-of-Sharon
Kerria	Japanese rose
Lonicera fragrantissima	Fragrant honeysuckle
Malus sargentii	Sargent crab apple
Philadelphus	Mock orange
Phoenix dactylifera	Date palm
Populus fremontii	Fremont cottonwood
Potentilla fruticosa	Bush cinquefoil
Robinia	Locust
Sophora japonica	Japanese pagoda tree
Spiraea × vanhouttei	Bridalwreath
Viburnum dentatum	Arrowwood
V. dilatatum	Linden viburnum
Washingtonia	Washington palm
Ziziphus jujuba	Common jujube

Some plants that will grow in acid soil (pH 4.5 to 5.5):

Botanical name	Common name

TREES AND SHRUBS

Botanical name	Common name
Amelanchier	Serviceberry
Arctostaphylos	Manzanita
Calluna	Heather
Camellia	
Cytisus	Broom
Erica	Heath
Gardenia	
Hydrangea	
Ilex	Holly
Kalmia	Mountain laurel
Lagerstroemia indica	Crape myrtle
Leucothoe	
Magnolia	
Picea	Spruce
Pieris	Andromeda
Pinus	Pine
Populus tremuloides	Quaking aspen
Quercus palustris	Pin oak
Rhododendron	Rhododendron, azalea
Salix babylonica	Weeping willow
Sorbus	Mountain ash
Tsuga	Hemlock

FLOWERS

Botanical name	Common name
Convallaria	Lily-of-the-valley
Coreopsis	
Gypsophila	Baby's-breath
Lupinus	Lupine

Climate Zone Map

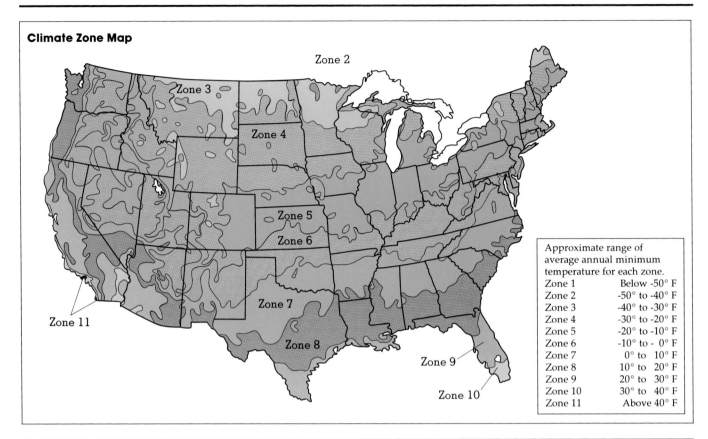

Zone 2
Zone 3
Zone 4
Zone 5
Zone 6
Zone 7
Zone 8
Zone 9
Zone 10
Zone 11

Approximate range of
average annual minimum
temperature for each zone.

Zone 1	Below -50° F
Zone 2	-50° to -40° F
Zone 3	-40° to -30° F
Zone 4	-30° to -20° F
Zone 5	-20° to -10° F
Zone 6	-10° to - 0° F
Zone 7	0° to 10° F
Zone 8	10° to 20° F
Zone 9	20° to 30° F
Zone 10	30° to 40° F
Zone 11	Above 40° F

U.S. Measure and Metric Measure Conversion Chart

		Formulas for Exact Measures			**Rounded Measures for Quick Reference**		
	Symbol	When you know:	Multiply by:	To find:			
Mass (Weight)	oz	ounces	28.35	grams	1 oz		= 30 g
	lb	pounds	0.45	kilograms	4 oz		= 115 g
	g	grams	0.035	ounces	8 oz		= 225 g
	kg	kilograms	2.2	pounds	16 oz	= 1 lb	= 450 g
					32 oz	= 2 lb	= 900 g
					36 oz	= 2¼ lb	= 1000 g (1 kg)
Volume	pt	pints	0.47	liters	1 c	= 8 oz	= 250 ml
	qt	quarts	0.95	liters	2 c (1 pt)	= 16 oz	= 500 ml
	gal	gallons	3.785	liters	4 c (1 qt)	= 32 oz	= 1 liter
	ml	milliliters	0.034	fluid ounces	4 qt (1 gal)	= 128 oz	= 3¾ liter
Length	in.	inches	2.54	centimeters	⅜ in.	= 1 cm	
	ft	feet	30.48	centimeters	1 in.	= 2.5 cm	
	yd	yards	0.9144	meters	2 in.	= 5 cm	
	mi	miles	1.609	kilometers	2½ in.	= 6.5 cm	
	km	kilometers	0.621	miles	12 in. (1 ft)	= 30 cm	
	m	meters	1.094	yards	1 yd	= 90 cm	
	cm	centimeters	0.39	inches	100 ft	= 30 m	
					1 mi	= 1.6 km	
Temperature	°F	Fahrenheit	⅝ (after subtracting 32)	Celsius	32°F	= 0°C	
	°C	Celsius	⅝ (then add 32)	Fahrenheit	212°F	= 100°C	
Area	in.²	square inches	6.452	square centimeters	1 in.²	= 6.5 cm²	
	ft²	square feet	929.0	square centimeters	1 ft²	= 930 cm²	
	yd²	square yards	8361.0	square centimeters	1 yd²	= 8360 cm²	
	a.	acres	0.4047	hectares	1 a.	= 4050 m²	

Apples

Variety	Pollination	Disease Resistance	2	3	4	5	6	7	8	9	10[2]
Anna	D								•	•	•
Baldwin	A	FB	•	•	•	•	•				
Corland	B	PM-			•	•	•	•			
Dorsett Golden	D							•	•	•	•
Ein Shemer	D								•	•	•
Empire	B	FB				•	•	•			
Golden Delicious	A					•	•	•	•		
Granny Smith	B								•	•	
Gravenstein	E	PM-						•	•	•	•
Idared	E	FB-,PM-			•	•	•	•			
Jonathan	B	CAR-,FB,PM-				•	•	•	•	•	
McIntosh	B			•	•	•	•				
Newton Pippin	B					•	•	•	•		
Northern Spy	B		•	•	•	•	•				
Prima	C	PM,S+,FB				•	•	•	•		
Priscilla	C	CAR+,S+,FB				•	•	•	•		
Red Delicious	B	BR, CAR-				•	•	•	•		
Red Rome Beauty	A	FB-,PM-				•	•	•	•		
Rhode Island Greening	E	FB-		•	•	•					
Sir Prize	C	S+,PM				•	•	•	•		
Stayman Winesap	E	BR,FB				•	•	•	•		
Winesap	E					•	•	•	•		
Winter Banana	B					•	•	•	•		
Yellow Transparent	B	FB-			•	•	•	•	•		

Zone Adaptation[1] (2 3 4 5 6 7 8 9 10[2])

[1] Based on USDA Plant Climate Zone Map. See page 348.
[2] Florida only.

POLLINATION KEY
A Self-fruitful, but crop is improved with a pollinator.
B Pollinate with any A or B.
C Prima and Priscilla cross-pollinate well. Sir Prize needs either Prima or Priscilla for pollination, but it will not pollinate them.
D Pollinate with another D.
E Not a pollinator. Pollinate with an A or a B.

DISEASE KEY
BR   Fairly resistant to bitter rot.
CAR+ Resistant to cedar-apple rust.
CAR- Highly susceptible to cedar-apple rust.
FB   Fairly resistant to fireblight.
FB-   Highly susceptible to fireblight.
PM   Fairly resistant to powdery mildew.
PM-   Highly susceptible to powdery mildew.
S+   Resistant to scab.

Apricots

Variety	Pollination	Disease Resistance	2	3	4	5	6	7	8	9[2]	10
Blenheim	A	BR-					•	•	•	•	
Goldcot	A					•	•	•	•		
Perfection	B						•	•	•		
Royal	A	BR-					•	•	•		
Stella	A					•	•	•	•		
Tilton	A	BR						•	•	•	•

Zone Adaptation[1] (2 3 4 5 6 7 8 9[2] 10)

[1] Based on USDA Plant Climate Zone Map. See page 348.
[2] California only.

POLLINATION KEY
A Self-fruitful. Needs no pollinator.
B Not self-fruitful. Pollinate with Blenheim or Royal.

DISEASE KEY
BR   Fairly resistant to brown rot.
BR-   Highly susceptible to brown rot.

Peaches

Variety	Pollination	Disease Resistance	2	3	4	5	6	7	8	9	10
Belle of Georgia	A	BLS+				•	•	•	•		
Desertgold	A								•	•	•
Early-Red-Free	A	BLS+				•	•	•	•		
Elberta	A	BLS-				•	•	•	•		
Flordasum	A									•	•[3]
J. H. Hale	B					•	•	•	•		
Madison[2]	A	BLS				•	•	•	•		
Redhaven	A	BLS				•	•	•	•		
Redskin	A	BLS				•	•	•	•		
Reliance[2]	A					•	•	•	•		
Rio-Oso-Gem	A	BLS-				•	•	•	•		
Sunhaven	A	BLS				•	•	•	•		

Zone Adapatation[1]

[1] Based on USDA Plant Climate Zone Map. See page 348.
[2] Does well in colder areas of Zone 5.
[3] Florida only.

POLLINATION KEY
A Self-fruitful, requires no pollinator.
B Requires pollinator. Use an A.

DISEASE KEY
BLS+ Resistant to bacterial leaf spot.
BLS Fairly resistant to bacterial leaf spot.
BLS- Susceptible to bacterial leaf spot.

Pears

Variety	Pollination	Disease Resistance	2	3	4	5	6	7	8	9[2]	10
Bartlett	B	FB-				•	•	•		•	
Bosc	B	FB-				•	•	•			
Clapp's Favorite	B	FB-				•	•	•			
Comice	B	(FB)				•	•	•		•	
D'Anjou	B	FB-				•	•	•			
Kieffer[3]	A	FB			•	•	•	•	•	•	
Moonglow	A	FB+				•	•	•	•		
Orient[3]	A	FB+				•	•	•	•	•	
Seckel	C	FB				•	•	•	•		

Zone Adaptation[1]

[1] Based on USDA Plant Climate Zone Map. See page 348.
[2] California only.
[3] Grown in Florida.

POLLINATION KEY
A Pollinate with another A.
B Pollinate with any B.
C Pollinate with any B except Bartlett.

DISEASE KEY
FB+ Resistant to fireblight.
FB Fairly resistant to fireblight.
(FB) Moderately susceptible to fireblight.
FB- Highly susceptible to fireblight.

Plums

Variety	Type	Pollination	Disease Resistance	4	5	6	7	8	9[2]	10
Blue Damson	E	B	BK-		•	•	•			
Burbank	J	D			•	•	•	•	•	
Ember	J	E		•	•	•	•	•		
Green Gage	E	B				•	•	•		
Italian Prune (Fellenberg)	EPP	F			•	•	•	•		
Methley	J	C	BK		•	•	•	•	•	
Ozark Premier	J	D			•	•	•	•	•	
President	E	A	BK+		•	•	•	•	•	
Santa Rosa	J	C	BK		•	•	•	•	•	
Shiro	J	D	BK		•	•	•	•	•	
Stanley	EPP	F	BK-	•	•	•	•	•		
Underwood	J	E			•	•	•	•	•	

Zone Adaptation[1]

[1] Based on USDA Plant Climate Zone Map. See page 348.
[2] California only.

TYPES
E European blue plum
EPP European prune plum
J Japanese red plum

POLLINATION KEY
A Not self-fruitful, pollinate with a B.
B Self-fruitful, no pollinator necessary.
C Self-fruitful, but crop is improved by a pollinator; use a D.
D Not self-fruitful, pollinate with another D.
E Ember and Underwood cross-pollinate well.
F Self-fruitful, but crop is improved by a pollinator; use an F.

DISEASE KEY
BK+ Resistant to black knot.
BK Fairly resistant to black knot.
BK- Highly susceptible to black knot.

Some bramble varieties, with regional adaptation and disease resistance:

Blackberries	Disease Resistance	Widely Adapted	North	South	Pacific Northwest	California
Black Satin				•		
Darrow		•				
Ebony King	OR	•				
Eldorado	OR	•				
Floridagrand*	LS			•		
Lawton	OR, V			•		
Oklawaha*				•		
Red Raspberries						
August Red			•			
Latham		•				
Meeker	PM	•			•	
Southland	LS, A, PM			•		
Sumner	PM	•			•	
Willamette	PM	•			•	
Trailing Blackberries						
Boysenberry					•	•
Loganberry					•	•
Ollaliberry	V, M					•
Youngberry					•	•

* Needs cross-pollination.

DISEASE KEY

A Resistant to anthracnose.
LS Resistant to leaf spot.
M Resistant to mosaic.
OR Resistant to orange rust.
PM Resistant to powdery mildew.
V Resistant to verticillium wilt.

Sweet Cherries

Variety	Pollination	Disease Resistance	Zone Adaptation[1] 2	3	4	5	6	7	8	9[2]	10
Bing	A	BC-				•	•	•	•	•	
Black Tartarian	B					•	•	•	•	•	
Corum	C	BC				•	•	•			
Early Burlat	C	BC+				•	•	•	•	•	
Lambert	A	BC-				•	•	•			
Royal Ann	A	BC-				•	•	•			
Sam	C	BC				•	•	•			
Sue	C	BC				•	•	•			
Van	B	BC-				•	•	•	•	•	
Sour Cherries											
Meteor	D	CLS			•	•	•	•			
Montmorency	D					•	•	•			
North Star	D	CLS			•	•	•	•	•		

[1] Based on USDA Plant Climate Zone Map. See page 348.
[2] California only.

POLLINATION KEY

A Pollinate with a B.
B Pollinate with an A.
C Pollinate with an A or a B.
D Self-fruitful, needs no pollinator.

DISEASE KEY

BC+ Resistant to bacterial canker.
BC Fairly resistant to bacterial canker.
BC- Susceptible to bacterial canker.
CLS Fairly resistant to cherry leafspot.

Some strawberry varieties, with regional adaptation and disease resistance:

Variety	Disease Resistance	Widely Adapted	South	North	California	Pacific Northwest
Blakemore	S+, LS, VW+	•				
Catskill	S+, VW+			•		
Darrow	LS, PM, S, RS+, VW	•				
Delite	RS+, VW+	•				
Earlibelle	LS, S		•			
Empire	VW+			•		
Fletcher	S+, VW+			•		
Florida 90*	V		•			
Guardian	RS+, VW+	•				
Hood	RS+, VW+, LS					•
Midway	RS			•		
Northwest	V, LS+					•
Ogallala	LS+	•				
Pocahontas	LS+		•			
Redchief	RS+, S+, VW	•				
Salinas	VW+				•	•
Sequoia					•	
Sparkle	RS+			•		
Surecrop	VW+, RS+	•				
Tioga	V				•	•

* Adapted to extreme southern regions.

DISEASE KEY
LS+ Resistant to leaf spot.
LS Moderately resistant to leaf spot.
PM Moderately resistant to powdery mildew.
RS+ Resistant to 1 or more races of red stele.
RS Moderately resistant to 1 or more races of red stele.
S+ Resistant to scorch.
S Moderately resistant to scorch.
V Moderately resistant to virus.
VW+ Resistant to verticillium wilt.
VW Moderately resistant to verticillium wilt.

Some grape varieties, with regional adaptation and disease resistance:

Variety	Disease Resistance	Northeast	Midwest	Pacific Northwest	Southeast	California Arizona
Aurore	DM	•		•		
Beta	BR+	•	•	•		
Campbell's Early	BR+	•		•		
Concord	DM	•	•	•		•
Delaware	PM	•	•	•		
Fredonia	BR+	•		•		
Magnolia					•	
Missouri Reisling	BR+	•				
Niagara	PM	•	•	•		•
Scuppernong*					•	
Thompson Seedless						•
Tokay						•
Worden	BR+	•	•	•		

* Needs pollinator; use Magnolia.

DISEASE KEY
BR+ Resistant to black rot.
DM Moderately resistant to downy mildew.
PM Moderately resistant to powdery mildew.

Earliest dates for safe spring planting of vegetables:

To find the average date of the last freeze, ask at your local nursery or Cooperative Extension Office.

Planting dates for localities in which average date of last freeze is:

Crop	Feb. 1	Feb. 15	Mar. 1	Mar. 15	Apr. 1	Apr. 15	May 1	May 15	June 1
Asparagus	—	—	—	2/1	2/15	3/15	3/15	4/15	5/1
Bean, lima	2/1	3/1	3/15	4/1	4/15	5/1	5/15	6/1	—
Bean, snap	2/1	3/1	3/15	3/15	4/1	4/15	5/1	5/15	6/1
Beet	1/1	1/15	2/15	2/15	3/1	3/15	4/1	4/15	5/1
Broccoli*	1/1	1/15	2/1	2/15	3/1	3/15	4/1	4/15	5/15
Brussels sprout*	1/1	1/15	2/1	2/15	3/1	3/15	4/1	4/15	5/15
Cabbage*	1/1	1/1	1/15	2/1	2/15	3/1	3/15	4/15	5/15
Carrot	1/1	1/15	2/1	2/15	3/1	3/15	4/1	5/1	5/15
Cauliflower*	1/1	1/15	1/15	2/1	2/15	3/1	4/1	4/15	5/15
Cucumber	2/15	2/15	3/1	4/1	4/15	5/1	5/15	6/1	—
Eggplant*	2/1	2/15	3/15	4/1	4/15	5/1	5/15	6/1	—
Lettuce	1/1	1/1	1/1	2/1	2/15	3/15	4/1	4/15	5/15
Muskmelon	2/15	2/15	3/1	4/1	4/15	5/1	6/1	—	—
Onion	1/1	1/1	1/1	2/1	2/15	3/1	3/15	4/15	5/1
Parsley	1/1	1/1	1/15	2/1	2/15	3/15	4/1	4/15	5/15
Pea	1/1	1/1	1/15	2/1	2/15	3/1	3/15	4/15	5/1
Pepper*	2/1	3/1	3/15	4/1	4/15	5/1	5/15	6/1	6/1
Potato	1/1	1/15	1/15	2/1	3/1	3/15	4/1	4/15	5/1
Radish	1/1	2/2	1/1	1/15	2/15	3/1	3/15	4/1	5/1
Spinach	1/1	1/1	1/1	1/15	2/1	2/15	3/15	4/1	4/15
Squash	2/1	3/1	3/15	4/1	4/15	5/1	5/1	5/15	6/1
Tomato*	2/1	3/1	3/15	4/1	4/15	5/1	5/15	5/15	6/1
Turnip	1/1	1/15	2/1	2/1	2/15	3/1	3/15	4/1	5/1
Watermelon	2/15	2/15	3/1	3/15	4/15	5/1	5/15	6/1	—

* Seeds may be started indoors 4 to 6 weeks before planting date.

Vegetable seed information:

	Optimum germination temperatures	Days to germination
Asparagus	70-75°	14-21
Bean, lima	70	7-10
Bean, snap	70	6-10
Beet	50-85	10-14
Broccoli	70-75	10-14
Brussels sprout	70-75	10-14
Cabbage	70-75	10-14
Carrot	50-85	14-21
Cauliflower	70-75	8-10
Cucumber	70	7-10
Eggplant	70	10-15
Lettuce	65-70	7-10
Melon	75	5-7
Onion	70-75	10-14
Parsley	70-75	14-21
Pea	40-75	7-10
Pepper	75-80	10
Radish	45-85	4-6
Spinach	70	8-10
Squash	70-75	7-10
Sweet corn	70	5-7
Tomato	70-75	5-8
Turnip	60-85	7-10

Regional adaptation of some onion varieties:

FOR THE SOUTH
Excel
Granex
Texas Grano
Tropicana Red
White Granex

FOR THE WEST
California Early Red
Early Yellow Globe
Southport Yellow Globe
Yellow Bermuda

FOR THE NORTH
Downing Yellow Globe
Early Yellow Globe
Empire
Nutmeg
Spartan lines

Some vegetables and fruits susceptible to fusarium wilt caused by various forms of *Fusarium oxysporum:*

Asparagus
Bean
Brussels sprout
Cabbage
Cauliflower
Celery
Cucumber
Melon
Okra
Onion
Pea
Pepper
Radish
Spinach
Sweet potato
Tomato
Turnip

Some vegetables and fruits susceptible to verticillium wilt:

Artichoke
Beet
Brussels sprout
Cabbage
Eggplant
Melon[1]
New Zealand spinach
Okra
Peanut
Pepper
Potato
Pumpkin
Radish
Rhubarb
Spinach
Strawberries[2]
Tomato

[1]Watermelon, cantaloupe, and honeydew become infected but are not seriously damaged. Persian, casaba, and crenshaw melons are very susceptible.

[2]See page 352 for strawberry varieties resistant to verticillium.

Adapted from *Plants Resistant or Susceptible to Verticillium Wilt,* University of California Cooperative Extension leaflet 2703.

Some vegetable varieties resistant to the southern root knot nematode (*Meloidogyne incognita*):

BEAN
Bountiful
Brittle Wax
Tender Pod
Wingard Wonder

CORN
Carmel Cross
Golden Beauty Hybrid
Golden Cross Bantam
Span Cross

PEA
Burpeeana Early
Wando

PEPPER
All Big
Bontoc Sweet Long
World Beater

TOMATO
All Round
Anahu
Anahu-R
Atkinson
Auburn 76
Beefeater
Beefmaster
Big Seven
Calmart
Chicogrande
Coldset
Eurocross
Extase
Monte Carlo
Nemared
Nematex
Patriot
Peto 662 VFN
Ponderosa
VFN-8

SWEET POTATO
Apache
Carver
Heartogold
Hopi
Jasper
Jewel
Nemagold
Nugget
Ruby
Sunnyside
White Bunch
White Triumph
Whitestar

Some tomato varieties, with regional adaptation and disease resistance:

EARLY SEASON	Disease Resistance	Widely Adapted	South	North	West
Early Cascade	V, F	•			
Jetfire	V, F				•
New Yorker	V			•	
Porter Improved					•
Small Fry	V, F, N	•			
Spring Set	V, F	•			

MIDSEASON					
Ace 55	V, F				•
Atkinson	F, N		•		
Better Boy	V, F, N	•			
Big Girl Hybrid	V, F	•			
Big Set	V, F, N	•			
Bonus	V, F, N	•			
Burpee's VF	V, F	•			
Columbia	V, F, Ct	•			
Floradel	F		•		
Floramerica	V, F	•			
Heinz 1350	V, F	•			
Jet Star	V, F			•	
Marglobe	F	•			
Park's Whopper	V, F, N, T	•			
Roma VF	V, F	•			
Rowpac	V, F, Ct				•
Roza	V, F, Ct				•
Salad Master	V, F, Ct				•
Supersonic	V, F			•	•
Terrific	V, F, N	•			
Tripi-Red	V, F		•		

LATE SEASON					
Beefeater	V, F, N	•			
Beefmaster	V, F, N	•			
Manalucie	F		•		
Ramapo	V, F			•	
Tropic	V, F, T		•		
Wonder Boy	V, F	•			
Vineripe	V, F, N	•			

DISEASE KEY
V   Resistant to verticillium wilt.
F   Resistant to fusarium wilt.
N   Resistant to nematodes.
T   Resistant to tobacco mosaic virus.
Ct   Resistant to curly top.

Some bean varieties resistant to rust:

Cape
Dade
Kentucky Wonder
Resisto

Some bean varieties resistant to mosaic:

Aristocrop
Astro
Bonanza Wax
Bush Blue Lake
Bush Blue Lake 47
Bush Blue Lake 274
Cape
Cherokee
Contender
Dade (pole)
Del Rey
Eagle
Early Gallatin
Early Harvest
Flo
Gallatin 50
Gator Green 15
Gold Crop
Golden Rod
Harvester
Improved Tendergreen
M.R.
Peak
Provider
Resistant Cherokee
Resisto
Roma II PVP
Romano
Spartan Arrow
Spurt
Strike
Stringless Blue Lake
FM-IK
Sungold
Tendercrop
Tenderlake
Topcrop
Win

Some beet varieties that produce round, smooth roots:

Albino White Beet
Detroit Dark Red
Earlisweet Hybrid
Early Wonder, Green Top
Early Wonder, Tall Top
Garnet
Golden Beet
Perfected Detroit
Red Ace Hybrid
Red Ball
Ruby Queen

Some corn varieties tolerant of smut (S), bacterial wilt (B), and maize dwarf mosaic (M):

Apache	S, B, M
Aztec	S, B
Bellringer	S, B
Calico	S, B
Calumet	S, B, M
Cherokee	B, M
Comanche	S, B
Comet	S, B
Gold cup	S, B
Merit	S, B, M
Mevak	S, B
Quicksilver	S, B, M
Seneca Sentry	B, M
Silver Queen	B
Sweet Sue	S
Wintergreen	S, B, M

Some corn varieties tolerant of or resistant to southern and northern leaf blights:

Apache
Atlantic
BiQueen
Capitan
Cherokee
Comet
Florida Staysweet
Guardian
Wintergreen

Some lettuce varieties resistant to or tolerant of tip burn:

Calmar
Climax
Empire
Empress
Fairton
Great Lakes 118, 366, 659, 659-700,
  and 6238
Green Lake
Ithaca
Merit
Mesa 659
Minetto
Montello
Montemar
New York 515 Improved
Oswego
Parris Island Cos
Pennlake
Salinas
Super 59
Vanguard
Vanguard 75
Vanmax

Some onion varieties resistant to or tolerant of pink root:

Autumn Spice
Beltsville Bunching
Brown Beauty
Buccaneer
Colossal
Copper Coast
Danvers
Early Supreme
El Capitan
Evergreen White Bunch
Fiesta
Granada
Granex Yellow
Henry's Special
Majesty
Red Commander
Rialto
Ringer
Spanish Main
White Granex
White Robust
Yellow Globe
Yellow Grano—New Mexico

Some spinach varieties resistant to downy mildew:

Aden
Badger Savoy
Basra
Bismark
Bouquet
Califlay
Chesapeake
Chinook
Dixie Market
Duet
Early Smooth
Grandstand
High Pack
Long Standing Savoy
Marathon
Melody
Nares
Salma
Savoy Supreme
Skookum
Vienna
Winter Bloomsdale

Some slicing cucumber varieties resistant to or tolerant of certain plant diseases:

A & C Hybrid Imp	L+, S+, A+, P+, D+, C+
A & C Hybrid 1810	L+, S+, A+, P+, D+, C+
Cherokee #7	L+, S+, A+, P, D, C+
Dasher	L, S, A, P, D, C
Dasher II	L, S+, A+, P+, D+, C+
Early Triumph	L, S, A, P, D, C
Gemini 7	L, S, A, P, D, C
Medalist	S+, P, D, C+
Poinsett	L+, A+, P+, D+
Poinsett 76	L+, S+, P+, D+
Roadside Fancy	L, S, A, P, D, C
Setter	L, S+, A, P+, D+
Shamrock	L, S, P, D, C
Slicemaster	L, S+, A, P, D, C
Slice-Mor	S+, A+, P, D+, C
Southernsett	L, S+, P, D, C+
Sprint 440	L, S, A, P, D
Sweet-Slice	L, S+, A, P, D, C
Sweet Success	S, P, D, C

Some pickling cucumber varieties resistant to or tolerant of certain plant diseases:

Addis	A, P, D, C, L
Bounty	S, A, P, D, C, L
Calypso	S, A, P, D, C, L
Carolina	S, A, P, D, C, L
Chipper	A, P, D, C, L
County Fair	S, A, P, D, C
Explorer	P, D, L
Flurry	S, A, P, D, C, L
Liberty	S, D, C, L
Lucky Strike	S, A, P, C
Multipik	S, A, D, C, L
Panorama	S, A, P, D, C, L
Peto Triplemech	S, A, P, D, C, L
Picarow	S, A, P, D, C, L
Premier	S, A, P, D, C, L
Salty	S, P, D, C
Sampson	A, P, D, C, L
Score	S, A, D, C, L
Spear-It	S, A, P, D, C, L
Sumter	S, A, P, D, C, L
Tamor	S, A, P, D, C, L
Triple Crown	S, A, P, C, L
V.I.P.	S, A, P, D, C, L

DISEASE RESISTANCE KEY

A variety's tolerance of a disease is indicated by the codes below. If a variety is resistant to the disease, the code is followed by a plus (+).

L	Angular leaf spot.
S	Scab.
A	Anthracnose.
P	Powdery mildew.
D	Downy mildew.
C	Cucumber mosaic virus.

Some peppers resistant to or tolerant of tobacco mosaic virus:

Ace
Allbig
Annabelle
Argo
Beater
Bell Boy
Big Bertha
Burlington
Early Canada Bell
Early Niagara Giant
Early Wonder
Emerald Giant
Gatorbelle
Gypsy
Hybelle
Lady Bell
Liberty Bell
Ma Belle
Merced
Mercury
Midway
Miss Belle
New Ace
Pennwonder
Pimientol
Puerto Rico Perfection
Puerto Rico Wonder
Resistant Florida Giant
Rutgers World Beater
Shamrock
Skipper
Staddon's Select
Thick Walled World Beater
Titan
Valley Giant
Yolo Wonder

Some canteloupe and muskmelon varieties resistant to or tolerant of certain plant diseases:

DOWNY MILDEW
Ambrosia
Dixie Jumbo
Early Dawn
Summet
Topmark
Topset

ANTHRACNOSE
Samson
Saticoy

POWDERY MILDEW
Ambrosia
Classic
Delicious 51
Early Dawn
Edisto
Saticoy
Summet

Some watermelon varieties resistant to or tolerant of anthracnose:
Blackstone
Calhoun
Charleston Gray
Crimson Sweet
Dixielee
Family Fun
Graybelle
Imperial
Madera
Smokylee
Sweet Favorite Hybrid
Verona
You Sweet Thing Hybrid

Potato varieties tolerant of common scab:
Alamo
Cascade
Cherokee
La Rouge
Lemhi
Nooksack
Norchip
Norgold Russet
Norland
Ona
Onaway
Ontario
Plymouth
Pungo
Russet Burbank
Shurchip
Sioux
Superior
Targhee

G

***Gaillardia* (Blanket flower)**
cultural information, 336
diseases of
aster yellows, 337
powdery mildew, 338
as verticillium-wilt resistant, 338

P

Pachysandra (Japanese spurge)
as acid tolerant, 66
iron deficiency in, 66
as shade tolerant, 335
Pacific coast tick, 319
Paeonia (Peony)
culture, 114
diseases of
fusarium wilt, 337
gray mold, 114
phytophthora blight, 115
failure to bloom in, 114
Pagoda tree, Japanese. *See*
Sophora japonica
Painted daisy. *See*
Chrysanthemum
Painted tongue. *See*
Salpiglossis
Pajaroello tick, 319
Palisade cells, defined, 16
Palms, indoors
growing locations for, 333
lace-cap hydrangea palm, 18
sago. *See Cycas*
salt-sensitive varieties of, 333
Palms, outdoors
as armillaria resistant, 345
as cotton-root-rot resistant, 339
as saline-soil tolerant, 341
sapsuckers and, 342
as verticillium-wilt resistant, 338
Pampas grass (*Cortaderia selloana*), as saline-soil tolerant, 341
Pandanus (Screw pine), as salt sensitive, 333
Panicgrass. *See* Barnyardgrass
PAN (Peroxyacetyl nitrate), 16, 84, 123, 125
Pansy. *See Viola*
Pantry pests. *See* Food products, pests in
Papaipema nebris (Common stalk borer), on corn, 279
Papaver (Poppy)
California poppy. *See*
Eschscholzia
as cotton-root-rot resistant, 339
diseases of, powdery mildew, 338
Paper products, pests in
booklice, 313
cigarette beetles, 331
cockroaches, 330
crickets, 311
drugstore beetles, 331
firebrats, 313
silverfish, 313
Paper wasps (*Polistes* species), 325
Parasite, defined, 16
Parasitic plants. *See* Mistletoe
Parking areas. *See* Sidewalks and driveways
Parkinsonia aculeata (Jerusalem thorn), as sandy-soil tolerant, 341
Parlor palm. *See Chamaedorea; Howea*
Parrotia persica (Persian parrotia), as disease and insect resistant, 342

Parsley
as aster-yellows susceptible, 337
germination of, 353
planting dates for, 353
Parsnip, diseases of
aster yellows, 337
scab, 293
Parthenocissus (Boston ivy; Virginia creeper), as sandy-soil tolerant, 341
Paspalum dilatatum. See Dallisgrass
Pasqueflower. *See Anemone*
Passiflora (Passion flower)
as full-light tolerant, 333
as powdery-mildew susceptible, 338
Pastinaca sativa. See Parsnip
Pathogen, defined, 17
Pathways, vegetable garden, 239
Patty pan squash. *See* Cucurbits
Paved areas. *See* Sidewalks and driveways
PCNB, 69, 94, 103, 110, 267, 274
Peace lily. *See Spathiphyllum*
Peach, flowering. *See Prunus* (flowering forms)
Peach blight
on almond, 214
on peach/nectarine, 227
Peach leaf curl, 228
Peach/Nectarine, 350
bacterial-leaf-spot-resistant varieties of, 228
blighted shoots on, 229
catfacing on, 229
culture, 226
diseases of
bacterial leaf spot, 228, 350
brown rot, 229
cytospora canker on, 207
fruit rot, 229
leaf curl, 228
phytophthora rot, 343
powdery mildew, 338
scab, 227
shothole fungus (coryneum blight; peach blight), 227
flowering. *See Prunus* (flowering forms)
gummosis on, 206
harvesting, 226
honeydew on, 230
insects on
aphids, 230
Mediterranean fruit flies, 346
peach twig borers, 228
plum curculios, 227
stinkbugs, 229
tarnished plant bugs, 229
nitrogen deficiency in, 212
planting locations for, 226, 350
pollination of, 350
regional adaptations of, 350
Peach twig borer (*Anarsia lineatella*)
on apricot, 220
on peach/nectarine, 228

Peanuts, diseases of
stem rot (southern blight; southern stem rot), 339
verticillium wilt, 353
Pear, 230
as armillaria resistant, 345
culture, 230
diseases of
bacterial blight, 343
Botryosphaeria ribis, 346
fireblight, 231, 345, 350
phytophthora rot, 343
powdery mildew, 338
scab, 230
insects on
codling moths, 231
Mediterranean fruit flies, 346
mites, 232
pear rust mites, 232
plum curculios, 227
San Jose scales, 232
two-spotted spider mites, 232
pollinators for, 350
poor-quality fruit on, 204
regional adaptations of, 350
ripening, 230
Pearleaf blister mite (*Phytoptus pyri*), on *Cotoneaster*, 165
Pear rust mite (*Epitrimerus pyri*)
on fruit and nut trees, 211
on pear, 232
Pearslug (*Caliroa cerasi*), on cherry, 221
Pear thrips (*Taeniothrips inconsequens*), on *Acer*, 159
Peas
climbing, supporting, 245, 246
diseases of
bacterial blight, 343
fusarium wilt, 353
powdery mildew, 290, 338
southern blight, 339
germination of, 353
insects on
cutworms, 253
onion thrips, 290
pea weevils, 290
seedcorn maggots, 280
southern root knot nematodes, 354
wireworms, 275
manganese deficiency in, 243
marsh spot in, 243
nematode-resistant varieties of, 354
planting dates for, 353
rabbits in, 252, 261
snail and slug baits for, 261
sweet. *See Lathyrus*
as verticillium-wilt resistant, 338
Peat
defined, 17
for iron deficiency in vegetables, 242
as lawn soil amendment, 33–34
as vegetable garden mulch, 244

Pea weevil (*Bruchus pisorum*), 290
Pecan
as armillaria resistant, 345
as *Botryosphaeria-ribis* susceptible, 346
insects on
hickory or pecan shuckworms, 233
pecan nut casebearers, 233
pecan weevils, 232
Pecan borer (*Synanthedon scitula*), on *Cornus*, 164
Pecan or hickory shuckworm (*Laspeyresia caryana*), 233
Pecan nut casebearer (*Acrobasis nuxvorella*), 233
Pecan weevil (*Curculio caryae*), 232
Pegomya hyoscyami
beet leafminer, 268
spinach leafminer, on spinach, 297
Pelargonium, indoors, 18, 333
Pelargonium, outdoors
budworms on, 116
in containers, watering, 115
culture, 115, 336
diseases of
bacterial stem rot and leaf spot, 116
black stem rot, 116
rust, 84
iron deficient, 83
oedema in, 115
planting locations for, 336
black stem rot and, 116
oedema and, 115
strawberry geranium. *See Saxifraga*
Pellicularia filamentosa, on *Vinca*, 71
Penicillium corm rot, on *Gladiolus*, 107
Penicillium gladioli, 107
Pennycress, clubroot harbored by, 274
Penstemon, as verticillium-wilt resistant, 338
Peonies. *See Paeonia*
Pepper plant. *See* Shepherd's-purse
Peppers, 291
blossom drop on, 291
blossom-end rot on, 291, 292, 302
culture, 291
diseases of
bacterial spot, 303
fusarium wilt, 353
southern blight, 339
tobacco mosaic virus (TMV), 356
verticillium wilt, 353
germination of, 353
harvesting, 291
insects on
Colorado potato beetles, 294
corn earworms (cotton bollworms; tomato fruitworms), 292